ISAIAH
The Lord Saves

Timothy L. Dane, Ph.D.

Copyright © 2022 Timothy L. Dane

All rights reserved. No part of this book may be reproduced or transmitted in any form or by any means, electronic or mechanical, including photocopying and recording, or by any information storage and retrieval system, without permission in writing from the publisher.

Published by:
Kress Biblical Resources
The Woodlands, TX 77393
www.kressbiblical.com

NASB: Unless otherwise indicated, all scripture quotations are from the New American Standard Bible® (NASB), Copyright © 1960, 1962, 1963, 1968, 1971, 1972, 1973, 1975, 1977, 1995 by The Lockman Foundation. Used by permission. www.Lockman.org

ESV: ESV® Bible (The Holy Bible, English Standard Version®), copyright © 2001 by Crossway, a publishing ministry of Good News Publishers. Used by permission. All rights reserved.

NIV: Scripture taken from the Holy Bible, NEW INTERNATIONAL VERSION®, NIV® Copyright © 1973, 1978, 1984, 2011 by Biblica, Inc.® Used by permission. All rights reserved worldwide.

Special thanks to Bev Greene, Howard Wilson, Dan Ziegler, and Marshall Winchester for their huge help in proofreading and creating the Topical and Scripture indexes.

ISBN: 978-1-934952-75-7

CONTENTS

    Section One: Judgment and Salvation Messages (1:1-39:8)   1

1   Introduction   1

2   Judgment and Salvation Messages to Jerusalem and Judah, 1 (1:1-6:13)   12

3   Judgment and Salvation Messages to Jerusalem and Judah, 2 (7:1-12:6)   66

4   Judgment and Salvation Messages to the Nations (13:1-23:18)   121

5   Judgment and Salvation Messages to the Whole World (24:1-27:13)   198

6   Trust in Flesh and You Will Fail (28:1-35:10)   227

7   Transition: Trust Yahweh and Prosper (36:1-39:8)   280

    Section Two: The Revealing of God's Great Salvation (40:1-66:24)   310

8   Salvation by Release from Babylon (40:1-48:22)   310

9   Salvation by the Servant of God (49:1-57:21)   402

10   Salvation to a Glorious Future (58:1-66:24)   486

11   Appendix One: A Concise Chart of Dispensational Premillennialism   570

12   Appendix Two: Topical Index   571

13   Appendix Three: Scripture Index   580

14   Bibliography   632

SECTION ONE: JUDGMENT AND SALVATION MESSAGES (1:1-39:8)

1
INTRODUCTION

It has been held that Isaiah is "the greatest of the major prophets, and arguably it is the greatest of all the prophets."[1] Isaiah is the third largest complete literary entity in the Bible, exceeded only by Jeremiah and the Psalms.[2] In addition to numerous allusions in the New Testament, Isaiah is quoted directly in the New Testament over 65 times (only the Psalms give more messianic prophecies or allusions). As Grogan puts it,

> Ignorance of any part of the Scripture is to be deplored, but this is particularly so with a book that gives such a manifold presentation of Christ . . . a view of Him that is most majestic and moving, one in which the virtually unknown contexts of the well-known passages shed a flood of light on those passages themselves.[3]

These truths remind us of the importance of a contextual meaning of the prophets in their own setting if we are to have a proper interpretation of the New Testament. Many writers also recognize that in Isaiah, "the literary grandeur is unequaled," the scope of its discussions is "unparalleled," and "its view of God is unmatched."[4] Grogan praises the literary style of Isaiah:

---

[1] Herbert M. Wolf, *Interpreting Isaiah* (Grand Rapids: Zondervan, 1985), 11.
[2] G. W. Grogan, "Isaiah," in *The Expositor's Bible Commentary*, ed. Frank E. Gaebelein, vol. 6 (Grand Rapids: Zondervan, 1986), 3.
[3] Ibid., 3-4.
[4] John N. Oswalt, *The Book of Isaiah: Chapters 1-39*, The New International Commentary On The Old Testament, R. K. Harrison, Gen. Ed. (Grand Rapids: Eerdmans, 1986), 3.

A survey of the whole book reveals the high literary quality of so much of its material—in its poetic style, in the wonderful way thought and language are matched to each other, in the plentiful and yet not forced use of devices like assonance and chiasm, and in the use of analogy and anthropomorphism.[5]

The literary devices Isaiah uses include alliteration, assonance, wordplay, hyperbole, chiasmus, inclusio, personification, as well as numerous forms of symbolism.[6] Isaiah is a literary masterpiece.

The first focus of this commentary will be given to five matters of Bible introduction: (1) authorship, (2) date and historical context, (3) major theological themes and purpose, (4) initial lessons for application, and (5) a suggested outline.

AUTHORSHIP

In Hebrew, the name Isaiah means Yahweh is salvation, or Yahweh saves, a fitting name for the prophet who speaks so much about the salvation Yahweh brings to His people. Archer explains,

Appropriately enough, the basic theme of Isaiah's message is that salvation is bestowed only by grace, by the power of God, the Redeemer, rather than by the strength of man or the good works of the flesh."[7] Indeed, there is only one God, and He alone is Savior.

Isaiah's calling was to declare the glory of Yahweh, the God of salvation.

The number of authors

This commentary teaches that there was one man named Isaiah (the son of Amoz) who wrote all parts of this prophecy in the eighth and seventh centuries B.C. These prophecies were received over many years, but they all came from the Spirit through this one single author (named in chs. 1; 2; 7; 13; 20; 37; 38; 39). In modern-day scholarship, there are those who believe that there were multiple authors (two or three), and that these different authors may have even lived in different times and places outside the land of Israel (such as in

---

[5] Grogan, "Isaiah," 10.
[6] Wolf, *Interpreting Isaiah*, 51-69.
[7] Gleason Archer, *A Survey of Old Testament Introduction* (Chicago: Moody, 1994), 333.

Babylon).⁸ Until the eighteenth century, however (with the exception of the twelfth century Jewish commentator Ibn Ezra), there was virtual universal acceptance of a single author. It was the rise of historical-critical theology in eighteenth-century Germany that began to challenge the unity of Isaiah with the theory of multiple authors. The initial challenges came from German critical scholars like (1) Johann C. Doederlein (1745-1792), a professor of theology at Jena who published an argument for a sixth century date of 40-66,⁹ (2) Ernest F. K. Rosenmueller (1768-1835), a professor of Arabic at Leipzig University, and (3) Bernard Duhm of Gottingen who proposed a theory of three Isaiahs.¹⁰

The main argument against the traditional view has been based on the rejection of supernatural inspiration,¹¹ with the corresponding argument that it would be impossible for an eighth century Isaiah to make such detailed predictions about the future as he did (e.g., the prediction that Babylon would overthrow Judah in 605, or the prediction that Cyrus would lead Persia to conquer Babylon in 539). These liberal objections have been refuted by scholars like Carl Paul Caspari (1814-1892), Heinrich Hahn (1821-1861), Franz Delitzsch (1813-1889), Rudolf E. Stier (1800-1862) and others. The present writer holds to the conviction that Isaiah wrote his prophetic messages under the direct inspiration of the Holy Spirit (cf. e.g., 1:1, 10, 24; 6:1; 7:3, 10; 8:1; 13:1, etc.), and that this is how he was able to give such predictions. Those who believe in the miraculous power of God have no trouble in accepting the idea that God has given futuristic prophecy.

The unity of the book

One can cite at least five reasons to hold to the unity of authorship. First, ancient Jewish writers always held that the book was a single unit (e.g., there are no known manuscripts with sections 1-39 and then 40-66, or 40-55 and 56-66). Second, the Dead Sea Scrolls support the unity of Isaiah. It is true that one of

---

⁸ For a summary of these views, see Oswalt, *The Book of Isaiah, Chapters 1-39*, 17-28.
⁹ Doederlein's reasoning was that an eighth century Isaiah could never have foreseen the fall of Jerusalem in 586 (nor Cyrus).
¹⁰ Duhm held that 40-55 were from Deutero Isaiah about 540 B.C. around Lebanon, and 56-66 (Trito Isaiah) were composed in Jerusalem around the time of Ezra around 450 B.C.
¹¹ Other objections include alleged differences in theme, language, style, or theology. These objections are unpersuasive. Differing historical contexts and differing theological purposes easily account for such differences.

the Isaiah scrolls (1Q Isaᵃ, dated ca. 150 B.C.) shows a small three-line gap between chapters 33-34, but there are no gaps elsewhere.¹² Third, other extra-biblical sources support the unity of Isaiah. For example, Ecclesiasticus (early second century B.C.) says, "By the Spirit of might, he (Isaiah), saw the last things, and comforted those who mourn in Zion" (Ecc. 48:24). Josephus (Ant. XI.3-6.1.1-2) wrote in the late first century A.D. that Cyrus read the prophecies about him in Isaiah and wished to fulfill them. Fourth, one finds significant overlap in style and content between 1-39 and 40-66, e.g., (1) expressions like "fire" for punishment (1:31; 10:17; 26:11; 33:11-14; 34:9-10; 66:24), and (2) numerous other notable verbal parallels (cf. 1:2/66:24; 1:5-6/53:4-5; 5:27/40:30; 6:1/52:13; 57:15; 6:11-12/62:4; 11:1/53:2; 11:6-9/65:25; 11:12/49:22; 35:10/51:11). Fifth, the New Testament usage of Isaiah suggests one Isaiah (Matt. 3:3; 12:17-21; Luke 3:4; John 12:37-41; Rom. 9:27, 29; 10:16, 20-21).

The personal life of Isaiah

It appears that Isaiah had a close connection with the Davidic monarchy and is also possible that Isaiah was of the family of David, and that he also had access to the kings of Judah (7:3; 37:21-22, et al.). He appears to have had a close relationship with Hezekiah and was well received into the royal court during his reign. He was also well-educated in issues of international affairs.¹³

In terms of marriage and family, there are interpretive issues involved here, but it appears that Isaiah was married and had a child, but his first wife died (from 7:3 we see Isaiah had a son named *She'ar Yashub*, "a remnant shall return"), and that he remarried after that and had at least one son with his second wife. Based on the prophecy that a young maiden was going to bear a prophetically significant son (the *almah* of 7:14 who would have a son called *Immanuel*), and the statement in 8:3 that Isaiah approached the prophetess and she bore a prophetically significant son (*Maher Shalal Hash Baz*), it seems best to understand that Isaiah's first wife died and Isaiah married a second time to a young lady that was still an unmarried virgin (an *almah*) at the time of the 7:14 prophecy.¹⁴ We also see that Isaiah understood that both he and his children had some sort of prophetic/typological significance (cf. 8:18). The New Testament makes many of these connections.

---

¹² Wolf, *Interpreting Isaiah*, 37-38.

¹³ Archer, *A Survey of Old Testament Introduction*, 336.

¹⁴ Wolf, *Interpreting Isaiah*, 12-13.

INTRODUCTION

The extra-biblical *Ascension of Isaiah* records a tradition that says Isaiah was killed by King Manasseh who reigned over Judah from 686-642 (with a co-regency beginning in 696). This tradition says that Manasseh had Isaiah put inside a hollow log and sawn in two (cf. Heb. 11:37). Since Isaiah records the death of Sennacherib in 37:37-38 (681 B.C.), it is fair to assume that he lived and prophesied until around 680 B.C.[15]

DATE AND HISTORICAL CONTEXT

The best estimate for Isaiah's ministry is that it stretched from 740-680 B.C., a tumultuous time for Israel because of the apostasy within the nation and also because of the advancing threat of the Assyrian empire. Pfeiffer notes,

> The high point of his political influence came in the crucial year 701 B.C. when the Assyrian invasion threatened to destroy the Kingdom of Judah and remove its inhabitants into slavery and exile. Through his intercession with God, the terrible danger was miraculously removed, and the remnants of Sennacherib's army fled.[16]

Israel faced two kinds of threats. One of these came from within the nation, but the other came from without by the threat of enemy invasions.

Trouble from within

The opening verse makes mention of four particular Judean kings who ruled during his ministry.[17] As noted by Martin,[18] "The reigns of these kings (including co-regencies) were: Uzziah (790–739),[19] Jotham (750–732),[20] Ahaz

---

[15] Archer, *A Survey of Old Testament Introduction*, 336.

[16] Charles F. Pfeiffer, *The Wycliffe Bible Commentary: The Old Testament*, cited in electronic form from Logos Libronix (Chicago: Moody Press, 1962).

[17] Isaiah's ministry began during the time of the divided monarchy (a division that came in 931 B.C.), but extended past the fall of the northern kingdom in 722.

[18] John A. Martin, "Isaiah," in *The Bible Knowledge Commentary: An Exposition of the Scriptures*, ed. J. F. Walvoord and R. B. Zuck, vol. 1, cited in electronic form from Logos Libronix (Wheaton, IL: Victor Books, 1985), 1027.

[19] Uzziah was a good king, though his pride became his undoing later in life when he tried to offer priestly incense, and God turned him into a leper (2 Kings 15:3-5; 2 Chron. 26:16-21).

[20] Jotham took over as a co-regent because of his father's leprosy. Like Uzziah, Jotham was a builder and a fighter. One of his downfalls was his own spiritual corruption and the corruption he allowed (2 Kings 15:34, 35; 2 Chron. 27:1-2).

(735–715),[21] and Hezekiah (715–686, with a co-regency that began in 729)." Hezekiah was not perfect, but arguably one of Judah's best kings.[22] Isaiah lived into the reign of Manasseh (686-642), but apparently did not have an active prophetic ministry during his reign. Manasseh was perhaps the worst of all the kings of Judah. The only ray of sunshine in Manasseh was a repentance that came later in life after a time in captivity (2 Kings 21; 2 Chron. 33). Although several of these kings demonstrated a certain amount of faith, their lack of complete trust would prove to be problematic for the nation. What the nation really needed was a wise king who would rule by the fear of the Lord. This was the only hope of the nation. This also was the promise that God had given to His people, a wise and just King who would deliver them not only from their physical enemies, but also from their own destructive sin (4:2; 7:13; 9:6-7; 11:1; 16:5; 22:22; 55:3).

The historical accounts in the Bible show that this era was prosperous outwardly due to strong leadership in both the northern and southern kingdoms (2

---

[21] Ahaz was a worthless king spiritually. On the positive side, he did reject a deal by Israel and Syria to join their alliance against Assyria (7:6; cf. 2 Kings 16:5), but he was quick to form a foreign alliance with Assyria because it was expedient (2 Kings 16:7). Assyria broke the deal and invaded Judah after overthrowing Gaza, Galilee, and Gilead, overthrowing Damascus in 732 and Samaria in 722. Samaria's fall resulted in many Jews being taken captive (2 Kings 17) and foreigners being settled there under Esarhaddon in 671, making the roots of the Samaritan people group (cf. Ezra 4:2). His fascination with Assyria led him to make an Assyrian altar in the temple (2 Kings 16:10-16; 2 Chron. 28:3).

[22] Spiritual reform was high on his priority list (2 Kings 18:4, 22; 2 Chron. 30:1). Hezekiah was forced at one point to pay tribute to Sennacherib (2 Kings 18:14), but he later resisted Assyria, trusted God, and was delivered (2 Kings 18:7). Assyria came in 701 and captured 46 Judean cities before laying siege to Jerusalem, but God struck the armies with a great plague that destroyed 185,000 of the Assyrian army (Isa. 36:2-37:8; cf. 2 Kings 18:17-19:8). The Greek historian Herodotus said that field mice invaded the Assyrian camps, bringing what might have been a fast-moving bubonic plague. The key point is that Isaiah and Hezekiah trusted the Lord, and the Lord delivered them (2 Kings 19:9ff.; Is. 37:9ff.). When an illness brought Hezekiah to the point of death in roughly 701, he prayed for healing and God gave him 15 more years till 686 (Isa. 38; cf. 2 Kings 20:1). After his recovery, Hezekiah proudly showed his treasures to Merodach-Baladan of Babylon who had congratulated him on his recovery and was seeking an alliance against Assyria (Isa. 39; cf. 2 Kings 20:12ff.). God told Hezekiah that these same Babylonians would one day be the ones to take these treasures away.

Kings 15-21; 2 Chron. 26-33). Under the reigns of Jeroboam II in the north (782-752) and Uzziah in the south (768-715) the economy was strong. In terms of defense, Uzziah had mounted a successful campaign against the Philistines and destroyed a number of their chief cities (2 Chron. 26:6). In terms of economic growth, Uzziah built a caravan route along the Mediterranean, and a significant port at Eilat at Red Sea (2 Chron. 26:2). He also fortified the walls of Jerusalem (26:9) and commissioned water projects and military outposts in the Negeb. Despite the external prosperity, they were also times of great apostasy. Idolatry was rampant, and social sins of injustice and oppression were rampant (Isa. 2:6-8; 5:8-10; cf. Micah and Hosea and Amos).[23]

Trouble from without

Outside the nation, a brief period of foreign weakness in the first half of the eighth century B.C. had allowed Israel to thrive, but all of that was quickly changing. Assyria was growing in power and beginning to push its empire westward, and Judah would soon face these Assyrian threats. During the ministry of Isaiah, Assyria was the most significant threat to both Israel and Judah.

Assyria's westward push

Tiglath Pileser III (aka Pul, 745-727) began pushing westward, conquering nations and deporting many. When he arrived at the Mediterranean coast, Menahem of Israel brought him tribute (2 Kings 15:19), along with Rezin of Aram. An anti-Assyrian coalition formed between Israel and Aram which resulted in these two powers attacking Judah in 735 for not joining their alliance. Their desire was to overthrow the Davidic dynasty and replace Ahaz with someone who would be loyal to this anti-Assyrian alliance (Isa. 7; cf. 2 Kings 16:2-6, ca. 734 B.C.). Against the impassioned protests of Isaiah (7:4, 16-17; 8:4-8; cf. 2 Kings 16:7-9), Ahaz paid tribute to Tiglath-Pileser to help him resist Israel and Syria. In 732 Assyria invaded Aram and Israel, and it was not long after this that Judah also became a vassal to Assyria (2 Kings 16:10; 2 Chron. 28:16, 20-22).

Tiglath-Pileser's successor was Shalmaneser V (727-722). Little is known about him except that he besieged Samaria for three years after Hoshea refused to pay tribute (2 Kings 17:3-5). According to 2 Kings 17:6; 18:9-12, the city finally fell to Shalmaneser who died at the time of the conquest. His successor was Sargon II (722-705), the one who actually took credit for bringing Samaria down (an Assyrian

---

[23] Wolf, *Interpreting Isaiah*, 18.

inscription speaks of his deporting 27,290). Second Kings 17 tells us that when Samaria fell, Hezekiah was tempted to join in a rebellion against Sargon when he attacked in Gaza, but Isaiah warned against this (ch. 18). In the meantime, Merodach-Baladan (721-710) was rising up in Babylon along with help from Elam, Assyria's enemy to the east. Sargon went to fight battles there, driving Merodach-Baladan from Babylon in 710, only to return some years later and regain power in 703.[24]

The siege of Jerusalem

Sennacherib (705-681) was the king of Assyria who attacked Hezekiah in 701 B.C. after subduing the Philistine plain and 46 cities of Judah (2 Kings 18-20). Hezekiah made many preparations for this attack (Isa. 22:8-11; 2 Kings 20:20; 2 Chron. 20:31-8, 30). The Prism of Sennacherib describes the siege against Judah and Jerusalem as he hemmed them in.

> As to Hezekiah, the Jew, he did not submit to my yoke. I laid siege to forty-six of his strong cities, walled forts, and to the countless small villages in their vicinity, and conquered them.... I drove out of them 200,150 people, young and old, male and female, horses, mules, donkeys, camels, big and small cattle beyond counting, and considered them booty. Himself I made a prisoner in Jerusalem, his royal residence, like a bird in a cage. I put watch posts closely round the city, and turned back to his fate anyone who came out of the city gate.[25]

This Assyrian account is a mirror of what we see in 2 Kings 18:13, including the account of his defeat of Lachish on the walls of the palace in Nineveh. Second Kings 18:17-37 describes how the Assyrian envoys used psychological warfare to try and get Judah to surrender. Despite the desperate situation, Isaiah and Hezekiah trusted the Lord, and the Lord delivered them from the hand of Sennacherib. Second Kings 19:37 tells us that eventually Sennacherib was murdered by his own sons: "It came about as he was worshiping in the house of Nisroch his god, that Adrammelech and Sharezer killed him with the sword; and they escaped into the land of Ararat. And Esarhaddon his son became king in his place."

---

[24] Merodach-Baladan is the Babylonian king who sent emissaries to Hezekiah to congratulate him on his recovery and seek assistance against Assyria (Isa. 39; cf. 2 Kings 20:12-19).
[25] Wolf, *Interpreting Isaiah*, 23-24.

INTRODUCTION

The fall of Assyria

Assyrian threats continued until later when the Medes joined Nabopolassar of Babylon to overthrow Nineveh in 612. This ended the tyranny of Assyria, but it also began the rise of Neo-Babylon who would eventually overthrow Judah under Nebuchadnezzar in 605 (cf. chs. 36-39).

What is the lesson in all this history?

One main lesson is that God exalts His people who trust Him. However, He also turns against those who refuse to believe. Because of their faithlessness, God allowed Israel to fall to enemy invasions, but their fall is not the end of the story. God not only promised judgment, but He also swore that one day He would restore them in the messianic Kingdom.

MAJOR THEOLOGICAL THEMES AND PURPOSES

Isaiah is a prophecy that is rich in theology, especially messianic prophecy. As Archer puts it, "Deeper Christological insights are to be found in his work than anywhere else in the Old Testament."[26]

Direct and indirect messianic predictions

Among these are: (1) the coming King (4:2; 7:10-15; 9:1-7; 11:1-16; 14:28-32; 22:15-25; 24:21-25; 32:1-8; 33:17-24), (2) an anointed Conqueror (55:3-5; 61:1-6; 63:1-6), (3) the Branch (4:1-4), (4) the Foundation (28:16), (5) the Teacher (30:19-26), and (6) the Servant (42:1-9; 49:1-13; 50:4-11; 52:13-53:12). Isaiah is filled with numerous prophecies about the coming messianic kingdom.

Other theological themes

Notable themes include: (1) the holiness of God (1:4; 5:16; 30:9-16; 37:23; 48:17-19; 57:15-21), (2) the title the "The Holy One of Israel" (found 25 times), (3) divine sovereignty (6; 24:1-3, 23; 37:15-20; 43:8-11; 46:8-11), (4) God's hatred of pride (2:11-18; 14:12-15; 37:23-25; 47:8-11; 66:1-3), and (5) God's hatred of idolatry (cf. e.g., ch. 44).

---

[26] Archer, *A Survey of Old Testament Introduction*, 333.

ISAIAH: THE LORD SAVES

The purpose

As with most of the prophets, at a most-basic level, one can identify a two-fold message: (1) God's warning to Israel to turn from their sin and to trust and follow Him, and (2) God's promise that even though they were going to experience an invasion and exile, God would one day restore them by sending them the promised Son of David. Terrible times were coming, but this is not going to mean the end of the nation. One day God will send the Promised One. Their calling was to believe in Him.

Summary and application

At this point, we can suggest at least two initial lessons for application. First, we see that God is always faithful and we can always trust Him. Second, we are reminded of this corollary truth that God will always fulfill His promises. Ultimately, this promise is that God will purge this world of sin and curse when He brings His kingdom. Yes, we will have trouble in this world (John 16:33), but we can always find rest in knowing that God uses trials and suffering to mold us into the image of His Son (Rom. 8:29).

SUGGESTED OUTLINE

Different outlines have been proposed for Isaiah. The following outline provides a reasonable picture of the structure. The chapter outlines provided in this book are organized around this more-detailed exegetical outline below with minor variations to create better chapter flows:

Section I: Various prophecies of judgment (1:1-39:8)
    Against Jerusalem and Judah (1:1-12:6)
        Judah's social sin (1:1-6:13)
        Judah's bad politics (7:1-12:6)
    Oracles of judgment and salvation (13:1-23:18)
        Babylon and Assyria (13:1-14:27)
        Philistia (14:28-32)
        Moab (15:1-16:14)
        Syria and Israel (17:1-14)
        Ethiopia (18:1-7)
        Egypt (19:1-20:6)
        Babylon (21:1-10)
        Edom (21:11-12)
        Arabia (21:13-17)
        Jerusalem (22:1-25)

INTRODUCTION

- Tyre (23:1-18)
- Redemption of Israel through worldwide judgment (24:1-27:13)
  - Devastation to the earth (24:1-23)
  - First song of thanksgiving for redemption (25:1-12)
  - Second song of thanksgiving for redemption (26:1-19)
  - Israel's chastisement and final prosperity (26:20-27:13)
- Warnings against alliances with Egypt (28:1-35:10)
  - Woe to drunken leaders (28:1-29)
  - Woe to religious formalists (29:1-14)
  - Woe to those who hide plans from God (29:15-24)
  - Woe to the pro-Egyptian army (30:1-33)
  - Woe to those who trust in horses and chariots (31:1-32:20)
  - Woe to the Assyrian destroyer (33:1-24)
  - A cry for justice against the nations, especially Edom (34:1-35:10)
- Transitional historical narrative (36:1-39:8)
  - Sennacherib's attempt to capture Jerusalem (36:1-37:38)
  - Hezekiah's sickness and recovery (38:1-22)
  - Babylonian emissaries to Jerusalem (39:1-8)

Section II: God's future salvation that is coming to earth (40:1-66:24)

- Deliverance from captivity (40:1-48:22)
  - Comfort to the Babylonian exiles (40:1-31)
  - The end of Israel's misery (41:1-48:22)
- Sufferings of the Servant (49:1-57:21)
  - The Servant's mission (49:1-52:12)
  - Redemption by the suffering of the Servant (52:13-53:12)
  - Results of the Suffering Servant's redemption (54:1-57:21)
- Future glory for God's people (58:1-66:24)
  - Two kinds of religion (58:1-14)
  - Plea for Israel to forsake sin (59:1-19)
  - Future blessedness of Zion (59:20-61:11)
  - Nearing of Zion's deliverance (62:1-63:6)
  - Prayer for Zion's deliverance (63:7-64:12)
  - The Lord's answer to the supplication (65:1-66:24)

2
JUDGMENT AND SALVATION MESSAGES TO JERUSALEM AND JUDAH, PART 1
(1:1-6:13)

Some people are shocked at the idea that God could hate religion, but this is what we see in Isaiah 1. However, it is not religious activity in itself that is the problem, for God Himself gives many commands for various kinds of religious duties. The problem comes when people carry out religious ritual that is divorced from a right relationship with God.

GOD'S CONDEMNATION OF HIS RELIGIOUS PEOPLE (1:1-31)

In this chapter, God confronts His people using what we would call courtroom language.[1] So to speak, He brings charges against people who know better than to practice empty religion, but do so because they refuse to turn from their sin.

Chapter 1 reads as follows: "The vision of Isaiah the son of Amoz concerning Judah and Jerusalem, which he saw during the reigns of Uzziah, Jotham, Ahaz *and* Hezekiah, kings of Judah. 2 Listen, O heavens, and hear, O earth, for the Lord speaks. Sons I have reared and brought up, but they have revolted against Me. 3 An ox knows its owner, and a donkey its master's manger, *but* Israel does not know; My people do not understand. 4 Alas, sinful nation, people weighed down with iniquity, offspring of evildoers, sons who act corruptly! They have abandoned the Lord; they have despised the Holy One of Israel; they have turned away from Him. 5 Where will you be stricken again as you continue in *your* rebellion? The whole head is sick and the whole heart is faint. 6 From

---

[1] Herbert M. Wolf, *Interpreting Isaiah* (Grand Rapids: Zondervan, 1985), 73.

the sole of the foot even to the head, there is nothing sound in it, *only* bruises, welts and raw wounds, not pressed out or bandaged, nor softened with oil. 7 Your land is desolate; your cities are burned with fire; your fields—strangers are devouring them in your presence; it is desolation, as overthrown by strangers. 8 The daughter of Zion is left like a shelter in a vineyard, like a watchman's hut in a cucumber field, like a besieged city. 9 Unless the Lord of hosts had left us a few survivors, we would be like Sodom, we would be like Gomorrah. 10 Hear the word of the Lord, You rulers of Sodom; give ear to the instruction of our God, you people of Gomorrah. 11 What are your multiplied sacrifices to Me? says the Lord. I have had enough of burnt offerings of ram and the fat of fed cattle; and I take no pleasure in the blood of bulls, lambs or goats. 12 When you come to appear before Me, who requires of you this trampling of My courts? 13 Bring your worthless offerings no longer; incense is an abomination to Me. New moon and sabbath, the calling of assemblies—I cannot endure iniquity and the solemn assembly. 14 I hate your new moon *festivals* and your appointed feasts; they have become a burden to Me; I am weary of bearing *them*. 15 So when you spread out your hands *in prayer*, I will hide My eyes from you; yes, even though you multiply prayers, I will not listen. Your hands are covered with blood. 16 Wash yourselves; make yourselves clean; remove the evil of your deeds from My sight. Cease to do evil. 17 Learn to do good; seek justice; reprove the ruthless; defend the orphan; plead for the widow. 18 Come now, and let us reason together, says the Lord, though your sins are as scarlet, they will be as white as snow; though they are red like crimson, they will be like wool. 19 If you consent and obey, you will eat the best of the land, 20 but if you refuse and rebel, you will be devoured by the sword. Truly, the mouth of the Lord has spoken. 21 How the faithful city has become a harlot, she *who* was full of justice! Righteousness once lodged in her, but now murderers. 22 Your silver has become dross; your drink diluted with water; 23 your rulers are rebels and companions of thieves; everyone loves a bribe and chases after rewards. They do not defend the orphan, nor does the widow's plea come before them. 24 Therefore the Lord God of hosts, the Mighty One of Israel, declares, Ah, I will be relieved of My adversaries and avenge Myself on My foes. 25 I will also turn My hand against you, and will smelt away your dross as with lye and will remove all your alloy. 26 Then I will restore your judges as at the first, and your counselors as at the beginning; after that you will be called the city of righteousness, a faithful city. 27 Zion will be redeemed with justice and her repentant ones with righteousness, 28 but transgressors and sinners will be crushed together, and those who forsake the Lord will come to an end. 29 Surely you will be ashamed of the oaks which you have desired, and you will be embarrassed at the gardens which you have chosen, 30 for you will be like an oak whose leaf fades away or as a garden that has no water. 31 The strong man will become tinder, his work also a spark. Thus they shall both burn together and there will be none to quench *them*" (1:1-31).

One way of dividing up this chapter is into three courtroom scenes: (1) the court's charge: God hates dead religion (vv. 1-17), (2) the court's mandate: Recognize the difference between dead religion and genuine righteousness (vv. 18-20), and (3) the court's sentence: Israel's dead religion demands swift and severe punishment (vv. 21-31).

First scene: The court's charge: God hates dead religion (vv. 1-17)

God tells His people that they have abandoned Him, and God will not accept their dead religion. Judgment is coming, but His true desire is that they would turn back to Him.

This is a prophetic message from God to man (v. 1)

God's message comes through the human source called Isaiah, but the reality is that this is a prophetic vision from the Lord Himself. We will first consider the divine character of this message.

The heavenly source of the vision. Isaiah identifies his message as a vision. A "vision" (*chazon*) can refer to something seen with physical eyes (cf. 33:20; 57:8), but in prophetic contexts it refers to perception in the human mind through the working of God's Spirit (cf. Obad. 1:1; Nah. 1:1), sometimes in the form of theophanies (Exod. 24:11; Job 19:26, 27; Pss. 11:7; 17:15).

The human source of the vision. Some traditions have suggested that Amoz was the brother of King Amaziah, the Father of Uzziah, but this is not certain. Isaiah had access to the royal court, suggesting that he may have been of the family of David.

The focus of the vision. The focus of his message was concerning Judah and Jerusalem. It was not many years earlier that Jonah took God's message to Assyria to call Nineveh to repentance (and they did), and only a short time earlier that Amos took God's message to the northern monarchy (which they ignored). Micah was a contemporary of Isaiah who took his message to Judah, but he had no positive response either. God is patient and desires men to live (cf. Ezek. 18:23, 30, 32), so God also sent Isaiah.

The time of the vision. Isaiah's ministry came during the days of four particular kings of Judah. Uzziah reigned from 790-739. Chapter 6 indicates that Isaiah's ministry began somewhere near the death of Uzziah. Uzziah was a good king, though pride became his undoing when he tried to offer incense and God turned him into a leper (2 Kings 15:3-5; 2 Chron. 26:16-21). To his credit, he did what was right in the eyes of the Lord (2 Chron. 26:4) and gave wise leadership. Uzziah built a strong military and developed a port for commerce at Eilat on the Red Sea (2 Chron. 26:3-15).

Jotham reigned from 750-731, taking over as a co-regent because of his father's leprosy. Jotham was also a builder, but his major failure was his own spiritual corruption and his willingness to allow such corruption to remain within the land (2 Kings 15:34; 2 Chron. 27:1-2).

Ahaz reigned from 735-715, but he was not a man of faith. When threatened by an overthrow from Syria and Israel, he did not trust Yahweh but paid the king of Assyria to save him from Syria and Israel (2 Kings 16:7-9). Despite a temporary intervention, this bribe did not stop Assyria from eventually invading. Ahaz sinned badly by having an Assyrian altar placed in the Jerusalem temple (2 Kings 16:10-16; 2 Chron. 28:3).

Hezekiah was a man of God. There is debate about the exact dates of his reign. One view is that he ruled from roughly 726-698 (29 years). Another view is that he reigned 715 to 686. Another view is that Hezekiah was a co-regent from 726–716 and sole king from 716–698.[2] Steinmann notes that Kitchen and Mitchell (*The New Bible Dictionary*), "propose to harmonize the synchronizations presented in 2 Kings 17 and 18 by postulating a thirteen-year co-regency of Hezekiah with his father Ahaz. This view is favored by Harrison as well [giving a 43+ year reign from 729-686]."[3] The Tyndale Bible Dictionary notes that,

> The chronology of Hezekiah's reign is difficult to establish with certainty. The Bible says the Assyrian siege of Samaria, capital of the northern kingdom of Israel, began in the fourth year of his reign and that Samaria fell in the sixth year (2 Kgs 18:9–10), which would make his reign begin about 728 bc and end about 699 bc. Assyrian king Sennacherib besieged the fortified Judean cities during Hezekiah's 14th year (2 Kgs 18:13), which would have been 714 bc. Assyrian records, however, indicate that Sennacherib came to the Assyrian throne in 705 bc and that his Judean campaign took place in 701 bc. The most generally accepted solution to the discrepancy is that Hezekiah came to the throne in 715 bc, probably after a co-regency with his father, Ahaz, that began in 728 bc.[4]

The precise dates of Hezekiah's reign are not a settled issue, but this has little bearing on the ultimate interpretation of Isaiah's messages. The present author sees 729-686 as the best understanding for the full reign.

---

[2] Charles F. Pfeiffer, *The Wycliffe Bible Commentary: Old Testament*, cited in electronic form with Logos Libronix (Chicago: Moody Press, 1962), Is 1:1.

[3] Andrew E. Steinmann, "The Chronology of 2 Kings 15-18," *JETS* 30:4 (1987): 393.

[4] Walter A. Elwell and Philip Wesley Comfort, *Tyndale Bible Dictionary*, Tyndale Reference Library, cited in electronic form in Logos Libronix (Wheaton, IL: Tyndale House Publishers, 2001), 601.

As noted earlier, Hezekiah was a godly man known for his reformation efforts (2 Kings 18:4, 22; 2 Chron. 30:1). Also notable was the way that Hezekiah trusted God when Assyria besieged Jerusalem and God delivered them (Isa. 37:9ff.; cf. 2 Kings 19:9ff.). Also notable was the way that God granted Hezekiah fifteen additional years of life when Hezekiah pleaded for healing, presumably from 703/2-686 B.C. (Isa. 38; cf. 2 Kings 20:1). The last notable detail in Hezekiah came after Hezekiah's recovery when Merodach-Baladan of Babylon sent messengers to congratulate Hezekiah on his recovery.[5] In his pride, Hezekiah showed the messengers his treasures. God told Hezekiah that it would be the Babylonians who would one day take these treasures away.

From within the Bible, the context of Isaiah is found within Israel's historical books (2 Kings 15-21; 2 Chron. 26-33). In general, this was a period of both prosperity and apostasy. Chapter 1 is probably the beginning of Isaiah's prophetic ministry right around 740 B.C. and it continued to about the year 680.

God lays out His case against Israel (vv. 2-17)

One thing that is clear is that God is very angry with His people. Isaiah lays out the case in verses 2-17 by exposing three major failures.

Israel's first failure: Israel failed to know her own God (vv. 2-3). Using courtroom language, God calls heaven and earth as witnesses that His people have forgotten Him. One finds similar courtroom language in various portions of the Old Testament (cf. e.g., Mic. 6; Ps. 50:3-23). The background for this courtroom language may come from Deuteronomy, especially the Song of Moses (Deut. 32) where God warned Israel about a future apostasy.[6]

The rebellion (v. 2: "revolted," *pāšaʻ*) is serious. Martin notes that this term "was often used in political treaties to describe a vassal state's disobedience to the covenant with its suzerain."[7] For Israel, it is even worse since Yahweh is

---

[5] Merodach-Baladan was also attempting to get Hezekiah to join an alliance against Assyria (Isa. 39; 2 Kings 20:12ff.).

[6] The flow of the background includes the following: (1) God announced these truths long before (30:15-19). (2) God warned the nation through Moses (31:14-16). (3) God told them He would judge (31:17-18). (4) God told Moses to write a song as a witness (31:19ff.). (5) God's faithfulness is always true (32:1-14). (6) The nation's rejection of the Lord will one day come (32:15-22). (7) God's rejection of the nation will be a certain response (32:23-27). (8) The folly of the people was predicted beforehand (32:28-43).

[7] John A. Martin, "Isaiah," in *The Bible Knowledge Commentary: An Exposition of the*

also their Father (Exod. 4:21-22) who has faithfully raised them up, even bringing them out of the slavery of Egypt. The description continues as God likens their rebellion as worse than an ox or donkey. Animals know their masters, but Israel does not know her God.

Israel's second failure: The failure to reap the blessings of covenant obedience (vv. 4-9). Instead of having the blessings of a proper relationship with her covenant God (cf. Deut. 28:1-14), Israel was now experiencing the curses of that covenant (Deut. 28:15-68). Here in vv. 4-9 we find three descriptions of Israel that highlight this failure.

Verse 4 describes the extreme misery the nation brought upon itself: "Alas, sinful nation, people weighed down with iniquity, offspring of evildoers, sons who act corruptly! They have abandoned the Lord; they have despised the Holy One of Israel; they have turned away from Him." Pfeiffer notes that this name "the Holy One of Israel,"

> is the most significant title employed by the prophet Isaiah [used 26 times in Isaiah]. In chapter 6 Jehovah reveals himself in a scene of heavenly glory as the Holy One (*Qādôsh*), i.e., the transcendent God, who is wholly separate from the frailty and finiteness of Creation (his majesty-holiness), and wholly separate from the sinfulness and defilement of man (his purity-holiness). But this Holy One has claimed the family of Abraham, Isaac, and Jacob as his covenant children. He has given himself to them and they have given themselves to him in a covenant undertaken nationally, on their part, and solemnized before Mount Sinai (Ex 19:5-8) ... Because he is the Holy One of Israel, he could not stand idly.[8]

From a familial perspective, Israel is completely faithless to her Father. Nevertheless, God still calls them "sons" even though they have "abandoned" (divorce in Mal. 2:15), "despised" (to look contemptuously on[9]), and "turned away" from the Lord (Isa. 30:1, 9; cf. Jer. 4:22; 2 Chron. 27:2).[10] Oswalt notes,

> What this points up is the intimate connection between the moral life and one's relationship to God. Morality without submission to the One from

---

Scriptures, ed. J. F. Walvoord and R. B. Zuck, vol. 1, cited in electronic form from Logos Libronix (Wheaton, IL: Victor Books, 1985), 1034.

[8] Pfeiffer, *The Wycliffe Bible Commentary: Old Testament*, Is 1:4. See the following passages for "The Holy One" (1:4, 5, 19, 24; 6:1ff.; 10:7, 20; 12:6; 17:7; 29:19, 23; 30:11, 12, 15; 31:1; 37:23; 40:25; 41:14, 16, 20; 43:3, 14, 15; 45:11; 47:4; 48:17; 49:7; 54:5; 55:5; 60:9, 14; only 6X in rest of OT).

[9] Ludwig Koehler et al., *The Hebrew And Aramaic Lexicon of the Old Testament*, cited in electronic form with Logos Libronix (Leiden: E.J. Brill, 1994–2000), 658.

[10] Edward J. Young, *The Book of Isaiah, vol. 1* (Grand Rapids: Eerdmans, 1965), 46.

whom morality stems may be merely another form of human pride. On the other hand, sin and evil, guilt and corruption, cannot be avoided when the vital link with the personal Lord is removed.[11]

The failure continues in verses 5-6. Because of its rebellion (*sarah*), the nation now looks like someone who has been beaten mercilessly with no one to give medical care (vv. 5-6). God asks the rhetorical question, "Where will you be stricken again?" In other words, where else can your body be struck more than it already has been? The nation is destroying itself with its sin. With descriptions like "the whole head is sick and the whole heart is faint," we get our first glimpse of the symbolism of sin and its consequences as being described by the imagery of sickness (Heb. *holiy*).[12] Sin has made the nation sick and faint (cf. Jer. 8:18; Lam. 1:22; Job 6:7). It is not just the head, though, for God says, "from the sole of the foot even to the head, there is nothing sound in it, *only* bruises, welts and raw wounds, not pressed out or bandaged, nor softened with oil."[13] The nation is incapable of saving itself from ruin, and humanly speaking there was no hope. Nevertheless, God's plan is that one day He will heal the "welts" (*chaburah*) of His people by placing one giant welt upon His Son who would give Himself to take away their sin (cf. Isa. 53:5).

The desperate situation continues in verses 7-9. Alexander explains, "The prophet brings distinctly into view foreign invasions as the instrument of vengeance, and describes the country as already desolated."[14] Israel and Judah were already beginning to feel the pain of foreign invasions. Among these were invasions from Egypt, Aram, Edom, and Philistia (cf. 2 Chron. 28:5-18), but the worst would come from Assyria and Babylon. These verses vividly show the devastation by making four verbless declarations: (1) the land has been stripped and made desolate; (2) the cities have been burned with fire; (3) the fields have been ravaged by the enemy; (4) all of it has become a desolation, overthrown by strangers (cf. Deut. 29:23).

Pitiful Jerusalem, i.e., the Daughter of Zion (Isa. 1:8; 10:32; Jer. 4:31; Lam.

---

[11] John N. Oswalt, *The Book of Isaiah, 1-39* (Grand Rapids: Eerdmans, 1986), 87.

[12] Especially notable is that God's Servant will one day become personally acquainted with such sickness (53:3) coming in human flesh to take the punishment for this sin/sickness upon Himself (53:4) as Yahweh crushes Him as a guilt offering in the place of His people (53:10).

[13] Common treatment would have included squeezing out infection followed by the pouring of oil and wrapping with bandages. No one has come to clean and wrap these wounds (cf. Hos. 5:13), but it is her own fault (Deut. 28:35).

[14] Joseph A. Alexander, *Commentary on Isaiah* (Grand Rapids: Kregel, 1992), 84.

1:6; 2:13; Mic. 1:13; 4:8; Zeph. 3:14; Zech. 9:9),[15] is now left like, "a shelter in a vineyard, like a watchman's hut in a cucumber field [cf. Job 27:18], like a besieged city." These structures were "temporary structures built to shade from the sun persons who guarded the crops against thieves and animals. Such huts were usually 'alone' and easily attacked."[16]

Humanly speaking the situation was hopeless,[17] but with Yahweh there is always hope. Isaiah thus declares, "Unless the Lord of hosts had left us a few survivors, we would be like Sodom; we would be like Gomorrah" (v. 9; cf. Gen. 19:24-29). Many generations would fall under the curses of the covenant, but this will not mean the end of Israel. By His own faithfulness (Gen. 12:1-3; 15; 35:9-12), Yahweh will not let His people become like Sodom and Gomorrah, for even in wrath there will be mercy (cf. Hab. 3:2), and God will restore His remnant (Isa. 10:20-23; cf. Rom. 9:29; 11:29).[18]

Israel's third failure: Israel failed to uphold true righteousness that is by faith (vv. 10-17). The rebuke begins in verse 10 when God gives a twofold, parallel call to listen. God likens Israel to Sodom and Gomorrah.[19] Israel had a sacrificial system that was commanded by Moses himself, but their religion was unacceptable because it was not out of faith. Oswalt explains, "In respect to the word and the teaching of not merely God, but their own God, they are no different from Sodom and Gomorrah."[20] In vv. 11-17 God singles out eight religious works they practiced with zeal, but could not bring them to God.

The first dead ritual was the "burnt offerings of rams." The burnt offering was an offering totally offered up on the altar, an offering that symbolically conveyed the idea of total consecration. Alexander explains:

> Male animals are mentioned, as the only ones admitted in the *alah* or burnt offerings; the fat and blood, as the parts in which the sacrifice essentially

---

[15] It is hermeneutically illegitimate to treat the name Zion (or Daughter of Zion or Virgin Daughter of Zion) allegorically by treating it as meaning heaven.

[16] Martin, "Isaiah," 1035.

[17] The problem is never that God is powerless to save (cf. 2 Kings 6:15-18).

[18] This is not the usual word "remnant," but means "one who has escaped" (*sarid*, someone fleeing and escaping death). See similar ideas in other passages (Isa. 1:27; 2:2-4; 4:2; 7:3; 10:18-23; 11:11, 16; 46:3; cf. Joel 2:32).

[19] God lambastes His people with these two expressions that would have curdled the blood of the self-righteous Jews (cf. Jer. 23:14; Rev. 11:8).

[20] Oswalt, *The Book of Isaiah, Chapters 1-39*, 96.

consisted, the one being always burnt upon the altar and the other sprinkled or poured around it.[21]

The second dead ritual was the "fat of fed cattle." This speaks about cattle that have been fattened up nice and plump for sacrifice. At the very least, it shows the religious zeal of the people. None of this, however, was out of faith, and therefore none of it was acceptable.

The third, fourth, and fifth dead rituals that God would not accept included the "blood of *bulls*," the "blood of *lambs*," and the "blood of *goats*." Martin comments, "the people assumed that merely by offering sacrifices at the altar they would be made ceremonially clean before God,"[22] but as God makes clear, such is not the case. God takes no pleasure in religion if it does not come out of a right relationship (v. 12).[23] Pfeiffer explains,

> These verses do not represent rejection of the validity of blood sacrifices (as some scholars have argued), for such an interpretation would entail also rejection of prayer (cf. v. 15). Rather, they make clear that even right and proper forms of worship are utterly offensive to the Lord when presented by unrepentant worshipers.[24]

Isaiah outlines a sixth, seventh, and eighth kind of ritual He would not accept. God tells them (1) to stop bringing their offerings (*minchah*, cf. Amos 5:21-27; Mic. 6:6), (2) that their incense (*qetoroth*) is an abomination, and (3) that all of their festivals (e.g., New Moon, Sabbath, Sacred Assemblies) are a burden. God did command these rituals (Exod. 20:8-11; 31:12-18; Lev. 23; Num. 10:10; 28:11), but as we see in Psalm 24:4 God does not accept worship from unclean hands and impure hearts. The problem, explains Wolf, was not the quantity of worship but the quality.[25] Thus, God wanted no more worship from them until they turn from their sins (vv. 15-17; cf. 8:17; 59:2; Ps. 32:6; Mic. 3:4).[26]

---

[21] Alexander, *Commentary on Isaiah*, 86.

[22] Martin, "Isaiah," 1035.

[23] We find a similar rejection of sacrifices elsewhere (1 Sam. 15:22-23; Ps. 51:16-17; Jer. 7:21-23; Hos. 6:6; Amos 5:22-24; Mic. 6:6-8). The key to acceptable worship is that it comes through repentant faith (1 Kings 8:23-53).

[24] Pfeiffer, *The Wycliffe Bible Commentary: Old Testament*, Is 1:11.

[25] Wolf, *Interpreting Isaiah*, 75.

[26] Blood is not necessarily a reference to physical blood, though this idea can be embraced by the expression. The idea is often that of violent injustice against others, i.e., doing hateful and violent injustice with what is effectively social murder. Many prophets mention such sin (Isa. 10:1-2; 58:6-7; 59:3; cf. Ezek. 9:9; 36:18; Mic. 3:10; Hab.

Throughout history, two of the most vulnerable classes of people have been widows and orphans. If the people really wanted to please God, they could start by loving and helping those who needed it most. Such deeds would be great outward marks of a truly changed heart (James 1:27). The religion God will accept must come from a changed life (cf. Isa. 66:18). Alexander explains, "It is religion which leaves iniquity unchallenged and unchanged that the prophet and, more importantly, God detest."[27]

Isaiah was not alone in calling Israel to repentance, for we find the same message in other prophets (cf. Mic. 6:8; Amos 5:21-24). The New Testament also shows that this is still the same message that applies today (Matt. 9:13; 12:7; James 1:27). True religion is a religion that produces changed lives (James 2:18), and if someone does not come to God with a pure heart, their religion is not acceptable (James 1:26).

Second scene: The court's mandate: A call to repentance (vv. 18-20)

The situation was grave, but still not hopeless.[28] God gives the people a three-fold ultimatum meant to offer them hope: (1) an invitation to repent (v. 18), (2) the promise for a right response (v. 19), and (3) a warning if they do not respond as they should (v. 20).

The invitation to repentance (v. 18)

This call to repentance should not be taken to mean, as suggested by some, that unsaved men have within themselves a spiritual capacity for reasoning themselves into a right relationship with God. The concept of reasoning together (a Niphal stem of *yakach*) carries the idea of disputing the legal case toward the goal of making a right judgment (cf. Gen. 20:16; Job 23:7).[29] God is pleading with His people to listen to His rebuke and repent. As Young describes it, what we have here is the "gracious condescension" of an amazing God,

---

2:12). The effective idea is that God is calling His people to true repentance. Isaiah's use of the Masoretic Text's Hithpael stem carries the force of "make yourself clean" (Oswalt, *The Book of Isaiah, Chapters 1-39*, 93).

[27] Alexander, *Commentary on Isaiah*, 97.

[28] Wolf, *Interpreting Isaiah*, 75.

[29] Ludwig Koehler et al., *The Hebrew and Aramaic Lexicon of the Old Testament*, cited in electronic form with Logos Libronix (Leiden: E.J. Brill, 1994–2000), 410.

calling His people to respond before it is too late.[30] God has exposed their sin, and now they are responsible to turn from it before it is too late.[31]

The promise that if they will repent, He will cleanse (v. 19)

By His grace, the sins that are scarlet and red will be white as snow and wool. The condition, however, is that there must be a true repentance. If they consent and obey, God will let them remain and be blessed (cf. Deut. 28:1-14)."[32] All they have to do is "consent to hear."[33] These promises remind us of timeless principles that relate to all of us. If we turn away from God, we can expect His displeasure, but if we will obey Him, we will always find forgiveness and restoration (cf. 1 John 1:9).

God's warning (v. 20)

Once again, the words of Isaiah flow out of the teaching God gave in the Law (Deut. 28:26, 25-36, 45ff., 64; 32:42). If they obey, they will find blessing, but if they do not, invaders will take them into exile. As Pfeiffer explains, "The destiny of the people depended upon their response."[34]

Third scene: The court's sentence: Judgment must fall (vv. 21-31)

Sadly, Israel is not going to listen, so judgment will come. It would be nice to see Judah repent and find blessing, and this is what God wants them to do (cf. Ezek. 18:23, 30-31). However, the tragic reality is that no matter what God says Judah will not repent.[35] Therefore, swift judgment is the only option. In

---

[30] Young, *The Book of Isaiah, vol. 1*, 77.
[31] If they will respond, they will find grace and healing (cf. Hos. 5:14-6:3).
[32] G. W. Grogan, "Isaiah," in *The Expositor's Bible Commentary*, ed. Frank E. Gaebelein, vol. 6 (Grand Rapids: Zondervan, 1986), 31.
[33] Cited by Alexander, *Commentary on Isaiah*, 90.
[34] Pfeiffer, *The Wycliffe Bible Commentary: Old Testament*, Is 1:19.
[35] A century later Jeremiah will denounce Judah for their miserable condition: "Can the Ethiopian change his skin or the leopard his spots? *Then* you also can do good who are accustomed to doing evil" (Jer. 13:23; cf. Hos. 4:4 with a similar rebuke to the northern kingdom: "Their deeds will not allow them to return to their God, for a spirit of harlotry is within them, and they do not know the way of the Lord. Moreover, the pride of Israel testifies against him, and Israel and Ephraim stumble in their iniquity").

verses 21-23 Judge Yahweh gives His indictment, and in verses 24-31 He pronounces the sentence.

God's indictment against His recalcitrant people (vv. 21-23)

Israel has failed to live according to the God-given standard that she once lived by (to some degree). Now, instead of being a city the reflects the glory of God, their sin had turned them into a breeding ground of wickedness, and the once-faithful city is now a faithless harlot. The city that used to practice righteousness is now filled with evil and corruption.

By design, Israel was to be a light of truth to all the world (41:8-9; cf. Gen. 12:1-3). God's desire for His people was that they would reflect His excellence so that others would see His glory and be drawn to Him. Unfortunately, Israel failed badly. In verses 21-23 we see five contrasts between God's right way and their present corrupted condition.

First contrast (v. 21). God says that the faithful city (*ne'emanah*) has become a harlot (*zonah*). There was a time when Jerusalem was a "faithful city" in a relative sense (Hosea hints at this in 2:15). All of this has changed, and now she is a harlot who has sold herself to her lovers (Jer. 2:20; 3:1ff.; Ezek. 16; Hos. 1:2; 2:2; 3:1).

Second contrast (v. 21). Jerusalem once was a city of justice (*mishpat*) and righteousness (*tsedeq*) with honest kings and judges, but now she has become a city of murders (*meratsechim*). Alexander notes that murder certainly was not the only sin, but as the worst all social sins it embraces all others.[36] We in America can relate to the way that our country was at one time largely characterized by a biblical worldview, but now is characterized by wickedness as the ruling norm.

Third and fourth contrasts (v. 22). Their silver has become dross and the drink diluted with water (*mahal*, mixed, corrupted). Just as the people were diluted with spiritual adultery, so too their silver and water have become diluted.

Fifth contrast (v. 23). Her early days had rulers (*sar* could include kings, princes, governmental officials, judges, or priests[37]) who characteristically

---

[36] Alexander, *Commentary on Isaiah*, 91.
[37] Ludwig Koehler et al., *The Hebrew and Aramaic Lexicon of the Old Testament*, cited in electronic form with Logos Libronix (Leiden: E.J. Brill, 1994–2000), 1350–1353.

strived to uphold the righteous character of Yahweh, but all that has changed. Now they are "rebels and companions of thieves; everyone loves a bribe and chases after rewards. They do not defend the orphan, nor does the widow's plea come before them." Oswalt notes that for the first time in his book, Isaiah "makes a connection which ought not to be overlooked—the connection between idolatry and social justice."[38] Apostasy from God and idolatry always lead to social evil, a theme we repeatedly find throughout the prophets (Isa. 29:17-21; 46:5-13; 48:17; 56:9-57:12; cf. Jer. 23:13, 14; Ezek. 16:47-52; Hos. 4:1-14; Amos 2:6-8; Mal. 3:5). Oswalt explains the problem that Israel could not see or understand:

> Social injustice is ultimately the result of refusal to entrust oneself to a fair and loving God. Whenever persons begin to believe that the cosmic order is basically uninterested in human welfare and that those who succeed are those who know best how to capture the cosmic forces for their own purposes (the underlying attitudes of idolatry), the relatively more helpless and vulnerable begin to be crushed.[39]

The result was a widespread demand for bribes with no concern for the helpless (Exod. 23:8; Deut. 27:25; Prov. 6:35; Amos 5:10; 8:4; Mic. 2:2; 3:1; 5:9; cf. esp. Mic. 7:1). Judah has passed the point of no return.

The sentence: God will continue His work (vv. 24-31)

God will continue His work, and God will fulfill His redemptive purposes. Verses 24-31 show us five purposes which God will accomplish by judging the nation. God will receive full satisfaction when sin has been dealt with, and in the end of His work He will use this chastising to bring His rebellious nation to repentance and restoration.

God's first purpose: He will satisfy His own anger by judging the wicked leaders of the land (v. 24).[40] In many contexts, God's adversaries are the pagan nations (Exod. 3:20; 15:6; Ps. 118:15-16), but here it is His own

---

[38] Oswalt, *The Book of Isaiah, Chapters 1-39*, 106.
[39] Ibid.
[40] The three-fold self-identification highlights His anger over sin: The Lord (the sovereign Lord, over 430 times in the OT), Yahweh of Hosts (i.e., the God of all the armies of heaven), The Mighty One of Israel (only here, although "Mighty One of Jacob" occurs 5 times in Isa. 49:26; 60:16; Gen. 5:24; Ps. 132:2, 5).

people. Isaiah uses assonance (homonyms) to show that the day is coming when God will get relief (*nacham*) from these who are defying Him by taking vengeance (*naqam*) on them (cf. Ezek. 5:13).

God's second purpose: God will use His judgment to purify the nation and bring the remnant to faith (v. 25). The end result will be purging and restoration, but this cannot happen until the nation repents. The sin (i.e., spiritual dross) must burned off (*tsaraph*, burn away) and taken away before a relationship with God can be restored (cf. Isa. 4:4; 48:10; Jer. 30:7; Ezek. 22:19; Hos. 3:4-5; Zeph. 3:1; Zech. 13:8-9; Mal. 3:1-3).

Just as the purifying of metals is a radical process, the purifying of Israel will also be a radical process.[41] Hermeneutically, we must note that God not only warns the nation that He is going to judge their sin, but He also promises that one day He will bring an eventual restoration to the whole nation. Theologically, this is the basis for what we call Dispensational Premillennialism, the view that the church is distinct from the nation of Israel (not a new or spiritual Israel), and that one day God will restore Israel in the kingdom. This purification/restoration has not yet happened, but God has promised that He will make it happen (Jer. 3:17; 30:7; 31:31-34; Ezek. 5:5; 36:20ff.; Mic. 4:2; Zech. 8:22; 13:1ff., 8-9; 14:16ff.).

God's third purpose: It will be a restoration of true righteousness in Jerusalem and all the land (vv. 26-27). The leaders of Isaiah's day were about as wicked as could be (vv. 21-23), but God promises that when His purification is completed, Zion will once again be a city of righteousness and faithfulness.[42] God says, "Zion will be redeemed (*padah*) with *justice* and her repentant ones with *righteousness*," a price that Yahweh pays by the exercise of His own covenant faithfulness (same terms in 9:7; 28:17; 32:16; 33:5; cf. 4:4; 5:16; 28:17).[43]

---

[41] Young, *The Book of Isaiah, vol. 1*, 87.

[42] This will include a Levitical priesthood (Jer. 30:20-21; 33:14-26; Ezek. 40-48).

[43] Ludwig Koehler et al., *The Hebrew and Aramaic Lexicon of the Old Testament*, cited in electronic form with Logos Libronix (Leiden: E.J. Brill, 1994–2000), 911–912. The basic force of *padah* is the idea of redeeming/ransoming/buying back by the payment of some kind of price (Exod. 13:13; Exod. 21:8: Slave; Num. 3:40: Levites; Num. 18:15-17). In sacrificial contexts, it is the expiation of guilt by the sacrifice of the animal, but in the present context, the price to be paid is the work of God exercising His

The price of sin is high, but faithful Yahweh will fulfill His promises (Isa. 53:4-6). Morris explains, "YHWH is bestirring Himself on His people's behalf; it is no ordinary activity."[44] All men have to do is repent and believe and restoration will be theirs (v. 27). Jerusalem will again be a city of righteousness and faithfulness (Isa. 33:5; 60:14; 62:1; cf. Zech. 8:3).

God's fourth purpose: Defiant sinners will be judged and excluded from His kingdom (v. 28). The absence of a copula verb makes the language quite vivid: "crushed together the transgressors and sinners" (cf. similar structure in 13:4; 52:8; 66:6).[45] Those who refuse to repent will be judged, excluded from the kingdom.[46]

God's fifth purpose: Israel will recognize the shame that comes when one turns from the Lord to embrace idols (vv. 29-31). Israel was habitually falling into idolatry—pagan worship that was typically carried out in places like sacred tree groves and sacred gardens (Isa. 17:8; 27:9; 57:5; 65:3; 66:17; cf. Deut. 7:5; 16:21; Judg. 3:7; 1 Kings 15; 2 Kings 17:10; Jer. 17:12; Ezek. 6:13; Hos. 4:13).[47] These idolaters believed "that divinity was attributed to the powers of nature, [so] worship was held under the trees."[48] One day they will be ashamed for trusting idols instead of Him (Isa. 41:24; 44:9; 65:11-12; 66:3).

Verses 30-31 tell what happens to those who refuse. Those who trust in dumb idols will become like them, dry up and shrivel away (Isa. 33:12-14; 34:8-12; 64:10; Jer. 17:6; Ps. 1:4). Eternal burning will come by the fires of an eternal hell that are never quenched (Isa. 66:24; Dan. 12:2; Rev. 14:9-11; 20:11-15).

Summary and application

The opening chapter confronts us with the reality that God will not tolerate dead religion. Outward ritual is worthless if it has not come out of a heart

---

justice and righteousness to buy back Israel (cf. Hos. 3:2).

[44] Leon Morris, *The Apostolic Preaching of the Cross* (London: Tyndale, 1955), 17.
[45] Young, *The Book of Isaiah, vol. 1*, 90.
[46] Cf. Isa. 65:8-15; Jer. 30:7-11; Ezek. 20:36-38; Amos 9:8-10; Zech. 5:3; Mal. 3:1-4; Matt. 8:11-12; 13:40-43, 49-50; 21:43; 22:1-14; 24:31, 40-41, 48-51; 25:1-13, 14-30, 31-46.
[47] Oswalt, *The Book of Isaiah, 1-39*, 110-111.
[48] Young, *The Book of Isaiah, vol. 1*, 91.

of faith. Let each one of us apply this truth to our hearts lest we fail as ancient Israel did in being religious without being righteous.

THE DESTINY OF THE PEOPLE, PT. 1 (2:1-22)

Chapters 2-4 form the second unit in the introductory section of chapters 1-6.[49] In this section, God warns His people that there will be only one of two destinies for all men. Those who repent and believe will obtain forgiveness and deliverance in the coming kingdom, but those who refuse will experience ruin. These chapters continue showing the contrast of how badly the people of Israel were failing to match up to what God had called them to be, but also give a first glimpse of the coming kingdom.

Chapter 2 reads as follows: "1 The word which Isaiah the son of Amoz saw concerning Judah and Jerusalem. 2 Now it will come about that in the last days the mountain of the house of the Lord will be established as the chief of the mountains, and will be raised above the hills, and all the nations will stream to it; 3 and many peoples will come and say, come, let us go up to the mountain of the Lord, to the house of the God of Jacob that He may teach us concerning His ways, and that we may walk in His paths, for the law will go forth from Zion and the word of the Lord from Jerusalem, 4 and He will judge between the nations, and will render decisions for many peoples; and they will hammer their swords into plowshares and their spears into pruning hooks. Nation will not lift up sword against nation, and never again will they learn war. 5 Come, house of Jacob, and let us walk in the light of the Lord, 6 for You have abandoned Your people, the house of Jacob, because they are filled *with influences* from the east, and *they are* soothsayers like the Philistines, and they strike *bargains* with the children of foreigners. 7 Their land has also been filled with silver and gold and there is no end to their treasures; 8 their land has also been filled with horses and there is no end to their chariots; their land has also been filled with idols; they worship the work of their hands, that which their fingers have made. 9 So the *common* man has been humbled and the man *of importance* has been abased, but do not forgive them. 10 Enter the rock and hide in the dust from the terror of the Lord and from the splendor of His majesty. 11 The proud look of man will be abased, and the loftiness of man will be humbled, and the Lord alone will be exalted in that day. 12 For the Lord of hosts will have a day *of reckoning* against everyone who is proud and lofty and against everyone who is lifted up, that he may be abased, 13 and *it will be* against all the cedars of Lebanon that are lofty and lifted up, against all the oaks of Bashan, 14 against all the lofty mountains, against all the hills that are lifted up, 15 against every high tower, against every fortified wall, 16 against all the ships of Tarshish, and against all

---

[49] Oswalt, *The Book of Isaiah, 1-39*, 113.

the beautiful craft. 17 The pride of man will be humbled, and the loftiness of men will be abased; and the Lord alone will be exalted in that day. 18 But the idols will completely vanish. 19 *Men* will go into caves of the rocks and into holes of the ground before the terror of the Lord and the splendor of His majesty, when He arises to make the earth tremble. 20 In that day men will cast away to the moles and the bats their idols of silver and their idols of gold, which they made for themselves to worship, 21 in order to go into the caverns of the rocks and the clefts of the cliffs before the terror of the Lord and the splendor of His majesty, when He arises to make the earth tremble. 22 Stop regarding man, whose breath *of life* is in his nostrils, for why should he be esteemed?" (2:1-22).

Judah could have restoration if only they would turn to the Lord. Sadly, they would not. For this reason, chapter two may be outlined as highlighting themes of both deliverance (vv. 1-4) and devastation (vv. 5-22).

Deliverance (vv. 1-4)

As noted by Martin, in verses 2-4 Isaiah, "introduced a concept which was to be a hallmark of his prophecy. A time will come when Jerusalem will have the primary position in the world."[50] Israel's sin would bring centuries of suffering, but God's promise is restoration in the kingdom. The opening words of 2:1 echo those of 1:1 and raise questions as to why this is so. Some would hold that this indicates a distinct prophetic section that Isaiah included as he grouped together all of his prophetic writings.[51] Interestingly, Isaiah calls it the word which he "saw" and not the word which he heard (cf. Amos 1:1). Culver notes that in prophetic contexts, this visionary term "saw" (*chazah*) refers to,

> the revelatory vision granted by God to chosen messengers, i.e. prophets. . . . This vision of the prophets took place sometimes in the waking state, but also in "the spirit" (see Num 24:2). Sometimes the experience of "seeing" a revelatory dream.[52]

---

[50] Martin, "Isaiah," 1037. Martin notes that Micah 4:1–3 is almost identical to Isaiah 2:1–4 and it is difficult to say who wrote first.
[51] Oswalt, *The Book of Isaiah, 1-39*, 113-114. Wolf sees these as being messages which came after his initial call in chapter 6 (Wolf, *Interpreting Isaiah*, 76).
[52] Robert D. Culver, "*chzh*," ed. R. Laird Harris, Gleason L. Archer Jr., and Bruce K. Waltke, *Theological Wordbook of the Old Testament*, cited in electronic form with Logos Libronix (Chicago: Moody Press, 1999), 274–275.

By His Spirit, God was revealing the coming kingdom to Isaiah.[53] Verses 2-4 reveal three features of what this kingdom will look like.

The first feature: the commencement of the kingdom (v. 2a)

God says the kingdom will commence in "the last days."[54] Many premillennial theologians hold that the last days will take place as follows: (1) the rapture of the church, (2) the establishing of a seven-year covenant by the Antichrist between Israel and Israel's enemies, (3) the seven-year tribulation period, (4) the return of Christ at the end of the seven years to destroy the Antichrist and his armies and save Israel from annihilation, (5) the establishing of the millennial kingdom,[55] (6) the final resurrection of all the unsaved at the end of the Millennium in preparation for a final judgment, (7) the destruction of the present material order, (8) the final judgment of all the unsaved, (9) the creation of a new heavens and new earth.

Generally speaking, post-millennial theologians have held that the kingdom began at some point in the past and that Christ will return at the end of the 1,000 years when the church has achieved a Christianization of the world. Amillennial theologians typically treat the 1,000 years as a figurative expression that simply means a long period of time. They typically assert that the church is the kingdom—a kingdom that began at the resurrection (or Pentecost) and continues until the new heavens and new earth. Young, for example, holds that the last days is, "the age of the Christian church which began its course with the first advent of Christ."[56] These explanations fail to give a proper explanation of the text.

It is true that in a broad sense, one can say that we entered into the "last days" when Messiah arrived some 2,000 years ago (Heb. 1:2; 1 Pet. 1:20; 1 John 2:8, 18). However, the Old Testament prophets did not have a clear understanding that the first coming of Christ would also include the rejection and death of the Messiah, and that the arrival of the kingdom (as here in 2:1-4) would not

---

[53] The multiple uses of the expression "in that day" support the view that this section is referring to the eschatological kingdom (2:11, 17, 20; 3:7, 18; 4:1, 2).

[54] This expression often refers to eschatological events, especially in the prophets, but it must be noted that some OT uses are not eschatological (cf. e.g., Gen. 49:1).

[55] The term millennium comes from Revelation 20:2-7 where we find 1,000 years spoken of six times in six consecutive verses. The inhabitants of the kingdom will include Christ, the resurrected church, the resurrected Old Testament saints, the resurrected Tribulation Martyrs, and the remnant of believing Jews and Gentiles who got saved during the Tribulation Period.

[56] Young, *The Book of Isaiah, vol. 1*, 99.

happen until His Second Coming. At the present time, we now live in the church age, an unforeseen time period that includes what Jesus called "the mysteries of the kingdom" (Matt. 13:11; cf. Rom. 16:25-26; Eph. 2:11-22; 3:1-9; Col. 1:26).[57] From an Old Testament perspective, the church age is part of a prophetic gap that was never seen by the Old Testament prophets. After the resurrection, the disciples were expecting Jesus to immediately establish Israel's kingdom (Acts 1:6; Phil. 4:6; James 5:8; 1 Pet. 4:7; 2 Pet. 3:9; Rev. 22:20-21), and this is what we are still waiting for today, i.e., the imminent return of Christ.

The second feature: The centrality of His kingdom (v. 2b)

The return of Christ is certain, and when He comes Isaiah says He will establish God's kingdom in Jerusalem, His chosen city (Ps. 48:1; Matt. 5:35).[58] The "the mountain of the house of the LORD" refers to the fact that the messianic kingdom will have its capital in the city of Jerusalem at the place that biblically is known as Mount Zion.[59] The whole world will belong to the Lord Jesus Christ in that day (Zech. 14:9), and in that day all the world will worship God's Son as He rules from Zion, for His kingdom will be the chief of all mountains/kingdoms (Zech. 14:16-21). Zion will be raised up not only physically (Zech. 4:7; 14:10), but also spiritually as the capital of the whole world (Zech. 8:3). Unger reminds us that this must not be allegorized away:

> As the religious center in the kingdom age, Jerusalem will be the site of the millennial Temple (Ezek. 40:1-47). . . . The result of the fulfillment of this great prophecy will not only involve the spontaneous inflow of the nations but also their eager seeking after Israel's God.[60]

The third feature: The changes His kingdom will bring (vv. 2c-4)

God is going to bring radical changes to this world when Christ returns. Verses 2-4 outline three kinds of radical changes this world will see.

A radical reversal (v. 2c). Life is going to change radically when Christ establishes His kingdom (a radical reversal of the curse Adam introduced), and all the nations "will stream" (*nahar*) to Jerusalem. Instead of looking with

---

[57] This would be "the last days" as seen by Isaiah.
[58] As Paul notes, God has not rejected His chosen people Israel (Rom. 11:1-2), for His gifts and promises are irrevocable (Rom. 11:25-29).
[59] See the multiple uses of this and similar expressions where kingdoms are referred to with mountain terminology (Isa. 4:1-6; 11:9; 25:6; 27:13; 56:7; 65:11, 25; 66:20; cf. Jer. 51:25 [Babylon]; Dan. 2:35; Mic. 3:12; 4:1; Zech. 8:3; 14:9-10; Rev. 17:9-10).
[60] Merrill F. Unger, *Unger's Commentary on the Old Testament, Vol. II: Isaiah-Malachi* (Chicago: Moody, 1981), 1145.

contempt on the Jews, all the nations (the *goyim*) will look to Jerusalem and its King as a source of blessing.

The centrality of Israel (v. 3). Verse 3 continues the imagery with a parallel statement: "many peoples will come and say, come, let us go up to the mountain of the Lord, to the house of the God of Jacob." The clear import of this prophecy is that the whole Gentile world will recognize Jerusalem and her King as the ruling center of the world, a promise that gets repeated throughout Isaiah (cf. e.g., Isa. 60:3-12; 61:5; 66:23). Post-exilic Zechariah looked ahead to that future age when Messiah would rule, and all the world would see Jerusalem as the capital of the world (Zech. 8:20-23). In Zechariah 8:13 God encouraged His downcast people by saying, "It will come about that just as you were a curse among the nations, O house of Judah and house of Israel, so I will save you that you may become a blessing." Here is a truth we must not miss: God will restore His fallen people.

The nations will stream to Jerusalem and seek the Lord so that He may teach them concerning His ways that they might walk in His paths. All the world will recognize that Yahweh is God, and that they need His instruction, i.e., His law (*torah*). In this present age, the world does all it can to cast off the ways of the Lord (Ps. 2:1-3), but when God brings His remnant into the kingdom (Jew and Gentile), these saints will recognize that these teachings are the truth they must learn (cf. Isa. 11:6-9).[61]

An end of war (v. 4). Christ will put an end to all war, and by His divine wisdom (cf. Isa. 9:6; 11:3-5), He will "judge between the nations, and will render decisions for many peoples." The result will be that all of the wealth that had been devoted to war will now be used for peaceful and productive purposes.[62] Israel's disobedience plunged the nation under one long age of warfare (spiritual and physical), but one day it will all come to an end (Isa. 40:1-2). Webb notes that, "it was this vision of the future which inspired [Isaiah]" and gave him hope for the future.[63]

Scripture shows us that God offered this restoration when He sent His

---

[61] Young, *The Book of Isaiah, vol. 1*, 105.
[62] The Apocalypse indicates that God will allow one final rebellion at the end of the Millennium when Satan and his hosts are released from the bottomless pit before they (and all unsaved men), are cast into the Lake of Fire (Rev. 20:7-10). Even though it is only the redeemed who are allowed entrance into the kingdom (Isa. 35:9; 62:12; cf. Matt. 25:34), these mortal saints will marry and have children in the Millennium (Isa. 65:20), and some of these children will refuse to believe in Jesus.
[63] Barry G. Webb, *The Message of Isaiah* (Downers Grove: IVP, 1996), 46.

Son 2,000 years ago (cf. Luke 19:41-44), but in the wisdom of God He used their rejection of Christ to bring forgiveness (Acts 2:23; 4:27-28). Verses 5-22 show the devastation that would come because of their refusal to listen.

Devastation on unrepentant sinners (vv. 5-22)

Isaiah 2:5-4:1 come as part of a sandwich in the middle of two other sections. In 2:1-4 we see for the first time the hope of the coming kingdom, and then in 4:2-6 we see this same promise for a second time. In between, however (vv. 2:5-4:1), we see a message of despair, for God is going to turn away from His people and bring a devastating judgment. This section may be outlined as follows: (1) a general warning of coming judgment (2:5-22), and (2) a specific warning of coming judgment (3:1-4:1). Isaiah highlights three dangers that led to their destruction.

The first danger was that of holding to a false trust (vv. 5-11)

It is easy to hold a false trust. For example, back in the 1920s America was filled with prosperity as the economy roared ("the roaring twenties"). Then came 1929, the stock market crash, and the Great Depression. In Isaiah's day, Judah had fallen into the trap of relying on false sources of trust. Wolf explains that unless Judah returns to the Lord, nothing is going to turn out well.[64] Verses 5-11 give a three-fold explanation of how their false trust was destroying the nation.

The plea to turn from false trust (vv. 5-6). Similar to 1:18-20, Isaiah calls on Judah to turn back to the Lord. Interestingly, he calls them by the name "house of Jacob." In his earlier years, Jacob was characterized as a man who trusted in his own devices, but in Genesis 32, God broke Jacob and gave him the name Israel to signify his new-found spiritual victories. Here, however, God calls them "house of Jacob" (vv. 5-6; cf. 8:17; 10:20; 14:1; 29:22; 46:3; 48:1). Isaiah's call to his people is that they should all walk in the light of the Lord (cf. Ps. 119:105; Prov. 6:23). Micah echoed the same idea when he wrote, "as for us, we will walk in the name of the Lord our God forever and ever" (Mic. 4:5). The problem was that Judah had turned away from the Lord, so the Lord had abandoned them (v. 6).[65]

Turning to the Lord would mean turning away from their false sources of trust, including all their idols and witchcraft.[66] Isaiah says, "they are filled *with*

---

[64] Wolf, *Interpreting Isaiah*, 77.
[65] Oswalt, *The Book of Isaiah, 1-39*, 121-122.
[66] These are deeds which were forbidden in the Torah (Lev. 19:26; Deut. 18:9-14).

influences from the east, and *they are* soothsayers like the Philistines, and they strike *bargains* with the children of foreigners."

Isaiah expands on Judah's false trust (vv. 7-8). They also had a false trust in their own wealth and military might,[67] something God had warned them about since the time of Moses (Deut. 17:16-17). Their trust was in their own strength and the idols they had come to worship—the work of their own hands (the term for idols ['*eliliym*] emphasizes the idea of weakness, emptiness, vanity, and futility; cf. Isa. 2:8, 18, 20; 10:10; 19:1, 3; 31:7; cf. Lev. 19:4; 26:1; Job 13:4; Ps. 96:5; Jer. 14:14; Zech. 11:7).[68] Kidner explains that Israel trusted everything but the living God (v. 8),

> The flood of superstition (6), alliances (6c), wealth (7a), armaments (7b), and idols (8), making cosmopolitan Judah anything but the light to the nations pictured just above, suggests the days of Jotham or Ahaz, early in Isaiah's career, between the prosperity of Uzziah and the reforms of Hezekiah. Thronged though it is, the land is destitute; it has everything but God (6a).[69]

These were terrible days for Judah, and little did they understand that their lack of trust in the Lord would lead to complete ruin (cf. Jer. 17:5-6). One cannot help but see how this same principle is working itself out in our time. America has had great light, but has turned away from it.

Four results that were about to fall on Judah (vv. 9-11). First, all the people would be severely afflicted regardless of economic or social status (v. 9). Second, God's terrifying judgment would drive them away from their homes and cities to find refuge in places like caves (v. 10). Delitzsch explains, "They would conceal themselves in holes of the rocks, as if before a hostile army"

---

[67] Horses and chariots could be powerful war weapons for any nation and God warned His people not to place their trust in these but in Him alone, but the people of Israel often disregarded these warnings and built up huge military reserves (cf. Deut. 17:14-17; 1 Kings 10:26-11:8).

[68] Ludwig Koehler et al., *The Hebrew and Aramaic Lexicon of the Old Testament*, cited in electronic form with Logos Libronix (Leiden: E.J. Brill, 1994–2000), 55–56. Isaiah attacks them for this sin in the later portions (40:18-20; 41:6, 7, 28, 29; 44:9-20; 45:16-20; 46:1, 2, 5-7). Oswalt explains, "How foolish to call divine what human hands have made" (Oswalt, *The Book of Isaiah, 1-39*, 123).

[69] F. Derek Kidner, "Isaiah," in *New Bible Commentary: 21st Century Edition*, ed. D. A. Carson et al., 4th ed., cited in electronic form with Logos Libronix (Leicester, England; Downers Grove, IL: Inter-Varsity Press, 1994), 635.

(Judg. 6:2; 1 Sam. 13:6; 14:11).[70] Third, God would bring an end to their pride and self-sufficiency (v. 11a; cf. 5:15; 10:12; 17:7). Fourth, God would show that He alone is exalted and worthy of trust (v. 11b). Oswalt explains,

> The God from whom their self-worship has alienated them will appear, and there will no more cause to glory in human greatness than there would be to praise a flashlight in broad daylight. . . . Having striven to become sovereigns of the universe, we have become meaningless victims of a vast cosmic bad joke.[71]

A second danger facing Judah (vv. 12-17)

God hates pride, and here in verses 12-17 God announces that the day is coming when He will judge all sin, including the pride of man, whether it is the pride of the Jew or the pride of the Gentile. The Old Testament repeatedly speaks about the time when God will break into human affairs to deal with the sin of man or, as Martin puts it, "a scheduled time of reckoning for sinners."[72] The Scripture often refers to this as "the day of the Lord" (cf. Isa. 13:6; Joel 1:15; 2:1, 11, 31; Amos 5:18; Zeph. 1:7, 14; Zech. 14:1; Mal. 4:5).[73] God first shows us a picture of Judah's pride (vv. 12-16), and follows this by showing the punishment He will bring (v. 17).

All the proud will be judged (vv. 12-16). God says this time of judgment will be against everyone who is proud [*ge'eh*] and lofty [*ram*] and lifted up [*nissa'*] that he may be abased. Isaiah uses numerous figures of speech in verses 13-16 to portray the arrogance of sinners. Although some take these references as being to literal, physical materials (like trees),[74] or even as referring to the destruction of buildings (such as the temple) that were constructed of these materials (cf. 2:15; 9:10), it seems best to understand that these are pictures of human

---

[70] F. Delitzsch, *Keil and Delitzsch Commentary on the Old Testament*, vol. 7 (Grand Rapids: Eerdmans, 1969), 121. See Rev. 6:16-17 how this terror will come upon the world during the future, seven-year tribulation period.

[71] Oswalt, *The Book of Isaiah, 1-39*, 123-124.

[72] Martin, "Isaiah," 1039.

[73] The NASB translates it as "a day of reckoning" in 2:12. Although certain uses of "the day of the Lord" speak about God's judgments in ancient times (cf. e.g., Isa. 10:3 and God's judgment against Assyria or Isa. 13:6, 9 and God's judgment against Babylon), a number of passages clearly indicate God's final intervention during the seven-year tribulation period (Joel 3:14; 1 Thess. 5:1ff.; 2 Thess. 2:1ff.).

[74] Lebanon was known for its large and beautiful cedars and Bashan was known for its large and beautiful oaks.

pride.⁷⁵ As Oswalt explains, these images are all figurative, though not an allegory.⁷⁶ Men build their towers, their castles, and their fortifications in which they think they will find strength and refuge (like in castles), but in reality all of these fortifications, including sources of wealth like maritime shipping (v. 16),⁷⁷ are all false sources of trust.⁷⁸

God will deal with the pride of Judah (v. 17). Sinners will be humbled, and the Lord alone will be exalted (Isa. 45:22-23; cf. Phil. 2:9-11). In context, it is best to understand this as referring to God's judgment on Judah in 605-586 in the ancient past. However, the same kind of judgment will fall upon Israel once again in the Tribulation period (cf. Dan. 9:27; 11:36; 12:7).

A third danger facing Judah (vv. 18-22)

This was the danger of seeking cheap substitutes to take the place of the living God. Anytime man puts his trust in something other than God, he is putting his trust in a cheap substitute. People today put their trust in cheap substitutes all the time with things like money, drugs, alcohol, immoral living, and false religions. Sinners today have a never-ending inclination to put their trust in all the wrong places; however, the same thing was true in the days of Isaiah. Here in verses 18-22 God shows the people the destiny of these cheap substitutes, and then He shows them that the only way to be delivered is to stop trusting in them and trust in Him.

Three destinies of cheap substitutes (vv. 18-21). All cheap substitutes will eventually be purged so that they might be seen for what they truly are (v.

---

[75] See similar ideas in other passages (Isa. 1:30; 6:13; 9:10; 10:33-11:1; 44:14; 60:16; cf. Ezek. 17:3, 4, 22-23; 31:2-14; Dan. 4:10, 20-23).

[76] Oswalt, *The Book of Isaiah, Chapters 1-39*, 126.

[77] Some have explained this expression as referring to ships that come from Spain (Tarshish), but careful studies suggest that Tarshish was also the name of Phoenician merchant ships (cf. NIV of Ezek. 27:25: "Every trading ship"). Tarshish was a Phoenician colony in the western Mediterranean and it was famous for its sea going vessels that sailed as far as Tarshish in the far western edge of the Mediterranean (Grogan, "Isaiah," 39, n. 16). Historical studies indicate that Kings Uzziah and Jotham recovered control of Eilat on the Red Sea and ships sailed from this port around the coast of Africa to the harbor of Tartessus, the ancient Phoenician emporium (cf. 2 Chron. 20:36).

[78] The expression "beautiful craft" appears to be a hapax legomenon derived from an Egyptian loanword, especially given its usage in the LXX (Oswalt, *The Book of Isaiah, Chapters 1-39*, 125, n. 2; Delitzsch, *Keil and Delitzsch Commentary on the Old Testament*, 124).

18). As Delitzsch explains, the idea here is that the idols "are one and all a mass of nothingness, which will be reduced to absolute annihilation: they will vanish."[79] Second, those who trusted in idols will seek in vain to flee from the terror of God's judgment (v. 19). Sinners delight in shaking their fists in God's face, but it will be different when God deals with their sin. Third, Isaiah says that men will seek in vain to abandon the idols they once trusted in (vv. 20-21). These once-arrogant sinners will "cast away to the moles and the bats their idols of silver and their idols of gold, which they made for themselves to worship." Even though there is debate about the precise meaning of the terms "moles" and "bats," it seems in context that these may be literal references to those animals that dwell under the earth, the digging creatures and bats that one finds in caves.[80]

Was there any way that the nation could have avoided this disaster? The answer is yes. Israel had the choice to repent and turn from sin (Ezek. 18:23, 30, 32). The same principle holds true today: Whether they are Jew or Gentile, God calls sinners to turn from sin and trust in Him (2 Pet. 3:9). Those who are willing to turn find grace and receive forgiveness.

The only true hope (v. 22). The only hope (then and now) is to turn to God in complete faith. The people needed to repent and trust in Yahweh. God says that if they would do this, they would find hope, so He tells them, "Stop regarding man, whose breath *of life* is in his nostrils, for why should he be esteemed?" Man, the one whose breath of life is in his nostrils (Gen. 2:7; cf. Job 34:14; Pss. 90:3-8; 104:29) is not the one to trust, and neither are the gods that he makes with his hands. The best thing sinners can do is, "turn to Him . . . and thus escape His severe judgment."[81]

Summary and application

In *Qoheleth*, King Solomon reminds us that there is nothing new under the sun. Truly that is the case with pride and false sources of trust. As Oswalt explains, "The tendency of human beings to make ourselves the center of all things and to explain all things in term of ourselves is the problem."[82] In the case of ancient Judah, it was the problem of trusting in idols, foreign alliances, and their own military strength.[83] May we be people who trust in nothing but the Lord and His redeeming grace.

---

[79] Ibid., 125.
[80] Grogan, "Isaiah," 39.
[81] Martin, "Isaiah," 1039.
[82] Oswalt, *The Book of Isaiah, Chapters 1-39*, 128.
[83] Wolf, *Interpreting Isaiah*, 79.

ISAIAH 1:1-6:13

THE DESTINY OF THE PEOPLE, PT. 2 (3:1-4:1)

God continues to unfold what Israel's destiny will look like. The Lord is pleading with His people to turn from their wicked ways and walk in the light of His Word, for His desire is to bless not destroy.

Verses 3:1-4:1 read as follows: "1 For behold, the Lord God of hosts is going to remove from Jerusalem and Judah both supply and support, the whole supply of bread and the whole supply of water, 2 the mighty man and the warrior, the judge and the prophet, the diviner and the elder, 3 the captain of fifty and the honorable man, the counselor and the expert artisan, and the skillful enchanter, 4 and I will make mere lads their princes, and capricious children will rule over them, 5 and the people will be oppressed, each one by another, and each one by his neighbor; the youth will storm against the elder and the inferior against the honorable. 6 When a man lays hold of his brother in his father's house, *saying,* you have a cloak; you shall be our ruler, and these ruins will be under your charge, 7 he will protest on that day, saying, I will not be *your* healer, for in my house there is neither bread nor cloak; you should not appoint me ruler of the people. 8 For Jerusalem has stumbled and Judah has fallen, because their speech and their actions are against the Lord, to rebel against His glorious presence. 9 The expression of their faces bears witness against them, and they display their sin like Sodom; they do not *even* conceal *it*. Woe to them! For they have brought evil on themselves. 10 Say to the righteous that *it will go* well *with them, f*or they will eat the fruit of their actions. 11 Woe to the wicked! *It will go* badly *with him,* for what he deserves will be done to him. 12 O My people! Their oppressors are children, and women rule over them. O My people! Those who guide you lead *you* astray and confuse the direction of your paths." 13 The Lord arises to contend, and stands to judge the people. 14 The Lord enters into judgment with the elders and princes of His people: It is you who have devoured the vineyard. The plunder of the poor is in your houses. 15 What do you mean by crushing My people and grinding the face of the poor? declares the Lord God of hosts." 16 Moreover, the Lord said, because the daughters of Zion are proud and walk with heads held high and seductive eyes, and go along with mincing steps and tinkle the bangles on their feet, 17 therefore the Lord will afflict the scalp of the daughters of Zion with scabs, and the Lord will make their foreheads bare. 18 In that day the Lord will take away the beauty of *their* anklets, headbands, crescent ornaments, 19 dangling earrings, bracelets, veils, 20 headdresses, ankle chains, sashes, perfume boxes, amulets, 21 finger rings, nose rings, 22 festal robes, outer tunics, cloaks, money purses, 23 hand mirrors, undergarments, turbans and veils. 24 Now it will come about that instead of sweet perfume there will be putrefaction; instead of a belt, a rope; instead of well-set hair, a plucked-out scalp; instead of fine clothes, a donning of sackcloth, and branding instead of beauty. 25 Your men will fall by the sword and your mighty ones in battle, 26 and her gates will lament and mourn, and deserted she will sit on the ground, 1 for seven women will take hold of one man in that day, saying, We will eat our own bread and wear our own clothes, only let us be called by your name; take away our reproach" (vv. 3:1-4:1).

The picture here is that of societal disintegration, with sin bringing a complete upheaval of life as they have known it.[84] Kidner calls this, "a study in disintegration, through the pressure of scarcity on a people without ideals. The scarcity, which is desperate, is twofold; of material things (*food* and *water*, v. 1; *clothing*, v. 7) and of leadership (vv. 2–4)."[85] God announces both how He will strike the nation (vv. 1-7) as well as why (vv. 3:8-4:1).

How God will strike the land (vv. 1-7)

God will bring Judah down by systematically striking it in a variety of ways to bring it to ruin. Yahweh, the sovereign Lord of the hosts, declares His intention in verse 1 and then fills in the specifics in verses 2-7.

The certain consequence of rebellion is judgment (v. 1)

Isaiah employs a four-fold use of the term "supply/support" to warn about the coming removal of life's basic provisions, namely food and water.[86] Once the judgment comes, nothing will be left to help or support the nation.[87] It is in 5:8ff. that God makes it clear that this will come by the hand of Assyrian and Babylonian invasions.

God will also strip them of their sinful leaders (vv. 2-3)

Verses 2-3 name out eleven kinds of leaders who had become false sources of trust—some of whom were legitimate God-ordained kinds of positions, some of whom were illegitimate and sinful by their very nature. The first two leaders (the mighty man and warrior) both refer to military warriors. Judges refer to civil officers who carried out governmental functions. In context, it is possible that prophets would include not only true prophets like Isaiah (cf. Amos 8:11),[88] but also the false prophets who plagued the nation (cf. Jer. 23:9-22). Diviners are by nature illegitimate professions involving sorcery and witchcraft (Deut. 18:10; 1 Sam. 28:38; 2 Kings 17:7; Hos. 3:4; Mic. 3:11). Elders were older men who gave guidance to local villages. Captains of fifty may be another military or governmental expression (Exod. 18:25; 1 Sam. 8:12; 2 Kings 1:9),

---

[84] The *kiy* clause that starts in 3:1 elaborates on 2:1-22.
[85] Kidner, "Isaiah," 636.
[86] Each word derives from the Heb. root *mash'en: mash'en, mash'enah, mish'an, mish'an*, all having the idea of support—such as even a walking stick.
[87] Grogan, "Isaiah," 41.
[88] Young, *The Book of Isaiah, vol. 1*, 139.

and honorable men and counselor both refer to governmental counselors. Up to this time, many such counselors had been godless leaders who were taking the nation to ruin, but God's promise is that one day He will bring them a truly wise counselor (Isa. 9:6-7; 11:1ff.). Expert artisans were those who were skilled in artistic skills (2 Kings 24:14; Jer. 24:1; 29:1), but sadly some of these were also the ones involved in making idols (Isa. 44:11; 45:16). This last leader, the skilled enchanter, comes from a root that speaks about the whispering of charms and spells, evil influences that had overtaken the whole land (Isa. 28:16; Jer. 8:17). God will destroy them all.

The third way God will strike the land (vv. 4-7)

There often are times when we wish that God would remove wicked leaders. Here in verses 4-7 Isaiah expands on the theme that there will be a complete removal of all qualified leaders, leaving them with only terrible leaders. In the case of Judah, God did remove some of these wicked leaders, but unfortunately, they ended up with more leaders in various roles who were young (*ne'ariym*), inexperienced, and foolish. In other words, explains Oswalt, Judah "will be ruled by incompetents."[89] Because these leaders are young and "capricious" (*ta'aluliym*), a term that speaks about the mischievousness of youth,[90] the end result will be a societal breakdown where the strong oppress the weak (v. 5). In our own times, this kind of breakdown shows itself in practices like abortion, euthanasia, and the use of wealth and political power for promoting evil values.[91] The dearth of leadership will be so bad that they will desperately search for anyone to lead them out of their descending spiral, but those with wisdom will refuse these roles knowing that they have no solution for the decay that has overcome the land (vv. 6-7). From this picture we are once again reminded of the ruin that sin produces.

Corrupt leadership is a prime cause of Israel's ruin (vv. 3:8-4:1)

Isaiah rebukes Judah for their brazenness and lack of shame. Martin explains, "The people defied God and were open about their sin much like the

---

[89] Oswalt, *The Book of Isaiah, Chapters 1-39*, 133.
[90] Ludwig Koehler et al., *The Hebrew and Aramaic Lexicon of the Old Testament*, cited in electronic form with Logos Libronix (Leiden: E.J. Brill, 1994–2000), 1768–1769. The root of this term conveys the idea of being whimsical and capricious (cf. Hos. 14:1; Mic. 2:9; Neh. 3:10), and this carries with it a "lack of maturity in judgment and decision (Young, *The Book of Isaiah, vol. 1*, 143).
[91] One evidence of God's judgment on a culture is when the youth are insolent and arrogant toward the elders (cf. Ps. 40:5; Prov. 6:3).

people of Sodom (cf. Gen. 18:20; 19:1–11; Isa. 1:9–10)."[92] Isaiah highlights three kinds of sin in 3:8-4:1.

First sin: The shamelessness of the nation (vv. 8-12)

Verse 8 begins with a *kiy* clause that connects the following section to 1-7, and why it is that God must judge. Everything they do, whether word or deed, is rebellious against God, and now they are stumbling and falling like a drunken man (v. 8). Why does no one want a leadership role (vv. 6-7)? The reason is because the whole society is collapsing. The nation does not even feel shame any more over their sin (v. 9). Despite the failure of the collective nation, God extends the promise that those who walk in His ways will be able to experience His favor (v. 10), an idea Ezekiel highlights (18:5-9). Nevertheless, for those who choose wickedness, the judgment will be horrific and fully deserved (v. 11). Isaiah continues by again emphasizing that the leaders of the nation have been especially guilty (v. 12). The reference to women ruling over them could be a reference to harems, queen mothers or, as some suggest, the weakness of the men who lead (cf. Amos 4:1ff). Horrible leaders were leading the country to ruin, but Yahweh saw it all. Pfeiffer explains, "These oppressive rulers and aristocrats might be immune from punishment by human courts for their ruthless exploitation of Jehovah's people; but God himself would bring them to judgment."[93]

Second sin: Ruthless leaders (vv. 13-15)

Isaiah again utilizes courtroom terminology to explain the coming judgment.[94] The leaders of Judah are guilty, and the judge is about to execute the sentence (vv. 13-14). Chapter 5 will introduce a parabolic song in which the vineyard symbolizes the nation whom God carefully planted (cf. Jer. 12:10; Ps. 80:8-16). God gave His people everything for prosperity, but evil leaders were bringing it to ruin, especially by their ruthless oppression of the weak and poor (cf. Job 19:2; Ps. 89:11; Amos 2:6-8; 3:4-15; 5:11-12; 6:4-11; 8:6; Mic. 2:1-2). God graphically portrays their evil by calling it "crushing My people" and "grinding the face of the poor."

All of this evil raises the question, how could God possibly forgive people who would ruthlessly crush (*daka'*) the innocent? The answer is that the Lord will send them a Redeemer whom He Himself will crush (*daka'*) to take away their sins (Isa. 53:10; Rom. 3:21-26). There is hope!

---

[92] Martin, "Isaiah," 1040.
[93] Pfeiffer, *The Wycliffe Bible Commentary: Old Testament*, Is 3:9.
[94] The psalmist pleaded with God, "Do not enter into judgment with Your servant, for in Your sight no man living is righteous" (Ps. 143:2).

Third sin: The arrogance and vanity of the women (vv. 3:16-4:1)

The focus turns to the perilous situation of having become a culture where the women were obsessed with sins of pride, narcissism, sensuality, and the flaunting of their sexuality (Prov. 11:22; 1 Pet. 3:1-6). As Motyer explains it, everything the women did was "designed to attract attention - posture, demeanour, movement, ornament."[95] Here in 3:16-4:1 God outlines thirty-one different areas of such sin.

The first two descriptions of Judah's godless women come in verse 16 where Isaiah says that they walk with "heads held high" and "seductive eyes" (a hapax legomenon, but cognate studies show it can include both painting of eyes with makeup and using seductive glances[96]). To "mince steps" (another hapax) carries the idea of "strutting along with swaying hips" (NIV). Fourth (vv. 16-17), Isaiah says they "tinkle the bangles on their feet" (NIV: "ornaments jingling on their ankles"). As Kidner explains, "Triviality has never been more mercilessly exposed, or more abruptly overtaken by tragedy."[97] God hates the arrogance of His women and tells them in verse 17, "therefore the Lord will afflict the scalp of the daughters of Zion with scabs, and the Lord will make their foreheads bare" (a removal of the natural beauty that comes from long hair). Verses 18-20 show nine kinds of seductive apparel used by the women of Judah in their attempt to flaunt their sexuality: "anklets" (cf. Prov. 7:22), "headbands, crescent ornaments" (moon symbols with Midianite or Astarte origins in the worship of Nanna or Sin; cf. Judg. 18:21, 26),[98] "dangling earrings" (Judg. 8:26), "bracelets" (a hapax of Persian origin), "veils" (hapax), "headdresses, ankle chains" (cf. 2 Kings 11:12), and "sashes" (cf. Jer. 2:32).

The NASB calls the fourteenth and fifteenth descriptions "perfume boxes" (v. 20),[99] and "amulets" (from the root that means to whisper). Verses 21-22 list six more kinds of apparel: "finger rings" (or signet ring), "nose rings" (Gen. 24:20; 35:4; Exod. 32:3; 35:22; Ezek. 16:2; Hos. 2:15), "festal robes" (cf. Zech. 3:4), "outer tunics" (hapax), "cloaks" (cf. Ruth 3:15), and "money purses." Descriptions 22-25 come in verse 23: "hand mirrors" (perhaps sheer undergarments), "undergarments" (linen undergarments; cf. Judg. 14:12; Prov. 31:24), "turbans" (cf. Job 29:14; Isa. 62:3; Zech. 3:5), and "veils" (cf. Song 5:7).

---

[95] J. Alec Motyer, *The Prophecy of Isaiah: An Introduction and Commentary* (Downers Grove: IVP, 1993), 63.
[96] Ludwig Koehler et al., *The Hebrew and Aramaic Lexicon of the Old Testament*, cited in electronic form with Logos Libronix (Leiden: E.J. Brill, 1994–2000), 1350.
[97] Kidner, "Isaiah," 636.
[98] Wolf, *Interpreting Isaiah*, 80.
[99] The expression literally says, "houses of breath" and appears to be some sort of amulet (Oswalt, *The Book of Isaiah, Chapters 1-39*, 142).

Verse 24 gives five more descriptions of how the women flaunted their sin—all of which God says He was about to take away:[100] "perfume" (putrefaction in the place of sweet balsamic perfumes, cf. Isa. 5:24), "belt" (a rope to lead away instead), "well-set hair" (instead a plucked out scalp, cf. Deut. 14:1; Isa. 15:2; Mic. 1:16; Amos 8:10;), "fine clothes" (only sackcloth), and "beauty" (only branding). God is taking it all away.

In 3:25-4:1 God tells them about one last thing (31st on the list) that He is about to take away from them—their "men" (a less common term *meth*). God will take away all the rich, handsome, young men they used to seduce, and He will kill them in battle. The death toll to the men will be so bad that it will leave a horrible disproportion of men to women (v. 25). The mourning will be great (v. 26), but this will only lead to the desperation of how to get a husband and children. In bold desperation "seven women will take hold of one man in that day, saying, We will eat our own bread and wear our own clothes, only let us be called by your name; take away our reproach!" (4:1). They don't care if they have to produce their own food, they just want a husband and children. Wolf explains, "What a change from the luxury and smug complacency described in 3:16-4:23."[101]

Summary and application

God wants us to understand that sin carries with it a costly price tag. It does not matter who we are, or where or when we live, sin has its wage (Rom. 6:23). May God stir our hearts to walk in obedient faith.

THE PROMISE OF A GLORIOUS RESTORATION (4:2-6)

As he often does, Isaiah quickly turns from scathing rebuke (2:5-4:1) to the promise of restoration. The focus in verses 2-6 turns to restoration.

Verses 4:2-6 read as follows: "2 In that day the Branch of the Lord will be beautiful and glorious, and the fruit of the earth *will be* the pride and the adornment of the survivors of Israel. 3 It will come about that he who is left in Zion and remains in Jerusalem will be called holy—everyone who is recorded for life in Jerusalem. 4 When the Lord has washed away the filth of the daughters of Zion and purged the bloodshed of Jerusalem from her midst, by the spirit of judgment and the spirit of burning, 5 then the Lord will create over the whole area of Mount Zion and over her assemblies a cloud by day, even smoke, and the brightness of a flaming fire by night; for over all the glory will be a canopy.

---

[100] Isaiah uses the word *tachath* (instead of) five times in v. 24 to stress the idea of removal and substitution.

[101] Wolf, *Interpreting Isaiah*, 81.

6 There will be a shelter to *give* shade from the heat by day, and refuge and protection from the storm and the rain" (4:2-6). Although Judah has fallen, Yahweh will certainly fulfill His covenant promises in His good time by restoring Israel under a new covenant when Messiah comes with the kingdom of God (cf. 2:2-4). Isaiah highlights four promises.

First promise: A righteous King (v. 2a)

Some people believe that the only hope for a better world is a new world order with some sort of one-world government. Their mistake is in thinking that fallen sinners are the ones who can achieve this better world. Only Christ can bring the righteous kingdom this world needs.

The time of the kingdom

God Himself is the only One who can bring in such blessings, and Isaiah tells us that it is "in that day" that He will do so—the end of the age when He sends His Son to restore a fallen world. Thus, the abrupt statement "in that day" has relation to the preceding context telling us how God will judge the world in a final period of "indignation" (Heb. *za'am*, cf. Isa. 10:25; 26:20; Dan. 8:19; 11:36),[102] but it is a judgment that comes at the end of the age.

The Ruler of the kingdom

God's promise for world restoration is that one day "the Branch of the Lord will be beautiful and glorious, and the fruit of the earth *will be* the pride and the adornment of the survivors of Israel." Who is this?

The origin of "Branch" terminology. This expression "Branch" (Heb. noun *tsemech*) is a messianic title with hundreds of years of biblical theology standing behind it. The origin of this messianic title appears to come from the lips of King David in his last psalm (cf. 2 Sam. 23:1-5). In these Spirit-inspired words, David was rejoicing over the covenant God had sworn to him many years earlier (2 Sam. 7:1-17). David was approaching death, but he knew that his "house" (i.e., his dynasty) was secure (23:5) since God had sworn to him an

---

[102] Oswalt, *The Book of Isaiah, Chapters 1-39*, 145-146. As Oswalt explains, destruction will come, but "God's coming day would only be complete when cleansing and restoration had taken place (cf. Zech. 12-14 for the same theme)." The judgment Israel has brought upon itself will not come to its end until God's chastisement has run its course in the seven-year tribulation period. The Scripture calls this eschatological climax of God's wrath "the final period of *indignation*" (*za'am*, Dan. 8:17, 19; cf. 11:36; 12:7), God's indignation against sin and transgression, especially that of His covenant people Israel (Isa. 10:5, 25; 13:5; 26:20; 34:20; 66:14).

everlasting covenant that the Savior of the world would come from his descendants. David declared that the covenant is ordered and secured, and then he asked the rhetorical question, "Will he not indeed *make it grow?*" (Heb. *tsamach*, the verbal form of the noun *tsemech*, meaning to sprout or branch out).

The development of "Branch" terminology. Commenting on the noun *tsemech*, Kaiser notes, "Especially significant are the passages related to the coming up of a shoot from the root or seed of David, i.e. the future messianic person."[103] David's certain hope was that one of his own sons would be the Son of God who would branch out from his line and restore this world and rule on the throne of David. Later prophets like Isaiah (4:2), Jeremiah (23:5-6; 33:15), Ezekiel (29:21), and Zechariah (Zech. 3:8; 6:12) all celebrated this same promise. God says in Psalm 132 that all of this will be fulfilled in the eschatological kingdom of God through "the horn of David": "There I will cause the horn of David to spring forth [*tsamach*]; I have prepared a lamp for Mine anointed [*maschiyach*]. His enemies I will clothe with shame, but upon himself his crown shall shine" (132:17-18). Here in 4:2 Isaiah declares that God's King will be "beautiful and glorious" when that day comes, the messianic King who is highly exalted (Isa. 52:13) and sought out by all His kingdom citizens (Hos. 3:5).[104]

Second promise: A fruitful prosperity (v. 2b)

God's kingdom will also be a time of great physical fruitfulness within the land of Israel (and the whole world),[105] a fruitfulness that will be enjoyed by the survivors of the tribulation period, the "ones who escape" (cf. *peleytath* in Isa. 10:20 and Joel 2:32). This statement may not be limited to the fruit that her own land produces, but perhaps also to the flow of blessings that the Gentiles bring to the Messiah and His kingdom (cf. Isa. 60:1-22).

Third promise: A purified people (v. 3)

The unrighteous will not inherit the kingdom of God (1 Cor. 6:9; Gal. 5:21), but only those who have been purified by faith through the grace of God.

---

[103] Walter C. Kaiser, "*tsmch*," ed. R. Laird Harris, Gleason L. Archer Jr., and Bruce K. Waltke, *Theological Wordbook of the Old Testament*, cited in electronic form with Logos Libronix (Chicago: Moody Press, 1999), 769.

[104] Young notes that the Targums recognized the messianic nature of this passage (Young, *The Book of Isaiah, vol. 1*, 176).

[105] Numerous verses speak about the literal fruitfulness of the land in the kingdom (Isa. 30:23-24; 32:14-20; 35:1-7; 41:17-20; 43:16-21; 51:3; 55:12; 60:13; cf. Num. 24:6; Ps. 104:16; Jer. 31:12; Ezek. 34:26-29; 47:1-12; Joel 3:18-21; Amos 9:13-15; Zech. 9:16-10:1; Mal. 3:11).

Only a remnant enters the kingdom

Numerous passages in the Old and New Testaments indicate that these kingdom blessings will be enjoyed only by those who have placed their faith in the Messiah (Jew and gentile). In this passage the focus is on the elect remnant of Israel who have trusted in Messiah. Isaiah calls them those who are "left in Zion" (another expression referring to the remnant; cf. Isa. 6:13; 7:3; 10:20-21; 28:5; 46:3; Rom. 9:27-28), the ones who are "recorded for life in Jerusalem," i.e., the elect who have been recorded for life (cf. Exod. 32:32; Dan. 12:1; Mal. 3:16; Rev. 13:8; 17:8; 20:15),[106] the ones who are now considered "holy" by the redeeming grace of God who has freely forgiven their sins (Isa. 35:8-10).

The remnant is an object of redeeming grace

This is the remnant of Israel whom God will save by a mighty outpouring of His Spirit in the midst of the tribulation period (Isa. 32:15; 44:3-5; cf. Joel 2:28-32; Zech. 12:10-13:1). Jesus referred to the salvation of this elect remnant in the Olivet Discourse (Matt. 24:22, 31; cf. Isa. 27:12-13) as being one of the reasons why the Great Tribulation would be no longer than three and a half years. During that time, Satan (the dragon) will do all he can through his agent the Antichrist to annihilate Israel (Joel 3:9-17; Zech. 12:1-9; 14:1-2; Rev. 12), but God will be at work to preserve His people and to use this persecution to bring the remnant to faith in Jesus Christ (cf. Dan. 12:7). Two thirds of the nation will die in disbelief (Ezek. 20:36-38; Zech. 13:8), but God will save His remnant so that they might enter His kingdom (Isa. 35:8-10; Matt. 25:34; Acts 13:48; Rom. 11:25-29; Rev. 7:1-8; 12:14-17).[107]

Fourth promise: A dwelling of Yahweh with His people (vv. 4-6)

One aspect of God's kingdom restoration includes the promise that He will once again dwell in the presence of His people. Isaiah assures us that God's saving grace will accomplish such a restoration.

---

[106] The statement "recorded" for life (a Qal Passive Participle *kathub*) conveys the force that these elect saints exercise saving faith because they were already recorded for life in the eternal purposes of God (cf. e.g., Rom. 8:28-29; 9:24; Eph. 1:3-4, 11; 2 Tim. 1:9; 2 Thess. 2:13; 1 Pet. 1:1-2). Similar ideas refer to citizen records or genealogical records as in Nehemiah [Neh. 7:5, 64] (Young, *The Book of Isaiah, vol. 1*, 179; Grogan, "Isaiah," 46, n. 3).

[107] Young explains that the doctrine of a remnant "is traced to its true and ultimate foundation in the doctrine of election" (Young, *The Book of Isaiah, vol. 1*, 180).

The dwelling of God will be in the midst of a purified people (v. 4)

God's promise to dwell in the midst of His people is one of the most precious promises in the Bible.[108] However, this cannot happen until the nation has been purified and restored under the New Covenant. The cleansing God brings comes through the fires of the Great Tribulation, the greatest tribulation the nation will have ever faced (Isa. 11:11-16; 27:12; Dan. 12:7; Mal. 3:1-4; Matt. 24:15-31).[109] God will accomplish this cleansing "by the spirit of judgment and the spirit of burning" (cf. Zech. 13:8-9; Mal. 3:1-4). There is some question about how we should take these two references to "spirit." It seems that the best explanation is what one calls "the abstract for the concrete,"[110] a statement that makes it clear that fiery judgments are coming. The result will be the glorious kingdom with the Lord dwelling in the midst of His people.

The dwelling of God will be a brilliant display of divine glory (vv. 5-6)

This dwelling of God is described in verses 5-6—a restoration of the shekinah glory as in days of old (Exod. 13:21-22; 24:16; Num. 9:15-23; 1 Kings 8:1ff.). The restoration of this glory will bring shelter and protection to the nation by the very presence of God. When the glory gets restored, Isaiah says that God will give His protective presence not simply within an inner sanctuary, but

---

[108] God's promises to dwell in the midst of His people (which actually began in Genesis 1-2) can be traced to the Exodus (the cloud and fire) and the subsequent command to build a sanctuary (Exod. 25:8-9; 29:45; 40:34-38). Because of Israel's sin, the glory of God departed from Solomon's temple shortly before its destruction (cf. Ezek. 10:1-4; 11:22-23). God's promise to Israel was that one day He would restore His people under a New Covenant and that He would once again dwell in their midst (Ezek. 37:21-28; 43:1ff.; 44:1ff.; Jer. 31:31-34; 33:14-26). An advance in God's plan included the Son coming to dwell (i.e., to "tabernacle") in the midst of man at the first coming of Christ (John 1:14). At the present time the Scripture shows that this indwelling is by the Spirit in the church (2 Cor. 6:14-18). The future dwelling of God starting with the return of Christ will include a dwelling of God with His people in a millennial temple (Ezek. 43:1ff.; 44:1ff.) as well as an eternal dwelling in the presence of His people in a new creation (Rev. 21:1-4).

[109] The term "filth" (*tso'ath*) is a strong word that can be used for things like vomit (Isa. 28:8; Prov. 30:12) or even excrement (Isa. 36:12; 2 Kings 18:27), a strong term to describe the sin of Israel (Young, *The Book of Isaiah, vol. 1*, 182, n. 48). The purging (see Jer. 51:34; Ezek. 40:38; 2 Chron. 4:6) of bloodshed, an idea that includes both literal murder as well as violent social injustice (cf. Isa. 1:15-23; Ezek. 9:9), conveys the idea that God will both make atonement for their past bloodshed and also bring a permanent removal of such sins for all time.

[110] See Oswalt for three views (Oswalt, *The Book of Isaiah, Chapters 1-39*, 148).

over the entire dwelling place of His city, the "whole area of Mt. Zion" and "all her assemblies" (cf. Isa. 24:23; 60:1-2, 19).[111] This canopy (cf. Exod. 13:21; 14:20; 40:34) will even produce an element of protection from any kind of harsh physical elements, a very welcome divine refuge (cf. Isa. 25:4; Pss. 14:6; 46:2) and protection (cf. Isa. 43:1-2; Amos 9:15).

Summary and application

One lesson for us all is the need to turn away from every form of false hope so that our trust would be only in the Lord and His saving grace. Our need is to keep our focus on two places. First, we need to look back to remember the cross and the resurrection. By His perfect sacrifice, our Jesus has won the victory over sin, curse, and death (and the resurrection is proof). Second, we need to look forward to the return of Christ when He brings a perfect consummation to this redemption process (Rom. 8:18-27).

THE DISAPPOINTING VINEYARD (5:1-30)

Chapter 5 continues the rebuke theme. Furthermore, as noted by Kidner, "this chapter has much in common with its predecessors. . . . It brings the book's long overture to a strong climax."[112]

Chapter 5 reads as follows: "1 Let me sing now for my well-beloved, a song of my beloved concerning His vineyard. My well-beloved had a vineyard on a fertile hill. 2 He dug it all around, removed its stones, and planted it with the choicest vine, and He built a tower in the middle of it, and also hewed out a wine vat in it; then He expected *it* to produce *good* grapes, but it produced *only* worthless ones. 3 "And now, O inhabitants of Jerusalem and men of Judah, judge between Me and My vineyard. 4 What more was there to do for My vineyard that I have not done in it? Why, when I expected *it* to produce *good* grapes did it produce worthless ones? 5 So now let Me tell you what I am going to do to My vineyard: I will remove its hedge and it will be consumed; I will break down its wall and it will become trampled ground. 6 I will lay it waste; it will not be pruned or hoed, but briars and thorns will come up. I will also charge the clouds to rain no rain on it. 7 For the vineyard of the Lord of hosts is the house of Israel and the men of Judah His delightful plant. Thus, He looked for justice, but behold, bloodshed, for righteousness, but behold, a cry of distress. 8 Woe to those who add house to house *and* join field to field, until there is no more room, so that you have to live alone in the midst of the land! 9 In my ears the

---

[111] Commentators disagree whether it is "those who assemble" or "places of assembly." Oswalt prefers the former more common use (ibid., 144, n. 2).
[112] Kidner, "Isaiah," 636.

Lord of hosts *has sworn,* surely, many houses shall become desolate, *even* great and fine ones, without occupants, 10 for ten acres of vineyard will yield *only* one bath *of wine,* and a homer of seed will yield *but* an ephah of grain. 11 Woe to those who rise early in the morning that they may pursue strong drink, who stay up late in the evening that wine may inflame them! 12 Their banquets are *accompanied* by lyre and harp, by tambourine and flute, and by wine, but they do not pay attention to the deeds of the Lord, nor do they consider the work of His hands. 13 Therefore My people go into exile for their lack of knowledge, and their honorable men are famished, and their multitude is parched with thirst. 14 Therefore *Sheol* has enlarged its throat and opened its mouth without measure, and Jerusalem's splendor, her multitude, her din *of revelry* and the jubilant within her, descend *into it.* 15 So the *common* man will be humbled and the man of *importance* abased; the eyes of the proud also will be abased. 16 But the Lord of hosts will be exalted in judgment, and the holy God will show Himself holy in righteousness. 17 Then the lambs will graze as in their pasture, and strangers will eat in the waste places of the wealthy. 18 Woe to those who drag iniquity with the cords of falsehood, and sin as if with cart ropes, 19 who say, let Him make speed, let Him hasten His work, that we may see *it;* and let the purpose of the Holy One of Israel draw near and come to pass, that we may know *it!"* 20 Woe to those who call evil good, and good evil, who substitute darkness for light and light for darkness, who substitute bitter for sweet and sweet for bitter! 21 Woe to those who are wise in their own eyes and clever in their own sight! 22 Woe to those who are heroes in drinking wine and valiant men in mixing strong drink, 23 who justify the wicked for a bribe, and take away the rights of the ones who are in the right! 24 Therefore, as a tongue of fire consumes stubble and dry grass collapses into the flame, so their root will become like rot and their blossom blow away as dust, for they have rejected the law of the Lord of hosts and despised the word of the Holy One of Israel. 25 On this account the anger of the Lord has burned against His people, and He has stretched out His hand against them and struck them down, and the mountains quaked, and their corpses lay like refuse in the middle of the streets. For all this His anger is not spent, but His hand is still stretched out. 26 He will also lift up a standard to the distant nation, and will whistle for it from the ends of the earth, and behold, it will come with speed swiftly. 27 No one in it is weary or stumbles; none slumbers or sleeps, nor is the belt at its waist undone, nor its sandal strap broken. 28 Its arrows are sharp and all its bows are bent; the hoofs of its horses seem like flint and its *chariot* wheels like a whirlwind. 29 Its roaring is like a lioness, and it roars like young lions; it growls as it seizes the prey and carries *it* off with no one to deliver *it,* 30 and it will growl over it in that day like the roaring of the sea. If one looks to the land, behold, there is darkness *and* distress, even the light is darkened by its clouds" (5:1-30).

The chapter breaks down into three major portions. It begins by telling a parabolic song about an unfruitful vineyard (vv. 1-7).[113] This is then followed with six woes against the people of Judah (vv. 8-23). Lastly, we see God's instruction about how to avoid His judgment (vv. 24-30).

The unfruitful vineyard (vv. 1-7)

One principle that runs throughout the Bible is that every person is accountable to worship God and bear fruit for His glory. If we are not doing these things, we are not fulfilling our purpose. This is true for individual Christians today, but it was also true for the nation Israel. Furthermore, we also recognize the principle that greater spiritual privilege increases one's responsibility before God (cf. Luke 2:48). This is a central idea in Isaiah 5. God gave Israel the privileged position of knowing Him and bearing fruit, but in spite of all that God did for them, they failed to produce fruit. By means of a parabolic story (a song), Isaiah tells the people that since they have failed to bear fruit, the only option left is for God to bring judgment. This song has two basic scenes.

First scene: Preparation of the vineyard (vv. 1-2)

In verse 1 Isaiah declares his passionate intention to sing a song about His "Beloved," the owner and builder of the vineyard. As noted, the major focus of Isaiah's song will be about the extraordinary effort to create a fruitful vineyard, and its subsequent failure to produce good fruit. Isaiah highlights six careful steps of preparation for the vineyard.

The first three steps (vv. 1-2a). The first thing this man did was to find the best possible location. The Hebrew text calls the location "a horn of a son of oil," an expression that means the soil was very rich and had good exposure to the sun (v. 1).[114] Next, he "dug it all around," meaning that he cultivated the dirt and dug furrows for good growth (v. 2). Third, the owner removed all of the stones.[115] The Arabs had a proverb that said that when God created the world an angel flew over it carrying a bag of stones under each arm, and when he flew over Palestine, one bag broke so that half of all the stones in the world are in Palestine. The key point is that the owner put great effort into making this an excellent vineyard.

The last three steps (v. 2b). Fourth, the owner planted the "choicest" kind of vine, a *sorek* vine. The *sorek* grape was noted as one of the choicest of

---

[113] We see the vineyard metaphor in Jeremiah 12:10 and Psalm 80.

[114] Oswalt, *The Book of Isaiah, Chapters 1-39*, 149, n 1.

[115] The "privative" use of the Piel expresses the idea of removal as seen in the Heb. of Ps. 51:9 (ibid., 149, n 2.).

all, and there is even a valley southwest of Jerusalem called The *Sorek* Valley (where Samson lived), a valley known for its excellent wine.[116] Fifth, he built a tower so that watchmen could protect against thieves and wild animals. Sixth, the owner hewed out a wine vat.[117] Wine vats consisted of two portions of ground that were carved into the bedrock (about 4-6 inches deep into the rock) with one being higher than the other and a channel connecting the two. Grapes were trampled in the upper vat, and then the juice flowed down the channel into the lower vat where it was collected and put into wine skins for fermenting.[118] The owner did everything possible to produce excellent fruit. Sadly, it produced only "worthless" grapes, grapes that were tasteless and sour (cf. Lam. 2:6).

Second scene: How God will deal with Judah (vv. 3-7)

In light of this, God calls upon His people to make a judgment about how the owner of the vineyard should deal with his dilemma (v. 3). Clearly there was nothing else the owner could have done (v. 4). God can no longer ignore their transgressions. Isaiah declares that nothing more can be done (vv. 5-6), then explains it more fully in verse 7.

Nothing more can be done (vv. 5-6). The time for patience has run its course, and the only thing that can be done is to destroy the worthless vineyard. The owner will remove its protective hedge and give the vineyard over to destruction. With no protection, wild animals will trample down the vineyard so that nothing can grow there (cf. 7:25).[119] Instead of rich fruit, the worthless vineyard will become a place of "briars and thorns," an expression Isaiah repeats five more times (7:23-25; 9:18; 10:17; 27:4; cf. Gen. 3:18 for the idea of curse with briars and thorns).[120]

Isaiah makes an explicit explanation (v. 7). The story is a parable that illustrates the failure of Israel and Judah to bear fruit for the Lord. God's people

---

[116] Wolf, *Interpreting Isaiah*, 82.

[117] The Hebrew *wegam* ("and even") emphasizes this as an extra, extraordinary step.

[118] An excellent example of such a wine vat can be seen in the place called Tel Avdat in the Negev of southern Israel.

[119] Young, *The Book of Isaiah, vol. 1*, 201. Young notes that "there was often a double enclosure, one of stones and the other of hedge. . . . When these protections are removed the cattle can enter the vineyard and so trample."

[120] The destruction to the fields and vineyards from the invading armies will be so bad that the remaining population will be forced to eat curds and wild honey (7:15, 19-25; 8:6-8). The impact of God bringing curse will also include the withholding of rain (Deut. 28:23-24; Ruth 1; 2 Sam. 1:21; Amos 4:4-11).

were His "delightful plant" from whom He expected rich fruit (e.g., righteousness and justice),[121] but instead they produced nothing but sin and wickedness (cf. Mic. 3:10; 7:2-4).[122]

What, then, is God to do? The answer is found in Isaiah's full prophetic message. For the present time there is no option but to bring a severe destruction. Terrible days are about to come, but even here God will not fully abandon His people. A restoration will come, but until long ages of judgment have run their course (cf. Deut. 30:1-10).

Six woes that bring the wrath of God (vv. 8-23)

Chapters 1-5 have already shown numerous reasons why God's judgment would fall upon Israel. This section continues exposing the sins of Israel with a series of woes why God must judge them. Weber explains,

[A woe is] an interjection, usually of lamentation. It occurs fifty times in the prophets and once elsewhere. Six usages refer to mourning for the dead (as I Kgs 13:30), and forty involve negative warnings or threats of God's physical chastisement. But in Isa 55:1 it introduces a positive invitation to come and buy good things without money or price.[123]

Isaiah exposes Judah's sin with a series of six woes that explain why the wrath of God would burn against Israel for a long time. Martin explains, "Though verses 8–30 are not a part of the song in verses 1-7, they fit into Isaiah's train of thought nicely because their six indictments ('woes') are against the 'bad fruit' the nation had been producing."[124]

The first of Isaiah's six woes: Unrestrained greed (vv. 8-10)

Greed is one of those ubiquitous sins that shows itself in every culture. The greed of Judah had become especially grievous.

---

[121] This term "delightful" (*sha'ashuyim*) is a rare term that conveys the idea of objects of pleasure or desire (Pss. 119:43, 77, 92, 174; Prov. 8:30-31). See 60:21 and 61:3 for similar imagery with different terms as God foretells His eschatological blessing upon Israel.
[122] The Hebrew text uses two pairs of rhyming terms (paranomasia) to vividly illustrate the failure: (1) justice, bloodshed [*mishpat, mispach*], (2) righteousness, cry [*tsedeqah, tse'aqah*]. See the same literary tool in 13:6; 24:17; 33:1; 57:6; 61:3.
[123] Carl Philip Weber, "*hoy*," ed. R. Laird Harris, Gleason L. Archer Jr., and Bruce K. Waltke, *Theological Wordbook of the Old Testament*, cited in electronic form with Logos Libronix (Chicago: Moody Press, 1999), 212.
[124] Martin, "Isaiah," 1042.

The nature of Israel's unrestrained greed (v. 8).[125] Israel had been overtaken by greed. Rather than finding contentment in their permanent land allotments given by the Lord (Lev. 25:23-25; Num. 27:7-11), many were relentlessly acquiring multiplied land possessions, often by means that were both sinful and illegal. Greed is a curious sin, for it does not matter whether one has little or much, the greedy man always wants more. Paul warns against this sin by reminding us that it is a form of idolatry (Col. 3:5), the kind of sin God's people should be very wary of (1 Tim. 6:17), for it is always at work to bring evil temptations (1 Tim. 6:9-11). Solomon warns, "He who loves money will not be satisfied with money nor he who loves abundance with its income. This too is vanity" (Ecc. 5:10).

The days leading up to Isaiah's time had been quite prosperous (the days of Jeroboam II and Uzziah), but still the people were not content. Pfeiffer explains that "by foreclosing mortgages or by forcing sales of land, the wealthy landowners acquired all the adjoining farms to form huge estates."[126] In reality, this greed showed a lack of faith in the Lord and a lack of love for their Israelite brethren, a sin that was illustrated supremely by King Ahab (1 Kings 21:17-24; cf. Mic. 2:1-9; Amos 2:6-7).

The result of Israel's unrestrained greed (vv. 9-10). Their sin infuriated God and lead Him to act.[127] The people found their delight in large, opulent estates, but God tells them that He would take it all away and make all those houses "desolate" (*shammah*, empty, uninhabited), even the largest and finest of the land. Amos gave the same warning when he wrote,

Therefore, because you impose heavy rent on the poor and exact a tribute of grain from them; *though* you have built houses of well-hewn stone, yet you will not live in them; you have planted pleasant vineyards, yet you will not drink their wine (5:11; cf. 6:4-7).

In other words, instead of a land that was populated and prosperous, it would be a land of ruin (v. 10).[128]

---

[125] Oswalt, *The Book of Isaiah, Chapters 1-39*, 157.

[126] Pfeiffer, *The Wycliffe Bible Commentary, Old Testament*, Is 5:8.

[127] The identification of God as "Lord of Hosts" highlights His anger over sin.

[128] For ten acres of vineyard to yield one bath of wine (about 6 gallons) was disastrous. For a field to yield one ephah of grain (an ephah was about 1/10 of a homer and the homer was equal to about 10 ½ bushels) was disastrous (about 1/10 of the norm), but all of it was God's judgment (Deut. 28:38-39; cf. Hag. 2:16-17).

Greed is still with us today, of course. Those who live in the West (esp. America) can testify that no matter how much money a person has, it will never be enough money if money is what is driving a person.

The second woe: The sin of drunken revelry (vv. 11-17)

Isaiah describes a nation that has been overcome not only with greed, but also by drunken revelry. The party life of Israel showed itself at both ends of the clock. Isaiah exposes their sin (vv. 11-12), and God follows this up by declaring how He will judge it (vv. 13-17).

Habitual drunkenness was a stumbling block (vv. 11-12). Whether it was strong drink (*sheker*) early in the morning,[129] or wine (*yayin*) late at night,[130] many had become enslaved to drunkenness. Young notes,

> It is not the fact of drinking in itself is here condemned, but the debauchery and waste of time that is connected with it. Those condemned rise early in the morning, not thereby to glorify the Lord in their daily work, but to satiate themselves with strong drink (a shameful way to live says Solomon in Ecclesiastes 10:16).[131]

Music has always been popular with all men. The lyre (*Kinneroth*) was a 10-stringed instrument and the harp (*nebel*) a 12-stringed instrument. Tamborines (*toph*) were among the percussion instruments, and flutes (*chaliyl*) were among the wind instruments. The problem was not music, but godless ease. Amos derided this kind of carefree living when he wrote about those who,

> improvise to the sound of the harp, and like David have composed songs for themselves, who drink wine from sacrificial bowls while they anoint themselves with the finest of oils, yet they have not grieved over the ruin of Joseph (Amos 6:5-6).

Again, the problem was not that music itself was bad, or that God was against His people having pleasure (cf. Ecc. 9:7-9), but it was an idolatrous view of hedonism and a lack of faith in the Lord Himself (v. 12).

---

[129] This term refers to the high sugar and high alcohol content of certain drink (cf. 28:7). The Greek equivalent is the word *sikera*, and both the Hebrew and Greek reflect themselves in our English word "sugar." Drunkenness is a sin that is condemned repeatedly (Isa. 5:22; 22:13; 28:1-8; Hos. 7:5; Joel 3:3; Amos 6:6).
[130] This is the most general of several terms for wine.
[131] Young, *The Book of Isaiah, vol. 1*, 208-209.

God's response (vv. 13-17). Verse 13 introduces the logical conclusions (*laken*) of their persistent rebellion—invasion and exile. Isaiah highlights five kinds of judgments that will be part of God's work. The first will be invasion and exile to a foreign land (v. 13). Exile should have come as no surprise since the Mosaic covenant said that this would be the punishment for covenant disobedience (Deut. 28:36, 64). God calls the problem "lack of knowledge" (cf. Isa. 1:3; 27:11). This is not an innocent lack of knowledge, but an intentional rejection of knowledge (cf. Hos. 4:6).

Second, none will escape this judgment, not even the highest classes in the land (v. 13b). Powerful sinners (the *kabod*) often see themselves as being immune to calamity, but God makes it clear that none will escape.

The third judgment will be death to the nation (v. 14). *She'ol*, i.e., death, is personified as standing with a wide-open mouth. Both Assyria and Babylon brought massive death to Israel, a death that seemed insatiable (Isa. 29:8; cf. Prov. 10:3). With this, God will bring an end to the sinful revelry.

The fourth judgment will be a complete reversal of the present, sinful order (vv. 15-16). The nation was so upside down that the only solution was a judgment so severe it would bring a radical reversal of the present order. As Young explains, this will mean "the complete and utter humiliation of man and the exaltation of the Lord" (cf. 17:7).[132] Israel will be humbled (v. 15), but Yahweh will be exalted by this judgment (v. 16). Up to this time, Israel had complete disregard for the righteousness of God, but all this was about to change with the visitation of the Holy God.[133]

The fifth and final judgment will be that the glorious land of Israel will become a desolate wasteland (v. 17). Instead of native Israelites farming their God-given inheritance and enjoying its fruit, the land will be overrun by animals and strangers from foreign lands.[134]

---

[132] Ibid., 214.

[133] When God speaks about vindicating His holiness and righteousness with judgments on sin, one is reminded of passages like Ezekiel 36:19ff. and Matthew 6:9ff. that speak not only of the judgments on sin historically, but also the eschatological restoration of Israel by which the world will know Yahweh.

[134] The MT has the term "strangers" (*gariym*), but LXX has the very similar word "kids" (*gadiym*, cf. similar terms in 5:14-17). Textual evidence and the parallel suggests that "goat" may be the correct text.

The third woe: Defiance against God (vv. 18-19)

The imagery Isaiah uses is that of dragging iniquity and sin with ropes like a cart (cf. Prov. 5:22). Instead of doing their labor by pulling a cart for work, they simply dragged around their iniquity and their sin. Their defiance showed itself in that they were taunting God to bring judgment (perhaps mocking Isaiah). Judgment was speeding toward them (cf. 8:1-4), but in their minds Isaiah's words were empty threats (cf. 30:8-11).

The fourth woe: Twisting and perverting moral truth (v. 20)

The sins that dominated Judah are the same today: "Woe to those who call evil good, and good evil, who substitute darkness for light and light for darkness, who substitute bitter for sweet and sweet for bitter!" The things that God said were good were being rejected. Pfeiffer explains, "they acclaimed depravity of character as manly strength, and sensuous impurity as true virtue and strength."[135] All of it is moral perversion.

The fifth woe: Extreme pride (v. 21)

God describes Judah as "wise in their own eyes" and "clever" in their own sight (empty pride). The Proverbs tell us that God hates haughty eyes (6:17) and that pride goes before destruction (16:18).

The sixth and final woe: Extremely wicked living (vv. 22-23)

For lack of a better label, the final woe might be characterized as that of extremely wicked living. The sin of drunkenness is vividly highlighted by calling them masters of making mixed drinks that became very strong through a combination of high alcohol and strong spices (cf. Ps. 75:9; Prov. 23:30; Song 8:2; Amos 6:6).[136] Not only were they master drunkards, but also master criminals who used their power and money to work the system for oppressing and robbing others. In all likelihood, Isaiah is referring to the princes and judges who, rather than dispensing justice, were using their powerful positions to enlarge themselves. Wrath will soon fall upon them.

The burning wrath of God (vv. 24-30)

Once God's patience runs its course, judgment is the only solution (cf. e.g., Gen. 6-9; 19). By the time of Isaiah, Israel had enjoyed God's patience for over seven-hundred years, but God's patience was about to be exhausted. Here in 5:24-30 we see three descriptions of how God will satisfy His wrath.

---

[135] Pfeiffer, *The Wycliffe Bible Commentary: Old Testament*, Is 5:20.
[136] Young, *The Book of Isaiah, vol. 1*, 221.

First description of God's burning wrath (v. 24)

The consequence of Israel's unrepentant sin will be divine anger that is likened to an unquenchable fire that consumes everything in its path. Israel rejected God, so He will reject them. Not only will the grass be burned up, but the root will rot and disappear (cf. Amos 2:9; Hos. 9:16; Mal. 4:1). They had the knowledge of God, but they willfully rejected Him (cf. 1:4), and now they will bear the consequences.

Second description of God's burning wrath (v. 25)

Because they rejected the Lord,[137] the anger of the Lord was burning against them. The vivid language of verse 25 portrays the invading armies of Assyria and Babylon who would lay waste to Judah and introduce a long age of covenant curses.[138] The judgments by Assyria and Babylon would be horrific, but God tells them that these invasions and wars would only be the beginning of a long period of wrath: "For all this His anger is not spent, but His hand is still stretched out." This is a fascinating expression that we find for the first time here, but recurs several times before it culminates with an end of the burning anger in chapter 12 when the anger of God has been fully spent (cf. 9:12, 17, 21; 10:4, 25; 12:1). God is showing His people that rebellion will bring judgments (Deut. 28:15-68).

A careful tracing of this theological theme (God's wrath on Israel) reveals a treasure of understanding about how God's judgments will fall on rebellious Israel, a wrathful anger that is often called the "indignation" of the Lord. This indignation began pouring down long ago (cf. Isa. 10:5, 25; 13:5; 30:27; 34:2), but it will not be exhausted until the end of the tribulation period. Isaiah 26:20-21 warns the future remnant of Israel to find shelter from the eschatological wrath in the tribulation period as God comes to destroy "the inhabitants of the earth."[139] All of this will come as God saves His remnant through the sufferings

---

[137] The Hebrew causal expression *'al ken* ("therefore") shows the direct connection between Judah's sin and the burning wrath of God.

[138] The string of waw consecutive imperfect verbs that follow the initial perfect stem verb ("burned") are all looking ahead to the imminent Assyrian and Babylonian invasions (Oswalt, *The Book of Isaiah, 1-39*, 166; Young, *The Book of Isaiah, vol. 1*, 225, n. 26). The idea of quaking mountains could be figuratively referring to the invading armies coming over the hills or, perhaps, to the earthquake that came during the days of Uzziah.

[139] The expression "the inhabitants of the earth" finds itself repeated in the Greek text of the apocalypse 11 times, always referring to a God-hating, Christ-rejecting world

of persecution and the regenerating work of the Spirit (cf. Zech. 12:10; 13:8-9; Mal. 3:1-6).

Daniel foretold that at "the time of the end" (Dan. 8:17)—the "appointed time of the end"—there would be a "final period of the indignation" (Dan. 8:19), and that it is through the fires of this tribulation that God would bring an end to Israel's covenant "transgression" (Dan. 9:24) and restore His fallen people. None of that can be fulfilled, however, until "the indignation is finished" (Dan. 11:36) and "that which is decreed" to fall upon Israel has been fulfilled (Dan. 11:36; cf. Dan. 9:27; Matt. 23:37-39). The fires of God's consuming wrath will bring Israel to its knees in the great tribulation period (cf. Dan. 12:7), but all of it will be part of God's gracious work to save His elect remnant (Isa. 1:9; 4:2; 6:13; 10:20-22; 11:11; 37:31-32; 43:5-6; 46:3; 49:6) and to restore His people (Rom. 11:25-36).

Third description of God's burning wrath (vv. 26-30)

God explains that He is about to bring in a fierce and impetuous nation who will not show any mercy.[140] The sovereignty of God is magnified as God makes it clear that He Himself is the One summoning this nation (cf. Isa. 9:11-12, 17, 21; 10:4).[141] God is the One raising the banner (Isa. 11:10, 12; 13:2; 18:3; 49:22; 62:10), and God is the One giving the whistle (Isa. 7:18; Zech. 10:8). Verses 26-30 show us four descriptions of these invasions.

First description of the invasions: It is a ready nation (v. 26). God is not describing events of the distant future, but events that would come soon and quickly, starting with invasions from far away Assyria, invasions, says Martin, that "seemingly come from the ends of the earth, a phrase Isaiah used frequently to suggest people everywhere (5:26; 24:16; 40:28; 41:5, 9; 42:10; 43:6; 45:22; 48:20; 49:6; 52:10; 62:11)."[142]

Isaiah began his prophetic ministry in 740 B.C. at a time when the Assyrian

---

that is now falling under God's judgments in the Day of the Lord (Rev. 3:10; 6:10; 8:13; 11:10bis; 13:8, 12, 14bis; 17:2, 8; cf. Isa. 66:14; Jer. 25:29; 30:10-17; 46:28; Amos 9:8).

[140] In the flow of Isaiah's messages, it is clear that the foreign invasions will commence with Assyria against Israel/Judah in 732, but continue with an invasion by Babylon against Judah in 605 (and the eventual fall of Jerusalem in 586).

[141] This is one of many passages where the Bible illustrates the sovereignty of God over human affairs without presenting any conflict between divine sovereignty and creaturely freedom (Isa. 40:21-24; 44:28-45:5; 46:8-11; cf. Dan. 1:2; 2:37).

[142] Martin, "Isaiah," 1043.

war machine was getting aggressive in a westward push. Tiglath Pileser III (aka Pul, 745-727) began pushing westward, conquering every nation in its path and deporting many of those he conquered. An anti-Assyrian coalition formed between Israel and Damascus which resulted in these two powers attacking Judah in 735 for not joining the alliance (cf. chs. 7-12). Their desire was to overthrow the Davidic dynasty and replace Ahaz with someone who would be loyal to this anti-Assyrian alliance (Isa. 7; cf. 2 Kings 16:2-6, ca. 734 B.C.). Here in these opening chapters Isaiah is warning the rebellious nation that all of this will soon come upon the nation.

Second description: It will be a powerful nation (v. 27). Assyria was a nation that showed no weakness, i.e., no weariness, no stumbling, no slumber, no sleep.[143] This is one powerful nation who is ready for battle with belts and sandals tightly bound for battle action.[144]

Third description: It is a prepared nation (v. 28). Every aspect of their weaponry is ready for action, whether it is sharp arrows (cf. Ps. 45:5-6), bent bows (bows were never bent until needed),[145] or powerful horses with sharp hooves. In the ancient world, chariots were a powerful military tool (like a modern tank). Isaiah describes these Assyrian tanks as having wheels like whirlwind (a blur of iron and loud sounds; cf. similar language referring to God in Isa. 66:15; Jer. 4:13).

Fourth description: It is a fierce nation (vv. 29-30). Isaiah uses two metaphors to describe Assyria. The first is that of a roaring lion (like a lioness making a kill, or a young, weaned lion in the prime of youth). Powerful lions make their kill, and none can stop it, and so it will be with Assyria. Secondly, Assyria is like the roaring of the sea, awesome in its force. Bad times are coming on Israel, very bad times. Nevertheless, by His saving grace, the day is coming when Messiah will bring light to the nation in the messianic kingdom (Isa. 2:3; 9:1ff.; 45:14, 22-25; 49:23; 58:10; 60:3), but this salvation cannot come until times of judgment and darkness come upon them for their sin (Isa. 8:22; 42:7; Amos 5:18). Pfeiffer explains, "The enemy warriors would be fierce and unsparing, and their armies would engulf Palestine like a tidal wave."[146]

---

[143] Curiously, God uses similar language to describe Himself and those whom He himself empowers through faith (cf. Isa. 40:28-31).
[144] Young, *The Book of Isaiah, vol. 1*, 228.
[145] Oswalt, *The Book of Isaiah, Chapters 1-39*, 169.
[146] Pfeiffer, *The Wycliffe Bible Commentary: Old Testament*, Is. 5:24.

Summary and application

God sees sin, and He certainly will judge it. That was true in ancient Israel, and it is still true today. As those who believe in Jesus Christ and the truthfulness of God's Word, we should apply this truth to ourselves by keeping ourselves from sin, for we know that God hates it and judges it.

THE CALL OF ISAIAH (6:1-13)

Chapter 6 brings us to Isaiah's call to prophesy. Although some authors have suggested that chapter 6 is an event subsequent to Isaiah's initial call, it seems preferable to follow the majority of writers who see chapter 6 as Isaiah's initial call.[147]

Chapter 6 reads as follows: "1 In the year of King Uzziah's death I saw the Lord sitting on a throne, lofty and exalted, with the train of His robe filling the temple. 2 Seraphim stood above Him, each having six wings: with two he covered his face, and with two he covered his feet, and with two he flew. 3 And one called out to another and said, Holy, Holy, Holy, is the Lord of hosts, the whole earth is full of His glory. 4 And the foundations of the thresholds trembled at the voice of him who called out, while the temple was filling with smoke. 5 Then I said, Woe is me, for I am ruined, because I am a man of unclean lips, and I live among a people of unclean lips! For my eyes have seen the King, the Lord of hosts. 6 Then one of the seraphim flew to me with a burning coal in his hand, which he had taken from the altar with tongs. 7 He touched my mouth *with it* and said, Behold, this has touched your lips; and your iniquity is taken away and your sin is forgiven. 8 Then I heard the voice of the Lord, saying, Whom shall I send, and who will go for Us? Then I said, Here am I. Send me! 9 He said, Go, and tell this people: Keep on listening, but do not perceive; keep on looking, but do not understand. 10 Render the hearts of this people insensitive, their ears dull, and their eyes dim, otherwise they might see with their eyes, hear with their ears, understand with their hearts, and return and be healed. 11 Then I said, Lord, how long? And He answered, until cities are devastated *and* without inhabitant, houses are without people and the land is utterly desolate, 12 The Lord has removed men far away, and the forsaken places are many in the midst of the land. 13 Yet there will be a tenth portion in it, and it will again be *subject* to burning, like a terebinth or an oak whose stump remains when it is felled. The holy seed is its stump" (6:1-13).

The Old Testament shows that many people hated the prophetic word of God in their own day just as unbelievers do today. Nevertheless, God's purpose was to tell the world His message. Isaiah's call contains two main elements.

---

[147] Wolf, *Interpreting Isaiah*, 85; Oswalt, *The Book of Isaiah, Chapters 1-39*, 171-176.

First element of Isaiah's call: Isaiah's cleansing (vv. 1-7)

God is holy and man is not. For Isaiah to prophesy as he needed to, this meant that Isaiah had to understand the holiness of God. Isaiah needed a vision of God's holiness, and that is what we see in verses 1-7. Verse 1 introduces what would properly be called the only actual vision of the book.[148] Isaiah tells us this vision took place in the year of King Uzziah's death.[149] Uzziah had been a good king, but years earlier he erred when he tried to offer priestly incense. God struck him with leprosy for his pride (2 Chron. 26:16-23). Uzziah has just died, but Pfeiffer reminds us that God was still in control:

> Uzziah's death in 740 or 739 B.C. marked the passing of a golden age of spiritual vigor in Judah (at least until the king's sin of presumption ten years before his decease); and his ungodly grandson, Ahaz, was perhaps already exerting an influence in Jotham's government. To the discouraged prophet, as he knelt in prayer at the Temple at Jerusalem, the Lord granted a transforming vision of His glory. He thus assured Isaiah that despite the apparent triumph of wickedness on earth, the Lord Jehovah still reigned omnipotent upon his heavenly throne.[150]

God's calling for Isaiah was to proclaim the word of heaven's holy King and call God's people to repentance. The foundation for this proclamation is going to be a right understanding of the nature of God. Two key attributes of Israel's sovereign God stand out here in verses 1-7.

First key attribute: The royal majesty of Yahweh (v. 1)

Throughout history men have been enamored with the majesty of earthly kings and the power they yield. However, no earthly king can ever match the power and sovereignty of the living God.

Israel's God is a sovereign God. Isaiah says that he "saw the Lord ['*Adonay*] sitting on a throne, lofty and exalted, with the train of His robe

---

[148] Wolf, *Interpreting Isaiah*, 86.

[149] Uzziah was a strong king who ruled from 792-740 B.C. (Jotham was co-regent for 12). We see several variant spellings of Uzziah: Uzziyahu (1:1; 7:1; 2 Kings 15:32, 34; 2 Chron. 26:1), Uzzah (2 Kings 21:18, 26), Uzziyah (2 Kings 15:13, 30; Amos 1:1; Zech. 14:5), Azariyah (2 Kings 14:21; 15:1, 7, 17, 23, 27; 1 Chron. 3:12), Azariyahu (2 Kings 15:6, 8) (Young, *The Book of Isaiah, vol. 1*, 235, n. 6).

[150] Pfeiffer, *The Wycliffe Bible Commentary, Old Testament*, Is 6:1.

filling the temple."[151] This is the holy God of Israel whose royal appearance highlights the sovereignty of His dominion, not only eternally in heaven (Pss. 93:2; 103:19; 145:13), but also over earth as well (Dan. 4:34-37). Heaven's King was clothed in a long-flowing robe, reminiscent of the one Jesus was wearing when John saw the glorified Christ (Rev. 1:13).

Israel's God is an exalted God. Isaiah says that the Lord was "lofty" and "exalted," two of the same terms Isaiah uses in 52:13 when he describes the eschatological exaltation and glorification of God's Servant (cf. Isa. 57:15). Yahweh is the King of Kings and nothing in this world is outside the dominion of heaven's King.

Second key attribute: The awesome holiness of Yahweh (vv. 2-7)

Isaiah not only saw the Lord, but he also saw the six-winged, angelic seraphim standing above the Lord. This is the only place where we see the mention of seraphim by name (the root *saraph* carries the idea of burning). It is hard to be dogmatic, but these are apparently a different class of angels from the cherubim which have four wings (cf. Ezek. 1:22; Rev. 4:6). They hold a highly privileged position of being in the immediate presence of the Lord and stand ready to worship and serve God at all times (cf. Dan. 7:10; 8:15-19; 9:20-27; 10:10ff.; Heb. 1:14; Rev. 4:4-11).

The angels of heaven stand in awe of the holiness of God (vv. 2-3). These seraphim give continual worship to their God by calling out with the three-fold praise, "Holy, Holy, Holy, is the Lord of hosts, the whole earth is full of His glory" (Num. 14:21; cf. Rev. 4:5-11; 5:8-14).[152] The root idea of being holy (*qadosh*) is that being set apart. This idea of being set apart can be spatial (physical separation), cultic (ritual separation), or ethical (conduct that corresponds to one's god). God is absolute and perfect in His own uncreated

---

[151] Oswalt notes that some have suggested emendation based on the supposition that the Masoretes would not have wanted to show it possible to see *Yahweh* so they changed it to *'Adonay* (vv. 1, 8, 11), but there is no objective basis for this reasoning (Oswalt, *The Book of Isaiah, Chapters 1-39*, 177). The use of *'Adonay* magnifies the sense of absolute sovereignty. The son of David has just died, but Israel's true King lives and reigns. As John 12:37-41 shows us, Isaiah was seeing Christ Himself in this vision.

[152] Some have suggested a trinitarian basis behind this praise, but it probably is better to simply see it representing an extremely emphatic declaration of holiness (cf. Jer. 22:29; Ezek. 21:27). The holiness of God Isaiah was allowed to see in this vision had a major impact on the prophet. His favorite title became "Holy One of Israel" (12 times in 1-39 and 14 times in 40-66; cf. 2 Kings 19:22; Pss. 71:22; 78:41; 89:18; Jer. 50:29; 51:5).

holiness, and for this reason the holy angels blush before Him and cover their own face and feet with their wings.

Heaven stands in awe of the holiness of God (v. 4). The thresholds of heaven's temple shook and filled with smoke (cf. Exod. 19:18; 33:9; Heb. 12:18-22; Rev. 15:8). God's holy presence is awesome—the kind of holiness that often puts his creation in terror (cf. Exod. 20:18-19). His glory—the sum total of His excellence—fills the whole earth, a glory that is seen in creation itself but sometimes manifest in what is called the *shekinah* glory (cf. Exod. 33:17-23; 34:6-7; 1 Kings 8). All of this was to prepare Isaiah to understand that Yahweh is a holy God who must judge sin.

Isaiah stands in awe of the holiness of God (vv. 5-7). The impact of this vision on Isaiah was overwhelming. God's holiness made him see not only the sin of the nation, but even his own sin in a whole new light so that he thought it would lead to his death (cf. Judg. 6:22-23; 13:22; Rev. 1:17).

God responded to Isaiah's sense of unworthiness by having one of the seraphim take one of the coals from the heavenly altar and touch his lips as a symbol of God's cleansing grace, the same kind of cleansing God gave other prophets (Jer. 1:9; Zech. 3:1-5).[153] Yes, Isaiah is a sinner unfit to serve holy Yahweh, but by His cleansing grace Isaiah can be a vessel fit for service (cf. 2 Tim. 2:21). Kidner explains, "The symbol, applied to Isaiah's lips . . . assures him of personal forgiveness."[154] Sin is great, but God's cleansing grace is always greater (Rom. 5:20-21). From this, we are reminded that God's saving grace is great enough to not only prepare us for heaven, but also great enough to prepare us for service to Jesus Christ. No one is worthy by their own spiritual resources, but by His cleansing and forgiveness we can serve Him (cf. Ps. 51:12-15).

Second element of Isaiah's call: Isaiah's commission (vv. 8-13)

Israel had turned its back on God, and that meant that Isaiah was going to have a difficult ministry and not be well received. Nevertheless, Isaiah was to prophesy and hold nothing back by the giving the message that would harden the nation even further. Isaiah's commission carries three main messages.

---

[153] It is best to understand this altar as being a heavenly altar of incense that stood immediately before the presence of God in the way that the altar of incense stood immediately before the curtain in the earthly temple (Exod. 30:1-8; Lev. 16:12; Num. 16:46-47; Heb. 9:11-14), the same imagery we see in Revelation (6:9; 8:3; 14:18; 16:7) (Oswalt, *The Book of Isaiah, 1-39*, 184).

[154] Kidner, "Isaiah," 638.

First main message: It is a message of hardening (vv. 8-10)

Typically, we think of the proclamation of God's Word as being for the positive aspect of turning men from sin to faith. No doubt God did use Isaiah's proclamation for this purpose, but in the present section we see the negative purpose of hardening sinners to intensify God's judgment against them. We see something similar when God commanded Moses to speak to Pharaoh, but God told Moses that He was going to harden the heart of Pharaoh so that He might make Himself known to Pharaoh and all Egypt (Exod. 4:21; 7:3, 13, 14; 9:12, 35; 10:1, 20, 27; 14:4, 8). Pharaoh had the opportunity to repent and avoid judgment, but God used Moses' message to harden the recalcitrant sinner in his rebellion. Now it is seven-hundred years later, and God is going to use Isaiah in a similar way.

Isaiah's call (v. 8). Yahweh asks who will go. Unlike Moses and Jeremiah, Isaiah immediately responds positively. Martin explains, "The prophet knew that the entire nation needed the same kind of awareness of God and cleansing of sin he had received."[155]

The hardening impact of Isaiah's ministry (vv. 9-10). Every preacher hopes to see positive fruit, but such was not going to be the case with Isaiah. Nevertheless, God's command was to prophesy and virtually taunt the nation with his message: "Go, and tell this people: Keep on listening, but do not perceive; keep on looking, but do not understand."[156] How is it that they could see and hear but not perceive and understand? The answer is that God's servant nation was sitting in a state of spiritual blindness and deafness (29:9; 42:19; 43:8),[157] and in this condition they were incapable of receiving God's truth.[158]

The idea in verse 10 is that of a judicial hardening from God, the kind of judgment God brings to people who habitually reject His Word (Rom. 1:18-21; 2 Thess. 2:11).[159] Israel has brought itself to the place where God has turned against His people, and the stated purpose of Isaiah's ministry is to keep them

---

[155] Martin, "Isaiah," 1045.
[156] In these words, we see the contempt God has toward these rebels (Isa. 8:6, 12; 9:16; 28:11, 14; 29:13, 14).
[157] One day the Messiah will reverse this condition (Isa. 29:18; 35:5; 42:7, 16; Matt. 11:5), but until that day this is where they are at spiritually (John 9:40-41).
[158] This is the same response Jesus Himself faced (cf. Matt. 13:10-17) as well as the Apostle Paul (Acts 28:25-27).
[159] Isaiah uses three vivid images to convey the sense of divine judgment: (1) rendering hearts "insensitive" (*shaman*, to make fat), (2) rendering "dull" (from *kabad*, to make heavy), and (3) rendering "dim" (from *sha'a'*, "to close").

from seeing, hearing, or understanding lest they repent and find healing (cf. 1:5-6).[160] Young explains, "In His mysterious wisdom, God had foreordained that this people would not respond to the blessed overtures of the Gospel."[161] The only solution left is that of destruction.

Second main message: It is a message of destruction (vv. 11-12)

For those who reject grace, the only thing left is judgment. For over seven-hundred years Israel had been rejecting the truth of God's Word. Now they were approaching the time of destruction.

The destruction will last for ages. Isaiah is heartbroken over this news and asks how long this judgment will last. God tells him that it will not end until a complete desolation overtakes the nation (Isa. 7:12; 9:22; 37:25; cf. Dan. 9:27; 11:36; 12:7; Matt. 23:37-39), and the land is utterly desolate (Lev. 18:25-27; Ezek. 21:27). The Law of Moses said that expulsion would be the penalty of rebellion (cf. Deut. 28:21, 26; 29:28), and the time has arrived for Israel to be cast out (Amos 3:15; 5:11; Mic. 3:12).

The destruction will not be permanent. Destruction will come, but it will not be permanent. God swore promises to Abraham and the people of Israel, and those promises mean that there will be a day of restoration.

Third main message: It is a message of promise (v. 13)

God will not utterly annihilate His people, but He will use the judgments to purify a remnant for a future restoration (a remnant which He calls a "tenth"). The restoration of a remnant is compared to oak tree that has been felled by fire, but later grows to become a strong tree once again (cf. 1:9; 4:2; 6:13; 7:3; 10:20-22; 37:4, 31-32; 46:3; 49:6).[162] The future remnant will face the fires of purification (Dan. 12:7; Zech. 12:10; 13:8-9; Mal. 3:1-5), but God will use it to restore His fallen nation (Rom. 11:25-32).

---

[160] The grammar (i.e., the telic particle) shows that God is not merely telling Isaiah what the negative results of his proclamation will be, but rather that of a divine purpose in keeping them from a positive response (Bruce K. Waltke and M. O'Connor, *An Introduction to Biblical Hebrew Syntax* [Winona Lake: Eisenbrauns, 1900], 661; J. C. L. Gibson, *Davidson's Introductory Hebrew Grammar-Syntax* [Edinburgh: T&T Clark, 1994], 160). God later told Jeremiah, "As for you, do not pray for this people, and do not lift up cry or prayer for them, and do not intercede with Me, for I do not hear you" (Jer. 7:16).

[161] Young, *The Book of Isaiah, vol. 1*, 259.

[162] Oswalt, *The Book of Isaiah, 1-39*, 190-191.

ISAIAH 1:1-6:13

Summary and application

What are the lessons for us today? Certainly, there are at least two major lessons for each one of us. The first one is the fact that God hates sin, and He will judge it. The entire Bible gives us the testimony that God judges all sin. This should move each one of us to turn from anything that God hates. Second, we find comfort in the truth that our God is a faithful God. Yes, He chastises sin, but His gracious promises are unbreakable. And for those who understand the cross of Christ, we know that this grace is only because of His Son.

3
JUDGMENT AND SALVATION MESSAGES TO JERUSALEM AND JUDAH, PART 2
(7:1-12:6)

Chapter 7 brings us to a new section that extends through chapter 12, a section that revolves around judgment and salvation messages against Jerusalem and Judah. When God gave Isaiah his call to prophesy in chapter 6, God warned Isaiah that the people were not going to listen. We now begin to see the outworking of this truth.[1] Will God's people put their faith in Yahweh or the powers of Assyria for deliverance?[2] Sadly, they are not going to trust Yahweh. Chapter 7 introduces us to their lack of trust and how this lack of trust would cost them dearly. Nevertheless, God has a plan to save His people one day through a very special promised child, a repeated focus of chapters 7-12.

THE PROMISED CHILD, Pt. 1 (7:1-25)

One of the most fascinating topics of biblical studies is that of messianic prophecy, the study of Old Testament prophecies that predict the coming of the Messiah. It has been estimated that there are over 60 specific prophecies that were fulfilled in the first coming of Christ alone. Josh McDowell cites Peter Stoner on the odds of fulfilling only eight prophecies in one individual. McDowell says, "we find that the chance that any man might have lived down to the present time and fulfilled all eight prophecies is one in ten to the seventeenth power. That is 1 in 100,000,000,000,000,000."[3] To illustrate, McDowell

---

[1] Herbert Wolf, *Interpreting Isaiah* (Grand Rapids: Zondervan, 1985), 89.
[2] John N. Oswalt, *The Book of Isaiah, 1-39* (Grand Rapids: Eerdmans, 1986), 192.
[3] Josh McDowell, *Evidence That Demands a Verdict* (San Bernardino: Here's Life

says this would be like covering the state of Texas with silver dollars two feet deep, marking one with a pen, randomly dropping a blindfolded man from a helicopter, and having that man pick out that one silver dollar on the first try. The odds are astronomical.

Isaiah 7-12 gives a number of messianic prophecies, but some of them take the form of what theologians call typology. Typology might be called a subset of prophecy where a historical person, place or institution serves to foreshadow some eschatological truth that is fulfilled in the Messiah.

Chapter 7 reads as follows: "1 Now it came about in the days of Ahaz, the son of Jotham, the son of Uzziah, king of Judah, that Rezin the king of Aram and Pekah the son of Remaliah, king of Israel, went up to Jerusalem to *wage* war against it, but could not conquer it. 2 When it was reported to the house of David, saying, The Arameans have camped in Ephraim, his heart and the hearts of his people shook as the trees of the forest shake with the wind. 3 Then the Lord said to Isaiah, Go out now to meet Ahaz, you and your son Shear-jashub, at the end of the conduit of the upper pool, on the highway to the fuller's field, 4 and say to him, Take care and be calm, have no fear and do not be fainthearted because of these two stubs of smoldering firebrands, on account of the fierce anger of Rezin and Aram and the son of Remaliah. 5 Because Aram, *with* Ephraim and the son of Remaliah, has planned evil against you, saying, 6 Let us go up against Judah and terrorize it, and make for ourselves a breach in its walls and set up the son of Tabeel as king in the midst of it, 7 thus says the Lord God: It shall not stand nor shall it come to pass. 8 For the head of Aram is Damascus and the head of Damascus is Rezin (now within another 65 years Ephraim will be shattered, *so that it is* no longer a people), 9 and the head of Ephraim is Samaria and the head of Samaria is the son of Remaliah. If you will not believe, you surely shall not last. 10 Then the Lord spoke again to Ahaz, saying, 11 Ask a sign for yourself from the Lord your God; make *it* deep as *Sheol* or high as heaven. 12 But Ahaz said, I will not ask, nor will I test the Lord! 13 Then he said, "Listen now, O house of David! Is it too slight a thing for you to try the patience of men, that you will try the patience of my God as well? 14 Therefore the Lord Himself will give you a sign: Behold, a virgin will be with child and bear a son, and she will call His name Immanuel. 15 He will eat curds and honey at the time He knows *enough* to refuse evil and choose good. 16 For before the boy will know *enough* to refuse evil and choose good, the land whose two kings you dread will be forsaken. 17 The Lord will bring on you, on your people, and on your father's house such days as have never come since the day that Ephraim separated from Judah, the king of Assyria. 18 In that day the Lord will whistle

---

Publishers, 1972), 167.

for the fly that is in the remotest part of the rivers of Egypt and for the bee that is in the land of Assyria. 19 They will all come and settle on the steep ravines, on the ledges of the cliffs, on all the thorn bushes and on all the watering places. 20 In that day the Lord will shave with a razor, hired from regions beyond the Euphrates (*that is,* with the king of Assyria), the head and the hair of the legs; and it will also remove the beard. 21 Now in that day a man may keep alive a heifer and a pair of sheep; 22 and because of the abundance of the milk produced he will eat curds, for everyone that is left within the land will eat curds and honey. 23 And it will come about in that day, that every place where there used to be a thousand vines, *valued* at a thousand *shekels* of silver, will become briars and thorns. 24 *People* will come there with bows and arrows because all the land will be briars and thorns. 25 As for all the hills which used to be cultivated with the hoe, you will not go there for fear of briars and thorns; but they will become a place for pasturing oxen and for sheep to trample" (7:1-25).

Chapter 7 introduces us to one of the most-famous passages of typology in the Bible, a passage where God is assuring the king of Judah that he can put his complete trust in the Lord. The signs God promises in this chapter are meant to encourage King Ahaz to trust in God's protection in the immediate crisis (the type), but they also contain long-term messianic implications as well (the antitype). God gives two signs to the king as proof that He would sustain the Davidic Dynasty and not let it fall.

First sign from God: The sign that comes when God promises and then destroys your enemy right before your eyes (vv. 1-9)

God tells Ahaz he has nothing to fear from two enemy powers (Syria, Israel) who were threatening to overthrow the throne of David, for God Himself would bring them down.[4] Isaiah gives Ahaz two reasons why he needed to trust.

First reason Judah needed the Lord's salvation (vv. 1-2)

Sound exegesis always searches for relevant historical data to help understand the setting. This is part of what is called Bible Introduction.

The historical context as being during the days of Ahaz (v. 1). Ahaz ruled as king of Judah from 735-715, but he was not a man of God (cf. 2 Kings 16:1-11). Jotham, the father of Ahaz, was an effective ruler (750-735), and in general "he did what was right in the sight of the Lord" (2 Kings 15:34). Ahaz

---

[4] As we have already seen, these two enemy powers were Syria and the northern kingdom of Israel who wanted to overthrow the Davidic dynasty so they could forcefully bring Judah into a military alliance against Assyria.

also had a second godly example in his grandfather Uzziah (ca. 792-750), not a perfect man, but one who trusted the Lord. Sadly, Ahaz had godly ancestors, but he himself did not trust the Lord.

Historical studies place the events of chapter 7 in 734 B.C., the year after Ahaz came to the throne.[5] Isaiah indicates that Judah was being attacked by a coalition of two nations, Aram, i.e., Syria (led by Rezin), and Israel (led by Pekah). These two nations had already tried to overthrow Judah in 735, but did not succeed (v.1). Ahaz then received another report that these two nations were making plans for another attack (v. 2).[6] Ahaz and the people of Judah were terrified (hearts shaking like trees). The goal of this invasion was to overthrow Judah and force them into a coalition to fight Assyria.

To state the problem bluntly, Ahaz was not a believer, and did not trust the Lord. Earlier he had done the right thing when he rejected a deal by Israel and Syria to join their alliance against Assyria (7:6; cf. 2 Kings 16:5), but then he turned right around and paid Assyria tribute money to help Judah against Israel and Aram (2 Kings 16:7). Assyria, however, eventually broke the deal and invaded Judah after overthrowing Gaza, Galilee, and Gilead, overthrowing Damascus in 732 and Samaria in 722. Samaria's eventual fall (722) resulted in many Jews being taken captive (2 Kings 17) and many foreigners getting settled in Israel in the days of Esarhaddon (671), making the beginnings of the Samaritan people group (cf. Ezra 4:2). Ahab's fascination with Assyria even led him to place an Assyrian altar in the Jerusalem temple (2 Kings 16:10-16; 2 Chron. 28:1-24).

Syria and Israel had already tried to overthrow Judah under Jotham, but they did not succeed (cf. 2 Kings 15:36-38). Second Chronicles 28:1-12 speaks about other battles involving Ahaz after he came to the throne where Judah suffered a massive defeat with the death of 120,000 troops (and even the king's son) and 200,000 people taken as slaves by Israel.[7] God intervened by sending the prophet Obed to order Israel to restore the captives, and they did. The dangers to Judah were real, but Judah's true need was to trust the Lord (Pss. 108:12; 118:8; Jer. 17:5-7).

---

[5] Oswalt, *The Book of Isaiah, 1-39*, 196.

[6] In the first year of Rehoboam (931 B.C.) the nation divided, with Judah and Benjamin staying faithful to the son of David in Jerusalem, and the other 10 tribes defecting to start a new kingdom in the north called Israel (Ephraim here).

[7] Young believes these events were probably prior to Isaiah 7 (Edward J. Young, *The Book of Isaiah*, vol. 1 (Grand Rapids: Eerdmans, 1965), 267. The captives were taken from Judah, but God intervened with a prophet named Oded and persuaded them to return them.

Another imminent threat (v. 2). Syria and Israel were preparing for another invasion of Judah, and Syria had already moved troops into Israel in preparation. The real problem, though, was that Ahaz did not trust in the Lord. God sent Isaiah to remind Ahaz that he really needed the Lord.

Second reason Judah needed the Lord's salvation (vv. 3-9)

Truth is what matters. Ahaz needed to know and believe the truth of God, so the Lord sent him the prophet Isaiah.

God sends Isaiah to assure Ahaz he need not fear (v. 3).[8] Ahaz was assessing the water supplies of Jerusalem at the end of the conduit of the upper pool on the highway to the fuller's field, a reservoir that may have held water from the Gihon Spring near Jerusalem.[9] The precise location of this pool has been debated with some placing it (1) at the confluence of the Kidron and Tyropean Valleys (cf. 36:2 where the King of Assyria would stand), or (2) at the foot of Zion in the Hinnom where we find Siloah–Gihon (8:6; cf. 1 Kings 1:33; 2 Chron. 32:30), or (3) that the stream divided making two pools, an upper pool (Neh. 2:15), and a lower pool (Isa. 22:9).[10] Regardless of the exact location, the issue at stake is this:

> An adequate water supply is imperative for a city under siege. The king was probably satisfying himself as to this or making arrangements for its improvement. He was therefore engaged in an activity directly related to the situation described in v. 1.[11]

Interestingly, God also told Isaiah to take along his son whose name was *She'ar Yashub*.[12] It is curious that Judah was in the midst of a national crisis and

---

[8] This event probably occurred in 734 B.C., sometime within the first year of Ahaz's reign (Wolf, *Interpreting Isaiah*, 89).
[9] John A. Martin, "Isaiah," in *The Bible Knowledge Commentary: An Exposition of the Scriptures*, ed. J. F. Walvoord and R. B. Zuck, vol. 1, cited in electronic form with Logos Libronix (Wheaton, IL: Victor Books, 1985), 1047.
[10] Oswalt, *The Book of Isaiah, 1-39*, 199.
[11] G. W. Grogan, "Isaiah," in *The Expositor's Bible Commentary*, ed. Frank E. Gaebelein, vol. 6 (Grand Rapids: Zondervan, 1986), 60.
[12] The name itself means "a remnant will return" and is one of several prophetically significant names we find in 7-12 (Isa. 8:18; cf. 7:14; 8:3; 9:6; Heb. 2:12-13). The good news is that Israel will one day have a restored remnant (cf. 1:9; 4:2; 6:13; 10:20-23; 11:11-16; 37:4, 31-32: 46:3; 49:6), but the bad news is that they must first suffer war, invasion, exile, and a huge reduction in their population.

yet God would have Isaiah take along his son to confront the king. As we shall see, there is prophetic significance in all these events.

God tells Ahaz not to fear (v. 4). Isaiah is to give Ahaz a four-fold command to not fear an attack by Rezin and Pekah (a murderer and usurper as seen in 2 Kings 15): "take care; be calm; have no fear; do not be fainthearted." He then mockingly calls these two kings "two stubs of smoldering fire brands." In God's estimation they are nothing but charred, smoldering sticks (cf. Amos 4:11; Zech. 3:2).

God exposes the plans of Rezin and Pekah (vv. 5-6). God tells Ahaz that their plan was to invade Jerusalem, overthrow the Davidic dynasty, and set up a puppet king named Tabeel whom they would control, thus forcefully bringing Judah into their anti-Assyrian coalition. God makes it clear that He already knew about their plans, and also that He was not going to let them succeed. In the meantime, however, Ahaz had sent the envoys to the king of Assyria with a bribe to have him turn aside Syria and Israel (2 Kings 16:7-9; 2 Chron. 28:16). His trust was not in the Lord.

The Davidic dynasty will not fall to Israel and Syria (v. 7). God makes it forcefully clear that He was not going to let these two powers succeed in overthrowing the Davidic Dynasty (cf. 2 Sam. 7:12-16; Pss. 2; 89; 132).[13] Now, the fact of the matter is that in a little over 100 years God would interrupt the Davidic dynasty by having the Babylonian armies of King Nebuchadnezzar overthrow Judah, but by the word of the Lord that overthrow of Judah was not going to happen by Syria and Israel.

God reinforces His message (vv. 8-9). God reinforces His message to King Ahaz by making it clear that Syria had its own capital (Damascus) and its own king (Rezin), and that Israel also had its own capital (Samaria) and its king (Pekah). That is, these two nations had their own spheres of power, and Judah and Jerusalem did not belong to them. Furthermore, within 65 years the people of Israel ("Ephraim") would be so diluted through exile and foreign repopulation that they would cease to exist as a distinct people group. Syria and Israel would soon fall to Assyria, but the eventual impact from Ashurbanipal (669-626) would also bring a death blow to Israel's national identity. Kidner notes that,

> Syria was crushed in 732, while Israel lost her northern territories as early as 734, her national existence in 722 [2 Kings 17], and her racial identity through a series of re-peoplings which continued to at least the reign of

---

[13] The forcefulness of the statement is emphasized by God's self-identification as the "Lord God," i.e., sovereign Yahweh who rules the affairs of man.

Esarhaddon (*cf.* Ezr. 4:2). By the end of this (669 bc) she was indeed *too shattered to be a people* (8).[14]

The main message for Ahaz was that God was not going to let the Davidic dynasty fall to Syria and Israel. All Ahaz had to do was believe God. The warning, though, is that a failure to believe the promise (Hiph. of *'aman*) would mean that they would also experience a military onslaught (Niph. of *'aman*).

Historical studies show us that it was very soon after this (in 734) that Tiglath Pileser began his westward movement and Ahaz allied himself with Assyria (2 Kings 16:7). Within two years, Damascus fell to Assyria in 732 (2 Kings 16:9; Isa. 17). After this, Assyria invaded the Philistine coastal plain, and many parts of Israel fell to Assyria (Isa. 14:28-32). Egypt instigated a revolt in 724 (2 Kings 17:4ff.) during the reign of Shalmaneser, but the revolt was short lived, and because of Israel's part in the revolt, Assyria came and overthrew Samaria in 722. Hosea explains it as being the judgment of God: "I gave you a king in My anger, and I am taking him away in My wrath." All that was left in Israel was a lowly residue. It was under Esarhaddon (65 years later) that Assyria re-located massive numbers of foreigners in Israel, putting an end to Israel's national identity (2 Kings 17:24; Ezra 4:2; 2 Chron. 33:11). At this moment in 734 B.C., though, God had given His promise to Ahaz that Syria and Israel would not overthrow the Davidic dynasty. Sadly, Ahaz refused to trust the Lord (cf. 2 Chron. 28:16-27). The result was an invasion that brought Judah to its knees (cf. Isa. 7:17-25; 8:5-8). Over the next 30 years Assyria ravaged Judah, and it was not until 701 B.C. during the reign of Hezekiah that God brought the Assyrians such a blow that they eventually pulled back (chs. 36-37). The promise was given (vv. 1-9), but Ahaz refused to trust the sign, leading God to give a second prophetic sign in verses 10-25.

Second sign from God: The sign that comes when God promises and then destroys your enemy right before your eyes (vv. 10-25)

Ahaz did not listen the first time, so God spoke in 10-25 with a second sign. This passage is filled with interpretive challenges which call for great care.

Interpretive challenges of the following section

Verses 10-25 reinforce the prophetic promises in verses 1-9, but this section includes one of the most-famous (and most-debated) prophetic passages

---

[14] F. Derek Kidner, "Isaiah," in *New Bible Commentary: 21st Century Edition*, ed. D. A. Carson et al., 4th ed., cited in electronic form with Logos Libronix (Leicester, England; Downers Grove, IL: Inter-Varsity Press, 1994), 638.

of the whole Bible. Numerous interpretive issues are involved.

New Testament use of the Old Testament. The New Testament uses the Old Testament in a variety of ways. One way is direct prophecy where the New Testament use reflects a direct and literal meaning of the Old Testament (e.g., Luke 19:42/Dan. 9:24-27; Matt. 2:6/Mic. 5:2). Second, sometimes the New Testament makes an application from a principle in the Old Testament (e.g., 1 Tim. 5:18/Deut. 25:24). Kaiser adds another category he calls "applications" where the New Testament applies something to Christ using some kind of specific term or theological concept (e.g., Rom. 8:32/Gen. 22).[15] A fourth kind takes place in typology wherein the New Testament makes reference to a real historical person, place, or institution in the Old Testament and shows that the historical event also serves as a shadow (a type) of something in the New Testament.[16] The authority for this connection comes from the Spirit-inspired New Testament prophet.

Matthew's use of Isaiah. How should we understand Matthew's use of Isaiah 7:14 (Matt. 1:18-25)? Is the virgin birth the fulfillment a direct prophecy?[17] This writer believes we should see this as typology. In other words, the "prophecy" of Isaiah 7:14 (which flows into ch. 8) was speaking about historical events fulfilled in the days of Isaiah, but God was using these events from Isaiah's day to typologically point to truths that would be fulfilled in Christ as revealed in the New Testament by the Holy Spirit.[18]

Ahaz rejects God's offer for a sign (vv. 10-13)

God told Ahaz to ask him for any kind of sign to prove that He was going

---

[15] Walter Kaiser, *The Messiah in the Old Testament* (Grand Rapids: Zondervan, 1995), 35.
[16] For example, Hebrews shows how in the Day of Atonement (Lev. 16) Christ was foreshadowed by both the High Priest (Heb. 9:11) and the sacrifice (Heb. 9:12).
[17] This commentary will not analyze the various alternative views that have been proposed. It is the hermeneutical conviction of this writer that the starting point for understanding its relationship must be the contextual exegesis of the passage in its own setting, and that the result will be that Matthew's use is typological. Grogan notes that there are many different ways people have interpreted this passage with numerous variations within those views (Grogan, "Isaiah," 62-63).
[18] We find four examples of typology in the first four chapters of Matthew: (1) 1:23: the birth of a son as sign of divine salvation (cf. Isa. 7:14), (2) 2:15: the protection of God's Son from enemy slaughter (cf. Hos. 11:1), (3) 2:18: the enemy attack to destroy the promised seed of Israel (cf. Jer. 31:15), (4) 2:23: God's Messiah would be despised as a "Nazarene" (as seen in all the OT). Given Matthew's pattern it is reasonable to see the present passage as being typological.

to deliver Judah from Syria and Israel (vv. 10-11), and the sign could be as big as Ahaz wants.[19] Ahaz feigns a pious façade by saying he did not want to tempt the Lord by asking for a sign (cf. Deut. 6:16), a sign that God already told him He would give.[20] Isaiah rebukes his empty piety (v. 13). The problem, explains Oswalt, is that "what they have rejected as foolish—reliance upon God's care and presence—is ultimate wisdom, while their wisdom—that Assyria can be trusted to look for Judah's interests—is errant nonsense."[21] Young explains, "[Ahaz was] a 'practical' man to whom the worship of Yahweh has little meaning,"[22] so he refused to ask.[23]

The giving of a sign of deliverance (vv. 14-16)

God then tells Ahaz that He Himself would provide the proof (i.e., the sign, *'oth*) that He would not let Judah fall to Syria and Israel.[24] As proof, God says,

> Therefore, the Lord Himself will give you a sign: Behold, a virgin will be with child and bear a son, and she will call His name Immanuel. He will eat curds and honey at the time He knows *enough* to refuse evil and choose good. For before the boy will know *enough* to refuse evil and choose good, the land whose two kings you dread will be forsaken (vv. 14-16).

---

[19] The sign could be from any of several means, perhaps a fulfilled prophecy (1 Sam. 2:34; 3:19-21; Jer. 44:29), or perhaps some other kind of miracle (Exod. 4:8-9; 7:8-12; Deut. 13:2-5; Judg. 6:36-40; 2 Kings 20:8-11; Isa. 38:7). The significance of this sign is that God is giving a visible indicator that He will not let the House of David fall to Syria and Israel.

[20] Wolf, *Interpreting Isaiah*, 90.

[21] Oswalt, *The Book of Isaiah, 1-39*, 203.

[22] Young, *The Book of Isaiah, vol. 1*, 280.

[23] Interestingly, when God told Hezekiah to ask for a sign a generation later, Hezekiah trusted the Lord and did ask . . . and was delivered (Isa. 38:7).

[24] The emphatic nature of God's promise concerning the House of David can be seen in that (1) God introduces the prophecy by saying "behold" (*hinneh*, a bold and dramatic statement). As Keil notes, this term is an exclamation that is meant to rivet attention to something spectacular (F. Delitzsch and C. F. Keil, *Keil and Delitzsch Commentary on the Old Testament*, vol. 7 [Grand Rapids: Eerdmans, 1969], 121). (2) It is a message from the sovereign Lord (*'Adonay*) of Israel—the One who rules heaven and earth (the DSS and a few other mss. read *YHWH* instead of *Adonay*). (3) Isaiah adds the third person pronoun "Himself" (*hu'*) placing emphasis on the subject. (4) It is a message spoken not merely to Ahaz, but to the entire House of David and people of Judah (*lakem*, "you" plural) (Young, *The Book of Isaiah, vol. 1*, 284). God's promise about the eternality of the Davidic Covenant is certain.

Let us make three initial observations about this promised child.

First observation: The promised child will be born to a young lady who is currently an unmarried maiden (v. 14a). The promise begins by saying that that a virgin will conceive and bear a child.[25] As recognized by all Hebrew scholars, the term used for "virgin" in 7:14 (*'almah*) is not the narrow Hebrew word for "virgin" (*bethulah*). *Bethulah* is the more precise term that means "virgin," so Oswalt explains that it is hard to see why Isaiah used the ambiguous *'almah* if he was wanting to make a prophecy about the virgin birth of Jesus.[26] The term *'almah* comes from a root that conveys the idea of coming to fullness or maturity. In the Bible it is frequently used to refer to young women who have arrived at a level of physical maturity so that they are now marriageable young ladies, i.e., unmarried maidens—young maidens who would also be expected to be sexually pure in the context of Old Testament Israel (cf. Gen. 24:43; Exod. 2:8; 1 Chron. 15:20; Ps. 46:1; 68:25; Prov. 30:19; Song 1:3; 6:8). It is true that the LXX translates *'almah* in 7:14 by the Greek term *parthenos*, the Greek word that means "virgin," but this translation must not be seen as the dominating point in seeking to understand the meaning of *'almah* in 7:14. Wolf notes that we find a parallel usage of two cognate Ugaritic terms in one Ugaritic document that sheds considerable light on how these two terms in Isaiah might properly be understood. Wolf explains that the Ugaritic text conveys the idea that,

> a particular virgin would soon be engaged and that after her marriage she would become the mother of a son. At the time the prediction was made, she was a virgin. This kind of announcement was a blessing on the upcoming marriage.[27]

Commenting on the implications of these parallels, Wolf states, "A close study of Isaiah 7 and 8 reveals the same picture. Isaiah was about to be engaged to a prophetess,"[28] and what we learn is that this future wife of Isaiah was the one who was currently the unmarried maiden (*'almah*) who would soon give birth to

---

[25] Notes on grammar: (1) The word "virgin" is articular ("the virgin" perhaps) and points us to think about someone particular. (2) The term conceive (*harah*) is in the form of a feminine adjective. (3) The term "bear" is in the form of a Qal feminine participle.

[26] Oswalt, *The Book of Isaiah, 1-39*, 210.

[27] Wolf, *Interpreting Isaiah*, 91. The Ugaritic term *glmt* is the cognate term with the Hebrew term *'almah*, both of which always refer to an unmarried, marriageable age maiden (Young, *The Book of Isaiah, vol. 1*, 287).

[28] Ibid.

another son to Isaiah.²⁹ This writer concurs with Wolf's explanation. Pfeiffer echoes these same ideas when he writes,

> This well fits the prospective mother alluded to in this situation. Judging from 8:1-4, the typical mother was the prophetess who became Isaiah's wife within a short time after this prophecy was spoken. Therefore she was a virgin at the time this promise was given. She serves as a type of the Virgin Mary, who remained a virgin even after her miraculous conception by the Holy Spirit. The son of this prophetess, correspondingly, is a type of the Messianic Immanuel, as will shortly be explained. 15.³⁰

In conclusion, the mother who would soon bear this child was still a young, unmarried virgin. However, she would soon marry Isaiah and bear the promised child, all of it as Syria and Israel were being weakened as a sign to unbelieving Ahaz.³¹

Second observation: The promised child will be given a symbolic name (v. 14b). The mother would name her child Immanuel. Many people in the ANE had names with some sort of spiritual significance, so it is not surprising that this child would also.³² The literal meaning of the name Immanuel is

---

²⁹ Isaiah's first wife had perhaps died, necessitating a remarriage. Webb posits the curious explanation that the *'almah* is Zion and that her son is the faithful remnant who will emerge from her sufferings (Barry G. Webb, *The Message of Isaiah* [Downers Grove: IVP, 1996], 63).

³⁰ Charles F. Pfeiffer, *The Wycliffe Bible Commentary: Old Testament*, cited in electronic form with Logos Libronix (Chicago: Moody Press, 1962), Is 7:14. Although Motyer does not prefer this explanation, he recognizes the strong contextual connections between 7:13-16 and 8:1ff. (J. Alec Motyer, *The Prophecy of Isaiah: An Introduction and Commentary* [Downers Grove: IVP, 1993], 86-87).

³¹ Thus, the sign to Ahaz had to be fulfilled within a few years or it would cease to be a sign (Wolf, *Interpreting Isaiah*, 91). A historical fulfillment of Isaiah 7:14 does not alter the reality that the Old Testament has a building body of prophetic truth revolving around one promised male child who would one day destroy God's enemy and bring a final restoration to this sin-cursed creation (Gen. 3:15; 4:1; 5:28-29; 9:27; 12:1-3; 15:1ff; 21:12; 22:18; 35:9-12; 49:10; Num. 24:17; 1 Sam. 2:1-10; 2 Sam. 7:12-16; Job 9:33; 16:19-21; 19:23-27; 33:23-28; Ps. 132:11; Isa. 42:1-9; 49:1-13; 50:4-11; 52:13-53:12; Jer. 23:5-6; 30:9-21; 33:14-26; Ezek. 17:22-24; 21:25-27; 34:23-31; 37:15-28; Dan. 7:13; Hos. 3:4-5; Joel 2:23; Amos 9:11-15; Mic. 2:12-13; 5:2; Zeph. 3:14-17; Hag. 2:6-9, 21-23; Zech. 3:8-10; 6:9-15; 9:9; 11:10-13; 12:10; 14:3-4, 9).

³² The father is often the one to name the child, but the Bible shows us that it is not uncommon for the mother to do so (Gen. 4:1, 25; 29:31; 30:13, 17-24; 35:18; Judg. 13:24; 1 Sam. 1:20; 4:21).

"God with us." What is the significance of this name? Matthew's application of Isaiah 7:14 to Jesus serves as a confirmation of the deity of the Son of God.[33] However, is this the idea being conveyed in the context of Isaiah? Perhaps not.

We see the name Immanuel used several times in this section (chs. 7-12). The most significant observations come from two uses in 8:8-10. What we see is the empty confidence of unsaved Judeans who thought that they would be exempt from invasion and defeat because of God's choice of Israel, David, Jerusalem, and the temple. The empty confidence of the unsaved Judeans reflected itself in open declarations that an overthrow of Jerusalem was impossible since God is "with us" ("Immanuel"). Their empty faith was not going to save them. When God tells Isaiah that his son would be called Immanuel, this was a form of sarcastic rebuke that He was not going to deliver them. Yes, Jesus is God in flesh, but this is not the original sense of how Isaiah was using the expression.[34]

Third observation: By the time the child reaches the age of moral awareness, the Syro/Israel threat will be gone (vv. 15-16). It is the flowing context of verses 15-16 which solidifies the solution proposed above. The two statements found in verses 15-16 make it clear that the promised child is one to be born in the immediate historical context.[35]

Here in verse 15, Isaiah states, "He will eat curds and honey at the time he knows *enough* to refuse evil and choose good." This statement is enigmatic on a first reading, but the flowing context explains it. God's promise is that by the time the promised child (Immanuel) is able to have the capacity for making

---

[33] Certainly, Matthew is correct when he indicates that Jesus is God in flesh—Yahweh the King of Israel who has come to save His people (Isa. 9:6-7; 10:20-23; cf. Jer. 23:5; 33:15; Zeph. 3:14-20).

[34] Oswalt correctly observes that the person who bears the symbolic name *Immanuel* is one in the same with the one who bears the symbolic name *Maher-Shalal-hash-baz* in 8:1-4 (Oswalt, *The Book of Isaiah, 1-39*, 213). Both symbolic names refer to the child that would soon be born to Isaiah and his soon-to-be wife.

[35] It is possible that "the boy" of verse 16 refers to Isaiah's son, She'ar Yashub, who was with Isaiah at that time (Isa 7:3). Matthew Poole writes: "… not the virgin's Son, but the prophet's child, *Shear-jashub*, whom in all probability the prophet, to prevent mistakes, pointed at, and who was brought hither by God's special command, ver. 3, and that for this very use; for otherwise his presence was wholly insignificant" (*Annotations upon the Holy Bible* [Vol. 2, p. 341]. New York: Robert Carter and Brothers). The context of the prophecy and further references to Immanuel in chapter 8 do not, however, favor his conclusion.

moral judgments (cf. similar wording in Gen. 2:17; Deut. 1:39; 1 Kings 3:9; Isa. 5:20; Jonah 4:11), his primary diet is going to be that of curds (*chem'ah*, sour milk, butter[36]) and honey (*debash*, probably bee honey, although the term was also used for honey made out of dates[37]). At what age do children develop the capacity for understanding moral instruction? This is probably best understood as being something roughly around two to three years of age.[38] But why will this child be eating curds and honey within two years? The answer is found in verses 17-25 where we read that within two to three years Assyrian armies were going to invade the land and so devastate the vineyards and fields that the only food source would be curds and honey.[39]

Verse 16 reinforces verses 14-15 with a second statement and makes it explicit what the essence of God's promise is: "For before the boy will know *enough* to refuse evil and choose good, the land whose two kings you dread will be forsaken." Not only will the Assyrian invasion mean devastation to the land of Judah, but it will also mean a complete weakening of Syria and Israel so that the danger of them overthrowing the Davidic dynasty will be gone forever.[40]

Historical sources show us that Tiglath Pileser began invading very soon after God gave these prophecies to Isaiah in 734 B.C., and very shortly after this time his armies both conquered Damascus and invaded Israel, all within a space of two years (Samaria fell in 722).[41] However, his invasions did not stop with the overthrow of Syria and Israel, but they came all the way into Judah as well.[42]

---

[36] Ludwig Koehler et al., *The Hebrew and Aramaic Lexicon of the Old Testament*, cited in electronic form with Logos Libronix (Leiden: E.J. Brill, 1994–2000), 325.

[37] Ludwig Koehler et al., *The Hebrew and Aramaic Lexicon of the Old Testament*, cited in electronic form with Logos Libronix (Leiden: E.J. Brill, 1994–2000), 212-213.

[38] Oswalt holds out the possibility that since Samaria did not fall until 12 years later in 722 B.C. the promise may be related to the idea of official accountability when the child would turn 12 (Oswalt, *The Book of Isaiah, 1-39*, 214).

[39] Ibid., 212.

[40] This is the same exact message conveyed in 8:1-8.

[41] As noted by Keil and Delitzsch, "Consequently, the birth of Immanuel apparently falls between the time then present and the Assyrian calamities, and his earliest childhood appears to run parallel to the Assyrian oppression" (Delitzsch, *Keil and Delitzsch Commentary on the Old Testament*, 223).

[42] The Assyrian oppressions began under Tiglath-Pileser III (745-727) in roughly 734-732 B.C. and continued through the reigns of Shalmaneser V (727-722), Sargon II (722-705), Sennacherib (705-681), Esarhaddon (681-669), and Ashurbanipal (668-631). Weaker kings followed, and within 20 years the Assyrian empire would fall to other rising powers.

As a result, the land of Judah was left in complete devastation (vv. 17-25; cf. 2 Kings 15:29; 16:9). Martin summarizes:

> Within about three years (nine months for the pregnancy and two or three years until the boy would know the difference between good and evil) the alliance would be broken. It was broken in 732 b.c. when Tiglath-Pileser III destroyed Damascus. After Tiglath-Pileser had defeated Aram and put Rezin to death Ahaz went to Damascus to meet the Assyrian monarch (2 Kings 16:7–10). Ahaz liked an altar he saw in Damascus, and had a sketch of it drawn so a similar altar could be set up in Jerusalem. No wonder Isaiah and God were angry with Ahaz. Even after the alliance had been broken by Tiglath-Pileser Judah had no peace. Though Assyria did not defeat Judah, she had to pay Assyria a heavy tribute.[43]

The consequences for disbelief (vv. 17-25)

God had given Ahaz the assurance that He would not let the Davidic dynasty fall, but Ahaz did not believe God, a disbelief that would have serious consequences (7:9).[44] Here in 17-25 God explains these consequences. We can break down 17-25 into five particular warnings.[45]

First warning: It will be one of the worst events in history (v. 17). Up to this time, one of the worst events in the history of Israel took place in 931 B.C. when the kingdom of Israel separated with ten of the tribes, breaking off to follow a false king and a false worship system in a separate kingdom called Israel (cf. 2 Kings 12). Judah and Benjamin stayed loyal to the son of David in Jerusalem and the worship of Yahweh in the temple of Jerusalem (the kingdom of Judah). Likewise, the coming calamity will be terrible for Israel—"the king of Assyria."[46] If Ahaz thought Syria and Israel were bad problems, he would soon find out how brutal the Assyrians were.[47]

Second warning: The coming invasion will leave nothing untouched (vv. 18-19). God makes it clear that He is the One who has planned this

---

[43] Martin, "Isaiah," 1048.
[44] Wolf, *Interpreting Isaiah*, 92.
[45] Isaiah repeats the expression "in that day" in vv. 18, 20, 21 and 23. In context it is clear that all of these are referring to near-term judgments that were going to fall on Judah and not to the eschatological Day of the Lord.
[46] The grammar is very bold in the way that the predicate accusative "the king of Assyria" is introduced by the marker *'eth* (cf. similar constructions in Gen. 4:1; 6:10; 26:34).
[47] Grogan, "Isaiah," 65.

invasion, for He is the One who will "whistle for the fly that is in the remotest part of the rivers of Egypt and for the bee that is in the land of Assyria" (v. 18).

Throughout its history, Israel was often caught in the middle between the power structures to the south (the fly in Egypt; cf. 18:1) and the powers to the north (the bee in Assyria/Babylon). Even though Ahaz thought he could summon aid from these powers, in reality God was the One at work who would bring in these powers for the purposes of judging His faithless people (cf. 5:26 for the same whistle metaphor).[48] God is bringing in enemy armies, and they will "come and settle on the steep ravines, on the ledges of the cliffs, on all the thorn bushes and on all the watering places" (v. 19). The timing of all these events is hard to pinpoint,[49] but clearly it will overwhelm the land.

Third warning: It will bring severe humiliation (v. 20). God already used two different metaphors to describe the invaders (flies and bees), but now he calls them a hired razor. Kidner explains, "The two metaphors in vs 18–20 make the swarms of looting soldiers not only an uncomfortably vivid prospect but clearly a divine scourge."[50] Here is the issue: God is at work to judge, and it will bring severe humiliation to faithless Judah. Ahaz thought he was hiring Assyrian mercenaries to save Judah from their enemies (2 Kings 16:7-8), but in reality, God was hiring them to shave the head, legs, and beard of the men of Judah, something that would have been severely shameful to a man in that culture (cf. 2 Sam. 10:4-5).[51]

Fourth warning: Loss of all food supplies (vv. 21-22). A massive invasion would mean devastation to the fields and vineyards. Bread and wine would become scarce, and that would mean a primary diet of curds and honey. Pfeiffer explains, "Here again we find butter and honey as the food of sparse survivors in a land of ruined fields and orchards."[52]

Fifth warning: It will leave total desolation (vv. 23-25). The last warning comes in verses 23-25: The well-cultivated land of Judah would see all its crops brought to ruin so that all that remains is a wasteland (the thousand vines valued at a thousand shekels is a hyperbolic way of expressing the former prosperity). The well-cultivated land will become a land of "briars and thorns" (Isa.

---

[48] Martin, "Isaiah," 1048.

[49] Oswalt, *The Book of Isaiah, 1-39*, 216.

[50] Kidner, "Isaiah," 639.

[51] It is also possible that Isaiah, by saying this, has exposed the king's plan before his very eyes (Oswalt, *The Book of Isaiah, 1-39*, 217).

[52] Pfeiffer, *The Wycliffe Bible Commentary: Old Testament*, Is 7:14.

5:1-7), wild animals (that require one to remain armed), and mere pastureland for oxen and sheep. The whole land will be one big mess—abandoned and left desolate.

Summary and application

These events took place some 2,700 years ago, but there are principles that apply today. Perhaps the greatest lesson is the importance of remembering that no matter what kind of trial we are facing, we should always trust the Lord and His Word.

THE PROMISED CHILD, Pt. 2 (8:1-22)

In chapter 7 God gave Ahaz a sign that revolved around the birth of a special son with a symbolic name. This same theme shows itself again in chapter 8. Martin explains, "This section is closely related to the previous chapter. It concerns the same event, namely, the deliverance from the Aram-Israel alliance and the subsequent Assyrian invasion that would eventually extend to Judah."[53]

Chapter 8 reads as follows: "1 Then the Lord said to me, Take for yourself a large tablet and write on it in ordinary letters: Swift is the booty, speedy is the prey. 2 And I will take to Myself faithful witnesses for testimony, Uriah the priest and Zechariah the son of Jeberechiah. 3 So I approached the prophetess, and she conceived and gave birth to a son. Then the Lord said to me, Name him Maher-shalal-hash-baz; 4 for before the boy knows how to cry out My father or My mother, the wealth of Damascus and the spoil of Samaria will be carried away before the king of Assyria. 5 Again the Lord spoke to me further, saying, 6 Inasmuch as these people have rejected the gently flowing waters of Shiloah and rejoice in Rezin and the son of Remaliah, 7 Now therefore, behold, the Lord is about to bring on them the strong and abundant waters of the Euphrates, *even* the king of Assyria and all his glory; and it will rise up over all its channels and go over all its banks. 8 Then it will sweep on into Judah, it will overflow and pass through; it will reach even to the neck, and the spread of its wings will fill the breadth of your land, O Immanuel. 9 Be broken, O peoples, and be shattered; and give ear, all remote places of the earth; gird yourselves, yet be shattered; gird yourselves, yet be shattered; 10 devise a plan, but it will be thwarted; state a proposal, but it will not stand, for God is with us. 11 For thus the Lord spoke to me with mighty power and instructed me not to walk in the way of this people, saying, 12 You are not to say, *It is* a conspiracy! in regard to all that this people call a conspiracy, and you are not to fear what they fear or be in dread of *it*. 13 It is the Lord of hosts whom you should regard as holy.

---

[53] Martin, "Isaiah," 1049.

And He shall be your fear, and He shall be your dread. 14 Then He shall become a sanctuary, but to both the houses of Israel, a stone to strike and a rock to stumble over, and a snare and a trap for the inhabitants of Jerusalem. 15 Many will stumble over them; then they will fall and be broken; they will even be snared and caught. 16 Bind up the testimony, seal the law among my disciples. 17 And I will wait for the Lord who is hiding His face from the house of Jacob; I will even look eagerly for Him. 18 Behold, I and the children whom the Lord has given me are for signs and wonders in Israel from the Lord of hosts, who dwells on Mount Zion. 19 When they say to you, Consult the mediums and the spiritists who whisper and mutter," should not a people consult their God? *Should they consult* the dead on behalf of the living? 20 To the law and to the testimony! If they do not speak according to this word, it is because they have no dawn. 21 They will pass through the land hard-pressed and famished, and it will turn out that when they are hungry, they will be enraged and curse their king and their God as they face upward. 22 Then they will look to the earth, and behold, distress and darkness, the gloom of anguish; and *they will be* driven away into darkness" (8:1-22).

Once again, God speaks about the birth of a special child who will be given a symbolic name. We can break chapter 8 down into four explanations of God's promise of another sign child.

First explanation: God offers Israel another sign (vv. 1-4)

The first sign was the Immanuel child in chapter 7. Chapter 8 carries on this same theme and gives us a second prophecy, one that is parallel to chapter 7.

God commands Isaiah to make a written prophecy (vv. 1-2)

God's command to Isaiah was that he was to write, "swift is the booty and speedy is the prey" on a large tablet (*gilllayon*)—a flat piece of wood or metal that can be posted as a placard (cf. Isa. 3:23; Ezek. 37:16).[54] God's intent is that this message was to be a prophecy of an imminent event,[55] so Isaiah took with himself two respected members of the community to be witnesses that he had made this prophecy (cf. Num. 35:30; Deut. 17:6; 19:15).

---

[54] Oswalt, *The Book of Isaiah, 1-39*, 221.

[55] The developing context says that this imminent event is the Assyrian invasion spoken of in chapter 7. The words themselves reflect the reality that in a very short time the armies of Assyria would be coming to take booty (*shalal*, the more valuable plunder) and prey (*baz*, the less valuable plunder).

The child is born and named (vv. 3-4)

One should not miss the similarity between this section and 7:14ff. The language and details strongly suggest the two passages are parallel and speak about the same child.

Isaiah had relations with his wife to conceive a child (v. 3). The expression "approached" (*qarab*: literally, "drew near"; NIV: "made love to") is a euphemism used several times in the Old Testament for the first intercourse between a man and his wife.[56] This idea is consistent with the explanation that Isaiah's first wife, the one who gave him *She'ar Yashub* (7:3), had died earlier and Isaiah was now about to have a remarriage to a young maiden (the *'almah* of 7:14) who would soon conceive and bear another son to Isaiah. Isaiah's new wife is called "the prophetess." Either this woman is actually a prophetess (cf. Exod. 15:20; Judg. 4:4; 2 Kings 22:14; Neh. 6:14) or she is being called this since she is the wife of Isaiah. Once the child was born, God instructed Isaiah to name him *Mahar-Shalal-Hash-Baz*, a name meaning "swift is the booty and speedy is the prey," the words Isaiah had written on the tablet.

The child's name will be symbolic (v. 4). God explains the reason for this symbolic name: "for before the boy knows how to cry out My father or My mother, the wealth of Damascus and the spoil of Samaria will be carried away before the king of Assyria." That is, within two to three years, Syria and Israel are going to be brought to ruin by Assyrian armies. Clearly, this is the same child of 7:14-16. Pfeiffer explains,

> This assault would crush both those kingdoms before the infant boy would be old enough to utter, "Mummy" or "Daddy," i.e., within three years. (This prophecy was fulfilled in the capture of Damascus and the spoliation of Samaria in 732 by Tiglathpileser III).[57]

Second explanation: God explains their rejection (vv. 5-8)

God warned Ahaz in chapter 7 that disbelief would bring tragedy. God's anger against Ahaz and Judah is evident again in the way God describes them as "these people" (literally, "this people," *ha'am hazzeh*).

The disbelief is like a rejection of the waters of *Shiloah* (vv. 5-6)

This statement refers to the waters that flowed out of the Gihon spring at the bottom of the Kidron Valley in the center of Zion, the City of David. Within

---

[56] Oswalt, *The Book of Isaiah, 1-39*, 222.
[57] Pfeiffer, *The Wycliffe Bible Commentary: Old Testament*, Is 8:1.

one generation Hezekiah would carve a tunnel that would bring all the Gihon waters into the Pool of Siloam (cf. John 9:7), but it is possible that natural conduits may have brought small amounts of water into storage pools even at that time.[58] Ahaz and Judah were rejoicing in the defeat of Syria and Israel, but they still were not trusting in the Lord.

The consequences of disbelief (vv. 7-8)

The key point is that Ahaz did not trust in God's promises to the House of David (i.e., the gentle waters of *Shiloah*), and for this reason God would bring upon Ahaz and Judah the mighty Euphrates River. That mighty river is the King of Assyria—the river that will completely overflow the land of Judah: "it will overflow and pass through; it will reach even to the neck, and the spread of its wings will fill the breadth of your land, O Immanuel." As noted earlier, God's use of the name Immanuel ("God is with us") is best understood as being a sarcastic taunt against the faithless people of Judah. The people made empty chants that they were safe from invasion because of their belief that God was with them (cf. Jer. 7:1-8). God makes it clear that their election was no guarantee against invasion.

Third explanation: God shows mercy despite disbelief (vv. 9-15)

Regardless of who it is, God will judge unrepentant sin. However, the Bible also shows us that He is also a God of mercy for those who are willing to repent and believe in Him. Judah was about to suffer a judgment, but this would not be the end of the story.

God interjects a message to Syria and Israel (vv. 9-10)

The heart of God's message to the nations in verses 9-10 is that they can make plans to overthrow His people, but no matter what they plot, it will not succeed.[59] Martin explains, "Even though they would carefully work out a strategy and a plan for battle they would not succeed."[60] The reason is because "God is with us." God is angry, but He will not let Judah fall.

---

[58] Oswalt, *The Book of Isaiah, 1-39*, 225.

[59] It is important that we recognize the distinction between God speaking about the efforts of Syria and Israel (to overthrow the Davidic dynasty) that were doomed to certain failure (vv. 9-10), versus the reality of an Assyrian invasion that would bring great devastation to the land (as seen in both chs. 7-8).

[60] Martin, "Isaiah," 1051.

God turns His message directly to Isaiah (vv. 11-12)

The immediate prophetic promises are now complete, so God turns his attention to His prophet. The Lord tells Isaiah that he is not to embrace the conspiracy theories that were circulating among "this people." Apparently certain people were circulating theories that obedience to Isaiah's prophecies were tantamount to a political conspiracy (*qesher*) against Judah, i.e., an alliance with foreign powers against your own country (cf. 2 Sam. 15:12; 2 Kings 11:14; 2 Chron. 23:13; Isa. 8:12).[61] God tells Isaiah that he was not to give heed to such folly. The real problem was that instead of looking to the root evils of their own hearts, the people were looking around for something to blame for their woes. God tells the people of Judah they were not to live with a fear and dread of man.

The cure will always be the fear of the Lord (vv. 13-14a)

The real cure, says God, is that, "It is the Lord of hosts whom you should regard as holy [*qadash*].[62] And He shall be your fear, and He shall be your dread."[63] The true solution to all of man's problems is to repent of sin and trust God (cf. Matt. 6:33). Believers are not to live in fear of man, but fear of God (Matt. 10:28). Those who live with such faith will find Him to be a safe sanctuary (*miqdash*).[64]

Those who refuse to trust the Lord will find ruin (vv. 14b-15)

For unbelieving Israel (God is not yet finished with the northern kingdom), the Lord will not be a sanctuary, but "a stone to strike and a rock to stumble over, *and* a snare and a trap for the inhabitants of Jerusalem." God is patient in calling sinners to repentance (cf. Amos 4), but those who harden their hearts will eventually fall under judgment (Prov. 29:1).

---

[61] Ludwig Koehler et al., *The Hebrew and Aramaic Lexicon of the Old Testament*, cited in electronic form with Logos Libronix (Leiden: E.J. Brill, 1994–2000), 1154. In particular, some were probably demanding that Judah join the alliance of Syria and Israel, and that any resistance to this idea was nothing but an anti-Judah conspiracy.

[62] The Hiphil use of *qadash* carries the force of declaring or regarding the Lord as holy. Ezekiel and Jesus both teach that one day a redeemed world will hold this holy view of God when Christ brings the kingdom (Ezek. 36:23; Matt. 6:9).

[63] The former term "fear" (*mora'*) conveys the idea of fear or awe, while the synonym "dread" (*'aratits*) conveys the idea of terror or dread. Both speak about genuine faith and trust in the living God (Pss. 25:12-14; 34:8, 12-15; Prov. 1:7).

[64] Young says the Lord surrounds them like a temple wall (Young, *The Book of Isaiah*, vol. 1, 312).

For the believer God is a Rock in the good sense of strength and stability (Deut. 32:4, 15, 18; Pss. 18:2; 71:3), but for those who disbelieve He becomes a Rock that people stumble over. So it is with Jesus Christ (Matt. 21:44; Luke 2:34; Rom. 9:33; 1 Pet. 2:8). Isaiah uses a second metaphor to describe the ruin that comes to the disbeliever: they get caught in the snare (*pach*) and trap (*moqesh*) of their own disbelief like an animal destined for slaughter (Isa. 24:17, 18; cf. Prov. 7:23). Pfeiffer applies it all:

> No matter how unfavorable present circumstances are, true believers will sanctify Jehovah by continuing to regard him as supreme in governing human affairs, and the fulfiller of his promises. They are to fear and revere him only; they are never to fear men.[65]

Fourth explanation: Israel's judgment for its disbelief (vv. 16-22)

Isaiah resigns himself to leave the messages of chapters 7-8 with the people. They will have to decide what to do with the Lord and His Word. Verses 16-22 reflect two kinds of responses.

First, we see the response of the believer (vv. 16-18)

Men need God's truth. Men need to preserve God's truth (v. 16), believe it (v. 17), and learn to appreciate its depths (v. 18).

Truth must be preserved (v. 16). Isaiah gives the command to preserve the prophetic instruction.[66] God's Word, i.e., His testimony and instruction, has been given, and now it must be preserved (cf. Jer. 32:14).[67]

Truth must be believed (v. 17). Isaiah knows God's Word will be fulfilled, so he is resigned to "wait" for the Lord (*chakah*, tarry[68]) and "look eagerly" (*qawah*, wait, hope) for the fulfilling of His promises (cf. Num. 6:25-26; Pss. 31:16; 80:3, 7, 19; Hab. 1:13). Isaiah knows God's Word never fails, so he is content to trust the Lord. Sin has separated Israel from God (Isa. 59:1-2), but God's promise is that one day He will restore them. Until that day, believers patiently wait on Yahweh (Isa. 30:18; 40:31; Ps. 118:8-9).

---

[65] Pfeiffer, *The Wycliffe Bible Commentary: Old Testament*, 8:9.

[66] These two verbs may be Qal imperatives. Oswalt sees them as Qal infinitive constructs used imperatively (Oswalt, *The Book of Isaiah, 1-39*, 230, n. 4).

[67] The act of binding and sealing was an affirmation of the message (Isa. 29:11; cf. Neh. 9:38; 10:1; Jer. 32:10-12, 14; Josh. 24:14-15).

[68] Ludwig Koehler et al., *The Hebrew and Aramaic Lexicon of the Old Testament*, cited in electronic form with Logos Libronix (Leiden: E.J. Brill, 1994–2000), 313.

Truth is very deep (v. 18). Part of Isaiah's faith is in knowing that in the life of himself and his own children (children with symbolic names), they have been part of God's prophetic messages here in chapters 7-8 as "signs" (*'oth*) and "wonders" (*mopheth*). As Martin explains, "Each one had a name that held significance for the nation's future."[69] Isaiah's own name means "the Lord saves." His first son's name (*She'ar Yashub*) speaks about the remnant who will return one day (cf. 10:20-22), and his second son's name (*Immanuel/Mahar-Shalal-Hash-Baz*) emphasized God's protection for His chosen people.

One of the challenges here is to understand how these historical concepts relate to the New Testament use of this passage in reference to Christ (cf. e.g., Heb. 2:13). What we see here is another one of the illustrations of the marvelous ways that God bears witness to the Messiah. By the Spirit, Isaiah understood that not only did his children have prophetic significance for prophetic events in the immediate context, but he also understood that these messages would also have an ultimate, typological fulfillment in Christ (cf. 1 Pet. 10-12). At a textual level, Isaiah's prophecies dealt with immediate near-term events, but the New Testament shows that they also had relationship to Christ (e.g., Isa. 7:14 and Matt. 1:18-25). Thus, the children born to Isaiah had prophetic significance to Israel's immediate future, but also to the ultimate salvation God would bring through Christ (Isa. 9:6-7; 10:20-22; 11:1-10). Furthermore, Hebrews (2:13-14) uses Isaiah to demonstrate the solidarity that Messiah has with the human race in that there is only one Father to all humanity, and that Messiah Himself came to share in this humanity to bring redemption by His own sacrificial death (Heb. 2:14-18). The key point is that God's people believe God's Word.

Consequences of disbelief (vv. 19-22)

Much of Isaiah's discussion revolves around God's truth. God's people believe His truth, but the unsaved reject His truth (vv. 19-20), and consequently pay a huge price (vv. 21-22).

The unsaved reject God's truth (vv. 19-20). Isaiah condemns those who reject God's Word and rely on the words of demonically-driven witchcraft. The terms "mediums" (*'ob*) and "spiritists" (*yidde'onim*), both speak about necromancers who try to gain power through communication with the dead (cf. Lev. 19:31; 20:6, 27; Deut. 18:11; 1 Sam. 28:7-8; 2 Kings 21:6; 1 Chron. 10:13; 2 Chron. 33:6; Isa. 8:19; 19:3).[70] The people should be listening to God's prophets

---

[69] Martin, "Isaiah," 1052.

[70] Ludwig Koehler et al., *The Hebrew and Aramaic Lexicon of the Old Testament*, cited in electronic form with Logos Libronix (Leiden: E.J. Brill, 1994–2000), 20. Such people used incantations and spells to seek occult knowledge by summoning the dead, but

(like Isaiah), so God severely rebukes them for consulting the dead, reminding them that they should be seeking God's Word as their source of light and truth (v. 19). He also makes it clear that if they reject the Word of God for witches (cf. 1 Sam. 28:13), the reason why is because they are not His people (i.e., there is no dawn within them).[71] Oswalt notes that "those who lack a truly transcendent perspective on their affairs, who succumb to the occult for their guidance, plunge themselves further into gloom, spiritual famine, and despair.[72]

The unsaved get judged for rejecting God's truth (vv. 21-22). The consequences of disbelief would mean invasion and exile (vv. 21-22). Famine and hopeless despair (cf. 3:1; 7:23-25) will eventually cause them to not only become enraged at their king, but also God. They rejected the Lord, so the curses of the covenant (Deut. 28:15-68) will come upon them with the result that they will look to the earth and find distress (*tsarah*), darkness (*chashekah*), and gloom of anguish (*me'uph tsuqah*), being driven away into darkness (*'aphelah*) (v. 22). These covenant judgments began with the Assyrian invasions, but they have continued to this very day. This is what happens when men reject God.

The consequences for Israel have included over 2,600 years in exile. Is there any hope? The answer is "Yes." One day God will lift the darkness off of His chosen people and place that darkness on the nations seeking their destruction (ch. 9; cf. Isa. 60:1-2), and this is what we see in chapter 9.

Summary and application

Israel was a nation with tremendous privilege, but sadly she would not trust the Lord. Her lack of trust eventually brought her under long ages of God's chastising judgment. God's people today should apply the lesson that we must never stop believing and obeying the Word of God.

THE PROMISED CHILD, Pt. 3 (9:1-10:4)

The warning for Israel in 8:22 was "distress" (*tsarah*), "darkness" (*chashekah*), "gloom of anguish" (*me'uph tsuqah*), and being driven away into "darkness" (*'aphelah*). Here, however, Isaiah announces in 9:1 a removal of the gloom (*me'uph*) and anguish (*tsuqah*) and darkness (*chashekah*) that had fallen on

---

Scripture indicates that this is the work of demons. It was a belief in the ANE that the dead spoke in birdlike, whispered voices, and it is to this that Isaiah refers (cf. Isa. 29:4) (Oswalt, *The Book of Isaiah, 1-39*, 230, n. 6, 237).

[71] A true believer hears (John 18:37) and listens to God (John 15:20; 1 John 4:5-6).
[72] Oswalt, *The Book of Isaiah, 1-39*, 238.

her in earlier ages. What we have here is a distinctive shift to the promise of an eschatological restoration.

Verses 9:1-10:4 read as follows: "1 But there will be no *more* gloom for her who was in anguish; in earlier times He treated the land of Zebulun and the land of Naphtali with contempt, but later on He shall make *it* glorious, by the way of the sea, on the other side of Jordan, Galilee of the Gentiles. 2 The people who walk in darkness will see a great light; those who live in a dark land, the light will shine on them. 3 You shall multiply the nation; You shall increase their gladness; they will be glad in Your presence as with the gladness of harvest, as men rejoice when they divide the spoil. 4 For You shall break the yoke of their burden and the staff on their shoulders, the rod of their oppressor, as at the battle of Midian. 5 For every boot of the booted warrior in the *battle* tumult, and cloak rolled in blood, will be for burning, fuel for the fire. 6 For a child will be born to us, a son will be given to us; and the government will rest on His shoulders; and His name will be called Wonderful Counselor, Mighty God, Eternal Father, Prince of Peace. 7 There will be no end to the increase of *His* government or of peace, on the throne of David and over his kingdom, to establish it and to uphold it with justice and righteousness from then on and forevermore. The zeal of the Lord of hosts will accomplish this. 8 The Lord sends a message against Jacob, and it falls on Israel. 9 And all the people know *it, that is,* Ephraim and the inhabitants of Samaria, asserting in pride and in arrogance of heart: 10 The bricks have fallen down, but we will rebuild with smooth stones; the sycamores have been cut down, but we will replace *them* with cedars. 11 Therefore the Lord raises against them adversaries from Rezin and spurs their enemies on, 12 the Arameans on the east and the Philistines on the west; and they devour Israel with gaping jaws. In *spite of* all this, His anger does not turn away and His hand is still stretched out. 13 Yet the people do not turn back to Him who struck them, nor do they seek the Lord of hosts. 14 So the Lord cuts off head and tail from Israel, *both* palm branch and bulrush in a single day. 15 The head is the elder and honorable man, and the prophet who teaches falsehood is the tail. 16 For those who guide this people are leading *them* astray, and those who are guided by them are brought to confusion. 17 Therefore the Lord does not take pleasure in their young men, nor does He have pity on their orphans or their widows; for every one of them is godless and an evildoer, and every mouth is speaking foolishness. In *spite of* all this, His anger does not turn away and His hand is still stretched out. 18 For wickedness burns like a fire; it consumes briars and thorns; it even sets the thickets of the forest aflame and they roll upward in a column of smoke. 19 By the fury of the Lord of hosts the land is burned up, and the people are like fuel for the fire; no man spares his brother. 20 They slice off *what is* on the right hand but *still* are hungry, and they eat *what is* on the left hand but they are not satisfied; each of them eats the flesh of his own arm. 21 Manasseh *devours* Ephraim, and Ephraim Manasseh, *and* together they are against Judah. In *spite of* all this, His anger does not turn away and His hand is still stretched out. 1 Woe to those who enact evil statutes and to those who constantly record unjust decisions, 2 So as to deprive the needy of justice and rob the poor of My people of *their* rights, so that widows may be their spoil and that they may plunder the orphans. 3 Now what will you do in the day of punishment, and in the devastation which will come from afar? To whom will you flee for help? And where will you leave your wealth? 4 Nothing *remains* but to crouch among the captives or fall among the slain. In *spite of* all this, His anger does not turn away and His hand is still stretched out" (9:1-10:4).

Chapter 9 brings a strong shift in tone, the kind of shift that is common in Isaiah. Whereas chapter 8 focused on judgments, the beginning of chapter 9 focuses on a future restoration. This chapter (ending in 10:4) divides broadly into two parts, first, a message of restoration (9:1-7), and second, a message of more judgments (9:8-10:4).

First message: The message of restoration (vv. 1-7)

Verses 1-7 all revolve around the eschatological restoration of Israel. This promise opens with a general declaration of this future restoration.

The general declaration of a future restoration (vv. 1-3)

The latter portion of chapter 8 warned that disbelief would bring distress (*tsarah*), darkness (*chashekah*), gloom of anguish (*me'uph tsuqah*), and being driven away into darkness (*'aphelah*). Isaiah now announces a future removal of the gloom (*me'uph*), anguish (*tsuqah*), and darkness (*chashekah*) that fell upon them in earlier days. Isaiah does not give a precise chronology for this restoration, but his statements about "earlier" and "later" times convey the idea that this restoration will not come until the distant future. The earlier days included the judgments that started with Assyrian invasions of the northern tribes,[73] but a future day is coming when God will "make *it* glorious" (cf. Zech. 9:16-17 for a post-exilic confirmation of this still yet-future restoration). Isaiah describes the land of Israel as from the perspective of the Babylon exile and calls it the region that

---

[73] Isaiah describes it as God treating the land of Zebulun (about 10 miles west of the Sea of Galilee) and Naphtali (northwest of the Sea of Galilee) with contempt (Hiph. of *qalal*). These judgments are the curses of the Sinaitic Covenant described in Deuteronomy 28:15-68, judgments that have continued to this present day, and which will not end until the nation repents and enters the messianic kingdom. The hatred and persecution of Israel is driven by satanic hatred (cf. Rev. 12), but all of it is also part of the just consequences of Israel's apostasy from Yahweh.

is "by the way of the sea, on the other side of Jordan, Galilee of the Gentiles,"[74] the regions in Galilee that were the first to experience the northern military invasions. Martin notes, "In 732 b.c. this northern portion of Israel became an Assyrian province under Tiglath-Pileser III, thus humbling the people there and putting them in gloom" (2 Kings 15:29 describes the events and the annals of Tiglath-Pileser III confirm them in ANET, 283-284).[75]

The promise of divine blessings (v. 1). God says that He will make the land glorious. This is the first of a string of "prophetic perfect" verbs that look ahead to Israel's eschatological restoration.[76]

The gospels cite this text at the first coming of Christ (v. 2). The restoration promises continue in verse 2 as God tells Israel that even though they had walked in a dark land,[77] one day they will see great light and that great light will shine upon them (cf. Matt. 4:12-16; Luke 1:79).[78]

This verse raises the question whether or not one should see the first coming of Christ as bringing a fulfillment of Isaiah 9. This is a great hermeneutical question that calls for careful explanation. The short answer is that Isaiah 9:1-7 is speaking about a literal, eschatological restoration of Israel—a restoration that will not be fulfilled until the second coming. At the same time, we also recognize that there was a literal aspect of fulfillment when Christ went out preaching at His first coming. The important piece to this puzzle that must not be left out is the fact that Isaiah also tells us in other places that the Messiah was going to be rejected and killed for the sins of His people (Isa. 52:13-53:12). The best hermeneutical explanation of Matthew's citation of Isaiah 9 is that it is an application of the literal meaning of the prophecy at His first coming, but the contextual fulfillment will not come until the second coming.

---

[74] The "the way of the sea" most likely refers to the plain that starts at Gennesaret and runs westward and southward from the Sea of Galilee (Grogan, "Isaiah," 73)
[75] Martin, "Isaiah," 1052.
[76] Wolf, *Interpreting Isaiah*, 96-97; Oswalt, *The Book of Isaiah, 1-39*, 242-243. See other passages that emphasize this eschatological restoration after ages judgment (Isa. 4:5; 24:23; 35:2; 58:8; 60:1-3; cf. Hos. 1:1-11; 3:4-5; 5:13-15).
[77] Regarding this expression "dark" (*tsalmaweth*, cf. Ps. 23:4 where it is often translated "shadow of death"), some today argue that this word simply means "deep shadow," but recent studies seem to support the "shadow of death" kind of translation (ibid., 240). The essential idea does seem to be that of deep darkness.
[78] God is compared to the sun in 60:1-3, 19-20 and Messiah is called a "Light" to the Gentiles in 42:6 and 49:6. The idea of God's favor shining on His people comes out in the Aaronic blessing (Num. 6:22-27; cf. 2 Sam. 22:29; Job 29:3; Ps. 139:11, 12; 1 John 1:5).

The promises continue (v. 3). Seen from the perspective of a nation already under the still future Babylonian exile, Isaiah assures the rejected nation that in the day of restoration God will once again (1) make the nation large and prosperous,[79] and (2) fill them with joy.[80] Some scholars (i.e., those who embrace supersessionism) find it hard to believe that these are literal promises to Israel, but such promises are repeated many times. Frequently these promises are tied to the coming of Israel's messianic King who will save an elect remnant from ruin (e.g., Isa. 4:2; 6:13; 10:20-25; cf. Zeph. 3:14-20; Zech. 2:10; 8:18-23; 9:9). One day all the oppression, gloom and despair will be gone forever and replaced with freedom, joy and hope.

The explanation of God's future restoration (vv. 4-7)

Verses 4-7 explain what this grand restoration is going to look like and how God will make it happen. This explanation comes in the form of three explanatory clauses in verses 4-6, each introduced with the word "for" (*kiy*).

The first explanation of how God will restore Israel: The promise that God will remove enemy oppressors (v. 4). Enemy oppression began coming against Israel with Assyria (cf. 10:27), and it has continued to this very day.[81] God's promise to Israel is that His day of restoration will bring a complete removal of all such oppression.[82] Isaiah says that God will break the yoke, the staff, and the rod of their oppressors and completely free Israel from all Gentile oppression.[83] What will it look like?

The second explanation of how God will restore Israel: A complete annihilation of all enemy powers (v. 5). Isaiah continues to explain how God

---

[79] Isaiah elaborates on this theme in ch. 54 where the "seed" of the Servant (Isa. 53:10) expands greatly in the restored land (cf. Zech. 10:10).

[80] There is some textual question over whether we should read a negation here as reflected in the Kethib of the MT (*lo'*, "you have not increased the joy"), or if the Qere is preferable (*loh*, "to it"). Though M, 1Q, the Vulg, and Sym. have the negative, it is better to go with B, Syr., the Targ, and Saadia and see it as "to him" and not "not" (Young, *The Book of Isaiah, vol. 1*, 326, n. 59).

[81] Daniel describes this as a sequence of godless Gentile powers starting with Babylon that would rule the world and oppress Israel until the Messiah comes and establishes the eternal kingdom of God (Dan. 2:31-45; 7:1-28).

[82] Even during times of relative freedom such as during the reign of Persia, the people of Israel still lived as slaves under oppressing Gentiles (cf. Neh. 9:36-37).

[83] The yoke is the large bar on the neck of an ox to pull the plow and wagon, but here it speaks metaphorically about Gentile oppression. God compares this future defeat to the defeat He gave when Gideon defeated Midian (Judg. 6:17-22; 7:22).

will save Israel. He will utterly destroy all enemy powers. The messianic kingdom will bring peace to the whole world (Isa. 2:4; Mic. 4:3; Ps. 46:9-10), but this peace cannot happen until God brings a final destruction to the godless world powers seeking the destruction of Israel (Rev. 16:12-21; 17:12-18; 19:11-21). Verse 5 graphically describes how every piece of military equipment, even the least of these items like boots and cloaks, will be burned in fire (cf. Ezek. 39:9-10).[84] The promise is wonderful, but still it leaves the reader asking how such a salvation could be possible. God answers that question with the third *kiy* clause in verses 6-7.

The third explanation of how God will restore Israel: Yahweh will send Israel its warrior King (vv. 6-7). Here in 6-7 we again find the promise of a special male child. As previously explained, this is not the same child who was promised to Isaiah back in chapters 7-8. This male child is one who is not going to be born until after long ages of darkness, gloom, and oppression (cf. 8:22; 9:1). Oswalt notes that, "this is clearly an eschatological figure, the Messiah," a fact recognized in the Targums.[85] Verses 6-7 give us seven explanations of this promised King and the kingdom He brings.

The first promise is that He will be a male child (*yeled*), a son (*ben*). God's salvation is not going to come through abstract, philosophical ideas, but through one promised son—the same son whom God promised from the moment humanity fell under the curse of sin and death (Gen. 3:15; 4:1; 9:27; 12:1-3; Num. 24:17). Oswalt explains, "Ultimately God's truth is not merely in the realm of ideas; ultimately it is meant to be incarnated."[86]

The second promise is that this boy will one day become the King of Israel, for the government will rest on His shoulders. Israel and Judah had many ungodly kings in its history, but this King will rule with the perfect wisdom of God since He Himself will be God in flesh (cf. Isa. 11:1-5).[87]

Third, this boy will not be a mere man, but somehow God in flesh as suggested by His four symbolic names. The name "Wonderful Counselor" refers to the fact that this King will rule with the wisdom of God, as opposed to the multitude of foolish, unsaved kings they had in past ages (1:26; 3:3; 5:21; 19:11-

---

[84] Oswalt, *The Book of Isaiah, 1-39*, 244. If the least of the equipment is destroyed, so too will the greatest. This catastrophic overthrow of godless world powers is precisely what one finds in many of the Psalms (cf. e.g., 2; 110).

[85] Ibid., 245.

[86] Ibid., 244.

[87] Some medieval Jewish commentators tried to say that this is speaking about Hezekiah, but Hezekiah was already born, and did none of these things (ibid., 245).

15; 28:7-10; 29:9-14; 30:1-2; 31:1-3; 47:10-13). Because the Messiah is divine and filled with the Spirit of God, He will give counsel that only God can give.[88] Second, this male child will be called "Mighty God" (*'El Gibbor*). Some writers have sought to treat this expression as simply meaning "mighty warrior," but parallel references that treat this expression as referring to God argue that the traditional rendering "Mighty God" is preferable (Isa. 10:21; cf. Deut. 10:17; Jer. 32:18). The third name, "Eternal Father," is best understood as meaning that the king is the everlasting father of the nation, the One who will rule forever.[89] Kidner explains, "*Everlasting Father* has no exact parallel but there is a paradox in so naming a child yet to be born. *Father* signifies the paternal benevolence of the perfect Ruler over a people whom he loves as his children."[90] The fourth and final name that connotes the idea of deity is the name "Prince of Peace." The never-ending peace He brings will come after He has brought a violent end to all sinful rebellion (cf. 32:17).[91] This is the promise of never-ending peace for the whole world, both Gentiles and Jews: "For the mountains may be removed and the hills may shake, but My lovingkindness will not be removed from you, and My covenant of peace will not be shaken, says the Lord who has compassion on you" (Isa. 54:10).

The fourth promise is that His kingdom will be one without any of the limitations of the kingdoms of men (Dan. 2:44). His government and peace will see no limitation as human kingdoms have limitations (cf. Ps. 72).

The fifth promise is that all of these blessings will fulfill the promises of the Davidic Covenant—the covenant God swore to King David that the Son of God would come from His own seed (2 Sam. 7:12-16; Pss. 2:7; 89; 110; 132:11). When Christ returns, He will rule the world from Zion, i.e., Jerusalem (Isa. 2:2-4; 16:5; 54:14; Mic. 4:1-5; Zech. 14:9-21; Pss. 48:2; 132:13-18; Matt. 5:35; 19:28; 25:31; Rev. 2:26; 3:21; 5:10; 14:1; 20:1-6). This messianic kingdom is not in force at the present time.[92] Amillennial and Progressive Dispensational theologians try to argue that Christ is ruling on the throne of David from

---

[88] This term "wonderful," literally "the one who counsels wonder" (*pele' yo'ets*), is only used of God and His supernatural ways (Isa. 28:29; cf. Ps. 78:12; Judg. 13:18).

[89] It was common for the king to be looked on as the father figure to an empire (Oswalt, *The Book of Isaiah, 1-39*, 247; Young, *The Book of Isaiah, vol. 1*, 339).

[90] Kidner, "Isaiah," 640.

[91] This peace will come between God and man (Rom. 5:1), man and man (Isa. 2:4; Mic. 4:3), and also between man and animals and animals and animals (Isa. 11:6-9). All of this is because He Himself made this peace on the cross (Isa. 53:5; 57:19; 66:12; Rom. 5:1; Eph. 2:11-22).

[92] This is not to deny the possibility of spiritual aspects of Christ's kingship at the present time during the church age (cf. e.g., Matt. 13:11; Rev. 1:6, 9).

heaven, but this theological concept has no valid, biblical support.

The sixth promise is that the kingdom of the God is one that will never see an end, for He will "establish it" and "uphold it with justice and righteousness from then on and forevermore."[93] Daniel 2:44 describes the eternality of this kingdom: "In the days of those kings the God of heaven will set up a kingdom which will never be destroyed, and *that* kingdom will not be left for another people; it will crush and put an end to all these kingdoms, but it will itself endure forever" (cf. Dan. 7:13-14; Mic. 4:7; Luke 1:33; Rev. 11:15). The messianic kingdom will first consist of 1,000 years upon this present earth (cf. Rev. 20:1-15), and then be followed by an eternal kingdom in a new heavens and new earth (cf. Rev. 22:5).

Seventh and lastly, the kingdom of the Messiah is one that God Himself will bring and establish: "The zeal of the Lord of hosts will accomplish this."[94] In other words, Christ's kingdom will be no mere human exercise, but it is the passion and zeal of God for His own truth and glory.

This sin-cursed world is constantly looking for an answer to this world's woes. Sadly, the vast majority will never find this answer, for they refuse to soften their hearts to believe in Jesus Christ. Sin is the root problem that separates men from God and creates the ruin that dominates this world (59:1). God made a provision for men to be saved when He sent His Son to die for the sins of mankind (John 1:29), but no one can share in the blessings of God's saving grace unless they are willing to receive Jesus Christ in personal faith (John 1:12). Those who refuse to believe remain in their sin and under the wrath of God (John 3:36), and as we see in the following section, sin always brings the judgment of God.

Second message: The message of judgment (vv. 9:8-10:4)

Once again, we see a sharp break in flow of Isaiah's messages, the kind of break that one finds in many portions of Isaiah (cf. e.g., 2:2-4 and 2:5-7). Verses 1-7 highlighted the promises of restoration through the Messiah, but now in 9:8-10:4 Isaiah abruptly returns to the theme of present judgment.[95] Severe wrath is coming on Judah, but why is this? This present section highlights four reasons why the wrath of God was coming on Israel.

---

[93] The Hebrew expression (*me'atah we'ad 'olam*) conveys the sense of "infinite duration" (Young, *The Book of Isaiah, vol. 1*, 344).

[94] God Himself will make all this happen because of His jealousy for what is true and right—His zeal and His jealousy (Isa. 37:32; cf. Exod. 20:5; 34;14; Deut. 4:24; 5:9; 6:15; Zech. 1:14; 8:2).

[95] Wolf, *Interpreting Isaiah*, 98.

The first reason for wrath: Arrogance and pride (vv. 8-12)

Once again, we are reminded of the ubiquitous problem of pride. Judah's pride was about to be judged.

God revisits Israel's pride (vv. 8-10).[96] The Bible makes many statements telling us that God hates pride (e.g., Prov. 6:16-17; 21:4; 30:13). Pride, so it would seem, is a universal sin. In the present context it is especially focused on the pride (*ga'awah*) and arrogance of heart (*godel*) of the northern kingdom as indicated by the name references (i.e., Jacob, Israel, Ephraim, Samaria). Assyria had already begun its invasion of the northern kingdom, but Israel was arrogant enough to suppose that they could simply rebuild with building materials that were even more glorious than before (vv. 8-10). Samaria was in fact a beautiful city as archeological excavations have indicated, but the people of Israel were being arrogant to think they could defy God and still find lasting prosperity with a rebuilding of their capital (cf. Amos 5:11-12). By the time God was finished with the northern kingdom, everyone would recognize that their destruction was the work of Yahweh to avenge Himself against Israel (Hos. 9:7; Ps. 14:4).

The northern kingdom will not recover (vv. 11-12). Not only will invading armies come from Assyria, but also from the east with the Syrians and from the west with the Philistines. With graphic language, God says they will "devour Israel with gaping jaws." Assyria, Syria, and Philistia are the ones invading, but interestingly God says that He Himself is the One raising them up (Piel of *sagab*, "to make high") and stirring them on (Pilpel of *sug*, "to provoke"). Once again, we are reminded of the absolute sovereignty of God. He is the One who rules His creation, and nothing happens outside of His perfect sovereignty and rule.

The destruction will be terrible, but God makes it clear that His judgments are nowhere near completed, so Isaiah finishes verse 12 with these words: "In *spite of* all this, His anger does not turn away and His hand is still stretched out." In other words, one painful blow is not going to be enough to bring them to repentance.[97]

A biblical theology of God's wrath on Israel. We have already noted in earlier sections that this idea of wrath we find in 9:12 gets repeated multiple times in Isaiah (Isa. 5:25; 9:12, 17, 21; 10:4, 23, 25; 12:1; 26:20).[98] God is going

---

[96] Ibid.

[97] Young, *The Book of Isaiah, vol. 1*, 350.

[98] We see similar ideas in other passages that show how God's ongoing indignation against Israel will climax in a final period of indignation during the tribulation period

to redeem His apostate nation, but He is going to do so by using the afflictions of war to bring them to faith in His Son, all by the work of the Holy Spirit to bring them to repentance (Zech. 12:10; 13:1).

The second reason for wrath: A refusal of leaders to listen (vv. 13-17)

God's chastising judgments had the purpose of bringing Israel to repentance, but Israel would not listen. Therefore, the judgments would get even harsher (Isa. 1:5; cf. Hos. 5:15-6:5; Amos 4:6-11). Martin explains,

> The prophet lamented that even though the Northern Kingdom had suffered at the hand of God, they still had not returned to Him. So their continued refusal would lead to more judgment. Israel was like a child who stubbornly refuses to obey his parents and therefore is punished more severely.[99]

In this present section we see a basic flow of thought where God (1) reviews the situation (vv. 13-16), (2) gives His response (v. 17a), and (3) states His resolve (v. 17b).

God reviews the situation (vv. 13-16). Israel has been struck (*nakah*) by the Lord, but they were still refusing to listen (v. 13).[100] For this reason, more severe judgments would come.[101] The foolish leaders of the land, i.e., the elders, honorable men, and prophets, would not listen, so God would bring a swift destruction upon them (vv. 14-15).

God gives further confirmation about the guilt of the northern-kingdom leaders in verse 16 when He says, "For those who guide this people are leading *them* astray; and those who are guided by them are brought to confusion." Godless leadership had already brought Israel to ruin, and the same problem in the south would also lead Judah into complete ruin (Jer. 6:13-14; 8:10-11; 12:10; 14:14; 28:1-17, esp. vv. 15-17).

(Dan. 8:17, 19, 23; 9:16, 27; 11:36; Matt. 23:38-39). In Daniel, it says that these horrific judgments on Israel will not come to an end until the last three and a half threes have passed and "they finish shattering the power of the holy people" (Dan. 12:7).
[99] Martin, "Isaiah," 1054.
[100] We see this same theme very clearly in Amos 4:6-11.
[101] The converted Waw Imperfect form of the verb in "cuts off" (v. 14) conveys a preterit force and indicates this is not merely a future warning, but events that have already begun falling upon them.

God's response: Judgment on all who refuse Him (v. 17a). The leaders had the greatest guilt, but the impact of their sin would bring ruin not only upon themselves, but also to the whole country. God identifies three groups who will be suffer great consequences. The young men (*bachur*) are those in the prime of life who get sent into battle and die. The orphans (*yathom*) and widows (*'almanah*) are the weakest and most-vulnerable elements of society (cf. 1:17). These will not be sent into battle, but they too will suffer, and all because of a wicked society (cf. Isa. 5:20-23).

God states His resolve (v. 17b). The whole land is godless, so God will bring all of them to ruin. Even now, however, they still will not repent, so God declares, "In *spite of* all this, His anger does not turn away and His hand is still stretched out." The solution is very simple: repent and believe. Why such wrath? Not only is it because of their arrogance (vv. 8-12), and refusal to listen to God's Word (vv. 13-17), but also because of their devotion to selfish self-exaltation (vv. 18-21).

The third reason for wrath: Devotion to self-exaltation (vv. 18-21)

Israel was consumed with selfish desires. For this reason, God reviews the situation and follows this with a statement about resolve.

God's review of the situation (vv. 18-21a). Verse 18 gives an explanation to the last portion of verse 17. Isaiah gives a four-fold picture of how the wickedness (*resh'ah*) of Israel was bringing them to ruin. Wickedness was burning and consuming the nation—even the briars and thorns (Isa. 5:6; 7:23-25; 10:17; 27:4; cf. Gen. 3:18)—but still the people had no idea that their miseries were because of their own sins. If only they would listen, they would recognize that their woes were "the fury of the Lord of hosts" burning up the land making the people fuel for fire (v. 19a).

Instead of repenting that God might heal their land (2 Chron. 7:14), they continued to harden their hearts and even began turning against one another (vv. 19-21a; cf. 1 Kings 14:30). These national conflicts in Israel would continue until the final overthrow of Samaria in 722,[102] and they would also be found in Judah, even up to the time of the Roman wars of A.D. 66-70 (cf. Zech. 11:14). It is curious, writes Martin, how the nation would eventually, "destroy itself by its own wicked deeds,"[103] the kind of self-ruin America seems to be

---

[102] The language of vv. 19-21 sounds like that of vicious wild animals devouring one another.

[103] Martin, "Isaiah," 1054. Oswalt notes that "in the north there was one bloody coup after another" (Oswalt, *The Book of Isaiah, 1-39*, 257).

experiencing at the present time. Kidner also observes that, "Sin, doubly destructive, first reduces society to a jungle, then spreads its fires through it—as our modern strifes still bear witness."[104]

God's resolve (v. 21b). For the third time here in chapter 9 (cf. vv. 12, 17), God says, "In *spite of* all this, His anger does not turn away and His hand is still stretched out." His judgment should have humbled them and brought them to repentance, but such was not the case.

The fourth reason for wrath: God hates oppression (vv. 10:1-4)

Isaiah introduces another woe in 10:1-4 (just like he gave in 5:8-23). The reason for this woe is because of oppression of the weak and helpless, a problem that was common in the northern kingdom as noted by Amos (2:6-7; 5:11-12; 8:4-6). Isaiah addresses this wicked oppression by (1) declaring a woe, (2) asking a question, and (3) restating God's resolve.

The woe (vv. 1-2). This woe is directed against evil leaders who were using their power and wealth to create unrighteous statutes that went against God's laws (Isa. 1:17; cf. Exod. 22:22; 23:6; Deut. 15:7–8; 24:17–18), but enabled them to legally steal from the poor and helpless (v. 1).[105] These wicked leaders used the system to claim legality, but God says that they were simply depriving the needy of justice (v. 2). God saw it all.

The question (vv. 3-4a). These powerful thieves will not prosper. God asks them what they will do once the invaders plunder them of all their possessions so that, "nothing *remains* but to crouch among the captives or fall among the slain."[106] Many will be slain and taken away, but no one will remain to enjoy their wickedly-obtained wealth. Pfeiffer explains,

> Those unrighteous judges and government officials who abused their power by oppressing their people and inscribing unjust sentences and decrees for their own personal gain would find their iniquities fittingly punished before God's bar of justice. They would lose all their tainted

---

[104] Kidner, "Isaiah," 640.
[105] Oswalt, *The Book of Isaiah, 1-39*, 258, n. 1
[106] Oswalt notes that the usage of the first Hebrew word in v. 4 ("nothing," *biltiy*) does not match up with its usual usage despite being rendered by "nothing" in the NASB, ESV, NIV, etc. The term typically means "except," so it appears that the usage here is somewhat elliptical (ibid., 260, n. 12).

possessions when foreign invaders would strip them of all they had and lead them off as miserable captives into bondage.[107]

One would think that these people would get the lesson. Instead, they continued in their sin and disbelief, and for this reason God repeats for a fourth time that His judgment would likewise continue.

The resolve (v. 4b). Here for the fourth time in this section (9:12, 17, 21; 10:4) God announces that His fiery judgments are going to continue against His unrepentant people: "In *spite of* all this, His anger does not turn away And His hand is still stretched out." Mercy and restoration could be theirs, but not unless they turn to the Lord. Sadly, they would not.

Summary for application

One thing is certain: No one who continues in sin and refuses to repent will prosper. Men may spurn the Lord for a time, but sooner or later their sins will catch up with them. By the time of Isaiah, the Jews had been living under the Mosaic covenant for over seven-hundred years, much of which involved serious transgressions of the covenant. For centuries the prophets had been calling the nation to repentance, but it was now in the days of Isaiah that those covenant curses were beginning to fall down on their heads.

THE PROMISED CHILD, Pt. 4 (10:5-34)

Isaiah again makes a rapid shift of focus. The last section (9:8-10:4) gave repeated reasons why God's wrath would continue coming on Israel, but now the focus shifts to His anger against Assyria. Assyria was indeed carrying out God's purpose by punishing rebellious Israel, but they themselves were sinning as they did so. For this reason, Assyria will eventually get judged and Israel will have a gracious restoration.

Chapter 10 reads as follows: "5 Woe to Assyria, the rod of My anger and the staff in whose hands is My indignation; 6 I send it against a godless nation and commission it against the people of My fury to capture booty and to seize plunder, and to trample them down like mud in the streets. 7 Yet it does not so intend, nor does it plan so in its heart, but rather it is its purpose to destroy and to cut off many nations. 8 For it says, Are not my princes all kings? 9 Is not Calno like Carchemish, or Hamath like Arpad, or Samaria like Damascus? 10 As my hand has reached to the kingdoms of the idols, whose graven images *were* greater than those of Jerusalem and Samaria, 11 shall I not do to Jerusalem and

---

[107] Pfeiffer, *The Wycliffe Bible Commentary: Old Testament*, Is 10:1.

her images just as I have done to Samaria and her idols? 12 So it will be that when the Lord has completed all His work on Mount Zion and on Jerusalem, *He will say,* I will punish the fruit of the arrogant heart of the king of Assyria and the pomp of his haughtiness. 13 For he has said, By the power of my hand and by my wisdom I did *this,* for I have understanding; and I removed the boundaries of the peoples and plundered their treasures, and like a mighty man I brought down *their* inhabitants, 14 and my hand reached to the riches of the peoples like a nest, and as one gathers abandoned eggs, I gathered all the earth; and there was not one that flapped its wing or opened *its* beak or chirped. 15 Is the axe to boast itself over the one who chops with it? Is the saw to exalt itself over the one who wields it? *That would be* like a club wielding those who lift it, *or* like a rod lifting *him who* is not wood. 16 Therefore the Lord, the God of hosts, will send a wasting disease among his stout warriors; and under his glory a fire will be kindled like a burning flame. 17 And the light of Israel will become a fire and his Holy One a flame, and it will burn and devour his thorns and his briars in a single day. 18 And He will destroy the glory of his forest and of his fruitful garden, both soul and body, and it will be as when a sick man wastes away. 19 And the rest of the trees of his forest will be so small in number that a child could write them down. 20 Now in that day the remnant of Israel, and those of the house of Jacob who have escaped, will never again rely on the one who struck them, but will truly rely on the Lord, the Holy One of Israel. 21 A remnant will return, the remnant of Jacob, to the mighty God. 22 For though your people, O Israel, may be like the sand of the sea, *only* a remnant within them will return; a destruction is determined, overflowing with righteousness. 23 For a complete destruction, one that is decreed, the Lord God of hosts will execute in the midst of the whole land. 24 Therefore thus says the Lord God of hosts, O My people who dwell in Zion, do not fear the Assyrian who strikes you with the rod and lifts up his staff against you, the way Egypt *did.* 25 For in a very little while My indignation *against you* will be spent and My anger *will be directed* to their destruction." 26 The Lord of hosts will arouse a scourge against him like the slaughter of Midian at the rock of Oreb; and His staff will be over the sea and He will lift it up the way *He did* in Egypt. 27 So it will be in that day, that his burden will be removed from your shoulders and his yoke from your neck, and the yoke will be broken because of fatness. 28 He has come against Aiath; He has passed through Migron; at Michmash he deposited his baggage. 29 They have gone through the pass, *saying,* Geba will be our lodging place. Ramah is terrified, and Gibeah of Saul has fled away. 30 Cry aloud with your voice, O daughter of Gallim! Pay attention, Laishah *and* wretched Anathoth! 31 Madmenah has fled. The inhabitants of Gebim have sought refuge. 32 Yet today he will halt at Nob; he shakes his fist at the mountain of the daughter of Zion, the hill of Jerusalem. 33 Behold, the Lord, the God of hosts, will lop off the boughs with a terrible crash; those also who are tall in stature will be cut down and those who are lofty will be abased. 34 He will cut down the thickets of the forest with an iron *axe,* and Lebanon will fall by the Mighty One" (10:5-34).

The Bible shows us that God settles scores with sinners, for He is a God, "who will render to each person according to his deeds" (Rom. 2:6). Furthermore, we see that God's eternal plan embraces and includes the sinful choices of men who will eventually be held accountable for their sin. Thus, writes Martin, "Even though God used the Assyrian Empire to punish Israel, He did not like the attitude Assyria displayed."[108] Assyria sinned by attacking Israel, and furthermore she was extremely arrogant about her own deeds, but still all of it was part of God's plan. Assyria did not understand that it was not by its own human power, but by God's sovereign purpose that Assyria attained power to chasten Israel. God was using Assyria, but once this work was accomplished Assyria would pay the price for its own sin (cf. Hab. 1:6-11; 2:6-17).

In 10:5-34, Isaiah outlines three facets of God's plan in settling the score with sinners. This reminds us that God's plan includes everything that happens in all places and all times, a wonderful truth that reminds us we can always trust Him no matter what life may bring (cf. Gen. 45:1-8; 50:20; Rom. 8:28).

First facet of God's plan in settling the score with sinners: God's punishment of Assyrian pride (vv. 5-19)

Assyria was a powerful, ruthless, and proud empire whom God was using for His purposes, but Assyria was completely ignorant that she was only a tool in the hand of Yahweh. Thus, none of their present crises were random chance, but actually an outworking of God's plan. This passage is one of the most-powerful texts that teaches about the absolute sovereignty of God. As Kidner explains it, this portion of Scripture is, "an important treatment of God's control of history, in the world at large and among his chosen people."[109] Here in verses 5-11 Isaiah gives us the first of three rebukes to Assyria, three rebukes that serve as a comfort that there is nothing that falls outside of the sovereignty of God.

First rebuke to Assyria: Assyria is a tool in God's hand (vv. 5-11)

God had a "woe" for His own people, but now the woe gets directed against Assyria. The reason is because God would soon be judging Assyria, just as He had Israel. Verses 5-11 show us both God's view of Assyria (vv. 5-6) as well as Assyria's view of itself (vv. 7-11).

God's view of Assyria (vv. 5-6). Assyria saw itself as the one in control, but God says they were a mere instrument—a rod (*shebet*, such as a battle ax)

---

[108] Martin, "Isaiah," 1055.
[109] Kidner, "Isaiah," 641.

and staff (*matteh*, a large stick) in God's hand to punish His own people.[110] God is the One who sent Assyria to punish and plunder Israel just as He would later use Babylon to punish Judah (cf. Jer. 50:23; 51:20; Nah. 2:9; Hab. 1:6).

God's alone is sovereign, and God alone controls human history. This does not preclude the reality of creaturely freedom and human responsibility. The Bible shows us that God created man in His image as a moral creature with a capacity for making free choices, but it also shows us that every event that takes place (including man's choices) falls under God's eternal plan.[111] This is not to say that God "manipulates people in a cynical way," but that He is "bringing out of them that which will most effectively serve goodness and truth."[112] Young explains that, "they thought they were acting in their own strength. [But] all that we do has been foreordained of God, and to Him we are responsible."[113]

Assyria's view of Assyria (vv. 7-11). Assyria had a different view. Assyria did not understand that were carrying out the will of God. Their only purpose was to destroy and plunder (v. 7). Assyria's arrogance is reflected in the way they claimed that their princes were more powerful and glorious than the kings they were conquering (a statement that finds corroboration in various Assyrian inscriptions with the king of Assyria seeing himself as the "king of kings" as reflected in Ezekiel 27:7).

Perhaps Assyria's most-serious sin was her failure to recognize that Yahweh is the true God (vv. 9-11). It is true that Assyria had completely overthrown a number of other pagan capitals so far (e.g., Calno, Carchemish, Hamath, Arpad, Samaria, Damascus; cf. 36:19),[114] but her worst sin was in thinking that Yahweh was just like the other pagan gods and their idols (it is true that many

---

[110] Concerning this term "indignation" (*za'am*), it is interesting to trace the usage of this term in various contexts as God speaks about His severe anger against covenant breaking Israel (Isa. 10:5, 25; 13:5; 26:20; 30:30; 34:2; 66:14; Dan. 8:19; 9:27; 11:36; Zech. 1:12).

[111] Theologians describe this relationship as "Compatibilism," i.e., the belief that God has given men a capacity to make free choices, but that God has an eternal purpose that He has planned and determined at the same time, i.e., the concept of "Determinism" (Isaiah 46:8-11 illustrates this truth very vividly).

[112] Oswalt, *The Book of Isaiah, 1-39*, 263.

[113] Young, *The Book of Isaiah, vol. 1*, 359.

[114] Carchemish is the farthest north on the bend of the Euphrates about 350 miles from Jerusalem (fell 717 B.C.). Calno is 50 miles from Carchemish and fell in 738 (cf. Amos 6:2). Arpad is not far away and fell in 740. Hamath is on the Orontes River 100 miles south of Arpad and fell in 738 and 720. Damascus is northeast of Israel and fell in 732 and Samaria in central Israel fell in 722 to Shalmaneser and Sargon (2 Kings 17:3-6).

idols of the ancient world were large and awe inspiring).[115] Assyria's great sin was in thinking that Yahweh was just another idol (Isa. 36; cf. 2 Kings 18:19-20, 22-23; 29-35), but Assyria would soon realize how wrong she was.

Second rebuke to Assyria: Once God has finished using Assyria to punish Israel, He will turn His punishment against Assyria (vv. 12-14)

God had a two-fold plan for Assyria. Assyria will pay the price for its own sin, but not until God was finished using her.

First part of God's plan for Assyria (v. 12a). The first part of God's plan was to use Assyria to bring a humiliating devastation to rebellious Judah—the kingdom ruled from Mount Zion. The judgments against the northern kingdom would be irreversible, but such would not be the case with Judah, for in the end Yahweh would crush Assyria and deliver Judah from complete ruin (chs. 36-37).

Second part of God's plan for Assyria (vv. 12b-14). Once God has finished using Assyria, His plan was to turn His anger against Assyria and "punish the fruit of the arrogant heart of the king of Assyria and the pomp of his haughtiness."[116] God hates pride (Isa. 2:11-17; 3:8-4:1; 5:15; cf. Prov. 6:16-17; 21:4).

Assyria reasoned that all of its victories were due to its own wisdom and power, not realizing that it was Yahweh who had raised her up. Assyria arrogantly compared her military activity to the plundering of a bird nest with eggs with not one bit of resistance (v. 14). Assyria was powerful and virtually unstoppable, but her time of punishment was about to come.

Third rebuke to Assyria: No one who raises itself up against Yahweh will prosper (vv. 15-19)

No one will ever raise himself up against God and prosper. Isaiah exposes the folly of the Assyrian pride (v. 15), then announces the penalty of that pride (vv. 16-19).

The folly of Assyria's pride (v. 15). Isaiah asks two absurd, rhetorical questions of Assyria to expose their arrogance in thinking that it was their own innate abilities that had given them such superiority. Axes, saws, clubs and rods

---

[115] Several terms are used for these false gods: vv. 10-11: "idols" (*'eliyl*, with a root meaning "worthless" or "good for nothing"), v. 10: "graven images" (*pasiyl*, carved stones to reflect divine images), v. 11: "images" (*'atsab*, effigy of a god).
[116] The term punish (*phaqad*) has a root idea "to visit." Sometimes this is visiting with a blessing (cf. Ruth 1:6), but often it is the idea of visiting with punishment.

are only tools yielded by the one who uses them. So it was with Assyria. Young asks, "Shall finite, human Assyria move the mighty God? . . . Yet, so do sinners constantly act, perverting the true nature of things."[117]

The punishment for Assyria's pride (vv. 16-19). Such pride cannot go unpunished, for no one can raise themselves up against Yahweh and prosper. Here in verses 16-19 Isaiah introduces two metaphorical pictures to describe the judgment God was about to bring upon Assyria.

The first picture: a wasting disease (v. 16a). Isaiah says, "The Lord, the God of hosts, will send a wasting disease among his stout warriors [*mishman*, lit. "fat ones"]." Though they are mighty according to the ranks of men, Yahweh of Hosts will strike down mighty Assyria by sending a "wasting disease" to bring them to the grave (Heb. *razon*: "emaciation, leanness, consumption"; cf. Ps. 106:15; Mic. 6:10[118]). This would be the plague that struck 185,000 Assyrians in 701 B.C. in the reign of Hezekiah (cf. 37:36).[119]

The second picture: a fire will be kindled like a burning flame (vv. 16b-19). Some hold that the expressions "light of Israel" and "Holy One of Israel may be references to the Messiah since similar language is used of God's Servant (Isa. 42:6; 49:6; cf. Ezek. 39:7-8; Luke 1:35; 4:34; John 6:69; 8:12; 9:5; Acts 3:14).[120] In any case, God is going to utterly destroy Assyria (cf. 1:29-31; 2:13; 6:13; 9:18; 37:24).

How did this violent overthrow of mighty Assyria take place? How could an empire that was so strong ever be brought down to ruin? One of the ways was a direct intervention from God with a disease that took the lives of 185,000 soldiers. Then, between the years of 629 and 605 God used the armies of Media and Babylon to take Assyria down to utter ruin. Nineveh fell in 612 B.C. as predicted by Nahum, and the Medes and Babylonians brought final death blow to Assyria at the Battle of Carchemish in 605 B.C. In the section that follows we see that God's punishment of the Jews will not include an utter annihilation. God's covenant with Abraham is an eternal covenant, so there will be an ultimate restoration of God's elect remnant and a restoration of the apostate nation.

---

[117] Young, *The Book of Isaiah, vol. 1*, 365.
[118] Ludwig Koehler et al., *The Hebrew and Aramaic Lexicon of the Old Testament*, cited in electronic form with Logos Libronix (Leiden: E.J. Brill, 1994–2000), 1209–1210.
[119] Wolf, *Interpreting Isaiah*, 101.
[120] Furthermore, the Lord of v. 16 (*Ha'Adon*) may find connection with the Lord of Isaiah 6:1-4 and John's identification of this being the Messiah in John 12:41.

Second facet of God's plan in settling the score with sinners: The restoration of Israel with salvation to an elect remnant (vv. 20-27)

Over the first ten chapters, Isaiah made it abundantly clear that God will settle the sin score with both Israel and Judah. The good news for the Jews, though, is that their sin will not bring a permanent ruin. The day is coming when God will restore His fallen nation. Here in verses 20-27, we see (1) the promise of salvation to an elect remnant (vv. 20-23), as well as the implications of this promise (vv. 24-27).

The promise of salvation to God's elect remnant (vv. 20-23)

Assyria was in the process of ravaging Israel and Judah, and within 100 years Babylon would overthrow Judah and take them into exile. Many Jews wrongly believed that there was no hope for restoration. God has sworn that even though His people might break the Sinaitic Covenant and go into exile (Deut. 28:15-68), His promise is that is that one day He will fulfill the Abrahamic Covenant and bring a final, eschatological restoration (Deut. 30:1-10). The consequences to unbelieving Israel would be horrific: (1) invasion by Babylon with the destruction of Solomon's temple and death to hundreds of thousands, (2) exile under Babylon for 70 years, (3) continual oppression by pagan nations for at least the next 2,500 years, (4) the destruction of Jerusalem and a second temple by the Romans in A.D. 70 with the death of over one million Jews, (5) another scattering of the Jews to every corner of the earth, (6) the ongoing hatred simply for being a Jew, (7) the murder of over six million Jews during World War II, and (8) the ongoing attempts by Islam to annihilate Israel. Satan's efforts to annihilate Israel have been relentless, but they will never for succeed, for God has sworn to bless the seed of Abraham (Gen. 12:1-3; 35:9-12). Verses 20-23 remind us of two, very-special restoration promises.

First promise: The people will abandon every false hope (v. 20). The people of Israel (both the northern and southern kingdoms) had an ongoing problem of not trusting Yahweh. At the present time, Judah had made the foolish decision to trust Assyria (2 Kings 16:7-9). As time would show, that would be a disastrous decision. God's promise here is that the day is coming when His people will never again make the foolish decision of putting their trust in anyone but Him.

Contextually speaking, there is good reason for treating the expression "in that day" (*bayom hahu*) as referring to events that take place after the rapture of the church during the tribulation period, in particular the last three and a half years (Isa. 2:11, 17, 20; 4:1-2; 10:20; 11:10, 16; 12:4; 19:16, 18, 19, 21, 23, 24;

22:20, 25; 24:21; 25:9; 26:1; 27:1, 2, 12, 13; 30:23; 52:6).[121] Thus, "that day" refers to the day of restoration when God brings Israel back to Himself and brings His kingdom to this earth. When that day of restoration comes, His people will never again put a false hope in earthly powers. Isaiah explains, "the remnant of Israel, and those of the house of Jacob who have escaped, will never again rely on the one who struck them, but will truly rely on the Lord, the Holy One of Israel" (cf. 10:17). That is, Israel will never again put their hope in someone like (1) the King of Assyria (immediate context) or (2) the Antichrist at the end of the age (Dan. 9:27; Zech. 11:15-17; 1 Thess. 5:1-2)—pagan leaders who promised help to Israel, but turned against them and struck them down. From this time on, their trust will only be in the Lord, i.e., Jesus Christ.

Isaiah makes it clear, however, that the promises he is talking about do not refer to every physical Jew, but only to those who have turned to Him in saving faith, the ones he describes as (1) "the remnant of Israel" and (2) "those of the house of Jacob who have escaped." Here is the promise: God has His chosen remnant (*she'ar*),[122] and these are the ones who will come to faith in the Messiah and escape (the *peleytah*) the ruin of the tribulation period (Isa. 4:2; cf. Joel 2:32). Those days are going to be the worst that Israel has ever experienced (Matt. 24:15-31), but God is going to save His remnant (Isa. 11:11-16; 27:12-13; cf. Matt. 24:31).

Second promise: The remnant will find restoration (vv. 21-23). The true Jew, i.e., the one who is not merely a physical descendant of Israel, but the one who also has saving faith in the Messiah, is the one who will inherit these kingdom promises (cf. Rom. 9:8).

What about the eschatological Jew who does not repent? The Bible says that their Jewish blood will avail them nothing,[123] for when the tribulation period comes God will "purge" every rebel (Ezek. 20:36-38), and two-thirds of the nation will die in disbelief (Zech. 13:8-9). Unbelievers will be cut off from the kingdom, but by His grace (cf. Zech. 12:10) God will save His elect remnant—every one of them (Ezek. 39:25-29; Hos. 1:10-12; 3:5; Mic. 2:12-13). This is the promise we see in verse 21: "A remnant will return, the remnant of Jacob, to the mighty God."

---

[121] Similar OT expressions also refer to the eschaton: e.g., "in the last days" (Isa. 2:2) or "in those days" (Jer. 3:16, 18; 5:18; 31:29; 33:15, 16; 50:4, 20) or "at that time" (Jer. 3:17; 30:7; 31:1; 33:15; 50:4, 20).

[122] For the "remnant" concept, see Isa. 1:9; 4:2; 6:13; 7:3; 10:20-22; 11:11, 16; 37:4, 31; 46:3; 49:6.

[123] The same message of The Baptist (Matt. 3:7-10).

This rich language calls for further comment. First of all, we must make comment on the statement "a remnant shall return." The expression itself comes from the Hebrew *she'ar Yashub* and, as we remember, this was the name of Isaiah's first son (Isa. 7:3). Isaiah's first son had the prophetically significant name that one day "a remnant shall return."

Secondly, we must make note of the One to whom this remnant shall return. Isaiah says this remnant of Jacob shall return to "the Mighty God" (*'El Gibbor*). The attentive reader will immediately recall that *'El Gibbor* is the name of the promised child in 9:6-7—the child who will deliver Israel from enemy oppression (9:1-5) and rule eternally on the throne of David (9:6-7). Unger comments on this connection: "That is the name by which Messiah was called in 9:6 and is parallel to **the Holy One of Israel** [bold original], which is an implied identification of the Messiah with God, since both God and Messiah are referred to as *El Gibbor* and the Holy One of Israel."[124] At the present time, most Jews hate Him, but by God's grace one day they will turn to Him in faith and find restoration.

The nation Israel may multiply at an external physical level, but in the end, it is only the believing remnant that obtains forgiveness and participation in the kingdom (vv. 20-23). One day they will become a mighty nation (Isa. 10:22a; cf. Gen. 15:5; 22:17; 26:4; 32:12), but only "a remnant will return" (*she'ar Yashub*) and find forgiveness (Rom. 9:27-28).

What about those who will not turn to Christ? Their fate is described in 22b-23. God will judge them severely: "a destruction is determined, overflowing with righteousness." A "destruction" (*killayon*, i.e., "decrease," "annihilation")[125] has been decreed for the rebels (*charuts*, Qal Pass. Pt.).

God has a plan to deal with this sinful world, in particular with His rebellious people Israel, and in this plan He will not only bring ruin to those who refuse to repent, but also salvation to those who open their hearts to His Son (Paul quoted this in Rom. 9:27-28 as proof of the future restoration of Israel). Like Isaiah 10:22-23, Daniel also described this period of judgment as "a complete destruction, *one that is decreed*" (Dan. 9:27; 11:36), the time of three-and-a-half years when "they finish shattering the power of the holy people" (Dan. 12:7 cf. Jer. 30:5-7). Thus, God will punish, but He will also bring salvation to His

---

[124] Merrill F. Unger, *Unger's Commentary on the Old Testament, Vol. II: Isaiah-Malachi* (Chicago: Moody, 1981), 1172.

[125] Ludwig Koehler, Walter Baumgartner, M. E. J. Richardson, et al., *The Hebrew and Aramaic Lexicon of the Old Testament*, cited in electronic form with Logos Libronix (Leiden: E.J. Brill, 1994–2000), 479.

remnant (Isa. 10:20-23). God's covenant love assures this final restoration. Pfeiffer explains,

> While pagan empires would have their day and pass away, the Lord declared, the weak and despised people of God were to live on down through history. By the divine discipline they would be taught to trust in the Lord alone for their salvation.[126]

The implications of God's promise (vv. 24-27)

God's promise is that He will preserve the nation by saving His elect remnant. Therefore (*laken*) says the Lord God of Hosts, "O, My people who dwell in Zion, do not fear the Assyrian who strikes you with the rod and lifts up his staff against you, the way Egypt *did*" (v. 24).[127] God continues this assurance in verses 25-27.

The promise: God will turn His anger to Assyria (vv. 25-26). The "indignation" God speaks of in verse 25 (*za'am*) is the indignation He has toward His own covenant breaking people (Isa. 10:5; 26:20; cf. Dan. 8:19; 11:36),[128] but once God has finished executing His indignation against His own people, He will then turn His anger (*'aph*) against the Assyrians and bring destruction (*tabliyth*, biblical hapax) upon them.[129] God compares the destruction of Assyria to two decisive victories in the history of Israel, Gideon's overthrow of Midian at the rock of Oreb (Judg. 7:25) and the overthrow of Egypt at the Red Sea (Exod. 14).

The result: Assyria's oppression will be gone forever (v. 27). Assyria took delight in enslaving other nations, but very soon God would break that oppressive yoke (Isa. 9:4; Jer. 30:8-9). The statement "because of fatness" could potentially refer (1) to the pride of Assyria or (2) to a fatness that God supplies to Israel in strengthening them to stand and resist (cf. Zech. 12:1-9). The certainty is that all that Israel has and all that she accomplishes will be through the undeserved grace of God.

---

[126] Pfeiffer, *The Wycliffe Bible Commentary: Old Testament*, Is 10:20.

[127] Take note how He now calls them "My people" in contrast to "this people" earlier in 6:9; 8:11, 12. Their rebellion to the Mosaic Covenant can never annul the unbreakable promises God made in the Abrahamic Covenant (Rom. 11:29).

[128] This is an indignation that is not fully spent until the end of the future tribulation period when Israel comes to repentance and faith in Jesus Christ.

[129] Young explains, "Against Israel Assyria had been a rod, but against Assyria a scourge is to be raised up" (Young, *The Book of Isaiah, vol. 1*, 372).

Third facet of God's plan in settling the score with sinners: Though Assyria was a terror to all, God will bring them to ruin (vv. 28-34)

Here we get reminded of the truth that ultimate salvation does not preclude the reality of temporal afflictions—especially for the disobedient nation of Israel. In this final portion of chapter 10 we see both the present terror of Assyria as well as the promise of divine ruin.

The terror of Assyria (vv. 28-32)

Assyria was a terror, but none of this is too much for God. God's command to His people is that they were to trust Him no matter what. Pfeiffer explains, "They were to trust in these promises of God and not fear the ruthless conquerors."[130] Verses 28-32 show us a list of 13 places in the kingdom of Judah that would become subject to Assyrian terror. One cannot be certain of the timing of when these towns were invaded but clearly they all got attacked (most evidence indicates Sennacherib attacked from the southwest from Lachish, but these might very well be earlier attacks that came after Sargon after he overthrew Samaria).[131]

Thirteen cities of Judah were about to be invaded (vv. 28-32). *Aiath* is the first town mentioned (v. 28). This is probably the town of Ai located northeast of Jerusalem in the territory of Benjamin, the second town invaded by Joshua (Josh. 7:2; cf. Neh. 11:31). The second town *Migron* would include a slight deviation from the main route. *Michmash* (third) is about seven miles northeast of Jerusalem and was separated from *Gibeah* (fourth) by the deep Wadi Suwenit. The armies stopped in the bottom before going up the hill to set up camp and leave off some of their equipment and hit the fifth city of *Geba* about six miles from Jerusalem (v. 29). *Ramah* is just to the west of *Geba*, only five miles north of Jerusalem. The seventh city named is *Gibeah* about three miles north of the capital. Isaiah tells the *Daughter of Gallim* to cry aloud for she is next (v. 30). The ninth city is *Laish*. Jeremiah's hometown of *Anathoth* is then told to pay attention, and *Madmeneh* (the eleventh city) is said to have fled, and the inhabitants of *Gebim* have also fled for refuge (v. 31). The twelfth stop is *Nob*, the town from which the King of Assyria will stop, look down on the slopes of Olivet at what is called Scopus, and shake his fists at *Jerusalem*, the thirteenth and final city named (v. 32).

From a human standpoint, it is hopeless. Judah is being overrun by the most powerful nation on the face of the earth and the situation is hopeless (at a human level). The good news, however, is that Yahweh has promised that Judah will not fall to Assyria.

---

[130] Pfeiffer, *The Wycliffe Bible Commentary: Old Testament*, Is 10:20.
[131] Oswalt, *The Book of Isaiah, 1-39*, 274.

The ruin of Assyria (vv. 33-34)

God will bring arrogant Assyria to ruin and teach them that He alone is God. The certainty and imminency of God's intervention are highlighted by both the expression "Behold" (*Hinneh*) and the expression "lop off" (a Piel participle of *saʻaph*, stressing the idea of certainty and imminency). The King of Assyria and his mighty armies might be likened to giant trees (Ezek. 17:22-24; Dan. 4), but Yahweh was about to chop them down (v. 33), for "The Mighty One" (*ʼAddiyr*, Isa. 33:21; Pss. 76:5; 93:4) will bring down every enemy power (See fulfillment in Isa. 37:24, 36-38; 2 Kings 19:35-37; 2 Chron. 32:21). Martin explains, "Even Lebanon, known for its thick forests of cedar trees, would fall before God. Certainly, then, Assyria should not think it could escape."[132]

Summary and application

Judah was in trouble, but there was hope. There are at least three major principles we can observe and apply to life today. The first is that God is perfect in holiness, and He will judge unrepentant sinners. The second is that God is faithful to His promises. Despite the fact that Judah was filled with unbelievers, God's promise was that He would not let them be destroyed. The third principle is that God is approachable, but only through sincere faith. Jesus said, "I am the way, the truth, and the life. No man comes to the Father except through Me" (John 14:6). Let each one of us who hears this truth respond by drawing (Heb. 10:19-25).

THE PROMISED CHILD, Pt. 5 (11:1-16)

As we have seen, one major theme in chapters 7-12 is that of a special, promised son (7:14ff.; 8:1ff.; 9:6-7; 10:20-23; 11:1ff.). Here in chapter 11, we continue to see the theme of a promised child for Israel. Assyria's mighty tree will be brought to ruin (10:33-34), but such will not be the case for Judah's fallen tree (Isa. 6:11-13). The fallen tree of Judah will one day see a glorious restoration. Kidner explains, "The tree, felled but not finished, makes a telling contrast to the razed forest of Assyria (10:33–34).... Here it is the house of David, and its growing-point is one man."[133]

Chapter 11 reads as follows: "1 Then a shoot will spring from the stem of Jesse, and a branch from his roots will bear fruit. 2 The Spirit of the Lord will rest on Him, the spirit of wisdom and understanding, the spirit of counsel and strength, the spirit of knowledge and the fear of the Lord; 3 and He will delight in the fear of the Lord, and He will not judge by what His eyes see, nor make a

---

[132] Martin, "Isaiah," 1056.
[133] Kidner, "Isaiah," 641.

decision by what His ears hear, 4 but with righteousness He will judge the poor, and decide with fairness for the afflicted of the earth, and He will strike the earth with the rod of His mouth; and with the breath of His lips He will slay the wicked; also righteousness will be the belt about His loins, and faithfulness the belt about His waist; 6 and the wolf will dwell with the lamb, and the leopard will lie down with the young goat, and the calf and the young lion and the fatling together, and a little boy will lead them; 7 also the cow and the bear will graze; their young will lie down together, and the lion will eat straw like the ox. 8 The nursing child will play by the hole of the cobra, and the weaned child will put his hand on the viper's den. 9 They will not hurt or destroy in all My holy mountain, for the earth will be full of the knowledge of the Lord as the waters cover the sea. 10 Then in that day the nations will resort to the root of Jesse, Who will stand as a signal for the peoples, and His resting place will be glorious. 11 Then it will happen on that day that the Lord will again recover the second time with His hand the remnant of His people, who will remain, from Assyria, Egypt, Pathros, Cush, Elam, Shinar, Hamath, and from the islands of the sea. 12 And He will lift up a standard for the nations, and assemble the banished ones of Israel, and will gather the dispersed of Judah. From the four corners of the earth. 13 Then the jealousy of Ephraim will depart, and those who harass Judah will be cut off; Ephraim will not be jealous of Judah, and Judah will not harass Ephraim. 14 They will swoop down on the slopes of the Philistines on the west; together they will plunder the sons of the east; they will possess Edom and Moab, and the sons of Ammon will be subject to them, 15 and the Lord will utterly destroy the tongue of the Sea of Egypt, and He will wave His hand over the River with His scorching wind, and He will strike it into seven streams, and make *men* walk over dry-shod, 16a and there will be a highway from Assyria for the remnant of His people who will be left. Just as there was for Israel. In the day that they came up out of the land of Egypt" (11:1-16).

Man's only hope lies in God's promised child, the child who will come through the nation of Israel. Verses 1-16 highlight four key messages to understanding the special significance of this promised child.

First key to understanding the promised child : This promised child is the One who fulfills the Davidic Covenant (v. 1)

Centuries earlier, God had made the promise to King David that He was at work to establish an eternal dynasty through David's family (2 Sam. 7:12-16; cf. Pss. 89; 132). Ultimately, it was the House of David that would give the world the King of kings, Jesus Christ. Verse 1 gives us two descriptions of this King.

ISAIAH 7:1-12:6

First description of the eschatological Son: The Shoot (v. 1a)

Adam's sin brought a curse and God is the only One who can fix it.[134] The good news is that God has promised to send a Savior to bring in this restoration. Three times already Isaiah has spoken about this coming Savior: (1) the beautiful Branch who will rule God's kingdom (4:2; cf. Jer. 23:5; 33:15; Zech. 3:8; 6:12; Ps. 132:17), (2) the typological reference to the virgin birth of Jesus (7:14; cf. Matt. 1:18-25), (3) the Child who will come to Israel as a baby, but one day rule in an eternal kingdom with His restored people (Isa. 9:6-7; cf. 10:20-23; Luke 1:32-33, 67-79; Rom. 9:27-29).

Isaiah calls the promised one "a Shoot" (v. 1a). This shoot (*choter*, here and Prov. 14:23) is the promised One who will spring forth from the stem of Jesse. Thus, Messiah is likened to a twig that shoots up from the stump of a fallen tree (cf. Job 5:6; 14:2, 8; Isa. 40:24). The House of David, i.e., the one descended from Jesse, will fall, but one day rise again (cf. Amos 9:11-15).[135]

Second description of the eschatological Son: The Branch (v. 1b)

Isaiah also says, "a Branch from his roots will bear fruit." The tree of David's kingdom was cut down long ago, but Isaiah says that there is hope, for one day a branch (*netser*) will come forth and bear fruit (Isa. 6:13; cf. Amos 9:11-15). The term for "branch" used here is neither the term used in Isaiah 53:2 (*yoneq*, a sapling twig), nor the term *tsemech* that we find in several other passages (Isa. 4:2; Jer. 23:5; 33:15; Zech. 3:8; 6:12; Ps. 132:17; 2 Sam. 23:5). The term *netser* carries the connotation of a little twig that is fresh and green (Isa. 14:9; 40:19; 60:21), e.g., a branch that springs from the side of the tree stump. Isaiah is talking about a "descendant" from David who offers the promise of new life for the nation.[136]

The key point is God's promise that one day He will bring life to fallen Israel through the promised One—the One who will rule with the wisdom and righteousness of God, not like "an ordinary judge who may be swayed by superficial knowledge. He will judge impartially and in righteousness."[137]

---

[134] As Solomon explains it, what is crooked cannot be made straight (Ecc. 1:5; 7:13).
[135] Revelation calls Jesus both the "root" and "descendant" of David (22:16).
[136] The Targum applied this passage to the Messiah, the One who will come to bring life to the nation (Young, *The Book of Isaiah, vol. 1*, 380).
[137] Martin, "Isaiah," 1056–1057.

Second key to understanding the promised child: The promised child lives and ministers by the power of the Holy Spirit (vv. 2-5)

The Messiah ministers by the power of the Spirit,[138] and for this reason His leadership reflects the wisdom of God Himself.[139] Many of the leaders in Isaiah's day were godless, foolish, and self-seeking, but the Messiah will rule by the Spirit according to the heart of Yahweh.[140] When Messiah comes, He will judge the righteous and the wicked (Ps. 2:9; 2 Thess. 2:8; Rev. 19:11-21), but all of it will be according to God's holiness and wisdom.

Third key to understanding the promised child: The promised child is the One who will cleanse the world of all curse (vv. 6-9)

God's King will purge this world of every trace of curse. In verses 6-9 we see how this purging will bring an end to all the enmity.

Enmity within the animal world will disappear (vv. 6-8)

We typically consider it natural when animals prey on one another for food. The truth is that none of this was part of God's original creation order. All of it is part of the "groanings" of this present age (Rom. 8:18-27). When Christ returns, He will purge this world of all curse and usher in an age of perfect restoration. Not only will God remove the enmity between the animals themselves, but He will also remove that enmity that exists between animals and humans.

The reason for harmony (v. 9)

The basis of this restoration is the worldwide redemption that Christ has

---

[138] Several of these genitive expressions attached to the word "spirit" speak about the character of the Messiah's leadership that comes from the empowering of the Spirit (cf. John 3:34). Young explains, "In the resting of the Spirit . . . [Yahweh provides] remarkable preparation" (Young, *The Book of Isaiah, vol. 1*, 381).

[139] Depending on how one outlines vv. 2-5, Isaiah gives at least eleven descriptions of the Spirit-anointed leadership of Messiah: His ministry is (1) by the Spirit of Yahweh (Isa. 48:16; 61:1; cf. John 1:33-34; 3:34), (2, 3, 4, 5) with the wisdom, understanding, counsel and strength of Yahweh, (6, 7) through the knowledge and fear of Yahweh (v. 2), (8) according to a delight in the fear of the Lord, (9) driven by the truth and righteousness of Yahweh (vv. 3-4), and (10, 11) based on the righteous of Yahweh so that the wicked and righteous receive what is just and fair.

[140] In the OT we see the Spirit empower men to serve God in various ways, e.g., craftsman (Exod. 31:3; 35:31), warrior (Judg. 6:34; 11:29; 13:25; 14:6), prophet (Num. 11:25), and king (1 Sam. 16:13).

accomplished: "For the earth will be full of the knowledge of the Lord as the waters cover the sea" (cf. Isa. 54:13; Hab. 2:14). When Jesus returns (1) all demons will be removed and cast into the bottomless pit for the Millennium (Rev. 20:1-3; cf. Zech. 13:2), (2) all the unsaved sinners will have been removed and cast into the bottomless pit awaiting the final judgment (Matt. 13:41-42, 49-50; 25:41; Rev. 20:11-15), and (3) only those who have trusted in Jesus will be allowed into His kingdom (Dan. 12:2-3, 12-13; Isa. 35:8-10; Jer. 31:34; Matt. 13:43, 25:43; Rev. 20:4). The enmity that curse introduced will gone forever (Isa. 65:25; Ezek. 34:25-29) and the world will experience rest from the curse.[141]

Fourth key to understanding the promised child : The promised child brings restoration to all the redeemed (vv. 10-16)

In verses 1-9 Isaiah's emphasis was on the eschatological restoration that Messiah will bring within the animal realm. Verses 10-16 make the emphasis on the restoration that Messiah will bring when He restores His elect remnant. This includes a restoration to both a Gentile remnant (v. 10) as well as a Jewish remnant (vv. 11-16).

The Gentile remnant (v. 10)

Twice in this context (vv. 10, 11), Isaiah indicates that this is an eschatological restoration that comes at the end of the age, i.e., "in the day" (*bayom hahu'*), and not anything that has taken place in history.[142]

The Gentile remnant will turn. Isaiah explicitly speaks about the restoration of God's Gentile remnant—"the nations" (*goyim*). The nations "will resort to the root of Jesse who will stand as a signal for the peoples; and His resting place will be glorious." The idea of "a signal" (*nes*) is that of a flag or ensign that serves as a rallying point (Isa. 5:26; 18:3; Jer. 4:21; 50:2). In the midst of the Great Tribulation, the Messiah Himself will be that rallying point—the One who calls the Gentile remnant to Himself (Zech. 8:20-23).

---

[141] Even though many Amillennial theologians might be considered "conservative" by certain definitions, they typically deny the plain meaning of God's Word in prophetic passages. Young typifies this error when he says, "the condition herein described cannot apply to a supposed millennium" (Young, *The Book of Isaiah, vol. 1*, 391). The plain meaning of the text speaks about a future kingdom on this earth, but the theological preunderstanding of these Reformed theologians hinders them from believing the plain meaning of the text.

[142] As noted by Oswalt, it is untenable to argue that this promised restoration was fulfilled in anything historically (Oswalt, *The Book of Isaiah, 1-39*, 286-289).

The result: All His people will seek Him in faith. These verses speak in particular about those Gentiles who turn to Messiah after the rapture. In the kingdom when Messiah rules from Zion, His resting place in His temple (his *menuchah*) will be glorious.[143]

The Jewish remnant (vv. 11-16)

God will also save a remnant from the Jews, as well. Here in verses 11-16 Isaiah gives four descriptions about this future restoration of Israel.

The first description of Israel's restoration (v. 11a). Christ's eschatological restoration of Israel will be comparable to the first regathering at the Exodus. Once again Isaiah takes the reader into the eschaton by telling us that these are events that will happen "in that day" (*bayom hahu'*) when the sovereign Lord regathers His people for a second time. This time, however, it will only be the scattered remnant (*she'ar*).

The second description of Israel's restoration (vv. 11b-12). Unlike the Exodus where all the people in Egypt were gathered, this restoration will gather only elect Jews from every corner of the earth. At the Exodus God brought His people back from Egypt (ca. 1446 B.C.), and when Babylon fell to Persia (539 B.C.), God did allow His people to migrate back to the land, but the restoration Isaiah speaks about here is one from every corner of the earth. Pfeiffer notes, "The Messianic kingdom will be ushered in by a second (v. 11) restoration of the Jews which clearly excludes reference to the return under Zerubbabel in 537 B.C."[144] Isaiah describes this restoration as coming from eight different regions of the ancient world—eight regions where basically no Jews lived during the days of Isaiah.[145] This regathering is future (Isa. 27:13; 49:22; 56:8; 62:10; 66:2). All of these promises are central to the New Covenant restoration of Israel which God promised through Jeremiah some 100 years after Isaiah (Jer. 31:31-

---

[143] Psalm 132 reads, "Arise, O Lord, to Thy resting place, Thou and the Ark of Thy strength. . . . This is my resting place forever. Here I will dwell for I have desired it" (cf. 1 Chron. 28:2; Isa. 40:5; 55:5; 60:19).

[144] Pfeiffer, *The Wycliffe Bible Commentary: Old Testament*, Is 11:10.

[145] (1) Assyria to the northeast of Israel, (2) Egypt to the west of Israel, (3) Pathros in the Nile valley, (4) Cush in Nubia or Ethiopia to the south of Egypt, (5) Elam to the east of Israel at the southern end of Persia, (6) Shinar in the region of Babylonia (Gen. 10:5; 11:1), (7) Hamath in Syria just north of Israel, (8) and the Islands of the regions of the Mediterranean world to the west (24:15; 40:15; 41:1, 5; 42:4, 10, 12, 15; 49:1; 51:5; 59:18; 60:9; 66:19).

34).[146] God says He will do this by raising up a standard (*nes*) for the nations, i.e., the Gentile nations who will assist in this restoration (cf. Isa. 14:1-2; 49:22-23; 62:10). God will raise this banner, and His people will return just as Moses predicted (Deut. 30:1-10). The trumpet will blow (Isa. 27:12-13), and the scattered elect of Israel will return (cf. Matt. 24:31). This is an eschatological restoration, one that must not be confused with the release from Babylon—a release that still included Gentile oppression (Neh. 9:36). Isaiah's restoration is an eschatological restoration—one also predicted by the post-exilic Zechariah (Zech. 8:1-8; 10:8-12).

The third description of Israel's restoration (vv. 13-14). This eschatological restoration will include a complete healing of the national breach that fell upon Israel when their kingdom split under Rehoboam in 931 B.C. Verse 13 tells us that this restoration will erase this internal division so that the people might reunite without conflict to possess the lands that God swore to Abraham (cf. Ezek. 37:15-28). This unity will enable the nation to resist any form of alien oppression such as they experienced in days of old (v. 14; cf. Isa. 25:10; 34:5; 49:23; 60:12; 63:1; Jer. 48:40; 49:22; Joel 3:19; Amos 9:11-12; Obad. 17-21).

The fourth description of Israel's restoration (vv. 15-16). Israel's restoration will be so complete that none will remain scattered, for no obstacle will stop this restoration. Pulling on imagery from the south (i.e., "tongue of the sea of Egypt"), and the north ("The River," i.e., Euphrates), Isaiah says they will come from every corner of the earth. Ezekiel writes,

When I bring them back from the peoples and gather them from the lands

---

[146] Biblical exegesis shows that the "New Covenant," an expression that occurs only once in the OT (Jer. 31:31), is a covenant that consists of the restoration of the nation of Israel from its covenant apostasy. This is the same eschatological restoration Moses wrote about in Deuteronomy 30:1-10 and referred to by virtually all the prophets. Jeremiah 30-33 has numerous promises about the elements of this New Covenant restoration: (1) It will be an eschatological restoration when Israel is regathered from being scattered across the earth (30:3, 10-11; 31:8-10; 32:37-39). (2) The entire land will be beautifully rebuilt (30:18; 31:3-4; 31:38-40; 32:15; 33:7). (3) The wrath of God that formerly sent Israel into exile will be turned against all the nations who had sought Israel's destruction (30:11; cf. Deut. 30:7; Isa. 10:25; 26:20; Ezek. 38-39; Dan. 2:34; 7:26; Joel 3:9-17; Zech. 14:1-3; Rev. 16:12-21). (4) The restoration of Israel's leadership will include both The Son of David ruling on His throne from Jerusalem as well as a restored Levitical Priesthood serving in a restored temple (33:14-26). (5) The former sorrow (31:15) will be replaced with eternal joy (31:12-14, 31-34; 32:40-44). (6) This restoration comes on the basis of the eternal forgiveness purchased by the Messiah (31:31-34). (7) This restoration is guaranteed by a God who is infinite in power (32:17-18, 27) and faithful to His promises (31:35-37; 33:14-26).

of their enemies, then I shall be sanctified through them in the sight of the many nations. Then they will know that I am the Lord their God because I made them go into exile among the nations, and then gathered them *again* to their own land; and I will leave none of them there any longer (Ezek. 39:25-29).

It is interesting to see the way that the Book of Revelation brings light to some of these passages into focus (Rev. 9:13-14; 16:12). Yes, there will be great human obstacles to God's promised restoration of Israel (Isa. 57:14; 62:10), but in the end, nothing will stop God from fulfilling His purposes.

Summary and application

Scripture makes clear that God will restore Israel by the redeeming work of His Son. Jesus is that promised Savior who gave Himself to save His people (Isa. 53:4-6). One day, He will return to finish the work.

THE PROMISED CHILD, Pt. 6 (12:1-6)

As noted earlier, chapters 7-12 form one large literary unit that contains a repeated emphasis on the idea of a promised child with prophetic significance. In chapters 7-8, we saw how two of Isaiah's own sons had prophetic significance. In chapter 9, God promised Israel one special Son who would come many days in the future (8:22-9:1). This male child will save Israel from ruin (9:1-5), rule on the restored throne of David (9:6-7), restore an elect Jewish remnant (10:20-23; 11:11-16), and usher in a worldwide restoration from the curse of sin and death (11:1-10). All of this will be the saving work of this promised child. Chapter 12 brings this unit to a close by showing the great joy Israel will experience in this day.

Chapter 12 reads as follows: "1 Then you will say on that day, I will give thanks to You, O Lord, for although You were angry with me, your anger is turned away, and You comfort me. Behold, God is my salvation. I will trust and not be afraid, for the Lord God is my strength and song, and He has become my salvation. 3 Therefore, you will joyously draw water from the springs of salvation, and in that day you will say, Give thanks to the Lord, call on His name. Make known His deeds among the peoples; make *them* remember that His name is exalted. 5 Praise the Lord in song, for He has done excellent things; let this be known throughout the earth. 6 Cry aloud and shout for joy, O inhabitant of Zion, for great in your midst is the Holy One of Israel" (12:1-6).

Israel does have a hope for future restoration, but only by turning to God's promised Savior. Chapter 12 reveals two reasons for Israel's great eschatological joy, each introduced the expression "in that day."

First reason for joy: God's anger has turned away (vv. 1-3)

Isaiah speaks in the first person singular ("I") as one representing the restored nation (v. 1)

Praise and thanks (*yadah* conveys both) belong to Yahweh because at long last His anger has turned away,[147] and the time of comfort has arrived (Isa. 40:1ff.; 49:13; 51:3, 12; 52:9; 61:2; 66:13). All who know the Lord rejoice over the precious truth that Yahweh is a God who is willing to turn away His anger because His Son took the wrath (Isa. 53:4-6, 10-12; cf. Rom. 3:21-26).[148]

The Lord is a God of salvation (vv. 2-3)

Because the Lord is a God of salvation (Jonah 2:9), Isaiah rejoices in Him, and says that He will trust and not be afraid (Rom. 8:31). Indeed, there is no place for fear, but only songs of praise (v. 2).[149]

A number of passages use water imagery to illustrate the saving grace of God, the grace that becomes effectual through the ministry of the Spirit (Isa. 32:15; 35:6-7; 43:18; 44:3-5; 55:1; Ezek. 36:25; Joel 2:28-32; Zech. 12:10; 13:1; John 3:5; 4:15; 7:37; Rev. 7:17; 21:6; 22:17). Israel will finally taste the sweet waters of saving grace, and she will not stay silent. Pfeiffer explains,

> This song of the Millennial believers furnishes assurance that despite the hindrances presented by the disobedient and backsliding ones of the chosen race, God's perfect plan for that race will be completely realized at the end of human history.[150]

---

[147] This is the same anger (indignation) that God began pouring out against His covenant-breaking people in the Assyrian and Babylonian invasions and has remained to this very day (Isa. 5:25; 9:12, 17, 21; 10:4, 25). This indignation (*za'am*) will continue until the end of the tribulation period (Isa. 10:5, 25; 13:5; 26:20; 66:14; cf. Dan. 8:19; 11:36). Oswalt notes that even though *kiy* often carries a causal force, the context shows that a concessive force is preferable, giving the idea "although you were angry" (Oswalt, *The Book of Isaiah, 1-39*, 289, n. 1).

[148] The shortened form *yashob* ("has turned") is not jussive here, but indicative as seen elsewhere at times (cf. Pss. 11:6; 18:13; 47:5; 107:29) (ibid., 290, n. 3).

[149] This is the only place in his prophecy where Isaiah refers to the Lord using a replicated form of God's name (*Yah Yahweh*). These particular words echo the words of praise that come from the Song of Moses after God's redemption at the Exodus (Exod. 15:2; 34:6; cf. Ps. 118:14).

[150] Pfeiffer, *The Wycliffe Bible Commentary: Old Testament*, Is 12:1.

Second reason for joy: God's full salvation has arrived (vv. 4-6)

Israel's calling as a nation flows out of the Abrahamic Covenant and includes the promise that all the families of the earth will get blessed through the people of Abraham (Gen. 12:1-3). Israel's very existence has always included a missionary mandate to make God known to the world.

God will fulfill His promises to Israel (v. 4)

When God completes His restoration of Israel, they will finally fulfill this purpose, for not only will they "give thanks to the Lord" and "call on His name," but they will also "make known His deeds among the peoples" and "make *them* remember that His name is exalted." Israel will fulfill the missionary purposes they failed to fulfill in earlier ages (cf. Isa. 26:17-18).

The praise of Yahweh must be universal (vv. 5-6)

The call for praise goes out to the whole earth (v. 5), but it will be a special form of praise for the people Israel, so Isaiah shouts out, "Cry aloud and shout for joy, O inhabitant of Zion, for great in your midst is the Holy One of Israel" (v. 6).[151] Isaiah uses a double command in calling Israel to rejoice with the synonyms *tsahal* (rejoice, shout aloud) and *ranan* (call loud, exult).[152]

Summary and application

One day the saving purposes of God are going to come to a final culmination. Two-thousand years ago God sent His Son into the world that He might "taste death for everyone" (Heb. 2:9). Jesus came to take the sin of all men by giving His life in their place (Isa. 53:6), and God's promise is that all who embrace Him with genuine, saving faith will experience this promised forgiveness (Acts 16:31; Rom. 10:13).

---

[151] The expression "The Holy One of Israel" occurs 29 times in the OT, 26 of which are in Isaiah, with the three others in Psalms 71:22; 78:41; 89:19 (Oswalt, *The Book of Isaiah, 1-39*, 295, n. 12). As progressive revelation makes clear, this Holy One of Israel is Jesus Himself (Isa. 6:1-3; 43:3, 10; 44:6; 48:17; cf. John 12:37-40).

[152] A comparison with other Old Testament passages shows a pattern where this double call to rejoicing is because the Messiah Himself will be in their very presence to rule as their King—the promise we see here in 12:6 (Zeph. 3:12-20; Zech. 2:10; 9:9; Ezek. 37:26-28; 48:35; Dan. 7:12-13, 27; Hos. 3:5; Mic. 2:12-13; Rev. 20:4).

4
JUDGMENT AND SALVATION MESSAGES TO THE NATIONS
(13:1-23:18)

Chapters 13-23 form a literary unit that brings oracles of judgment against the nations.[1] God judges the sin of all men, not only covenant-breaking Israel. God identifies 12 nations that will fall under His judgment, the first of which is Babylon in chapters 13-14.

JUDGMENT ON NATIONS: BABYLON (13:1-22)

The beginning of this message against Babylon here in chapter 13 reads as follows: "1 The oracle concerning Babylon which Isaiah the son of Amoz saw. 2 Lift up a standard on the bare hill; raise your voice to them; wave the hand that they may enter the doors of the nobles. 3 I have commanded My consecrated ones; I have even called My mighty warriors, My proudly exulting ones, to *execute* My anger. 4 A sound of tumult on the mountains, like that of many people, a sound of the uproar of kingdoms, of nations gathered together! The Lord of hosts is mustering the army for battle. 5 They are coming from a far country, from the farthest horizons, the Lord and His instruments of indignation, to destroy the whole land. 6 Wail, for the day of the Lord is near! It will come as destruction from the Almighty. 7 Therefore all hands will fall limp, and every man's heart will melt. 8 They will be terrified, pains and anguish will take hold of *them;* they will writhe like a woman in labor; they will look at one another in astonishment, their faces aflame. 9 Behold, the day of the Lord is coming,

---

[1] Herbert Wolf, *Interpreting Isaiah* (Grand Rapids: Zondervan, 1985), 109. We see similar ideas elsewhere when the nations are all singled out for judgment (cf. Jer. 46-51; Ezek. 25-32; Amos 1-2; Zeph. 2:4-15).

cruel, with fury and burning anger, to make the land a desolation; and He will exterminate its sinners from it. 10 For the stars of heaven and their constellations will not flash forth their light; the sun will be dark when it rises and the moon will not shed its light. 11 Thus I will punish the world for its evil and the wicked for their iniquity; I will also put an end to the arrogance of the proud and abase the haughtiness of the ruthless. 12 I will make mortal man scarcer than pure gold and mankind than the gold of Ophir. 13 Therefore I will make the heavens tremble, and the earth will be shaken from its place at the fury of the Lord of hosts in the day of His burning anger. 14 And it will be that like a hunted gazelle, or like sheep with none to gather *them;* they will each turn to his own people, and each one flee to his own land. 15 Anyone who is found will be thrust through, and anyone who is captured will fall by the sword. 16 Their little ones also will be dashed to pieces before their eyes; their houses will be plundered and their wives ravished. 17 Behold, I am going to stir up the Medes against them, who will not value silver or take pleasure in gold. 18 And *their* bows will mow down the young men; they will not even have compassion on the fruit of the womb, *nor* will their eye pity children. 19 And Babylon, the beauty of kingdoms, the glory of the Chaldeans' pride, will be as when God overthrew Sodom and Gomorrah. 20 It will never be inhabited or lived in from generation to generation; nor will the Arab pitch *his* tent there, nor will shepherds make *their flocks* lie down there. 21 But desert creatures will lie down there, and their houses will be full of owls; ostriches also will live there, and shaggy goats will frolic there. 22 Hyenas will howl in their fortified towers and jackals in their luxurious palaces. Her *fateful* time also will soon come and her days will not be prolonged" (13:1-22).

History of Babylon

Just as seen in chapters 1-12 with its messages of judgment against Judah, Babylon will also fall under the wrath and judgment of God. No sinners are exempt from God.

Origins of Babel

Babylon was located in the Plain of Shinar and had a long history in the Bible. Genesis 10:10 indicates us that this city was founded after the Noahic flood (ca. 2458 B.C.) by a man named Nimrod. Babylon was the place at which God scattered the languages of all the descendants of Noah at The Tower of Babel (ca. 2357 B.C.) as a judgment against their refusal to spread out across the earth (cf. Gen. 10:25; 11:1ff.).[2] Nimrod was a man of pride, and from the days of its beginning Babylon was an arrogant city.

---

[2] The original term means "gate of god," but the Bible makes a play on this term to mean "confusion" when it speaks about the confusion of human languages.

Babylonian dynasties

Early dynasties. One of the most notable first-dynasty rulers of early Babylon was an Amorite king named Hammurabi (1792-1750 B.C.). A second dynasty began when the Hittites took control of Babylon in roughly 1595. After this, Kassite tribes established a third dynasty that lasted until roughly 1160 when Elamite armies invaded Babylon and overthrew the Kassites. After the Elamites pulled back, natives from the Babylonian city Isin established a fourth dynasty. Babylon entered a kind of dark ages from roughly 1103 onward, the era when Assyria rose up as a dominating power.

Neo-Babylon. In 626 B.C., Neo-Babylon began to rise in power under the leadership of the Chaldean King Nabopolassar. In 612 Babylon formed an alliance with the Medes to overthrow Nineveh, with Assyria suffering further major defeats at Haran in 609, and a final defeat at Carchemish in 605 (Jer. 46:2-12). From this time onward, Babylon exercised dominion like never before, especially under King Nebuchadnezzar II (605-562). Under Nebuchadnezzar, Babylon overthrew Judah in 605 (2 Kings 24:1-5) and brought the nation to complete ruin with two more invasions in 597 (2 Kings 24:6-12) and 588, culminating with the destruction of Solomon's temple in 586 (2 Kings 25).

The rule of Nebuchadnezzar. Under Nebuchadnezzar, Babylon rose up to become a powerful empire with a well-fortified capital. The city of Babylon spanned the Euphrates River and was surrounded by an eleven-mile-long outer city wall plus an inner wall that was wide enough to accommodate chariot races two chariots abreast. Entrance to the city came from any of eight city gates, the greatest of which was called the (northern) Ishtar Gate. It was through the Ishtar Gate that an annual procession was made for a New Year festival in honor of Marduk, the chief god of Babylon.[3] Nebuchadnezzar devoted great resources to make Babylon into a great city that honored the gods of Babylon.[4] Speaking of the beauty and greatness of Babylon, the Greek Historian Herodotus who visited the city in 460 B.C. said, "it surpasses in splendor any city of the known world." Babylon would not, however, survive the judgment of Yahweh. God's oracle against Babylon in chapter 13 may be divided into three sections that tell us about God's mighty army who was coming to overthrow Babylon.

---

[3] During this annual festival there was a celebration of "Enuma Elish," the Babylonian creation account in which Marduk slew Tiamat the sea goddess of chaos. From the blood of another slain god, Ea, mankind was created. Through this, Marduk became the chief god and was installed in Esagila, his temple in the city of Babylon.

[4] Great portions of the excavated city, the Procession Way, and the city wall, are found today in the Pergamon Museum in Berlin.

God's oracle against Babylon (vv. 1-22)

God has a message of judgment against mighty Babylon. This begins with a call for God's mighty army to come forth.

The call for God's mighty army (vv. 1-5)

The first oracle is introduced by the word "oracle" (vv. 1-2).[5] To deal with the sin of Babylon, God calls for a standard to be lifted up (*nes*, the banner that rallies the troops; cf. 5:26; 11:12; 18:3; 33:23; 62:10) that will summon His chosen warriors. These are the armies who will overthrow all the "haughty and elegant" nobles of proud Babylon (v. 2).[6]

These warriors are very special warriors (vv. 3-5). These warriors are special in that they have been consecrated by the Lord to carry out His special plan to punish proud Babylon (cf. Isa. 10:6-7; 45:4-6; 46:8-11; Jer. 22:7; Joel 2:2, 11). God says, I myself have commanded them, and they are my mighty warriors who will execute My anger (v. 3).

God describes His mighty army as "the sound of the tumult on the mountains."[7] It is the uproar of powerful kingdoms who have come to crush proud Babylon.[8] Sinful hearts are at work in this military invasion, but in an ultimate sense this gathering of powerful nations is nothing less than the work of the Lord who is preparing His army for battle (v. 4).

The Lord's armies are coming from a great distance to carry out His purpose so that they would become His "instruments of indignation."[9] Babylon

---

[5] This term directly introduces most, but not all of the following oracles against the nations (Isa. 14:28; 15:1; 17:1; 19:1; 21:1, 11, 13; 22:1; 23:1; cf. Nah. 1:1; Hab. 1:1; Zech. 9:1; 12:1; Mal. 1:1; Lam. 2:14). Scholars debate the exact sense of the term, but it seems to carry the idea of a weighty prophetic message given by God and lifted up by the prophet (John N. Oswalt, *The Book of Isaiah, 1-39* [Grand Rapids: Eerdmans, 1986], 296, n. 1).

[6] Ibid., 302.

[7] Some have suggested that these "mountains" are the Zagros Mountain of the Iranian Plateau (ibid., 302-303). The Zagros chain parallels the Tigris and forms the eastern boundary of Mesopotamia, making a natural barrier between Media/Elam and Babylon.

[8] When King Cyrus of the Persian empire overthrew Babylon in 539 B.C. he did so with the help of the Medes.

[9] Charles F. Pfeiffer, *The Wycliffe Bible Commentary: Old Testament*, cited in electronic

has already been used to bring wrath upon the land of Judah, but now she herself will become the target of His wrath. In like manner, Assyria had been the rod of God's anger who brought wrath upon the people of Israel (10:5), but subsequently fell under God's judgment once they had completed His purposes (10:12). So it will be with Babylon (v. 5).

The job for God's mighty army (vv. 6-16)

Devastation is coming (v. 6). By their own wicked purposes, these armies will wreak havoc on Babylon, but all of it is the work of God. Babylon should wail (*yalal*), for this is "the day of the Lord" (*yom Yahweh*) that has finally drawn near (cf. 2:12; 10:3; 13:9; 34:2, 8; 61:2; Ezek. 30:3; Amos 5:18; Zeph. 1:7), destruction from the Almighty (v. 6).[10]

Babylon will be helpless (vv. 7-9). Babylon was powerful, but when God's judgment comes, she will be left helpless with impotent, limp hands (cf. Isa. 35:3; 2 Sam. 4:1; Job 4:3; Jer. 6:24; 50:43; Ezek. 7:17; 21:12; Zeph. 3:16) and melting hearts (cf. Isa. 19:1; Ezek. 21:7; Nah. 2:10). The terror will leave Babylon writhing "in extreme distress, in pain like a woman's labor pains" (cf. Isa. 21:3; 6:17; Jer. 4:31; 6:24; 13:21; 22:23; 30:6; 48:41; 49:22, 24; 50:43; Micah 4:9–10).[11] This is the cruel and merciless day (Deut. 32:33; Job 30:21; 41:2; Lam. 4:3) when Yahweh exterminates sinners in Babylon (v. 9).

Stellar disturbances (v. 10). Verse 10 introduces what modern commentators sometimes label as "apocalyptic elements" with the language of stellar disturbances.[12] A full survey of prophetic passages shows that such language should not automatically be taken as mere metaphors, but as pointing to actual, literal disturbances in the heavenly realms that come at the end of the age (Zech. 14:6-7).[13] God created these heavenly luminaries to produce order in His

---

form with Logos Libronix (Chicago: Moody Press, 1962), Is 13:1. Persia lay to the east of Elam, over 350 miles from Babylon.

[10] The Heb. reads *shod* from *Shaday* (cf. Isa. 10:5; 14:23; Ezek. 1:24; 10:5; Joel 1:15; Ruth 1:21; Ps. 68:14).

[11] John A. Martin, "Isaiah," in *The Bible Knowledge Commentary: An Exposition of the Scriptures*, ed. J. F. Walvoord and R. B. Zuck, vol. 1, cited in electronic form with Logos Libronix (Wheaton, IL: Victor Books, 1985), 1059.

[12] Wolf, *Interpreting Isaiah,* 110. Day of the Lord judgments are found in various other places (Isa. 34:4; Ezek. 32:7; Joel 2:10, 30-31; 3:15; Zech. 14:6-7; Matt. 24:29; Rev. 6:12-14).

[13] For example, in the fourth and fifth bowls (Rev. 16:8-11), we see how extreme solar activity brings scorching heat to the earth and produces what is probably best seen as

universe (Gen. 1:14-19), but in the day of the Lord, even these will be struck.

This raises an important question. Are these prophecies speaking about God's judgment on Babylon some 2,500 year ago when the Medes and Persians overthrew Babylon in 539 B.C., or are they speaking about a final judgment on the whole world that comes during the tribulation period at the end of the age? The contextual setting in chapters 13-23 deals with judgments God brought on these nations in ancient times, but one has to recognize that some of these ancient judgments appear to telescope into the eschaton in also describing how God will bring one final judgment at the return of Jesus Christ. For example, Kidner explains, "While *Babylon* is the focal point of the chapter (1, 19), it stands for something much bigger. . . . This is a setting of cosmic upheaval such as the NT uses to depict the last days (*cf.* vs 10, 13 with Mt. 24:29)."[14] Also, Pfeiffer comments, "Here the day of Jehovah . . . is clearly not eschatological, but refers to the events of 539. . . . Yet this fall of Babylon is prophetically typical of the overthrow of latter-day Babylon (Rev 14:8)."[15] These are hermeneutical challenges that must be recognized. The immediate context tells us that these are judgments that got fulfilled historically, and this must be our starting point.

Universal themes (vv. 11-16). The universal/eschatological themes seem to flow into verses 11-12 where God says that He will "punish the world for its iniquity." The term "world" (*tebel*) is a word that is always used in poetic literature for referring to the entire world.[16] One day, God will deal with all sin, especially the sin of pride which seems to be so universal to all (v. 11; cf. 2:11, 17). Oswalt explains, "Instead of the earth being full of the presence and glory of human kind, it will be emptied by humanity.[17] This is always the result of defiance against God."[18]

---

a severe darkening due to the failure of the earth's electrical systems. Some scholars disregard these prophecies and treat them metaphorically based on the presupposition that this is "apocalyptic" literature that should not be understood literally.

[14] F. Derek Kidner, "Isaiah," in *New Bible Commentary: 21st Century Edition*, ed. D. A. Carson et al., 4th ed., cited in electronic form with Logos Libronix (Leicester, England; Downers Grove, IL: Inter-Varsity Press, 1994), 642.

[15] Pfeiffer, *The Wycliffe Bible Commentary: Old Testament,* Is 13:1.

[16] John N. Oswalt, *The Book of Isaiah, 1-39* (Grand Rapids: Eerdmans, 1986), 303.

[17] "Mortal man" (*'enosh*) connotes the idea of man in his weakness, and "mankind" (*'adam*) connotes the idea of man in a general sense. "Pure gold" speaks about gold that has been well refined (cf. Pss. 19:11; 21:4; 119:127; Song 5:11, 15; Prov. 8:19) and "gold of ophir" refers to "fine gold." An ostracon from Tell Qaileh bears an inscription "gold of Ophir for Beth Horon and may refer to east Africa as referred to in 1 Kings 9:26-28.

[18] Ibid., 307.

Sin had an impact that was universal to the whole creation (cf. Rom. 5:12ff.; 8:18ff.), so God's judgment on sin must also be universal. Isaiah's descriptions of God's judgment include heavens that tremble and an earth that is shaken (v. 13). The judgment on Babylon will be unrelenting like that of a hunter coming against helpless gazelle or sheep, so intense that mercenary soldiers will flee (vv. 14-15). Mercy will be shown to none, not even to their little ones who will be dashed to pieces,[19] nor their wives who will be raped by the invading soldiers (cf. Deut. 28:30; Jer. 3:2). Who could bring such a judgment?

The identity of God's mighty army (vv. 17-18)

Despite any possible eschatological implications we may perceive in verses 1-16, the historical grounding of these prophecies finds confirmation when God identifies the invading armies as those of the Medes and Persians. The Medes were Iranian peoples who came to the Iranian Plateau in the first millennium B.C. (a constant threat to Assyria), the ones who joined forces with the Babylonians in 612 to overthrow Nineveh. However, it was also the Medes who helped form a coalition with the Persians to overthrow Babylon in 539 under the leadership of Cyrus of Persia. Isaiah predicted that the Medes would not even demand money to enter into this coalition. The overthrow of Babylon would be enough reward (v. 17).[20] Not even the young (cf. 2 Kings 8:12; Hos. 10:14; 14:1; Nah. 3:10)—will be exempt from the wrath of the Medes and Persians (v. 18).

The deeds of God's mighty army (vv. 19-22)

The mighty Babylonians overthrew Judah and the Davidic dynasty (605 B.C.), but in time the Medes and Persians would likewise bring destruction to Babylon (539 B.C.). Great Babylon that brought havoc to the world would one day be gone forever (v. 19a). The overthrow will be so great that it will be like the overthrow of Sodom and Gomorrah (vv. 19b-22).

One historical challenge here is the fact that the city of Babylon did not experience an immediate and complete destruction by the Medes and Persians.[21] One way of explaining this is to say that the prophecies here do speak about the Persian/Median invasions, but that the final results were not immediate and did

---

[19] The term "little ones" (*'olel*) speaks about little playful children like one sees in ages like 2-5 year olds.

[20] Xenophon verified that the Medes assisted Cyrus in bringing down Babylon and did not even ask for monetary reward (G. W. Grogan, "Isaiah," in *The Expositor's Bible Commentary*, ed. Frank E. Gaebelein, vol. 6 [Grand Rapids: Zondervan, 1986], 103).

[21] The walls of Babylon stood until 518 B.C., and the city itself did not become uninhabited until the 7th century A.D. when Islamic invasions left the city desolate (Wolf, *Interpreting Isaiah*, 111-112).

not get fulfilled until a complete desolation came some 1100 years later when not even Bedouin Arabs would dwell there (cf. Neh. 2:19; 4:7; 6:1).[22] A second way of explaining these prophecies is to say that these prophecies really find their ultimate fulfillment in the eschaton when Jesus Christ brings a final overthrow to Babylon (Isa. 47; cf. Rev. 17-18). Perhaps Babylon will become so desolate in the messianic kingdom that no humans will ever live there, but only wild animals like owls, ostriches, goats, hyenas, and jackals (Isa. 34:13; 43:20; cf. Mic. 1:8; Job 30:29). A third way of understanding these prophecies is to recognize that they are fully fulfilled in the invasion and overthrow by Persia. Prophetic language is frequently very graphic and dominated by vivid imagery, and such might be the case here (cf. Zeph. 2:9-10).

Summary and application

We have seen that there are some significant interpretive questions about whether these prophecies speak strictly about events of ancient history, or whether they could include some aspect of eschatological fulfillment. One thing is certain: Clearly, we cannot ignore the historical setting of the message which speaks about the historical overthrow of Babylon by the Medes and Persians in 539 B.C. At the same time, we cannot forget that what happened in ancient history also reminds us about one final judgment that God will bring at the end of the age, a final judgment (which makes mention of "Babylon" in Revelation 17-18) that will also bring a restoration of Israel as intimated in chapter 14. In any case, these prophecies clearly remind us all of the need to trust in the Lord for our own salvation.

JUDGMENT ON NATIONS: BABYLON CONT. (14:1-23)

Sometimes it is hard for people who live in a place like modern America to relate to the horrible sufferings that other nations have experienced over human history due to invasion and war. Israel is a nation that has experienced these kinds of sufferings many times over the ages.[23] The Bible tells us, however, that one day God will bring these sufferings to a final end. Isaiah 13 predicted a historical judgment on Babylon and chapter 14 continues this message of judgment with what appears to be more hints of eschatological significance.

---

[22] Cyrus conquered Babylon in 539 B.C., but did not destroy it at all. The walls of Babylon were not destroyed until 518 B.C. Alexander the Great had great plans for it before he suddenly died there in 323 B.C.

[23] For example, we can think about persecutions from Egypt, Assyria, Babylon, Persia, Greece, Rome, medieval Europe, and even the Islamic world up to this day.

Chapter 14 reads as follows: "1 When the Lord will have compassion on Jacob and again choose Israel, and settle them in their own land, then strangers will join them and attach themselves to the house of Jacob. 2 The peoples will take them along and bring them to their place, and the house of Israel will possess them as an inheritance in the land of the Lord as male servants and female servants; and they will take their captors captive and will rule over their oppressors. 3 And it will be in the day when the Lord gives you rest from your pain and turmoil and harsh service in which you have been enslaved, 4 that you will take up this taunt against the king of Babylon, and say, "How the oppressor has ceased, *and how* fury has ceased! 5 The Lord has broken the staff of the wicked, the scepter of rulers 6 which used to strike the peoples in fury with unceasing strokes, which subdued the nations in anger with unrestrained persecution. 7 The whole earth is at rest *and* is quiet; they break forth into shouts of joy. 8 Even the cypress trees rejoice over you, *and* the cedars of Lebanon, *saying,* Since you were laid low, no *tree* cutter comes up against us. 9 *Sheol* from beneath is excited over you to meet you when you come; it arouses for you the spirits of the dead, all the leaders of the earth; it raises all the kings of the nations from their thrones. 10 They will all respond and say to you, Even you have been made weak as we; you have become like us. 11 Your pomp *and* the music of your harps have been brought down to *Sheol*; maggots are spread out *as your bed* beneath you, and worms are your covering. 12 How you have fallen from heaven, O star of the morning, son of the dawn! You have been cut down to the earth, you who have weakened the nations! 13 But you said in your heart, I will ascend to heaven; I will raise my throne above the stars of God, and I will sit on the mount of assembly in the recesses of the north; 14 I will ascend above the heights of the clouds; I will make myself like the Most High. 15 Nevertheless you will be thrust down to *Sheol*, to the recesses of the pit. 16 Those who see you will gaze at you, they will ponder over you, *saying,* Is this the man who made the earth tremble, who shook kingdoms, 17 who made the world like a wilderness and overthrew its cities, who did not allow his prisoners to *go* home?' 18 All the kings of the nations lie in glory, each in his own tomb. 19 But you have been cast out of your tomb like a rejected branch, clothed with the slain who are pierced with a sword, who go down to the stones of the pit. Like a trampled corpse. 20 You will not be united with them in burial. Because you have ruined your country, you have slain your people. May the offspring of evildoers not be mentioned forever. 21 Prepare for his sons a place of slaughter because of the iniquity of their fathers. They must not arise and take possession of the earth and fill the face of the world with cities. 22 I will rise up against them, declares the Lord of hosts, and will cut off from Babylon name and survivors, offspring and posterity," declares the Lord. 23 I will also make it a possession for the hedgehog and swamps of water, and I will sweep it with the broom of destruction, declares the Lord of hosts" (14:1-23).

A reversal of ancient oppression (vv. 1-2)

In the opening verses of chapter 14 we see that one day God is going to bring a radical reversal to Israel's oppression, oppression from nations like Babylon. This is the future time when "the Lord will have compassion on Jacob and again choose Israel, and settle them in their own land." In other words, one day God will completely and finally fulfill the promises He swore to Abraham, Isaac, and Jacob and settle them in the land of Canaan from whence they will worship Him forever (cf. Luke 1:67-79).

The centrality of Israel in the kingdom

When this restoration takes place, "strangers will join them and attach themselves to the house of Jacob" (v. 1). In other words, the oppressors who took them into captivity will eventually attach themselves to Israel. Not only will they attach themselves to Israel, but they will also assist in bringing them back from the places where they have been dispersed.

The peoples will take them along and bring them to their place, and the house of Israel will possess them as an inheritance in the land of the Lord as male servants and female servants; and they will take their captors captive and will rule over their oppressors (v. 2). Israel will no longer be a subjugated nation.

The end of Israel's covenant punishments

God describes these eschatological events as the time when the Lord will at long last have compassion on Jacob and again choose Israel (v. 1).[24] Israel's transgression of the covenant brought a merciless judgment (Ezek. 9:4-10), but God's promise is that her restoration will be one of intense mercy and compassion (Isa. 40:1ff.; cf. Rom. 11:25-36). This "choosing" of Israel speaks not of God's initial choosing (cf. Gen. 12), but the effectual outworking of this choosing when He brings a final restoration in the messianic kingdom (Zech. 1:17; cf. Deut. 7:4-6; Ps. 74:1). In the kingdom, God will not only settle Israel in the land that He swore to Abraham, Isaac, and Jacob (Gen. 12:1-3; 13:14-17; 15; 35:9-12), but He will also bring the nations to submission to Christ (Isa. 45:14; 49:23; 54:23; cf. Zech. 8:20-23). At long last Israel will become the light to the world

---

[24] The expression "again choose" is driven by second Exodus imagery, i.e., the idea that God chose Israel once before when He delivered them from Egypt (Deut. 4:37; 7:6-9; Ps. 135:4), but one day there will be a second Exodus with a final eschatological restoration. When this takes place, all the Gentile nations will seek to attach themselves to the people of Israel (Isa. 2:3; 11:10-12; 45:14; 49:23; 60:1-3; 61:5-7; cf. Zech. 8:20-23) (Oswalt, *The Book of Isaiah, 1-39*, 312-313).

that God had intended from the beginning (Isa. 42:6; 49:6; 60:1-3). Not only will the Gentile remnant attach itself to Yahweh, but they will also bring the scattered people of Israel back to the land, a reversal from earlier days of oppression (Isa. 43:5-7; 49:22-23; 60:4; 66:20; cf. Joel 3:1-8; Amos 9:12; Obad. 19-21).

The taunt song against God's enemy (vv. 3-23)

The final fall of Babylon will mean the rise of Israel with an eternal rest from long ages of Gentile oppression.[25] Such restoration calls for mockery against the one who brought her into exile—a taunt song to celebrate God's vengeance against Babylon. We break this taunt song into three main sections all of which highlight the joy over Babylon's fall.

The earth's joy over Babylon's destruction (vv. 3-8)

The time of Israel's eschatological rest will also be the time for Babylon's final judgment—a day of retribution against the arrogance and cruelty of Babylon (v. 3). This judgment will lead Israel to make a taunt song against Babylon for what she had done to her in ancient times.[26] Babylon brought great oppression and fury, but all of it has now ceased, for the Lord will have shattered their tyrannical rule and power (vv. 4-6),[27] and the whole world will finally find rest and joy (Isa. 12:4-6). Isaiah personifies this great joy: "Even the cypress trees rejoice over you, *and* the cedars of Lebanon, *saying,* since you were laid low, no *tree* cutter comes up against us" (vv. 7-8).[28] Not only will earth rejoice over the

---

[25] Wolf, *Interpreting Isaiah*, 112; Oswalt, *The Book of Isaiah, 1-39*, 311. Numerous prophecies speak about this eschatological day of rest for Israel (Deut. 30:1-10; Jer. 30:3, 18; 31:23; 32:44; Ezek. 34:23-31; 37:21-28; 39:25-29; Zech. 10:8-12).

[26] The term for "taunt song" (*mashal*) can speak about something like a wisdom saying (e.g., 1 Kings 15:12) or proverb (e.g., Prov. 1:6), but the context here calls for the idea of taunt song (e.g., Deut. 28:37; Mic. 2:4). This "taunt" is directed against the power behind Babylon, "The King of Babylon." Some suggest that this may not be referring to a single king of Babylon, but perhaps even Babylon as representative of wicked world dominion. It is hard to know for certain.

[27] Isaiah describes this as a full cessation of activity (cf. Rev. 18:21-24 where we see the eschatological realization). Daniel's says that this final rest takes place in the kingdom of God with a final end to all godless rule on earth (Dan. 2:34-35, 44-45).

[28] Young notes that, "Nebuchadnezzar had built a special road for obtaining cedars for his building activities, and it may be that some such activities as this lay at the base of the prophet's thought, even though the Babylonians were to carry on their activities long after Isaiah's death (Edward J. Young, *The Book of Isaiah, vol. 1* [Grand Rapids: Eerdmans, 1965], 437-438).

fall of Babylon, but so, too, will the netherworld (vv. 9-12) and even God Himself (vv. 13-21).

The netherworld's joy over Babylon's destruction (vv. 9-12)

This section emphasizes the great joy that will come because the fall of Babylon's king. This section will address the special interpretive questions that arise from these prophecies.

The departed kings in *Sheol* rejoice.[29] Isaiah says that *Sheol* below is excited (*ragaz*, trembling in excitement) because the one who brought them to ruin is now also in *Sheol* (vv. 9-10).[30] The ones to welcome him include many departed kings, leaders, and "spirits," a rather unusual term as noted by Kidner: "The word for *spirits of the departed* (9) is of uncertain derivation. The poetic description here and in 26:14 and Ps. 88:10 suggests a virtual suspension of existence."[31] All the gaiety of a wicked life on earth has come to an end (v. 11),[32] and all that awaits now is the rot of never-ending death symbolized by maggots and worms. These departed kings in *Sheol* speak about the former glory of the King of Babylon by calling him "star of the morning" (*helel*, lit. "shining one") and "son of the dawn" (*ben shachar*).[33] Yes, he was a glorious king, but now he is in ruin just like them.

Is this a reference to the fall of Satan? Some theologians believe that these expressions carry a veiled reference to the work of Satan who stands as the root power behind the king of Babylon, and that verses 1-11 speak about the human King of Babylon, but that verses 12ff. speak about a primordial fall of Satan—the demonic power who stood behind the human king. In the

---

[29] These kings are called "the leaders" of the earth, literally "goats" (the *'attudim*; cf. Jer. 50:8; Zech. 10:3).

[30] In the OT, the dominant idea of *Sheol* is that of death/the grave, but this context it certainly carries with it the dark and negative connotation found in certain passages (cf. Job 7:9; 17:16; 26:6; Pss. 6:5; 31:17; 88:11-12; 115:17).

[31] Kidner, "Isaiah," 643.

[32] Cf. Dan. 5; Amos 6:5-6; Rev. 18:21-24.

[33] The first term means shining one (*halal*: to shine, be bright; cf. Isa. 13:10; Job 29:3; 31:26; 41:18) may be a reference to Venus which never reaches its zenith before the sun rises to extinguish it. The second expression "son of the dawn" (*ben shachar*) may show how both expressions find their meaning in Canaanite mythology. In Ugaritic *shacharu* (dawn) is the name of the one of the children born to a woman seduced by the god *'El* (Young, *The Book of Isaiah, vol. 1*, 440, n. 77). One thing that seems to be inescapable is that there seems to be allusion to Canaanite mythology.

opinion of this writer, such could be the case, but it is difficult to be dogmatic on this point.[34] Martin explains,

> Who is this king of Babylon? Many expositors hold the view that he is Satan, the ultimate personification of pride. Tertullian (ca. a.d. 160–230) and Gregory the Great (ca. 540–604) were the first to present this view, now widely accepted. Though verses 12–14 seem to support the view, little else in the chapter does. Though many hold that verses 12–14 refer to the entrance of sin into the cosmos by Satan's fall, that subject seems a bit forced in this chapter. (However, Ezek. 28:12–19 *does* refer to Satan's fall; see comments there.).[35]

Even if this passage does not refer to the fall of Satan, we have other passages which do speak about his fall (2 Pet. 2:4; Jude 6; Rev. 12:3ff.).

Which king is this? Assuming this is speaking about the human King of Babylon, which king is it referring to? This is not an easy question. One suggestion is that it may be referring to one of the early Assyrian kings under whom Babylon served as a vassal nation until the overthrow of Assyria in 612. According to Martin,

> It seems more natural to view this proud tyrant as Sennacherib (705–681). ... He was king of both because Babylon was a vassal of Assyria from the end of the 10th century b.c. ... Sennacherib's death by assassination (2 Kings 19:37) eight years after he destroyed Babylon would give great joy and comfort to the surrounding nations, especially Judah. (Sennacherib was the king who had failed in his attempt 12 years earlier, 701 b.c., to capture Jerusalem, Isa. 37; 2 Kings 18:13–19:36.).[36]

Martin's suggestion is possible, but it may be better to see the references to the kings of Neo-Babylon.

God's joy over Babylon's destruction (vv. 13-23)

Not only will the earth and the netherworld rejoice, but so will the Lord Himself. The judgment will be severe, but it is well-deserved.

The arrogance of Babylon (vv. 13-14). The focus shifts from the

---

[34] The same argument could be made in Ezekiel 28 where vv. 1-10 appear to be speaking about the human king of Tyre but vv. 11ff. appear to be referring to the demonic powers who stood behind the human king.

[35] Martin, "Isaiah," 1061.

[36] Ibid.

response of the kings in *She'ol* to the arrogance of the king of Babylon. Five times in these verses the king of Babylon shows his arrogance with bold assertions of how he will be supremely exalted, even to heaven itself with his throne above the stars of God.[37] The claim of sitting in the Mount of the Assembly in the far north is probably a reference to Mount Zaphon (Mount Cassius) about twenty-five miles northeast of Ugarit, the dwelling place of the gods in Canaanite mythology.[38] What we see here is a claim by the king of Babylon to become greater than all the gods of the land. Archeological finds at Ugarit have demonstrated such challenges from other Canaanite gods, but never from a human king as here.[39] As Webb explains, this language points to the essence of human pride, "self-deification."[40] These assertions reflect the extreme arrogance of the king of Babylon and why God is going to bring him to judgment. As already noted, most contemporary scholars resist the idea that these words are speaking about the fall of Satan, but that opinion is not universal, as reflected by Pfeiffer:

> This title is addressed to the king of Babylon, not so much as a specific human individual (like Belshazzar, for example), but as a representative or embodiment of Satan, who is regarded as the power behind the king's throne. The titanic pride and ambition expressed in verses 13, 14 are out of place on any lips but Satan's.[41]

Even if this passage does contain a secondary allusion to the fall of Satan (and it may),[42] the immediate context demands we see this as a reference to the extreme arrogance of the King of Babylon. He sees himself as supreme.

The King of Babylon is not supreme (vv. 15-21). With the strong adversative "nevertheless" (*'ak*), Isaiah gives a sharp rebuttal to the arrogant views

---

[37] It is doubtful that this is an assertion of achieving divinity since neither Assyrian nor Babylonian kings ever claimed to be divine (Wolf, *Interpreting Isaiah*, 113). The claim to have a throne above the stars of God uses the term *'El* (the high god in Canaanite religion) and not *'Elohim* as commonly used for God in the Bible.

[38] Ibid. This is the place presided over by *'El*.

[39] Oswalt, *The Book of Isaiah, 1-39*, 320-321. Oswalt notes, "In Canaanite mythology the god Athtar, with whom the gods attempt to replace Baal at one point, may also be the morning star. In that story however, Athtar does not seek the position and upon finding himself unsuited for it, voluntarily leaves it" (ibid., 321).

[40] Barry G. Webb, *The Message of Isaiah* (Downers Grove: IVP, 1996), 83.

[41] Pfeiffer, *The Wycliffe Bible Commentary: Old Testament*, Is 14:12.

[42] Grogan echoes Pfeiffer: "Nothing could be more appropriate, for the pride of the king of Babylon was truly satanic. When Satan works his malign will through rulers of this world, he reproduces his own wicked qualities in them, so that they become virtual shadows of which he is the substance" (Grogan, "Isaiah," 105).

of the king. Like all men, he too will be cast down to *She'ol*,[43] the place of eternal judgment in "the recesses of the pit" (*bor*) (v. 15). Those who have preceded him will marvel that this once-powerful, marauding potentate who brought ruin to the world (poetic *tebel*) has now been reduced to ruin like themselves (vv. 16-17).[44] Because of the arrogance and cruelty of this king, he will not be given an honorable burial like other rulers, but cast out like a rejected branch (vv. 18-20).[45] Oswalt explains, "He who had exiled hundreds of thousands from their homes and would not let them return now is himself homeless."[46] Even worse will be the slaughter of his sons with the result that his name will be blotted out. The sin of Babylon has been so great (beginning in Gen. 10:8-11; 11:1ff.), there must be a complete destruction of all their seed (v. 21). The language is severe, and it is no surprise that God's message about Babylon, both here and in other Old Testament passages (like Jeremiah), would find echoes in Revelation when God describes the final overthrow of evil.

God's joy over Babylon's destruction (vv. 22-23). One day, Babylon will be brought to complete ruin without even a remaining remnant, and it is here where we learn that it is the work of the Lord Himself (Isa. 47:9; cf. Jer. 51:53-56).[47] All that will remain from Babylon is an uninhabited, swampy wasteland that is given over to wild beasts (Isa. 13:17-19; 21:19; 34:11; cf. Jer. 50:38-39; 51:37; Zeph. 2:14; Rev. 18:2).

At the beginning of this chapter (vv. 1-3), Isaiah connected the extermination of Babylon with the time when Israel will experience her restoration to the Lord.[48] This indicates that God's prophecies against Babylon seem to deal in some way with an ultimate judgment on evil that goes beyond the historical fall of Babylon to Persia in 539 B.C. Clearly God did predict the historical overthrow of Babylon, but all of this also points to one final overthrow of evil at the end of the age (cf. Rev. 17-18).

---

[43] Motyer notes that the essence of *She'ol* is "the home of the departed in the next world," which in context is a place of eternal damnation (J. Alec Motyer, *The Prophecy of Isaiah: An Introduction and Commentary* [Downers Grove: IVP, 1993], 144).

[44] Both Assyria and later Babylon practiced deportation of conquered nations, a cruel punishment on surviving populations.

[45] Though some explain this as an "abortion," this idea is probably not correct (taken so by Symmachus and Targum based on the reading *nephel* instead of *netser*). Lack of proper burial is a great disgrace (Young, *The Book of Isaiah, vol. 1*, 444). The burial clothes for this one shall be those corpses whom he slaughtered.

[46] Oswalt, *The Book of Isaiah, 1-39*, 323-324.

[47] Ibid., 326.

[48] We see a similar pattern in Jeremiah (50:1-5) and post-exilic Zechariah (2:6-13).

Summary and application

Despite the interpretive difficulties one finds in 13-14, several points are clear, and the implications for personal application are also clear. Interpretively, we see the absolute certainty that God will judge Babylon for its evil. We can say that this was true historically when God used the Persians to bring ruin to Babylon in 539 B.C., and that these verses also hint at a final, eschatological ruin to Babylon. Many passages in both the Old (Zech. 5:5-11; Jer. 50-51) and New Testaments (Rev. 17-18) speak about these eschatological judgments. As these passages also show, it will not be only Babylon that falls under God's judgment at the end of the age, but every wicked power that rises up against the Lord and His people. For this reason, each of us should take note of the reality that God judges all sin, and that one of the sins that really angers God is that of pride. We would do well to always be examining our own hearts as it comes to pride.

JUDGMENT ON NATIONS: ASSYRIA (14:24-27)

Some see it better to consider verses 24-27 as being part of the message against Babylon in verses 13:1-14:23 since (1) this section is still dealing with ancient Mesopotamian empires, (2) it is possible that both 13 and 14 are all addressing Assyria since Assyria was lord over Babylon during Isaiah's day, (3) chapter 21 is fully devoted to Babylon, and (4) the term "burden" does not introduce God's message against Assyria.[49] In any case, verses 24-27 bring a message of judgment against Assyria.

This short section reads as follows: "24 The Lord of hosts has sworn saying, Surely, just as I have intended so it has happened, and just as I have planned so it will stand, 25 to break Assyria in My land, and I will trample him on My mountains. Then his yoke will be removed from them, and his burden removed from their shoulder. 26 This is the plan devised against the whole earth; and this is the hand that is stretched out against all the nations. 27 For the Lord of hosts has planned, and who can frustrate *it*? And as for His stretched-out hand, who can turn it back?" (14:24-27).

History of Assyria

Before the rise of Neo-Babylon in 626 B.C. (the empire who overthrew Assyria in 612), Assyria had been the major power in the region for roughly 400 years. Earlier in Isaiah, God had already announced a severe judgment on

---

[49] Accounting vv. 24-27 as part of the message against Babylon could be best, but one should note that Isaiah does distinguish between Babylon and Assyria, and the term "burden" does not always stand at the head of each nation in chapters 13-23.

Assyria (cf. 10:5-34), but this section once again highlights God's coming judgment.

God's oracle against Assyria (vv. 24-27)

Just as 10:5-34 made emphatic statements about the sovereignty of God, these four verses also highlight the same theme. This section makes three declarations of the sovereignty of God in judging Assyria.

First declaration of God's sovereignty in judging Assyria (vv. 24-25)

The sovereignty of God first shows itself as God uses an oath formula (*'im lo'*; cf. 45:23; 62:8) to say, "Surely, just as I have intended so it has happened, and just as I have planned [*ya'ats*] so it will stand."[50] In other words, God has made His certain plan, and it will stand.[51] That purpose is to break Assyria so that Israel might be saved from his yoke (cf. 9:4; 10:27). Yes, Assyria was a powerful empire, but Yahweh is the sovereign Lord who rules the earth, and His counsel will stand (Isa. 43:13; 46:8-11; cf. Ps. 33:6-11; Prov. 19:21).

Second declaration of God's sovereignty in judging Assyria (v. 26)

For the second time, Isaiah uses terminology that speaks about God's determined plan (*e'tsah* and the cognate *ya'ats*). God will bring Assyria to complete ruin, and nothing will stop His plan. As noted by Pfeiffer, "As a confirmation beforehand of this promise concerning Babylon, the Lord foretold the more immediate disaster to the armies of Assyria . . . which took place upon Sennacherib's invasion of 701 B.C."[52]

Third declaration of God's sovereignty in judging Assyria (v. 27)

Verse 27 makes a third declaration about the sovereignty of God in judging Assyria using the term "planned" (*ya'ats*). Yahweh has planned this destruction of Assyria, and no one will stop it (cf. 37:36-37).

---

[50] The first term "intended" is a Piel form of *damah* which carries the force of "to intend" or "to being inclined to," while the second term "planned" comes from the verb *ya'ats* which means to "plan" or "decide." Numerous passages in Isaiah convey the certainty of God's plan and purpose (5:19; 10:6, 15; 19:12, 17; 23:9; 25:1; 34:2; 41:2, 3, 21-29; 42:5-9; 43:8-21; 44:28; 46:10-11).

[51] In 46:8-11 we find similar language about the absolute sovereignty of God in all human affairs since He is the One who has an eternal plan and purpose.

[52] Pfeiffer, *The Wycliffe Bible Commentary: Old Testament*, 14:21.

Summary and application

God's people need to appreciate the beauty of God's absolute sovereignty. Young explains, "There's nothing that comes to pass but He has purposed, and everything He has purposed does come to pass."[53] A comprehensive theology forbids us from holding to any form of fatalism, but this truth does give the believer a firm source of peace and security, knowing that he can put complete trust in the goodness and sovereignty of God no matter what kinds of trials life may bring.

JUDGMENT ON NATIONS: PHILISTIA (14:28-32)

Isaiah now turns his attention to an enemy power who lived within their own borders, the Philistines.

God's message against Philistia reads as follows: "28 In the year that King Ahaz died this oracle came: 29 Do not rejoice, O Philistia, all of you, because the rod that struck you is broken; for from the serpent's root a viper will come out, and its fruit will be a flying serpent. 30 Those who are most helpless will eat, and the needy will lie down in security; I will destroy your root with famine, and it will kill off your survivors. 31 Wail, O gate; cry, O city; melt away, O Philistia, all of you, for smoke comes from the north, and there is no straggler in his ranks. 32 How then will one answer the messengers of the nation that the Lord has founded Zion, and the afflicted of His people will seek refuge in it?" (14:28-32).

The history of the Philistines

The Philistines lived along the Mediterranean coast just to the west of Jewish occupations. There is some uncertainty concerning the origins of the Philistines.

Ancient origins

Ancient Egyptian records refer to them by the consonants *prst*, and called them part of a larger movement of people known as "the Sea Peoples." These documents say that they invaded Egypt about 1188 B.C. both by land and by sea. Amos 9:7 and Jeremiah 47:4 suggest that they migrated from Caphtor (Crete), but other sources suggest that their initial migrations might have been from Egypt soon after the Tower of Babel.

---

[53] Young, *The Book of Isaiah, vol. 1*, 450.

Biblical background

In the Bible we first encounter the Philistines in Genesis 21:32 in the days of Abraham and Isaac (where they appear to be relatively friendly). In later days after Israel took Canaan, the Philistines were aggressive enemies during the times of the Judges (13-16), prompting the tribe of Dan to leave its inheritance and move north to Laish (Judg. 18:11, 29).

The Philistine nation revolved around five city states: Ashdod, Gaza, Ashkelon, Gath, Ekron, with each city state having its own "lord" (1 Sam. 6:17). During the days of Samuel, Israel dealt a number of blows to Philistia (1 Sam. 7:5-11; 14; 16-23), but they never defeated them soundly until the reign of David (2 Sam. 5:17-25). The Philistines were in submission under Jehoshaphat, in rebellion under Jehoram, in submission under Uzziah, but again in rebellion under Ahaz.

God's message against the Philistines (vv. 28-32)

Aside from Egypt (ch. 20), this is the only other oracle of 13-23 that contains a date. That date is the year that King Ahaz died when Hezekiah became (sole) king (v. 28).[54] Although it is tempting to identify Ahaz as the broken rod in verse 29 (as held by some like Pfeiffer), it seems preferable to identify the broken rod as an Assyrian King (or Assyria in general). If this oracle came in 715 B.C., the giving of the oracle might coincide with Philistine preparations for revolt against Assyria as seen in 20:1-6.[55] God's warning is clear: Philistia will face a severe judgment for its own sin.

First message of judgment (vv. 29-30)

Prior to the death of Ahaz, the Philistines had seized four large Jewish

---

[54] There is no firm consensus on the exact year of death of Ahaz. Second Kings 18:1, 9, 10 suggest that Hezekiah (the son of Ahaz) began ruling in ca. 729 B.C. but 18:13 places the Sennacherib invasion of 701 B.C. as Hezekiah's fourteenth year which would make his reign begin in roughly 715 B.C. (Oswalt, *The Book of Isaiah, 1-39*, 331). One possibility is that Hezekiah began serving as a co-regent in 729 B.C. but became sole king in 715 B.C. It is tempting to date this oracle at 727 B.C., the year of death for Tiglath-Pileser III, but there are considerable challenges to this view. If this were the correct position, this passage would be speaking about the rejoicing of Philistia over the death of one who had done considerable harm to the Philistines (ibid., 332). The specific mention of the death of Ahaz still lends considerable weight to the empty Philistine rejoicing over his death.
[55] Ibid.

cities (2 Chron. 28:18), and then came the death of Ahaz with no opportunity for retribution. God tells Philistia not to rejoice over the fact that the rod who had struck them was now broken (perhaps a recent defeat). As already noted, it is difficult to give a precise identity of the rod, but the implications are clear: Philistia may feel safe for the moment, but another aggressive enemy will rise up from the broken rod. Sennacherib may be that viper/flying serpent, the one who invaded Philistia in 701 B.C. and soundly put down all rebellions (29).[56]

Verse 30 may be directed to the people of Judah, "the most helpless" (lit. the "firstborn of the poor"; cf. Job. 18:13) and the "needy" (cf. Zech. 11:7, 11). Aggressive Philistia will suffer continued judgments, and this will ease the pressure on Judah. To Philistia, though, God promises, "I will destroy your root with famine, and it will kill off your survivors" (v. 30). A temporary setback for Assyria will not mean safety for Philistia.

Second message of judgment (vv. 31-32)

God tells Philistia to wail, cry, and melt away (cf. 13:6; 15:2; 16:7; 23:1), for the Assyrian armies will make their invasions by coming down from the north like smoke, storming the gates of their cities. None of these soldiers will come with slackness (cf. 5:27-28), for the Assyrians are strong (v. 31). Philistia has no hope in itself. Should messengers come to Judah, the message they need to hear is that the only hope is in Yahweh and Zion (v. 32). The "afflicted" will find security in Him (28:16), so Philistia should stop trusting in itself and turn to Zion, for Zion does have a future as promised by the Lord (2:2; 4:2; 14:1-2; 16:5; 18:7; 19:17; Ps. 87:1-5).

Summary and application

God's warning to Philistia reminds us that all men need to repent of their sin and trust in the Lord Jesus (Pss. 46:1-7; 48:8; 62:7; 87:5; 91:2, 9; 142:5). Why is this so? The answer is because there is only one Savior, and that is Jesus Christ the One all men need to trust (John 14:6; Acts 4:12).

JUDGMENT ON NATIONS: MOAB (15:1-9)

The fourth nation singled out for judgment is Moab. Wolf notes that even though Moab was not a major world power, Isaiah interestingly had two chapters devoted to Moab.[57]

---

[56] Wolf, *Interpreting Isaiah*, 116. Alternatively, if the broken rod/serpent is identified as Ahaz, then the viper/flying serpent would be Hezekiah.
[57] Ibid.

Chapter 15 reads as follows: "1 The oracle concerning Moab. Surely in a night Ar of Moab is devastated *and* ruined; surely in a night Kir of Moab is devastated *and* ruined. 2 They have gone up to the temple and *to* Dibon, *even* to the high places to weep. Moab wails over Nebo and Medeba. Everyone's head is bald *and* every beard is cut off. 3 In their streets they have girded themselves with sackcloth; on their housetops and in their squares Everyone is wailing, dissolved in tears. 4 Heshbon and Elealeh also cry out; their voice is heard all the way to Jahaz. Therefore the armed men of Moab cry aloud; his soul trembles within him. 5 My heart cries out for Moab. His fugitives are as far as Zoar *and* Eglath-shelishiyah, for they go up the ascent of Luhith weeping; surely on the road to Horonaim they raise a cry of distress over *their* ruin, 6 for the waters of Nimrim are desolate. Surely the grass is withered, the tender grass died out; there is no green thing. 7 Therefore the abundance *which* they have acquired and stored up they carry off over the brook of Arabim. 8 For the cry of distress has gone around the territory of Moab; its wail *goes* as far as Eglaim and its wailing even to Beer-elim, 9 for the waters of Dimon are full of blood. Surely I will bring added *woes* upon Dimon, a lion upon the fugitives of Moab and upon the remnant of the land" (15:1-9).

The history of Moab

Moab had a very ignoble origin

Moab's beginning came when each of Lot's daughters got their father drunk so that he could impregnate them (Gen. 19:30-38).[58] The Moabites lived on the tableland land east of the Dead Sea (ca. 3,000 feet elevation) with a border that went from the Arnon River on the north (the southern border of Ammon) to the Zered River on the south at the northern border of Edom (cf. Num. 21:10-13).[59] Their total land was about 50 miles from north to south and 30 miles from east to west with its two chief cities being Ar and Kir Haresheth (2 Kings 3).

Biblical relationship to Israel

Moab was related to the people of Abraham, but despite this blood relationship they showed much animosity against Israel.[60] Early antagonism started

---

[58] The two nations who came out of this were the Ammonites and the Moabites.

[59] Oswalt, *The Book of Isaiah, 1-39*, 335. Moab was somewhat isolated since the Arnon canyon on the north was 2,000 feet deep, the Dead Sea was on the west, and the Arabian deserts were on the east. The Arnon canyon left the cities north of the Arnon, Heshbon, Medeba, and Dibon, susceptible to attacks since they were cut off from the rest of the land (cf. Judg. 11:12; Josh. 13:15-28).

[60] God's initial instruction to Israel was to not harm Moab since they were family to

when King Balak of Moab hired the pagan prophet Balaam to curse Israel, but God would not let him curse Israel (Num. 22-25). The Moabite Stone with the Mesha Inscription (found in 1868, and dating to ca. 840 B.C.) shows that Moabite aggression continued throughout the ages (1 Sam. 14:47; 2 Kings 13:20).[61] Because of Moab's relentless hostility against Israel, Zephaniah wrote, "Surely Moab will be like Sodom and the sons of Ammon like Gomorrah, a place possessed by nettles and salt pits, and a perpetual desolation. The remnant of my people will plunder them" (Zeph. 2:9-10).

Isaiah's message against Moab (vv. 1-9)

Moab was about to suffer great ruin.[62] Chapter 15 names out sixteen of these cities that were headed for ruin by the hand of Assyria.

Ar and Kir (v. 1)

Great mourning will come to Moab when God's swift judgment falls upon her, and the destruction is certain as reflected in God's message to the two chief cities of Moab.[63] Many of the cities highlighted for judgment had previously been part of Israel's possession from the time of the conquest, but subsequently

---

Israel: "Do not harass Moab, nor provoke them to war, for I will not give you any of their land as a possession, because I have given Ar to the sons of Lot as a possession" (Deut. 2:9). According to Numbers 21:25-30, Sihon of the Amorites had taken land from the Moabites, but after Israel defeated Sihon when he attacked them, Israel took the land from him. After this, according to Numbers 32:1-5; 33-38, the land of Ammon—that which was north of Arnon—was given to the tribes of Reuben and Gad and this became a continual source of conflict between the two nations (cf. Num. 21:24-30; Judg. 3:12-30; 11:22-26; 1 Sam. 14:47; 2 Kings 3:4-27).

[61] King Mesha is the one who sacrificed his own son to gain the favor of the gods for battle victory, and subsequently took vessels of Yahweh and placed them before his god Chemosh (2 Kings 3). Despite the national hostility, Elimelech and Naomi went to Moab (Ruth), and David sent his parents there for safety (1 Sam. 22:3-4; cf. 1 Kings 11:1-8).

[62] Such judgment may have already begun, but 16:13-14 makes a reference to judgment coming in three years.

[63] The certainty of this coming destruction is reflected in Isaiah's two-fold use of the particle *kiy* ("Surely," "Certainly"). *Ar* was on the edge of the Arnon River and *Kir* was a central fortress about fifteen miles south of *Ar* (Oswalt, *The Book of Isaiah, 1-39*, 337).

taken away by the Moabites.⁶⁴ They too will have great mourning when the armies of Assyria come and crush them.⁶⁵

Dibon, Nebo, and Medeba (vv. 2-3)

Weeping over Dibon (v. 2). The parallel statement in verse 2 suggests that the "house" and "high place" are both referring to a place of worship. Dibon was about three miles north of the Arnon in the area that had previously belonged to Israel and was more difficult to protect due to its isolation (Num. 32:34; 33:45-46; Josh. 13:17). Dibon was also home to King Mesha as well as a temple dedicated to Chemosh. The weeping was great as Chemosh could not save them from Assyria (cf. Jer. 48:35).⁶⁶

Weeping over Nebo and Medeba (v. 3). Nebo is the great mountain northeast of the Dead Sea, the mountain from which Moses looked across to the promised land before he died (Deut. 34:1). Nebo was about 12 miles east of the mouth of the Jordan River, about 2740 feet in elevation, making it a defensive strongpoint for Moab (documented in the Mesha inscription, line 14).

Medeba was about five miles southeast of Nebo. According to Joshua 13:9, Medeba belonged to Reuben at one time (cf. Num. 21:30; 1 Chron. 19:7). Nebo became famous because of the discovery of a remarkable mosaic map that archeologists discovered there.⁶⁷ These cities would be utterly destroyed, and nothing would remain but intense mourning.⁶⁸

Heshbon and Elealeh and Jahaz (v. 4)

At one time, Heshbon was the capital of King Sihon (Num. 21:25), the city whose fish-pools are mentioned in Song of Songs (7:4). Elealeh was about two miles north of Heshbon and was built by the tribe of Reuben (Num. 32:3, 37). Both of these are the northernmost cities of Moab, among the ones disputed by Israel and Moab. Jahaz was located about ten miles south of these two. The mourning that overtook these northern cities will be so bad that it would reach

---

⁶⁴ Wolf, *Interpreting Isaiah*, 117.

⁶⁵ Eleven times Isaiah uses words for wailing, weeping, and crying, even mourning that comes from himself. Yes, Moab was an inveterate enemy to Israel, but the human carnage made the Israeli prophet mourn (ibid.).

⁶⁶ Oswalt, *The Book of Isaiah, 1-39*, 337.

⁶⁷ Young, *The Book of Isaiah, vol. 1*, 457, n. 8.

⁶⁸ Typical forms of intense mourning included shaving the head, shaving the beard, and wearing rough sackcloth (46x in the OT) made out of goat's hair (Lev. 21:5; 2 Sam. 3:31; Job 16:5; Isa. 22:12; Jer. 4:8; 41:5; 48:37; Lam. 2:10).

all the way down to Jahaz. Even the soldiers are overtaken with fear.

Zoar, Eglath-shelishiyah, Luhith, Horonaim, and Nimrim (vv. 5-7)

Moab was no tender ally to Israel, but Isaiah was heartbroken over the human misery he foresaw (v. 5). Pfeiffer explains, "The prophet could only weep with compassion at the spectacle of the bloody cruelty of the conqueror and the wretched lines of refugees streaming away from their doomed cities."[69]

Isaiah highlights five additional cities that would fall. Zoar, one of the Canaanite cities of the plain (Gen. 13:10; 14:2; 19:22), was located at the southern end of Moab near the southern end of the Dead Sea in what was actually Edomite territory, and Eglath-shelishiyah (lit. a calf of three years) was located somewhere near Zoar (cf. Jer. 48:34). Fugitives from the far north were fleeing as far south as they could to escape the invading Assyrians. Isaiah saw the refugees ascending to the ascent of Luhith (location unknown, but it may be the "King's Highway" of Num. 21:21-30). Cries of distress were on the road to Horonaim, a location mentioned by King Mesha (1.31), but presently unknown (v. 5).

Nimrim was an oasis near the southeastern end of the Dead Sea, possibly Wadi en-Numeira (cf. Num. 32:3, 36; Josh. 13:27).[70] Isaiah says they will be weeping because the springs that used to supply the river have now been destroyed and everything has withered (v. 6). All they can do is grab a few possessions and flee by crossing the brook of Arabim (the "brook of willows," perhaps the Wadi Zered which forms the border of Edom) at the southern end of the Dead Sea, a tragic picture of people uprooted and driven away (v. 7).

Eglaim, Beer-elim, and Dimon (vv. 8-9)

Deep misery and loud wailing will overtake the entire land of Moab from the Zered in the south to Eglaim (near Kir) and Beer-Elim in the north of the Arnon (v. 8). The reason is that the "waters of Dimon are full of blood." Dimon cannot be identified, but this may to be a wordplay on the major city of Dibon (v. 2) by replacing the "b" with an "m" to rhyme with the term blood (*dam*).[71] The enemy will be like a tireless lion that will not allow the fugitives to flee (v. 9). Assyria is the human agent (cf. Isa. 5:29), but all of it is the wrath of God (cf. Amos 3:3, 8; Hos. 5:14-15).

---

[69] Pfeiffer, *The Wycliffe Bible Commentary: Old Testament*, Is 15:1.
[70] Martin notes how, "the destruction of Moab described in Isaiah 15–16 caused the Moabites, under Assyrian attack, to flee south to Edom" (Martin, "Isaiah," 1063).
[71] King Mesha had described Dibon as a center for politics and religion, so this would be a good climax to the prophecies (Oswalt, *The Book of Isaiah, 1-39*, 339).

ISAIAH 13:1-23:18

Summary and application

There is only one hope for Moab: Zion. They must trust in the God of Israel. This, of course, is the timeless lesson that still applies. The Day of the Lord is going to come like a thief in the night (1 Thess. 5:1ff.), and Paul tells us the unbelieving world is going to be caught in this coming judgment. The only hope is Christ who delivers from the coming wrath (1 Thess. 1:10; 5:9).

JUDGMENT ON NATIONS: MOAB, CONT. (16:1-14)

The judgment oracle against Moab continues into chapter 16. Moab has no hope in their own power nor in fleeing to the land of Edom, but there is hope in Judah.

Chapter 16 reads as follows: "1 Send the *tribute* lamb to the ruler of the land, from Sela by way of the wilderness to the mountain of the daughter of Zion. 2 Then, like fleeing birds *or* scattered nestlings, the daughters of Moab will be at the fords of the Arnon. 3 Give *us* advice; make a decision; cast your shadow like night at high noon; hide the outcasts; do not betray the fugitive. 4 Let the outcasts of Moab stay with you; be a hiding place to them from the destroyer, for the extortioner has come to an end, destruction has ceased, oppressors have completely *disappeared* from the land. 5 A throne will even be established in lovingkindness, and a judge will sit on it in faithfulness in the tent of David; moreover, he will seek justice and be prompt in righteousness. 6 We have heard of the pride of Moab, an excessive pride, *even* of his arrogance, pride, and fury; his idle boasts are false. 7 Therefore Moab will wail; everyone of Moab will wail. You will moan for the raisin cakes of Kir-hareseth as those who are utterly stricken. 8 For the fields of Heshbon have withered, the vines of Sibmah *as well;* the lords of the nations have trampled down its choice clusters which reached as far as Jazer *and* wandered to the deserts; its tendrils spread themselves out *and* passed over the sea. 9 Therefore I will weep bitterly for Jazer, for the vine of Sibmah; I will drench you with my tears, O Heshbon and Elealeh, for the shouting over your summer fruits and your harvest has fallen away. 10 Gladness and joy are taken away from the fruitful field; in the vineyards also there will be no cries of joy or jubilant shouting, no treader treads out wine in the presses, *for* I have made the shouting to cease. 11 Therefore my heart intones like a harp for Moab and my inward feelings for Kir-hareseth. 12 So it will come about when Moab presents himself, when he wearies himself upon *his* high place and comes to his sanctuary to pray, that he will not prevail. 13 This is the word which the LORD spoke earlier concerning Moab. 14 But now the LORD speaks, saying, Within three years, as a hired man would count them, the glory of Moab will be degraded along with all *his* great population, and *his* remnant will be very small *and* impotent" (16:1-14).

Is there hope in Judah? (vv. 1-5)

To escape Assyria, Moab fled south to Sela (i.e., Petra), the capital of their ally Edom (cf. 2 Kings 14:7). However, Moab needs to understand that there is a better hope in Judah. Pfeiffer explains, "From their asylum in Edom they are bidden to make submission to the people of God, for Jehovah is their only sure refuge."[72]

A lamb for the King of Judah (v. 1)

The plea to Judah will take the form of a "tribute lamb" (NASB) as a request for asylum, the equivalence of saying, "We will submit to you. Here is our token of submission. Now save us from our enemy" (as Mesha did when he sent Ahab 100,000 lambs per year in 2 Kings 3:4). There is some question about the source of these words. Are these the words of the Moabites, or is this the counsel of the Edomites to the Moabites, or are these words of counsel from Isaiah to Moab.[73] Given the sorrow that Isaiah felt over the overthrow of Moab, it may be that Isaiah is pleading with Moab in this verse to find refuge in the God of Israel.[74]

The desperation of the plea to Judah (vv. 2-4)

Moab is fluttering for safety like a bird out of its nest. "Daughters of Moab" could be referring to the cites of Moab (Isa. 3:16, 17; cf. Ezek. 16:55-57) but may be better understood as the women themselves (v. 2). In desperation, Moab is seeking refuge in Judah, a refuge that is like shade from the scorching heat of the sun (v. 3; cf. Isa. 4:6; 30:2, 3; 32:3; 49:2; Ps. 91:1).[75] Assyria was a brutal foe, but one day this enemy—even all enemies—will be brought to an end.[76] In the end, Moab's only hope is found in these words: "Let the outcasts of Moab stay with you [*gur*, reside as an alien]; be a hiding place to them from

---

[72] Pfeiffer, *The Wycliffe Bible Commentary: Old Testament*, Is 15:1.
[73] Oswalt prefers this view (Oswalt, *The Book of Isaiah, 1-39*, 341). Could the Moabites themselves have a messianic Christology like v. 5 indicates?
[74] In view of the possibility that Isaiah was part of the royal family (he did have considerable access to the palace), it could be that he was related to David and also had family roots in Moab like David.
[75] Moab needed a wise and godly counselor as bad as Judah (cf. Isa. 9:6-7; 11:1ff.).
[76] This statement sounds eschatological, and certainly will have an ultimate eschatological fulfillment, but in context it probably refers to the death of a brutal Assyrian king (cf. Isa. 33:1).

the destroyer" (v. 4).⁷⁷ Judah can be an immediate refuge to Moab, but the larger principle is that there is only one hope for sinners, the King of Judah. Kidner explains, "The prospect of Zion as a refuge and rallying point (*cf.* 14:32; 2:3–4) leads in vs 4b–5 to another of Isaiah's visions of a perfect king to come."⁷⁸

The true hope is in the King of Judah (v. 5)

True hope is found in the King of Judah, a hope not only for Judah, but also for Moab and all the nations.⁷⁹ Isaiah names four reasons why Judah's future King is the only hope (cf. Isa. 9:6-7; Amos 9:11; Hos. 3:4-5).⁸⁰

First reason why Judah's King is the true hope. Judah's promised King will have a throne established "in lovingkindness" (*chesed*, i.e., loyalty, faithfulness, graciousness).⁸¹ We do not know if Judah was willing to show compassion to their enemy Moab, but Israel's promised King was their only hope.

Second reason why Judah's King is the true hope. Israel's Messiah is the Judge (*Shophet*) who will sit in the tent of David "in faithfulness" (*'emeth*, i.e., truth, trustworthiness).⁸² The true hope of the world is the coming King who rules in *chesed* and *'emeth* (Isa. 2:2-4; cf. Ps. 89:13-37; John 1:14).⁸³

Third and fourth reasons why Judah's King is the true hope. Moab needed compassion. Once again, the ultimate answer for Moab, and for all men, is in the King of Judah, for He will "seek justice" (*mishpat*) and "be prompt in righteousness" (*tsedeq*), two themes that are common in Isaiah (cf. Isa. 9:7; 11:4; 28:6; 32:16; 33:5; 42:1–4; 51:5).⁸⁴

---

⁷⁷ Israel had a moral responsibility to show compassion to such refugees (Deut. 5:14; 10:19). The NASB calls them "*the* outcasts" but the MT calls them "*my* outcasts" (*niddachay*). This could be God speaking or perhaps the Moabite leaders.

⁷⁸ Kidner, "Isaiah," 644.

⁷⁹ The waw that introduces the verb "established" (*hukan*, a Hophal prophetic perfect of *kun*) is probably best seen as carrying a causal force like *kiy*. Ultimately, the reason why oppression will cease and destruction will come to an end is because of God's King who rules from Zion.

⁸⁰ Later prophets would speak even more of this promised messianic King (Ezek. 34:24; 37:24; Jer. 23:5; 33:15; Hag. 2:20; Zech. 3:9; 6:9-15; 12-14).

⁸¹ Ludwig Koehler et al., *The Hebrew and Aramaic Lexicon of the Old Testament*, cited in electronic form with Logos Libronix (Leiden: E.J. Brill, 1994–2000), 336–337.

⁸² Ibid., 68–69.

⁸³ These two are God's self-ascribed attributes in Exodus 34:6 (cf. John 1:14 where they are ascribed to Jesus Christ).

⁸⁴ Martin, "Isaiah," 1063.

The end of Moab's pride (vv. 6-12)

The solution to Moab's dilemma is found in verses 1-5, but verses 6-12 show us why they would not repent and seek refuge in Israel. They were too proud.[85] In this section we see not only the excess of Moab's pride (v. 6), but also the consequences of Moab's pride (vv. 7-12).

The excess of Moab's pride (v. 6)

This verse introduces a significant change in tone. Some think these words are out of place since up to this point Moab has been portrayed as the victim of oppression. At a human level this is true, but it does not change the basic truth about Moab's arrogant character, a pride Jeremiah described as being against the Lord Himself: "Moab will be destroyed from *being* a people because he has become arrogant toward the Lord" (Jer. 48:29, 42; Isa. 25:10-11; Zeph. 2:8). God tells us He hates pride.[86] Moab's pride was no secret, with verse 6 alone making six statements about this pride. Verses 7-12 tell us the consequences.

The consequences of Moab's pride (vv. 7-12)

Mankind has a tendency to forget about the consequences of sin until God's judgment comes. The misery is going to be so bad that it will strike both the people of Moab (vv. 7-8), and even Isaiah himself (vv. 9-12).

Moab's misery (vv. 7-8). Chapter 16 has once again revealed the devastation that is coming because of Moab's unrepentant heart.[87] This leads Isaiah to once again describe the misery. Raisin cakes were small blocks of pressed raisins that were considered a delicacy and often used in festivals (2 Sam. 6:19; Song 2:5; Hos. 3:1). The wailing (*yalal*) and moaning (*hagah*) will be great and nationwide for all the vineyards will be destroyed by the invading hoards, the same devastation Judah would experience from the Assyrians (Isa. 7:17-25).[88]

---

[85] Wolf, *Interpreting Isaiah*, 118.

[86] Cf. e.g., "There are six things which the Lord hates, yes seven which are an abomination to Him: Haughty eyes" (Prov. 6:16); "Thou dost save an afflicted people, but haughty eyes Thou dost abase" (Ps. 18:27); "No one who has a haughty look and an arrogant heart will I endure" (Ps. 101:5); "God is opposed to the proud, but gives grace to the humble" (James 4:6).

[87] The "therefore" (*laken*) of v. 7 probably connects Moab's unrepentant pride with the inevitability of judgment.

[88] These expressions about the spreading vines may include a reference to an end of the massive grape and wine exports that were central to Moab's economy.

Isaiah's misery (vv. 9-12). The misery felt by Moab was also felt by Isaiah himself for, "the prospect of the destruction of rich land [and the people] reduces the prophet to tears"[89] (v. 9). All of this is the work of Yahweh (v. 10).

Despite the reality that Moab was an enemy and this destruction was the judgment of God, Isaiah is broken over the human misery, so he says, "Therefore my heart intones like a harp for Moab and my inward feelings for Kir-hareseth" (v. 11).[90] Young explains, "it was a profound, soul-stirring emotion resulting from a deep affection for those to whom he was to preach."[91] How interesting that Isaiah did not rejoice and say, "Yeah, they deserved it!" Rather, he was heartbroken over the human misery. This, dear friends, is the heart of God (cf. Hos. 11:1-9).

Despite Isaiah's sympathy, all these woes would certainly come upon Moab for her refusal to seek refuge in the Son of David. Moab will plead with Chemosh at the high places to save them, but Yahweh, the true Sovereign, will not let Moab find mercy in her idols (Isa. 44:9; 47:13; cf. 1 Kings 18:25-29; Mal. 1:12-13).

Three years until God's judgment (vv. 13-14)

Moab's days are numbered, namely three years. Wolf suggests this devastation might have been carried out by Sargon (715 B.C.),[92] but others, like Pfeiffer, see it later: "The time was doubtless revealed in 704 B.C. and referred to the coming of Sennacherib three years later."[93]

Summary and application

There at least two major points of application we can pull away from God's oracle against Moab. The first one would be that we should examine our own hearts for unrepentant sin, especially pride. Second, each one of us should learn the lesson about being people of compassion. God has compassion over the ruin of sinners (Hos. 11:1-9); Christ has compassion over the ruin of sinners

---

[89] Oswalt, *The Book of Isaiah, 1-39*, 346. The intensity of this weeping comes through the verb "weep" (*bakah*) combined with the cognate noun "weep" (*bekiy*).

[90] The use of "heart" (*me'ay*), the term for innards like kidneys, and the parallel term "inward feelings" (*qereb*) which refers to entrails/inward parts, speaks about the gut-wrenching agony Isaiah felt (cf. Isa. 63:15; Song 5:4; Jer. 31:20; Lam. 1:20; 2:11).

[91] Young, *The Book of Isaiah, vol. 1*, 467.

[92] Wolf, *Interpreting Isaiah*, 119. Sargon conducted a major operation against Arabia in 715.

[93] Pfeiffer, *The Wycliffe Bible Commentary: Old Testament*, Is 15:1.

(Matt. 9:36; Luke 19:41); even Isaiah had compassion over the ruin of sinners (chs. 15-16). We should also.

JUDGMENT ON NATIONS: DAMASCUS/ISRAEL (17:1-14)

God's messages against the nations continues. Chapter 17 brings us a fifth judgment oracle, this one against Damascus and Syria.

Chapter 17 reads as follows: "1 The oracle concerning Damascus. Behold, Damascus is about to be removed from being a city and will become a fallen ruin. 2 The cities of Aroer are forsaken; they will be for flocks to lie down in, and there will be no one to frighten *them*. 3 The fortified city will disappear from Ephraim, and sovereignty from Damascus and the remnant of Aram. They will be like the glory of the sons of Israel, declares the Lord of hosts. 4 Now in that day the glory of Jacob will fade, and the fatness of his flesh will become lean. 5 It will be even like the reaper gathering the standing grain as his arm harvests the ears, or it will be like one gleaning ears of grain in the valley of Rephaim. 6 Yet gleanings will be left in it like the shaking of an olive tree, two *or* three olives on the topmost bough, four *or* five on the branches of a fruitful tree, declares the Lord, the God of Israel. 7 In that day man will have regard for his Maker and his eyes will look to the Holy One of Israel. 8 He will not have regard for the altars, the work of his hands, nor will he look to that which his fingers have made, even the Asherim and incense stands. 9 In that day their strong cities will be like forsaken places in the forest, or like branches which they abandoned before the sons of Israel; and the land will be a desolation. 10 For you have forgotten the God of your salvation and have not remembered the rock of your refuge. Therefore you plant delightful plants and set them with vine slips of a strange *god*. 11 In the day that you plant *it* you carefully fence *it* in, and in the morning you bring your seed to blossom, *but* the harvest will *be* a heap in a day of sickliness and incurable pain. 12 Alas, the uproar of many people who roar like the roaring of the seas, and the rumbling of nations who rush on like the rumbling of mighty waters! 13 The nations rumble on like the rumbling of many waters, but He will rebuke them and they will flee far away, and be chased like chaff in the mountains before the wind, or like whirling dust before a gale. 14 At evening time, behold, *there is* terror! Before morning they are no more. Such *will be* the portion of those who plunder us and the lot of those who pillage us" (17:1-14).

This oracle opens by addressing Damascus (capital of Aram), but by verse 3 Israel is included in the oracle.[94] Pfeiffer explains,

---

[94] The northern kingdom were Jews, but from the time they broke away in 931 B.C. they were characterized by both political and religious apostasy (2 Kings 12:25-33).

This chapter is contemporaneous with Isaiah 7, and predicts the downfall of the northern coalition in the reign of Ahaz. Tiglath-pileser was to leave Damascus a heap of ruins in 732 B.C., likewise its vassal cities, like Aroer near Rabbath-Ammon. The glory of Damascus would be removed along with that of North Israel (which had risen to such power under Jeroboam II, 782–753 B.C.). Only a pitifully small remnant of the ten tribes would remain.[95]

From our studies in chapters 7-12 we learned that in 734 B.C. Syria and Israel were plotting to overthrow the Davidic dynasty and bring Judah into a military alliance against Assyria—an effort that crumbled when Tiglath-Pileser III began invading Aram and Israel in 732 B.C.[96] Chapter 17 may be broken into three major sections, each of which highlights the work of Yahweh to protect Judah and to punish those aggressor nations.

Yahweh will bring Aram and Israel to ruins (vv. 1-3)

This oracle is against Damascus, the capital of the ancient Arameans (Syria) just north of Israel. Let's first look at the history of Aram.

The history of Aram

Genesis tells us that the Arameans were descendants of Shem (thus, relatives to Abraham) who settled in the area that today is called Syria at the upper regions of the Euphrates and Tigris Rivers. Once source tells us,

> [The country name Aram Naharaim, i.e.,], Aram of the two rivers, appears in title of Psalm 60 in KJV. Transliterated from Hebrew also in Gen. 24:10; Deut. 23:4; Judg. 3:8; and 1 Chron. 19:6 by NIV. It refers to the land between the Tigris and Euphrates Rivers. Nahor, Abraham's brother and Rebekah, Isaac's wife, came from there.[97]

Genesis 10 tells us about the ancestry of Aram:

> Also to Shem, the father of all the children of Eber, *and* the older brother of Japheth, children were born. The sons of Shem *were* Elam and Asshur and Arpachshad and Lud and Aram. The sons of Aram *were* Uz and Hul and Gether and Mash. Arpachshad became the father of Shelah; and Shelah became the father of Eber [the ancestor of the Hebrews] (Gen. 10:21-24).

---

[95] Ibid., 17:1.
[96] Wolf, *Interpreting Isaiah*, 119; Oswalt, *The Book of Isaiah, 1-39*, 349.
[97] Chad Brand, Charles Draper, et al., eds., "Aram-Naharaim," *Holman Illustrated Bible Dictionary*, cited in electronic form with Logos Libronix (Nashville, TN: Holman Bible Publishers, 2003), 95.

Aram migrated to this region after Babel (Gen. 10:25; 11:1ff.), and the chief city of Aram was called Damascus. Damascus was a major city located northeast of Mount Hermon about 60 miles east of Sidon at about 2300 feet above sea level. Damascus sat in a strategic location with major international highways running through the city. Some believe that Damascus may be longest continuously-occupied city in the world (cf. Gen. 12:4; 14:15; 15:2; 24:4ff., etc.). Although the Arameans were relatives to the Israelites and early relationships with them were good, later relationships were often hostile.[98] Aramean aggression would not go unpunished.

The judgment of Aram (vv. 1-2)

Another oracle of judgment (v. 1). Isaiah introduces yet another message of ruin to those who oppose God—a message of ruin first for the people of Aram (vv. 1-2), but secondly to the northern kingdom of Israel (v. 3). Here in verse 1, God announces that "Damascus is about to be removed from being a city and will become a fallen ruin" (v. 1), and that the cities of Aroer will be forsaken with such desolation that "they will be for flocks to lie down" and there will be "no one to frighten *them*" (v. 2).

Assyria's destruction of Aram (v. 2). Around 735/734 B.C. Rezin of Syria joined with Pekah of Israel to try and force Judah into their alliance against Assyria. Ahaz did not join, but he committed a different sin by paying a bribe to the King of Assyria to help him against this threat (Isa. 7-12; 2 Kings 16:7-9). At this time Ahaz saw an Assyrian altar in Damascus and had a replica placed in the Jerusalem temple (2 Kings 16:10-16). God's anger was now against Syria and Israel, but also Ahaz and Judah. The judgment on Aram would bring a severe decimation of its cities. Damascus was left in ruins.[99]

---

[98] This ongoing hostility is found throughout the OT: David exercised lordship over the Arameans (2 Sam. 8:5-6); Rezon hassled Solomon (1 Kings 11:23-25); Asa King of Judah (910-869) paid tribute to Ben Hadad to attack Basha the King of Israel (1 Kings 15:16-23); Ben Hadad attacked King Ahab at Samaria (1 Kings 20, 874-853); Naaman found help from the prophet Elisha to get healing (2 Kings 5); Elisha captured the Syrian army (2 Kings 6-7); Shalmaneser the Assyrian King (858-824) defeated Ben Hadad, and Hazael and gained dominion (2 Kings 8:25-9:26); after battles in 853 at Qarqar, Damascus fell under Assyrian power; Jehoash of Israel (798-782) gained some independence from Damascus (2 Kings 13:3-25); Jeroboam II (793-753) expanded Israeli control over Damascus (2 Kings 14:28). It was 20 years after this that Damascus fell to Assyria.

[99] A complete annihilation did not take place leading some to consider this as having a final, eschatological fulfillment, but this is not a necessary conclusion.

The identity of Aroer (v. 2). With reference to Aroer, Martin notes that, "Since Aroer was a city in Moab, the words the cities of Aroer are difficult to understand. Some Septuagint manuscripts read that Damascus and her cities will be 'abandoned forever.'"[100] In any case, Damascus was about to feel the weight of Assyrian invasions and it would leave Aram in desolation.

The judgment of Israel (v. 3)

Because of her union with Aram and her opposition to Judah, God also announced a judgment for the northern kingdom. This would include a destruction to the fortified cities of Israel and the eventual fall of Samaria (722 B.C). The invasions began under Tiglath Pileser III (745-727), starting with his invasion of Damascus in 732 B.C., but very quickly they flowed into Israel. In the end, the "glory" of both Aram and Israel would be brought to nothing. As one source explains, "Damascus would be reduced to a heap of ruins and lose its power . . . and the prestige of the Northern Kingdom would be diminished."[101] Verses 4-11 give four warnings to Aram and Israel.

Yahweh's warnings to Aram and Israel (vv. 4-11)

Each of these four warnings are introduced with the expression "in that day" (*bayyom hahu'*), an expression that frequently introduces an eschatological prophecy. Here, however, Martin explains that the phrase, "refers to the situation mentioned repeatedly throughout the first portion of Isaiah, the invasion of Aram and Israel by Assyria,"[102] events that have already been fulfilled in history.

First warning to Aram and Israel (vv. 4-6)

The message of verses 4-6 is directed specifically to Israel (as might be the rest of ch. 17) using three metaphors to describe the coming ruin.

First metaphor to describe Israel's ruin (v. 4). God announces that the glory of Jacob "will fade," i.e., the former strength of the northern kingdom will

---

[100] Martin, "Isaiah," 1064. Oswalt notes that since Aroer (1) is a Moabite city (2 Kings 10:32-33), (2) is not contained in the Targum and (3) the Hebrew *resh* and *daleth* are easily confused, it seems best to not read this Aroer but as "forever" (Oswalt, *The Book of Isaiah, 1-39*, 348, n. 3).

[101] David S. Dockery, ed., *Holman Bible Handbook*, cited in electronic form with Logos Libronix (Nashville, TN: Holman Bible Publishers, 1992), 392.

[102] Martin, "Isaiah," 1064.

become poor, thin, and scarce.[103] The fatness, i.e., prosperity, they enjoyed in recent years under Jeroboam II would come to an end. Oswalt's language is vivid: "Folds of gray skin hang from the man who once was fat and shining."[104]

Second metaphor to describe Israel's ruin (vv. 5-6a). The Valley of Rephaim (Josh. 15:8; 18:16; 2 Sam. 5:18-25) was a fertile valley to the southwest of Jerusalem noted for its rich grain harvests (and hence in Judah and not Israel). The fertility of former ages was about to come to an end, and the prosperity of the populace will become like a field after it has been stripped bare in the harvest (cf. Isa. 7-8).

Third metaphor to describe Israel's ruin (v. 6b). Not only will the grain harvests come to ruin, but so too will the olive harvests. The people of Israel will pay a high price for its refusal to trust the Lord, and they will be like an olive tree shaken bare, reminding us of the truth that we should never trust in self (cf. 1 Tim. 6:17-19).

Second warning to Aram and Israel (vv. 7-8)

God's judgment would serve a purpose of not only punishing evil, but also of bringing sinners to brokenness.[105] Sinful pride would be crushed, and men would turn in brokenness to the Lord. Up to this time Israel trusted everything but the Lord, e.g., military might, military alliances, and their idols (Isa. 2:6-22; 44:9-18; cf. Jer. 17:5). All of this was folly and great sin against the Lord (v. 7). God's warning was that He would break this false trust: "He will not have regard for the altars, the work of his hands, nor will he look to that which his fingers have made, even the Asherim and incense stands" (v. 8).[106] Martin notes, "In the Northern Kingdom of Israel, widely influenced by Baalism, were many Asherah-worshipers. But when under Assyrian attack, Israel would realize that only the Lord could deliver them."[107] Better it is to trust in Yahweh alone (Pss. 118:6-9; 146:3).

---

[103] Ludwig Koehler et al., *The Hebrew and Aramaic Lexicon of the Old Testament*, cited in electronic form with Logos Libronix (Leiden: E.J. Brill, 1994–2000), 223. This may be referring ultimately to the population of Israel, especially men of war.
[104] Oswalt, *The Book of Isaiah, 1-39*, 350.
[105] Following the overthrow of the northern kingdom there were some who fled to Judah because of their faith in the Lord.
[106] Asherah was the female consort of El, the Canaanite high god, and as such the goddess mother (sometimes she was the consort of Baal). These fertility cults often worshipped on high hillsides in groves of poplar trees which had phallic significance (Isa. 27:9; cf. Exod. 34:13; Deut. 16:21; Judg. 6:25, 28; Mic. 5:14).
[107] Martin, "Isaiah," 1064.

Third warning to Aram and Israel (vv. 9-10)

The language of verse 9 is slightly obscure, but the point is clear: Israel will come to ruin (v. 9), for they refused to trust the Lord (v. 10). They had "forgotten" the God of their salvation (Deut. 8:10-14; Jer. 2:11-13, 17-19; Hos. 2:13; 13:4-6). They stopped trusting the Lord—their Rock of Refuge (Deut. 5:15; 7:18; 8:2; 31:4; Ps. 18)—and were trusting in everything but Him.[108]

Fourth warning to Aram and Israel (v. 11)

The fourth and final warning to Aram and Israel builds off of the delightful plant metaphor in verse 10. The people will diligently pursue their false gods in hope of prosperity and victory, but in the end it would disappoint (a "heap" with only "sickliness" and "incurable pain"). Israel had every reason to trust the Lord, but they didn't. Their refusal to trust cost them greatly. This reminds us that our great need is to always trust the Lord (cf. Matt. 6:25-34; 10:28).

Yahweh is Lord of the nations (vv. 12-14)

This next section expands the warnings to a universal level by using plural terms when speaking about the nations, but at a more-immediate level it appears that Isaiah may be taking the message back to Assyria where he began in 17:1-3. This section breaks down into one unit that highlights the rage of the nations (vv. 12-13a) and a second unit that highlights God's rebuke of the nations (vv. 13b-14).

The rage of the nations (vv. 12-13a)

This fallen world is characterized by non-stop "uproar" (*hamon*: noise, turmoil).[109] Isaiah uses two metaphors to describe this incessant turmoil.

First description of the nations (v. 12a). Isaiah likens the nations to the uproar of the roaring of seas. The seas are always agitated and never cease to

---

[108] The "delightful plants" metaphor is obscure, but may refer to the machinations of man driven by trust in self. Oswalt suggests that this relates to the Adonis Cult where potted plants were force bloomed then allowed to die as symbolic of the fertility cult cycle, a Greek version of Tammuz worship seen in Ezekiel 8 (Oswalt, *The Book of Isaiah, 1-39*, 354).

[109] Ludwig Koehler et al., *The Hebrew and Aramaic Lexicon of the Old Testament*, cited in electronic form with Logos Libronix (Leiden: E.J. Brill, 1994–2000), 250–251.

rage (cf. Ps. 2).[110] This is the world we live in, and it will continue to be this way until Jesus Christ returns to establish the kingdom of God.

Second description of the nations (v. 12b-13a). Isaiah then describes the nations like the roar of rumbling waters. The way of the world is to rage with mighty armies like a tsunami. Man may be helpless to withstand such forces, but none of these powers are greater than God.

The rebuke of the nations (vv. 13b-14)

A mighty rebuke is coming from God (v. 13b). God will respond to the arrogance of the nations with a mighty "rebuke" (*gu'r*; cf. Pss. 9:6; 106:9; Nah. 1:4; Zech. 3:2; Mal. 3:11) and put them in their place. When He does, they will flee and be like chaff (Isa. 29:5; cf. Pss. 1:4; 88:13) or dust (Isa. 40:15) that gets taken away in the wind.

A mighty reversal is coming from God (v. 14). Verse 14 portrays the idea that the enemy is convinced that his terror is going to prevail over Israel: "At evening time, behold, *there is* terror!" (*balahah*: sudden terror; cf. Ezek. 26:21; 27:36; 28:19; Ps. 73:19; Job 18:11; 27:20). The enemy is certain of victory, but then the Lord brings a mighty reversal that brings them to naught: "Before morning they are no more. Such *will be* the portion of those who plunder us and the lot of those who pillage us" (v. 14b).

We have good reason for seeing this prophecy as getting fulfilled by God's judgment on Sennacherib in 701 B.C. (Isa. 37:21-38; 2 Kings 19:35).[111] Sennacherib had Jerusalem completely surrounded, and Hezekiah and Jerusalem were helpless to fight back, but God struck the Assyrian armies with a severe plague that wiped out 185,000 in one night, forcing Sennacherib to retreat to Assyria where he was murdered by his own sons.

Summary and application

Once again, our study of Isaiah shows us that one of the biggest principles for application comes down to the need for every man to trust the Lord Jesus Christ as personal Savior no matter what kinds of life trials we might be facing. In this section, we are reminded how Hezekiah and Jerusalem were in a situation that was utterly hopeless at a human level. God, however, was there to deliver them because they trusted Him.

---

[110] Many religions, such as seen Canaanite mythology, saw the chaos of the seas as being driven by powerful gods (cf. Isa. 27:1; 51:9).
[111] Wolf, *Interpreting Isaiah*, 121; Oswalt, *The Book of Isaiah, 1-39*, 357.

ISAIAH 13:1-23:18

JUDGMENT ON NATIONS: ETHIOPIA (18:1-7)

The judgments against the nations continue. Chapter 18 brings us to a sixth nation named for judgment, Ethiopia (*Cush*).[112]

Chapter 18 reads as follows: "1 Alas, oh land of whirring wings which lies beyond the rivers of Cush, 2 which sends envoys by the sea, even in papyrus vessels on the surface of the waters. Go, swift messengers, to a nation tall and smooth, to a people feared far and wide, a powerful and oppressive nation whose land the rivers divide. 3 All you inhabitants of the world and dwellers on earth, as soon as a standard is raised on the mountains, you will see *it,* and as soon as the trumpet is blown, you will hear *it.* 4 For thus the Lord has told me, I will look from My dwelling place quietly like dazzling heat in the sunshine, like a cloud of dew in the heat of harvest. 5 For before the harvest, as soon as the bud blossoms and the flower becomes a ripening grape, then He will cut off the sprigs with pruning knives and remove *and* cut away the spreading branches. 6 They will be left together for mountain birds of prey, and for the beasts of the earth; and the birds of prey will spend the summer *feeding* on them, and all the beasts of the earth will spend harvest time on them. 7 At that time a gift of homage will be brought to the Lord of hosts from a people tall and smooth, even from a people feared far and wide, a powerful and oppressive nation, whose land the rivers divide—to the place of the name of the Lord of hosts, *even* Mount Zion" (18:1-7).

This message is introduced by the term "woe" (*hoy*), but is less severe than the other oracles. Interestingly, this message contains no direct statements of condemnation. We will first give some general background of who Ethiopia was before commenting on God's message.

History of Ethiopia

We should not make an exact equation of ancient Ethiopia with modern Ethiopia. Although there is some overlap in territory, the two lands are not exactly the same. Modern Ethiopia is a very poor country in central Africa. The ancient name for Ethiopia is the name "Cush" (Gen. 2:13; 10:6-8; 1 Chron. 1:8-10; Isa. 11:11), the land along the Nile River south of the fourth cataract in the region of the White and Blue Nile, just south of Upper Egypt ("the ends of the earth"). Because of its location and political interaction, Ethiopia is often

---

[112] Oswalt suggests this is not a judgment oracle since the term "burden" is not used although the word "woe" is employed (Oswalt, *The Book of Isaiah, 1-39*, 359). Certainly, this message does not contain harsh judgment statements like seen in the oracles to the other nations.

associated closely with Egypt in the Bible (Ps. 68:31; Isa. 20:3-5; Ezek. 30:4).

Ethiopia actually gained control over Egypt in 715 B.C. when an Ethiopian leader named Shabako ("So" in 2 Kings 17:4) became king over Egypt, founding Egypt's twenty-fifth dynasty (715 B.C. to 633 B.C.).[113] Although we cannot be certain of the time of Isaiah's message, it is possible that they were already ruling over Egypt and Ethiopia were sending envoys to Judah, attempting to encourage an alliance with them for rebellion against Assyria.[114]

God's message to Ethiopia (vv. 1-7)

God's message to Ethiopia is short and obscure. The first part comes in verses 1-3 where God announces a message for Ethiopia with a lengthy description of the nation.

The heralding of God's message to Ethiopia (vv. 1-3)

A land of buzzing (v. 1). God describes Ethiopia as the land of "whirling wings" (*tsiltsal kenaphim*), the kind of buzzing one hears from locusts or crickets or flies.[115] This expression is best understood as describing the massive numbers of "tsetse flies" that live (even to this day) in that region of the Nile "beyond the rivers of Cush."

A land of envoys (v. 2). Isaiah also describes them as the land "which sends envoys by the sea, even in papyrus vessels on the surface of the waters." These are envoys looking to form alliances to fight against Assyria. These boats were made of papyrus reeds (cf. Job 9:26) which were able to travel very quickly down the Nile River, i.e., "the sea" (cf. Isa. 19:5; Nah. 3:8). Verse 2 is difficult, but it may be that Ethiopia was afraid of Assyria and they were sending envoys to Judah ask for help. Isaiah describes the Ethiopians as tall and smooth (which they are), but they were not known as being particularly powerful or oppressive. Again, the message to Ethiopia is different from the others in 13-23 in that Ethiopia is not singled out for any special message of condemnation.

The envoys are not necessary (v. 3). What seems to be happening is that Isaiah is talking about the way that messengers (presumably from Israel) needed to go back to the Ethiopians to tell them that their fear of Assyria was not necessary. Ethiopia will realize this as soon as the standard is raised (5:26; 11:10;

---

[113] Wolf, *Interpreting Isaiah*, 121.
[114] Oswalt, *The Book of Isaiah, 1-39*, 360.
[115] Ludwig Koehler et al., *The Hebrew and Aramaic Lexicon of the Old Testament*, cited in electronic form with Logos Libronix, (Leiden: E.J. Brill, 1994–2000), 1031.

13:2) and the trumpet sounds. Martin explains, "The prophet exhorted the Cushites to go back home and not try to form an alliance because the Lord would defeat the enemy at the proper time."[116]

The heart of God's message to Ethiopia (vv. 4-6)

The heart of God's message to Ethiopia comes out in verses 4-6. There is no need to fear, for Assyria will fall (v 4), and fall quickly (vv. 5-6).

Assyria will fall (v. 4). The Lord looked down from heaven and gave Isaiah the message that Assyria will fall. At the moment, God was still using Assyria to accomplish His purposes (cf. Isa. 10:12, 25, 32), but it would not be long until He would visit them for their own sins.

Assyria will fall quickly (vv. 5-6). God's wrath is coming quickly. Isaiah likens this judgment to the way that one might clip off fresh buds immediately before the blossoms can produce fruit. Right at that time when all is ripe, God will then cut off the sprig with His knife and bring an end to Assyria. The carnage described in verse 6 suggests that this overthrow of Assyria is that which took place when God brought the armies of Sennacherib to ruin in 701 B.C. (Isa. 36-37).

The hope of God's message to Ethiopia (v. 7)

Isaiah concludes this section by predicting that Ethiopia will celebrate Yahweh's victory over Assyria by sending a gift to Israel. Second Chronicles says that after God destroyed Assyria, "many were bringing gifts to the Lord at Jerusalem and choice presents to Hezekiah king of Judah" (2 Chron. 32:23). This appears to be the fulfillment of the words of Isaiah.

Summary and application

Israel's Shema declares that there is only one God (Deut. 6:4). From the Torah, it is clear that Yahweh chose Israel (and no other) to be His own special nation (Exod. 19:5-6; Deut. 7:6-9; cf. Amos 3:2), but truly we also know that He is God of all the nations (Rom. 3:30). Ethiopia recognized this victory of Yahweh by sending gifts to Hezekiah, but one day this worship will be universal and driven from sincere saving faith (cf. Ps. 72).

JUDGMENT ON NATIONS: EGYPT (19:1-25)

God's message to the nations continues. Chapter 19 brings us to God's oracle against Egypt, a message that flows into chapter 20.

---

[116] Martin, "Isaiah," 1065.

ISAIAH: THE LORD SAVES

Chapter 19 reads as follows: "1 The oracle concerning Egypt. Behold, the Lord is riding on a swift cloud and is about to come to Egypt; the idols of Egypt will tremble at His presence, And the heart of the Egyptians will melt within them. 2 So I will incite Egyptians against Egyptians, and they will each fight against his brother and each against his neighbor, city against city *and* kingdom against kingdom. 3 Then the spirit of the Egyptians will be demoralized within them, and I will confound their strategy, so that they will resort to idols and ghosts of the dead and to mediums and spiritists. 4 Moreover, I will deliver the Egyptians into the hand of a cruel master, and a mighty king will rule over them, declares the Lord God of hosts. 5 The waters from the sea will dry up, and the river will be parched and dry. 6 The canals will emit a stench; the streams of Egypt will thin out and dry up; the reeds and rushes will rot away; 7 the bulrushes by the Nile, by the edge of the Nile and all the sown fields by the Nile will become dry, be driven away, and be no more. 8 And the fishermen will lament, and all those who cast a line into the Nile will mourn, and those who spread nets on the waters will pine away. 9 Moreover, the manufacturers of linen made from combed flax and the weavers of white cloth will be utterly dejected. 10 And the pillars *of Egypt* will be crushed; all the hired laborers will be grieved in soul. 11 The princes of Zoan are mere fools; the advice of Pharaoh's wisest advisers has become stupid. How can you *men* say to Pharaoh, I am a son of the wise, a son of ancient kings? 12 Well then, where are your wise men? Please let them tell you, and let them understand what the Lord of hosts Has purposed against Egypt. 13 The princes of Zoan have acted foolishly, the princes of Memphis are deluded; *those who are* the cornerstone of her tribes have led Egypt astray. 14 The Lord has mixed within her a spirit of distortion; they have led Egypt astray in all that it does, as a drunken man staggers in his vomit. 15 There will be no work for Egypt which *its* head or tail, *its* palm branch or bulrush, may do. 16 In that day the Egyptians will become like women, and they will tremble and be in dread because of the waving of the hand of the Lord of hosts, which He is going to wave over them. 17 The land of Judah will become a terror to Egypt; everyone to whom it is mentioned will be in dread of it, because of the purpose of the Lord of hosts which He is purposing against them. 18 In that day five cities in the land of Egypt will be speaking the language of Canaan and swearing *allegiance* to the Lord of hosts; one will be called the City of Destruction. 19 In that day there will be an altar to the Lord in the midst of the land of Egypt, and a pillar to the Lord near its border. 20 It will become a sign and a witness to the Lord of hosts in the land of Egypt; for they will cry to the Lord because of oppressors, and He will send them a Savior and a Champion, and He will deliver them. 21 Thus the Lord will make Himself known to Egypt, and the Egyptians will know the Lord in that day. They will even worship with sacrifice and offering, and will make a vow to the Lord and perform it. 22 The Lord will strike Egypt, striking but healing; so they will return to the Lord, and He will respond to them and will heal them. 23 In that day there will be a highway from Egypt to Assyria, and the Assyrians will come into Egypt and the

Egyptians into Assyria, and the Egyptians will worship with the Assyrians. 24 In that day Israel will be the third *party* with Egypt and Assyria, a blessing in the midst of the earth, 25 whom the Lord of hosts has blessed, saying, Blessed is Egypt My people, and Assyria the work of My hands, and Israel My inheritance" (19:1-25).

This message to Egypt is particularly fascinating due to the eschatological promises made in the final section. Here in chapter 19, we will first look at the history of Egypt before examining God's oracle.

History of Egypt

The English name "Egypt" comes from the Greek word *Aigyptos*, but in the Old Testament it is the Hebrew name *Mizraim*. The Bible tells us that *Mizraim* was one of the four grandsons of Noah through his son Ham: "The sons of Ham *were* Cush and Mizraim and Put and Canaan" (Gen. 10:6). The initial formation of Egypt as a people group and nation would have begun when God scattered the nations at the Tower of Babel in roughly 2357 B.C. (cf. Gen. 10:25; 11:1ff.).[117]

Secular scholarship typically suggests that the founding of Egypt began long before the Noahic Flood (biblically ca. 2458 B.C.) and the subsequent Tower of Babel dispersion (biblically ca. 2357 B.C.). As recognized by many scholars (biblical and secular), there are serious flaws with the dates often proposed by secular Egyptology. It is beyond the scope of this work to deal with this topic in detail, but the author affirms a biblical view of Egyptian dating and encourages further studies from those that affirm the authority of Scripture like Answers in Genesis below:

> Though traditional Egyptian chronology dominates modern understanding of ancient history, traditional chronology is inconsistent with the Bible. . . . Though many claim that traditional chronology is indisputable, a close look at this chronology reveals its shaky foundation. . . . Accepting traditional Egyptian chronology necessitates rejection of biblical truth. Accepting biblical chronology allows a reconstruction of ancient chronology on a foundation of truth. . . . For further studies of revised chronologies,

---

[117] Secular chronologies for the history of ancient Egypt contain serious flaws that would place Egypt's origins as early as the fourth millennium B.C., but these dates should not be seen as holding more authority than the Scriptures.

because the Bible is the ultimate standard, I suggest consulting Dr. Floyd Jones' book *The Chronology of the Old Testament*.[118]

In terms of geography, Egypt is located on the northeastern corner of the African continent, the closest nation to the southwest edge of Israel. Historically, Egypt has been divided into Lower Egypt (the northern portion on the edge of the Mediterranean) and Upper Egypt (the southern portion which extends to the region where the Nile begins). Historically, Upper Egypt was considered the beginning of its power, but over the ages Egypt was ruled over as two lands under one rule. The Pharaohs were always considered the king of Upper and Lower Egypt, a land that was divided into various provinces or "nomes."

The Nile is the longest river in the world and has always been the dominant feature of Egypt. The Nile begins deep in Upper Egypt and flows north for over 4200 miles to empty into the Mediterranean. The course of the Nile gets interrupted at six different locations because of six different granite rock outcroppings that the Nile must pass through. These six granite outcroppings are called "the cataracts," and their presence made a hindrance to ancient navigation on the Nile. Moving southward, the first cataract comes at Aswan, with the sixth coming in modern day Sudan. The Nile is what brings life to Egypt, for apart from it the land is a barren wasteland.[119] The annual pattern of the Nile was to overflow its banks from roughly August to November. These floods brought irrigation and life to all of Egypt. Kill the Nile, and you strike a death blow to Egypt.

God's oracle to Egypt (vv. 1-25)

Chapter 19 breaks down into two major sections. In the first, God tells Egypt she has no hope in the flesh (vv. 1-15). In the second, He tells Egypt there is only one place to find hope, and that is in the people of Judah and her warrior King (vv. 16-25).[120]

Egypt has no hope in the flesh (vv. 1-15)

Egypt was doomed to fall, which also means it was no place for Judah to look for help. Isaiah singles out three areas that would be no hope.

---

[118] Elizabeth Mitchell, "Doesn't Egyptian Chronology Prove That the Bible Is Unreliable?" (<https://answersingenesis.org/archaeology/ancient-egypt/doesnt-egyptian-chronology-prove-bible-unreliable/>, accessed Oct. 23, 2019).

[119] Of the 386,000 square miles of Egypt, 96% of that terrain is desert.

[120] Ch. 20 also talks about Egypt by showing the futility of trusting in Egypt.

No hope in its ancient religion (vv. 1-4). The oracle begins with a vision of Yahweh riding on a swift cloud, imagery that is often found where God announces that He is coming in judgment (cf. Deut. 33:26; Pss. 18:10; 68:33; 104:3; Dan. 7:13; Matt. 24:30; 26:64; Rev. 1:7). Yahweh is the sovereign Lord of the earth on His way to judge Egypt.[121]

Terror in the religious leaders (v. 1). The idols of Egypt,[122] and the pagan priests who minister to them, will provide no hope to Egypt (nor did they for Judah, cf. Isa. 8:19-20).[123] Once God begins His judgment, the idolaters will tremble, and all hearts will melt in fear and despair.

Internal strife within the nation (vv. 2-3). Egypt will fall into a state of great internal strife—the same kind of internal strife that God brought upon His own people when He judged them (Isa. 9:21; cf. Zech. 11:14). Egypt was prone to this kind of internal disunity since each of the nomes had its own god.[124] God's judgment included the use of the nation's own sin to bring itself to ruin (cf. 1 John 2:15-17).[125] Egypt will be desperate, but none of its sorcery will bring relief.

Overthrow (v. 4). The end result of this internal disintegration will come when a powerful tyrant brings Egypt to ruin. From 740 B.C. onward, Assyria made numerous invasions against Egypt, but the greatest of these victories came from Esarhaddon in 670 B.C., the one who may be the "cruel master" (*'Adoniym Qasheh*) Isaiah speaks of.[126] This much is clear: Egypt's religious leaders and their idols will be absolutely no help to them.

No hope in its economic might (vv. 5-10). Not only will the religious leaders provide no hope, but neither will Egypt's mighty Nile.[127] The Nile was

---

[121] Oswalt, *The Book of Isaiah, 1-39*, 367.

[122] The term "idols" (*'eliyliym*) carries the connotation of "nothings" (cf. 2:8, 18, 20; 10:10, 11; 19:3; 3:7). Note: It is not as though Isaiah has sanctioned such idols to even have life (Isa. 44:8-20; cf. Jer. 43:12, 13; 46:25; Ezek. 30:13).

[123] These practices were absolutely forbidden (Lev. 19:31; 20:6, 27; Deut. 18:9-14).

[124] Ibid., 367-368.

[125] God's wrath shows itself in different ways: (1) eternal wrath (Rev. 14:9-11), (2) eschatological tribulation wrath (1 Thess. 1:10; ; 2:16; 5:9), (3) wrath from foreign nations (Luke 21:23, 26-35), (4) natural disaster (Amos 4:4-13), (5) wrath when God abandons people to sin (Rom. 1:18-32). One ancient source said, "even the winds are said to oppose one another" (Ipu-wer, cited by Young, *The Book of Isaiah, vol. 2*, 15-16, n. 8).

[126] Wolf, *Interpreting Isaiah*, 123; Grogan, "Isaiah," 126. Grogan describes Esarhaddon as a tyrant of unusual cruelty and ferocity.

[127] All of these terms, sea (cf. 18:2; Job 14:11), river, canals, streams, are references to

the heart of Egypt's prosperity, but God will bring Egypt to its knees with a drought that strikes every aspect of Egypt (farming, fishing, flax [cf. Exod. 9:31], linen/cotton). God will withhold the snow/rain that creates the Nile's overflow, and it will become a foul stench (vv. 5-9). Egypt will come to ruin (v. 10).[128]

No hope in its powerful leaders (vv. 11-15). Third, God will give Egypt over to wicked leaders whose foolish counsel will lead the nation to ruin. Martin notes that, "Egypt was well known in the ancient world for its wisdom writings and its wise men [cf. 1 Kings 4:30]. But Isaiah warned Egypt not to count on her wise men to save the nation."[129] Verses 11-15 follow an alternating pattern of exposing the folly of the leaders, but that it was all part of God's judgment.

The folly of the Leaders (vv. 11-12a). Zoan (Tanis) was a capital city on the northeastern edge of Egypt (Num. 13:22; Ps. 78:12; Isa. 30:4; Ezek. 30:14),[130] and Noph (Memphis) was a second major city located south of Zoan (Jer. 2:16; 44:1; 46:14, 19; Ezek. 30:13, 16; Hos. 9:6). God derisively rebukes them for their folly and inability to be of any help to Pharaoh.

The judgment of God (v. 12b-13). The folly of Egypt's leaders is part of their ignorance in not knowing how to deal with the coming enemy and economic catastrophes.[131] These judgments will come just as God has "purposed" (cf. Isa. 14:24). The leaders were fools who had no wisdom to stay off the invasions—the fate of those who reject God. (v. 13).

The judgment of God (vv. 14-15). Once again, we see that the folly of the leaders is really part of God's judgment.[132] God Himself is the One who brings judgments on those who reject Him and turn to idols:

> I, the Lord, am the maker of all things, stretching out the heavens by Myself and spreading out the earth all alone, causing the omens of boasters to

---

Egypt's Nile. The term Egypt in v. 6 is the rare singular term *Mazor* (which looks at Egypt as one unit) and not the usual Dual form *Mizraim* which speaks about both Upper and Lower Egypt as a unit.

[128] These "pillars" are probably referring to the mighty ruling class and the "hired laborers" all the working class.

[129] Martin, "Isaiah," 1066.

[130] Zoan was built seven years after Hebron (Num. 13:22).

[131] God's mockery of Egypt comes out through the question, "Where is your wise men" (cf. 1 Cor. 1:20).

[132] The worthless "cornerstones" included advisors like princes, nobles, and priests who were no more help than a drunk man, staggering in his vomit (cf. Isa. 28:7).

fail, making fools out of diviners, causing wise men to draw back and turning their knowledge into foolishness (Isa. 44:24-25).

The end result of Egypt's failed leadership will be complete economic failure, a failure so bad that no one will find any means of work or support (v. 15). All-powerful, all-beautiful Egypt will now be out of business. Oswalt graphically describes the situation: "[Egypt is] like an ancient whore who does not know that her beauty is gone."[133] Nevertheless, despite the fact that Egypt has no hope in herself, the Lord will extend hope to her. This is the hope of redemption through the warrior King of Judah.

Egypt will find a hope in the warrior King of Judah (vv. 16-25)

Verses 16-25 bring a radical change in focus. Whereas verses 1-15 were about judgment that left no hope, verses 16-25 extend a wonderful promise to Egypt. The passage is utterly fascinating as noted by Wolf: "It is the longest and most remarkable passage of this kind in this section on the nations and also one of the most difficult to interpret."[134] This section contains five eschatological promises of salvation and restoration for the nation of Egypt, each of which gets introduced by the expression "in that day" (*bayyom hahu'*).[135]

First promise of salvation to the people of Egypt (vv. 16-17). The day is coming when Egypt is going to fall under a great dread that is likened to helpless women trembling in fear (cf. Jer. 50:37; 51:30; Nah. 3:13). The dread will be intense, but all of it part of God's eschatological work of salvation for Egypt (v. 16),[136] a salvation to His elect, but only through great tribulation.

Isaiah continues in verse 17 by explaining that the land of Judah will become a "terror" (*chagah*) to Egypt (shame, confusion).[137] After ages of hatred against Israel, Egypt will have a holy fear that these are the people of God (cf.

---

[133] Oswalt, *The Book of Isaiah, 1-39*, 372.

[134] Wolf, *Interpreting Isaiah*, 124.

[135] Isaiah uses this expression forty-two times, one fourth of all uses in the Old Testament. As already observed, this expression frequently introduces eschatological truth, but such is not always the case (cf. e.g., 17:7). The sensitive exegete recognizes the not-infrequent pattern where God's prophets jump from events of ancient history to the eschaton, often using the expression "in that day" (Isa. 2:2; 4:2; 9:7; 10:20; 12:1; cf. Jer. 30:3; 50:4; Dan. 2:34-35; 7:13; 8:23; 11:36; Hos. 3:5; Amos 9:11; Obad. 15; Mic. 7:9-20; Zeph. 3:8; Hag. 2:20; Zech. 3:10).

[136] Kidner, "Isaiah," 645; Grogan, "Isaiah," 128.

[137] Ludwig Koehler et al., *The Hebrew and Aramaic Lexicon of the Old Testament*, cited in electronic form with Logos Libronix, 290.

Deut. 2:25). All of this is part of the "purpose" of the Lord (cf. Isa. 14:24; 19:12) to bring redeeming grace to the land of Egypt.

Second promise of salvation to the people of Egypt (v. 18). Isaiah now announces that the work of God's redeeming grace is going to move Egypt to make a major change of spiritual alliance. By a mighty outpouring of saving grace, Egypt will abandon her empty trust in idols for faith in Yahweh the living God: "In that day five cities in the land of Egypt will be speaking the language of Canaan and swearing *allegiance* to the Lord of hosts; one will be called the City of Destruction." We face interpretive challenges over certain details, but the message is clear: God is going to bring a great salvation to Egypt.[138] The reference to "five" cities speaks about a major turning to the Lord in such a way that they even embrace the language of the Hebrews and swear allegiance to the God of Israel."[139]

Third promise of salvation to the people of Egypt (vv. 19-22). The people of Egypt are going to experience a new revelation of the Lord that will lead them to worship Him. Isaiah singles out two places where they will have memorials to the Lord for worship. One will be an altar (cf. Gen. 12:8; 28:22) in the midst of Egypt (v. 19).[140] The second is called "a pillar to the Lord near its border." The term "pillar" often referred to items of pagan worship (Exod. 23:24; Lev. 26:21; Deut. 7:5; 1 Kings 14:23; Hos. 3:4), but here is direct toward Yahweh with a memorial purpose to celebrate Yahweh's saving grace (cf. Josh. 4:3, 20-22; 7:26; 8:29; 10:27). Grogan explains that this pillar at the border, "probably symbolizes the claiming of the land for the true and living God, the Almighty."[141]

---

[138] The number five could simply be a round number (Gen. 45:22; Exod. 22:1), but perhaps it speaks about specific cities (e.g., Leontopolis, Heliopolis, Mogdol, Daphne, Memphis). We cannot be sure of the significance of the statement.

[139] With regards to "the city of destruction," the MT reads "destruction," but there is a textual variant here that suggests that the reading could be "city of the sun" as found in 1QIs[a] and many other textual sources like Symm., Targ., Vulg., Arab. (Oswalt, *The Book of Isaiah, 1-39*, 373, n. 6). If the poetic use of *cheres* is referring to the sun and not destruction (cf. Job 9:7; Judg. 14:18) this may be speaking of Heliopolis, the City of the Sun (cf. Gen. 41:45), the place called *On* in the Bible. If this is correct, then what we see is that even the city of Ra would be turning to the worship of Yahweh.

[140] Some commentators have suggested that these events find fulfillment in the second century B.C. when a Jewish priest named Onias erected an altar in Egypt, but this prophecy is about Egyptian worship and not Jewish worship.

[141] Grogan, "Isaiah," 129.

This altar (and pillar?) will provide a memorial for Egypt (a "sign and witness") to perpetually remind them about the way the Lord saved them (cf. Isa. 18:7; 60:7; Zeph. 3:10; Zech. 14:16-21; Mal. 1:11). The Lord will bring this salvation because "oppressors" will be afflicting them,[142] but when they turn to Him and cry for help,[143] He will send them a "Savior" (*moshiya'*) and a "Champion" (*Rayb*) to deliver them.[144] Indeed, this is one of the most-powerful messianic prophecies of the Bible (v. 20).

Through this great deliverance, the Lord will "make Himself known to Egypt" (v. 21).[145] This message surely served as a rebuke to self-righteous Israel. In the beginning of Isaiah's prophecies (cf. 1:3) we saw that Israel does not know Yahweh her God, but one day Egypt and all the nations (including Israel herself) will know Him (Isa. 60:16). The result will be a true worship of Yahweh the living God.[146] In the kingdom, Egypt will give full allegiance to the Lord, the God of Israel.[147] All of this is a beautiful picture of the saving grace of Jesus Christ (v. 22). Yes, redemption will require "striking" (*nagaph*, to injure by striking), but the striking is such that it ultimately brings repentance, faith, and healing.

This is the same wonderful saving grace God works in His people Israel to bring them to repentance and faith (Jer. 30:11, 17; Dan. 12:7; Hos. 5:14-6:1). The promises are so wonderful that they are hard to fathom, but this is the truth of God's saving grace: "This situation was almost unbelievable for the people of Judah in Isaiah's day, but it *will* occur after the Messiah has returned and

---

[142] One day God will send oppressors—ones who squeeze and afflict (as in Judg. 1:34; 2:18). Interestingly, *lachats* is the same Hebrew word used in Exodus to describe the way Egypt oppressed Israel (Exod. 3:9; 22:20; 23:9).

[143] God will give afflicted Egypt a Savior just like he did Israel in the days of the Judges (Judg. 3:9, 15; 6:7; 10:10).

[144] It is fascinating to ponder the eschatological connections with this passage and how Daniel predicts a huge military invasion into Egypt (led by the Antichrist, the king of the north?) during the tribulation period (Dan. 11:42-43). This could be describing Christ saving elect Egyptian saints from the ravages of Antichrist.

[145] The language reminds us how in the beginning Pharaoh did not "know" the Lord, but through God's great redemption all Egypt and Israel came to know the Lord (Exod. 5:2; 7:5, 17; 9:28; 10:2; cf. Jer. 9:23-24).

[146] The terms "sacrifice" (*zebach*, blood sacrifice) and "grain offering" (*minchah*) should be taken literally (Isa. 56:7; 60:7; cf. Ezek. 45:21-25; Zech. 14:16-21).

[147] Even their oaths will be in the name of Yahweh as a reflection of their gratitude for His grace (cf. Num. 30:1ff.; Pss. 22:25; 50:14; 61:8; 65:1; 66:13; 116:14, 18).

established His millennial kingdom."[148] When we consider the present state of the Middle East, these promises are hard to fathom, but it will happen.

Fourth promise of salvation to the people of Egypt (v. 23). God's saving grace will create an interesting union between all of His saints in the millennial kingdom with a "highway" that runs from Egypt to Assyria (Isa. 2:2-4; 11:16; 27:12-13; 33:8; 35:8; 40:3; 49:11; 60:10-14; 62:10; 66:23). Is this a literal, physical highway? It could be. At the very least, this verse tells us that when His kingdom comes, God is going to create a union between all saints, even those that were inveterate enemies during the days of Isaiah:

> In a remarkable statement Isaiah sees the ancient enmity between Assyria and Egypt dissolved. No more will Israel be merely a pawn between these warring powers. Now she will take her place beside them to fulfill the ancient promise (Gen. 12:3).[149]

These will be glorious days, and this knowledge should move us to long for the return of Christ to usher in the consummation of His redeeming work.

Fifth promise of salvation to the people of Egypt (vv. 24-25). At the present time, Israel is hated with the utmost hatred by the Islamic world that dominates most of the land of Egypt and most of the Middle East. When Egypt's elect come to faith in Christ, they will recognize God's mediatorial work through His chosen nation Israel—a "blessing in the midst of the earth" (v. 24). She who had been hated and despised will no longer be a curse, but a blessing (cf. Zech. 8:11-13).

This section closes with one of the most amazing statements in the Bible. Not only is Israel a nation that has been blessed by God (vv. 24-25a), but so are Assyria and Egypt: "Blessed is Egypt My people, and Assyria the work of My hands, and Israel My inheritance" (v. 25b). In the day of redemption, the Lord will declare favor on all the nations of world whose elect citizens have come to faith in His Son. The language is staggering when God calls *Egypt* "My people" (Isa. 10:24; 43:6, 7; Hos. 1:10; 2:23; Jer. 11:4), *Assyria* "the work of My hands" (29:23; 60:21; 64:8; Pss. 119:73; 138:8), and *Israel* "My inheritance" (Deut. 32:9).[150] God's redemption is not limited to Israel alone (cf. 42:6; 49:6).

---

[148] Martin, "Isaiah," 1067.

[149] Oswalt, *The Book of Isaiah, 1-39*, 380.

[150] The statements about Egypt and Assyria were so hard for Jewish scribes that the Targum altered these passages to try and eliminate what they said (ibid., 381, n. 28).

Summary and application

Without exaggeration, the previous section of eschatological prophecy contains one of the grandest statements of God's redeeming grace in the entire Bible. This portion of Scripture reminds us once again that God is not only the God of the Jews, but also God of the Gentiles. Regardless of ethnicity, if we trust in Jesus Christ, God will save us.

JUDGMENT ON NATIONS: EGYPT/CUSH (20:1-6)

Chapter 20 introduces another message about Cush, i.e., Ethiopia to the south of Egypt (cf. ch. 18). Chapter 19 was about Egypt, but both Egypt and Ethiopia are part of the context here.[151]

Chapter 20 reads as follow: "1 In the year that the commander came to Ashdod, when Sargon the king of Assyria sent him and he fought against Ashdod and captured it, 2 at that time the Lord spoke through Isaiah the son of Amoz, saying, Go and loosen the sackcloth from your hips and take your shoes off your feet, and he did so, going naked and barefoot. 3 And the Lord said, Even as My servant Isaiah has gone naked and barefoot three years as a sign and token against Egypt and Cush, 4 so the king of Assyria will lead away the captives of Egypt and the exiles of Cush, young and old, naked and barefoot with buttocks uncovered, to the shame of Egypt. 5 Then they will be dismayed and ashamed because of Cush their hope and Egypt their boast. 6 So the inhabitants of this coastland will say in that day, Behold, such is our hope, where we fled for help to be delivered from the king of Assyria; and we, how shall we escape?" (20:1-6).

The essence of this message is that shame will come to all who refuse to trust the Lord. Even though Egypt will have an eschatological redemption in Israel's Messiah, this section shows that she will first experience heaps of shame and humiliation for her ages of sin and idolatry. Furthermore, the people of Judah should never put their trust in other nations like Egypt, but only in the Lord their God, for anyone who does otherwise will experience terrible disappointment and shame.

To symbolize this message, God instructs His prophet to do a three-year drama skit where he walks around through the land of Israel naked to symbolize such shame (cf. similar symbolism in Ezek. 4; Jer. 13; 1 Kings 11:29; Zech. 11). The meaning of the sign is that shame will come to those who do not trust in the Lord. Isaiah tells us four facts about this sign.

---

[151] Wolf explains that this chapter portrays the intense hatred between Assyria and Egypt in his own day and that this chapter serves as a sort of epilogue to 18-19 (Wolf, *Interpreting Isaiah*, 126).

First fact about Isaiah's sign: Time of the sign (v. 1)

God gave Isaiah this command "the year that the commander came to Ashdod when Sargon the king of Assyria sent him and he fought against Ashdod and captured it." This commander was the senior general to the King of Assyria (cf. 2 Kings 18:17 for the same term). It was in 711 B.C. that Sargon sent troops to put down Philistine rebellions that had begun in 713 B.C. under King Azuri.[152] Judah would have sided with Ashdod over Assyria, but all of this is a message to Judah to trust in no one but the Lord. When the Ethiopian Shabako took control of Egypt in 715/714 B.C., one of the things he did was to inspire Ashdod to rebel against Assyria.[153]

Second fact about Isaiah's sign: Nature of the sign (v. 2)

God's way of teaching Judah to trust in no one but Himself was to have Isaiah walk about naked for a three-year time period—the three years that led up to the fall of Ashdod. It would have been tempting for Judah to join the Ashdod rebellion (with promises from Edom, Moab, and Egypt), but to do so would bring much shame. It is possible that Isaiah was completely naked, but it is probably preferable to understand that Isaiah was wearing a loin cloth and not completely naked (an action that was still very shameful; cf. 2 Sam. 10:4). Despite the shame, Isaiah did as the Lord commanded. Verses 3-4 show us the object of this sign.

Third fact about Isaiah's sign: Object of the sign (vv. 3-4)

The only way to avoid shame is to trust the Lord. Martin explains, "This object lesson was to show how the Egyptians and Cushites would be treated by the victorious Assyrian forces,"[154] for at a primary level this symbolic action was "a sign and token against Egypt and Cush" (cf. Isa. 8:18; Deut. 13:1; 28:46; 29:3; 34:11; Ps. 135:9; Jer. 32:20-21). The real message is this: Ashdod is going to fall to Assyria, but so are Egypt and Cush (v. 3). For Egypt, the end result was watching her people get taken away into captivity by Assyria (v. 4).[155] Kidner explains,

> An inscription by Sargon fills out this picture. The Philistine city of Ashdod had revolted against Assyria, which promptly deposed its king. A new

---

[152] Ibid.

[153] Oswalt, *The Book of Isaiah, 1-39*, 382-383. The king of Ashdod had been the pro-Assyrian Ahimiti, but in 713 B.C. he was deposed and his brother, the anti-Assyrian Yamani, was made king. Assyria retaliated, Yamani fled to Egypt, and Ashdod fell in 711.

[154] Martin, "Isaiah," 1067.

[155] This was literally fulfilled in 671 B.C. when Assyria began deporting conquered Egyptian Cushites (Isa. 37:38; 2 Kings 19:37; Ezra 4:2).

ringleader, Yamani, carried on the struggle with pledged support from Egypt and Ethiopia and had also approached Judah. Isaiah's powerful dissuasion turned out to be fully justified: Egypt failed to fight, Ashdod was subjugated, and Yamani, who had fled to Ethiopia, was handed over to the Assyrians' tender mercies.[156]

Judah was to trust in none of these nations, not even Egypt with its new Ethiopian rule (Isa. 30:1-5; 31:1-13). Egypt did try to come to help Judah in 701 B.C., but they were so badly defeated at Eltekeh they were useless. The Psalmist wrote, "It is better to take refuge in the Lord than to trust in man. It is better to take refuge in the Lord than to trust in princes" (Ps. 118:8-9).

Fourth fact about Isaiah's sign: Significance of the sign (vv. 5-6)

God's message for Judah was to not put their trust in Egypt, but sadly they did. For this reason, God says, "they will be dismayed and ashamed because of Cush their hope and Egypt their boast" (v. 5).

Verse 6 indicates that this kind of empty trust was not limited to Israel, but also the inhabitants of "the coastland" (*ha'iy*).[157] None of the coastlands, not even Ashdod at the eastern end of the coastlands, should trust in anyone but the Lord—not even mighty Egypt. Any alliance with foreign nations to fight off Assyria—even with mighty Egypt—would bring them nothing but shame.[158]

Summary and application

In ancient times Egypt was perhaps the most powerful and wealthy nation on the face of the planet, but it did not take long before they fell from this status and became weak and impoverished when God brought His judgments on their sin. This is a tremendous lesson for all of us lest we become proud and secure in our own prosperity and ease. For many generations the nation of America has been enjoying a time of unprecedented peace and prosperity. Sadly, America has chosen to reject Jesus Christ and embrace the ways of evil.

JUDGMENT ON NATIONS: BABYLON (21:1-10)

The focus now shifts eastward. Babylon was already the focus in chapters 13-14, but God has more to say about this once-powerful empire.

---

[156] Kidner, "Isaiah," 645.

[157] This expression, here singular but often in the plural, refers to the entire Mediterranean coastlands as far as Tarshish in the far west (cf. Isa. 11:11; 13:22; 20:6; 23:2, 6; 24:15; 34:14; 40:15; 41:1, 5; 42:4, 10, 12, 15; 49:1; 50:1; 51:5; 59:18; 60:5; 66:1, 19).

[158] Martin, "Isaiah," 1067.

God's oracle against Babylon reads as follows: "1 The oracle concerning the wilderness of the sea. As windstorms in the Negev sweep on; it comes from the wilderness, from a terrifying land. 2 A harsh vision has been shown to me; the treacherous one *still* deals treacherously, and the destroyer *still* destroys. Go up, Elam, lay siege, Media; I have made an end of all the groaning she has caused. 3 For this reason my loins are full of anguish; pains have seized me like the pains of a woman in labor. I am so bewildered I cannot hear, so terrified I cannot see. 4 My mind reels, horror overwhelms me; the twilight I longed for has been turned for me into trembling. 5 They set the table, they spread out the cloth, they eat, they drink; rise up, captains, oil the shields, 6 For thus the Lord says to me, go, station the lookout, let him report what he sees. 7 When he sees riders, horsemen in pairs, a train of donkeys, a train of camels, let him pay close attention, very close attention. 8 Then the lookout called, O Lord, I stand continually by day on the watchtower, and I am stationed every night at my guard post. 9 Now behold, here comes a troop of riders, horsemen in pairs. And one said, Fallen, fallen is Babylon, and all the images of her gods are shattered on the ground. 10 O my threshed *people,* and my afflicted of the threshing floor! What I have heard from the Lord of hosts, The God of Israel, I make known to you" (21:1-10).

This is the first of two oracles which do not begin by naming the nation targeted (the other is ch. 22), but the target of the message becomes clear in verse 9.[159] Chapter 21 is about God's promise to purge this world of all evil (including Babylon), but this chapter also highlights the agonies that are a part of this purging. This chapter gives us four descriptions of God's plan as clues about how God's judgment on Babylon will unfold.

First description of God's plan: The description of Babylon (v. 1)

Isaiah calls Babylon the "wilderness of the sea."[160] The meaning is not especially clear,[161] but from verse 9 we can see that the entire passage is actually about Babylon (with later discussions about Babylon in 40-47). Here Isaiah sees a judgment coming against Babylon "from the wilderness, from a terrifying land." The appearance of this judgment was like a howling dust storm coming from Israel's Negeb (Job 1:19; Jer. 4:11; 13:24; Hos. 13:15; Zech. 9:14). These are the armies of Media and Persia (i.e., Elam) bringing ruin to Babylon.

---

[159] Wolf, *Interpreting Isaiah*, 126-127.
[160] "Sea" could be the Persian Gulf or better the alluvial plains of southern Babylon, some of which are covered with marsh lands.
[161] The DSS reads "the burden of the word of the sea."

As already noted, Babylon's history traces back to Genesis 10:10, but it was during the Neo-Babylonian empire (626-539 B.C.) that Babylon became the dominant empire of the ANE.[162] What makes Babylon especially prominent in Scripture is that it was Babylon who invaded Judah and overthrew the Davidic dynasty in 605 B.C. This overthrow of Judah introduced an extended era of judgment against the people of Israel that will not end until the arrival of the messianic kingdom. These judgments are the outworking of the covenant curses spoken of in the Law of Moses (Deut. 28:15-68). The "times of the Gentiles" (Luke 21:24) began when Nebuchadnezzar overthrew Judah in 605 B.C. (other defeats in 597 and 586), and this period of God's "indignation" against Israel (cf. Isa. 10:5, 25; 13:5; 26:20; 34:2; 66:14; Dan. 8:19; 11:36; Zech. 1:12), will not end until the return of Christ.

Second description of God's plan: The destroyer of Babylon (v. 2)

Isaiah identifies the conquering enemy as Elam and Media. Elam was located in southern Persia and later got incorporated as part of the Persian empire. The overthrow of Babylon came in October 539 B.C. when Cyrus led the combined forces of Media and Persia to overthrow the treacherous destroyer Babylon (cf. Dan. 5:30-31). Jeremiah uses similar "destroyer" language for Babylon (51:25), but God tells us here that He has another destroyer in Persia and Elam

---

[162] It is helpful to understand the history of Assyrian and Babylonian relations from the time of Isaiah onward: Tiglath-Pileser (745-727) left the native Nabu-nasir on the throne of Babylon till his death in 734, then the southern tribes of Babylon seized the city of Babylon. Tiglath regained power until the death of Shalmaneser V in 722 when Merodach Baladan proclaimed himself as "king of Babylon" (Isa. 39:1). With the help of Elam, Baladan was able to hold off Assyria for the next 10 years. In 710 Sargon II led a successful attack and was welcomed in Babylon as "viceroy of Marduk" at the New Year celebration in 710, leaving Marduk-apla-iddina (Baladan) as sheikh of his tribe. In 703, Baladan rebelled, seeking the help of Hezekiah (2 Kings 20:12-17). Assyria brought defeat to Babylon, but rebellions continued with Sennacherib mounting a major offensive in 700 and again in 695. In 689, Sennacherib destroyed Babylon (some think this is fulfillment of Isaiah 21). In 681, Sennacherib got murdered by his own sons, and power passed to Esarhaddon (Isa. 37:38). Esarhaddon ruled Assyria from 681-669, and one of his sons (Shamash shum ukin) became crown prince of Babylon while his brother Ashurbanipal became crown prince of Assyria. Dissension between the two brothers led to a three-year attack on Babylon beginning in 651 till the king of Babylon set the palace on fire and took his own life. After a period of semi-independence, Babylon rose to great power under the leadership of Nabopolassar (626-605). In 612, the Babylonians teamed up with the Medes to overthrow Nineveh. Assyrian defeats in 609 (2 Kings 23:29-30) and 605 (Jer. 46:2-12) left Babylon the dominant empire.

who will destroy Babylon and put an end to all the groaning Babylon has caused (cf. Jer. 51:1, 6, 11, 20, 25, 48, 53, 55, 56).

Third description of God's plan: The dread over Babylon (vv. 3-4)

We again see the intense pain Isaiah suffered because of the human suffering God showed him. The physical impact was so intense he could not even function (Isa. 13:8; 26:7). Truly Isaiah was a compassionate man: "To a man of Isaiah's sympathetic nature, the vision of bloody carnage in the captured cities of Babylonia, as Cyrus' forces advanced toward the capital, had a deeply disturbing effect, like that of a fearful nightmare."[163]

Fourth description of God's plan: The destiny of Babylon (vv. 5-10)

This section tells us the destiny of Babylon and how God's purpose against her would unfold. We are going to break this unit down into four smaller sections that show the destiny of Babylon.

First destiny of Babylon: Preparation of the armies (v. 5)

Interestingly, the first detail Isaiah talks about is Babylonian feasting, an ironic comment in light of the agony we saw in Isaiah. Apparently proud Babylon did not take the Persian threat seriously (cf. Isa. 14:11; 47:1, 8).[164] We cannot help but think of the feasting in Daniel 5 as reflecting what we see here, feasting up to the moment of invasion.

The last statement is an interesting command to the captains to rise up and oil their shields (to deflect blows and keep them from cracking). Is this command coming from the King of Babylon, or better is it one from God Himself giving them the warning that they had better prepare for war?

Second destiny of Babylon: Anticipation of Judah (vv. 6-8)

God speaks again, but this time to Isaiah and Judah. The command is to set up a watchman who can watch the east for messengers to come and tell the outcome against Babylon (v. 6). The watchman is to be especially attentive if a larger military company appears with horses (cf. 43:17; Jer. 46:9, horses and

---

[163] Pfeiffer, *The Wycliffe Bible Commentary: Old Testament*, Is 21:1.
[164] Young calls it "a description of the arrogant, worry-free enemy" (Young, *The Book of Isaiah, vol. 2*, 66).

charioteers), donkeys and camels (v. 7).[165] The watchman replies to God that he is diligently fulfilling his charge (v. 8).[166]

Third destiny of Babylon: Overthrow by invaders (vv. 9-10)

Suddenly the messengers appear with the good news: "Fallen, fallen is Babylon, and all the images of her gods are shattered on the ground" (v. 9). This is great news: The destroyer has been destroyed and the images of her gods have been shattered (Isa. 52:7 shows how this good news means an end of war for the people of Israel). This is the prophetic message God gave Isaiah, and this was the message he gave to the threshed (cf. 28:27, 28; 41:15, 16; Amos 1:3; Mic. 4:13), i.e., trampled and afflicted Israel (v. 10).

The fall of Babylon was near. Isaiah announced the fall of Babylon, and just as Jeremiah would prophesy 100 years later, Israel's captivity to Babylon would end after 70 years, and with the fall of Babylon Judah would be allowed to return home (Jer. 25:11-12; 29:10-14). This fall of Babylon came in 539 B.C., and within two years a remnant from Israel began migrating back home.[167]

The fall of Babylon has eschatological implications. Other portions of Scripture indicate that there are broader implications to these prophecies. Yes, Babylon fell to northern Persian armies in 539 B.C. and this passage is a direct prophecy about those events. However, we also recognize that there is also going to be an eschatological fall of "Babylon" as other Scriptures indicate. It is beyond the scope of this commentary to give an exhaustive treatment to that topic, but it is important that we make some brief comment about how these eschatological events are portrayed.

First of all, we should note that the eschatological events prophesied in this, and other, passages do not require one to ever abandon the basic hermeneutical principle of the single meaning of language. That is, we must not treat this passage as having a "double fulfillment," one which took place in 539 B.C.

---

[165] The historian Xenophon told how the Persian armies advanced by twos (Oswalt, *The Book of Isaiah, 1-39*, 395). If this is representing Persia, this could indicate that it may be Persians approaching Judah as foreseen by Isaiah or perhaps Persians approaching Babylon.

[166] The MT carries the reading "lion" (*'aryeh*) instead of "watcher" (*haro'eh*) as found in 1QIs^a. The latter is probably preferable (ibid., 388, n. 9).

[167] Historically these things came upon Babylon when the Medes teamed up with Persia in 539 B.C. Herodotus wrote that the overthrow was swift when Persia diverted the Euphrates and entered under the city walls. Drunken Babylon never realized till it was too late.

and another which will come at the end of the age. This passage has a meaning that finds fulfillment historically. Other prophetic passages do, however, tell us about an eschatological fall to Babylon as well.

Having said this, we also recognize that the order and fulfillment of prophetic visions were not always clearly laid out in the Old Testament prophets. One good illustration is the fact that Jesus read from Isaiah 61:1-2 in Luke 4:18. Jesus read 61:1-2a and declared that those events were being fulfilled at that present time (the first coming of Christ). However, He did not read from verse 2bff. since those events refer to God's eschatological judgments at the second coming (cf. Isa. 9:1-7).

From other prophetic passages we see that a very malevolent Babylon will rise up at the end of the age, and this Babylon will also experience one final, catastrophic overthrow at the second coming of Christ. We suggest that the following passages are some of these texts which appear to speak to this eschatological fall of Babylon (Isa. 14:1-2 [cf. Jer. 50:1-5]; 47 [could all of this chapter be eschatological?]; Jer. 50:1-5, 17-20, 38-40; 51:8, 24-26, 59-64; Zech. 2:6-13; 5:5-11; Rev. 14:8; 17; 18).[168]

Summary and application

Evil must be judged, and one day God will bring a final judgment to all of it. This truth should stir each believer to cleanse himself from the things he knows God hates, since these are the things that put Christ on the cross, and these are the things that bring wrath on the unsaved (Eph. 5:6-8).

JUDGMENT ON NATIONS: EDOM (21:11-12)

The next country singled out for judgment is Edom. Edom was to the south of Moab to the east of Israel.

God's oracle against Edom reads as follows: "11 The oracle concerning

---

[168] We must also note that this eschatological rise of Babylon appears to have elements that refer to both (1) a literal, geopolitical Babylon as well as (2) a figurative aspect that is somehow global and universal. With reference to the former aspect, we see that the literal elements are present (cf. Zech. 5:5-11; Rev. 16:12; , et al.). With reference to the latter aspect, we see other passages that are global and universal, especially in Revelation 17-18 as John describes "Mystery Babylon" (17:5) who sits on "many waters." However, unlike literal Babylon who sat on the many water canals of the Euphrates (cf. Jer. 51:13), the "many waters" on which "Mystery Babylon" sits are "peoples, multitudes, tongues and nations" (Rev. 17:1, 15).

Edom.[169] One keeps calling to me from Seir, Watchman, how far gone is the night? Watchman, how far gone is the night? 12 The watchman says, Morning comes but also night. If you would inquire, inquire, come back again" (21:11-12).

Edom is a country with an ancient history. Before making comments on Isaiah's oracle against Edom, we will first examine its history.

History of Edom

Edom's origin and character

Edom has its origin in Genesis, descending from Isaac's son Esau (Gen. 25:19-26). Esau was actually the firstborn twin brother of Jacob; however, during Rebekah's pregnancy God told Rebekah that the younger child would be the one through whom He would fulfill His promises (Gen. 25:23). Esau despised the promises of the Abrahamic covenant (Gen. 25:27-34) and showed dishonor to his parents with shameful living (Gen. 26:34-35; 27:46; Heb. 12:16-17), but God still allowed Esau to prosper and grow into a mighty nation.

Edom's location

Edom settled on the eastern side of the Jordan Valley (Gen. 36), east and southeast of the Dead Sea. Their northern border was the Brook Zered, and their southern border was the Brook of Egypt. Sometimes the name Seir is used for Edom. Mt. Seir was originally inhabited by a group called the Horites (Gen. 36:20-30), but they were eventually incorporated into the people of Esau (Gen. 36:40-43; 32:3; Num. 24:18; Judg. 5:4).

Edom's hostility to Israel

Because Esau was family to Israel, God told Israel not to wage war against Edom as they made their way to Canaan (Deut. 23:7-8). Despite Israel's kindness to Edom, Edom showed much enmity to Israel over the ages, an enmity God would not ignore (2 Sam. 8:14; 1 Kings 11:15; 2 Kings 14:7; 2 Chron. 20). Over time, the judgment of God on Edom came through enemy invasions that virtually wiped it out of existence (Mal. 1:1-4). These invasions came from the Assyrians, the Babylonians, the Arabians (Nabateans) and others. Isaiah's oracle speaks about their coming ruin (chs. 34 and 63 speak more about their doom).

---

[169] The MT reads "Dumah" ("silence") while the LXX reads "Edom." Even though there is a name called Dumah (Gen. 25:14; 1 Chron. 1:30; and Josh. 15:52) and a place called Dumah (250 miles east of Petra), Isaiah's use of this name appears to be a wordplay on the name Edom, for God will bring Edom to "silence." The LXX recognized that the oracle is about Edom, and used the actual name Edom.

The Oracle against Edom (vv. 11-12)

The fearful anticipations (v. 11)

The background of this oracle is the growing threat of Assyrian invasion. An unidentified voice calls out to the watchman how far gone the night is. The people of Edom see Assyria gaining dominion, and by this symbolic vision, God shows the uncertainty of Edom's future.

The bad news for Edom (v. 12)

The answer. The watchman (Isaiah) answers in verse 12: "Morning comes but also night. If you would inquire, inquire; come back again." Pfeiffer explains, "Isaiah, as the watchman, announces to the Edomites of Mount Seir that the morning of deliverance is breaking for Israel, but the night of defeat and bondage will soon fall upon Edom. Let the Edomites, therefore, seek Jehovah."[170]

The unfolding of God's message. Assyrian invasions started in 732 B.C., and Tiglath Pileser III made Kaush-malku his tributary. The tribute drained Edom to the point of poverty. In 604 B.C. Babylon gained lordship over Edom. Edom later joined with Babylon in 586 B.C. to invade Judah and help Babylon overthrow her brother Israel (Ps. 137:7; Lam. 4:21, 22). Eventually, Nabatean tribes overran Edom and forced the Edomites to migrate into Hebron and begin the Idumean people group which was eventually crushed by John Hyrcanus. Edom's future is not bright (Isa. 34; 63; Jer. 49; Ezek. 35), but there is always hope for those who turn to Christ (Amos 9:12; Obad. 19).

Summary and application

Once again, we are reminded about the truth that God judges sin. Edom was a relatively small player in terms of world powers, but this oracle reminds us that all men and all nations are accountable to God. We are also reminded that salvation can always be found by turning to the living God.

JUDGMENT ON NATIONS: ARABIA (21:13-17)

Arabia is the target of Isaiah's next oracle. Arabia is another ancient people group with origins from the early days of Genesis.

Isaiah's message against Arabia reads as follow: "13 The oracle about Arabia. In the thickets of Arabia you must spend the night, O caravans of

---

[170] Pfeiffer, *The Wycliffe Bible Commentary: Old Testament*, Is 21:11.

Dedanites. 14 Bring water for the thirsty, O inhabitants of the land of Tema, meet the fugitive with bread. 15 For they have fled from the swords, from the drawn sword, and from the bent bow and from the press of battle. 16 For thus the Lord said to me, In a year, as a hired man would count it, all the splendor of Kedar will terminate; 17 and the remainder of the number of bowmen, the mighty men of the sons of Kedar, will be few, for the Lord God of Israel has spoken" (21:13-17).

Arabia has a very ancient history with a great future that awaits it. We will first present a concise history of Arabia before making comments about Isaiah's oracle.

History of Arabia

The people of Arabia find their roots in the earliest stages of human history. We will first look at the origin of the Arab people groups and then see where they are located at geographically.

Origins of the Arab people groups

Most scholars recognize Ishmael, the son of Abraham and Hagar, as one of the key progenitors of the Arab world (Gen. 16). During Hagar's pregnancy, the Angel of the Lord indicated that Ishmael would grow up to be a "wild donkey of a man," i.e., one who was inclined to conflict (Gen. 16:12). Ishmael and Hagar fled to this eastern region when Abraham sent them away, but this was also the region to where the descendants of Keturah later migrated (Gen. 25). Even though Isaac was the son of promise (Gen. 21:12), God nevertheless promised Abraham that He would raise up twelve princes out of Ishmael and make him into a great nation (Gen. 17:15-21; 25:12-18: Nebaioth, Kedar, Abdeel, Mibsam, Mishma, Dumah, Massa, Hadad, Tema, Jetur, Naphish, and Kedemah). The Arab world had many other elements of intermarriage to make it what it is today, including other descendants of Abraham through Keturah (Gen. 25:1-4), descendants of Esau (Gen. 28:8-9), and other descendants of Ham.

Geography of Arabia

Arabia lies to the east and south of Israel. Arabia is a massive peninsula east of the Red Sea (some 1200 by 600 miles). In terms of borders, Arabia is a land mass whose northern border reaches to Israel, whose southern border is the Arabian Sea, whose north-eastern border is Mesopotamia, whose western border is the Red Sea, and whose eastern border is the Persian Gulf. The modern nation is called Saudi Arabia. This entire part of the world has been dominated by Islam since its rise in seventh century A.D., but prior to this, various forms of polytheism dominated the land. With regard to Islam, it is very interesting how this religion has come to dominate the Arab world. In this section, Isaiah declares that Arabia will eventually be judged for its sin.

The oracle against Arabia (vv. 13-17)

Arabia sat on the southern edge of Edom. This region was sometimes spoken of simply as the land to the east. Here in verses 13-17, Isaiah gives us two descriptions of Arabia's judgment.

First description of Arabia's judgment (vv. 13-15)

Just as experienced by other nations, Arabia (three particular cities highlighted) will also be forced to flee from Assyrian invaders (v. 13).[171] They will be forced into the wilderness where they will have no food or water (v. 14), but that will be better than being slain by the invaders (v. 15). Young explains, "Caravans that were able to travel undisturbed in normal conditions and times would now have to leave the main road and lie in hiding."[172] Invasions began under Tiglath-Pileser III (732 B.C.) and grew under Sargon II (726 B.C).[173]

Second description of Arabia's judgment (vv. 16-17)

These invasions will come in one year and bring an end to the glory of Kedar (v. 16).[174] Arabian bowmen, as good as they were, would be no match for the Assyrians, for God has said this is what will happen (v. 17).[175] Assyria fulfilled the purposes of Yahweh exactly as predicted.

---

[171] Dedan, Tema, and Kedar are mentioned several times in the OT (Isa. 21:16-17; 42:11; 60:7; cf. Gen. 10:7; 25:3; Jer. 2:10; 49:8; Ezek. 25:13; 27:21; 1 Chron. 1:9; Job 6:19; Ps. 120:5; Song 1:5). Dedan and Tema were both located in a region called Kedar (Oswalt, *The Book of Isaiah, 1-39*, 400). Kedar was the second son born to Ishmael (Gen. 25:13) and one of the 12 princes who formed one particular tribe in Arabia (Joseph A. Alexander, *Commentary on Isaiah* [Grand Rapids: Kregel, 1992], 378). The use of Kedar here is probably a general use of Kedar for all Arabia and not the specific tribe (cf. Isa. 42:11; 60:7; Jer. 2:10 [Grogan, "Isaiah," 138, n. 16]). Of special interest is the fact that Nabonidus of Babylon (556-539) left his son Belshazzar to rule Babylon around 553 B.C. and spent the remainder of his time living in the oasis city of Tema.

[172] Young, *The Book of Isaiah, vol. 2*, 79-80.

[173] Wolf, *Interpreting Isaiah*, 129.

[174] The idea "as a hired man would count it" speaks about the idea of a strict accounting of time.

[175] A relief from the palace wall of Ashurbanipal in Nineveh (7th century) depicts the

Summary and application

Whatever God says in His Word is true. This is a message every man should believe and apply. If God says it is sin, it is sin. If He says He judges sin, we know that He will judge sin. If He says He will forgive us if we trust in His Son, we can also be sure that He will do just as He said.

JUDGMENT ON NATIONS: JERUSALEM (22:1-25)

Chapters 1-12 were dominated by messages of judgment against Judah. God has another message for Judah here in chapter 22.

The oracle against Jerusalem reads as follows: "1 The oracle concerning the valley of vision. What is the matter with you now, that you have all gone up to the housetops? 2 You who were full of noise, you boisterous town, you exultant city, your slain were not slain with the sword, nor did they die in battle. 3 All your rulers have fled together, *and* have been captured without the bow; all of you who were found were taken captive together, though they had fled far away. 4 Therefore I say, turn your eyes away from me; let me weep bitterly; do not try to comfort me concerning the destruction of the daughter of my people. 5 For the Lord God of hosts has a day of panic, subjugation and confusion in the valley of vision, a breaking down of walls and a crying to the mountain. 6 Elam took up the quiver with the chariots, infantry *and* horsemen, and Kir uncovered the shield. 7 Then your choicest valleys were full of chariots, and the horsemen took up fixed positions at the gate, 8 and He removed the defense of Judah. In that day you depended on the weapons of the house of the forest, 9 and you saw that the breaches in the *wall* of the city of David were many, and you collected the waters of the lower pool. 10 Then you counted the houses of Jerusalem and tore down houses to fortify the wall, 11 and you made a reservoir between the two walls for the waters of the old pool. But you did not depend on Him who made it, nor did you take into consideration Him who planned it long ago. 12 Therefore in that day the Lord God of hosts called *you* to weeping, to wailing, to shaving the head and to wearing sackcloth. 13 Instead, there is gaiety and gladness, killing of cattle and slaughtering of sheep, eating of meat and drinking of wine: Let us eat and drink, for tomorrow we may die. 14 But the Lord of hosts revealed Himself to me, surely this iniquity shall not be forgiven you until you die, says the Lord God of hosts. 15 Thus says the Lord God of hosts, come, go to this steward, to Shebna, who is in charge of the *royal* household. 16 What right do you have here, and whom do you have here, that you have hewn a tomb for yourself here, you who hew a tomb on the height, you who carve a resting place for yourself in the rock? 17 Behold, the Lord is

---

infantry and cavalry of Assyria pursuing Arabs fleeing on camelback, with each camel holding two men, one guiding with a stick and one armed with a bow.

about to hurl you headlong, O man, and He is about to grasp you firmly 18 *and* roll you tightly like a ball, *to be cast* into a vast country; there you will die and there your splendid chariots will be, you shame of your master's house. 19 I will depose you from your office, and I will pull you down from your station. 20 Then it will come about in that day, that I will summon My servant Eliakim the son of Hilkiah, 21 And I will clothe him with your tunic and tie your sash securely about him. I will entrust him with your authority, and he will become a father to the inhabitants of Jerusalem and to the house of Judah. 22 Then I will set the key of the house of David on his shoulder, when he opens no one will shut, when he shuts no one will open. 23 I will drive him *like* a peg in a firm place, and he will become a throne of glory to his father's house. 24 So they will hang on him all the glory of his father's house, offspring and issue, all the least of vessels, from bowls to all the jars. 25 In that day, declares the Lord of hosts, the peg driven in a firm place will give way; it will even break off and fall, and the load hanging on it will be cut off, for the Lord has spoken" (22:1-25).

Of all nations, Israel has had the greatest of spiritual privileges, for it was Israel whom God chose to be His own covenant nation, and they are the ones through whom God chose to bring redemption to the world (Gen. 12:1-3; Rom. 9:1-5). Israel's election also carried with it a greater accountability to obey God (Amos 3:2). Covenant blessings would come through faith and obedience (Deut. 28:1-14), but curses would come from disobedience (Deut. 28:15-68). Chapter 22 once again focuses on the judgments caused by covenant disobedience. The four sections of chapter 22 show that judgment must come, but they also show that there is hope for a final restoration. The need is to trust the Lord, and in Him alone.

First message to Judah: The fall of Judah (vv. 1-3)

There is a question about the immediate historical context of this chapter.[176] In this writer's opinion, it seems reasonable to date this oracle at the same time as the events we see in chapters 36-37 (ca. 701 B.C.).[177] However, even

---

[176] Some place it during the days of Hezekiah (729-686 B.C.) especially around 711 B.C. when Sargon made attacks against Ashdod; others would place these events around the time of Sennacherib's invasion in 701 B.C.; others (Young, Clements) would place these events around 586 B.C.

[177] Oswalt, *The Book of Isaiah, 1-39*, 407. Oswalt notes that this appears to be the majority opinion. Some of the supports for this view include the following: Hezekiah had made wall and water preparations and was ready for invasion (2 Chron. 32:1-5). There was general destruction but not total overthrow. There may have been mercenary troops who fled. Even though there was a degree of outward change in Hezekiah's

though Isaiah's initial comments revolve around the Assyrian defeat (in 701 B.C.), it appears that this vision also reveals future events that would come upon Jerusalem over 100 years later with the Babylonian invasions and conquest that would extend until 539 B.C.

There is also a question about the meaning of this expression "Valley of Vision." The word "vision" probably refers to visions which Isaiah has been receiving from God, and the term "valley" may be referring to the fact that Jerusalem was surrounded by several valleys, the Kidron, the Tyropean, and the Hinnom. It may be that God was giving this vision to Isaiah from his location right on the edge of the city, perhaps from the Kidron Valley which sat on the eastern edge of the temple mount. Jerusalem rejoiced over the fall of Assyria, but it was an inappropriate rejoicing since it was not accompanied by a true, national repentance.

Inappropriate rejoicing (vv. 1-2a)

God asks the people of Jerusalem why they have gone up onto the housetops. It may be that the people of Jerusalem were looking out in the horizon to see how the battle was faring. Humanly speaking, it did not look good for Jerusalem.[178] Assuming a date of 701 B.C., we know that God struck down 185,000 Assyrian soldiers in that year (Isa. 36-37; 1 Kings 19:35). If this is the background, it could be that the city had begun to rejoice when they saw the overthrow of the enemy (cf. vv. 12-13). Jerusalem rejoiced over its deliverance, but unfortunately it was a city in whom there was no repentance, a city of continual tumult, and revelry (cf. 5:11-12; 32:13).[179]

Death, but not by sword (vv. 2b-3)

The interpretation of this passage continues to be difficult. What does it mean that the people did not die by the violence of war? Does this mean that they died by some other means like starvation (cf. e.g., Lam. 4:9 and the starvation that came during the Babylonian siege)? We know that the eventual fall of Jerusalem in 586 B.C. was one characterized by great starvation.[180] For this

---

day, it really was only superficial. Mention of Shebna and Eliakim places this during the days of Hezekiah.
[178] Sennacherib's war annals told how Assyria had subjugated 46 walled cities of Judah and how the armies had Jerusalem surrounded in a mighty siege.
[179] Ibid., 409.
[180] Young, *The Book of Isaiah, vol. 2*, 90. Jerusalem did experience horrific starvation in the Babylonian siege (2 Kings 25:3; Jer. 25:6; Lam. 1:19, 20; 2:12, 19; 4:3-5, 9, 10;

reason, some see certain events as being fulfilled later during the Babylonian siege. This much is clear: Jerusalem has been faithless and is continuing to be faithfulness, and at this point her real need was repentance. Kidner explains,

> There is a clear contrast between the city's gaiety (2a, 13) and its grim future. It is not so clear whether the revels are in progress as Isaiah speaks (perhaps after the retreat of Sennacherib; 37:37) or whether we should supply a past verb in v 2a: 'you who were full ...', as in the lament of 1:21. Either way, Isaiah alone sees where this escapism ... will end.[181]

Verse 3 indicates that the failure of Jerusalem to trust in the Lord would lead to ultimate ruin. The capture of fleeing rulers sounds similar to what happened during the Babylonian siege when Zedekiah and his house tried to flee (2 Kings 25:4-7). On the other hand, these events may have been fulfilled during Sargon's attack on Ashdod in 711 B.C.[182]

In terms of worthless leaders, a look at the history of Judah in the eighth and seventh centuries B.C. shows us that many her leaders were godless men who cared only for themselves (1:23; 3:2; 5:13; 7:2; 28:7, 14; 29:15; cf. Mic. 2:1ff.; 3:1ff., 9-12).[183] Clearly, great misery is coming upon Judah.

Second message to Judah: The misery over Judah (vv. 4-11)

Isaiah pleads for the people to turn away, for he cannot bear to have people gazing on his sorrow, and he wants no comfort him for the coming destruction (v. 4).[184] Verses 5-11 show us three reasons for Isaiah's misery.

First reason for misery: A hoard of invaders have arrived (vv. 5-7)

God's judgment will come through a hoard of invaders bringing panic, subjugation, and confusion (v. 5).[185] Elam had become an ally with Babylon to fight against Assyria, and we see them here as part of the invading forces along

---

5:10), a judgment Moses predicted (Lev. 26:25; 26:29; Deut. 28:21, 48, 52). This interpretation would probably change our view of what Isaiah was predicting.

[181] Kidner, "Isaiah," 646.

[182] Oswalt, *The Book of Isaiah, 1-39*, 408.

[183] What they should have been doing was trusting God (Isa. 30:15; Jer. 17:5-6).

[184] This specific expression "daughter of my people" is found only here and represents the people of Israel as a beloved daughter who has gone astray (Isa. 47:1; Jer. 8:12; Lam. 1:8-9; 2:13; Amos 5:2; Mic. 1:13 [Grogan, "Isaiah," 403, n. 4]).

[185] The three terms come with terrifying alliteration and assonance: *Mehumah, Mebusah, Mebukah.*

with another Babylonian ally called Kir (v. 6).[186] The result was a massive force that completely overran the land of Israel (v. 7). Isaiah is overcome with the sorrow of seeing his homeland ravaged.

Second reason for misery: No preparation can help (vv. 8-11a)

Judah tried to defend itself against the invaders, but it would all be to no avail, for Yahweh is the One who "removed the defense of Judah."[187] Isaiah exposes four sources of false trust in the people of Judah.

First false hope (v. 8). The "House of the Forest" was a weapons storage facility (1 Kings 7:2-6; 10:17; Isa. 39:2). Trust in weapons would be no help.

Second false hope (v. 9). Walls were falling, so the people sought to collect water to hold off the invaders. None of it would save them.[188]

Third false hope (v. 10). The people knew that the city walls were vulnerable, so they tore down houses so they could fortify (*batsar*) the walls. All of it would be a futile effort to stave off the wrath of God.[189]

Fourth false hope (v. 11a). Isaiah says, "you made a reservoir between

---

[186] Wolf, *Interpreting Isaiah*, 130. Kir appears to be located in Aram (Amos 1:5; 9:7). Some identify "Kir" with Kuros, the name of a river rising in the Caucasus, and emptying into the Caspian Sea (Alexander, *Commentary on Isaiah*, 381-382). This Kir was subject to Assyria at this time as seen by the fact that Assyria exported people from the 10 tribes into this area.

[187] The term "defense" (*masak*) is like a veil or curtain (Isa. 47:2; Nah. 3:5; Lam. 1:8). Jerusalem will now be fully exposed.

[188] If the proper understanding of these events goes back to the Assyrian invasions of 701 B.C. (which is possible), these preparations could be explained by the preparations of Hezekiah when he made a tunnel and a new pool from the Gihon spring to a place inside the city walls (2 Kings 20:20; 2 Chron. 32:1-5). Oswalt says that the Old, or Upper Pool was the one which had been built earlier at Gihon to capture the water of the spring (Isa. 7:3; 36:2; 2 Kings 18:17). The Lower Pool was one which had been constructed by Ahaz at the foot of the Tyropean Valley and was incorporated by Hezekiah in the larger construction related to the reservoir between the walls—the Pool of Siloam (Oswalt, *The Book of Isaiah, 1-39*, 413). The exact location of the lower pool is not certain. Alexander thinks it is the reservoir still in existence in the Valley of Hinnom (Alexander, *Commentary on Isaiah*, 383).

[189] The evidence for this is available today in the Old City where the author has seen below the top levels how the expanded city wall ran right through some existing houses (2 Chron. 32:5).

the two walls for the waters of the old pool." If these events are taking place in the days of Hezekiah rather than the later Babylonian invasions, this could refer to The Pool of Siloam which was located between a pair of walls.

Third reason for misery: Judah did not trust in the Lord (v. 11b)

The root problem was that Judah did not trust the Lord: "But you did not depend on Him who made it, nor did you take into consideration Him who planned it long ago." God is the One who "made" and "formed" "it" (fem. suffix, prob. the plan). This lack of faith would cost Judah greatly.

Third message to Judah: The unrepentance of Judah (vv. 12-14)

The solution was to repent of her sin and trust in the Lord. This is the true need, but sadly Judah had no desire to do so.

The need for repentance and faith (v. 12)

God's command was repentance, a genuine kind of repentance that was often characterized by weeping, wailing, the shaving of the head, and the wearing of sackcloth. Outward actions were not the real issue, though, but genuine repentance and genuine faith were. This is the kind of repentance Joel spoke about: "Rend your heart and not your garments. Now return to the Lord your God" (Joel 2:13; cf. Isa. 32:11-13; Amos 8:10; Mal. 1:8-11; Ps. 51:15-19).

The lack of repentance and faith (vv. 13-14)

The command was there, but the righteous response was not. Isaiah explains two basic problems.

A party spirit (v. 13). The people of Judah did not see their need, so instead of turning to God they turned to revelry. They knew it was a desperate situation, but their attitude was, "Let us eat and drink, for tomorrow we may die."

God's anger (v. 14). This lack of repentance angered God all the more. Therefore, there will be no remedy except death, a judgment announced with an oath formula (*'im* . . .). The sense of the oath would be something like, "Surely this iniquity will not be expiated for you until you die" (cf. Isa. 14:24; Deut. 1:34; Jer. 22:6). Martin notes, "They did not believe God was powerful enough to save them and to follow through on His promises. Therefore, a pronouncement of woe came to the people."[190] There was hope for Judah, but that hope was only in the promised Son of David.

Fourth message to Judah: The hope of Judah (vv. 15-25)

Judah's selfish faithlessness is exemplified through one particular man named Shebna.[191] Shebna characterized the faithless leaders of the land (vv. 15-19), but God's promise to Isaiah was that one day He would bring in One who would faithfully bring salvation to His people Israel (vv. 20-25).

The faithless man Shebna (vv. 15-19)

The call to visit Shebna (v. 15). God commands Isaiah to go visit a man named Shebna, the steward of the House of David (v. 15). Shebna held a high position in the royal court,[192] but he was not a man of God, and certainly not one whom God esteemed. Kidner explains,

> Every nuance in God's message to him is scornful, from *this steward* (15) to *you disgrace* (18). It exposes the human craving for recognition and power and the worldly love of status symbols (*grave* and *chariots*) and the trappings of office, all of them mere husks. A large tomb-lintel of just such an official, describing him as 'over the house' (*cf.* v 15), has been found at Siloam and could be Shebna's; but a mortice hole has destroyed the name.[193]

The problem here is that Shebna was a man of high position, but his focus was only on himself and not the Lord or His people. The absence of any mention of his father's name could suggest that he might have even been a foreigner, perhaps an Egyptian (cf. Isa. 28:14-15; 30:1-5).

God rebukes Shebna for his sinful selfishness (v. 16). God challenges his right to be where he is, especially as one who is hewing out a fresh tomb in the royal city. Shebna is a man who wanted an eternal dwelling place (a tomb) with the kings of David (cf. 2 Chron. 16:14). This, however, was not his right since he was not of the House of David. His attitude showed great disregard

---

[190] Martin, "Isaiah," 1070.

[191] Wolf, *Interpreting Isaiah*, 131.

[192] The term "steward" is not exactly clear since it is a hapax in this exact form (but cf. 1 Kings 1:2, 4; 16:9; 18:3; 2 Kings 15:5; Job 15:3; 22:2; 34:4; 35:3; Isa. 40:20 where the "service" idea is part of the root). Cognate terms in other languages indicate that it was a very high official government position, perhaps only second to the king himself (Oswalt, *The Book of Isaiah, 1-39*, 418).

[193] Kidner, "Isaiah," 646.

for Judah during this time of invasion. God saw the selfish faithlessness of this man, and would judge him.

God declares his complete rejection of Shebna (vv. 17-19). Not only will God reject Shebna,[194] and remove him from his office, but He will also cast him from the land of Judah (vv. 17-18a). Shebna the man of shame will die in a foreign land, perhaps Assyria or Egypt (v. 18b), and God will remove him (v. 19).[195]

Judah's hope in God's chosen man (vv. 20-25)

Eliakim is going to replace faithless Shebna. Eliakim is also going to serve as a type who foreshadows Messiah, the One who will be perfectly faithful.

The messianic hints in God's chosen one (v. 20). Isaiah first hints at the messianic/eschatological nature of God's work by announcing this section with the words "in that day" (*bayyom hahu'*). Furthermore, the Lord speaks approvingly of Eliakim by calling him "My servant."[196]

The glory of God's chosen one (v. 21). God will take the glory and authority that he stripped from faithless Shebna, and He will place it all upon His servant Eliakim,[197] a man of high authority over the people of God.

The high authority of God's chosen one (v. 22). The high authority is further emphasized by God giving Eliakim "the key of the house of David," the key representing authority over the entire household. Young explains:

Just as the master possesses the key to that house, and has complete

---

[194] The expression "hurl" combines a Pilpel participle of the verb *tul* and a cognate noun *taltelah* to emphatically express God's complete rejection of Shebna. Likewise, the expression "grasp" combines a participle and infinitive absolute of the verb *'atah* to expression the intensity of how God would "grasp" Shebna. Thirdly, the expression "roll tightly" combines an infinitive absolute, followed by an Imperfect form of verb followed by a noun all from the root *tsanaph*. The language is extremely intense.

[195] Later verses indicate that by 701 B.C. Shebna had gotten demoted to what was at that time a lower office within the royal court, and Eliakim took his position (Isa. 36:3, 11, 22; 37:2; 2 Kings 18:18, 26, 37). Apparently Shebna was exiled after this initial demotion.

[196] Of special interest are those four sections of Isaiah which speak very directly about the promised Son of God whom God addresses as the Servant (Isa. 42:1-9; 49:1-13; 50:4-11; 52:13-53:12).

[197] This includes Shebna's tunic (in Exod. 28:4 this term applies to the priest's garments), and also his sash.

authority with respect to permitting anyone to enter or to leave, and so entire authority over the house, so God will give to Eliakim a key to the house or dynasty of David [cf. Matt. 16:19].[198]

God is granting His servant Eliakim great authority over the entire House of David and the entire land of Judah,[199] a kind of authority that foreshadows the Messiah as we learn in the New Testament. In other words, just as God gave Eliakim authority to open or shut the royal house, the Messiah will give authority to believers to entire into the messianic kingdom (Rev. 3:7-8).

The permanence of God's chosen one (vv. 23-24). When God says that He will drive Eliakim like a peg in a firm place, this conveys the idea of stability and permanence.[200] The God-given glory will never pass away.

The typological nature of God's chosen one (v. 25). Eliakim was a faithful man chosen by God, but even he is not permanent, for all of this ultimately points to the Son of David.[201] God announces that when He brings judgment on the House of David (through Babylon), this man too would lose his position of prominence as God brings justice to His royal house. Nothing temporal, not even a faithful man like Eliakim, was of any eternal hope. Our only true hope is in God's Son, the Lord Jesus Christ.

Summary and application

Isaiah's prophecies once again remind us that there is only one real hope, and that is Jesus Christ. Christ's promise is that He is the One who opens, and no one can close (Rev. 3:7-8). If you trust in Him, God will give you entrance into the kingdom, and no one can ever take that away.

JUDGMENT ON NATIONS: TYRE (23:1-18)

Chapter 23 brings us to the final oracle of this section—an oracle against Tyre. With the exception of chapter 22 that was directed against Judah, all of the oracles in chapters 13-23 were directed against the Gentiles. Chapter 23 now turns back to the last pagan nation, Tyre.

---

[198] Young, *The Book of Isaiah, vol. 2*, 114.

[199] Oswalt, *The Book of Isaiah, 1-39*, 422.

[200] Some think that this may refer to the big pole in the center of the tent that holds the tent up (Judg. 4:22). Others think it is a peg driven into a wall. It is possible that this is the center pole driven into firm ground from where belongings would hang (Ezra 9:8; Zech. 10:4).

[201] As Wolf explains, "Eliakim's effectiveness was only temporary at best" (Wolf, *Interpreting Isaiah*, 132).

Chapter 23 reads as follows: "1 The oracle concerning Tyre. Wail, O ships of Tarshish, for *Tyre* is destroyed, without house *or* harbor; it is reported to them from the land of Cyprus. 2 Be silent, you inhabitants of the coastland, you merchants of Sidon; your messengers crossed the sea 3 And *were* on many waters. The grain of the Nile, the harvest of the River was her revenue, and she was the market of nations. 4 Be ashamed, O Sidon, for the sea speaks, the stronghold of the sea, saying, I have neither travailed nor given birth, I have neither brought up young men *nor* reared virgins. 5 When the report *reaches* Egypt, they will be in anguish at the report of Tyre. 6 Pass over to Tarshish; wail, O inhabitants of the coastland. 7 Is this your jubilant *city* whose origin is from antiquity, whose feet used to carry her to colonize distant places? 8 Who has planned this against Tyre, the bestower of crowns, whose merchants were princes, whose traders were the honored of the earth? 9 The Lord of hosts has planned it, to defile the pride of all beauty, to despise all the honored of the earth. 10 Overflow your land like the Nile, O daughter of Tarshish. There is no more restraint. 11 He has stretched His hand out over the sea; He has made the kingdoms tremble; the Lord has given a command concerning Canaan to demolish its strongholds. 12 He has said, You shall exult no more, O crushed virgin daughter of Sidon. Arise, pass over to Cyprus; even there you will find no rest. 13 Behold, the land of the Chaldeans—this is the people *which* was not; Assyria appointed it for desert creatures—they erected their siege towers, they stripped its palaces, they made it a ruin. 14 Wail, O ships of Tarshish, for your stronghold is destroyed. 15 Now in that day Tyre will be forgotten for seventy years like the days of one king. At the end of seventy years it will happen to Tyre as *in* the song of the harlot: 16 Take *your* harp, walk about the city, O forgotten harlot, pluck the strings skillfully, sing many songs that you may be remembered. 17 It will come about at the end of seventy years that the Lord will visit Tyre. Then she will go back to her harlot's wages and will play the harlot with all the kingdoms on the face of the earth. 18 Her gain and her harlot's wages will be set apart to the Lord; it will not be stored up or hoarded, but her gain will become sufficient food and choice attire for those who dwell in the presence of the Lord" (23:1-18).

It is interesting that Tyre was not a powerful, tyrannical empire like Assyria or Babylon, but still she was also given a judgment oracle. Why is this? The answer is that the people of Tyre were sinners like all other men, and as such they were accountable to a holy God.[202] What made Tyre especially notable was her fabulous wealth and prosperity from her vast maritime, commercial activities. Wolf explains,

---

[202] Thus, God's focus on Tyre was not due to relentless imperialistic warfare, but obsessive pre-occupation with wealth and commercial activity. The message for application is that we must not trust in anything other than the Lord God.

Because of their excellent harbors and seamanship, the Phoenician cities of Tyre and Sidon had carved a commercial empire far beyond that which their size deserved. Tyre was the "Babylon" of the sea, and Revelation 18 seems to combine some of the qualities of ancient Babylon and Tyre to portray the commercial "Babylon" of end times.[203]

This entire section (chs. 13-23) opened with an oracle against the great city at the eastern edges of the world (Babylon), and closes with an oracle against the great city at the western edges of the world (Tyre).[204] We will introduce our study of Tyre by first looking at its history.

History of Tyre

Tyre was an ancient Canaanite city

Tyre and Sidon were ancient Canaanite cities on the Mediterranean coast. Tyre was about 35 miles north of Mt. Carmel, and Sidon was about another 20 miles north of Tyre. Our first biblical reference to these peoples (Tyre/Sidon) comes in Genesis 10:15 where we see that Sidon was the son of Canaan (the one who had been cursed by Noah in Genesis 9:25). These Canaanite settlements began soon after the scattering of the nations at the Tower of Babel around 2357 B.C. As noted by one historian,

> Sidon and Tyre were ancient cities, having been founded long before the Israelites entered the land of Canaan. Extrabiblical sources first mention Sidon before 2000 b.c. and Tyre just after 2000 b.c. While Sidon seems to have been the more dominant of the two cities during the early part of their histories, Tyre assumed this role in the latter times. Both cities were known for their maritime exploits and as centers of trade. One of Tyre's most coveted exports was purple dye.[205]

Tyre had a unique existence with two cities

Tyre had one city on both the mainland (city called Palwetyrus) and a second seaport city on two rocky islands just off the coast (cf. Ezek. 28:2). King

---

[203] Ibid., 132-133. The clear emphasis on Babylon in chapter 18 is upon the end of Babylon as the center of godless commercialism (vv. 9-20). These descriptions seem to follow the OT descriptions of Tyre as seen in Isaiah 23 and Ezekiel 26-28.
[204] Oswalt, *The Book of Isaiah, 1-39*, 427.
[205] Scott Langston, "Sidon and Tyre," ed. Chad Brand et al., *Holman Illustrated Bible Dictionary*, cited in electronic form with Logos Libronix (Nashville, TN: Holman Bible Publishers, 2003), 1499.

Hiram was the one who connected the two islands with an embankment and also brought water to the larger island. The two cities gave them a strategic location for commerce as well as a good place of refuge in times of mainland invasions.

Early relations with Israel

Although God's command for Israel was to drive out every trace of the Canaanites from the land (Exod. 33:2; Deut. 20:16-17), Israel did not succeed in fully carrying out God's commands (Josh. 13:3-4). If we fast-forward 400 years from Joshua, we see that King David had a good friendship with King Hiram of Tyre, and Hiram even supplied skilled workers and cedar trees for the temple (2 Sam. 5:11). Ahab (ca. 870 B.C.) did great evil by marrying the Canaanite princess Jezebel, and these two wicked people were responsible for bringing widespread Baal worship into the northern kingdom.

Until the strong westward expansions of Assyria in the eighth century B.C., Tyre had been allowed to do its own thing and become very prosperous.[206] It was Sennacherib (705-701 B.C.) who brought an end to this period of relatively undisturbed commerce and prosperity. There is some scholarly debate about which specific judgments Isaiah is speaking about here in chapter 23.[207]

The oracle against Tyre (vv. 1-18)

Tyre had enjoyed ages of great prosperity and ease, but she did so with no reverence to the living God. Isaiah's oracle announces that the days of gaiety were about to come to an end, an end that began coming even in the days of Isaiah. Martin explains,

> As in the other prophecies (chaps. 13–22) this one about Tyre also pertains to the Assyrian aggression at the end of the eighth century b.c. Though Tyre was not destroyed until some 200 years later, the trade of this great city was cut off between about 700 and 630 b.c.[208]

---

[206] Grogan, "Isaiah," 146.

[207] The possibilities are (1) invasions under Sennacherib in 705-701 (the preferred view), (2) invasions under Esarhaddon (679-671), (3) invasions under Nebuchadnezzar (585-573), (4) invasions under Artaxerxes III Ochus (343), or (5) invasions under Alexander (ca. 332). Alexander destroyed the coastal city then used the rubble to build a causeway reaching the two islands (Oswalt, *The Book of Isaiah, 1-39*, 428).

[208] Martin, "Isaiah," 1070–1071.

Tyre will be judged (vv. 1-14), but this will not include a complete annihilation. One day she will find rest from her invaders (vv. 15-18).

The overthrow of Tyre (vv. 1-14)

Nebuchadnezzar was the first invader to actually conquer the mainland city, but prior to this the armies of Assyria had exacted heavy tribute from these coastland cities. Isaiah describes these invasions in verses 1-14 as being part of the work of Yahweh. This divides into four calls to wail.

A first call for wailing (v. 1). God's judgment on Tyre begins with a call to wail.[209] Just who are these ships of Tarshish? There is some debate about the location of Tarshish but, as noted by Oswalt, history gives us enough basis for saying that it refers to "Tartessus on the Guadalquivir in Spain. Phoenician colonies in this area are reported to have existed as early as the twelfth century B.C."[210] The "ships of Tarshish" were large trading ships that originated in Tyre (Albright saw them as "ore" ships) and traveled on the open sea carrying out huge commercial shipping ventures (1 Kings 10:22; 22:48; Ps. 48:7; Isa. 2:16; 23:14; 60:9; Ezek. 27:25; Jonah 1:3).[211] The reason why the ships of Tarshish are to wail is because Tyre has been destroyed and her harbors are in ruins. These ships heading back to Tyre from the western parts of the Mediterranean have now been told from messengers at Kittim (Cyprus, Gen. 10:4) that they Tyre has fallen under God's judgment, and they are not going to be able to return home. This is terrible news for Tyre.

A second call for wailing (vv. 2-3). The inhabitants of the coastland are commanded to "be silent."[212] As we have already seen, the "coastland(s)" refers to entire Mediterranean world which lay to the west of Israel.[213] These are the ones who have been the "merchants" (*socher*) of Sidon (Isa. 23:3, 18; 45:14; Ezek. 27:12-21; Prov. 3:14; 31:18). Sidon is brought into the picture because anything that happens to Tyre is surely going to happen to Sidon as well (v. 2). God is

---

[209] Even though the command is given to the ships (feminine), the verb agrees according to sense and is masculine plural.
[210] Oswalt, *The Book of Isaiah, 1-39*, 429.
[211] Tarshish (Spain) at the western edge of the Mediterranean world was very rich in minerals like silver (Jer. 10:9) and iron, and tin, and lead (Ezek. 27:12), and all these riches made her a wonderful trade partner for Tyre.
[212] Textual critics suggest that the term "be silent" may actually be better understood as a term that means "to mourn" (Oswalt, *The Book of Isaiah, 1-39*, 430, n. 23).
[213] Cf. Isa. 11:11; 13:22; 20:6; 23:2, 6; 24:15; 34:14; 40:15; 41:1, 5; 42:4, 10, 12, 15; 49:1; 50:1; 51:5; 59:18; 60:5; 66:1, 19.

judging the Phoenician coast, and none will be exempt.[214] God has brought an end to shipping of Mediterranean goods like Egyptian wheat, so the only appropriate response is mourning (v. 3).[215]

A third call for wailing (vv. 4-5). If Tyre is doomed to fall, so is her sister city Sidon, twenty miles up the coast. Isaiah commands Sidon to be ashamed because Assyria would leave none un-touched. Up to this time, Sidon had never experienced this kind of violation, so Isaiah describes her as one who has never travailed nor given birth.[216] Despite scholarly debate about certain details, the point is clear: The destruction and death of Tyre will be as a total loss, a frequent picture in Isaiah (7:14; 8:3; 9:6; 17:1-2; 26:16-18; 37:3; 44:3-5; 45:10, 11; 47:8; 49:21; 54:1; 66:9). The impact to the Mediterranean world will be so great that Egypt will be in anguish (v. 5). If Tyre has suffered, surely they will be next.

A fourth call for wailing (vv. 6-14). Verse 6 may be saying that the people of Tyre are going to have to flee from the wrath of Assyria, but some think this may find fulfillment in later centuries. History tells us that several hundred years later during the siege of Alexander, the Tyrians "sent their children and old people to Carthage for safety, for at that time Carthage was probably a Tyrian colony."[217] This much is clear: Tyre will come to ruins.[218] Why? Isaiah answers in 8-14: This is the judgment of Yahweh as seen three times in verses 8-14.[219]

Isaiah's first declaration that this is the work of Yahweh comes in 8-9. Isaiah rhetorically asks who could bring such devastation against the bestower of crowns,[220] and then he answers his own question. It is Yahweh of Israel (cf. Isa. 14:27; 19:23). Once again, we see Isaiah's use of the term for "plan" (*ya'ats*), the term he has repeatedly used to emphasize the sovereignty of God over

---

[214] The transporters were oftentimes the brokers. Thus, all got affected, the producers, the shippers, and the brokers.
[215] "Grain [seed] of the Nile" comes from a word *shihor*, a word which may mean "black" as in reference to the muddy black water (cf. Jer. 2:18; Josh. 13:3).
[216] Young, *The Book of Isaiah, vol. 2*, 125.
[217] Ibid., 127.
[218] The Greek historian Herodotus died in 425 B.C., but claimed that the temple of Tyre was over 2000 years old. The Ugaritic Keret Epic reports that Keret made a special visit to the Tyrian Ashtoreth on his way to reclaim his wife, suggesting that a shrine existed there by 1350 B.C. (Oswalt, *The Book of Isaiah, 1-39*, 431, n. 29).
[219] Ibid., 432. Oswalt explains, "He, the God of a small country whose size is exceeded by many counties in the United States, is in fact God of the whole world, including mighty Tyre, and He will call her to account for her pride."
[220] Tyre's power to bring wealth to others (like modern-day America) made her a desirable ally.

human history (cf. e.g., Isa. 14:24, 26, 27; 19:27). The God of Israel is the author of all history, for history is actually the outworking of His plan and purpose.[221]

Isaiah's second declaration that this is the work of Yahweh comes in verses 10-11. Verse 10 has a degree of obscurity,[222] but within the flowing context the idea becomes clear: Tyre's economic lordship has been great, but soon it would end, for mighty Tyre would soon come to ruin.[223] How could such a mighty power come to naught? Pfeiffer explains, "Jehovah would be the author of this doom . . . which would serve as a judgment not only upon Tyre but upon the whole world view it represents."[224] Once again, the sovereignty of God shows itself in verse 11, for "He is the one who has put the nations into upheaval."[225] Yahweh is the One who "stretches out His hand" to exercise dominion (5:25; 10:4; 31:3). Thus, "No kingdom on its coasts could reckon itself immune from God's righteous wrath, and He is the One judging the people of Canaan."[226]

Isaiah's third declaration that this is the work of Yahweh comes in verses 12-14. Sidon, the "crushed virgin daughter" (used of Zion in 37:22 as one who had never been violated), will come to such ruin that the people will be forced to flee across the waters to Cyprus (as King Lulli of Sidon did), but not even here will they find rest from the relentless Assyrians (v. 12).[227] Resistance against Assyria would be futile if powerful Babylon could not resist them (v. 13). The attacks of Sargon (710) and Sennacherib (689) on Babylon brought it to naught, and it would take sixty-five years before they would eventually rise up under Nabopolassar and Nebuchadnezzar (v. 13).[228] Tyre and Sidon should recognize that they would not be able to stand. With a form of inclusio, Isaiah issues one final call for the people of Tyre to wail (v. 14). Tyre's stronghold fortress will be destroyed, and nothing will give them safety from the Assyrians. Things look dark, but Isaiah leaves a ray of good news that it will not be a total annihilation.

---

[221] One major purpose of God's work with Israel and the nations was to show that He is the sovereign God, and that no one should place their trust in anyone or anything but Him (Isa. 2:11, 17; 4:2, 5; 5:15-16; 13:19; 14:12-20; 28:1-6; 60:15).

[222] This could mean that there is "no more restraint," or it could mean, literally, that "there is no more girdle." Some take this as meaning that the "removal of girdle" looks at a total plunder of all possessions. Young thinks that the idea of "girdle" is "to symbolize the restraining force of Tyre" (Young, *The Book of Isaiah, vol. 2*, 131).

[223] Oswalt, *The Book of Isaiah, 1-39*, 433.

[224] Pfeiffer, *The Wycliffe Bible Commentary: Old Testament*, Is 23:1.

[225] Oswalt, *The Book of Isaiah, 1-39*, 434.

[226] Grogan, "Isaiah," 147.

[227] Oswalt, *The Book of Isaiah, 1-39*, 434.

[228] Wolf, *Interpreting Isaiah*, 134. The "desert creatures" (*tsiyim*) would be animals such as wild cats (Isa. 13:21; 23:13; 34:14; Jer. 50:39; Ps. 72:9).

The future of Tyre (vv. 15-18)

Prosperous Tyre will be brought to ruins, but that does not mean a total annihilation, for there will be a future after seventy years of ruin.[229] Nevertheless, Isaiah compares Tyre's latter prosperity to that of an old, undesirable prostitute who now must roam the streets singing her harlot's song to attract customers for her meager earnings (vv. 15-16).[230] The glory days will be gone for many ages.

Verse 17, however, indicates a brighter future after seventy years of dismal existence when the Lord will "visit" her and bring a degree of restoration after seventy hard years.[231] Following the ravages of the Assyrians and Babylonians, the Persians allowed Tyre to rebuild and grow, and later during the days of the Ptolemies, Tyre regained a level of autonomy.[232]

Verse 18 may be another one of those passages that takes the reader into the eschaton of the messianic kingdom. Verse 18 indicates that a day is coming when the prosperity of Tyre, i.e., her harlot's wages from godless commerce, will be "set apart to the Lord."[233] God's purpose in allowing Tyre to recover is ultimately so that all of this wealth might be brought to Yahweh Himself in His kingdom.

The Son of God, the One who redeemed all creation from the curse of sin and death by His vicarious sacrifice on Calvary's cross, is the One who will inherit His redeemed creation (Isa. 53:10-12; Col. 1:16; Heb. 1:1-3). When Jesus Christ brings His kingdom to this world, the surviving nations will retain their distinct identities, but all of them will belong to the King of Kings, for the

---

[229] This use of seventy years does not equate to the seventy years God appointed for Judah to be under Babylonian exile. Under the rise of the Persian empire (539 B.C.), Tyre did experience a slight amount of recovery, but never such as it was before. This could be like the expression "like 70 years of a hired man" (precise counting; cf. 16:14; 21:16). This idea is better than looking at 70 as some kind of allegorical or ideal number (Oswalt, *The Book of Isaiah, 1-39*, 435).

[230] In former times she was the young and desirable prostitute who did great trade with all the nations (cf. Nah. 3:4), but now she is old and must scrape by to attract a man.

[231] This verb "visit" (*phaqad*) is often used to mean "to punish," but it can also be used positively as here (Gen. 50:24, 25; Exod. 3:16-17; Ruth 1:6; Zech. 10:3).

[232] Ibid., 436.

[233] At a literal level, this was something forbidden in Law of Moses in the Old Testament (Deut. 23:18), but in the messianic kingdom all will be sanctified and set apart to Messiah (Zech. 14:20-21).

kingdom is the Lord's, and He rules over the nations (Isa. 4:2; 60:1-14; 61:6-7; 66:20-23; Pss. 2:8; 22:28; 72:10-11; Mic. 4:13; Obad. 19-21; Hag. 2:6-9; Zech. 2:8; 14:20).

Summary and application

Once again, we are reminded of the amazing grace of God. Yahweh is a holy God who must judge evil, but He is also a God who extends grace and forgiveness to anyone who is willing to trust in His Son (the message we see so clearly in John 3:15ff.). As the Scripture makes clear, even though sin brings condemnation and ruin, God's desire is to restore this fallen world in a kingdom that will never again be tyrannized by sin and death. In terms of personal application, this is the key question: Am I willing to repent of my sin and put my faith in Jesus Christ as my personal Lord and Savior. The Bible says that if we are willing to repent of our sins and trust Jesus Christ as our personal Savior, God will save us and deliver us into His eternal kingdom. Let us all praise God for His grace.

5

JUDGMENT AND SALVATION MESSAGES TO THE WORLD
(24:1-27:13)

Many writers have noted that God's judgment at a national level in 13-23 takes on a global character in 24-27.[1] For this reason, some have called this section "the Apocalypse of Isaiah,"[2] for the focus in this unit is on the worldwide triumph of God at the end of the age, the day of the Lord.[3] Pfeiffer explains, "The judgment that has been particularized in chapters 13–23 for each of the nations involved with Palestine now is represented as about to be poured out upon the earth as a whole."[4] No one will be exempt from the day of the

---

[1] Herbert Wolf, *Interpreting Isaiah* (Grand Rapids: Zondervan, 1985), 137.

[2] G. W. Grogan, "Isaiah," in *The Expositor's Bible Commentary*, ed. Frank E. Gaebelein, vol. 6 (Grand Rapids: Zondervan, 1986), 149; John N. Oswalt, *The Book of Isaiah, 1-39* (Grand Rapids: Eerdmans, 1986), 1. This section has repeated uses of the expression "in that day" in contexts that call for an eschatological interpretation (24:21; 25:9; 26:1; 27:1, 2, 12, 13).

[3] Webb explains that in many ways Isaiah's mini apocalypse "anticipates that better-known apocalypse, the book of Revelation, which serves as the grand finale of the Bible as a whole" (Barry G. Webb, *The Message of Isaiah* [Downers Grove: IVP, 1996], 105).

[4] Charles F. Pfeiffer, *The Wycliffe Bible Commentary: Old Testament,* cited in electronic form with Logos Libronix (Chicago: Moody Press, 1962). Grogan suggests that chapter 24 might be considered somewhat of an introduction to the three chapters that follow in that, "It speaks of a judgment that is universal. Not only does it make no reference to particular nations or specific historical events, [but] it does not even restrict the judgment to the earth" (Grogan, "Isaiah," 151; Oswalt, *The Book of Isaiah, 1-39*,

Lord, for it will be the "desolation and ruin of the whole earth."[5] For the unsaved it will be horrific, but in reality this the good news believers have been waiting for since the beginning: God is going to judge evil and put an end to the tyranny of Satan (cf. Rev. 14:6-8).[6] Not only does this section speak about judgment on evil, but also on the blessings that will come to God's saints including, "one of the two clear promises in the OT of bodily resurrection [cf. 26:19]."[7]

Isaiah 24-27 gives a sneak preview of what the day of the Lord is going to look like after Christ raptures His church. According to the progressive revelation available to the early church, these were events that the apostles believed might imminently fall upon the world even in their own generation (Acts 1:6-8; Rom. 13:12; 1 Cor. 7:29; 10:11; 16:22; Phil. 4:5; 1 Thess. 1:9-10; 2:16; 5:1-9; Heb. 10:25, 37; James 5:8; 1 Pet. 4:7; 2 Pet. 3:9, 11; 1 John 2:18; Rev. 1:3; 22:10, 20). In God's plan, there would be at least 2,000 years of church history to take the name of Jesus into the world before these events would come.

JUDGMENT ON THE WORLD, PT. 1 (24:1-23)

Chapter 24 introduces the whole section. The context suggests that much of this message (all?) are eschatological events that come after the rapture.

Chapter 24 reads as follows: "1 Behold, the Lord lays the earth waste, devastates it, distorts its surface and scatters its inhabitants. 2 And the people will be like the priest, the servant like his master, the maid like her mistress, the buyer like the seller, the lender like the borrower, the creditor like the debtor. 3 The earth will be completely laid waste and completely despoiled, for the Lord has spoken this word. 4 The earth mourns *and* withers, the world fades *and* withers, the exalted of the people of the earth fade away. 5 The earth is also polluted by its inhabitants, for they transgressed laws, violated statutes, broke

---

443).

[5] John A. Martin, "Isaiah," in *The Bible Knowledge Commentary: An Exposition of the Scriptures*, ed. J. F. Walvoord and R. B. Zuck, vol. 1, cited in electronic form with Logos Libronix (Wheaton, IL: Victor Books, 1985), 1072. Through 24-27, the expression "the earth" (*'erets*) is used seventeen times, and Isaiah also uses the term *tebel* ("world," v. 4) a poetic term for the "inhabited world" (the whole world).

[6] The Bible reminds us of the tyranny of Satan when it uses expressions like the "ruler of this world" (John 12:31; 14:30; 16:11; cf. 1 John 5:19; Heb. 2:14) and the "god of this world" (2 Cor. 4:4).

[7] F. Derek Kidner, "Isaiah," in *New Bible Commentary: 21st Century Edition*, ed. D. A. Carson et al., 4th ed., cited in electronic form with Logos Libronix (Leicester, England; Downers Grove, IL: Inter-Varsity Press, 1994), 646.

the everlasting covenant. 6 Therefore, a curse devours the earth, and those who live in it are held guilty. Therefore, the inhabitants of the earth are burned, and few men are left. 7 The new wine mourns; the vine decays; all the merry-hearted sigh. 8 The gaiety of tambourines ceases; the noise of revelers stops; the gaiety of the harp ceases. 9 They do not drink wine with song; strong drink is bitter to those who drink it. 10 The city of chaos is broken down; every house is shut up so that none may enter. 11 There is an outcry in the streets concerning the wine. All joy turns to gloom; the gaiety of the earth is banished. 12 Desolation is left in the city and the gate is battered to ruins. 13 For thus it will be in the midst of the earth among the peoples, as the shaking of an olive tree, as the gleanings when the grape harvest is over. 14 They raise their voices, they shout for joy; they cry out from the west concerning the majesty of the Lord. 15 Therefore glorify the Lord in the east, the name of the Lord, the God of Israel, in the coastlands of the sea. 16 From the ends of the earth we hear songs, lory to the Righteous One. But I say, Woe to me! Woe to me! Alas for me! The treacherous deal treacherously, and the treacherous deal very treacherously. 17 Terror and pit and snare confront you, O inhabitant of the earth. 18 Then it will be that he who flees the report of disaster will fall into the pit, and he who climbs out of the pit will be caught in the snare; for the windows above are opened, and the foundations of the earth shake. 19 The earth is broken asunder; the earth is split through; the earth is shaken violently; 20 the earth reels to and fro like a drunkard and it totters like a shack, for its transgression is heavy upon it, and it will fall, never to rise again. 21 So it will happen in that day, that the Lord will punish the host of heaven on high, and the kings of the earth on earth. 22 They will be gathered together *like* prisoners in the dungeon, and will be confined in prison; and after many days they *will be* punished. 23 Then the moon will be abashed and the sun ashamed, for the Lord of hosts will reign on Mount Zion and in Jerusalem, and *His* glory will be before His elders" (24:1-23).

Chapter 24 divides into the following units: (1) the desolation of the earth (vv. 1-6), (2) the end of revelry (vv. 7-13), (3) the joy and grief of God's judgments (vv. 14-16), (4) the hopelessness of this present world (vv. 17-20), and (5) the reign of the Lord (vv. 21-23).

The desolation of the earth (vv. 1-6)

Verses 1-6 introduce us to the global ruin that will come to this earth during the tribulation period. This section reminds us that not only is the Day of the Lord God's work to judge sin (vv. 1-3), but also that the human cause of it is the sin of a wicked world who hates God (vv. 4-6).

The divine side: God is at work to judge (vv. 1-3)

God is going to totally overturn things from the way that we now know them. Verse 1 makes four statements to emphasize the horrific ruin God will bring (lay waste, devastate, distort, scatter).[8] The "inhabitants of the whole earth" are about to see their world turned upside down (v. 1).[9] Isaiah highlights six pairs of persons from opposite stations of life to show how God's judgment will totally erase the class distinctions that used to separate men from one another (v. 2). In the day of the Lord, "No advantage will come from having a high rather than a low position, for all will come under God's hand of judgment (v. 2)."[10] The devastation will be like the world has never seen, for the Lord "has spoken His word,"[11] and it will devastate like never seen before (v. 3).[12]

The human side: Wicked men are reaping from their sin (vv. 4-6)

Verses 1-3 made several statements which emphasize that this is the judgment of God, but verses 4-6 make several statements which highlight the human evil which has evoked the wrath of God. Isaiah communicates this with a string of "prophetic perfects" which remind us that this day is coming and is coming quickly.

The world will wither (v. 4). The idea of withering reminds us of the judgments God brought on Moab (15:6; 16:8; 34:4). The withering and mourning of the earth convey the idea of drought and the loss of all fertility (cf. 1 Sam. 2:5; Jer. 15:9; Isa. 3:26; 16:8; 19:8; 24:9; 33:9; Joel 1:12). When Isaiah speaks of "the world" fading and withering (1:30; 28:1, 4; 34:4; 40:7, 8; 64:5), he uses a poetic term for world (*tebel*) that speaks about the entire inhabited world. Arrogant sinners will now fade into eternal judgment, and no one will be immune from the coming wrath.

Sinners are to blame (v. 5). It is the "inhabitants" of the earth who have polluted God's earth,[13] unsaved sinners who have, "transgressed laws, violated statutes, [and broken] the everlasting covenant." There is some debate about how to interpret this last expression. Some think it may refer to the Noahic

---

[8] The first two terms are in the form of participles which, in association with "behold," emphasize imminence and certainty (cf. 3:1; 17:1; 19:1; 30:27).

[9] In the Apocalypse, John repeatedly pulls from this terminology when speaking about the unsaved "earth dwellers" (Isa. 24:4-6; 26:9, 21; Mic. 7:13; Zeph. 1:18; cf. Rev. 3:10; 6:10; 8:13; 11:10; 11:10; 13:8; 13:12; 13:14; 13:14; 17:2; 17:8).

[10] Martin, "Isaiah," 1072.

[11] Cf. 1:2, 20; 16:13, 14; 21:17; 22:25; 25:8; 37:22; 39:8; 40:25; 46:11; 48:15, 16; 58:14.

[12] The expression "completely laid waste" employs the term *baqaq* in a participle form followed by a finite verb emphasizing the idea of certainty and totality.

[13] Isaiah uses the term "pollute" (*chanaph*, pollute, defile) several times (Isa. 9:16; 10:6; 32:6; 33:14; cf. Num. 35:33; Deut. 21:19; Ps. 106:38; Jer. 3:2, 9).

Covenant and the shedding of blood (Gen. 9:8-17),[14] while others think it refers to Adam in the Garden of Eden,[15] while yet others still think it could be referring to the Abrahamic Covenant (cf. Gen. 17:7, 13, 19; 1 Chron. 16:15, 17; Pss. 105:8, 10; 111:5, 9).

Sin has a price tag (v. 6). In any case, the price of this pollution is the wrath of God as expressed in two major declarations. First, the idea of curse was something very familiar to people living in the Ancient Near East (cf. Lev. 26:14ff.; Deut. 28:15ff.). These horrific events are not mere chance, but rather the outworking of a violation of God's laws.

Isaiah adds, "Therefore, the inhabitants of the earth are burned, and few men are left." Looking to the eschaton, we do not know precise numbers of how many people will perish during the tribulation period, but from Revelation we know it will be huge. Revelation contains twenty-one judgments as symbolized by seven seals, seven trumpets, and seven bowls. The fourth seal judgment alone (Rev. 6:7-8) predicts the death of one fourth of the earth and the sixth trumpet judgment (9:13-21) speaks about the death of one third of the earth.

The end of wine and revelry (vv. 7-13)

Worldwide judgment continues, but in verses 7-13 the emphasis turns to the idea that God's judgment will bring an end to all revelry. With this in mind, we see five comments about the harvest, the produce of the vine, and the joy that was typically associated with a successful harvest.

First mention of the end of wine and revelry (v. 7)

The harvest has always been a time of rejoicing, but Isaiah prophecies that such joy is coming to an end, and the new wine (*tiyrosh*) will mourn (*'abal*),[16] and the vine (*gephen*) will decay (*'amal*, dry out, dwindle; cf. 16:8; 19:8; 24:4, 7; 33:9; Joel 1:10-12). Just like the earth (vv. 4-6), the vine will wither and dry up "because it partakes in the sorrow of the land."[17]

Second mention of the end of wine and revelry (v. 8)

All the party music will come to an end when the Day of the Lord comes

---

[14] Oswalt, *The Book of Isaiah, 1-39*, 446; Wolf, *Interpreting Isaiah*," 138.
[15] Edward J. Young, *The Book of Isaiah, vol. 2* (Grand Rapids: Eerdmans, 1965), 158).
[16] "New wine" is the sweet fresh grape juice that has just come off the vine (unfermented). There is no joy here, only sighs and mourning (cf. Rev. 18:9ff.).
[17] Young, *The Book of Isaiah, vol. 2*, 161.

(cf. Amos 6:4-7 and God's judgment on Samaria).[18] "Gaiety" (*masos*), another favorite word for Isaiah (24:8, 11; 32:13; 60:15; 62:5; 65:18; 66:10; cf. Jer. 49:25; Ezek. 24:25; Hos. 2:13; Lam. 2:15; 5:15; Ps. 48:3) has fled from the earth. The "revelers" (*'aliyz*) speaks about the arrogant sinners of the world whose life is dominated by wanton pleasure (Isa. 13:2; 22:2; 23:7; 24:8; 32:13; cf. Zeph. 2:15; 3:11).[19] God is bringing an end to the world's sin party.[20]

Third mention of the end of wine and revelry (v. 9)

God's judgment will bring an end not only to wine (*yayin*) and song, but the misery will be so bad that men will not even desire "strong drink" (*shekar*). The Day of the Lord will put an end to such celebration of sin: "When God pours out His wrath on the unbelieving world in the Tribulation, all will be desolate and gloomy."[21]

Fourth mention of the end of wine and revelry (vv. 10-11)

The expression "city of chaos" (*tohu*)[22] could represent a global idea similar to the way Babylon receives a universal usage in Revelation 17-18.[23] For long ages the world rejoiced in rejecting God, and now it has the "chaos" its sin was producing. The wine, joy, and gaiety of sin-driven living is now gone forever.

Fifth mention of the end of wine and revelry (vv. 12-13)

When God's judgment has run its course, there will be nothing left but a world in ruins (cf. Rev. 18:9-19). Just as nothing is left after the people have completed a thorough harvest, so it will be when the Lord has finished His judgment: All sin "in the midst of the earth" (cf. 5:8; 6:12; 7:22; 10:23; 19:24) will be judged and purged away forever (vv. 12-13).[24]

---

[18] Young says, "Isaiah is not condemning music as such, for music in itself is one of God's most wondrous gifts" (ibid., 162).
[19] Ludwig Koehler et al., *The Hebrew and Aramaic Lexicon of the Old Testament*, cited in electronic form with Logos Libronix (Leiden: E.J. Brill, 1994–2000), 833.
[20] Perhaps we might see it represented by places like Mardi Gras, Carnival, Oktoberfest, Las Vegas or anywhere else where sin rules.
[21] Martin, "Isaiah," 1072.
[22] Isaiah 29:21; 34:11; 40:17, 23; 41:29; 44:9; 45:18; 49:4; 59:4; cf. Gen. 1:2 where the first use of the term speaks about the world as being "formless" prior to God's shaping it for habitation.
[23] Grogan, "Isaiah," 153; Young, *The Book of Isaiah, vol. 2*, 163-164.
[24] As Oswalt explains, the whole thing is going to be brought down to virtually nothing (Oswalt, *The Book of Isaiah, 1-39*, 449).

ISAIAH: THE LORD SAVES

The joy and grief of God's judgments (vv. 14-16)

The following verses raise several interpretive questions. First of all, the "they" who raise voices and shout for joy with shouts from the west raises interpretive questions (vv. 14ff.).[25] Perhaps the best answer is that it is all those from "the midst of the earth" from "among the peoples" (v. 13). God's eschatological wrath will leave no corner of the earth untouched (Rev. 6:15-17), but this same work of God will also bring salvation to God's elect (cf. Rev. 5:9; 7:9).

These judgments will leave the unsaved world in mourning (vv. 1-13; cf. Rev. 18:9-19), but out of this God will save His remnant who will rejoice over His awesome deeds (Rev. 18:20; Jer. 51:48), and these will be the ones who glorify the God of Israel across the face of the whole earth (v. 15). Many who place their faith in Jesus during that tribulation period will be martyred for their faith in Christ (Rev. 7:9-17; 13:7-10; 15:1-4; 20:4), but there will also be those who believe and survive until the coming of Christ (cf. e.g., Rev. 14:1-5). God's elect will give glory to "the Righteous One,[26] but Isaiah's day was still a day of evil,[27] and all he could say was "woe to me" (v. 16).[28]

The hopelessness of this present world (vv. 17-20)

The unsaved world habitually suppresses the knowledge of God (Rom. 1:18ff.), but one day they will give an account to God. When the Day of the Lord comes, these men will try to hide from God, but they will not be able to (Rev. 6:15-17). There be no escape for the earth-dwellers (vv. 17-18), and the earth will be brought to ruin (vv. 19-20).

---

[25] The term "west" (*yam*) means the sea. The "east" (*'ur*) is the region of light. The term "islands" (*'iy*) speaks of the Mediterranean world to the west (11:11; 24:15). The whole world will give praise to the Lord (Isa. 42:4, 10; 51:5; 59:18, 19; Pss. 96:1-13; 97:1, 6; 98:2-4). The "ends of the earth" (*kenaph ha'erets*) takes one to the farthest imaginable places one could travel from the land of Israel (Isa. 11:12; Ezek. 7:2; Job 37:3). God's work of judgment and salvation will be universal.

[26] The "Righteous One" (*Hatsadiyq*) is God and not the people (as held by Young, *The Book of Isaiah, vol. 2*, 172, n. 60). All of this is praise for what Yahweh has done in saving His people from ruin (Isa. 60:2, 3; 62:2; cf. Phil. 2:9-11).

[27] The "treacherous" (*bogediym*) could be a reference to enemy Gentile powers (cf. 21:2; 33:1) or perhaps the treacherous within Israel. Isaiah uses a form of the word (*bagad*) five times to emphasize this idea of "treachery" or "unfaithfulness."

[28] The term "woe" (*raziy*) carries the idea of "leanness" (Isa. 17:4; 10:16; cf. Ps. 106:15; Zeph. 2:11). Like Daniel (7:28; 8:27; 10:8-9), Isaiah was overwhelmed by the terrifying visions God showed him (cf. Isa. 22:4).

No escape for the earth dwellers (vv. 17-18)[29]

Isaiah's language vividly announces the terror men will face with "pounding assonance" in the opening words of verse 17, terror, pit, and snare (*pachad, pachath, pach*).[30] God the Hunter is pursuing His prey. They can run, but they cannot hide (v. 17). The one who tries to run will fall into the pit, and the one who climbs out of the pit will be trapped in the snare (cf. Amos 5:18-20). God has opened the window of heaven (cf. same term in Gen. 7:11), and He is coming down to shake the world (v. 18; cf. Hag. 2:20-23).[31]

The end of the earth dwellers home (vv. 19-20)

The poetic impact is magnified by the multiple parallels.[32] Isaiah makes five declarations how God is going to shake the world to pieces. First, Isaiah says the earth will be broken asunder (*ra'a'*, smashed, shattered; cf. Deut. 28:27; Isa. 8:9; 24:19; Jer. 15:2; Mic. 5:9; Ps. 2:9).[33] Second, the earth will be "split through" (perhaps "convulsed" or "totter" is a better rendering for *parar*). Third, the earth will shake (*mut*) and be made to stagger and totter (v. 19). Fourth, the earth will reel to and fro like a drunkard (v. 20; cf. Isa. 29:9; Ps. 107:27), and fifth, it will "totter like a shack." These descriptions certainly center around the judgment of God on sinful man, but the multitude of references to disturbances on the earth and in the heavens do not preclude a literal, physical meaning as well.

Why such destruction? It is because the transgression of man has been great. For millennia, the curse of sin has been at work ravaging God's creation, and now the time for judgment has finally come (cf. Rev. 17-18).

The reign of the Lord (vv. 21-23)

The events Isaiah has been describing are what we call the Day of the

---

[29] We saw the first expression "those who dwell upon the earth" (*yosheb ha'erets*) in 24:1, and it gets used repeatedly to describe a Christ-hating world (24:1, 5, 6; 26:9, 21; cf. Zeph. 1:18; Mic. 7:13; Rev. 3:10; 6:10; 8:13; 11:10; 13:8, 12, 14; 17:2, 8).
[30] Oswalt, *The Book of Isaiah, 1-39*, 453 (cf. 2 Sam. 22:6; Pss. 18:5; 64:5; 106:36; 124:6; Jer. 48:43, 44; Lam. 3:47; Amos 5:19; Job 18:5-11; 22:10).
[31] The Old and New Testaments predict that massive earthquakes will come all throughout the tribulation period with the worst coming in the closing portion.
[32] The strength of these parallels is magnified in that all of them begin with Hebrew infinitives followed by finite verbs.
[33] Ludwig Koehler et al., *The Hebrew and Aramaic Lexicon of the Old Testament*, cited in electronic form with Logos Libronix (Leiden: E.J. Brill, 1994–2000), 1270–1271.

Lord—that eschatological era that commences after the rapture of the church when the wrath of God brings the world to ruins, and Christ brings His kingdom to this world (cf. 1 Thess. 1:10; 2:16; 5:1ff.). Isaiah highlights the targets of wrath (v. 21), the punishment of wrath (v. 22), and the impact of wrath (v. 23).

The targets of God's wrath (v. 21)

Isaiah introduces this final section with the eschatological expression "in that day" (4:2; 11:10; 17:7; 19:23; 25:9; 26:1). Isaiah highlights the way that God brings punishment (*phaqad*) on two particular groups of sinners.

First group of sinners: sinners in heaven (v. 21a). The language and context suggest that Isaiah is announcing the long-awaited punishment of Satan and all fallen angels.[34] Progressive revelation shows us that Satan and his demons will be cast into the bottomless pit for 1,000 years at the beginning of the Millennium (Zech. 13:2; Rev. 20:1-3; cf. perhaps Isa. 14:9ff.), but that they are punished eternally at the end of the Millennium when they are cast into the Lake of Fire (2 Pet. 2:4; Jude 6; Rev. 20:7-10).

Second group of sinners: sinners on earth (v. 21b). The return of Christ will bring destruction to the godless leaders of this world and all who follow them. These tribulation period judgments are spoken of in various prophecies (Ezek. 38-39; Dan. 7:15-28; Joel 3:1-17; Zech. 12:1ff.; 14:1ff.), but Revelation gives us the final picture with the return of Christ (Rev. 19:11-21). Demonic powers have led these unsaved world leaders to destroy Israel (Rev. 16:13-16; 17:12-14), but Jesus will triumph over them all. Those unsaved men that are killed will go directly into hell and immediate judgment in "the bottomless pit" (Dan. 7:12).[35] The unsaved who survive the tribulation will not be allowed entrance into God's kingdom (Isa. 35:8-10; Matt. 25:41). Rather, the angels will remove them from the earth and cast them into judgment (Matt. 8:12; 13:39-43, 49-50; 21:44; 22:13; 24:37-41, 48-51; 25:12-13, 30, 41, 46).

The punishment of God's wrath (v. 22)

As already described in verse 21, immediate punishment comes to all who

---

[34] The expression "host of heaven" (*tseba'*, literally "the host in the height") can refer to the physical stellar realm (Isa. 34:4; 40:26; 45:12; cf. Jer. 33:22; Neh. 9:6), but Isaiah is speaking about the punishment of rational creatures, fallen angels (cf. 1 Kings 22:19; 2 Chron. 18:18; Matt. 24:29; Rom. 8:38; Eph. 3:10; 6:12; Col. 1:13 16; 2:15; Rev. 12:4, 9), just as the following judgment on kings suggests.

[35] The only exception is that the Antichrist (i.e., "the beast") and False Prophet are cast into the Lake of Fire at the beginning of the Millennium instead of at the end when every other unsaved man is judged (Dan. 7:11; Rev. 19:20-21).

perish without Christ. Isaiah further describes the punishment by saying, "They will be gathered together *like* prisoners in the dungeon,[36] and will be confined in prison; and after many days they *will be* punished."

The Book of Revelation indicates that the immediate judgment of the unsaved awaits a final judgment that comes at the end of the Millennium. This is the time when all the unsaved are brought into resurrection and given a final judgment for eternal torment in the Lake of Fire (Rev. 14:9-11; 20:11-15). This is also the time when all demons are cast into the Lake of Fire for eternal judgment (Rev. 20:10). Grogan summarizes it well: "The spiritual powers of evil are bound in prison during the reign of Christ on earth, after which they-along with the unsaved dead-suffer eternal punishment in the Lake of Fire."[37]

The impact of God's wrath (v. 23)

God's eschatological judgment will shake all creation when Jesus returns in His resurrection glory (Matt. 16:27; 25:31; Mark 9:1-3; Rev. 1:7). This is apparently the basis for the statement that the sun and moon will be ashamed in that day, for the glory of Christ will eclipse both of them (Isa. 60:19; Zech. 14:7; Rev. 21:23; 22:5).[38] All of this is what the world will see when Jesus brings the kingdom of God to rule the world from Jerusalem (Isa. 30:33; 32:1; 33:17, 22; 41:21; 43:15; 44:6; 52:7; Ps. 48; Matt. 5:35).[39]

Summary and application

These promises should terrify the unsaved and remind them about their need to trust in Christ. On the other hand, these promises bring great comfort to all believers. They are both bitter and sweet (Rev. 10:9-11).

JUDGMENT ON THE WORLD, PT. 2 (25:1-12)

Chapter 24 portrayed the global ruin God will bring to the world and the mourning that comes with it. Chapter 25 continues this global focus, only now on the great rejoicing God's people will enjoy in that day.

---

[36] This "dungeon" is the term for "pit" (*bor*), seen parallel with *she'ol* in Isaiah 14:15-19. Revelation 20:1-3 calls it "the bottomless pit" (cf. Rev. 9:2, 11; 11:7; 17:8). This pit is the place of temporary punishment before the Lake of Fire at the end of the Millennium (Oswalt, *The Book of Isaiah, 1-39*, 455).

[37] Grogan, "Isaiah," 155.

[38] Young, *The Book of Isaiah, vol. 2*, 181.

[39] There is some question about the identity of the "elders." This could refer potentially to angels (Rev. 4:4), resurrected saints (OT saints, church saints, tribulation martyrs; cf. Rev. 20:4), or mortal saints (cf. Exod. 24:9-10).

Chapter 25 reads as follows: "1 O Lord, You are my God; I will exalt You, I will give thanks to Your name, for You have worked wonders, plans *formed* long ago, with perfect faithfulness. 2 For You have made a city into a heap, a fortified city into a ruin; a palace of strangers is a city no more; it will never be rebuilt. 3 Therefore a strong people will glorify You; cities of ruthless nations will revere You. 4 For You have been a defense for the helpless, a defense for the needy in his distress, a refuge from the storm, a shade from the heat; for the breath of the ruthless is like a *rain* storm *against* a wall. 5 Like heat in drought, You subdue the uproar of aliens; *like* heat by the shadow of a cloud, the song of the ruthless is silenced. 6 The Lord of hosts will prepare a lavish banquet for all peoples on this mountain, a banquet of aged wine, choice pieces with marrow, *and* refined, aged wine. 7 And on this mountain He will swallow up the covering which is over all peoples, even the veil which is stretched over all nations. 8 He will swallow up death for all time, and the Lord God will wipe tears away from all faces, and He will remove the reproach of His people from all the earth, for the Lord has spoken. 9 And it will be said in that day, Behold, this is our God for whom we have waited that He might save us. This is the Lord for whom we have waited. Let us rejoice and be glad in His salvation, 10 for the hand of the Lord will rest on this mountain, and Moab will be trodden down in his place as straw is trodden down in the water of a manure pile, 11 and he will spread out his hands in the middle of it as a swimmer spreads out *his hands* to swim; but *the Lord* will lay low his pride together with the trickery of his hands. 12 The unassailable fortifications of your walls He will bring down, lay low *and* cast to the ground, even to the dust" (25:1-12).

As we have seen, God's eschatological work is going to touch every corner of the earth. Chapter 25 may be broken into two units: God's perfect plan (vv. 1-5), and God's kingdom blessings (vv. 6-12).

God's perfect plan (vv. 1-5)

Our God is a sovereign God who rules over the earth, and nothing is outside of His sovereignty (Isa. 46:8-11; cf. Gen. 45:5-9; 50:20; Acts 2:23; 4:27-28; Rom. 8:28). At the same time, the Bible never allows one to hold to any form of fatalism, for God's sovereign plan always operates in perfect harmony with the moral responsibility of His rational creations. Verses 1-5 speak about the praise that God's people bring to the Lord for His good and perfect plan, even though it was a plan that would bring the world into great ruin for a temporary period. Verses 1-2 show us Isaiah's own praise, and this is followed in 3-5 with praise that comes from all God's redeemed.

Isaiah's praise of God's perfect plan (vv. 1-2)

God's plan is a perfect plan (v. 1). Isaiah is committed to exalting (Pss.

54:8; 118:28; 145:1) and praising God (Isa. 12:1, 4; 38:18) because of "the wonders" (*pele'*) He works. The Hebrew term for "wonders" always refers to something marvelous, such as the wonders that God alone accomplishes (Exod. 15:11; Pss. 40:5; 77:11, 14; 78:12; 88:10, 12; 89:5; Isa. 9:6). These wonders are "the plans formed long ago with perfect faithfulness." Isaiah often emphasizes the truth that God has a plan that is good, perfect, and formed in eternity past, and that the outworking of history is really the outworking of His eternal plan (Isa. 5:19; 14:24-27; 25:1; 28:29; 44:26; 46:8-11; cf. Jer. 49:20; 50:45; Mic. 4:12) with "perfect faithfulness."[40] These plans will also include the overthrow and exile of his own people to bring ultimate redemption, but they are nonetheless in "perfect faithfulness." Young explains, "What He does is not precipitate nor rash, but is the outworking of His eternal purpose and decrees."[41]

God's plan is a ruinous plan (v. 2). In the present context, these faithful plans include turning a city into a heap. Some have suggested that the (wicked) city that has been overthrown could be Jerusalem or Babylon (cf. Isa. 21:9; Jer. 51:37; Rev. 17-18), but in context this appears to be "enunciating a general truth, namely, that God's wondrous counsels have been carried out in that He has completely overthrown the order of things."[42] That is, the term "city" may be symbolizing the whole world that has fallen under God's judgment, and evil will never again rule the world.[43] The ruin that God brings is horrific, but Isaiah is overflowing with praise.[44]

The world's praise of God's perfect plan (vv. 3-5)

The necessity of praise from a redeemed world (v. 3). God's judgment will lead all to praise God, both men (Rev. 15:1-4) and angels (Rev. 16:4-7). For long ages, the saints have longed for this day of retribution (Rev. 6:9-11), and now it has finally arrived (Rev. 18:20; 19:1-10). Evil cannot go unpunished, and for this reason the day of judgment is a day for rejoicing (Isa. 17:7-9; 19:19-20; 23:18; 24:15). Isaiah says it will also usher in an age of reverence. Nations that used to mock and despise God will now be filled with a redeemed remnant who will worship the Lord and give Him glory (cf. Ezek. 36:23, 38; 38:16; 39:7-8, 21-

---

[40] The expression represents the combination of two different nouns both, from the root *'aman*.
[41] Young, *The Book of Isaiah, vol. 2*, 186.
[42] Ibid., 187.
[43] Grogan, "Isaiah," 158. The "palace of *strangers* (Heb. *zariym*)" might actually be a "place of the *arrogant*" (Heb. *zediym*) as indicated by the LXX *asebos* ("wicked, ungodly"). The possibility is that a resh was accidently used for the daleth.
[44] Cf. Rev. 18:20 and the call to praise God, and the four hallelujah choruses which follow in Rev. 19:1-6.

23, 27-29). Jesus said we should pray for this day (Matt. 6:9-10).

The reason for praise from a redeemed world (vv. 4-5). The judgment will be severe, but in reality this judgment is the outworking of divine compassion for the afflicted—tender compassion for the saints who have been afflicted by the "ruthless" (*'ariyts*)—the violent and powerful sinners who trample the weak (Isa. 11:4; 13:11; 25:3-5; 29:5, 20; 49:25; cf. Ezek. 28:7; 30:11; 31:12; 32:12).[45] At long last, God has stepped in to become the defense, refuge and shade of the "needy" and "helpless" (v. 4).[46] Neither raging rain (v. 4) nor scorching heat will hinder God from giving His saints the comfort they have longed for (v. 5; Matt. 5:3-12; cf. Rev. 7:16).

God's kingdom blessings (vv. 6-12)

Not only is the Lord to be praised for the removal of wickedness, but He is also to be praised for the glorious blessings He gives His saints in His kingdom. Isaiah praises God for three marvelous kingdom blessings.

First kingdom blessing: Universal prosperity (v. 6)

The curse of sin introduced long ages of hardship (cf. Gen. 3:17-19), but the arrival of God's kingdom ("this mountain"; cf. 2:2-4; Ps. 48) will bring an end to curse—an age of prosperity symbolized by a lavish banquet.[47] It has been suggested that this lavish banquet could symbolize the coronation of Christ the King who has now begun to reign.[48] In any case, this lavish banquet with the

---

[45] Ludwig Koehler et al., *The Hebrew and Aramaic Lexicon of the Old Testament*, cited in electronic form with Logos Libronix (Leiden: E.J. Brill, 1994–2000), 884.

[46] The "helpless" (*dal*) are the low, poor and insignificant of society, and the parallel "needy" (*'ebyon*) are likewise those who are miserably poor and oppressed, those who are lowest of all and most vulnerable of all.

[47] The Hebrew word for "lavish" is the term *shemen* (lit. "fat"), with the plural form conveying the idea that this will be the richest of all foods and wines (Oswalt, *The Book of Isaiah, 1-39*, 457, n. 7 from GKC, 124e). The meat is the richest cut, and the wine has been aged for high fermentation and filtered to remove all dregs (Jer. 48:11; Zeph. 1:14). In ch. 24, the "city of chaos" mourned that their wine was no more, but God's people will have the best in the kingdom (Grogan, "Isaiah," 159).

[48] Oswalt, *The Book of Isaiah, 1-39*, 463; Wolf, *Interpreting Isaiah*, 140. Such feasts were held at coronations (1 Sam. 11:15; 1 Kings 1:9, 19, 25; 2 Sam. 6:18) and at other joyous events like weddings (Judg. 14:10; Rev. 19:9). It is difficult to decide whether the marriage supper of the Lamb in Revelation 19:7-10 takes place during the Millennium (as seen in this banquet) or during the seven-year tribulation period before the church

richest of all foods certainly indicates that the messianic kingdom will usher in an age of universal prosperity and blessing to "all peoples" who believe in Christ, not only the nation of Israel (Matt. 8:10-12).[49] Whoever believes will share in that messianic banquet (Rev. 3:20).

Second kingdom blessing: Universal life (vv. 7-9)

Not only will Christ's kingdom will bring universal prosperity (v. 6), but it will also usher in the age where life, not death, is the rule. We must not forget that death was not part of God's original order. It was Adam's sin that introduced death (Gen. 2:17; Rom. 5:12-21; 8:18-27), but one day the Lord will end the tyranny of death. Isaiah gives five vivid descriptions of how God will end the tyranny of death.

First description of how God will end death's tyranny (v. 7). First, God will swallow up "the covering" (*lot*) which is over all the peoples—a covering that is further described as "the veil" (*massekah*) which is stretched out over all the nations. The following statements make it clear that Isaiah is talking about a removal of "the shroud of death."[50]

Second description of how God will end death's tyranny (v. 8a). God will swallow up death for all time. It was on the cross that Jesus defeated Satan and the curse of sin and death (2 Tim. 1:10; Heb. 2:9, 14-15). Those who trust in Christ will one day share in this victory with resurrection glory (John 11:25-26; 1 Cor. 15:12-57; 1 Thess. 4:14).

Third description of how God will end death's tyranny (v. 8b). God will wipe away all tears. This is a supremely tender picture of how the Creator will step down like a gentle mother in wiping away the tears of death (Isa. 35:10; cf. Rev. 21:4).

Fourth description of how God will end death's tyranny (v. 8c). God will take away the reproach of His people. One day, the reproach of death will be gone forever.

---

returns with Christ at the end of the seven years (Rev. 19:11ff.). This author thinks there is a slightly stronger case for seeing it as in heaven.

[49] These "choice pieces" of meat were the fattest pieces that were used for certain "peace offerings" (Lev. 3:3; 4:8, 9; 7:25; cf. Gen. 49:20; Ps. 63:6; Job 36:16; Neh. 8:10; Isa. 55:2; Jer. 31:14). Here, though, they are not offerings to God, but they are blessings enjoyed by all saints.

[50] Oswalt, *The Book of Isaiah, 1-39*, 464.

In order to have a proper understanding of these promises, it is crucial that we allow progressive revelation to inform our systematic theology. At the present time, all men still experience physical death. At the moment of death, the unbeliever passes immediately into the realm of judgment (Luke 16:22-23) where he awaits a final judgment at the second resurrection (Rev. 20:11-15). Believers, however, go directly into the presence of Jesus Christ (2 Cor. 5:8; Phil. 1:21-23), awaiting the day when Christ will return and bring them into bodily resurrection (Rom. 8:23; Eph. 4:30; 1 Thess. 4:13-18; Dan. 12:2-3; Rev. 20:4). When God brings in the New Heavens and New Earth (Rev. 21-22), all of God's saints will be in resurrection glory, and God will bring a final end to all sin and death (Rev. 21:1-4; 22:3). During the Millennium, this world will still be populated by mortal saints who still possess a sin nature. Open sin and rebellion will not take place during the Millennium, but sin and death will still be experienced in a suppressed way (cf. Isa. 65:20) until the new creation arrives. God's redemptive plan has stages, and we do not see the final stage until we come to the New Creation (Rev. 21-22).

Fifth description of how God will end death's tyranny (v. 9). Martin explains, "The certainty of future prosperity and joy and absence of death would encourage Judah in Isaiah's day to trust in the Lord and not lose heart."[51] Isaiah records the response of the people to this great news: "And it will be said in that day, Behold, this is our God for whom we have waited that He might save us. This is the Lord for whom we have waited;[52] let us rejoice and be glad in His salvation." The promises are certain, and it is only a matter of time before they are realized.

Third kingdom blessing: Universal peace (vv. 10-12)

War has been ravaging mankind since the entrance of sin. It is hard to imagine how much pain and misery this world has seen from the evils of war. When Jesus Christ returns, He will make an end of all war (Isa. 2:2-4; 11:6-9; 32:17-19; 40:1ff.; Mic. 4:3). Zion will be the place from which these blessings flow, but this cannot happen until evil has been subdued. Here in verses 10-12 God singles out one particular nation for His focus as the one whom He will utterly bring down, Moab. Certainly Moab was not the largest nation, nor the most hostile nation, but in this passage it seems that Moab may be serving illustratively as representative of all the adversaries, and God is using Moab to represent the overthrow of all who oppose Him. Isaiah gives us both the declaration of Moab's overthrow (v. 10), as well as the description (vv. 11-12).

The declaration of Moab's overthrow (v. 10). God's hand of blessing

---

[51] Martin, "Isaiah," 1074.
[52] Cf. 26:8; 33:2; 40:31.

will be on Zion, but first evil must be thrown down. Moab must be trodden down just as the straw in the animal pen is trodden in the mire. Even though Moab was not the most formidable enemy, we do see indications that during the tribulation period those who dwell east of the Jordan (with both Moab and Edom singled out) will show hostility and become targets of the Messiah's judgments (Isa. 34:5-17; 63:1-6; cf. Obad. 1-9). Kidner explains, "*Moab*, startlingly local in so universal a scene (*cf.* Edom in 34:5), is introduced as the embodiment of pride (11b; *cf.* 16:6)."[53]

The description of Moab's overthrow (vv. 11-12). Moab has been trampled in the mire of mud, manure and urine, scrambling for someone to pull him out (perhaps some of this will include invasions by the Antichrist and his forces as we see in Dan. 11:41). It will be desperate times for Moab, all part of God's judgment on the "pride" (*ga'awah*, arrogance; cf. Isa. 9:8; 13:11; 16:6; 25:11) and "trickery" (*'arbah*, hapax) of Moab (v. 11).[54] Striving will be in vain, for God's judgments will destroy their "unassailable fortifications,"[55] and the unsaved of Moab will be brought to ruin (v. 12; cf. Ps. 2).

Summary and application

It is ultimate folly for sinners to strive against his God. Isaiah 25 shows us the wonderful kingdom promises that God has stored up for His people. These promises, says Peter, are the kinds of things we should eagerly long for (1 Pet. 1:13). God's present world certainly has blessings, but the blessings of Christ's kingdom are going to eclipse the very best that a fallen world can offer. Let us fix our eyes on these promises.

JUDGMENT ON THE WORLD, PT. 3 (26:1-21)

Isaiah continues to unfold God's marvelous eschatological plan for the world. This chapter might rightly be described as Judah's Song of Praise.[56]

Chapter 26 reads as follows: "1 In that day this song will be sung in the land of Judah: We have a strong city; He sets up walls and ramparts for security. 2 Open the gates, that the righteous nation may enter, the one that remains faithful. 3 The steadfast of mind You will keep in perfect peace, because he trusts in You. 4 Trust in the Lord forever, for in God the Lord, *we have* an everlasting Rock. 5 For He has brought low those who dwell on high, the

---

[53] Kidner, "Isaiah," 648.

[54] Grogan notes that this word is a hapax legomenon, though the root does appear elsewhere in the sense of "ambush" (Grogan, "Isaiah," 161, n. 11).

[55] Moab was noted for having strong fortified walls.

[56] Wolf, *Interpreting Isaiah*, 142.

unassailable city; He lays it low; He lays it low to the ground; He casts it to the dust. 6 The foot will trample it, the feet of the afflicted, the steps of the helpless. 7 The way of the righteous is smooth. O Upright One, make the path of the righteous level. Indeed, *while following* the way of Your judgments, O Lord, we have waited for You eagerly; Your name, even Your memory, is the desire of *our* souls. 9 At night my soul longs for You; indeed, my spirit within me seeks You diligently, for when the earth experiences Your judgments, the inhabitants of the world learn righteousness. 10 *Though* the wicked is shown favor, he does not learn righteousness; he deals unjustly in the land of uprightness, and does not perceive the majesty of the Lord. 11 O Lord, Your hand is lifted up *yet* they do not see it. They see *Your* zeal for the people and are put to shame; indeed, fire will devour Your enemies. 12 Lord, You will establish peace for us, since You have also performed for us all our works. 13 O Lord our God, other masters besides You have ruled us; *But* through You alone we confess Your name. 14 The dead will not live, the departed spirits will not rise; therefore You have punished and destroyed them, and You have wiped out all remembrance of them. 15 You have increased the nation, O Lord; You have increased the nation; You are glorified; You have extended all the borders of the land. 16 O Lord, they sought You in distress; they could only whisper a prayer; your chastening was upon them. 17 As the pregnant woman approaches *the time* to give birth, she writhes *and* cries out in her labor pains; thus were we before You, O Lord. 18 We were pregnant; we writhed *in labor,* we gave birth, as it seems, *only* to wind; we could not accomplish deliverance for the earth, nor were inhabitants of the world born. 19 Your dead will live; their corpses will rise. You who lie in the dust, awake and shout for joy, for your dew *is as* the dew of the dawn, and the earth will give birth to the departed spirits. 20 Come, my people, enter into your rooms and close your doors behind you; hide for a little while until indignation runs *its* course. 21 For behold, the Lord is about to come out from His place to punish the inhabitants of the earth for their iniquity, and the earth will reveal her bloodshed and will no longer cover her slain" (26:1-21).

Chapter 26 continues the theme of good news for God's people. In this chapter, Isaiah predicts a happy future for Judah. This chapter may be broken down into three units: Judah's song of salvation (vv. 1-6), Judah's prayer for salvation (vv. 7-18), and Judah's realized salvation (vv. 19-21).

Judah's song of salvation (vv. 1-6)

Israel is often in the news in our modern world, but typically it is with harsh condemnation from the world. When Christ returns, God will reverse all of this. Zechariah tells us, "It will come about that just as you were a curse among the nations, O house of Judah and house of Israel, so I will save you that you may become a blessing. Do not fear; let your hands be strong" (Zech. 8:13). Here in chapter 26, we see another "song" that celebrates this eschatological day of salvation—a salvation that will mean a permanent end of the exiles, inquisitions, pogroms, and holocausts. This is an eschatological salvation that Moses himself wrote of (cf. Deut. 30:1-10). Isaiah's song of salvation portrays this salvation as a perfect city which God will bring to His people to replace the evil city that He has just judged and removed (Isa. 24:10; 25:2).[57] God's city can be known by four key truths.

First key truth: A city of safety (v. 1)

Isaiah again uses the expression "in that day" to introduce God's eschatological work. God's city will be a safe city for it is one whose walls and ramparts make her strong and unassailable. Martin describes the impact of the Messiah's presence: "[Isaiah] pictures the security of the world's redeemed inhabitants. Because of the Messiah's presence there, that city is figuratively said to have salvation for its walls and ramparts."[58]

Second key truth: A city of faith (v. 2)

Second, God's city (i.e., God's kingdom and Zion its capital) will be characterized by faith. When Christ brings the kingdom, only believers will be allowed to enter,[59] the "righteous" and "faithful" (Isa. 35:8-10; 51:10-11; 60:21; Matt. 5:3-12; 25:34). David wrote, "Who may ascend into the hill of the Lord? And who may stand in His holy place? He who has clean hands and a pure heart, who has not lifted up his soul to falsehood and has not sworn deceitfully" (Pss. 24:3-4; 37:9, 11, 18, 27, 29, 34). Entrance into God's city is not for Jews only, but for all who believe (Matt. 8:10-12). What a day it will be when the whole world knows the Lord (Isa. 11:9; Jer. 31:34)!

Third key truth: A city of peace (v. 3)

God promises that He will keep His redeemed saints in perfect peace.[60] The peace God brings in that day will be untouchable (Isa. 55:3; Ezek. 37:24-26), but this is a peace that believers can apply to themselves today no matter what problems they face (Phil. 4:5-6; 1 Pet. 5:7). The psalmist echoes Isaiah by telling us that the believer who fears the Lord "will not fear evil tidings; his heart

---

[57] Revelation says that harlot Babylon must be removed (Rev. 17-18) before the bride New Jerusalem can come (Rev. 21:1ff.).

[58] Martin, "Isaiah," 1074.

[59] Entrance by the gates of God's city brings to mind the annual pilgrimage festivals (Grogan, "Isaiah," 163).

[60] This is the one whose "heart" is fixed because He "trusts" in the goodness and sovereignty of God.

is steadfast, trusting in the Lord. His heart is upheld, he will not fear" (Ps. 112:7-8). Our need today is to be completely sold out to the lordship of Jesus Christ so that no matter what the world brings, His peace will be our peace (John 14:27; 1 Pet. 3:13-15).

Fourth key truth: A city of refuge from all dangers (vv. 4-6)

One day God will bring perfect salvation to those who trust Him. Isaiah highlights the need and reason for such unshakable trust.

The need for unshakable trust (v. 4). God's redeeming grace should lead every believer to unshakable trust, for Yahweh is an "everlasting Rock" (Isa. 30:29; cf. Deut. 32:4; 1 Sam. 2:2; 2 Sam. 22:2, 32; Pss. 19:14; 61:2).[61] The Rock is the One we can trust.

The reason for unshakable trust (vv. 5-6). Every believer needs to trust the Lord because He is the God who saves us from every enemy, the God who brought down the "unassailable city" (cf. 25:12) and cast it into the dust (v. 5). He is the One who crushed all evil so that the afflicted might be lifted up to inherit salvation (cf. Matt. 5:5; Luke 1:50-53, 71-74).[62] Jesus is the God of salvation who defeated the curse and death, and one day He will purge this world of every trace of sin and curse.

Judah's prayer for salvation (vv. 7-18)

The focus shifts from celebration to intense prayer.[63] We must not forget that even though Isaiah was giving His people glimpses of a glorious future, in His own day the situation was desperate. Isaiah's petitions may be broken down as a prayer for the Lord to make a straight path (vv. 7-8) and a prayer for the Lord to bring His ways to the world (vv. 9-18).

A prayer for the Lord to make a straight path (vv. 7-8)

Isaiah says that the path of the righteous is a "smooth" path (*yashar*, level, straight), and then he follows this with the declaration that God, the "Upright One" (same root),[64] will clear the path of the righteous (v. 7). Young explains, "Isaiah does not wish to place attention upon the path on which the righteous

---

[61] The NASB "in God the Lord" is actually "in Yah Yahweh" (*beYah Yewah*), a beautiful and poetic way of portraying Israel's covenant God.

[62] Believers are often characterized as those who are afflicted or helpless because of their dedication to godly virtues (Ps. 37:11; Zeph. 3:12; Zech. 11:11; Matt. 5:5).

[63] Wolf, *Interpreting Isaiah*, 142.

[64] The vocative sense of the NASB seems best although not found in this form elsewhere.

must travel but rather upon the blessedness that comes to the righteous who travel this path."[65] The righteous who walk in God's level paths are the ones who wait patiently on the Lord for Him to come and give them the straight path of His kingdom (v. 8; cf. Isa. 40:1-4).[66]

A prayer for the Lord to bring His ways to the world (vv. 9-18)

God's people must live in the same fallen world as everyone else, but they have always been characterized by a longing for God to fulfill His promise of fixing this broken world. They even learn how to draw closer to the Lord in the midst of afflictions. Not so with the wicked. This is the contrast we find here in verses 9-18.

The righteous long for the Lord's ways (v. 9). Isaiah longs for the Lord to bring His kingdom, and confesses that God's judgments are His way of demonstrating His righteousness. Sometimes the unsaved respond in repentance when judged, but most do not and fall into eternal ruin. Martin explains, "Those who refuse to heed God's ways learn of God's righteousness when they are eventually judged."[67]

The wicked never long for the Lord's ways (vv. 10-11). Isaiah expands on the bitter path of the wicked by explaining how they characteristically refuse the goodness of the Lord, i.e., His common grace. Peace and prosperity are not enough to turn a wicked heart to the Lord (vv. 10-11). As we see in Revelation 20, a millennium of earthly paradise that ends with rebellion by the unsaved is the supreme illustration.

The righteous pray for the Lord's ways (vv. 12-13). Although times were very dark, Isaiah's faith in God never wavered that the Lord would fulfill His promises just as He had in the past (v. 12). Their rebellion against God had caused other nations to rule over them (Deut. 28:15-68; Isa. 7:17-25; 8:5-8, 21-22; 52:4; Neh. 9:26-31), but Isaiah still had faith in the Lord (v. 13). Just as Paul wrote to the Philippians (1:6), Isaiah knew that God would perfect His good work with Israel. Judah's peace, however, will never come without The Prince of Peace (Isa. 9:6-7), the One who will remove all spiritual war (Isa. 40:1-2).

Those who reject the Lord's ways descend into ruin (v. 14). Verse 14 is obscure, but in the flowing context it appears to refer to the wicked leaders

---

[65] Young, *The Book of Isaiah*, vol. 2, 212-213.
[66] The essence of this desire is the Lord Himself—His name, His memory (Exod. 3:15; Ps. 30:4; Hos. 12:6; 14:8).
[67] Martin, "Isaiah," 1075.

who tried to destroy Israel, but have now passed into death and judgment.[68] Kidner explains, "[these are] the tyrants who have trespassed on the crown rights of Yahweh . . . *departed spirits*" who are now under the judgment of Yahweh.[69]

God's promise is that He will bring His ways to the world (v. 15). Despite their failures, Judah will survive, and in the end God will prosper them and multiply them (Isa. 9:3; 10:20-23; ch. 54).[70] This is His promise.[71]

Judah failed to accomplish the Lord's ways (vv. 16-18). Isaiah recognizes that they did seek the Lord in prayer, but he also recognizes that the Lord would not hear their prayer because His judgment was upon them (v. 16). Oswalt notes that even though verse 16 is obscure (and textual questions create questions), "the sense is that the hard experiences of Israel's history are seen as chastisements from God" (v. 16; cf. Isa. 59:1-2).[72] Ultimately, God is the One causing her grief, and until Judah repents, the Lord will not hear their pleas (Isa. 41:23-24; 45:7; Amos 3:6).

Isaiah vividly illustrates the failures of Judah by comparing the nation to a woman in labor (vv. 17-18).[73] Israel "might have been a source of blessing for the world at large but the people of Israel admitted their failure (v. 18)."[74] God's design was for Israel to be a light to the Gentiles, and thus she was like a woman in the midst of labor. Unfortunately, she gave birth only to wind,[75] and the

---

[68] Young explains, "He is not denying that in the general resurrection they too shall arise unto everlasting punishment. On that particular subject he is not now speaking. What he is saying, however is of comfort to the Israelites, for it teaches them that in the kingdom founded on Zion, they shall be free from those who formerly had oppressed them" (Young, *The Book of Isaiah, vol. 2*, 220).

[69] Kidner, "Isaiah," 649.

[70] In that day they Israel will eternally possess the land God swore to Abraham, Isaac, and Jacob (Gen. 12:1-3; 13:15; 15:18-21; 25:12), and Israel will be a mighty and numerous people who needs an expanded land (Deut. 4:6; Isa. 9:3; 49:19-21; 54:1ff.; Jer. 7:28; Mic. 7:11; Hag. 2:14; Zeph. 2:9; Pss. 33:12; 106:5).

[71] Young explains, "Adding to the nation would be an action of blessing, in that the nation would become increased through the inclusion of more members. This would rebound to God's honor" (Young, *The Book of Isaiah, vol. 2*, 221; Oswalt, *The Book of Isaiah, 1-39*, 482). Thus, these perfect stem verbs are best taken as prophetic perfects looking ahead to that day when all these blessings will be realized, and not seen as having been fulfilled in the past.

[72] Ibid., 484.

[73] Cf. similar childbirth imagery in Isa. 13:8; 21:3; 42:14; Hos. 9:14; Mic. 4:10.

[74] Wolf, *Interpreting Isaiah*, 144.

[75] This may mean that all laboring Israel did was pass gas.

inhabitants of the world (*tebel*) were not born.[76] Her spiritual harvest was a failure. Unger explains, "They will experience the pangs of childbirth without obtaining the salvation for which they hope."[77] Fortunately, God's Servant will bring a spiritual victory, and He will have His own "offspring" (Isa. 53:10; 54) and God's purpose will be accomplished (cf. Isa. 66:7-9).

Judah's realized salvation (vv. 19-21)

Even though Judah failed to fulfill God's spiritual purposes, the Lord will not fail. This includes God's promise of an eschatological resurrection (v. 19), as well as the promise of an eschatological deliverance (vv. 20-21).

The promise of eschatological resurrection (v. 19)

Isaiah's promise of resurrection. Verse 18 leaves us with the message of death and failure. Is there any hope? The answer is Yes. Three times in verse 19 God assures His people that their dead will have an ultimate resurrection victory at the end of the age.[78] Isaiah had already given us the promise that God will bring an eventual end to death in the kingdom (25:7-8), but here he adds the promise of resurrection to those who have already experienced death.

Other promises of resurrection. Other prophets give us further confirmation of the promise of a future resurrection.[79] The prophet Job lived some

---

[76] Another interpretive possibility is that the expression "born" (NASB, Heb. *naphal*, "to fall") is not referring to Israel giving spiritual childbirth but to Israel failing to see her enemies "fall" in battle (cf. 9-11 for this concept). The preceding parallel expression "salvation" (*yeshuah*) for the earth helps persuade this writer that Isaiah is speaking about a spiritual salvation to the world that was part of God's calling to the nation Israel (Isa. 42:6; 49:6).

[77] Merrill F. Unger, *Unger's Commentary on the Old Testament, Vol. II: Isaiah-Malachi* (Chicago: Moody, 1981), 1212.

[78] The first term is the broad term "the dead" (*muth*). The second term is the very physical term "corpses" (*nebelah*). The MT literally reads "my corpse" (a singular noun) but with a plural verb. This could a collective idea, though the Targum, BHS, and most modern translations make it "their corpses." LXX drops the suffix altogether (Oswalt, *The Book of Isaiah, 1-39*, 486). The third term "departed spirits" (*repha'iym*, cf. v. 14) is a term that highlights the immaterial aspect.

[79] Some passages speak about the resurrection of all men without delineating distinctions about the differences in timing between the saved and unsaved (John 5:28-29). Other passages make it explicit that the departed righteous are raised to enter the kingdom of God (Dan. 12:2; 1 Cor. 15:21-24, 50-58; 1 Thess. 4:13-18), but the unsaved are all raised at the end of the Millennium (Rev. 20:11-15).

1400 years before Isaiah, but God revealed this truth to him (Job 19:25-27). The prophet Abraham lived around the same time as Job, and God had also revealed the promise of resurrection to him (Gen. 22:5; cf. John 8:56; Heb. 11:17-19). In the sixth century B.C. Ezekiel gave the promise of resurrection as he revealed the promise that national Israel would rise in resurrection at the end of the age (Ezek. 37:1-14). Daniel prophesied in sixth century B.C. that God will bring a resurrection to His saints that they might share in the kingdom (Dan. 12:2-3, 13). The way to share in this resurrection is through faith in Christ (John 11:25-26).

The implications of God's resurrection. Isaiah illustrates the beauty of this precious promise by comparing God's resurrected saints to the glimmering "dew of the dawn" (cf. Ps. 110:3). Indeed, God's promises are meant to encourage His people that even though this is an age of sin, suffering, curse, and death, one day He will bring us a final victory (Rom. 8:18-30). Before this can happen, though, there must be one final period of horrific earthly conflict, one from which Israel will find deliverance.

The promise of eschatological deliverance (vv. 20-21)

Because of its transgression against God, Israel brought covenant curses upon itself (Deut. 28:15-68). The Babylonian exile introduced an extended time of judgment that Jesus described as "the times of the Gentiles" (Luke 21:24). These covenant curses will not end until Christ returns.

Various passages emphasize the idea that God's "indignation" (*za'am*) against Israel will remain until it is fully exhausted during one final period of time that God has decreed—the time period we call the great tribulation (Matt. 24:21-22).[80] After the rapture, great wrath will fall on Israel (1 Thess. 1:10; 2:16; 5:1-3; 2 Thess. 1:6-9; 2:8-12), but not in a way so as to destroy the nation completely (Jer. 30:11). Rather, it will destroy the unrepentant earth-dwellers (Jew and Gentile), cutting them off from entrance into the kingdom (Ezek. 20:36-38; Matt. 25:41, 46; Luke 21:35), but purging the elect (Jew and Gentile) to bring them to saving faith in the Messiah (Isa. 10:20-23; 27:12-13; cf. Ezek. 36:16-28;

---

[80] Daniel calls it "the time of the end" (8:17), the "final period of the indignation" (8:19), the "appointed time of the end" (8:19), the complete destruction that has been "decreed" (9:27), the period of time when the Antichrist will prosper "until the indignation is finished" and "that which is decreed is finished" (11:36), and the time, times, and half a time that must come until God has finished shattering the power of the holy people and all these events will be completed (12:7). As pointed out in previous comments, Israel's sin has produced a severe judgment that will not end until it has been fully spent (Isa. 5:25; 9:12, 17; 21; 10:4, 25; 12:1).

37:21-28; 39:25-29; Zech. 12:10; 13:8-9; Mal. 3:6; Matt. 25:34). In the end, the full force of God's wrath will turn from Israel to the nations that are seeking their destruction (Deut. 30:7; Isa. 10:25; 28:28-29; 40:1-2; Joel 3:1-17; Zeph. 3:8; Zech. 14:3; Rev. 19:11-21). Isaiah highlights two promises how God will save Israel.

God's first promise: Protection to the remnant of Israel (v. 20). The language is fascinating: "Come, my people, enter into your rooms and close your doors behind you; hide for a little while until indignation [the *za'am*] runs *its* course." The final period of indignation is coming, and Israel will not be left untouched. However, God's indignation will bring a purging to Israel, and then turn itself against the pagan nations who are seeking Israel's destruction. God's command to the remnant is to seek refuge in their "rooms" (inner chambers) and close the doors until the indignation has run its course.[81] One cannot help but think about the way that The Apocalypse shows how God will shelter His remnant from the murderous rage of the Antichrist at that time (Rev. 7:1-8; 9:4; 11:1-2; 12:6, 14-17; 14:1; cf. Zeph. 2:3; 3:12; Zech. 14:2b).

God's second promise: Destruction to the earth-dwellers (v. 21). God will save the remnant of Israel, but the nations that were seeking Israel's destruction will come to ruin, and the Lord will "come out from His place to punish the inhabitants of the earth for their iniquity."[82] The earth-dwellers will receive their just due in full measure and "the earth will reveal her bloodshed and will no longer cover her slain."[83]

Summary and application

One day God will make right all the wrongs. Our part is to keep our eyes focused on these promises to find strength to persevere until the sorrows of this world get eclipsed by the glories of His salvation (1 Pet. 1:13).

JUDGMENT ON THE WORLD, PT. 4 (27:1-13)

---

[81] Motyer notes how the language of hiding inside while God judges "recalls Exodus 12:22-23 and the safety of the Passover community while judgment was in process" (J. Alec Motyer, *The Prophecy of Isaiah: An Introduction and Commentary* [Downers Grove: IVP, 1993, 220).

[82] The statement "about to come out" (*yotse'*) stands in the form of a participle which brings out the idea of unexpectedness and imminence—an eschatological judgment that will come upon the world just like a thief in the night (Matt. 24:43-44; Luke 21:34-36; 1 Thess. 5:1-3; 2 Pet. 3:10; Rev. 3:3; 16:15).

[83] For the wicked, the return of Christ will mean no more escape from their murderous deeds, for the blood of the victims will cry out, and vengeance will come swiftly (cf. Gen. 4:10-11; 37:26; Job 16:18; Ezek. 24:7, 8; Rev. 6:10; 16:4-7).

Chapter 27 brings a close to Isaiah's focus on eschatological world judgments, so we find some minor debate on whether a chapter division was appropriate after chapter 26.[84] Regardless of outlines, the theme of God's eschatological work is what dominates the chapter.

Chapter 27 reads as follows: "1 In that day the Lord will punish Leviathan the fleeing serpent, with His fierce and great and mighty sword, even Leviathan the twisted serpent; and He will kill the dragon who *lives* in the sea. 2 In that day, a vineyard of wine, sing of it! 3 I, the Lord, am its keeper; I water it every moment. So that no one will damage it, I guard it night and day. 4 I have no wrath. Should someone give Me briars *and* thorns in battle, *then* I would step on them, I would burn them completely. 5 Or let him rely on My protection; let him make peace with Me; let him make peace with Me. 6 In the days to come Jacob will take root; Israel will blossom and sprout, and they will fill the whole world with fruit. 7 Like the striking of Him who has struck them, has He struck them? Or like the slaughter of His slain, have they been slain? 8 You contended with them by banishing them, by driving them away. With His fierce wind He has expelled *them* on the day of the east wind. 9 Therefore through this Jacob's iniquity will be forgiven; and this will be the full price of the pardoning of his sin: when he makes all the altar stones like pulverized chalk stones; *when* Asherim and incense altars will not stand. 10 For the fortified city is isolated, a homestead forlorn and forsaken like the desert. There the calf will graze, and there it will lie down and feed on its branches. 11 When its limbs are dry, they are broken off; women come *and* make a fire with them, for they are not a people of discernment; therefore their Maker will not have compassion on them, and their Creator will not be gracious to them. 12 In that day the Lord will start *His* threshing from the flowing stream of the Euphrates to the brook of Egypt, and you will be gathered up one by one, O sons of Israel. 13 It will come about also in that day that a great trumpet will be blown, and those who were perishing in the land of Assyria and who were scattered in the land of Egypt will come and worship the Lord in the holy mountain at Jerusalem" (27:1-13).

Chapter 27 may be broken down into four eschatological promises: a final end of the enemy (v. 1), a final end of the curse (vv. 2-6), a final end of covenant judgments (vv. 7-11), and a final end of the diaspora (vv. 12-13).

A final defeat of the enemy (v. 1)

Chapter 27 continues to be about the restoration of Israel, but verse 1

---

[84] The options include (1) 27:1 concludes the promises begun at 26:1, (2) 27:1 continues promises beginning at 26:20 and ending at 27:13, or (3) 27:1 is an independent section based on "in that day" (Oswalt, *The Book of Isaiah, 1-39*, 490).

reminds us about the need for God to defeat every one of his enemies. The Lord is going to punish (*phaqad*) the inhabitants of the earth (26:20), but there stands one enemy named Leviathan who also must be punished (*phaqad*) before God's work can be complete. As Grogan notes, "This fascinating verse presents a graphic picture of God the Great Warrior, going into battle against fearsome and monstrous enemies and utterly defeating them."[85] Just who or what is Leviathan the fleeing serpent?[86]

It would appear that Isaiah is using language of Canaanite mythology to convey the promise of Yahweh's sovereignty over everything, with an eventual defeat of all evil.[87] Thus, this reference to the defeat of Leviathan, the dragon, the fleeing serpent (*nachash*, cf. Gen. 3:1), is speaking about God's universal eschatological overthrow of all evil (cf. Deut. 32:41-42).[88]

It seems best, however, to not restrict this to simply to the overthrow of evil at an abstract level, but to see this as ultimately speaking about the overthrow of Satan and his demonic hosts. Yahweh is the Sovereign God who brings down every enemy, even Satan himself, the dragon, the great serpent of old (2 Cor. 11:3; Rev. 12:3, 9, 15; 20:2). Satan and his hosts will be bound in the bottomless pit during the Millennium (Rev. 20:1-3), but sent into permanent destruction in the Lake of Fire at the end of the Millennium (Rev. 20:10).

A final end of the curse (vv. 2-6)

For the second time, God introduces His promise with the expression "in that day." The promise of verses 2-6 revolves around the theme that one day God will reverse the curse that sin introduced.

God will care for His vineyard (vv. 2-3)

---

[85] Grogan, "Isaiah," 169.

[86] The Bible has several references to Leviathan (*liweyathan*, Job 3:8; 41:1; Pss. 74:14; 104:26) and a sea monster or dragon (*taniyn*, Job 7:12; Ezek. 29:3; 32:2). The references to Leviathan in Job and Psalm 104 appear to speak about giant water creatures, but the references in Ezekiel using *taniyn* seem to be speaking about an Egyptian crocodile as symbolizing Pharaoh (prob. also in Ps. 74; the author recalls a National Geographic article from 2002 about a skeleton they found of a 40-foot-long crocodile in the middle of the Sahara Desert; what a frightful foe he must have been). Pharaoh is also called *Rahab* in Isaiah 51:9.

[87] For example, in one Ugaritic passage it says, "When Thou dost smite *Lothan* the fleeing serpent and shall put an end to the tortuous serpent *Shalyat* of the seven heads" (Young, *The Book of Isaiah, vol. 2*, 233).

[88] Oswalt, *The Book of Isaiah, 1-39*, 491.

Back in chapter 5, Isaiah metaphorically described Israel as God's vineyard. Sadly, it was a vineyard that produced nothing but worthless grapes (5:2, 4) and briars and thorns (5:6). God's promise is that one day He is going to reverse Israel's apostasy so that they will bear fruit and become a vineyard worth singing over (v. 2; cf. 24:9; 25:5; 26:1, 19).[89] Thus, Israel need not fear, for the Lord Himself will keep the vineyard so that none should harm it (*phaqad*) that it might bear fruit (v. 3). All of this reminds us of the words of Jesus that He is the Vine, His Father is the Vinedresser, and all who abide in Him bear fruit (John 15).

Wrath will be gone forever (vv. 4-5)

When God's restoration of Israel is completed in The New Covenant, the ages of wrath and indignation will come to an end, and never again will Israel fall under such judgments as when she broke the Sinaitic Covenant (Jer. 31:31-34). The end of wrath means that the curse of "briars and thorns" (Isa. 5:6; 7:23, 24, 25; 10:17) will never again come upon Israel (v. 4). Should someone consider introducing briars and thorns, they should make peace with Yahweh (v. 5).

Israel can now bear fruit as God intends (v. 6)

Here in verse 6, we are once again reminded of God's promise to make His people bear fruit. By His grace, God will cause Jacob to "take root" (*sharash*), "blossom" (*tsuts*), and "sprout" (*parach*) so that Israel might become a fruitful nation that makes the very finest of fruit (*tenubah*; cf. Deut. 32:13; Ezek. 36:30; Isa. 11:1ff.; 37:31ff.; Hos. 14:5-7).

A final end of covenant judgments (vv. 7-11)

The tone now makes an abrupt shift. It is true that Israel will one day bear fruit for God (v. 6), but before this can happen, she must first be restored. Martin explains, "Because the Lord cares for His people, He will judge them and purify them so they can be fruitful."[90] Pfeiffer notes that in this passage, "God reveals his plan for Israel's future: survival through trial; purgation through suffering; and destruction for all her foes."[91]

---

[89] The reading of Leningradensis and 1QIs[a] is a word that means "wine" (*chemer*: not the common word for wine). However, the BHS follows other Heb. mss. and the LXX and Targums by reading the term "pleasant" vineyard (*chemed*)," a reading that matches passages like Isaiah 32:12 and Amos 5:11 (Ibid., 493; Grogan, "Isaiah," 174, n. 2). It may be preferable to follow Leningradensis and the DSS.
[90] Martin, "Isaiah," 1076.
[91] Pfeiffer, *The Wycliffe Bible Commentary: Old Testament*, Is 27:7.

Chastisement for repentance and not annihilation (v. 7)

Can God's judgment of the unbelieving world be compared to His chastisements against Israel? The answer is No. His judgment on the wicked nations will mean ruin, but for the elect of Israel it will mean purging and restoration as the chosen nation.

Extended exile is part of the plan (vv. 8-9a)

Thus, when the Lord strikes His people, it will include a banishing from His land by the "east wind" in the Babylonian exile (cf. Deut. 28:64).[92] Ultimately, however, this banishing will not lead to destruction, but a final restoration. Thus, exile and extended chastisement are part of the means how God will bring Jacob to repentance (cf. Isa. 50:1; 54:6-8; Jer. 31:31; Heb. 12:11). Young explains, "By sending Judah away into exile in moderation, thou art trying to contend or reason with her."[93]

The Babylonian exile is only the beginning (vv. 9b-11)

As history and progressive revelation reveal, the release from Babylon in 539 B.C. did not mean an end of God's chastisements. God's chastisements against Israel will not end until the return of Messiah. For Israel to be restored, God must bring Israel to complete repentance from every form of idolatry—an idolatry that had come to permeate the fortified city of Jerusalem in ancient times (vv. 9b-10; cf. Hos. 3:4-5; Zech. 13:1ff.).[94] All idolatry must be purged, and this is what Christ will accomplish in the great tribulation (Isa. 44:1-5; 57:17-19; 59:15-20). Desolations have been decreed for Israel (Dan. 9:27), but "desolations" are not the end of the story.

A final end of the diaspora (vv. 12-13)

A final harvest (v. 12)

God will restore His scattered people to their own land once again and put an end to the diaspora that began with the Babylonian exile. Isaiah describes

---

[92] "East winds" were the scorching scirocco winds off of the eastern desert (Job 27:21; Ps. 48:8; Jer. 18;17; Ezek. 27:26; Hos. 13:15), but here it is Babylonian exile.

[93] Young, *The Book of Isaiah, vol. 2*, 243. Young continues: "The basic thought seems to be that God has punished Judah according to measure, determining precisely this measure so that Judah will not perish by a punishment that exceeds this measure [cf. Matt. 24:22]" (ibid., 244). (interesting words for an Amillennialist)

[94] The utter desolation is symbolically portrayed as Jerusalem being a pasture field where all limbs are stripped and dead (cf. Ezek. 31; Matt. 23:39).

this eschatological restoration of Israel as God's harvest work,[95] another one of God's assurances that He will not abandon His people (cf. Isa. 49:14-16). The elect of Israel will be threshed, but then they will be gathered up "one by one" (v. 12; cf. Is. 11:11-12; 43:5-7; 66:20; Ezek. 39:25-29; Zech. 10:11). The harvest of elect Israel will be widespread and universal, beginning with threshing from the flowing stream of the Euphrates River,[96] and extending southward to the Brook of Egypt.[97]

A remnant will return (v. 13)

God's restoration of Israel will bring them to the place they should have been all along, a nation who worships Yahweh. The trumpet will sound for God's restoration (cf. Matt. 24:31), and at long last the redeemed remnant of Israel will worship the Lord in Zion (Isa. 2:2-4; 24:23; 25:6, 10). Restored Israel will include a remnant from every nation from every corner of the earth, even Assyria and Egypt (cf. Isa. 19:23-25).

Summary and application

Our God is worthy to be worshipped since He is the One who has purchased the redemption of His people by the blood of His only Son. This message of redemption is one over which we need to rejoice, and it is one we need to keep proclaiming until the Lord returns or calls us home.

---

[95] Young explains: "The Lord will beat so that the fruit or grain falls, and the re-gathering may then be compared to such a falling. This will be done so as to re-gather men so that they will occupy the once promised land" (ibid., 250).

[96] The term "flowing stream" (Heb. *shibbeloth*) is best seen as a flowing stream and not grain heads as elsewhere—the flowing stream of the Euphrates River in Assyria (Josh. 24:15; Isa. 8:7).

[97] This is not the Nile, but the Wadi 'El 'Arish on the border between Israel and Egypt, the southern border of the promised land (Gen. 15:18; 1 Kings 8:56; Ezek. 47:15-19).

6
TRUST IN THE FLESH AND YOU WILL FAIL (28:1-35:10)

Chapters 28-35 turn the focus from God's judgment on the nations (chs. 13-27) back to a primary focus on Israel and Judah.[1] Chapters 28-29 emphasize the folly of Israel's leaders; 30-31 emphasize their folly of trusting in Egypt; 32-33 emphasize how God will judge them for not trusting Him; 34 brings a special focus on God's judgment of Edom, a judgment that may symbolically represent a universal overthrow of evil such as seen in 24-25; 35 focuses on the arrival of the kingdom and the restoration of Israel, the eschatological restoration we saw back in 26-27.

WOE TO THE DRUNKARDS OF ISRAEL (28:1-29)

Chapter 28 contains repeated references to the drunkenness of Israel's leaders. These statements have literal realities behind them, but they also represent broader spiritual principles as well, i.e., spiritual drunkenness.

Chapter 28 reads as follows: "1 Woe to the proud crown of the drunkards of Ephraim, and to the fading flower of its glorious beauty, which is at the head of the fertile valley of those who are overcome with wine! 2 Behold, the Lord has a strong and mighty *agent;* as a storm of hail, a tempest of destruction, like a storm of mighty overflowing waters, He has cast *it* down to the earth with *His* hand. 3 The proud crown of the drunkards of Ephraim is trodden under foot. 4 And the fading flower of its glorious beauty, which is at the head of the fertile valley, will be like the first-ripe fig prior to summer, which one sees, *and* as soon as it is in his hand, he swallows it. 5 In that day the Lord of hosts will become a beautiful crown and a glorious diadem to the remnant of His people; 6 a spirit

---

[1] Herbert Wolf, *Interpreting Isaiah* (Grand Rapids: Zondervan, 1985), 147.

of justice for him who sits in judgment, a strength to those who repel the onslaught at the gate. 7 And these also reel with wine and stagger from strong drink: The priest and the prophet reel with strong drink; they are confused by wine, they stagger from strong drink; they reel while having visions; they totter *when rendering* judgment. 8 For all the tables are full of filthy vomit, without a *single clean* place. 9 To whom would He teach knowledge, and to whom would He interpret the message? Those *just* weaned from milk? Those *just* taken from the breast? 10 For *He says,* Order on order, order on order, line on line, line on line, a little here, a little there. 11 Indeed, He will speak to this people through stammering lips and a foreign tongue, 12 He who said to them, Here is rest, give rest to the weary, and, Here is repose, but they would not listen. 13 So the word of the Lord to them will be, order on order, order on order, line on line, line on line, a little here, a little there, that they may go and stumble backward, be broken, snared and taken captive. 14 Therefore, hear the word of the Lord, O scoffers, who rule this people who are in Jerusalem, 15 because you have said, We have made a covenant with death, and with *Sheol* we have made a pact. The overwhelming scourge will not reach us when it passes by, for we have made falsehood our refuge and we have concealed ourselves with deception. 16 Therefore thus says the Lord God, Behold, I am laying in Zion a stone, a tested stone, a costly cornerstone *for* the foundation, firmly placed. He who believes *in it* will not be disturbed. 17 I will make justice the measuring line and righteousness the level; then hail will sweep away the refuge of lies and the waters will overflow the secret place. 18 Your covenant with death will be canceled, and your pact with *Sheol* will not stand; when the overwhelming scourge passes through, then you become its trampling *place.* 19 As often as it passes through, it will seize you; for morning after morning it will pass through, *anytime* during the day or night, and it will be sheer terror to understand what it means. 20 The bed is too short on which to stretch out, and the blanket is too small to wrap oneself in. 21 For the Lord will rise up as *at* Mount Perazim; He will be stirred up as in the valley of Gibeon, to do His task, His unusual task, and to work His work, His extraordinary work. 22 And now do not carry on as scoffers, or your fetters will be made stronger, for I have heard from the Lord God of hosts of decisive destruction on all the earth. 23 Give ear and hear my voice; listen and hear my words. 24 Does the farmer plow continually to plant seed? Does he *continually* turn and harrow the ground? 25 Does he not level its surface and sow dill and scatter cummin and plant wheat in rows, barley in its place and rye within its area? 26 For his God instructs and teaches him properly. 27 For dill is not threshed with a threshing sledge, nor is the cartwheel driven over cummin; but dill is beaten out with a rod, and cummin with a club. 28 *Grain for* bread is crushed, indeed, he does not continue to thresh it forever. Because the wheel of *his* cart and his horses *eventually* damage *it,* He does not thresh it longer. 29 This also comes from the Lord of hosts, *Who* has made *His* counsel wonderful and *His* wisdom great" (28:1-29).

Chapter 28 has a message that is first directed against Israel (vv. 1-13), and then against Judah (vv. 14-29).

God's message to the people of Israel (vv. 1-13)

This section opens with a "woe" upon the leaders of Israel. This woe, however, is only the beginning of a series of woes in 28-33. Martin notes,

> Isaiah continued his theme of judgment with a series of "woes" against various groups who were opposing his words. Here he was attacking primarily the rulers of the Northern and Southern Kingdoms for their failure to heed God's Word and for looking to other means for protection.[2]

By this woe, Isaiah is declaring the anger of God against those who should trust Him but do not. The leaders of Ephraim, i.e., the northern kingdom, are likened to drunkards who refuse to listen. It is a dangerous thing to hear God, but then refuse to listen. For this reason, an overwhelming judgment is coming to Israel (vv. 1-4). Messiah is their only hope (vv. 5-8), but will the people listen (vv. 9-13)?

An overwhelming judgment is coming to Israel (vv. 1-4)

As this woe indicates, impending disaster is coming against the still-standing northern kingdom. This disaster will leave them with no answer or solution.[3] The city is beautiful (v. 1), but it is headed for doom (vv. 2-4).

A beautiful city (v. 1). Physically speaking, Samaria, the capital of the northern kingdom (which had broken from Judah in 931 B.C.), was a very beautiful place.[4] Jeroboam I made his capital at Shechem (1 Kings 12:25) and Tirzah

---

[2] John A. Martin, "Isaiah," in *The Bible Knowledge Commentary: An Exposition of the Scriptures*, ed. J. F. Walvoord and R. B. Zuck, vol. 1, cited in electronic form with Logos Libronix (Wheaton, IL: Victor Books, 1985), 1076. Six times in this section we see a unit introduced by the expression "Woe" (28:1; 29:1, 15; 30:1; 31:1; 33:1; cf. 1:4, 24; 5:8, 11, 18, 20, 22, 22; 10:1, 5; 16:4; 17:12; 18:1; 45:9, 10; 55:1).

[3] Edward J. Young, *The Book of Isaiah, vol. 2* (Grand Rapids: Eerdmans, 1965), 263. Many commentators acknowledge that this is a difficult verse for translation. The NIV renders it as, "Woe to the coronet of pride of the drunkards of Ephraim and to the fading flower of its glorious beauty that is on the head of the fat valley of those who are stunned with wine."

[4] Despite the physical beauty, spiritually it was apostate from the beginning. The northern kingdom was built on a false king (19 kings in 200 years) and a false system of worship (idols at Dan and Bethel).

(1 Kings 14:17), but it was Omri the sixth king of Israel (885-874), and later Ahab (874-853), who built Samaria into a grand capital (1 Kings 16:23-24).[5] The city rose up above the surrounding fertile valley (Heb. "fat valley"; cf. 2 Josh 8:11; Chron. 15:8), a hill "which bore a crown, even the city itself."[6]

A city destined for doom (vv. 2-4). Isaiah compares Samaria to a beautiful, flowery garland (a crown or wreath) whose beauty is very short-lived.[7] Mighty Assyria was coming like a flood, and in a short time they would kill thousands and take 27,290 into captivity, leaving behind only a small remnant (vv. 2-3; cf. 2 Kings 17). To the Assyrians, Samaria would be like a tasty early fig desired by all. Over time, Assyria also imported masses of foreigners to minimize future rebellions (Isa. 7:8; Ezra 4:9-19).[8] They should have recognized that their demise was drawing near, but they would not listen.[9] When Assyria finally came, it might have seemed that Samaria was cut off in its prime, but "signs of a descent into decay were already present."[10]

---

[5] This mountaintop capital whose name means "mountain of watching" was located in central Israel 42 miles north of Jerusalem. Samaria was a rich city (Hos. 9:6; 12:9; 13:15) and a strong city (Isa. 17:3). Ahab had built a magnificent ivory palace in Samaria, one for which Amos denounced him (Amos 6:1, 4; cf. 1 Kings 22:39). This palace was the center of godlessness and Baal worship (1 Kings 16:29-33) and a place where Jezebel killed many prophets of Yahweh (1 Kings 18:2-4).

[6] Ibid., 264. Fertile Shechem lay on the southeast edge and fertile Sharon lay to the west.

[7] Samaria was a very brilliant city whose shining could be seen from the Mediterranean. Because Israel was quite powerful in its early days, they could afford to be seen by those at sea without fear of being conquered, and in their pride they hated the rebuke of God's true prophets (Amos 3:11-15; 4:1-3; 5:10; 6:1). Isaiah likens Samaria to a beautiful, flowery garland (*'atarah*, cf. v. 5).

[8] These mixed people groups became the beginning of what would be called The Samaritans (Ezra 4:1-3; Neh. 4:7; Luke 9:52-54; 10:25-37; 17:11-19; John 4:1; 8:48). The Greeks conquered Samaria in 331 B.C. and in 119 B.C. John Hyrcanus led the Hasmoneans and destroyed the entire city. Samaria did not become a city again until 63 B.C. in the days of Pompey. In 30 B.C. Herod the Great rebuilt it and made it one of his chief cities, renaming it *Sebaste* (reverend) in honor of the emperor (Greek for *Augustus*). Rome destroyed it again around A.D. 66 only to be rebuilt again and remain as it has till this day as *Sebaste*. Modern-day Samaritans live there and carry out Samaritan worship, even carrying out a Passover Sacrifice.

[9] Wolf estimates that Isaiah's warnings were around 725 B.C. (Wolf, *Interpreting Isaiah*, 148).

[10] G. W. Grogan, "Isaiah," in *The Expositor's Bible Commentary*, ed. Frank E. Gaebelein, vol. 6 (Grand Rapids: Zondervan, 1986), 178.

Messiah is the only hope (vv. 5-8)

There is a hope for the people of God in the promised Messiah (vv. 5-6). Sadly, they would not listen, and judgment would be the result (vv. 7-8).

A promise to heed (vv. 5-6). Isaiah introduces God's messianic promise with an eschatological hint by using the expression "in that day" (cf. 4:1ff.). Samaria's crown was the empty crown of sin and pride, but the One they should have trusted in was the true Crown, the Lord Himself who would become a glorious diadem for His remnant (v. 5). Young explains, "When the false object of pride has been removed through the sovereign work of the God of Israel, then it will appear that the Lord Himself, the Lord of Hosts, will be the crown of glory."[11]

Isaiah further describes Messiah by calling Him a "spirit of justice for him who sits in judgment" and a "strength to those who repel the onslaught at the gate" (v. 6; cf. 11:1-5). In other words, the Spirit of Messiah will enable Him to carry out perfect justice when He is here to judge His people (cf. 32:1) and repel the enemy (Zech. 14:3ff.).

A promise rejected (vv. 7-8). There comes a point when God ceases to strive with men and brings judgment (e.g., Gen. 6; 11; 19). King David reminds the people that they should listen to God before it is too late: "For this cause everyone who is godly shall pray to You in a time when You may be found; surely in a flood of great waters they shall not come near him" (Ps. 32:15). Even though God's promise was there, their refusal to listen demanded judgment. Their rebellion is characterized by a severe abuse of alcohol, both wine (*yayin*) and strong drink (*shekar*),[12] a severe drunkenness that even characterized the priests and the (false) prophets (v. 7).[13]

The condition was widespread: "all the tables are full of filthy vomit,[14] without a *single clean* place" (v. 8). The people had God's promises, but as the

---

[11] Young, *The Book of Isaiah, vol. 2*, 269. Messiah is likened not only to a garland (*atarah*), but also a glorious diadem (*tsepiyrah*, a plaited wreath; cf. Judg. 7:3; Ezek. 7:7). This blessing will belong to the remnant (*she'ar*; Isa. 4:3; 10:19, 20, 21, 22; 11:11, 16; 14:22; 16:14; 17:3, 6; 21:17; 24:6, 12; 28:5; 37:31; 49:21; cf. Zech. 13:8-9; Rom. 11:25-26).

[12] Strong drink was a high sugar, high alcohol drink that was always condemned in Scripture (Prov. 20:1; 31:4-6).

[13] The abuse was so bad that that the people would "stagger" (*ta'ah*, go astray, wander) and "reel" (*shagah*, stagger)

[14] The term "vomit" (*tso'ah*) speaks of refuse, vomit, or excrement (Isa. 4:4; 36:12; Ezek. 32:6; Prov. 32:12).

New Living Translation puts it, "now, however, Israel is led by drunks who reel with wine and stagger with alcohol" (cf. Mic. 3:9-12). With a condition like this, you would think that Israel would surely listen to Isaiah, but sadly they wanted nothing to do with that pesty prophet of Yahweh.

What kind of speech will the people listen to? (vv. 9-13)

Unsaved people hate the truth of God's Word, but they love the lies of the world (John 8:40, 45). Here in 9-13, we see how Israel rejected the word of the Lord through Isaiah (vv. 9-10), and how God would respond for rejecting His prophet (vv. 11-13).

The people's rejection of Isaiah's plain speech (vv. 9-10). Those speaking appear to be the unsaved leaders whom Isaiah has been rebuking. Martin explains,

> The speakers in verse 9 are probably the priests and prophets mentioned in verses 7–8. They were angry that Isaiah was treating them as if they were young children. They felt they were adults who could think for themselves; they had no need for someone to tell them what to do or think. So they mimicked Isaiah as if he were speaking "baby talk" to them (v. 10).[15]

In light of the Assyrian threat, the unsaved leaders saw Isaiah's command to trust the Lord like an adult teaching a little child with pedantic language (v. 10; cf. similar mockery in 5:19).[16] In other words, "Come on, Isaiah, stop harping on us with your simplistic message about trusting Yahweh." These wicked leaders despised God's simple message of trust and obedience, and they could not even recognize how badly they had turned away from truth (Isa. 5:18-23). Because the people would not listen to Isaiah's straightforward language, God tells them that He would speak to them in a language they would have to listen to.

God's reply with a language they will have to listen to (vv. 11-13). The "stammering lips" and "foreign tongue" God would speak through would be through the mouths of the Assyrian soldiers whom God was about to bring upon His rebellious people (v. 11; cf. Deut. 28:45; Jer. 5:15).[17] Isaiah tells them

---

[15] Martin, "Isaiah," 1077.
[16] Their words have a repetitious assonance in Hebrew: "order on order" (*tsaw letsaw tsaw letsaw*), "line on line" (*qaw leqaw qaw leqaw*), and a "little here and a little there" (*zeyar sham zeyar sham*).
[17] The Akkadian language was Semitic, but quite garbled and strange to the Hebrews.

that God's word about "rest" and "repose" really was a passionate plea to listen to God that they might find true relief from their woes (cf. Matt. 11:27ff.), but the sad reality is that they would not listen to this offer of rest (v. 12; cf. 8:12-14; Matt. 23:37). Instead, they were running to Egypt for help just as Ahaz had run to Assyria for help a decade earlier (Isa. 30:1-3; 31:1-15). Therefore, because God spoke but they would not listen, God will speak to them with the most basic of words that will get their attention, a foreign invasion that would crush them and take them into captivity (v. 13).[18]

God's message to the people of Judah (vv. 14-29)

The focus shifts to Judah and Jerusalem. If God judged the northern kingdom, "therefore" (v. 14) Judah had better listen or it will be no different for her. As history would show, she too would be overthrown by foreign invaders (Babylon 100 years later). This section may be outlined as follows: (1) A true hope will save (vv. 14-17), (2) a false hope will fail (vv. 18-22), and (3) a saving hope will come (vv. 23-29).

A true hope will save (vv. 14-17)

Pride is a stumbling block (v. 14). Hope in the Lord is a saving hope, but the pride of man is always opposed to such trust.[19] Because Judah was refusing to listen to God, Isaiah addresses them as being "scoffers" (*'anshey latson*, sinners who hear God, but refuse to listen; cf. Ps. 1:1; Prov. 1:22, et al.).[20] The scoffer, explains Grogan, is the one who is "utterly contemptuous of the ways of God."[21] God exposes their empty hope and reveals what the true hope is.

The empty hope of the people (v. 15). Isaiah recites the false hope of Judah as being a covenant with death (i.e., a pact with *Sheol*). Isaiah is using symbolic imagery to express the thoughts of the leaders who thought they were

---

Paul used this passage in 1 Corinthians 14:21-22 to illustrate how tongues in the apostolic age carried with them a "sign" function.

[18] Motyer explains, "When the simple intelligibility of the word of God is refused, divine judgment falls in the shape of the unintelligible" (J. Alec Motyer, *The Prophecy of Isaiah: An Introduction and Commentary* [Downers Grove: IVP, 1993], 232).

[19] Unfortunately, men end up trusting in their own wisdom, their own power, or the power of some other earthly source and they end up severely disappointed (cf. Jer. 17:5; Pss. 118:8-9; 146:3).

[20] Oswalt, *The Book of Isaiah, 1-39*, 516.

[21] Grogan, "Isaiah," 180.

immune from disaster because of their own military planning, especially their alliance with Egypt (cf. Jer. 2:13-19).[22] Kidner explains,

> The *covenant with death* and *with the grave* (lit. *Sheol*) could perhaps allude to an invocation of gods of the underworld, *e.g.* in necromancy (*cf.* 8:19) or in a treaty with Egypt. It is, however, more probably to be understood like the boast in v 15b of *a lie* and *falsehood, i.e.* as God's estimate of their hope, put into their mouths.[23]

They thought that the Assyrian "scourge" (*shot*, an outburst and flood of water) could not touch them,[24] but they were fooling themselves.

The true hope (vv. 16-17). The true hope would be the promised Messiah, the costly cornerstone God would one day place in Zion v. 16).[25] He is the tested Stone, the true Foundation, the One they needed to trust.[26] God promises that the one who believes in Him will never be disturbed (v. 16b; cf. 8:17; 25:9; 26:8; 30:18; 33:2), for He is the One who will usher in the age of justice and righteousness that will purge away the lies and ruin of sin (v. 17). For those who refuse, "the false foundation of the worldly wise was to be violently swept away in the catastrophe of Assyrian invasion, and Judah's treaty of alliance would prove to be a false refuge."[27]

A false hope will fail (vv. 18-22)

The failure of Judah's false hope (vv. 18-20). Their empty sources of trust would bring them to ruin (v. 18; cf. 5:5; 7:25; 10:6). God again warns them

---

[22] Oswalt, *The Book of Isaiah, 1-39*, 516.

[23] F. Derek Kidner, "Isaiah," in *New Bible Commentary: 21st Century Edition*, ed. D. A. Carson et al., 4th ed., cited in electronic form with Logos Libronix (Leicester, England; Downers Grove, IL: Inter-Varsity Press, 1994), 650.

[24] The imagery is that of a military invasion that comes like a mighty flood (Isa. 8:8; 10:22, 26; cf. Dan. 11:10, 26, 40; Rev. 12:15-16 [Young, *The Book of Isaiah, vol. 2*, 283, n. 26]).

[25] The "therefore" (*laken*) shows how the promise of Messiah comes immediately on the heels of Judah's disbelief just as it did earlier in 7:14. We find the same foundation stone imagery in Isa. 8:14; 26:4; Rom. 9:33; 10:11; 1 Pet. 2:6-8. For other stone imagery (Gen. 49:24; Deut. 32:4; Dan. 2:34-35; Zech. 3:9; Ps. 118:22; Matt. 21:42; Mk. 12:10; Luke 20:17; Acts 4:11; Eph. 2:20).

[26] Joseph A. Alexander, *Commentary on Isaiah* (Grand Rapids: Kregel, 1992), 455.

[27] Charles F. Pfeiffer, *The Wycliffe Bible Commentary: Old Testament*, cited in electronic form with Logos Libronix, Is 28:17.

that this military scourge will envelop the whole land and bring "sheer terror" to all (v. 19). The endless assaults (which started with Assyria but have continued to this present day) will leave Israel stripped of all its former sources of false hope like a bed and blanket that are too small to keep one warm (v. 20).[28]

God will judge the enemy (vv. 21-22). Nevertheless, God will intervene as a Judge against His enemies as indicated by two illustrations from Israel's history: (1) Mount Perazim was the place where God defeated the Philistines by the hand of David (2 Sam. 5:20; 1 Chron. 14:11). (2) Gibeon was the great hailstorm victory God gave Joshua over the Canaanites during the conquest (Josh. 10:11). The Lord will once again arise and judge His enemies in an "unusual task" and "extraordinary work" (v. 21).[29] God will judge Assyria, but the people of Judah needed to recognize that if they would not repent and believe, they too would be reckoned as worthy of judgment (Isa. 5:12; Hos. 5:14-15; Amos 5:18).[30] Therefore, Isaiah commands the "scoffers" to listen (v. 22).

A saving hope will come (vv. 23-29)

Judgment is coming, but God still extends the hope of salvation. With this idea, we are once again reminded of the reality that God's eternal plan always involves elements of human responsibility (v. 23) as well as divine sovereignty (vv. 24-29).

Human responsibility (v. 23). Isaiah uses four simple commands to plead with the people lest judgment intensify (cf. 1:18-20). Man's responsibility is to obey the will of God. If he does this, he will find blessings instead of judgment. Unfortunately, Israel was not going to listen. Even this, however, was part of God's plan to bring an eventual restoration.

Divine sovereignty (vv. 24-29). Many theologians have wrestled with the relationship of human freedom and divine responsibility. One of the key truths we find in Scripture is that our God has an eternal plan that He is working out, and His good and perfect plan embraces every event in human history, including the choices of men. Isaiah uses the illustration of farm work (vv. 24-28) to convey the spiritual principle that God's judgment on Israel is according to His plan for their eventual restoration.

Farmers plow and plant, but plowing and planting are only one part of the work (vv. 24-26). Likewise, harvesting is carried out for a limited time and only

---

[28] Wolf, *Interpreting Isaiah*, 149.
[29] Kidner notes that Luther found much comfort in that while judgment is Christ's *strange work*, salvation is his *proper work* (Kidner, "Isaiah," 650).
[30] Oswalt, *The Book of Isaiah, 1-39*, 524.

in a certain manner to accomplish the harvest goal. Harvesting must be done with care and the proper tools otherwise the harvest will be ruined (vv. 27-28).[31] Martin explains, "Caraway and cumin (aromatic herbs) are beaten out with a rod or stick (not threshed) because their seeds are so small. Grain is ground by millstone after the wheat stalks are threshed."[32] Thus, these judgments are not designed for ultimate destruction, but redemption (Isa. 26:20; 54:7-8; Hab. 3:2; Lam. 3:21ff.).

For Judah this means there must be a period of wrath (Isa. 5:25; 9:12, 17, 21; 10:4, 25), but in the end there will be a restoration when God's wrath has turned away (Isa. 12:1-6; cf. chs. 40-66). All of this, says Isaiah, "comes from the Lord of hosts, *Who* has made *His* counsel wonderful and *His* wisdom great" (v. 29; cf. Rom. 11:25-36).[33]

Summary and application

The Apostle Paul marveled over the wisdom of God as he pondered the future restoration of Israel (Rom. 11:25-36). Paul quotes from Isaiah 59 with the reminder that Christ will come from Zion and save His people. We know that the promises of God are certain and true. This is true for both corporate Israel as well as every individual who places their trust in Jesus Christ. The faithfulness and sovereignty of God give us great assurance that no matter what life may bring, we are safe in His hands.

ARIEL: THE CITY OF DEAD RELIGION (29:1-24)

God's rebuke against defiant Judah flows into chapter 29. Blessings could come to Judah if they would just obey the Lord, but they won't come as long as she is defiant to Yahweh.

Chapter 29 reads as follows: "1 Woe, O Ariel, Ariel the city *where* David *once* camped! Add year to year, observe *your* feasts on schedule. 2 I will bring distress to Ariel, and she will be *a city of* lamenting and mourning; and she will be like an Ariel to me. 3 I will camp against you encircling *you,* a*nd* I will set siegeworks against you, and I will raise up battle towers against you. 4 Then you will be brought low; from the earth you will speak, and from the dust *where* you are prostrate your words *will come.* Your voice will also be like that of a spirit from the ground, and your speech will whisper from the dust. 5 But the

---

[31] Wolf, *Interpreting Isaiah*, 150.
[32] Martin, "Isaiah," 1078.
[33] The roots for both "counsel" (*'etsah*) and "wonderful" (*pele'*) are found in describing the Messiah in 9:6 (cf. 25:1).

multitude of your enemies will become like fine dust, and the multitude of the ruthless ones like the chaff which blows away; and it will happen instantly, suddenly. 6 From the Lord of hosts you will be punished with thunder and earthquake and loud noise, *with* whirlwind and tempest and the flame of a consuming fire. 7 and the multitude of all the nations who wage war against Ariel, even all who wage war against her and her stronghold, and who distress her, will be like a dream, a vision of the night. 8 It will be as when a hungry man dreams—and behold, he is eating; but when he awakens, his hunger is not satisfied, or as when a thirsty man dreams—and behold, he is drinking, but when he awakens, behold, he is faint and his thirst is not quenched. Thus the multitude of all the nations will be who wage war against Mount Zion. 9 Be delayed and wait, blind yourselves and be blind; they become drunk, but not with wine, they stagger, but not with strong drink. 10 For the Lord has poured over you a spirit of deep sleep; he has shut your eyes, the prophets; and He has covered your heads, the seers. 11 The entire vision will be to you like the words of a sealed book, which when they give it to the one who is literate, saying, Please read this, he will say, I cannot, for it is sealed. 12 Then the book will be given to the one who is illiterate, saying, Please read this, and he will say, I cannot read. 13 Then the Lord said, Because this people draw near with their words and honor Me with their lip service, but they remove their hearts far from Me, and their reverence for Me consists of tradition learned *by rote*, 14 Therefore behold, I will once again deal marvelously with this people, wondrously marvelous; and the wisdom of their wise men will perish, and the discernment of their discerning men will be concealed. 15 Woe to those who deeply hide their plans from the Lord, and whose deeds are *done* in a dark place, and they say, Who sees us? or Who knows us? 16 You turn *things* around! Shall the potter be considered as equal with the clay, that what is made would say to its maker, He did not make me; or what is formed say to him who formed it, He has no understanding? 17 Is it not yet just a little while before Lebanon will be turned into a fertile field, and the fertile field will be considered as a forest? 18 On that day the deaf will hear words of a book, and out of *their* gloom and darkness the eyes of the blind will see. 19 The afflicted also will increase their gladness in the Lord, and the needy of mankind will rejoice in the Holy One of Israel. 20 For the ruthless will come to an end and the scorner will be finished; indeed all who are intent on doing evil will be cut off, 21 who cause a person to be indicted by a word, and ensnare him who adjudicates at the gate, and defraud the one in the right with meaningless arguments. 22 Therefore thus says the Lord, who redeemed Abraham, concerning the house of Jacob: Jacob shall not now be ashamed, nor shall his face now turn pale; 23 But when he sees his children, the work of My hands, in his midst, they will sanctify My name; indeed, they will sanctify the Holy One of Jacob and will stand in awe of the God of Israel. 24 Those who err in mind will know the truth, and those who criticize will accept instruction" (29:1-24).

Jesus told us that God is looking for true worshippers (John 4:23-24), i.e., people of sincere faith. True worship is not a matter of religious ritual (cf. 1 Sam. 15:22), but humble faith that recognizes the need for grace and mercy (Isa. 1:11; 57:15; 66:1-2). True believers live out their faith (Isa. 33:13-17; 58:6-7; Hos. 6:6; Mic. 6:8), but all of this was far from ancient Judah. For this reason, God announces two woes.

First woe: Religious Jerusalem will be brought low (vv. 1-14)

Jerusalem was blessed with many spiritual privileges, but privileges without faith are worthless. This section may be outlined as follows: Jerusalem will be brought low (vv. 1-4); the brutal enemy will be brought low (vv. 5-8); the spiritual drunkards will be brought low (vv. 9-14).

Jerusalem will be brought low (vv. 1-4)

The religious formalists will be judged, and God will bring great degradation to Judah (v. 1). Four times in verses 1-2 God speaks to Jerusalem by calling her with the name "Ariel" (which literally means "lion of God"). It is not quite clear why God calls Jerusalem by this name, but it appears that this is a reference to Jerusalem by virtue of the parallel statement that calls it "The City where David once camped" (this could be the idea that David had camped against the city in capturing it, or better that he camped in it by living in it as his capital city).[34]

Regardless of how one understands "Ariel," one thing is sure: Jerusalem is the city in question. God is going to judge Jerusalem severely and it will become like an "altar hearth" to God (v. 2). Enemy armies will surround the city and bring it so low all they will be able to do is whisper for help (vv. 3-4; cf. 26:16). The reason is pride and disbelief. Young paraphrases: "Celebrate your feasts

---

[34] One idea is that the term "lion" hearkens back to the prophecies to Judah (Gen. 49:8-12; 2 Sam. 23:20; 1 Kings 10:19-20; 1 Chron. 11:22; Isa. 31:4; Mic. 5:7), while others suggest that the expression could be taken to mean "altar hearth" since the Hebrew term for "hearth" resembles Ariel, and the Targum reads the "altar of God" (Oswalt, *The Book of Isaiah, 1-39*, 526; Young, *The Book of Isaiah, vol. 2*, 305, n. 1). Grogan adds, "The name Ariel does possess a certain naturalness if in fact it actually means altar hearth, so that in all four occurrences (two in v. 1 and two in v. 2) it would bear the same meaning. Its naturalness derives from the fact that Jerusalem was a place of sacrifice, with an altar hearth in the temple where sacrifices were always burning" (Grogan, "Isaiah," 187). Webb notes that "there is no doubt that *Ariel* in verses 1-2 is a code word for Jerusalem" (Barry G. Webb, *The Message of Isaiah* [Downers Grove: IVP, 1996], 123).

regularly, year by year as you have been doing. It will be of no avail,"[35] for you will be brought to judgment (Isa. 35:10; 51:11; cf. Lam. 1:22; 2:5).

The brutal enemy will be brought low (vv. 5-8)

Judah will be brought low, but the enemy will be brought to complete ruin. We see this in verses 5-8 as Isaiah declares that "not only can God save them now, he can also save them after they will have experienced the consequences of their refusal to trust Him."[36] Isaiah makes four declarations about how the Lord will deliver them from their enemies.

First declaration of how God will judge the enemy (v. 5a). Jerusalem will be brought low into the dust (v. 4, *'aphar*), but the enemies will be judged so severely that they will become like "fine dust" (*'abaq daq*). Mighty Assyria will not have the final victory. Martin explains,

> Jerusalem's protection described in these verses refers to her deliverance from Assyria, recorded in chapter 37. It would have seemed impossible to hope that the Assyrians would not take the city. Only by God's sovereign intervention was Jerusalem spared.[37]

Second declaration of how God will judge the enemy (v 5b). The enemy will be made like fine dust, but also like "chaff" (*mots*) which the wind blows away. God's anger against Jerusalem will turn and bring sudden ruin upon the ruthless enemies of Jerusalem.

Third declaration of how God will judge the enemy (v. 6). Isaiah likens God's judgment to the tempests of nature with theophany imagery (cf. Exod. 19:16-19; Judg. 4-5; Ps. 18:7-15; Ezek. 20:47-48; Hab. 3:3-7; Rev. 8:5; 11:19; 16:18). A storm is coming upon the enemies of Israel.

Fourth declaration of how God will judge the enemy (vv. 7-8). Lastly, God's judgment is likened to a bad dream. The imagery is difficult to understand. It is possible the dream belongs to Judah and "the nations and their might will seem but a bad dream,"[38] i.e., the bad dream that threatened ruin to Jerusalem would be gone when one awakes (v. 7; cf. chs. 36-37). Pfeiffer understands verse 7 with this sense:

---

[35] Young, *The Book of Isaiah, vol. 2*, 306.
[36] Oswalt, *The Book of Isaiah, 1-39*, 528.
[37] Martin, "Isaiah," 1078–1079.
[38] Oswalt, *The Book of Isaiah, 1-39*, 529. Mighty Assyria will be brought to ruin, but this will not mean the end of Judah's misery as Isaiah continues his description.

The Lord would suddenly disperse and destroy these heathen besiegers. Sennacherib's forces lifted the siege to fight the Egyptians at Eltekeh. It was on their return from that victorious engagement that the devastating stroke of God here predicted fell upon them. The loss of 185,000 troops in one night was like the shattering devastation of a mighty thunderstorm and whirlwind. To the Jews the sudden disappearance of the enemy would be like the fading of a nightmare when the dreamer awakes from his tortured sleep.[39]

Alternatively, Oswalt thinks it is better understood that the dreamer might actually be the Assyrians.[40] Yes, the hungry dreamer will think that he is feasting, but when he awakens, he will realize that he still is hungry and has no food (v. 8). They thought they would feast on Judah, but it would soon be gone—the same kind of great reversal that the invading nations will face at the end of the age when they seek the destruction of Israel in the tribulation period (Joel 3:1-17; Zech. 14:1ff.; Rev. 17:14-18). This latter view has better support from the immediate context.

Spiritual drunkards will be brought low (vv. 9-14)

Despite the past faithfulness of God, Judah still refused to trust the Lord. The result would be a hardening from God (Isa. 6:1ff.; cf. Prov. 29:1).[41] God's judgment would show itself in three forms of hardening, (1) an inability to see (vv. 9-10), (2) an inability to read (vv. 11-12), and (3) an inability to reason (vv. 13-14).

An inability to see (vv. 9-10). God taunts Judah by provoking them to continue in their present path, a path that is against His will and will lead to destruction (Isa. 51:17, 21, 22; 63:6; cf. Rev. 22:11). God does this with the command to delay and blind themselves (v. 9).[42] In other words, explains Young, "Don't act, don't speak, continue in your state of wonder and hesitation."[43] This judgment is further explained as spiritual drunkenness, spiritual sleep, and spiritual deception through the false prophets (v. 10). Oswalt reminds us, "it is God who gives enabling grace, and if a people stubbornly misconstrue

---

[39] Pfeiffer, *The Wycliffe Bible Commentary: Old Testament*, Is 29:1.
[40] Ibid.; Wolf, *Interpreting Isaiah*, 151.
[41] Young, *The Book of Isaiah, vol. 2*, 314.
[42] Both initial verbs in this pair of commands are in the Hithpael imperative form (followed by Qal imperatives) emphasizing the reflexive nature of these human choices. Their willful choices are going to bring judgment back upon themselves.
[43] Ibid., 315.

His words, then that enabling grace is withdrawn" (Isa. 6:9-10 [Acts 28:26-28]; Mic. 3:6; Ps. 69:23; Rom. 11:8; 2 Thess. 2:11).[44]

An inability to read (vv. 11-12). Isaiah uses two analogies to illustrate these hardening judgments. First, it is like giving someone a book that is sealed so that it cannot be read (v. 11). Second, it is like giving an open book to one who is illiterate (v. 12). Because of God's judicial blinding, the people will be absolutely insensitive to God.[45]

An inability to reason (vv. 13-14). Isaiah highlights a third way that God was hardening Judah. He was blinding their minds in their ability to think and reason. A refusal to heed God leads to a darkening of the mind (Rom. 1:19; cf. Dan. 4:28-33). The nation had rote tradition, but in the heart they were far from God (v. 13).[46] Empty religion is never acceptable (1 Sam. 15:22; Hos. 6:6; Matt. 15:8-9; John 4:24).

The result will be that "the wisdom of their wise men will perish, and the discernment of their discerning men will be concealed" (v. 14). God's "marvelous" and "wonderful" work (both from Heb. *pele'*; cf. Isa. 9:6; 25:1; 28:29) will be to further blind the minds of the rebellious nation so that judgment will certainly fall upon them (Isa. 44:24-25; Jer. 8:9; 49:7; Matt. 13:11ff.; 1 Cor. 1:9). Verse 14 brings the end of the first woe.

Second woe: One's response determines one's destiny (vv. 15-24)

The Bible gives ample evidence for God's absolute sovereignty. God, the eternal God, has a plan and purpose that He is working, and nothing will stop or frustrate Him (Isa. 46:8-11; Acts 2:23; 4:27-28; Eph. 1:11). At the same time, the Bible compels us to embrace the truth that God created human beings with a capacity for making free moral choices.[47] We understand that man's will is a fallen will that is captive to sin's domination; nevertheless, it is a will that men freely exercise, and it is on this basis that God judges. Here in verses 15-24, we find that one's response is what determines one's destiny, the defiant will find ruin (vv. 15-16), but the righteous will find relief (vv. 17-24).

---

[44] Oswalt, *The Book of Isaiah, 1-39*, 531.

[45] Young, *The Book of Isaiah, vol. 2*, 318.

[46] God's real desire is love and obedience from a thankful heart (Exod. 35:5; Deut. 10:16; 1 Sam. 10:9; 1 Kings 3:9; 1 Chron. 28:9; Ps. 66:18; Is. 6:10; 51:7; 57:15; Joel 2:13, [Oswalt, *The Book of Isaiah, 1-39*, 532, n. 12]).

[47] When one embraces both divine sovereignty and human freedom as being true, he is embracing a doctrine called Compatibilism.

The defiant will find ruin (vv. 15-16)

Unrepentant sinners will eventually come to ruin. Isaiah highlights two defiant sins of Judah that would eventually bring them to ruin.

First defiant choice that called for judgment (v. 15). Isaiah exposes the folly that Judah thought that God would not see their sinful plans. So to speak, Judah saw themselves as doing their deeds in the dark where no one could see them: "Who sees us? Who knows us?" No, the Lord saw all of it (Ps. 139; Job 14:16; 31:4). Oswalt explains the context:

> Probably this is in reference to the decision to break the vassal covenant with Assyria and to rely on help from Egypt. . . . [and the Lord is contesting] the idea that a nation calling itself God's people should endeavor to insure its own freedom and security through a system of secret compacts with other nations (2 Kings 18:7b).[48]

Judah thought it could get away with the sin of trusting in foreign alliances. This choice would be disastrous.

Second defiant choice that called for judgment (v. 16). Isaiah further exposes Judah's sin as being a failure to recognize the sovereignty of Yahweh. In effect, Judah was turning things around as though she were the one who possessed sovereignty.[49] Pfeiffer summarizes the problem well:

> They were attempting to reverse true values, putting man at the top of the scale and God at the bottom, and supposing that the thing created matters more than the Creator. But God will not be subject to man's puny judgment nor tolerate his behaving as if he existed for his own sake, independently of the divine will.[50]

The righteous will find relief (vv. 17-24)

Isaiah quickly shifts the focus from present judgment to the future blessings of the kingdom. Isaiah highlights three such blessings.[51]

---

[48] Ibid., 536.

[49] Paul uses this text in Romans 9 (esp. vv. 20-21) to demonstrate the truth that God is absolutely sovereign in the salvation of sinners through the exercise of His grace in election.

[50] Pfeiffer, *The Wycliffe Bible Commentary: Old Testament*, Is 29:9.

[51] Martin, "Isaiah," 1079. Martin explains, "The phrase in a very short time refers to the coming kingdom. Some think it refers to the time when the Assyrian army was slaughtered (37:36), but the conditions described in 29:20–21 seem to nullify that interpretation."

First blessing: A great reversal (vv. 17-19). One aspect of reversal includes a total transformation to the land, so much so that the wild mountainous regions of Lebanon will become like a fertile field and the fertile field will become like a forest (v. 17).[52] The deaf will hear, the blind will see (v. 18), the afflicted will experience gladness, and the needy will experience joy. All of this will come from the Holy One of Israel (v. 19).

These promises raise the question whether Isaiah's words should be taken literally, figuratively, or perhaps a combination of both. Is Isaiah speaking about a physical restoration to those who are literally deaf and blind, or this is figurative? Back in 29:10-14, Isaiah had spoken about those whose eyes were shut because they were not listening to God, a reference that appears to be figurative (cf. 6:10). It is true that some of these statements are using figurative language, but there is no reason for ruling out a literal meaning as many passages suggest (Isa. 32:3; 35:5). When the kingdom comes, not only will all spiritual blindness be obliterated, but even the physical blindness will be taken away so that all traces of curse are gone forever. As Young explains it, the coming of God's restoration will mean, "a complete reversal"[53] of the miseries of this fallen world.

Second blessing: The wicked will be judged (vv. 20-21). Before all these kingdom blessings can come, evil must be judged. This is what Christ will do during the tribulation period when the ruthless, scorners, and evil-doers who harm God's people fall under His judgment (vv. 20-21).[54] When Christ returns, He will put an end to evil forever. Earlier, Isaiah said, "He will not judge by what His eyes see, nor make a decision by what His ears hear; but with righteousness He will judge the poor, and decide with fairness for the afflicted of the earth" (11:3-4).

Third blessing: Israel will have a final restoration (vv. 22-24). Israel's covenant rebellion made the nation especially despised by the nations. God's promise is that He, the One "who redeemed Abraham,"[55] will one day take away

---

[52] Young, *The Book of Isaiah*, vol. 2, 325.

[53] Ibid., 326.

[54] The "ruthless" (*'ariyts*) are oppressors who heartlessly extract what they can from the weak (13:11; 25:3-5; 29:5; 49:25); the "scorners" (*lets*) are those who mock God and bring evil to the world (Isa. 28:15; Prov. 1:22; 13:1); evil-doers is a general expression that embraces all unrepentant sinners. Those who un-righteously indict the innocent, ensnare the innocent with legal manipulation, or who defraud the innocent with legal manipulation, will eventually be judged by Righteous Yahweh when Messiah brings the kingdom of God to this world.

[55] This is an interesting expression found only here in the Bible. This could be

this reproach from His chosen people (v. 22). Two hundred years later Zechariah looked with anticipation to this day:

> But now I will not treat the remnant of this people as in the former days, declares the Lord of hosts. For *there will be* peace for the seed: the vine will yield its fruit, the land will yield its produce and the heavens will give their dew; and I will cause the remnant of this people to inherit all these *things*. It will come about that just as you were a curse among the nations, O house of Judah and house of Israel, so I will save you that you may become a blessing. Do not fear; let your hands be strong. For thus says the Lord of hosts, just as I purposed to do harm to you when your fathers provoked Me to wrath, says the Lord of hosts, and I have not relented, so I have again purposed in these days to do good to Jerusalem and to the house of Judah. Do not fear! (Zech. 8:11-15).

Here is the promise we find in the Bible: One day, God will take away Israel's shame and reproach. Isaiah repeats this promise several times in the latter portions of his prophecies: "You shall not be put to shame or confounded to all eternity" (Isa. 45:17). "Those who wait for me shall not be put to shame" (Isa. 49:23). "Do not fear, for you will not be ashamed; do not be discouraged, for you will not suffer disgrace; for you will forget the shame of your youth, and the disgrace of our widowhood you will remember no more" (Isa. 54:4). Wow!

These promises will be realized in the day that Jacob sees his children, the work of God's hands (v. 23). This statement refers to the eschatological redemption of God's Jewish remnant to create and restore a redeemed Israel (Isa. 49:20-21; 53:10; 54:1-2; cf. Ps. 110:3). These are the ones at the end of the age who will sanctify the name of Yahweh, the Holy One of Israel (cf. Ezek. 36:19-23). This is the kingdom restoration God has promised, the restoration Jesus told us to pray for (Matt. 6:9-15).

Restoration and blessing will come to all who embrace the promised Messiah. Many of these will be those who previously had erred in mind and been critical of the truth of God's Word (v. 24). These are the sinners who previously had been "the deaf and blind" (v. 18), but have now been touched by redeeming grace.[56] When God's eschatological work comes, the rebellious will be cut off in their rebellion (Ezek. 20:36-38), but by the grace of God the remnant shall be saved (Zech. 13:8-9; Rom. 11:25-36). Pfeiffer explains, "The Redeemer will

---

referring to the way that God took Abraham out of Ur from a life of idolatry (Josh. 24:2-3), but is better understood as the way that God bought Israel out of her bondage to slavery in Egypt (Exod. 6:6; 15:13; Isa. 43:1, 3, 14).
[56] Ibid., 333.

surely bring to pass his perfect plan for Israel, and forge them into a godly and reverent people, after they have repented and opened their hearts to the truth of Christ."[57]

Summary and application

The Bible tells a marvelous story of redemption for Israel. The truth, though, is that it is a message that applies to every man who receives forgiveness through Jesus Christ. The fabulous news is that sinners who believe receive eternal forgiveness and redemption, and in the end all of it brings glory to God (Eph. 1:6, 12, 14).

THE FOLLY OF TRUSTING EGYPT (30:1-33)

Chapter 30 gives the fourth "woe" of chapters 28-35. This woe is directed against those who advocated a military alliance with Egypt, something God never approved of (Exod. 13:17; Deut. 17:16).[58]

Chapter 30 reads as follows: "1 Woe to the rebellious children, declares the Lord, who execute a plan, but not Mine, and make an alliance, but not of My Spirit, in order to add sin to sin, 2 who proceed down to Egypt without consulting Me, to take refuge in the safety of Pharaoh and to seek shelter in the shadow of Egypt! 3 Therefore, the safety of Pharaoh will be your shame and the shelter in the shadow of Egypt, your humiliation. 4 For their princes are at Zoan and their ambassadors arrive at Hanes. 5 Everyone will be ashamed because of a people who cannot profit them, *who are* not for help or profit, but for shame and also for reproach. 6 The oracle concerning the beasts of the Negev. Through a land of distress and anguish, from where *come* lioness and lion, viper and flying serpent; they carry their riches on the backs of young donkeys and their treasures on camels' humps, to a people who cannot profit *them,* 7 even Egypt, whose help is vain and empty. Therefore, I have called her Rahab who has been exterminated. 8 Now go, write it on a tablet before them and inscribe it on a scroll, that it may serve in the time to come as a witness forever. 9 For this is a rebellious people, false sons, sons who refuse to listen to the instruction of the Lord, 10 who say to the seers, You must not see *visions,* and to the prophets, You must not prophesy to us what is right; speak to us pleasant words; prophesy illusions. 11 Get out of the way; turn aside from the path; let us hear no more about the Holy One of Israel. 12 Therefore thus says the Holy One of Israel, Since you have rejected this word and have put your trust in oppression and guile, and have relied on them, 13 therefore this iniquity will be to you like a breach about to fall, a bulge in a high wall, whose collapse comes suddenly in

---

[57] Pfeiffer, *The Wycliffe Bible Commentary: Old Testament*, Is 29:17.
[58] Wolf, *Interpreting Isaiah*, 153.

an instant, 14 whose collapse is like the smashing of a potter's jar, so ruthlessly shattered that a sherd will not be found among its pieces to take fire from a hearth or to scoop water from a cistern. 15 For thus the Lord God, the Holy One of Israel, has said, In repentance and rest you will be saved; in quietness and trust is your strength. But you were not willing, 16 and you said, No, for we will flee on horses; therefore you shall flee! and we will ride on swift *horses;* therefore those who pursue you shall be swift. 17 One thousand *will flee* at the threat of one *man;* you will flee at the threat of five, until you are left as a flag on a mountain top and as a signal on a hill. 18 Therefore the Lord longs to be gracious to you, and therefore He waits on high to have compassion on you. For the Lord is a God of justice; how blessed are all those who long for Him. 19 O people in Zion, inhabitant in Jerusalem, you will weep no longer. He will surely be gracious to you at the sound of your cry; when He hears it, He will answer you. 20 Although the Lord has given you bread of privation and water of oppression, *He,* your Teacher will no longer hide Himself, but your eyes will behold your Teacher. 21 Your ears will hear a word behind you, This is the way, walk in it, whenever you turn to the right or to the left. 22 And you will defile your graven images overlaid with silver, and your molten images plated with gold, you will scatter them as an impure thing, *and* say to them, Be gone! 23 Then He will give *you* rain for the seed which you will sow in the ground, and bread *from* the yield of the ground, and it will be rich and plenteous; on that day your livestock will graze in a roomy pasture. 24 Also the oxen and the donkeys which work the ground will eat salted fodder, which has been winnowed with shovel and fork. 25 On every lofty mountain and on every high hill there will be streams running with water on the day of the great slaughter, when the towers fall. 26 The light of the moon will be as the light of the sun, and the light of the sun will be seven times *brighter,* like the light of seven days, on the day the Lord binds up the fracture of His people and heals the bruise He has inflicted. 27 Behold, the name of the Lord comes from a remote place; burning is His anger and dense is *His* smoke; His lips are filled with indignation, and His tongue is like a consuming fire; 28 His breath is like an overflowing torrent, which reaches to the neck, to shake the nations back and forth in a sieve, and to *put* in the jaws of the peoples the bridle which leads to ruin. 29 You will have songs as in the night when you keep the festival, and gladness of heart as when one marches to *the sound of* the flute, to go to the mountain of the Lord, to the Rock of Israel. 30 And the Lord will cause His voice of authority to be heard, and the descending of His arm to be seen in fierce anger, and *in* the flame of a consuming fire, in cloudburst, downpour and hailstones. 31 For at the voice of the Lord, Assyria will be terrified, *when* He strikes with the rod, 32 and every blow of the rod of punishment, which the Lord will lay on him, will be with *the music of* tambourines and lyres; and in battles, brandishing weapons, He will fight them. 33 For Topheth has long been ready; indeed, it has been prepared for the king. He has made it deep and large, a pyre of fire with plenty of wood; the breath of the Lord, like a torrent of brimstone, sets it afire" (30:1-33).

At a principle level, all who refuse to trust the Lord will come to ultimate ruin. The history of Israel shows that they had a repeated pattern of failing to trust the Lord (cf. ch. 1), a problem that was compounded by trusting in unreliable Egypt. Martin comments, "At this time Egypt was waning as a world power and could be of no real assistance to Israel and Judah in their fight against the strong Assyrian Empire."[59] This unit can be broken down as follows: ruin to those who trust in flesh (vv. 1-5), disappointment to those who reject God (vv. 6-14), salvation to those who trust God (vv. 15-26), and wrath to the unrepentant (vv. 27-33).

Ruin to those who trust in the flesh (vv. 1-5)

God pronounces a woe on Judah for making plans to form a new military alliance with Egypt to fight against Assyria (vv. 1-2). Assyria was a powerful enemy, but Judah was compounding her problems by failing to trust the Lord, something she had done years earlier (vv. 3-4). Kidner explains:

> Ten years earlier, Isaiah had dissuaded Judah from playing Egypt's game against Assyria (ch. 20); now the mood has hardened, and Judah's envoys are on their way. The *officials* (4) seem to be Pharaoh's, in which case *Hanes* seems implied to be near *Zoan* (which is Tanis, the nearest important town to the Israel border), rather than 50 miles (80 km) further up the Nile, as commonly identified.[60]

There is some question about the context for this prophetic rebuke. As noted by Kidner above, it seems best to understand this as referring to events leading up to the siege by Sennacherib in 701 B.C.[61] This much is certain: Egypt will fail them, and they will be put to shame (v. 5).[62]

Disappointment to those who reject God (vv. 6-14)

Once again, we are reminded that all who reject the Lord will be put to shame, yet Judah thought she could get away with such disobedience. Isaiah outlines both the deception of God's rebellious children (vv. 6-11) as well as the disappointment of God's rebellious children (vv. 12-14).

---

[59] Martin, "Isaiah," 1079.

[60] Kidner, "Isaiah," 651. Zoan, i.e., Tanis, was the first city they would reach in the Delta region, and Hanes ("House of the child of the king") was further south in the region that was later called Fayyum (Young, *The Book of Isaiah, vol. 2*, 338).

[61] Oswalt, *The Book of Isaiah, 1-39*, 544. Others have seen this as events in time of Sargon (ca. 714-711 B.C.) in the early days of the Saite Dynasty of Egypt before the Ethiopian Shabako had unified Egypt under his control (cf. Isa. 20).

[62] Egypt was stopped 100 miles from her border by an Assyrian army that was 600 miles from its own home (ibid., 546).

The deception of God's rebellious children (vv. 6-11)

This message is introduced as being an oracle—an oracle concerning the beasts of the Negev. The Negev was the southern portion of Israel between Israel and Egypt—a land that was hot, dry, and full of dangers.[63]

A trip to Egypt will be disappointing (vv. 6-7). If Judah wants to make a trip down to Egypt with a big bribe, it is not going to be easy (v. 6). As a matter of fact, it will be "vain" (a breath) and "empty" (void). Egypt was so unreliable, God says He has given her the name "Rahab who has been exterminated" (v. 7). Many believe that Rahab is "the monster of popular legend. She is the ancient chaotic Matter against whom the gods struggled for survival, only subduing her by dint of the last bit of effort."[64] The tragedy is that Rahab is the terrible foe Yahweh has already overthrown at the Exodus, but now his people are crawling through the Negev to look to her for help.[65] Egypt is nothing but a broken reed (Isa. 36:6).

Judah needed to understand her own self-deception (vv. 8-11). Judah's real problem was self-deception. God instructs Isaiah to make a permanent record of His message by writing his prophecies down on a tablet for permanent record to remind them later (cf. Isa. 8:1-16; Deut. 32-33). We cannot be certain about all the contents,[66] but it was about "Rahab the Do-Nothing," a rebuke to remind them later that this is what he had warned.[67] They were so hard hearted they rejected this truth and wanted nothing but flattering messages (vv. 9-10).[68] They were disgusted with Isaiah always telling them to trust in the Holy One of Israel (v. 11; cf. 5:19; Amos 7:12).[69] Pfeiffer explains, "Very modern is this demand of the congregation that their clergy temper their messages to the desires and preferences of the people, rather than preach some unpopular doctrine derived from God's Word."[70]

---

[63] Lions, vipers, and fiery serpents (Num. 21:6; Deut. 8:15) would be but a few of the dangers.

[64] Ibid., 548. Isaiah was probably using the Rahab legend as a literary allusion to speak of the way that God had overcome Egypt to set them free (Isa. 51:9; Job 9:13; 26:12; Pss. 87:4; 89:10).

[65] Young, *The Book of Isaiah, vol. 2*, 340-341.

[66] Oswalt, *The Book of Isaiah, 1-39*, 550.

[67] Wolf, *Interpreting Isaiah*, 155. Trust in Egypt will bring ruin (Grogan, "Isaiah," 195).

[68] A wise son listens to his father (Prov. 2:1), but Israel was not wise (Isa. 1:1-3).

[69] They hated the prophets of Yahweh who gave truth, but loved the false prophets who made them feel good (cf. Jer. 6:13; 8:10; 14:14).

[70] Pfeiffer, *The Wycliffe Bible Commentary: Old Testament*, Is 30:6.

The disappointment of God's rebellious children (vv. 12-14)

Because God's people had rejected (*ma'as*) His truth and relied on lies, i.e., "oppression and guile" (cf. Prov. 29:15), they would be greatly disappointed (v. 12). This disappointment would be like having a great wall collapse on them (v. 13). They will be crushed by the collapse and scattered by the enemy (v. 14). Grogan reminds us that, "sin contains the seeds of its own punishment, and Judah's trust in a foreign power rather than in God would bring about her downfall."[71] The message for every man is that he must not rely on anything but God's Word (v. 10; cf. 10:20; 31:1; 50:10; Prov. 12:15; 28:26; 29:1; Matt. 24:36-44; 2 Pet. 3:3-10).

Salvation to those who trust God (vv. 15-26)

Ruin comes to those who reject God, but salvation comes to those who trust. Isaiah first makes this clear at a general level (vv. 15-18), and then he makes it clear at a particular level by showing that God saves through trust in the promised Messiah (vv. 19-26).

Trust in the Lord saves (vv. 15-18)

Judah rejected trust in the Lord (vv. 15-17). Judah's disbelief was going to bring great ruin (vv. 13-14), but God once again reminds them that they could have salvation by turning to Him (v. 15; cf. 28:12, 16).[72] Salvation was not going to come by their own human efforts, but this was where they kept turning despite Isaiah's pleas (v. 16). Egypt might supply fast horses, but they will not be fast enough (v. 17; cf. Hos. 14:3; Amos 2:14).[73] Their military efforts will be a lone flagpole on a hill.

God's desire was to have them trust Him (v. 18). Verse 18 is transitional from the idea of judgment to the promise of a hope. God's desire has always been that they would trust Him and find salvation (cf. Matt. 23:37). Isaiah stresses God's compassion by saying that He "longs" to be gracious to them

---

[71] Grogan, "Isaiah," 196.

[72] Salvation is characterized as requiring repentance, rest, quietness, and trust in Yahweh.

[73] To put this into a contemporary perspective, Oswalt compares it to America rejecting the rule of Jesus Christ but putting its hope in things like F-16s (Oswalt, *The Book of Isaiah, 1-39*, 555).

(*chakah*, wait, tarry, be patient for),[74] and "waits" to have compassion on them (*rum*, lit. rise up),[75] for this is what kind of a God He is.

Grace from Messiah (vv. 19-26)

The compassion of God seen in verse 18 turns into a promise of restoration in verses 19-26, a restoration for Israel that God will accomplish through the Messiah, for Israel's disobedience can never annul God's promises (Jer. 33:14-26; Rom. 11:29). God will send Messiah, and He will restore them. In verses 19-26 we find four kinds of kingdom blessings God will bring them.

First kingdom blessing: An end of sorrow (v. 19). The NASB reads, "O people in Zion, inhabitant in Jerusalem, you will weep no longer," but the ESV (following the Masoretic text more closely) is preferable: "For a people shall dwell in Zion; in Jerusalem; you shall weep no more."[76] God will remove all weeping and sorrow, for grace will be abundant when they turn to Messiah (Isa. 9:1-7; 25:8; 61:2-5; cf. Pss. 30:5; 126:1-6).

Second kingdom blessing: An end of meager living (v. 20). Covenant curses brought hard times (cf. Isa. 8:21-22), but this will end in the kingdom. Even though "teacher" is in a plural form, it may be better to understand it as referring to the Messiah Himself (*'Adonay*), the One who gave them affliction when they broke the covenant (*Yahweh* of v. 18).[77]

Third kingdom blessing: An end of spiritual lostness (vv. 21-22). Disbelief plunged Judah into great lostness (cf. Isa. 53:6), but God will reverse this lost condition when they turn to Him (v. 21). Israel will despise the idolatry of former ages (cf. Exod. 32:20; Deut. 7:25; 2 Kings 23:4-14; Ezek. 7:19-24), and at long last they will reject idols forevermore (v. 22).[78]

---

[74] Ludwig Koehler et al., *The Hebrew and Aramaic Lexicon of the Old Testament*, cited in electronic form with Logos Libronix (Leiden: E.J. Brill, 1994–2000), 313.

[75] Ludwig Koehler et al., *The Hebrew and Aramaic Lexicon of the Old Testament*, cited in electronic form with Logos Libronix (Leiden: E.J. Brill, 1994–2000), 1202–1205.

[76] Oswalt, *The Book of Isaiah, 1-39*, 557, n. 1. The verb "to dwell" (*yashab*) is Qal Imp. in the MT and LXX, but the Targum supports an emendation to a participle.

[77] The noun is plural, but the verb "hide" is singular. The reference about seeing their teacher with their own eyes strongly suggests a messianic meaning. The Messiah is probably called their Teacher in Joel 2:23 as well. Alternatively, this could be a reference to their prophets or priests (28:9-13).

[78] Idols will no longer be sacred and holy but common and unclean. "Impure" comes from the term *dahah* which can refer to flows of menstrual blood as in Lev. 15:33; 20:18 (Young, *The Book of Isaiah, vol. 2*, 359).

Fourth kingdom blessing: An end of desperate living (vv. 23-26). Disobedience brought desperation (cf. Deut. 28:15-68), but grace will reverse it. Copious rain will cause the land to be rich (*dashen*, fat; cf. Pss. 22:30; 92:15) and plenteous (*shamen*, fat; cf. Ezek. 34:14, 16), for all creation "will participate in the blessings of a restored Zion" (v. 23).[79] Even work animals will be blessed as they "eat salted fodder which has been winnowed with shovel and fork" (v. 24).

Verse 25 is one of many passages that speak about the abundant waters God will pour out in the kingdom (Isa. 32:15; 35:6-7; 41:17-18; 43:18-21; 44:3-5). Some of these references speak about the eschatological outpouring of the Holy Spirit (Isa. 32:15; 44:3-5; Zech. 12:10; 13:1), but there is no reason to not see a literal reference to these passages as well. The land that had been parched from curse will be blessed with many waters and great productivity (Joel 3:18; Ezek. 47:1ff.).[80]

The messianic kingdom will be a day when ages of darkness come to an end (cf. Isa. 8:21-22; 9:1ff.). Verse 26 probably contains elements of hyperbolic language, but the message is clear: The age of darkness is over, and the age of light has begun (cf. 60:19-22).[81] Israel's wounds were deep (Hos. 5:13-15), but now they will be healed (Isa. 1:6; Ezek. 34:16; Hos. 6:1-3; Mal. 4:2). Pfeiffer suggests that the intensified light of 30:26, "is symbolic of glorious deliverance and peace as the kingdom of David is established on earth,"[82] an end of the curse.

Wrath to the unrepentant (vv. 27-33)

Redemption comes to those who believe (vv. 15-26), but verses 27-33 remind us that wrath and judgment will be the end of those who disbelieve. Isaiah describes the intensity of God's judgment (vv. 27-28), the joy over God's judgment (v. 29), and the justice of God's judgment (vv. 30-33).

The intensity of God's judgment on the unrepentant (vv. 27-28)

The oppressor (Assyria in Isaiah's day) was fierce, but God's wrath would soon consume all enemies.[83] Isaiah describes the coming judgment with

---

[79] Wolf, *Interpreting Isaiah*, 156.

[80] The fall of towers may speak about the complete failure of Israel's prideful trust in its own power to fight for survival (cf. 2:12-17; 32:14, 15; 57:15).

[81] Isaiah's poetic language calls the moon "the white one" and the sun "the burning one."

[82] Pfeiffer, *The Wycliffe Bible Commentary: Old Testament*, Is 30:23.

[83] The anthropomorphisms (God's lips, tongue, breath) paint a very vivid picture of God's wrath. The name of Yahweh comes in anger later in 59:15-21.

theophany language (Isa. 28:2; 29:6; Pss. 18:7-15; 50:3; Nah. 1:3-8; Hab. 3:3-15) that reminds us of the fury of God's wrath (v. 27). This storm will consume the unrepentant (v. 28). The nations made their choices to attack God's people, but all of this is part of God's work leading them to judgment as with a bridle in the jaws (cf. Isa. 10:5-6, 15; 37:29). These prophecies had their fulfillment in the destruction of Assyria in the eighth century B.C., but they also remind us of one final judgment at the end of the age, as noted by Kidner: "While these verses survey the immediate situation, naming 'Assyria' (31), they further apply to the end time" (cf. Ezek. 38:4; Joel 3:2; Rev. 16:13-16; 17:13-17).[84]

The joy over God's judgment on the unrepentant (v. 29)

God's judgment on Assyria will bring great joy to Israel (Isa. 9:1-3; 35:10; 54:1; 65:14, 18, 19; 66:10; cf. Ps. 96). This is the kind of joy used to have at their annual festivals when they made their pilgrimage to Mount Zion for worship, i.e., the mountain of the Lord (Isa. 2:1-4; 27:13; 66:20).

The justice of God's judgment on the unrepentant (vv. 30-33)

God's judgment on sinners is always harsh, but it is also fully just. Isaiah describes this fierce wrath as the voice of the Lord which comes with "the flame of a consuming fire" and a "cloudburst, downpour and hailstones" (v. 30). His voice will terrify the enemy (cf. Isa. 10:12; 11:4; 14:25; 31:8), and once this day comes there will be no escape (v. 31). God's rod of judgment will bring sinners to ruin, but the righteous will rejoice (v. 32; cf. Exod. 15:20; 1 Sam. 18:6; Rev. 18:20; 19:1-6). God's saints waited long ages for this divine retribution, and it is one that has been fully deserved. Isaiah likens this judgment to "Topheth" (v. 33). Topheth ("place of burning") was the altar in the Hinnom Valley on the southern edge of Jerusalem where apostate Jews sacrificed their children to the Ammonite God Molech (2 Kings 23:10; Jer. 7:31-32; 19:6).[85] This is the place where King Ahaz sacrificed his own son to Molech with the hope of military and economic prosperity. God has His own Topheth prepared for the King of Assyria and for all who refuse to heed His Word.

Summary and application

God's promise of judgment carries with it several principles of application that apply to all saints in every generation. First, it should move every man to

---

[84] Kidner, "Isaiah," 652.
[85] The "Valley of Hinnom" (Heb. *Gey Hinnom*) is the place which came to be called *Gehenna*. This is the cursed place where perpetual fires consumed refuse and dead carcasses, and came to symbolize the eternal fires of hell (Isa. 66:24; Matt. 5:22, 29, 30; 10:28; 18:9; 23:15, 33; Mark 9:43, 45, 47; Luke 12:5; Jas. 3:6).

be quick to listen to the Word of God. Second, it should give us comfort and encouragement as we remember that one day God will bring a perfect and final judgment on all sin. Third, these promises should give us encouragement to persevere in following and serving the Lord Jesus Christ, for His promises will never fail.

THE RUIN OF NOT TRUSTING THE LORD (31:1-9)

Chapter 31 repeats the themes of chapter 30, only in a condensed fashion. In short, it is folly to trust in Egypt rather than God. Oswalt explains, "Not only will Egypt not be able to help, but going to her necessarily involves a rejection of God."[86] God has already told His people that He will fight for them. All they need to do is trust Him.

Chapter 31 reads as follows: "1 Woe to those who go down to Egypt for help *and* rely on horses, and trust in chariots because they are many and in horsemen because they are very strong, but they do not look to the Holy One of Israel, nor seek the Lord! 2 Yet He also is wise and will bring disaster and does not retract His words, but will arise against the house of evildoers and against the help of the workers of iniquity. 3 Now the Egyptians are men and not God, and their horses are flesh and not spirit; so the Lord will stretch out His hand, and he who helps will stumble and he who is helped will fall, and all of them will come to an end together. 4 For thus says the Lord to me, As the lion or the young lion growls over his prey, against which a band of shepherds is called out, *and* he will not be terrified at their voice nor disturbed at their noise, so will the Lord of hosts come down to wage war on Mount Zion and on its hill. 5 Like flying birds so the Lord of hosts will protect Jerusalem. He will protect and deliver *it*; He will pass over and rescue *it*. 6 Return to Him from whom you have deeply defected, O sons of Israel. 7 For in that day every man will cast away his silver idols and his gold idols, which your sinful hands have made for you as a sin. 8 And the Assyrian will fall by a sword not of man, and a sword not of man will devour him. So he will not escape the sword, and his young men will become forced laborers. 9 His rock will pass away because of panic, and his princes will be terrified at the standard, declares the Lord, whose fire is in Zion and whose furnace is in Jerusalem" (31:1-9).

Judah looked for salvation from its own strength and foreign alliances. Because Judah was not trusting the Lord, she would pay the price. Isaiah introduces this section with another "woe," the fifth of six woes in chapters 28-35 (28:1; 29:1, 15; 30:1; 31:1; 33:1; cf. 1:4; 5:8, 11, 18, 20-22; 10:1; 17:12; 18:1; 45:9; 55:1). Chapter 31 shows us three reasons for this woe.

---

[86] Oswalt, *The Book of Isaiah, 1-39*, 570.

First reason for Judah's woe (vv. 1-3)

Judah needed to trust the Lord, for trust in self brings disaster.[87] The psalmist writes, "It is better to take refuge in the Lord than to trust in man. It is better to take refuge in the Lord than to trust in princes" (Ps. 118:8-9).

Judah's role (v. 1)

The immediate problem was that Judah was sending messengers to Egypt to ask for help. God told Judah they would be ashamed for trusting in "do-nothing-Rahab" (30:5, 7), but Judah would not listen (cf. 1 Kings 10:28-29).[88] Verse 2 shows us how God would deal with this.

God's role (v. 2)

Isaiah sarcastically responds by saying that God "also is wise" and would arise with disaster for those who rebel against Him.[89] The "wise" counselors of Judah thought they knew more than God, but it would ultimately bring ruin upon both themselves and the whole nation.[90]

Egypt's role (v. 3)

Egypt had promised help, but it would not happen for the Lord was going to bring judgment on them as well. The real error in trusting in Egypt is that unlike Yahweh, Egypt is flesh and not spirit—mere men and horses. True wisdom would have trusted in sovereign God and not puny flesh (cf. Jer. 17:5-9). The truth is that Egypt would fall badly so that both Judah and Egypt would fall together under mighty Assyria.

Second reason for Judah's woe (vv. 4-5)

Judah was failing to trust in the Mighty One of Israel whose passion had always been to care for His people and protect them from the enemy. Zechariah reminds us of this when he writes, "whoever touches you touches the apple of his eye" (Zech. 2:8). Verses 4-5 use two animal metaphors to give confirmation of those promises in verses 1-3.

---

[87] This is why God told His people to not build standing armies (Deut. 17:14-20).

[88] In modern terms, it is like having an army with numerous tanks and war planes.

[89] The waw consecutive imperfect stem verb ("bring") is part of the future narrative of how God will judge in the future and does not look back at an action already fulfilled in Isaiah's day (Oswalt, *The Book of Isaiah, 1-39*, 569, n. 2).

[90] Paul used similar imagery with the Corinthians who saw themselves as "wise" (1:18-3:23) (Grogan, "Isaiah," 202).

First metaphor: A lion with its prey (v. 4)

God first compares His protective care to that of a lion who is passionately guarding over its fresh kill. Just as the young, growling lion will not be frightened away from its prey, neither will Yahweh be frightened away from protecting His people Judah.[91]

Second metaphor: A bird watching over its own (v. 5)

The metaphor changes to birds, but the idea is still the same: God will care for His own people. The imagery here carries the idea of tenderness where Isaiah reminds us that God's desire is to care for His people as a bird protects her own little chicks (cf. Matt. 23:37). Kidner explains, "The growling *lion* and the *birds* in flight both depict . . . the formidable and the tender aspects of the Lord as protector (*cf.* Dt. 32:11)."[92]

Third reason for Judah's woe (vv. 6-9)

Judah failed to understand that God hates and judges all evil. For Judah, this meant they needed to turn back to the Lord with full trust.

Israel's defection was deep (v. 6)

Isaiah describes Judah's lack of trust by saying that they have "deeply defected" from the Lord (cf. same terms in Hos. 9:9).[93] The sin was bad, and the only solution was to turn back to the Lord (cf. Isa. 1:18).

God's judgments will eventually bring men to see their sin (v. 7)

As we have seen, there will be a final restoration of Israel at the end of the age. This passage, however, is best seen as referring to a near-term salvation God would bring with the overthrow of Assyria. For Judah, the immediate application of this message would be to repent now and trust the Lord and not the idols (cf. Isa. 2:8, 20; 17:8; 30:22). Trust in the Lord is always the safe path.

---

[91] It has been suggested that God is making war against the people of Zion, but it is preferable in context to see Him waging war against the enemies of Judah.

[92] Kidner, "Isaiah," 652.

[93] As Oswalt describes it, "Literally, this expression 'deeply defected' says that they have 'made apostasy deep' or 'have deepened the turning away' (Oswalt, *The Book of Isaiah, 1-39*, 575).

God will destroy those who seek the death of His people (vv. 8-9)

Assyria is going to fall (v. 8; cf. Isa. 10:5, 12; 14:24-28), but it will not be a human agent who brings their ruin but God Himself. Historically speaking, Assyria did experience a final overthrow by an alliance of the Babylonians and the Medes (626, 612, 609, with a final fall at Haran in 605). This defeat, however, is speaking about one which God would bring against Assyria in 701 B.C. Isaiah makes six declarations on how God will destroy Assyria, and in the end every enemy of His people.

First and second declarations (v. 8a). Twice Isaiah prophesies that the fall of Assyria will not be by the sword of a man.[94] The source of defeat will be God Himself (cf. 24:21; 27:1; 34:3). Young explains that, "Assyria represented the kingdom of man, which would attempt to dominate all the earth. It is significant that the kingdom of man will be brought to an end by the sword not of a man."[95]

Third and fourth declarations (v. 8b). The destruction will be brutal, but those young men (*bachur*, young, choice men) who do survive will be cast into slavery. How could this be? The answer is that it will be a direct blow from God Himself. Pfeiffer notes that this is "a most remarkable prediction that no human army would shatter the enemy, but rather a direct stroke of God,"[96] the stroke that is described in 37:36 when the Angel of the Lord struck down 185,000 Assyrian soldiers in one night.

Fifth and sixth declarations (v. 9). There is some debate about the meaning of "rock," but the parallel with "princes" in the next clause suggests it is referring to the extreme confidence King Sennacherib had in his own military might.[97] When God's judgment comes, terror and dread will overtake Assyria (cf. Jer. 6:25; 20:3; Lam. 2:22 for the same usage).

One challenge to seeing this fulfilled in 701 B.C., says Young, is that we do not have evidence that the young men of Assyria,

> actually became tribute to Judah. It would seem that the prophet is speaking in wider and grander tones of the final destruction of power that, were that possible, would have destroyed the theocracy. To say that the young

---

[94] The first reference to "man" uses *iysh* (a common term for individual men) and the second reference uses the term *'adam* (a general term for humanity).
[95] Young, *The Book of Isaiah, vol. 2*, 381.
[96] Pfeiffer, *The Wycliffe Bible Commentary: Old Testament*, Is 31:1.
[97] Oswalt, *The Book of Isaiah, 1-39*, 576-577. Oswalt notes that Driver shows Arabic examples where "hill" or "rock" can refer to a ruler/leader (ibid., 577, n. 18).

men of Assyria will become tribute is to say that Assyria herself will be completely destroyed.[98]

Even though some of Assyria's men might have been taken away in 701 B.C., his explanation seems reasonable. The key issue is that the Lord came and saved His people and brought Assyria to utter defeat.

Summary and application

Those who seek to harm Israel will find themselves fighting against God, for the Lord will avenge. Zechariah communicated this truth two-hundred years later when he wrote, "I myself will be a wall of fire around it, declares the Lord, and I will be its glory within" (Zech. 2:5). This promise to Israel does not mean that believers today will be exempt from persecution (cf. Matt. 5:11-12; John 15:18-19), but it does remind us that no matter what the Lord allows, we can entrust ourselves into the hand of God as always doing what is good and best (1 Pet. 3:13; 4:19).

THE BLESSINGS OF A LEADER FROM GOD (32:1-20)

Whereas chapters 30-31 highlighted the folly of trusting in Egypt, chapters 32-33 highlight God's promise that one day He will bring His people a good King to lead the nation in truth and righteousness. Their King will be the Lord Himself (33:22).[99]

Chapter 32 reads as follows: "1 Behold, a king will reign righteously and princes will rule justly. 2 Each will be like a refuge from the wind and a shelter from the storm, like streams of water in a dry country, like the shade of a huge rock in a parched land. 3 Then the eyes of those who see will not be blinded, and the ears of those who hear will listen. 4 The mind of the hasty will discern the truth, and the tongue of the stammerers will hasten to speak clearly. 5 No longer will the fool be called noble, or the rogue be spoken of *as* generous. 6 For a fool speaks nonsense, and his heart inclines toward wickedness: To practice ungodliness and to speak error against the Lord, to keep the hungry person unsatisfied and to withhold drink from the thirsty. 7 As for a rogue, his weapons are evil; he devises wicked schemes to destroy *the* afflicted with slander, even though *the* needy one speaks what is right. 8 But the noble man devises noble plans; and by noble plans he stands. 9 Rise up, you women who are at ease, *and* hear my voice; give ear to my word, you complacent daughters. 10 Within a year and *a few* days you will be troubled, O complacent *daughters, for* the vintage is ended, *and* the *fruit* gathering will not come. 11 Tremble, you *women* who are at ease; be troubled, you complacent *daughters;* strip, undress and put *sackcloth* on

---

[98] Young, *The Book of Isaiah, vol. 2,* 382.
[99] Oswalt, *The Book of Isaiah, 1-39,* 578-579; Wolf, *Interpreting Isaiah,* 159.

your waist; 12 beat your breasts for the pleasant fields, for the fruitful vine, 13 for the land of my people *in which* thorns *and* briars shall come up, yea, for all the joyful houses *and for* the jubilant city, 14 because the palace has been abandoned, the populated city forsaken. Hill and watch-tower have become caves forever, a delight for wild donkeys, a pasture for flocks, 15 until the Spirit is poured out upon us from on high, and the wilderness becomes a fertile field, and the fertile field is considered as a forest. 16 Then justice will dwell in the wilderness and righteousness will abide in the fertile field. 17 And the work of righteousness will be peace, and the service of righteousness, quietness and confidence forever. 18 Then my people will live in a peaceful habitation, and in secure dwellings and in undisturbed resting places; 19 and it will hail when the forest comes down, and the city will be utterly laid low. 20 How blessed will you be, you who sow beside all waters, who let out freely the ox and the donkey" (32:1-20).

In terms of flowing structure, chapters 28-35 consist of a series of six woes (28:1; 29:1; 29:15; 30:1; 31:1; 33:1). The possibility has been suggested that this would make chapters 31-32 part of one woe unit and 33-35 part of the final woe unit. To whatever extent this might be true, we have already noted that chapters 32-33 both speak about the hope of future godly King. Chapter 32, then, still deals in part with the folly of trusting in man rather than God. Chapter 32 emphasizes the theme that we need to trust in the Lord alone. Isaiah outlines three aspects of the coming kingdom: a righteous King (vv. 1-8), the need to be ready (vv. 9-14), and an outpouring of grace (vv. 15-20).

First aspect of God's kingdom: A righteous King (vv. 1-8)

Verses 1-5 boldly ("behold," Heb. *hen*) introduce God's promise to bring a righteous king. God is reminding Judah of its need to recognize that He is going to reverse the present order of curse by sending the promised Messiah. Isaiah reveals three radical changes that God will bring.

First radical change: An end of all wicked rulers (vv. 1-2)

One of the biggest reasons countries suffer is because of wicked rulers. God's Messiah and all who rule under Him will do so with perfect justice and righteousness (v. 1; cf. Isa. 11:1-5; Jer. 23:5). Righteous Hezekiah may have been ruling at the time of this prophecy, but even then the nation was still plagued by unrighteous leaders who used their power to oppress for personal gain (Isa. 1:10-15; Mic. 3:1-9; 7:1ff.). One day God will completely purge all such wickedness,[100] and only the righteous will rule with Him.[101] After ages of oppression (cf. Isa. 1:21-23; 29:20-21), these rulers will be like a refuge from wind, a shelter from storm, streams in the desert (cf. Isa. 35:1-2; 43:18-44:5), and shade in a parched land (v. 2).

Second radical change: An end to all spiritual blindness (v. 3)

We find the theme of blindness, deafness, and stammering speech multiple times in Isaiah. Although we have reason to say that the Messiah will bring an end to all physical afflictions (35:5-6; 42:7), we also have good reason for seeing these expressions as speaking about the removal of all spiritual blindness (6:9-10; 28:7, 8; 29:9, 10, 14; 30:1, 2; 31:1).

Third radical change: An end to the tyranny of godless men (vv. 4-8)

The lifting of all spiritual blindness will also mean an end to the tyranny of godless leaders. The expression "the mind of the hasty" refers to those leaders of Judah who were fearful because they did not trust Yahweh. The coming of the Messiah will put an end to all such destructive disbelief (v. 4). Never again will "fools" (*nabal*) and "rogues" (*kiylay*) have lordship nor be exalted to places they do not belong (v. 5). Pfeiffer explains:

> Under his government and influence, men will no longer be deceived by the prince of lies but will clearly see the difference between moral wisdom and folly, appreciating how fatuous is a life bent upon evil. God's standards of judgment will at last become man's standards.[102]

Having declared that fools and rogues will no longer have noble roles, Isaiah gives three reasons why in verses 6-8.

First reason fools will not rule (v. 6). The term "fool" is one of the strongest Hebrew terms for fool.[103] This is the kind of person who knows the truth, but "has consciously rejected the ways of God."[104] Fools speak nonsense and have no place for ruling in God's kingdom. Wicked hearts lead only to

---

[100] Young, *The Book of Isaiah, vol. 2*, 385.

[101] Some of those who reign with Christ will be resurrected saints from the Old Testament (Dan. 12:2-3, 13; Rev. 20:4), the church (2 Tim. 2:12; Rev. 2:26; 3:21; 5:10), and the tribulation martyrs (Rev. 20:4). Other saints include the righteous, mortal saints who got saved during the tribulation period and survived to enter the messianic kingdom (Dan. 7:13-14, 18, 27; Ezek. 45:21-25).

[102] Pfeiffer, *The Wycliffe Bible Commentary: Old Testament*.

[103] This is the term *nabal* as found in 1 Samuel 25.

[104] Oswalt, *The Book of Isaiah, 1-39*, 581.

wicked conduct—the kind of wicked conduct that leads to oppression and affliction. Christ will not allow this in His kingdom.

Second reason fools will not rule (v. 7). The word "rogue" (*kilay*) might rightly be translated as "knave" or "scoundrel" (cf. 32:5). The rogue is the person who is dedicated to destroying the righteous with slander to take advantage of them. Micah wrote about these same kinds of evil doers:

> Concerning evil, both hands do it well. The prince asks, also the judge, for a bribe, and a great man speaks the desire of his soul; so they weave it together. The best of them is like a briar; the most upright like a thorn hedge (Mic. 7:3-4).

This is the kind of evil that ruled over the land of Judah in the days of Isaiah. God's promise is that He will put an end to such evil.

Third reason fools will not rule (v. 8). Verse 8 presents a contrast to the evil leaders of verses 6-7 by telling us that the coming of God's kingdom will bring godly leaders who will rule in righteousness. The "noble" man (*nadib*) should be one of exalted character that cares for the rights of others (cf. Isa. 11:4-5).[105]

Second aspect of God's kingdom: The warning to be ready (vv. 9-14)

For Israel to enjoy God's blessings, they must first turn to the Lord (Hos. 5:15; 10:12; 11:11). Isaiah has already demonstrated the sin of many segments of Jewish society, but in verses 9-14 he singles out the godless women of the land.[106] The call is to repentance, but it is also a call to mourning because of the impending destruction they are about to face. Isaiah gives two calls to repentance.

First call to repentance (vv. 9-10)

This first call is addressed to the "women at ease," the "complacent daughters" of the land (cf. Amos 4:1ff.; 6:1ff.). Isaiah is exposing the way that godlessness had so permeated the land that the women of Israel had no fear of God and cared for nothing but ease and pleasure. Young describes them as, "women

---

[105] Oswalt says that the noble man is the "man of character, someone who is generous and large hearted" (Oswalt, *The Book of Isaiah, 1-39*, 582).
[106] Though not apparent in English, we can note that Isaiah varies his verb forms several times: vv. 9-10: fem. pl., fem. pl., fem. pl., fem. pl., v. 11: 2 masc., pl, 2 masc. sing., 2 masc. sing., 2 masc. sing., 2 masc. sing., v. 12: masc., pl. part.

who have a false confidence as to their security and therefore believe themselves to be protected from harm."[107] As in Amos 4, it is likely that Isaiah is focusing especially on wives in aristocratic circles who had great power and influence over their husbands and others.[108]

Isaiah commands these women to rise up and listen, for in shortly over one year catastrophe is going to bring an end to their prosperity and ease. These words were probably spoken about 703-702 B.C., for it would come about in 701 B.C. that Sennacherib would bring a siege on Jerusalem. This siege brought Judah to the verge of destruction and prevented Judah from going into their fields and vineyards to collect any harvest.[109]

Second call to repentance (vv. 11-14)

Isaiah repeats this call to repent: "Strip, undress and put *sackcloth* on *your* waist, beat your breasts for the pleasant fields, for the fruitful vine" (vv. 11-12; cf. 3:24-26). The days of gaiety were coming to an end, and the time to put on garments of mourning were coming. Beating the breasts reflects another way of expressing misery and mourning in the ancient near east. Oswalt explains, "It was typical for women in the ancient near east to bare their breasts in mourning and to put sackcloth about their waists . . . [although] there is no indication that complete nakedness was intended."[110] The days of godless celebration will come to an end, leaving the land desolate and covered with briars and thorns (1:7; 5:6, 17; 7:23-25; cf. Gen. 3:18) and overrun with wild animals (5:17; 7:25; 27:10). Self-confidence will be replaced by misery (v. 13; cf. 22:1-2). Pfeiffer notes that during the Assyrian invasions, "virtually every Jewish city besides Jerusalem was looted and burned in the campaign of 701, and the country districts were laid waste by Assyrian foragers."[111] The whole land suffered terribly because of its refusal to trust Yahweh.

The palace (*'armon*) may be referring to the royal palace in the City of David, but it could include houses belonging to other royal figures (v. 14; cf. Isa. 23:13; 25:2; 32:14; 34:13; 1 Kings 16:18; 2 Kings 15:25; Jer. 6:5; 9:20; 17:27; 30:18; 49:27; Amos 6:8; Pss. 18:19; 122:7),[112] while The Hill (*'ophel*) speaks about the hill that is on the southeast edge of Jerusalem near the palace, and The

---

[107] Young, *The Book of Isaiah, vol. 2*, 392.

[108] Grogan, "Isaiah," 206.

[109] Ibid.

[110] Oswalt, *The Book of Isaiah, 1-39*, 585.

[111] Pfeiffer, *The Wycliffe Bible Commentary: Old Testament*, Is 32:9.

[112] Ludwig Koehler et al., *The Hebrew and Aramaic Lexicon of the Old Testament*, cited in electronic form with Logos Libronix, 89.

Watchtower (*bachan*) was located nearby (Neh. 3:25-27).

These judgments began with the Assyrian invasions, but continued with the Babylonian invasions starting in 605 B.C., culminating with the destruction of Solomon's temple in 586 B.C. Martin reminds us that the desolations that fell on Jerusalem would last for many ages, but as verses 15-20 show, they will not last forever: "This Hebrew word ['*olam*] does not always carry the same force as the English word 'forever.' From verse 15 it is obvious that Isaiah saw a day when the desolation would cease."[113] The day of eschatological restoration will come when God does a mighty work to bring His people to repentance and faith in the messianic kingdom.

Third aspect of God's kingdom: An outpouring of grace (vv. 15-20)

One day this world is going to see a reversal back to glory. This reversal back to glory is never going to come by the efforts of man, but only the intervention of God with the return of Jesus Christ. Unger explains, "Jerusalem's restoration will be accomplished by the pouring of the Spirit from on high upon Israel (32:15; 44:3; 59:21; Ezek. 39:29; Joel 2:28-29; Zech. 12:10-13:1) as the saved and Spirit-filled remnant enters the kingdom."[114] The return of Christ and the pouring out of the Holy Spirit will bring the greatest reversal this world has ever seen. Verses 15-20 show us three areas where these reversals will take place.

First area: Frustration will be replaced by fruitfulness (v. 15)

The preceding section focused on judgments, but this section focuses on blessings—blessings that cannot take place until God pours out His Spirit. This outpouring will bring both spiritual and physical restoration. We have good reason to believe that the physical transformations described will be literal (Isa. 35:1; 41:18; 43:18-21; 55:12; cf. Ezek. 47:1-12; Joel 3:18-21; Amos 9:13; Zech. 14:8), but behind it all is the spiritual transformation God's Spirit will work to bring regeneration to God's elect, both Jewish (Isa. 11:11-16; 27:12-13; 44:3-5; 49:22; 56:8; Ezek. 11:17-20; 36:22-32; Joel 2:28-32; Zech. 12:10; 13:1) and Gentile (Isa. 11:10; 42:6; 49:6; 51:4; 56:1-8). The present devastation that sin has brought on the world will be replaced by "unparalleled fertility" in the days of the kingdom.[115]

---

[113] Martin, "Isaiah," 1082.

[114] Merrill F. Unger, *Unger's Commentary on the Old Testament, Vol. II: Isaiah-Malachi* (Chicago: Moody, 1981), 1229.

[115] Wolf, *Interpreting Isaiah*, 162.

Second area: Oppression will be replaced by righteousness (vv. 16-17)

Ancient Israel was overrun with oppression and unrighteousness, but this is what the world has been like since the entrance of sin. God's promise is that the messianic kingdom will usher in a righteous rule that will bring blessings to the whole world (Isa. 9:7; 11:4; 16:5; 33:5).

Third area: Covenant curses will be replaced by blessings (vv. 18-20)

The Law warned that rebellion to the covenant would bring expulsion from the land (Deut. 28:15-68). God's promise was that even though Israel broke that covenant, He would one day bring in a day of restoration under a New Covenant (Deut. 30:1-10; Jer. 31:31-34). The result of this covenant restoration would mean peace, everlasting peace, not only for Israel but also for the whole world (Isa. 2:4; Jer. 30:18; 31:23; 32:37-44; 33:7, 14-26; Amos 9:11-15; Mic. 4:3). God's promise to Israel is that one day they will live eternally in their land with no one to ever disturb them again (v. 18).

Verses 19-20 are enigmatic, but the context makes it clear enough how to understand them: Judgment must come before the blessings of restoration.[116] Kidner explains, "*Peace* is not a thing God superimposes on a corrupt society: the ground must be cleared and re-sown with *righteousness*, of which peace is the fruit (vv. 16–17)."[117] Have the blessings of verses 15-20 been realized? Oswalt says that some may argue that these promised blessings were fulfilled after the return from Babylon or perhaps at Pentecost, but it is best to see them all fulfilled in the future with a "complete fulfillment at the final day."[118]

Summary and application

The day is coming when God will purge out all curse and usher in the day of restoration. An eternal age of blessing is coming to all who place their faith in His Son, whether Jew or Gentile. This promise reminds us that even though we will have tribulation in this world, Jesus Christ has overcome it all, and we know that we can always trust Him (John 16:33).

---

[116] The forest that must come down (v. 19) could be symbolic of Assyria and all other forces of evil (cf. 10:33-34; 30:31), though it could refer to the pride and arrogance of Judah since it is said to be the city that is laid low (1:29-31; 2:13; 29:2-4) and not the whole world as elsewhere (24:10; 25:2; 26:1, 5).
[117] Kidner, "Isaiah," 652.
[118] Oswalt, *The Book of Isaiah, 1-39*, 589.

DESTRUCTION OF THE DESTROYER (33:1-24)

Chapter 33 contains the sixth and final woe of chapters 28-35 (28:1; 29:1; 29:15; 30:1; 31:1; 33:1). In a break from the previous woes, however, this woe is not directed against the rebellious leaders of Judah, but against the Assyrian invaders who were seeking Judah's destruction.[119]

Chapter 33 reads as follows: "1 Woe to you, O destroyer, while you were not destroyed, and he who is treacherous, while *others* did not deal treacherously with him. As soon as you finish destroying, you will be destroyed; as soon as you cease to deal treacherously, *others* will deal treacherously with you. 2 O Lord, be gracious to us; we have waited for You. Be their strength every morning, Our salvation also in the time of distress. 3 At the sound of the tumult peoples flee; at the lifting up of Yourself nations disperse. 4 Your spoil is gathered *as* the caterpillar gathers, as locusts rushing about men rush about on it. 5 The Lord is exalted, for He dwells on high; He has filled Zion with justice and righteousness. 6 And He will be the stability of your times, a wealth of salvation, wisdom and knowledge; the fear of the Lord is his treasure. 7 Behold, their brave men cry in the streets, the ambassadors of peace weep bitterly. 8 The highways are desolate, the traveler has ceased; He has broken the covenant, he has despised the cities; He has no regard for man. 9 The land mourns *and* pines away; Lebanon is shamed *and* withers; Sharon is like a desert plain, and Bashan and Carmel lose *their foliage*. 10 Now I will arise, says the Lord; now I will be exalted; now I will be lifted up. 11 You have conceived chaff, you will give birth to stubble; My breath will consume you like a fire. 12 The peoples will be burned to lime, like cut thorns which are burned in the fire. 13 You who are far away, hear what I have done, and you who are near, acknowledge My might. 14 Sinners in Zion are terrified; trembling has seized the godless. Who among us can live with the consuming fire? Who among us can live with continual burning? 15 He who walks righteously and speaks with sincerity, he who rejects unjust gain and shakes his hands so that they hold no bribe, he who stops his ears from hearing about bloodshed and shuts his eyes from looking upon evil; 16 he will dwell on the heights; his refuge will be the impregnable rock; his bread will be given *him*; his water will be sure. 17 Your eyes will see the King in His beauty; they will behold a far-distant land. 18 Your heart will meditate on terror: Where is he who counts? Where is he who weighs? Where is he who counts the towers? 19 You will no longer see a fierce people, a people of unintelligible speech which no one comprehends, of a stammering tongue which no one understands. 20 Look upon Zion, the city of our appointed feasts; your eyes will see Jerusalem, an undisturbed habitation, a tent which will not be folded; its stakes will never be pulled up, nor any of its cords be torn apart. 21 But there the majestic *One*, the Lord, will be for us, a place of rivers *and* wide canals on which no boat with

---

[119] Wolf, *Interpreting Isaiah*, 162; Grogan, "Isaiah," 210.

oars will go, and on which no mighty ship will pass—22 For the Lord is our judge; the Lord is our lawgiver; the Lord is our king; He will save us. 23 Your tackle hangs slack; it cannot hold the base of its mast firmly, nor spread out the sail. Then the prey of an abundant spoil will be divided; the lame will take the plunder, 24 and no resident will say, I am sick. The people who dwell there will be forgiven *their* iniquity" (33:1-24).

Judah was facing terrible woes, but the leaders of the land were still refusing to trust the Lord, the one thing that would save them. Oswalt explains: "The leaders of Judah have tried every other avenue to extricate themselves from Assyria's grip. But each has been fruitless."[120] Judah's ultimate hope was for God their King to save them. Chapter 33 presents us with the prayer for the king's salvation (vv. 1-9), and the promise of the king's salvation (vv. 10-24).

The prayer for the King's salvation (vv. 1-9)

Judah was afflicted by the powerful Assyrians. Their need was to seek the Lord. God was ready to hear their prayers if they would only turn to Him. One reason why God would answer was because Assyria was guilty of great sin for doing harm to His people.

Assyria the destroyer will be punished (v. 1)

A good way to anger someone is to harm to their child (Gen. 12:1-3; Exod. 4:22-23; cf. Zech. 2:8-9; 2 Thess. 1:6-9; Rev. 15:1-4; 16:4-7). The Assyrians (and other successive nations) brought great harm to God's people, and Isaiah makes it clear that the Lord will bring retribution. Assyria the treacherous destroyer would experience destruction with no remedy (cf. Isa. 10:12-19, 24-25; 14:24-27; 30:30-33; 31:8-9).[121]

Judah's real need is to turn to the Lord in faith and trust (vv. 2-9)

Assyria would never be satisfied with anything less than total domination. Judah's only hope against this war machine was the Lord.

---

[120] Oswalt, *The Book of Isaiah, 1-39*, 590.

[121] It may be best to date this prophecy about 702 B.C., about one year before the catastrophic defeat God brought to Sennacherib in chs. 36-37. The participial form of the word "Destroyer" conveys the sense that Assyria's destructive behavior was an ongoing pattern, a fact well-attested by history (cf. 2 Kings 18:13-16; 19:32-37). We see the idea of "treachery" (*bagad*) may be seen in the fact that King Hezekiah had tried to pay off Assyria with a bribe of 300 talents of silver and 30 talents of gold (2 Kings 18:14), but Sennacherib broke the agreement and invaded.

Judah's (Isaiah's) prayer to the Lord (v. 2). We cannot be certain if the prayer in verse 2 is coming from the people of Judah, or (better) from Isaiah. It is a plea for the Lord to bring grace and salvation to a nation that has no other hope. Judah's sin had brought it to this time of desperation, but perhaps desperation was the best thing that could have happened, for the people of God were being forced to trust in the Lord. Their great need (and ours) was "the strength" (*zeroa'*, arm) of the Lord (cf. 51:9; 52:10; 53:1; 59:16; 63:5). Young explains, "the prayer is a refutation of the idea that deliverance can come from man. God must be their salvation."[122]

The anticipation of how the Lord will scatter the enemy (vv. 3-4). Isaiah knew God would bring a fierce judgment on the enemy, one that would scatter the enemy (v. 3; cf. Isa. 37:37; 2 Chron. 32:21). This scattering would give Judah the opportunity to collect all the spoil (v. 4).[123]

God must bring this reversal (vv. 5-9). The promise of reversal was great, and Isaiah emphasizes that it is one only the Lord can accomplish. Therefore, the Lord is the One who will be exalted, for He is the One who brings justice, righteousness (v. 5), stability and salvation (v. 6).

Judah thought they could find peace by paying off the Assyrians, but they would soon realize that treacherous Assyria could not be trusted. Judah's only hope was the Lord, the One being mocked by the king of Assyria. The Jewish ambassadors had sought peace terms with Sennacherib at Lachish, but he rejected it all (v. 7; cf. 2 Kings 18:17; 19:8-13). As Grogan explains, the messengers "who have been sent out to parley with the enemy return weeping, for their words would not penetrate his hard heart."[124] The highways have now been left empty and desolate (7:3; 11:16; 19:23; 40:2; 49:11; 59:7; 62:10), for none would dare to venture outside the fortified city with the enemy controlling the land (v. 8). The result was that the entire land, even the rich plains of Sharon (35:2; 65:10), would shrivel due to the invading armies (v. 9). Martin helps us understand the greatness of this desolation that came to four particular places of great fertility:

> Lebanon, north of Israel and well known for its cedar forests, would wither. Sharon was the coastal plain south of Mount Carmel extending inland to the hill country of Ephraim. A fertile area, Sharon would become

---

[122] Young, *The Book of Isaiah*, vol. 2, 406.
[123] The caterpillar (cf. 1 Kings 8:37; Josh. 1:4; 2:25; Ps. 78:46; 2 Chron. 6:28) and locust imagery are meant to convey the idea that Israel will gather up the spoil of the enemy like the work of a caterpillar or locust.
[124] Grogan, "Isaiah," 211-212.

a desert like the Arabah (which means "arid" or "dry"), the desolate rift valley extending from the Dead Sea south to the Gulf of Aqabah. Bashan ("fertile plain"), east of the Sea of Kinnereth (later named the Sea of Galilee), was productive agriculturally (cf. Jer. 50:19) and known for its oak trees (Isa. 2:13; Ezek. 27:6; Micah 7:14; Zech. 11:2). Carmel ("fruitful land") was a mountain range thickly forested and well watered at that time. This destruction would show that the people could not save themselves. When the Lord would use the Assyrians against Judah, Judah's plans for peace would come to nothing. It was as if the people gave birth like a mother to nothing but chaff and straw, which can easily be burned up.[125]

These four regions were the richest and most fertile of all, yet look at them now: desolate and ruined waste lands. All men need to trust the Lord!

The promise of the king's salvation (vv. 10-24)

The prayer for God to act was given (vv. 1-9). God now answers with five declarations that He will save His people.

First declaration: God will exalt Himself (v. 10)

Twice God declares that when He rises up to judge the proud Assyrians, His judgments will bring Him glory by "exalting" (*rum*) and "lifting" (*nasa'*) Him up before His enemies (6:1; 33:5).[126] We see something similar when God told the Pharaoh, "But, indeed, for this reason I have allowed you to remain, in order to show you My power and in order to proclaim My name through all the earth" (Exod. 9:16). God will exalt Himself.

Second declaration: God will bring the enemy to ruin (vv. 11-12)

Hosea tells us that those who sow wind will reap a whirlwind (Hos. 8:7). Verses 11-12 give us four vivid pictures that remind us that the sin of Assyria will come back on their own heads.[127] The massive blow that was about to come

---

[125] Martin, "Isaiah," 1083.
[126] These two terms that speak about the exaltation of the Lord are two of the four terms used in 52:13 in connection with the suffering Servant. The present exaltation does not come by the forgiving of sins, but by the judging of sins.
[127] The NASB follows the LXX with the reading "My breath" will consume, but the MT and DSS support "your breathe," probably a reference to the Assyrians bringing destruction upon themselves (cf. 26:11; 29:6; 30:27, 30; 33:14 For other uses of the fire metaphor)

in 701 B.C. would eventually culminate in one final, devastating blow 100 years later, leaving Assyria in irreparable ruins.[128]

Third declaration: God calls on all to recognize His greatness (v. 13)

God is about to accomplish a great victory, one that the whole world near and far needs to hear about, for the whole world needs to recognize the saving grace of Yahweh (Isa. 49:1; 52:13-15; 57:19). The impact of this judgment will be that, "the unconverted sinners of Judah would be thrown into consternation at this proof of God's power, for it implies a threat that their own iniquities would be visited."[129]

Fourth declaration: God says only the righteous will stand (vv. 14-15)

One day soon, the sinners of Judah who had not been trusting in the living God, i.e., the sinners and the godless (*chaneph*, cf. Isa. 9:16; 10:6), were going to realize that Yahweh really does judge evil. Young notes that up to this time, there were many within Judah who, "felt no need for God, who neglected His ways and commands, walking securely in their own power, breaking His law, when they felt it was for their own profit."[130] All of that false thinking was about to change, for God's furious judgment would lead the people to ask these two very important questions.[131]

The two important questions (v. 14). The two questions are (1) Who among us can live with the consuming fire? and (2) Who among us can live with continual burning? In verse 15 Isaiah gives us the description of who will be able to stand.

The description of who will stand (v. 15). The only ones who will stand are those who have faith in the living God (Isa. 58:6-12; Hab. 2:4). Isaiah identifies these true believers according to the righteous lives they live (cf. Pss. 15; 24; Matt. 5:1-12). The true believer is the one who is dedicated to righteous conduct and speech that is not harmful to others.[132] Unjust gain through oppression was rampant in the days of Isaiah (1:16, 17, 23; 3:14, 15; cf. Mic. 3:9-10; 7:1-6), but this kind of person will be excluded from the kingdom. God's delight is that of genuine righteousness, a message repeated by all the prophets (Amos 5:24; Mic. 6:8).

---

[128] Oswalt, *The Book of Isaiah, 1-39*, 598.
[129] Pfeiffer, *The Wycliffe Bible Commentary: Old Testament*, Is 33:13.
[130] Young, *The Book of Isaiah, vol. 2*, 417.
[131] Other prophets ask the same kind of question (Ezek. 22:14; Mal. 3:2; Rev. 6:17).
[132] Ibid., 419.

Fifth declaration: Kingdom blessings to the righteous (vv. 16-24)

Isaiah describes five kinds of blessings that will come to those who trust the Lord and enter into the kingdom.

First kingdom blessing: Safety from all enemies (v. 16a). Dwelling on the *height* (*marom*) and *impregnable* rock (*metsad*) conveys the idea of security from every enemy. Eternal security will be the first blessing.

Second kingdom blessing: Abundant life provisions (v. 16b). God's people will also have every form of provision as expressed by the promise of abundant food and water. We see this same promise repeated when Isaiah says, "They will not hunger or thirst, nor will the scorching heat or sun strike them down, for He who has compassion on them will lead them and will guide them to springs of water" (49:10).

Third kingdom blessing: Dwelling with Messiah (v. 17). Some have suggested that this reference to seeing "the King" (the absence of the article may convey the idea of an ideal king) may be a reference to Hezekiah, but contextually it is best seen as the promise of the Messiah. True peace and blessing cannot come until Christ returns. Oswalt explains, "If we have discovered an ultimate One who is truly for us, then we may be secure, no matter what."[133]

Here, as elsewhere, we see that Israel's true King is Lord Himself. Martin notes, "The King (cf. 32:1; 33:22; 43:15; Micah 2:13; Zeph. 3:15; Zech. 14:9), the Messiah, will be there (Isa. 33:17), and the people will see Him" (cf. Isa. 6:1-3; 9:6; 10:20-21; 12:6; Jer. 23:5; 33:15; Ezek. 37:24-28; 48:35; Zeph. 2:14-17; Zech. 12:10; 14:9; Matt. 24:29-31; 25:31-46).[134] The last phrase conveys the idea that their eyes will also behold a land that has been stretched and extended way beyond anything that has ever been seen before (NIV: "a land that stretches afar"). All of this is part of the blessing of being with the King in His fruitful kingdom (cf. 26:15; 32:1ff.; 54:1ff.).

Fourth kingdom blessing: A removal of all miseries (vv. 18-19). God warned that disobedience would bring misery (Gen. 2:17). For Israel, this would include "the curses" of the covenant (Deut. 28:15-68). God promises He will remove those miseries to be nothing more than memories.

No longer will the people be forced to figure ways of escaping the plights of a fallen world,[135] for those days will be gone forever (v. 18; cf. Rev. 21-22 for

---

[133] Oswalt, *The Book of Isaiah, 1-39*, 602-603.

[134] Martin, "Isaiah," 1084.

[135] Counting and weighing may refer to the weighing of tribute money for oppressing kings, and counting towers may have a reference to military strategizing.

the final removal). All the miseries of a fallen world will be gone forever, for the fierce foreigners,[136] the invading armies with strange-sounding languages, will be gone forever (v. 19; cf. Deut. 28:49; Isa. 28:11; 36:11; Jer. 5:15).

Fifth kingdom blessing: Eternal restoration (vv. 20-24). The language in verses 20-24 uses some interesting metaphors to describe the blessings of restoration, but the point is clear enough. Zion, God's chosen city Jerusalem (Deut. 12; 2 Sam. 5; 1 Kings 8; Ps. 132), the place where she held her annual feasts (Lev. 23), will see eternal security and peace.[137]

The restoration language used here includes that of calling Jerusalem the tent that will never again get folded up (v. 20), the place of rivers and canals where no (foreign) boats will ever pass (v. 21), and the boat whose tackle will be fully seaworthy, a condition that is in stark contrast to its present condition (v. 23a),[138] the place where spoils previously taken will become spoils returned (v. 23b; cf. 2 Sam. 5:6), and forgiven saints will never again experience the sickness that comes from life in a fallen world (v. 24; cf. Isa. 57:18-19; 58:8; Jer. 31:31-34; 33:6-8; 36:3; 50:20).[139]

How can all these things be true? It is because Judah's Savior-King will deliver them: "For the LORD is our judge; the LORD is our lawgiver; the LORD is our king; He will save us." Messiah Jesus will be the final realization of a Champion-Judge (Isa. 2:4; 11:4; 19:20), a perfect Lawgiver (Isa. 23; 51:4; cf. Gen. 49:10; Deut. 33:21; Judg. 5:13, 14), and a righteous King (Isa. 11:1ff.; 32:1). Everything the people ever have needed they will find in God's kingdom when Messiah is in their midst.

Summary and application

We remind ourselves that the wonderful restoration promises given to Israel include a perfect restoration for all who trust in the redeeming work of Christ. As John explains it, "there will no longer be any curse" (Rev. 22:3). The cost of this redemption was the blood of God's only Son, and the promise is that this redemption will be freely given to any who ask for it (Isa. 55:1-3; cf. Rev. 22:17).

---

[136] "Fierce" connotes barbarous (Oswalt, *The Book of Isaiah, 1-39*, 601, n. 1).

[137] These land promises were first made to Abraham and the patriarchs (Gen. 12:1-3; 13:14-15; 17:7-8; 28:13; 35:11-12; 48:4), but get repeated over the ages (cf. Deut. 30:1-10; 2 Sam. 7:10; Jer. 30:10, 17-18; 31:38-40; 32:15, 37-44; Ezek. 37:25; 39:25-29; Joel 3:17-21; Amos 9:14-15; Zech. 14:11; Mic. 4:4-7).

[138] Young, *The Book of Isaiah, vol. 2*, 426.

[139] Wolf, *Interpreting Isaiah*, 164.

THE OVERTHROW OF WICKED EDOM (34:1-17)

Chapters 34-35 appear to form a summary and climax to the preceding section (chs. 28-33) somewhat in the same way that chapters 24-27 form a summary and climax to 13-23.[140] One of the truths that comes out in chapter 34 is that the end of this age is going to usher in a period when God will bring a severe judgment on all the nations of the world—especially those nations that were seeking the destruction of Israel. The ancient nation called Edom is highlighted as one of those nations.

Chapter 34 reads as follows: "1 Draw near, O nations, to hear, and listen, O peoples! Let the earth and all it contains hear, and the world and all that springs from it. 2 For the Lord's indignation is against all the nations, and *His* wrath against all their armies; He has utterly destroyed them; He has given them over to slaughter. 3 So their slain will be thrown out, and their corpses will give off their stench, and the mountains will be drenched with their blood. 4 And all the host of heaven will wear away, and the sky will be rolled up like a scroll; all their hosts will also wither away as a leaf withers from the vine, or as *one* withers from the fig tree. 5 For My sword is satiated in heaven; behold it shall descend for judgment upon Edom and upon the people whom I have devoted to destruction. 6 The sword of the Lord is filled with blood; it is sated with fat, with the blood of lambs and goats, with the fat of the kidneys of rams. For the Lord has a sacrifice in Bozrah and a great slaughter in the land of Edom. 7 Wild oxen will also fall with them and young bulls with strong ones; thus their land will be soaked with blood, and their dust become greasy with fat, 8 for the Lord has a day of vengeance, a year of recompense for the cause of Zion. 9 Its streams will be turned into pitch, and its loose earth into brimstone, and its land will become burning pitch. 10 It will not be quenched night or day; its smoke will go up forever. From generation to generation it will be desolate; none will pass through it forever and ever. 11 But pelican and hedgehog will possess it, and owl and raven will dwell in it, and He will stretch over it the line of desolation and the plumb line of emptiness. 12 Its nobles—there is no one there *whom* they may proclaim king—and all its princes will be nothing. 13 Thorns will come up in its fortified towers, nettles and thistles in its fortified cities; it will also be a haunt of jackals *and* an abode of ostriches. 14 The desert creatures will meet with the wolves; the hairy goat also will cry to its kind; yes, the night monster will settle there and will find herself a resting place. 15 The tree snake will make its nest and lay *eggs* there, and it will hatch and gather *them* under its protection. Yes, the hawks will be gathered there, every one with its kind. 16 Seek from the book of the Lord, and read: Not one of these will be missing; none will lack its mate, for His mouth has commanded, and His Spirit has gathered them. 17 He

---

[140] Ibid., 165.

has cast the lot for them, and His hand has divided it to them by line. They shall possess it forever; from generation to generation they will dwell in it" (34:1-17).

Many prophets predicted a worldwide judgment in an eschatological tribulation period (Isa. 26:20-21; cf. Ezek. 38-39; Dan. 7:23-28; Joel 3:1-17; Zech. 12:1ff.; 14:1ff.; Rev. 16:12-16). Isaiah 34 tells us about a judgment on all the nations (vv. 1-4), and follows this with a section singling out Edom as representative of this universal judgment (vv. 5-17).

Judgment on all the nations (vv. 1-4)

God has a plan for this world, and He wants men to know what this plan is. God first announces that He has a plan for all to hear (v. 1), and then He tells us the nature of how this plan will unfold (vv. 2-4).

The announcement of God's eschatological plan (v. 1)

Isaiah uses a four-fold repetition to announce God's plan for the world, a message for the nations, peoples, earth, and whole world. God's plan will embrace every corner of human existence.

The nature of God's eschatological plan (vv. 2-4)

God feelings (v. 2a). God is angry with sinners, and He is going to judge them. "Indignation" (*qetseph*) conveys the broad idea of anger, while "wrath" (*chemah*) conveys the sense of heated rage. As noted elsewhere, God's wrath and indignation is against all sin (Isa. 10:5, 25; 13:5; 26:20-21; 27:4; 42:25; 59:18; 66:14-15).

God's deeds (vv. 2b-4). God will devote (*charam*) the world to destruction and slaughter as one slaughters an animal (v. 2b; cf. Josh. 6:21; 1 Sam. 15:3). On earth, the impact of this wrath will show itself by the massive slaughter of sinners, especially those who were seeking the destruction of Israel. Many will be slaughtered and left unburied on the open ground (v. 3; cf. Ezek. 39:18-20; Pss. 2; 110; Rev. 19:11-21).

The impact of God's wrath will be so severe that it will even impact the physical creation (v. 4). Some interpret these statements as simply being metaphors of God's judgment on the nations,[141] but there is no reason for not seeing this to include the idea that the physical universe will experience intense convulsions during the tribulation period, as noted here and elsewhere (cf. Isa.

---

[141] Young, *The Book of Isaiah, vol. 2*, 431.

13:13; 24:4; 51:6; Ezek. 32:7; Joel 2:31; Zech. 14:6-7; Matt. 24:29; Acts 2:20; Rev. 6:12-14; 16:8-11).[142] God will judge all evil.

Judgment on Edom (vv. 5-17)

Through the rest of the chapter, the focus shifts to Edom. Edom was founded by Esau the brother of Jacob (Gen. 36:8), and was located on the eastern edge of the Jordan Valley, just south of Moab. The Edomites were close relatives to Israel (Gen. 25:23), but had a long history of hostility against them (cf. e.g., Num. 20:14-21). Their treachery was exemplified when they chose to turn against Judah and aided the Babylonians when they invaded Jerusalem in 588-586 B.C. (Lam. 4:21; Ezek. 35:1-15; Obad. 11-14; Ps. 137:7; 2 Chron. 21:8-10; 25:11; 28:17; Joel 3:19; Amos 1:11-12; Mal. 1:2-3). Even though Edom was not a particularly powerful empire like Assyria, their hostility against Israel was a source of great wrath for the Lord (Isa. 25:10; 63:1ff.). The remaining section announces both the carnage (vv. 5-15) and certainty of Edom's fall (vv. 16-17).

The carnage of Edom's fall (vv. 5-15)

God's revenge will be a great sacrifice (vv. 5-8). The message against Edom begins with the promise that God's sword will be "satiated" (Heb. *ruah*, filled with abundant drink; cf. Isa. 16:9; Prov. 5:19; 7:18; Jer. 46:10),[143] for it will be "filled" (*male'*) with blood of Edom and "sated" (Heb. *dashan*, made fat; cf. Deut. 31:20) from the multitude of slaughtered victims (vv. 5-7; cf. Jer. 46:10; 51:40; Ezek. 39:18-20; Zeph. 1:7-9). The repetition of the name Edom, and the mention of Bozrah,[144] reinforce the idea that this country will become an object of God's eschatological wrath. All sin has a payday, especially for those who sought the harm of Israel (Gen. 12:3). Edom will have her payday when God brings vengeance and recompense for Edom's violence and arrogance (v. 8; cf. 35:4; 59:17-18; 61:2; 63:4). Martin explains, "Having promised to bless His Chosen People, He must fulfill His promises."[145]

---

[142] Oswalt suggests this usage of the term "host" (*tseba'*) may go beyond the physical host of heaven to include the demonic hosts as well (2 Kings 17:16; 21:3, 5; 23:4-5 [Oswalt, *The Book of Isaiah, 1-39*, 609, n. 14])

[143] Ludwig Koehler et al., *The Hebrew and Aramaic Lexicon of the Old Testament*, cited in electronic form with Logos Libronix (Leiden: E.J. Brill, 1994–2000), 1194–1195.

[144] Bozrah was the leading city of the Edomites (Gen. 36:33; Jer. 49:13, 22) and is identified with the modern town of Buseirah, located about 20 miles southeast of the lower end of the Dead Sea (Oswalt, *The Book of Isaiah, 1-39*, 612).

[145] Martin, "Isaiah," 1084–1085. The language (the "cause" of Zion, Heb. *riyb*) carries the idea of a legal dispute where wrongs must be made right (Young, *The Book of Isaiah, vol. 2*, 435).

Historically, Edom fell to the Nabatean Arabs around 500 B.C., but the events spoken of here appear to reach beyond ancient history to describe a destruction that is eschatological and cataclysmic. Pfeiffer notes that the language here seems to go beyond events of history to show "a description of the coming utter desolation of the Edomite domains and, by implication, the ruin of all the God-denying civilization of unregenerate mankind."[146] In terms of present-day inhabitants, this region is populated by the nation called Jordan. It will be interesting to see how this and other prophecies find fulfillment at the end of the age (cf. Isa. 63:1-6; Dan. 11:41).

God's revenge will bring utter desolation (vv. 9-15). The following section paints a picture of utter desolation to the land of Edom. The desolation resembles two other severe judgments. The first is the one that fell upon Sodom and Gomorrah (Gen. 19:24-28; Deut. 29:23; Ps. 11:6; Jer. 49:18; Rev. 14:10-11). Just as Sodom and Gomorrah were left in perpetual ruins, Edom will see its streams turned to pitch and the earth into brimstone, a fire that will not be quenched (vv. 9-10).

The second similar judgment is the one that falls upon Babylon (vv. 11-15; cf. Isa. 13:20-22). God's measured out destruction will bring such a destruction that the "desolation" (*tohu*) and "emptiness" (*bohu*) will be like an utter reversal from God's purposes of shaping and filling his creation with life and habitation (cf. Gen. 1:2 where the two terms *tohu* and *bohu* show the earth before God's creative purposes were fully accomplished, and Jeremiah 4:23 where the terms describe God's devastations to Judah).

In verses 11-15, Isaiah names out twelve kinds of wild creatures that will overtake desolated Edom because of God's judgment,[147] including the mythical creature the NASB calls "the night monster."[148] As with Babylon, the judgments will be severe and irreversible (cf. Rev. 18:18; 19:3) and arrogant Edom will never rise again with the proud aristocracies of the past (Gen. 36:40-43). Young explains, "all the former nobles of Edom have disappeared, and there are none at all remaining who might constitute a kingdom."[149]

---

[146] Pfeiffer, *The Wycliffe Bible Commentary: Old Testament*, Is 34:8.

[147] The identification of some of these animals is hard to pinpoint, though we do seem to have a good idea what most of them are. All of the birds mentioned would have been considered unclean in the Law of Moses (Deut. 14:14-17).

[148] The Hebrew term *lyliyth* appeared in Babylonian literature as a night demon (Wolf, *Interpreting Isaiah*, 167), but is also found in the Jewish work Tobit 3:8 (Oswalt, *The Book of Isaiah, 1-39*, 616, n. 18).

[149] Young, *The Book of Isaiah, vol. 2*, 439.

The certainty of Edom's fall (vv. 16-17)

Isaiah does not explain what "the book of the Lord" is, but it appears to speak about God's determined plan (Pss. 40:7; 139:16; Dan. 7:10; Mal. 3:16).[150] God has planned every detail, including the animals that will overtake the land, and none of it will lack fulfillment. Pfeiffer says that we see "a strong affirmation that these predictions recorded in writing in Jehovah's book, i.e., the inspired prophecies of Isaiah, would be literally fulfilled."[151] God spoke, and it will happen just as He spoke it.

Summary and application

The unsaved world lives in utter disregard of God, but one day they will realize the folly of their disbelief. Believers must make sure that they do not allow the worries and cares of this world to divert their affections from eternity and the things of the Lord (Matt. 6:25-34; 2 Cor. 3:18).

THE FRUIT OF GOD'S KINGDOM (35:1-10)

God's first warning was that disobedience would bring tragic consequences (Gen. 2:17; Rom. 8:20). The entrance of sin and death plunged creation into a state of immeasurable suffering and misery (Rom. 5:12-21). God's promise, however, has always been that one day He would send a Savior to destroy the enemy and bring in a restoration (Gen. 3:15). This restoration will come ultimately when Jesus returns and brings the Kingdom of God. Chapter 35 describes the coming kingdom.

Chapter 35 reads as follows: "1 The wilderness and the desert will be glad, and the Arabah will rejoice and blossom; like the crocus 2 it will blossom profusely and rejoice with rejoicing and shout of joy. The glory of Lebanon will be given to it, the majesty of Carmel and Sharon. They will see the glory of the Lord, the majesty of our God. 3 Encourage the exhausted, and strengthen the feeble. 4 Say to those with anxious heart, Take courage, fear not. Behold, your God will come *with* vengeance; the recompense of God will come, but He will save you. 5 Then the eyes of the blind will be opened and the ears of the deaf will be unstopped. 6 Then the lame will leap like a deer, and the tongue of the mute will shout for joy, for waters will break forth in the wilderness and streams in the Arabah. 7 The scorched land will become a pool and the thirsty ground springs of water; in the haunt of jackals, its resting place, grass *becomes* reeds and rushes. 8 A highway will be there, a roadway, and it will be called the Highway

---

[150] Oswalt, *The Book of Isaiah, 1-39*, 617-618.
[151] Pfeiffer, *The Wycliffe Bible Commentary: Old Testament*, Is 34:8.

of Holiness. The unclean will not travel on it, but it *will* be for him who walks *that* way, and fools will not wander *on it*. 9 No lion will be there, nor will any vicious beast go up on it; these will not be found there, but the redeemed will walk *there,* 10 and the ransomed of the Lord will return and come with joyful shouting to Zion, with everlasting joy upon their heads. They will find gladness and joy, and sorrow and sighing will flee away" (35:1-10).

The messianic kingdom will be unlike anything this world has seen since the fall of man in the Garden of Eden. Isaiah presents a concise, three-fold picture of the blessings that will characterize this kingdom.

It will be a kingdom of rejoicing (vv. 1-2)

The nature of the coming transformation (vv. 1-2a)

Isaiah foresaw a day when the earth would break into great joy (gladness, rejoicing) and fruitfulness (blossoming in the desserts). All the areas that were barren and desolate like the wilderness, the desert, and the Arabah,[152] will be radically transformed to become like the rich regions of Lebanon, Carmel, and Sharon. These promises are best understood as including not only a physical transformation, but also the underlying spiritual transformation. Smith explains,

> The prophet was far more concerned with the theological effect of God's work than the botanical, but the two ideas work together rather than against one another. God's work will remove the curse from every part of the earth.[153]

God's Word tells us that a perfect restoration is coming, the perfect restoration that Paul described in Romans 8:21 where we read that, "the creation itself also will be set free from its slavery to corruption into the freedom of the glory of the children of God."

The reason for the coming transformation (v. 2b)

The reason for this transformation is the redeeming grace of God. His people will see the "glory" and "majesty" of the God of Israel (Isa. 32:17), and the messianic kingdom will transform the whole earth (Isa. 9:1-7). The plain

---

[152] The wilderness (*midbar*) refers to open land areas such as the Sinai and Negeb, while the desert (*tsiyah*) conveys the idea of dry and parched land, while the Arabah (*'arabah*) speaks about the Jordan Valley.

[153] Gary V. Smith, *Isaiah 1-39*, ed. E. Ray Clendenen, The New American Commentary, cited in electronic form with Logos Libronix (Nashville: B & H Publishing Group, 2007), 579.

meaning of the text within its flowing context tells us that these are literal promises that will get fulfilled in the Millennium, and "God's people who will have long asked for him to show himself will see his glory"[154] (cf. Matt. 25:31-46; Rev. 19:11-20:15). Smith explains that this promise,

> could simply refer to the glory of God reflected in the glorious changes in nature (41:19–20; 51:3; 60:13), but other similar texts seem to indicate that God himself will appear in splendor in a visible theophany (cf. 4:5; 24:23; 40:5; 52:10; 60:1–2; 66:18).[155]

We have every reason to believe that this is the Son of God who has returned in glory at the end of the tribulation period to establish His kingdom on this earth (Matt. 16:27; 24:27-31; 25:31; 26:64; Acts 1:11; Rev. 1:7).

It will be a kingdom of restoration (vv. 3-7)

One of God's purposes in giving prophecy is to give His people hope. Here in verses 3-4, Isaiah says, "encourage the exhausted," "strengthen the feeble," and "take courage" and "fear not," for the Savior is coming with a twofold mission of both judging evil (cf. same two terms in 34:8),[156] and saving His people. When Christ returns, He will not only bring an end to all human suffering (vv. 5-6a), but also to the suffering that afflicts the earth itself (vv. 6b-7).

The coming kingdom restores a suffering humanity (vv. 5-6a)

Four times Isaiah speaks about restoration from physical suffering. As noted previously, there are times when some expressions (like blindness language) appear to be speaking about spiritual blindness (cf. Isa. 6:9-10), but we have good reason to see these as literal promises that the messianic kingdom will bring a purging of all physical disease and deformity (28:7; 29:9-10, 18; 30:20-21; 32:3-4; 42:7, 16; 50:4; Matt. 8:14-17; 11:5).[157]

The coming kingdom restores a suffering world (vv. 6b-7)

The reason for this restoration is a mighty outpouring of God's grace, an

---

[154] Oswalt, *The Book of Isaiah, 1-39*, 623.
[155] Smith, *Isaiah 1-39*, 579.
[156] The OT uses both "vengeance" (*naqam*, Isa. 47:3; Deut. 32:41, 43; Ezek. 25:14; Mic. 5:14; Ps 79:10) and "recompense" (*gemul*, to requite and reward according to deeds) elsewhere to tell us that one day God will make every wrong right. God will repay sinners according to their sins (2 Thess. 1:6-9; Rev. 16:4-7).
[157] Wolf, *Interpreting Isaiah*, 168.

outpouring that is often symbolized by a mighty outpouring of waters (Isa. 32:15; 43:18-19; 44:3-5). It will not be a little dribbling of grace, but a mighty outpouring of grace that breaks forth (*baqa'*, cleave, break open) and brings complete restoration. As a result, the dry and scorched land will blossom and thrive from the restoring grace of God. Martin explains,

> Though some interpreters take these statements as figurative of spiritual blessings, it seems preferable to take them as literal statements, especially in view of the covenant promises (Deut. 28:1–14). With the Lord living among His people and with righteousness being practiced by them, the Lord will provide physical healing and agricultural fecundity.[158]

It will be a kingdom of righteousness (vv. 8-10)

Isaiah gives a final description of the kingdom. Evil will not be allowed in, for only the righteous will enter. Isaiah uses one of his favorite terms, "highway" (Heb. *maslul*; cf. 11:16; 19:23; 35:8; 40:3; 49:11; 62:10), to convey the idea that the kingdom will be a place of holiness, and that nothing unclean will enter. The unsaved, i.e., the "fool" (Heb. *'ewiyl*; cf. Prov. 1:7; 10:8, 10; 27:22; 29:9),[159] will not enter (Matt. 25:41).

Just as desolation was the consequence of judgment (Isa. 7:23-25; 8:21-22), blessing will be the consequence of restoration (Isa. 9:1-7). Isaiah does not intend to convey the idea that animals will be absent, but that the present ferocity of wild animals (*pariyts*) will be gone forever (cf. 11:6-9). Nothing morally evil or physically harmful will enter, but only those who have been redeemed and ransomed from curse (v. 9b-10).[160] Each of these two synonyms carries its own distinctive connotation as noted by Smith:

> "Redeemed" is used when a person delivers a blood relative from some obligation (legal, financial, social). . . . "Ransom" comes from the legal practice of making a payment to deliver someone from a debt, obligation,

---

[158] Martin, "Isaiah," 1085.
[159] Ludwig Koehler et al., *The Hebrew and Aramaic Lexicon of the Old Testament*, cited in electronic form with Logos Libronix (Leiden: E.J. Brill, 1994–2000), 21. Oswalt says that the fool means "not merely a simpleton but that morally perverse person who knowingly chooses the opposite to God's truth" (Oswalt, *The Book of Isaiah, 1-39*, 625). God's highway will not only give entrance to all the saints, but it will also bring them together as one people (19:23-25).
[160] This term for "redeemed" (*ga'al*) is found 21 times in chs. 40-66 and the term "ransomed" (v. 10, *padah*) is used twice in 40-66. Both terms convey the idea of being bought back out of bondage and ruin.

or punishment. . . . Both terms emphasize that the people's status as the redeemed or ransomed is based on an act of divine grace.[161]

These who enter the kingdom are those who trusted in God's Servant (Isa. 52:13-53:12). These are the sheep on the right hand of the King: "Come, you who are blessed of My Father; inherit the kingdom" (Matt. 25:34).[162] These redeemed saints, "will return and come with joyful shouting to Zion with everlasting joy upon their heads" and they will find "gladness and joy" and "sorrow and sighing will flee away" (v. 10; cf. Isa. 25:6-9; 30:29; 51:11; 65:19). The kingdom will usher in an age of everlasting blessing that ultimately will culminate after the Millennium with a new creation and a complete removal of every trace of sin, curse and death (Rev. 21:1-5; 22:1-5).

Summary and application

Living in a fallen world, it is easy to forget that things will one day be different. God's promises are here to encourage us to keep trusting the Lord. He faithful, and He is strong enough to fulfill it (cf. chs. 36-39).

---

[161] Smith, *Isaiah 1-39*, 580–581.

[162] It will be helpful to make a clarifying point about who all enter the Millennium: (1) Christ will return at the end of the seven-year tribulation period to rule over His millennial kingdom (Pss. 2:7-9; 110; Dan. 7:13-14; Mic. 2:12-13; Zeph. 3:14-20; Zech. 14:9; Matt. 19:28; 25:31; 26:29, 64). (2) The resurrected church will return with Christ at the end of the tribulation period to rule with Christ (Matt. 19:28; Rev. 2:26; 3:21; 5:10; 19:7-8, 14; 20:4a). (3) OT saints will be raised to rule with Christ (Dan. 12:2-3, 13). (4) Tribulation martyrs will be raised and rule with Christ (Rev. 20:4b). (5) The mortal saints who got saved after the rapture and survived will enter the kingdom to live, marry, and repopulate the earth (Isa. 11:10-16; 27:12-13; Ezek. 20:33-38; Zech. 8:14-23; Matt. 25:31-46).

7
TRUST IN YAHWEH AND PROSPER
(36:1-39:8)

Chapters 36-39 bring the reader to what most consider a close to the first half of Isaiah. These four chapters introduce the reader not only to the demise of mighty Assyria (chs. 36-37), but also to the ominous rise of the next dominating empire, mighty Babylon who will take Judah into exile.[1] As noted by Kidner, the significance of these historical transitions is reflected in the reality that "apart from Hezekiah's psalm (found only in 38:9–20), these chapters coincide almost word for word with 2 Ki. 18–20."[2] A radical transition is coming to Judah that will result in long ages of exile, an exile Moses warned of 800 years earlier (Deut. 28:15-68). All of these events stand as the backdrop for the restoration promises in chapters 40-66.

These four chapters may be explained as having four major themes: the invasion by Assyria (ch. 36), the destruction of Assyria (ch. 37), the recovery of Hezekiah (ch. 38), and the rise of Babylon (ch. 39). The major lesson is that no matter what life may bring, we need to keep trusting the Lord.[3] Oswalt explains that these chapters,

> demonstrate that it is not necessary to revoke one's dependence on God

---

[1] Herbert M. Wolf, *Interpreting Isaiah* (Grand Rapids: Zondervan, 1985), 171.

[2] F. Derek Kidner, "Isaiah," in *New Bible Commentary: 21st Century Edition*, ed. D. A. Carson et al., 4th ed., cited in electronic form with Logos Libronix (Leicester, England; Downers Grove, IL: Inter-Varsity Press, 1994), 654.

[3] Webb notes that the real issue at stake is "the issue of trust, and where that trust should ultimately be placed" (Barry G. Webb, *The Message of Isaiah* [Downers Grove: IVP, 1996], 147).

and turn to human powers in order to survive. In this way they constitute a lived-out example of the truths taught in chs. 13-35. The nations of mankind are under God's hand; he is their ruler and those who trust in him need not, indeed, must not, bow down to those nations.[4]

Chapter 36 opens this section by showing us how the faith of Hezekiah and all of Judah will soon be tested by the Assyria invasion. The big question is who they are going to trust.

THE HUMILIATING INVASION BY ASSYRIA (36:1-22)

For several hundred years, Assyria had been a power to be feared, but this threat had become especially bad in recent decades. At this point in time (ca. 701 B.C.), Hezekiah is the king of Judah, and the armies of Assyria are trying to overthrow Jerusalem. Is Hezekiah going to trust in human power by asking the help of foreign armies, or is he going to turn to the Lord? The Scripture is clear: "It is better to take refuge in the LORD than to trust in man. It is better to take refuge in the LORD than to trust in princes" (Ps. 118:8-9; cf. Prov. 3:5-6; Jer. 17:5-8). As we have already noted, trusting in God does not preclude the concept of exercising human responsibility, but it does mean that our ultimate confidence and hope must always come from seeking God and trusting in Him to save us.

Chapter 36 reads as follows: "1 Now in the fourteenth year of King Hezekiah, Sennacherib king of Assyria came up against all the fortified cities of Judah and seized them. 2 And the king of Assyria sent Rabshakeh from Lachish to Jerusalem to King Hezekiah with a large army, and he stood by the conduit of the upper pool on the highway of the fuller's field. 3 Then Eliakim the son of Hilkiah, who was over the household, and Shebna the scribe, and Joah the son of Asaph, the recorder, came out to him. 4 Then Rabshakeh said to them, Say now to Hezekiah, Thus says the great king, the king of Assyria, What is this confidence that you have? 5 I say, Your counsel and strength for the war are only empty words. Now on whom do you rely, that you have rebelled against me? 6 Behold, you rely on the staff of this crushed reed, *even* on Egypt, on which if a man leans, it will go into his hand and pierce it. So is Pharaoh king of Egypt to all who rely on him. 7 But if you say to me, We trust in the Lord our God, is it not He whose high places and whose altars Hezekiah has taken away and has said to Judah and to Jerusalem, You shall worship before this altar'? 8 Now therefore, come make a bargain with my master the king of Assyria, and I will

---

[4] John N. Oswalt, *The Book of Isaiah: Chapters 1-39*, The New International Commentary On The Old Testament, R. K. Harrison, Gen. Ed. (Grand Rapids: Eerdmans, 1986), 629.

give you two thousand horses, if you are able on your part to set riders on them. 9 How then can you repulse one official of the least of my master's servants and rely on Egypt for chariots and for horsemen? 10 Have I now come up without the Lord's approval against this land to destroy it? The Lord said to me, Go up against this land and destroy it. 11 Then Eliakim and Shebna and Joah said to Rabshakeh, Speak now to your servants in Aramaic, for we understand *it;* and do not speak with us in Judean in the hearing of the people who are on the wall. 12 But Rabshakeh said, Has my master sent me only to your master and to you to speak these words, *and* not to the men who sit on the wall, *doomed* to eat their own dung and drink their own urine with you? 13 Then Rabshakeh stood and cried with a loud voice in Judean and said, Hear the words of the great king, the king of Assyria. 14 Thus says the king, Do not let Hezekiah deceive you, for he will not be able to deliver you, 15 nor let Hezekiah make you trust in the Lord, saying, The Lord will surely deliver us; this city will not be given into the hand of the king of Assyria. 16 Do not listen to Hezekiah, for thus says the king of Assyria, Make your peace with me and come out to me, and eat each of his vine and each of his fig tree and drink each of the waters of his own cistern, 17 until I come and take you away to a land like your own land, a land of grain and new wine, a land of bread and vineyards. 18 *Beware* that Hezekiah does not mislead you, saying, The Lord will deliver us. Has any one of the gods of the nations delivered his land from the hand of the king of Assyria? 19 Where are the gods of Hamath and Arpad? Where are the gods of Sepharvaim? And when have they delivered Samaria from my hand? 20 Who among all the gods of these lands have delivered their land from my hand, that the Lord would deliver Jerusalem from my hand? 21 But they were silent and answered him not a word; for the king's commandment was, Do not answer him. 22 Then Eliakim the son of Hilkiah, who was over the household, and Shebna the scribe and Joah the son of Asaph, the recorder, came to Hezekiah with their clothes torn and told him the words of Rabshakeh" (36:1-22).

Chapter 36 can be broken down into a pair of interactions between the messenger of the king of Assyria and Hezekiah and the royal officials of Judah who are trapped inside the city of Jerusalem. Assyria is trying to humiliate and demoralize the people of Judah, but all of these interactions remind us not to fear the foolishness of a wicked world.

First set of interactions (vv. 1-12)

Jerusalem was a heavily fortified city, one that could not be easily conquered, even by the strongest of armies. Assyria's initial strategy was to employ psychological warfare to discourage the Jews and persuade them to surrender. This section includes an introduction to the context (vv. 1-3), a record of the blasphemous ragings of Rabshakeh (vv. 4-10), and the response from Judah (vv. 11-12).

ISAIAH 36:1-39:8

The historical context (vv. 1-3)

These events took place in the fourteenth year of King Hezekiah. In earlier comments we have already noted that 2 Kings 18 (vv. 1, 9, 10) suggests that Hezekiah (the son of Ahaz) may have begun ruling in 729 B.C. as a co-regent, but 2 Kings 18:13 places the Sennacherib invasion at 701 B.C. If Hezekiah became sole king in 715 B.C., that would place Isaiah 36 in the fourteenth year of his reign.[5]

At one point, Hezekiah had been forced to pay tribute to Sennacherib (2 Kings 18:14), but he later rebelled against him. For this reason, Assyria came and captured 46 Judean cities before laying siege to Jerusalem. The well-documented annals of Sennacherib place this attack on Judah in 701 B.C., the fourteenth year of Hezekiah. Sennacherib's father (Sargon II) died in 705 B.C., and it was not long until Sennacherib (705-681) began his aggressive policy of westward expansion.

Lachish is Jerusalem's last hope (v. 1). By the time we come to 701 B.C., Sennacherib had just finished a sweep down the coast of Palestine from north to south, a sweep which brought the fall of all the cities along the coastline, including the Egyptian forces which were stationed at a place called Eltekeh about 20 miles west of Jerusalem. It was during these invasions that Sennacherib brought down 46 fortified cities of Judah.[6] Historical sources tell us that the Assyrian armies made one of their last stops at the fortified city called Lachish (Jer. 34:7), but before this they laid siege to Azekah. When Lachish looked north and saw smoke rising from Azekah, they knew it would not be long before they themselves would fall.[7]

Jerusalem is all that is left (v. 2). With the fall of Lachish, Jerusalem was the only city of Judah left. Sennacherib sent Rabshakeh (cf. Neh. 1:11), his "field commander" (NIV), to try and talk Jerusalem into a surrender. According to 2 Kings 18:17, there were also two other important officials with him that day, Tartan and RabSaris. Tartan appears to be second only to the king, and RabSaris (unattested elsewhere) seems to mean chief eunuch or officer (cf. Gen. 39:1; 2 Kings 25:19; Jer. 39:3, 13).[8]

---

[5] Ibid., 331. Perhaps the easiest solution is to hold that Hezekiah began serving as a co-regent in 729 B.C. and became sole king in 715 B.C.

[6] G. W. Grogan, "Isaiah," in *The Expositor's Bible Commentary*, ed. Frank E. Gaebelein, vol. 6 (Grand Rapids: Zondervan, 1986), 227.

[7] The fall of Lachish is depicted on an Assyrian bas-relief which is now located in the British Museum. This author has stood on the mound that used to be Lachish from which they watched the smoke of Azekah begin to rise.

[8] Oswalt, *The Book of Isaiah: Chapters 1-39*, 632.

Rabshakeh (and his forces) stood by the conduit of the upper pool on the highway of the fuller's field, the same place Isaiah came to meet Ahaz some thirty-three years earlier (a virtual repeat from when God had told Ahaz to simply trust Him). We see that thirty-three years earlier, "Isaiah had told Ahaz that he would not fall to his enemy, that the Lord would deliver him.... Now Hezekiah was also confronted with a message of deliverance from the same man of God."[9] Would Hezekiah trust the Lord?

It is time to talk (v. 3). Three representatives came out to talk with Rabshakeh. Just as predicted in 22:20-23, Shebna has been demoted and is now a scribe (cf. Jer. 36:12), and Eliakim is now the prime minister over the House of David. Joah the recorder (2 Sam. 8:16; 1 Kings 4:3) was another one of the king's servants. Will Hezekiah capitulate like his father Ahaz?

The blasphemous raging of Rabshakeh (vv. 4-10)

Assyria's strategy was to use psychological warfare to demoralize Judah into surrender. Rabshakeh makes a series of six verbal attacks on Hezekiah, Judah, and Yahweh to get them to surrender.[10]

First attack: Arrogant mockery (v. 4). In this first attack—one which lacked any form of diplomacy—Rabshakeh exalted the greatness of Sennacherib over any confidence Judah might have in Yahweh or their armies. The Assyrians were noted for such arrogance (cf. 10:15-19).

Second attack: Assyria is too powerful (v. 5). Rabshakeh says that mere words would be no match for Assyrian power. Any military plans would be empty words and empty hope.[11]

Third attack: Judah's allies are unreliable (v. 6). Rabshakeh tells Judah that Egypt was unreliable as a military ally, a true statement in itself (Isa. 19:14-16; 30:3-7; 31:3; cf. Ezek. 29:6-7). He compares Egypt to a crushed reed that will pierce your hand if you lean on it.

---

[9] John A. Martin, "Isaiah," in *The Bible Knowledge Commentary: An Exposition of the Scriptures*, ed. J. F. Walvoord and R. B. Zuck, vol. 1, cited in electronic form with Logos Libronix (Wheaton, IL: Victor Books, 1985), 1086.

[10] Grogan, "Isaiah," 228.

[11] Rabshakeh uses the term rebellion (*marad*) because Judah had already agreed to submit to Assyria, but at this time they decided to break off the covenant (2 Kings 17:4; 18:7, 14). The covenant with Assyria probably originated in 2 Kings 16:10 when Ahaz brought back an Assyrian altar for sacrifice in Jerusalem.

Fourth attack: Yahweh is angry at them (v. 7). Rabshakeh makes the (false) claim that Judah could not depend on Yahweh to save them because Hezekiah had made Him angry by tearing down his altars. The reality was that Jerusalem was the only legitimate place for corporate worship (Deut. 12:5ff.; 1 Kings 8:10, 18, 27-29; 11:32), and the altars that Hezekiah had torn down were false shrines (Canaanite altars) that he was right to destroy (cf. 2 Kings 18:4; 2 Chron. 31:1).

Fifth attack: Judah has poor military skills (vv. 8-9). Rabshakeh claims that the people of Judah were unskilled in the latest military technology and not able to defend with chariots or cavalry. The fact is that Israel did not have a strong cavalry, and their efforts to get Egypt as an ally were to build up such defenses. Rabshakeh mocks Judah by telling them that he would give them 2,000 horses if they could provide men who could ride them (v. 8). Chariots might have been the best in military equipment, but none of it would help Judah (v. 9).

Sixth attack: Assyria was carrying out a divine mandate (v. 10). Rabshakeh tells the ambassadors that Assyria was there at the command of Yahweh. Smith notes, "It was traditional for kings to justify their action by claiming that the gods of a vanquished land had directed them to conquer that territory."[12] They did not understand, however, that even though Yahweh was using Assyria to punish His own people (cf. Isa. 10:5-6), He was not going to let Jerusalem fall. Instead, they would be the ones to fall. Did the king of Assyria really believe all these words? The answer is "Yes," as noted by Smith, who reminds us that, "these are the words of a self-deluded Assyrian king who thinks that God has no power and should not be trusted."[13] How wrong he was.

The response from Judah (vv. 11-12)

An eventual response (v. 11). Eliakim and his associates called out asking Rabshakeh to speak to them in Aramaic instead of their native Hebrew. The reason why, explains Pfeiffer, is that by the time of the eighth century, Akkadian (the original language of Assyria) was on the decline, and "the Syrian language—was already becoming the lingua franca of the Near East ... But the average Jew, untrained for foreign commerce, was ignorant of it."[14] The Jewish leaders did not want their people to understand the Assyrian propaganda.

---

[12] Gary V. Smith, *Isaiah 1-39*, ed. E. Ray Clendenen, The New American Commentary, cited in electronic form with Logos Libronix (Nashville: B & H Publishing Group, 2007), 599.

[13] Ibid., 600–601.

[14] Charles F. Pfeiffer, *The Wycliffe Bible Commentary: Old Testament*, cited in electronic form with Logos Libronix (Chicago: Moody Press, 1962), Is 36:1.

Rabshakeh's reply (v. 12). Rabshakeh understood their motive and refused to comply. Instead, he made it clear he had come to address the multitudes. The siege would be so bad that they would be doomed to eat their own dung (*charaim*) and drink their own urine (*shayin*), extreme measures in desperate times (cf. 2 Kings 6:25).[15]

Second set of interactions (vv. 13-22)

Rabshakeh was not about to stop. Again and again, we see the ragings of Rabshakeh (vv. 13-20) followed by the response of Judah (vv. 21-22).

Rabshakeh's ragings (vv. 13-20)

Taking Jerusalem without an extended siege would be to Assyria's advantage, so Rabshakeh continued his efforts to demoralize the people. In the present section he launches three different kinds of verbal attacks.

First attack: Hezekiah was deceiving the nation (vv. 13-15). Assyria was noted for its arrogance, and this is no exception (v. 13). This time Rabshakeh was trying to get the people to believe that Hezekiah was leading them to a standoff they could never win (v. 14). Hezekiah had rightly been telling the people to trust (*batach*) the Lord, but Rabshakeh wanted them to believe that this was a fatal mistake (v. 15). The fact, though, is that the Lord had promised that He would defend His city (10:12-34; 14:24-27; 31:8-9; 33:17-21). As noted by Smith, Hezekiah was completely convinced in the faithfulness of God:

> The Hebrew sentence is constructed using an infinitive absolute from the verb "deliver" (*nāṣal*), followed by the imperfect verb of the same root, lit. "delivering, he will deliver," which is an emphatic way of promising that God will certainly, surely, completely deliver them.[16]

Hezekiah was bringing great glory to God with such unshakable faith.

Second attack: Assyria will treat them favorably (vv. 16-17). Rabshakeh's second effort was to convince the people that if they were to surrender without a fight, the Assyrians would treat them favorably (v. 16; cf. 1 Kings 4:25; Mic. 4:4; Zech. 3:10). Eventually, though, they would still be taken away in exile as was the common practice (v. 17).

---

[15] The Qere softens the terms from the Kethib, indicating that the sense of the Kethib was quite strong and offensive.

[16] Smith, *Isaiah 1-39*, 603.

Third attack: Yahweh is not strong enough to deliver (vv. 18-20). Rabshakeh now combined arguments from theology and history by telling the people that no nation had been able to withstand Assyria and her gods.[17] Biblically speaking, this is probably where the Rabshakeh erred since he was making a public mockery of Yahweh, treating Him like the idols of the nations (v. 18). As a sampling, he names out four of the nations that had recently fallen to Assyria (v. 19).[18] No god had been able to deliver from Assyria, and neither would Yahweh be able to deliver Jerusalem (v. 20). They would soon learn differently.

Hezekiah's response (vv. 21-22)

Rabshakeh's words were arrogant and blasphemous, but Hezekiah's orders were to stay silent (v. 21). The only response of the Judean ambassadors was to tear their clothes (Isa. 37:1; cf. Gen. 37:29; Josh. 7:6; 2 Kings 11:14; 19:1; 22:11; Job 1:20; 2:12), and to bring Hezekiah the report.

Summary and application

You and I are reading about events that took place 2,700 years ago, but in this story, we have a marvelous lesson about trusting God. Hezekiah was completely convinced that God could, and would, deliver His people from ruin. Hezekiah was convinced that the Lord would be faithful to His Word. We, too, need to trust the promises of God.

THE MIRACULOUS DESTRUCTION OF ASSYRIA (37:1-38)

Rabshakeh's goal was to demoralize Hezekiah to the point of surrender, but it was not going to work. God had been at work in all of these circumstances to bring Hezekiah to the place where he was stripped of all external sources of trust so that he would have to trust in God alone.[19]

Chapter 37 reads as follows: "1 And when King Hezekiah heard *it*, he tore his clothes, covered himself with sackcloth and entered the house of the Lord. 2 Then he sent Eliakim who was over the household with Shebna the scribe and the elders of the priests, covered with sackcloth to Isaiah the prophet, the

---

[17] Wolf, *Interpreting Isaiah*, 173.
[18] Hamath was a major Syrian city on the Orontes River about 150 miles north of Damascus (cf. Gen. 10:18). Arpad was another Syrian city about 85 miles north of Hamath. The location of Sepharvaim is uncertain, but it may be at a place called Sippar in southern Mesopotamia (cf. 2 Kings 17:24, 31). Samaria was the capital of Israel and fell to Assyria in 722 B.C.
[19] Oswalt, *The Book of Isaiah: Chapters 1-39*, 643.

son of Amoz. 3 They said to him, Thus says Hezekiah, This day is a day of distress, rebuke and rejection, for children have come to birth, and there is no strength to deliver. 4 Perhaps the Lord your God will hear the words of Rabshakeh, whom his master the king of Assyria has sent to reproach the living God, and will rebuke the words which the Lord your God has heard. Therefore, offer a prayer for the remnant that is left. 5 So the servants of King Hezekiah came to Isaiah. 6 Isaiah said to them, Thus you shall say to your master, Thus says the Lord, Do not be afraid because of the words that you have heard, with which the servants of the king of Assyria have blasphemed Me. 7 Behold, I will put a spirit in him so that he will hear a rumor and return to his own land, and I will make him fall by the sword in his own land. 8 Then Rabshakeh returned and found the king of Assyria fighting against Libnah, for he had heard that the king had left Lachish. 9 When he heard *them* say concerning Tirhakah king of Cush, He has come out to fight against you, and when he heard *it* he sent messengers to Hezekiah, saying, 10 Thus you shall say to Hezekiah king of Judah, Do not let your God in whom you trust deceive you, saying, Jerusalem will not be given into the hand of the king of Assyria. 11 Behold, you have heard what the kings of Assyria have done to all the lands, destroying them completely. So will you be spared? 12 Did the gods of those nations which my fathers have destroyed deliver them, *even* Gozan and Haran and Rezeph and the sons of Eden who *were* in Telassar? 13 Where is the king of Hamath, the king of Arpad, the king of the city of Sepharvaim, *and of* Hena and Ivvah? 14 Then Hezekiah took the letter from the hand of the messengers and read it, and he went up to the house of the Lord and spread it out before the Lord. 15 Hezekiah prayed to the Lord saying, 16 O Lord of hosts, the God of Israel, who is enthroned *above* the cherubim, You are the God, You alone, of all the kingdoms of the earth. You have made heaven and earth. 17 Incline Your ear, O Lord, and hear; open Your eyes, O Lord, and see; and listen to all the words of Sennacherib, who sent *them* to reproach the living God. 18 Truly, O Lord, the kings of Assyria have devastated all the countries and their lands, 19 and have cast their gods into the fire, for they were not gods but the work of men's hands, wood and stone. So they have destroyed them. 20 Now, O Lord our God, deliver us from his hand that all the kingdoms of the earth may know that You alone, Lord, are God. 21 Then Isaiah the son of Amoz sent *word* to Hezekiah, saying, Thus says the Lord, the God of Israel, Because you have prayed to Me about Sennacherib king of Assyria, 22 this is the word that the Lord has spoken against him: She has despised you and mocked you, the virgin daughter of Zion; she has shaken *her* head behind you, the daughter of Jerusalem! 23 Whom have you reproached and blasphemed? and against whom have you raised *your* voice and haughtily lifted up your eyes? Against the Holy One of Israel 24 through your servants you have reproached the Lord, and you have said, With my many chariots I came up to the heights of the mountains, to the remotest parts of Lebanon, and I cut down its tall cedars *and* its choice cypresses. And I will go to its highest peak, its thickest forest. 25 I dug *wells* and drank waters, and with the sole of my feet I dried up all the rivers of Egypt. 26 Have you not heard? Long ago I did it; from ancient times I planned it. Now I have brought it to pass, that you should turn fortified cities into ruinous heaps. 27 Therefore their inhabitants were short of strength; they were dismayed and put to shame; they were *as* the vegetation of the field and *as* the green herb as grass on the housetops is scorched before it is grown up. 28 But I know your sitting down, and your going out, and your coming in, and your raging against Me. 29 Because of your raging against Me, and because your arrogance has come up to My ears, therefore I will put My hook in your nose and My bridle in your lips, and I will turn you back by the way which you came. 30 Then this shall be the sign for you: you will eat this year what grows of itself, in the second year what springs from the same, and in the third year sow, reap, plant vineyards and eat their fruit. 31 The surviving remnant of the house of Judah will again take root downward and bear fruit upward. 32 For out of Jerusalem will go forth a remnant and out of Mount Zion survivors. The zeal of the Lord of hosts will perform this. 33 Therefore, thus says the Lord concerning the king of Assyria, He will not come to this city or shoot an arrow there; and he will not come before it with a shield, or throw up a siege ramp against it. 34 By the way that he came, by the same he will return, and he will not come to this city, declares the Lord. 35 For I will defend this city to save it for My own sake and for My servant David's sake. 36 Then the angel of the Lord went out and struck 185,000 in the camp of the Assyrians; and when men arose early in the morning, behold, all of these were dead. 37 So Sennacherib king of Assyria departed and returned *home* and lived at Nineveh. 38 It came about as he was worshiping in the house of Nisroch his god, that Adrammelech and Sharezer his sons killed him with the sword; and they escaped into the land of Ararat, and Esarhaddon his son became king in his place" (37:1-38).

Externally things were bleak, but Hezekiah maintained his trust, and his trust paid off. Beyond all human expectations, God delivered Jerusalem from the Assyrians. Chapter 37 can be broken down by showing us the faith of Hezekiah (vv. 1-20), the speedy response of God (vv. 21-35), and the ignoble end of proud Sennacherib (vv. 36-38).

The marks of Hezekiah's faith (vv. 1-20)

Hezekiah was a man of true faith whose faith showed itself in both words and deeds. Here in verses 1-20 we find four distinct marks of Hezekiah's great faith.

First mark of faith: Great personal brokenness (v. 1)

Hezekiah heard the blasphemous words of Rabshakeh and was completely broken, not because he feared Assyria would overthrow Jerusalem, but because of the mockery of God (cf. Ezek. 9:4; Matt. 5:3-4). Hezekiah tore his clothes (a sign of great grief), covered himself with sackcloth (1 Kings 20:31; 21:27; Neh.

9:1; Dan. 9:3; Joel 1:13; Jonah 3:6; Matt. 11:21), and went into the temple to pray, the place Solomon called God's "house of prayer" (Isa. 56:7; cf. 1 Kings 8; Matt. 21:13). As noted by Motyer, "Hezekiah realized that the Lord was his only resource," so he immediately sought him in prayer.[20]

Second mark of faith: The call for intercessory prayer (vv. 2-7)

It is time for lots of prayer. Hezekiah makes a call for intercession from Isaiah (vv. 2-5), and Isaiah immediately responds (vv. 6-7).

The call for intercession (vv. 2-5). Hezekiah sent a delegation to tell Isaiah what Rabshakeh was saying so that Isaiah could intercede (v. 2).[21] Hezekiah likened their situation to a woman who has come to the time of childbirth, but has no strength to deliver (v. 3).[22] His hope was that God would hear Isaiah and save the nation (vv. 4-5). This prayer was on behalf of the remnant, but more than this, it was one that dealt with silencing blasphemous sinners (cf. 1 Sam. 17:26-30). This invasion will mean the death of the nation unless God intervenes.[23] Hezekiah trusted Yahweh.

God's reply (vv. 6-7). Isaiah's reply came from a direct word from the Lord. God's assurance was that He had already heard the blasphemies, and that Judah had nothing to fear (v. 6; cf. 7:4; 35:4).[24] God had two plans. First, God would cause Sennacherib to follow a demonic influence that would eventually send him back to Assyria,[25] and then He would cause him to die by the sword in His own land (cf. same prophecy in 30:8-9).[26]

Third mark of faith: The willingness to wait on the Lord (vv. 8-13)

---

[20] J. Alec Motyer, *The Prophecy of Isaiah: An Introduction and Commentary* (Downers Grove: IVP, 1993), 279.
[21] Cf. notes from 36:3 and 22:15.
[22] Isaiah calls the present humiliation a day of "distress" (*tsarah*, be in distress), "rebuke" (*yachach*, reproof), and "rejection" (*na'ats*, disgrace).
[23] Ibid., 645.
[24] The term God uses for the servants (*na'ar*) is the word that means lad or young boy. These young punks were no one to fear and neither was their master.
[25] The "spirit" reference could be understood as an attitude or disposition (cf. Isa. 19:14; Num. 5:14; Hos. 4:12) rather than a demon.
[26] This statement could be telling us that the Assyrian commander rejoined Sennacherib at Libnah (not far from Lachish) due to reports that Tirhakah of Egypt was approaching to fight against them (Wolf, *Interpreting Isaiah*, 175). Tirhakah was the most-famous ruler of the so-called Ethiopian Dynasty of Egypt (the 25th Dynasty), ruling over Egypt from 690-664.

God had given his promise, and now it was time to simply wait on the Lord. This would include two further military steps by the Assyrians.

Rabshakeh left Jerusalem to join Sennacherib at Libnah (v. 8). Verse 8 seems to fit with the idea that verses 6-7 are referring to Rabshakeh pulling away from Jerusalem. Libnah was a city in the Judean foothills in the Valley of Elah, not far from Lachish from whence Sennacherib had just departed (Josh 10:29, 31; 12:15; 15:42; Jer. 52:1).[27] Whether it was by the order of the king or by personal choice based on his own feelings (spirit), Rabshakeh left Jerusalem to join Sennacherib there at Libnah, and with his departure, the verbal blasphemies ceased for the moment.[28]

Sennacherib sent more demoralizing messages (vv. 9-13). Rabshakeh's departure did not mean an end to the blasphemies, for Sennacherib soon had letters sent back to call Hezekiah to surrender (vv. 9-10). With the news about Egypt making an advance, it would be much better for Assyria to get Hezekiah to surrender quickly. Not only did these most-recent messengers once again accuse Hezekiah of deceiving the people (vv. 9-10), but he also had the messengers recount the fall of all of the other cities who had tried to resist (vv. 11-13). Sennacherib wanted Israel to believe that nothing could stop Assyria in this holy war.[29] Humanly speaking, Judah was in a hopeless situation. Smith explains,

---

[27] Edward J. Young, *The Book of Isaiah, vol. 2* (Grand Rapids: Eerdmans, 1965), 479. Young notes that, "although Sennacherib himself in his inscription does not mention Lachish, a relief in the British Museum shows the king besieging that city before pulling away due to the Egyptian advances (ibid., 478). These advances meant that Assyria would potentially be facing a battle on two opposing fronts.

[28] This departure appears to be incidental to the dangers facing Jerusalem, but reminds us about the accurate historicity of the Bible (Grogan, "Isaiah," 231).

[29] He even gives a list of nine cities that had already fallen: (1) Gozan (cf. 2 Kings 17:6; 18:11) was a river by which exiles were placed, and known to be Guzana east of Haran from Assyrian texts. (2) Haran on the River Balikh (cf. Gen. 11:31; 12:5; 27:43) had been home to Abraham for a time. (3) Rezeph was between Palmyra and the Euphrates. (4) The Sons of Eden in Telassar was along the middle of the Euphrates, also known as the Chaldean people of Bit-Adini. (5, 6) Hamath and Arphad (cf. Isa. 10:9) were two other cities of Syria that had fallen. (7) Sepharvaim had been completely wiped out by Assyria. According to 2 Kings 17:24, captives from Hamath and Sepharvaim were resettled in Samaria. (8, 9) Hena and Ivvah (2 Kings 18:34; 19:13) cannot be identified. See Young, *The Book of Isaiah, vol. 2*, 480-481; Grogan, "Isaiah," 234, n. 12; Oswalt, *The Book of Isaiah: Chapters 1-39*, 651. Oswalt notes, "They, too, may have trusted oracles from their gods and they had been flayed alive, impaled, mutilated, and killed."

Hezekiah must make a life and death decision. Is God truly stronger than these other gods, and is it his plan to deliver Jerusalem from the Assyrians at this time? Although most believers today make daily decisions on much more trivial issues than these, the answer to these two fundamental questions—Is God able? Is it God's will?—must still be answered by all who desire to walk by faith.[30]

Wisely, Hezekiah was willing to keep trusting the Lord.

Fourth mark of faith: Complete dependence (vv. 14-20)

Hezekiah needed to completely depend on the Lord, and this is what we. Having read the scroll, Hezekiah went into the temple and laid himself down to pour out his heart to God. We can identify four key elements to his prayer.

First key element: A recognition of God's majesty (vv. 15-16). One of the central features of great prayers in the Bible is that they characteristically center around the greatness and glory of God (Dan. 9:15-19; Matt. 6:9). Isaiah identifies God as the Lord of Hosts,[31] the God of Israel who is enthroned above the cherubim (Exod. 40:34; Num. 7:89; 1 Sam. 4:4; 2 Sam. 6:2; 1 Kings 8:10-13; Ps. 80:2). This is the God of Israel whose glory hovered over the cherubim who covered the *kapporeth* (the Ark lid). He alone is God (Isa. 40:26, 28; 42:5; 45:12). Hezekiah rightly acknowledged the greatness of God's glory and majesty.

Second key element: A recognition of Assyria's blasphemy (v. 17).

Secondly, Hezekiah pleaded with God to silence the blasphemies. Unlike pagan gods who have no ability to respond (Isa. 43:8), Yahweh has eyes to see and ears to hear (cf. Deut. 5:26; Josh. 3:10; 1 Sam. 17:26, 36; Pss. 42:2; 84:2; Jer. 10:10; 23:36; Dan. 6:20, 26; Hos. 1:10). Very soon the Assyrians would learn that, "God does hear and see; he does act to rule creation and human history. [Furthermore] it is a blasphemous insult to classify the glorious God who rules the universe as just another useless god."[32]

Third key element: A recognition of Assyria's might (vv. 18-19). Hezekiah's confidence in the Lord did not mean that he was unaware of Assyria's might. Hezekiah acknowledges that the Assyrians had ravaged other nations,

---

[30] Smith, *Isaiah 1-39*, 616.

[31] The Lord of the armies (prob. best understood as the armies of Israel, but perhaps also of the angels in heaven).

[32] Ibid., 619.

but the gods of those nations were nothing but dead idols (cf. Isa. 44:9-20).[33] Things would be different with the God of Israel.

Fourth key element: A recognition of God's worthiness (v. 20). The God of Israel is worthy of perfect praise from every man. For this reason, Hezekiah, "grounded his petition on the need for vindication of God's glory, not upon his own personal need or that of his people (he knew they deserved no favor)."[34] With this truth in mind Hezekiah beseeches God to take action so that all men might recognize His greatness.

The speedy response of God (vv. 21-35)

Hezekiah gave his prayer, and God's response was immediate. This gives us a wonderful reminder of Jesus' words: "Whatever things you ask in prayer, believing, you will receive" (Matt. 21:22). Our real need is to pray according to the moral will of God as stated in Scripture, and then entrust ourselves into His hand. In this case, Hezekiah asked God to save them from a wicked enemy, and the Lord was ready to answer (cf. Dan. 3:17-18; Matt. 26:42; John 16:23; James 1:6; 1 John 5:14). Here in verses 21-35, we see five facts about Assyria's mockery and why it was that God would bring a speedy answer to punish arrogant Assyria.

First fact: Mockery of Judah is mockery of Yahweh (vv. 21-25)

The Lord gave Hezekiah a swift response through Isaiah (perhaps written), and God made it clear that Assyria's mockery against Judah was really a mockery against Him (v. 21).[35] God makes it clear that His reply was because Hezekiah had sought the Lord in prayer. Smith reminds us that this teaches us about the importance of prayer, and that "one of the key values in prayer is that it requires the person praying to humbly admit that they cannot successfully control the future and need God's help."[36] God tells Hezekiah that He has heard Assyria's

---

[33] Psalm 115:4-7 reads, "But their idols are silver and gold, made by the hands of men. They have mouths, but cannot speak, eyes, but they cannot see; they have ears, but cannot hear, noses, but they cannot smell; they have hands, but cannot feel, feet, but they cannot walk; nor can they utter a sound with their throats."

[34] Pfeiffer, *The Wycliffe Bible Commentary: Old Testament*, Is 37:1.

[35] The mockery was intense: "despised" (*buz*; cf. 2 Kings 19:21), "mocked" (*la'ag*; cf. 2 Kings 19:21), "shaken her head" (cf. Job 16:4), "reproached" (*charaph*; cf. Isa. 36:3-15, 18, 20; 37:34), "blasphemed" (*gadaph*; cf. 2 Kings 19:6, 22; Isa. 37:6), "raised your voice" (cf. Isa. 37:17), "haughtily lifted up your eyes" (cf. Isa. 2:11; 5:15, 21).

[36] Smith, *Isaiah 1-39*, 623.

mockery, and He has a message for them, the kind of message we call a "taunt song."[37]

In this taunt song, both Jerusalem and Assyria are personified as females (fem. grammar), and in verses 22-25 God uses multiple expressions to convey the mockery that Assyria had heaped upon Jerusalem and Judah.[38] In reality, this mockery was ultimately against Yahweh, "the Holy One of Israel" (v. 23; cf. Ps. 2:1). Because Hezekiah cared about the glory of the Lord, God promised action.[39] Assyria would face the judgment of Yahweh not only for their mockery of Yahweh, but also for their unrestrained arrogance (vv. 24-25).[40]

Second fact: Assyria's deeds were all part of God's plan (vv. 26-27)

Assyria was powerful, but what she did not understand was that all of her power was entirely within the eternal purposes of Yahweh. The kings of Assyria were men who made free moral choices, but as the Scripture shows us, all of these choices were embraced under the eternal plan of God (Isa. 10:5-15; 46:8-11; cf. Gen. 45:1-8; 50:20; Acts 2:23; 4:27-28).[41]

God informs the King of Assyria that the deeds they are bragging about are the deeds that God Himself had planned (*yatsar*, "formed") from ancient times (v. 26). The immediate cause of these devastations were the evil plans of Assyria (cf. Isa. 8:6-8), but all of it was within the larger plan of God, the plan

---

[37] Grogan, "Isaiah," 232. God is going to mock those who have mocked Him.
[38] It is common in the prophets to see feminine grammar used for cities and nations. The use of the term virgin conveys the idea that Jerusalem was a city that had never before been violated through invasion and overthrow (1:8; 47:1). Thus, writes Oswalt, Jerusalem may be getting represented, "as a young girl rebuffing with contempt the unwelcome advances of a churl. Perhaps there is a suggestion that she is betrothed to the Holy One of Israel, for Isaiah later uses the figure of marriage and divorce in relation to Israel (50:1)" (Oswalt, *The Book of Isaiah: Chapters 1-39*, 660).
[39] Therefore, writes Oswalt, "Isaiah can look to a day when Jerusalem, now a prone maiden helpless before a swaggering rapist, will mock her would be conqueror's impotence. . . . So as the oppressor slinks away, the intended victim will stick out her tongue at him and wag her head from side to side in derision" (ibid.).
[40] The heavily forested mountains of Lebanon were beautiful, but steep and difficult to climb (cf. Isa. 10:34). All of these statements represent the extreme arrogance of the Assyrians. The Imperfect tense verbs may indicate the plans of the Assyrians and not necessarily deeds already accomplished, especially since we know that Sennacherib never reached as far as the Delta of Egypt.
[41] Theologically, this is a doctrine we call Compatibilism: divine sovereignty and human responsibility (i.e., creaturely free will) are both biblical and true.

that ultimately works all things for good for His own people (v. 27; cf. Rom. 8:28). Sennacherib saw himself as the lord of his own destiny, but "it was God who planned it all and brought it all about."[42]

Third fact: God sees it all, and He will soon repay (vv. 28-29)

Again, we see the comprehensive character of God's eternal plan, and that He sees all things, knows all things, and controls all things (cf. Deut. 28:6; 1 Kings 3:7; Pss. 121:8; 139:2). God has perfect knowledge of every movement, and even every thought of Sennacherib (v. 28). God's solution is that he will work in such a way that He will send Sennacherib back to Assyria without the overthrow of Jerusalem (v. 29; cf. 2 Kings 19:28; 2 Chron. 33).[43] What we have here is an excellent illustration of a theological view of history: Man looks at life with the view that man is the ultimate sovereign, but in Scripture God makes it clear that He is the only Sovereign.

Fourth fact: They will never return (vv. 30-32)

In the event of an enemy retreat, one fear was always that they would return again. God assures His people that this will not happen. God gave Hezekiah a three-year sign by promising him that by the end of this time period Judah would be back in a normal pattern of planting and harvesting, the same three-year promise given in earlier prophecies (v. 30; cf. 20:3).[44] Not only will the crops have a chance to prosper, but so too will the people themselves as we see in verses 31-32: The remnant of Judah, "will again take root downward and bear fruit upward. For out of Jerusalem will go forth a remnant and out of Mount Zion survivors."[45] What a promise.

Remnant language is a significant theme in Isaiah,[46] and it calls for some brief comment. In the present context, it is best to see this promise as speaking about a recovery from the Assyrian invasions. Nevertheless, the immediate

---

[42] Smith, *Isaiah 1-39*, 625.

[43] The hook in the nose and bridle in the lips remind us of similar language in Ezekiel's prophecies (Ezek. 29:4; 38:4). Part of justice here is that Assyria frequently led away its captives by attaching ropes to rings that were placed into the prisoner's noses (Wolf, *Interpreting Isaiah*, 176).

[44] First, they will eat this year from what grows of itself. In the second year, they will also eat from what grows from the same. In the third year, though, God commands that they resume planting. In the end, Assyria will be gone, and God will meet their need despite the immediate Assyrian threat.

[45] The promise bears striking resemblance to 27:6.

[46] Cf. 1:9; 4:2; 6:13; 7:3; 10:20-23; 11:11; 37:4, 31-32; 41:17; 43:5-6; 46:3; 49:6.

promise of restoration cannot be separated from the promise of an ultimate rescue from the seven-year tribulation period, and the eschatological restoration of God's elect remnant at the end of the age (Isa. 2:1-4; 4:1-4; 9:1-7; 10:20-25; 11:11; 12:1-6; 27:12-13; 42:6; 46:3; 49:6; 53:10; 54:1ff.; cf. Deut. 30:1-10; Jer. 31:31-34; Ezek. 36:22-32; Hos. 3:1-5; Joel 2:28-32; Amos 9:11-15; Mic. 2:12-13; Zech. 8:20-23; 10:9-12). The zeal of God guarantees it will be fulfilled.[47]

Fifth fact: God will save Jerusalem from Sennacherib (vv. 33-35)

God makes a clear promise that Sennacherib will not personally come against Jerusalem, but rather he will return to Assyria never to return again (vv. 33-34). Even though Rabshakeh had made all these threats, there would be no extended siege and overthrow of Jerusalem. Young notes that in the annals of Sennacherib, he never said that he took Jerusalem, but only that he had Hezekiah caged up like a bird.[48]

God says the reason for this salvation is that, "I will defend this city to save it for My own sake and for My servant David's sake" (v. 35; cf. same concept in Ezek. 36:22-32). In other words, because God's reputation was at stake (Isa. 43:1, 21), and David was the king to whom God promised an eternal dynasty (2 Sam. 7:12-16; 1 Kings 11:13-36; 2 Kings 8:19; 18:3; Ps. 132:11-12; Isa. 7:2, 13, 17; 9:6-7; 11:1; 16:5; 22:22; 55:3), and Jerusalem was God's chosen city (Ps. 48:1; 78:68; 132:13-18; Isa. 31:5; 38:6; 60; 62) God would act. Within 100 years God would use Babylon to punish Judah for its rebellion, but that would not be in Hezekiah's day.

The ignoble end of Sennacherib (vv. 36-38)

This last portion of chapter 37 shows how God brought an end to Assyria. First, we see the nature of God's protective care of Jerusalem (v. 36), and then we see the results of God's protective care (vv. 37-38).

The nature of God's protective care (v. 36)

As noted by Oswalt, "this verse is the crux of the entire account, so it is not surprising that it has come under severe scrutiny by biblical scholars."[49] God's way of dealing Assyria was by striking its army with a plague so powerful that it left 185,000 dead in a single night. Although it is distinctly possible that God used some kind of natural plague to strike them down (e.g., bubonic plague),[50] the text tells us that it was a miraculous work of God carried out by

---

[47] Cf. Isa. 9:6-7; 59:16-21; Zech. 1:14; Rom. 11:25-36.

[48] Young, *The Book of Isaiah, vol. 2*, 502.

[49] Oswalt, *The Book of Isaiah: Chapters 1-39*, 668.

[50] A possibility recognized by Wolf (Wolf, *Interpreting Isaiah*, 177).

"the Angel of the Lord."[51] It is possible (but not certain) that this "Angel of the Lord" was none other than Christ Himself who came to rescue His people from ruin (Isa. 63:9) although He was the One they habitually spurned. In any case, the Lord promised salvation, and He did it exactly as He said He would (cf. same promise earlier in 30:27-33; 31:8-9; 33:1, 18-19).

One explanation that has been given for what happened is based on the writings of Herodotus, the fifth-century Greek historian. Herodotus wrote that a plague of mice had eaten Sennacherib's bowstrings when they were at Pelusium on the edge of the Nile Delta, forcing them flee Egypt. The conjecture is that the mice gave the Assyrians the bubonic plague which killed them several days later.[52] This probably was not at Jerusalem since Isaiah tells us that Sennacherib was not going to come to Jerusalem. The end result was that the arrogant king of Assyria met the true King face to face (6:5; 31:8, 9; 33:17).

The result of God's protective care (vv. 37-38)

With this decimation of his armies, Sennacherib signaled a retreat back to Assyria. Smith notes that by this supernatural work of God, Assyria realized that, "they were not fighting against an enemy that they could defeat. . . . This was an act of a divine power. . . . The only sensible thing for Sennacherib to do was to break camp and head for home in Nineveh,"[53] and that is precisely what Assyria did (v. 37). Interestingly, God even tells us about Sennacherib's final end:

> It came about as he was worshiping in the house of Nisroch his god [an unknown god, but perhaps known as Nusku elsewhere], that Adrammelech and Sharezer his sons killed him with the sword; and they escaped into the land of Ararat, and Esarhaddon his son became king in his place (v. 38).[54]

Smith adds a final note about his end:

---

[51] A thorough study on "the Angel of the Lord" is beyond the scope of this commentary, but we believe this was the preincarnate Christ as seen elsewhere (Gen. 16:7-14; 17:1; 18:1; 22:11; 32:24; Exod. 3:2; 23:20-21; Josh. 5:13-15; Judg. 6:11-25; 13:3ff.; Isa. 63:9; Zech. 3:1-6; Mal. 3:1).

[52] Oswalt, *The Book of Isaiah: Chapters 1-39*, 669.

[53] Smith, *Isaiah 1-39*, 633.

[54] Assyrian records show us that this murder took place in 681 B.C. The death of Hezekiah is disputed but usually seen as being somewhere around 686 B.C., about five to six years before the death of Sennacherib.

The Assyrian record of Esarhaddon's reign verifies what this account says and also adds some new information. It records that Esarhaddon was the youngest son, but the gods of Assyria chose him to succeed Sennacherib. When he was made the crown prince, his older brothers realized they would not rule so they plotted against Esarhaddon by making false statements against him, so he went into hiding for a time. After his older brothers killed Sennacherib and fought each other for the right to rule, Esarhaddon re-entered the scene, defeated them, and rose to power.[55]

Summary and application

One of the biggest lessons for application is that no matter what is happening in the world around us, our God is the Living God who is always in control. He is in control, and we can always trust Him no matter what is happening around us. We will have tribulation, but we can be assured that He is victorious over it all (John 16:33).

THE MIRACULOUS RECOVERY OF HEZEKIAH (38:1-22)

As noted earlier, chapters 36-39 are transitional chapters with chapters 36-37 focusing on the demise of Assyria and chapters 38-39 focusing on the rise of Babylon.[56] Assyria will be gone, but that does not mean that Judah will not face threats in the future. Judah has broken the covenant, and Babylon will be the nation to inflict the curses of the covenant.

Chapter 38 reads as follows: "1 In those days Hezekiah became mortally ill, and Isaiah the prophet the son of Amoz came to him and said to him, Thus says the Lord, Set your house in order, for you shall die and not live. 2 Then Hezekiah turned his face to the wall and prayed to the Lord, 3 and said, Remember now, O Lord, I beseech You, how I have walked before You in truth and with a whole heart, and have done what is good in Your sight, and Hezekiah wept bitterly. 4 Then the word of the Lord came to Isaiah, saying, 5 Go and say to Hezekiah, Thus says the Lord, the God of your father David, I have heard your prayer, I have seen your tears; behold, I will add fifteen years to your life. 6 I will deliver you and this city from the hand of the king of Assyria, and I will defend this city. 7 This shall be the sign to you from the Lord, that the Lord will do this thing that He has spoken: 8 Behold, I will cause the shadow on the stairway, which has gone down with the sun on the stairway of Ahaz, to go back ten steps. So the sun's *shadow* went back ten steps on the stairway on which it

---

[55] Ibid.

[56] Chapter 38 follows the chapter 37 account of Assyria's defeat, but 38:6 makes it clear that these events took place very soon before the defeat of Assyria.

had gone down. 9 A writing of Hezekiah king of Judah after his illness and recovery: 10 I said, In the middle of my life I am to enter the gates of *Sheol*; I am to be deprived of the rest of my years. 11 I said, I will not see the Lord, the Lord in the land of the living; I will look on man no more among the inhabitants of the world. 12 Like a shepherd's tent my dwelling is pulled up and removed from me; as a weaver I rolled up my life. He cuts me off from the loom; from day until night You make an end of me. 13 I composed *my soul* until morning. Like a lion—so He breaks all my bones; from day until night You make an end of me. 14 Like a swallow, *like* a crane, so I twitter; I moan like a dove; my eyes look wistfully to the heights. O Lord, I am oppressed, be my security. 15 What shall I say? For He has spoken to me, and He Himself has done it. I will wander about all my years because of the bitterness of my soul. 16 O Lord, by *these* things *men* live, and in all these is the life of my spirit. O restore me to health and let me live! 17 Lo, for *my own* welfare I had great bitterness. It is You who has kept my soul from the pit of nothingness, for You have cast all my sins behind Your back. 18 For *Sheol* cannot thank You; death cannot praise You; those who go down to the pit cannot hope for Your faithfulness. 19 It is the living who give thanks to You, as I do today; a father tells his sons about Your faithfulness. 20 The Lord will surely save me; so we will play my songs on stringed instruments all *the* days of our life at the house of the Lord. 21 Now Isaiah had said, Let them take a cake of figs and apply it to the boil, that he may recover. 22 Then Hezekiah had said, "What is the sign that I shall go up to the house of the Lord?" (38:1-22).

Chapter 38 tells us about an event that took place sometime during the Assyrian invasions of chapters 36-37 (which ended with a defeat in 701 B.C.).[57] One of the difficulties we have already seen is that scholars do not all agree on the years in which Hezekiah reigned. This commentary has taken the position that Hezekiah began ruling as a co-regent with his father in 729 B.C. and reigned as sole king from 715-686 (hence, a 29-year reign). Hezekiah's sickness took place during the time that Merodach-Baladan II was the King of Babylon. Merodach-Baladan II ruled Babylon twice, once from 721-710 B.C. and a second time for nine months in 703 B.C.[58] If Hezekiah's sickness and recovery took place around 703/702 B.C., these dates would match up with an Assyrian invasion around that same time and a death of Hezekiah around 686 B.C.[59]

---

[57] One cannot be dogmatic on what year these events took place.
[58] Editors, "Merodach-Baladan II," Encyclopaedia Britannica Online, <https://www.britannica.com/biography/Merodach-Baladan-II>, accessed March 20, 2020.
[59] These dates also correspond to those of Assyrian records themselves. Assyrian chronology places the third campaign of Sennacherib in 701 B.C., when he came

Putting aside chronological challenges, one thing is clear: Hezekiah had more than one major trial to face during his reign, but he faced them all as a man of faith. Chapter 38 may be broken down as God's warning of imminent death (vv. 1-3), God's healing promise (vv. 4-18), Hezekiah's poem (vv. 9-20), and Isaiah's final word (vv. 21-22).

God's warning of imminent death (vv. 1-3)

All people know death can come at any time, but few people expect it to come soon. Early death catches people off guard, and so it was when God gave this news to Hezekiah (cf. 2 Kings 20:1-11; 2 Chron. 32:24-26).[60]

God's warning of imminent death (v. 1)

Hezekiah had become mortally ill, and God sent Isaiah to tell him to get his affairs in order. We do not know what kind of sickness it was, but clearly it was serious as reflected in the two-fold promise of death.[61] From 2 Chronicles 32:25 we get a hint that this sickness might have been due to pride. God's message was to prepare for death.

Hezekiah's plea for life (vv. 2-3)

As a man of faith, Hezekiah's immediate response was to seek God in prayer despite the word that death was certain (v. 2). Hezekiah's plea began with a strong plea that the Lord remember the good things he had done (v. 3).[62]

---

against Hezekiah. The Assyrian sources put 152 years from the sixth year of Shalmaneser III's battle against Ahab at Qarqar in 853 B.C. According to the reconstructed history of the Hebrews, it was also 152 years from the death of Ahab to the fourteenth year of Hezekiah in 701 B.C. One alternative chronology reasons as follows: (1) Hezekiah's reign started in 727/726 B.C. and ended with his death in about 696 B.C. (appx. 29 years). (2) His illness and recovery took place in about 712/711 B.C. (3) His extension of life for 15 years places his death in 696 B.C. (See Oswalt, *The Book of Isaiah: Chapters 1-39*, 674; Wolf, *Interpreting Isaiah*, 178). This view would require that the king in 38:6 would be Sargon.

[60] If Hezekiah was born in 740/739 B.C. and the year was now 703 B.C. that would make Hezekiah about 36 years of age.

[61] All we are told is that Hezekiah had a boil and it would be fatal (38:21).

[62] The Hithpael verb stem of "to walk" (*halak*) conveys the idea of habitual, back and forth conduct. Despite any personal weakness, the Scripture shows us that Hezekiah truly was a man of God (cf. 2 Kings 18:3-6). This stood in radical contrast to his father Ahaz (2 Kings 16:10). Some of Hezekiah's righteous deeds included the fact that

Hezekiah reasoned that the Lord might hear his prayer because of his piety.[63] Smith makes an apt observation about trials:

> Possibly Hezekiah's bitter weeping (38:2b) eventually caused him to realize his own unworthiness (rather than trumpeting his piety) and his need to trust in God, rather than his own good works. This episode is instructive for believers who are suffering a life-threatening illness. It is evident that good works will not prevent an early death, that all one can do is to confess one's sins and cry out to God for mercy, and that God may sometimes choose to miraculously heal the sick if it is fits into his greater purposes.[64]

God's healing promise (vv. 4-8)

God not only gave Hezekiah the promise that He would heal him (vv. 4-6), but He also gave the king a wondrous sign to assure him (vv. 7-8).

God's promises (vv. 4-6)

God's word to Hezekiah was swift and simple (v. 4).[65] With this answer, God made two amazing promises to King Hezekiah.

---

he had the temple reopened, and he demolished and cast out all foreign idols, pagan shrines, pillars, Asherim, high places, destroyed the bronze serpent (Num. 21:4-9) that had become an idol, put the priests and Levites back into ministry, gave public worship through offerings and music, invited the northern tribes to join in the Passover Feast (the first in many years), restored the nation's military from years of neglect, and established a water supply for the city by digging a long tunnel (1777 feet long) from the Gihon Spring (which was outside the walls) to the Pool of Siloam (inside the city walls). Hezekiah truly was a good king.

[63] Another one of Hezekiah's fears might have been that of succession. His son Manasseh came to the throne at twelve years of age and ruled for fifty-five years. Once again, we see scholarly debate on how to understand the chronologies. If Manasseh was born in about 709 B.C., he could have become a coregent with Hezekiah at twelve years of age in 696 B.C. Based on this chronology, his sole reign would have been from 686-642. Thus, Manasseh's fifty-five years of reign would have begun in 696 and ended in 642 (cf. 2 Kings 21:1-9; 2 Chron. 33:1-9). Others would see Manasseh's reign extending from 696-642 (2 Kings 20:21), a chronology that would place the death of Hezekiah in 696 and not 686. This author prefers to understand that Manasseh had a coregency with Hezekiah from 696-686 and a sole reign from 686-642.

[64] Smith, *Isaiah 1-39*, 640.

[65] Second Kings 20:4 tells us that Hezekiah had not even left the palace before God gave him this message.

First promise: Fifteen years of additional life (v. 5). God told Isaiah to turn around and inform Hezekiah that He had heard Hezekiah's prayer and seen his tears, and for this reason he would take away the sickness and give him fifteen additional years.[66]

How could it be that the message had been death, but through answered prayer it would not be death? In His eternal purpose, God had already ordained the answer to this prayer knowing that His child would pray such a prayer. The appearance to us is that change has taken place in the purpose of God, but in reality it was all part of the outworking of a larger plan (cf. Exod. 32:7-14; Jonah 4:2).[67] Our part is to seek God with a whole heart according to His Word, and to trust Him for those things that we need, remembering that in many cases the real change that needs to take place is a change in our own hearts as reflected with the response of Hezekiah. Oswalt reminds us that this does not always mean that matters will turn out the way we want, but "it does mean that prayer can change the course of events,"[68] and we should always be seeking God.

Second promise: Salvation from the Assyrians (v. 6). God also told Hezekiah that He would deliver Jerusalem from the hand of the king of Assyria. Based on our estimate that this prophecy was given in about 703 B.C., this helps us to understand why Hezekiah had such unshakable faith when surrounded by Assyria two years later even though the Jerusalem siege in 701 was preceded by the fall of 46 fortified Judean cities and the taking of 200,000 Jewish prisoners.[69]

God's sign (vv. 7-8)

These were two wonderful promises, but as an added measure, at his request (cf. 38:21-22), God also gave Hezekiah a sign (*'oth*) that would assure him of their fulfillment (v. 7). Unlike the signs in 7:14, 20:3, and 37:30, this one involved a miracle. The purpose of this sign was not to increase the certainty of the promise (for God cannot lie), but to provide a miraculous attestation that would encourage the faith of His king, as is consistent most of the eighty uses of *'oth* (cf. Isa. 7:11, 14; 20:3; Exod. 7:3; Deut. 4:34; 6:22; 7:19; 26:8; Judg. 6:17; Neh. 9:10).[70] God told Hezekiah that He would cause the shadow on "the

---

[66] When God identified Himself as the God of His father David, He was impressing upon Hezekiah the covenant promises made to King David.
[67] Young, *The Book of Isaiah, vol. 2*, 512.
[68] Oswalt, *The Book of Isaiah: Chapters 1-39*, 675.
[69] Wolf, *Interpreting Isaiah*, 179.
[70] Robert Alden, "*'oth*," ed. R. Laird Harris, Gleason L. Archer Jr., and Bruce K. Waltke, *Theological Wordbook of the Old Testament*, cited in electronic form with Logos

stairway" which had already gone down to go backward ten steps, and this is exactly what happened.

We have two questions to answer. First, what is this stairway?[71] One can speculate, but in the end, we simply cannot be sure.[72] Second, what actually happened in this miracle? Since a reversal of the earth's rotation is a difficult idea to sustain,[73] it may be best to understand this as some sort of light refraction there at the palace that caused this reversal (cf. 2 Chron. 32:31).[74] Martin holds that, "Apparently a special stairway had been built as a time device, a kind of sundial. As the sun went down in the west, a shadow would move upward on the staircase so that people could ascertain the time of the day."[75] Hezekiah trusted God and God answered him.

Hezekiah's poem (vv. 9-20)

Life in a fallen world brings tough blows to everyone. No one is exempt, not even kings. How are we to respond? Hezekiah was in great despair over the news that he was going to die (vv. 9-19), but he maintained his confidence in the Lord (v. 20).

Hezekiah's despair over his situation (vv. 9-19)

Hezekiah was a man of God who delighted in the Psalms (cf. 2 Chron. 29:30), so it should not surprise us that one of his songs would also get recorded in the Scriptures. Scholars have debated what kind of label they should apply to this psalm, but that is not critical.[76] Verse 9 forms the introduction to the prayer that opens with Hezekiah's lament over the prospect of imminent death (though written after his recovery).

A lament over death (vv. 10-14). The main theme is Hezekiah's

---

Libronix (Chicago: Moody Press, 1999), 18–19.

[71] Oswalt notes that the Saint Mark's Dead Sea Scroll (1QIsa) has "the steps of the upper chamber of Ahaz" and the LXX has the "steps of the house of Ahaz" and refers to 2 Kings 23:12 where reference is made to the pagan altars associated with such an upper chamber. If this view is correct, it is tempting to relate the steps to some form of sun worship (Oswalt, *The Book of Isaiah: Chapters 1-39*, 672, n. 2).

[72] Ibid., 678.

[73] We do see something similar in Joshua 10:12-14. This author does not deny that God could have worked in this manner if He so willed.

[74] Wolf, *Interpreting Isaiah*, 179.

[75] Martin, "Isaiah," 1089.

[76] Smith, *Isaiah 1-39*, 643–644.

complaint that he should be taken out of this world in the prime of life. Hezekiah makes eight complaints that cry out to God for another chance. The first two complaints deal with being deprived of his remaining years in this life by being forced into death, i.e., having to enter into the gates of *Sheol* (v. 10; cf. Job 38:17; Pss. 9:13; 107:18; Matt. 16:18).

Hezekiah's third and fourth complaints speak about not being able to look up to men or to "the Lord the Lord" (a double *Yah Yah*, cf. 12:2; 26:4), "in the land of the living" (v. 11). Hezekiah has no fear of annihilation or soul sleep; rather, he simply does not want to die yet (cf. 2 Cor. 5:1ff.).[77]

Hezekiah's fifth and six complaints use two metaphors to restate the point (v. 12). The first is a Bedouin having his tent removed, and the second is a weaver whose life has been rolled up and cut off from the loom.

Hezekiah's seventh complaint is that he feels like God is a lion breaking all his bones (v. 13; cf. Job 3:23-26). Hezekiah did what he could to quiet his spirit (cf. Ps. 131:2), but the prospect of death was overwhelming.

In Hezekiah's final complaint, he compares himself to some kind of bird that just sits there making noises. Smith comments, "It almost appears that he is so weak that he cannot address God with a traditional prayer and that he is in such physical and emotional anguish that he can only groan out a few words."[78] In all of this agony, the king cries out, "O Lord, I am oppressed, be my security" (v. 14b; cf. Gen. 43:9).

Hezekiah's thanks (vv. 15-19). The theme of thanksgiving begins to flow. Hezekiah first recognizes that God's message had left him with nowhere to turn (cf. Ps. 39:9).[79] Verse 16 is difficult to understand,[80] but could refer to

---

[77] The MT has *chadel* ("cessation") so many emend this to *cheled* ("world"), but some still read the idea of cessation (Young, *The Book of Isaiah, vol. 2*, 519, n. 18).

[78] Smith, *Isaiah 1-39*, 648.

[79] Oswalt explains that some take v. 15 to have a negative sense (as does this author), but others think it could have a positive tone in that Hezekiah is overwhelmed with a sense of gratitude for the promise of recovery as in Psalm 116:12 (Oswalt, *The Book of Isaiah: Chapters 1-39*, 686).

[80] The difficulty accounts for why the LXX and Targum both differ from the MT (ibid.). The LXX reads, "O Lord, yes, it was told you concerning it and you roused up my breath and I was comforted and came to life," and the Targum reads, "My Lord, with regard to the dead you have declared that you would bring them back to life: but before them all you have caused my spirit to live and have preserved me alive and established me."

the idea of God's gracious acts of mercy as seen in his restoration to life, for it is by these things that men live.[81] Hezekiah is begging God for mercy, so he cries out, "O Lord . . . restore me to health and let me live!" (v. 16).

Hezekiah's heart was broken, but he reflects on the reality that his present trials were having the positive effect of making him reflect on life, acknowledging that "God's love was with him, and that God had not punished him in accord with his sins"[82] (v. 17). By His grace, God had "kept" (*chashaq*) him from the "pit of nothingness" (*beliy*; cf. Ps. 55:23), and not given him over to be judged (v. 18; cf. 1 Kings 14:9; Ezek. 23:35).[83] By His grace, God had cast all his sins behind His back and Hezekiah is praising God for it (Isa. 43:25; 44:22; cf. Pss. 51:1, 9; 103:12; Jer. 31:34; Mic. 7:18-19). Our God is a forgiving God.

Hezekiah's praise continues with the claim that dead men do not praise God (v. 18), but it is only the living who can do this (v. 19; cf. Job 10:21-22; Pss. 6:5; 30:9; 88:10-12; 115:17; Ecc. 9:10). Hezekiah is making no statement about annihilation, but simply that dead people do not praise God (in this world).[84] God showed mercy so that Hezekiah and others might praise God.

Hezekiah's confidence in the Lord (v. 20)

The praise and joy that began in verses 17-19 become bold confidence in verse 20: "The Lord will surely save me; so we will play my songs on stringed instruments all *the* days of our life at the house of the Lord." Just as with David (cf. Ps. 23:6), Hezekiah's passion was to be in the temple of Yahweh (cf. 2 Chron. 29:25-30; Rev. 5:9-10). Smith reminds us, "All believers should have a similar commitment to praise and glorify God even if they have not gone through such a traumatic near-death experience."[85]

Isaiah's final word (vv. 21-22)

These last two verses serve as an epilogue showing the healing of the king. Isaiah commanded fig cakes to be applied to the wound, a form of treatment that apparently was often efficacious (v. 21).[86] Based on what we read in 2 Kings

---

[81] Young, *The Book of Isaiah*, vol. 2, 524.

[82] Martin, "Isaiah," 1090.

[83] The Hebrew term for "kept" actually has the idea of "loved" in the sense of attaching oneself to another (Gen. 34:8; Deut. 7:7; 10:15; 21:11).

[84] Old Testament saints certainly believed in an afterlife when we will praise the Lord (cf. Ps. 23:6; Isa. 26:19; Job 19:25-26; Ecc. 12:13-14).

[85] Smith, *Isaiah 1-39*, 651–652.

[86] Evidence from Ras Shamra shows this (Grogan, "Isaiah," 238, n. 21). Of course, in

20:7, these events may have taken place earlier when Hezekiah first got the promise of healing but before he got the sign from God. Isaiah closes with Hezekiah asking what kind of sign God might give to assure him that he would live to worship the Lord in His temple (v. 22).

Summary and application

From this account, we learn the following lessons. First, we need to always be on guard against the sins that so easily ensnare us (Hezekiah's sin was pride). Second, we must remember that our God is the God of the impossible (Mark 9:23). Third, we must remember to keep our hearts tender, and keep seeking the Lord for grace (Matt. 7:7-8), and give Him the praise He deserves no matter what life might bring (Hab. 3:16-19).

THE PROMISED RISE OF BABYLON (39:1-8)

Throughout the last several chapters we have been faced with a common topic: Who are we going to trust? In chapters 36-39, Hezekiah faced two major trials. The first trial was that the most powerful empire in the world was trying to overthrow his kingdom. The second trial was that right in the middle of these military threats, God told Hezekiah that he was going to die. Both were huge trials, but as we saw in chapter 38, God heard Hezekiah's prayer and removed both of these trials. Chapter 39 brings a final message how all these events would work together in God's plan.

Chapter 39 reads as follows: "1 At that time Merodach-Baladan son of Baladan, king of Babylon, sent letters and a present to Hezekiah, for he heard that he had been sick and had recovered. 2 Hezekiah was pleased, and showed them *all* his treasure house, the silver and the gold and the spices and the precious oil and his whole armory and all that was found in his treasuries. There was nothing in his house nor in all his dominion that Hezekiah did not show them. 3 Then Isaiah the prophet came to King Hezekiah and said to him, What did these men say, and from where have they come to you? And Hezekiah said, They have come to me from a far country, from Babylon. 4 He said, What have they seen in your house? So Hezekiah answered, They have seen all that is in my house; there is nothing among my treasuries that I have not shown them. 5 Then Isaiah said to Hezekiah, Hear the word of the Lord of hosts, 6 Behold, the days are coming when all that is in your house and all that your fathers have laid up in store to this day will be carried to Babylon; nothing will be left, says the Lord. 7 And *some* of your sons who will issue from you, whom you will beget, will be taken away, and they will become officials in the palace of the king of Babylon. 8 Then Hezekiah said to Isaiah, The word of the Lord which you

---

the end, God Himself was the agent in this healing, but at this moment they were doing the best they could with the best medical options available (cf. James 5:14).

have spoken is good, for he thought, for there will be peace and truth in my days" (39:1-9).

Assyria is now out of the picture, but that does not mean an end to Israel's dangers, for Babylon would soon rise up. At this moment, however, Babylon was not yet a threat. That is why we see the favorable response from the King of Babylon when Hezekiah recovered from his sickness.

Babylon's response to Hezekiah's recovery (v. 1)

The chronological context

The expression "at that time" indicates that the events of chapter 39 took place very shortly after Hezekiah's recovery (ca. 703/702 B.C.). As noted, Merodach-Baladan II ("Marduk has given a son") ruled over Babylonia two different times, once from 721-709 (deposed by Sargon II) and a second time for nine months around 703-702 (deposed by Sennacherib).[87]

Baladan's deed

Baladan heard that Hezekiah had recovered, and sent him letters of congratulations and a present to celebrate his recovery. At this time, relations were good between Babylon and Judah, and Baladan certainly wanted to maintain a good relationship with Judah as a potential ally against mighty Assyria.[88]

The work of God

As we pull back the curtains, we find that there was more at work than the eye could see, for God was at work in the entire situation as well. From our studies of Hezekiah's sickness and recovery, we saw that God's king had a problem with pride. It appears that his recovery did not solve the problem, for this is what we read in 2 Chronicles. After his recovery,

> Hezekiah gave no return for the benefit he received, because his heart was proud; therefore wrath came on him and on Judah and Jerusalem.... Even *in the matter of* the envoys of the rulers of Babylon, who sent to him to inquire of the wonder that had happened in the land, God left him *alone only* to test him, that He might know all that was in his heart (2 Chron. 32:25, 31).

---

[87] Grogan, "Isaiah," 239.
[88] Wolf, *Interpreting Isaiah*, 181. No doubt Baladan had political and military reasons behind the gesture.

As we have seen, Hezekiah was a good man of God, but how interesting it is how pride could be such a downfall.

Hezekiah's response to Babylon (vv. 2-4)

Verses 2-4 expose Hezekiah's pride by the way he responded to the envoys (v. 2). His proud ways received a speedy rebuke (vv. 3-4).

Hezekiah's pride (v. 2)

The text simply says that Hezekiah showed the envoys all of his treasures. At first glance, we might not see any particular sin. However, the Bible shows us that God, the One who knows the heart, knew better. These deeds were another manifestation of Hezekiah's pride. Whether or not Hezekiah was looking to Babylon as an ally against Assyria, he demonstrated pride in his riches. Isaiah even gave a description of what these riches consisted of (cf. 2 Chron. 32:27-29).

God's rebuke (vv. 3-4)

Even if no one else saw Hezekiah's pride, God saw it, and He sent Isaiah to address it. Isaiah asked where the strangers had come from, and Hezekiah told them from Babylon (v. 3). Next, Isaiah asked Hezekiah what they saw, and Hezekiah explained that he showed them everything (v. 4). Hezekiah had no idea what kind of impact his deeds would have.

Isaiah's ominous warning to Hezekiah (vv. 5-7)

The words "Hear the word of the Lord of hosts" must have made Hezekiah's heart race (v. 5).[89] Isaiah gave Hezekiah two somber messages.

All the riches will be taken away (v. 6)

Isaiah tells Hezekiah that all of the riches he just showed the Babylonians will one day be taken away by them. At this point, the time frame is left vague ("days are coming"),[90] but with certainty these will be the ones to overthrow Judah. Thus, it is here for the first time in Isaiah we are told that Babylon will be the nation to overthrow Judah.[91]

---

[89] This form of address is one which typically carries great weight and authority.
[90] The first invasion came a little less than 100 years later when Nebuchadnezzar invaded Judah in 605 B.C. Babylon made a second attack in 597 and a third and final attack in 586 when they destroyed Jerusalem and Solomon's temple.
[91] Ibid.

Hezekiah's own heirs will be taken away (v. 7)

The Babylonians will also take large numbers of captives, including some of Hezekiah's own family members. Isaiah indicates that some of these captives will even become "officials" (*saris* can refer to a eunuch or simply an official or officer) in the palace of Babylon. No doubt, we are correct in recognizing Daniel as being one such person (Dan. 1:1-3; cf. 2 Kings 24:12-16; 2 Chron. 33:11).

Hezekiah's less than honorable response (v. 8)

Isaiah's message was terrible, but Hezekiah gave a curious response: "The word of the Lord which you have spoken is good." Hezekiah said this because he knew this invasion would not come in his lifetime. Some have seen Hezekiah's response as being the words of a man who truly trusts the Lord, but this may be better understood as showing some self-centered thinking.[92] Despite all the good, we are once again reminded that he is nothing but a mere man.

Summary and application

What kind of lessons can we learn from all this? Certainly, we are reminded of the truth that God hates pride (Prov. 6:16-17). Smith explains,

> The final Hezekiah narrative illustrates how easy it is for even the greatest of God's people to momentarily slip in their thinking. . . . Hezekiah had a great opportunity to tell the Babylonians about his sickness, his pious prayer, his letter about his experience, God's miraculous sign, and God's healing because his healing was one of the reasons why the Babylonians came.[93]

Hezekiah could have given all the glory to God, but he let his pride get the best of him, a sin that did not go unnoticed by God. Let us remember this truth as we seek to live a life that is fully pleasing to the Lord.

---

[92] Why not break down in tears and prayer as he did when God told him he was going to die soon? (Oswalt, *The Book of Isaiah: Chapters 1-39*, 697).
[93] Smith, *Isaiah 1-39*, 660.

SECTION TWO: THE REVALING OF GOD'S GREAT SALVATION (40:1-66:24)

8

SALVATION BY RELEASE FROM BABYLON (40:1-48:22)

Chapters 40-66 portray numerous events that lay many years in the future from Isaiah's own time.[1] This would include not only the exile to Babylon (some 80 years later), and an eventual release from Babylon (some 150 years later), but also numerous events that will not get fulfilled until the end of the age when Jesus Christ returns to establish His kingdom. Liberal scholars typically reject the idea that Isaiah could have prophesied these future events, so they often hold that 40-66 must have been written later.[2] Those who believe in supernatural inspiration have no problem in believing that one author prophesied all these things, but even here we recognize a shift in tone. Young comments on this shift: "When one turns from the thirty-ninth to the fortieth chapter it is as though he steps out of the darkness of judgment into the light of salvation. The contrast is great, and yet is evident that thirty-nine is a preparation for forty."[3] Thus, even if one rejects the theory of multiple authors,[4] we recognize that the

---

[1] As noted in the Introduction, some writers see this as a basis for positing multiple authors with this portion being written after these events were fulfilled.

[2] Because of the liberal refusal to accept divine inspiration and a unity of authorship, Grogan notes that chs. 40-66 have produced "more scholarly literature than any other part of the OT. The number of different views as to authorship, structure, and other related matters of introduction is bewildering" (G. W. Grogan, "Isaiah," in *The Expositor's Bible Commentary*, ed. Frank E. Gaebelein, vol. 6 [Grand Rapids: Zondervan, 1986], 240).

[3] Edward J. Young, *The Book of Isaiah, vol. 3* (Grand Rapids: Eerdmans, 1972), 17.

[4] Unity of the whole book and single authorship were commonly held until 1895 when

tone does shift in broad terms from messages that were primarily messages of judgment to messages that were primarily of comfort and restoration. Martin explains, "Whereas the first portion of the book (chaps. 1–39) is filled with messages of judgment, this portion emphasizes restoration and deliverance."[5]

I would like to assign a broad description to each of the major sections in 40-66 to help us see how the book unfolds. Section I, chapters 40-48, *The purpose of peace*, could break down as follows: 40: The Majesty of Yahweh the Comforter; 41: God's challenge to the unbelieving world; 42: The Servant of Yahweh; 43: Redemption by grace; 44:1-23: The folly of idolatry; 44:24-45:25; God uses sinful man for His own glory; 46:1-13: Babylon's idols; 47:1-15: The fall of Babylon; 48: Israel's resistance to the Lord's grace. Section II, chapters 49-57, *The good news of the Servant*, could break down as follows: 49: The Servant restores elect Jew and Gentiles; 50: The disobedient nation and the obedient Servant; 51:1-16: Trust in God and depart from evil; 51:17-52:12: Be alert and turn to the Lord; 52:13-53:12: The suffering Servant; 54: Israel's glorious and fruitful future; 55: The freedom of God's redeeming grace; 56:1-8: Gentile inclusion in the blessings of the Lord; 56:9-57:21: Condemnation upon the wicked. Section III, chapters 58-66, *The program of peace*, could break down as follows: 58: The "true fast" (true vs. false worship); 59: Confession brings salvation; 60: The glory of redeemed Zion; 61: Redemption and the Spirit-filled Messiah; 62: Zion's glorious future; 63:1-6: Yahweh the Avenger; 63:7-64:12: Prayers and praises; 65: God's mercy on redeemed Israel; 66: Restoration of true worship.

GOD'S MESSAGE OF HOPE (40:1-31)

Chapter 40 breaks on the scene by introducing us to a multitude of promises revolving around the way God will bring restoration to this world. This includes a perfect restoration to fallen Israel as well as the whole world.

Chapter 40 reads as follows: "1 Comfort, O comfort My people, says your God. 2 Speak kindly to Jerusalem, and call out to her, that her warfare has ended, that her iniquity has been removed, that she has received of the Lord's

---

Bernard Duhm posited three authors, one each for 1-39 (ca. 739-700 B.C.), 40-55 (ca. 545-535 B.C.), and 56-66 (ca. 520-500 B.C.) (John N. Oswalt, *The Book of Isaiah: Chapters 40-66*, The New International Commentary On The Old Testament, R. K. Harrison, Gen. Ed. [Grand Rapids: Eerdmans, 1998], 3).

[5] John A. Martin, "Isaiah," in *The Bible Knowledge Commentary: An Exposition of the Scriptures*, ed. J. F. Walvoord and R. B. Zuck, vol. 1, cited in electronic form with Logos Libronix (Wheaton, IL: Victor Books, 1985), 1091. However, both sections include messages of judgment and messages of restoration.

hand double for all her sins. 3 A voice is calling, Clear the way for the Lord in the wilderness; make smooth in the desert a highway for our God; 4 let every valley be lifted up, and every mountain and hill be made low, and let the rough ground become a plain, and the rugged terrain a broad valley. 5 Then the glory of the Lord will be revealed, and all flesh will see *it* together, for the mouth of the Lord has spoken. 6 A voice says, Call out. Then he answered, What shall I call out? All flesh is grass, and all its loveliness is like the flower of the field. 7 The grass withers, the flower fades when the breath of the Lord blows upon it. Surely the people are grass. 8 The grass withers, the flower fades, but the word of our God stands forever. 9 Get yourself up on a high mountain, O Zion, bearer of good news; lift up your voice mightily, O Jerusalem, bearer of good news; lift *it* up, do not fear. Say to the cities of Judah, Here is your God! 10 Behold, the Lord God will come with might, with His arm ruling for Him. Behold, His reward is with Him and His recompense before Him. 11 Like a shepherd He will tend His flock; in His arm He will gather the lambs and carry *them* in His bosom; He will gently lead the nursing *ewes*. 12 Who has measured the waters in the hollow of His hand, and marked off the heavens by the span, and calculated the dust of the earth by the measure, and weighed the mountains in a balance and the hills in a pair of scales? 13 Who has directed the Spirit of the Lord, or as His counselor has informed Him? 14 With whom did He consult and *who* gave Him understanding? And *who* taught Him in the path of justice and taught Him knowledge and informed Him of the way of understanding? 15 Behold, the nations are like a drop from a bucket, and are regarded as a speck of dust on the scales; behold, He lifts up the islands like fine dust. 16 Even Lebanon is not enough to burn, nor its beasts enough for a burnt offering. 17 All the nations are as nothing before Him; they are regarded by Him as less than nothing and meaningless. 18 To whom then will you liken God? Or what likeness will you compare with Him? 19 *As for* the idol, a craftsman casts it, a goldsmith plates it with gold, and a silversmith *fashions* chains of silver. 20 He who is too impoverished for *such* an offering selects a tree that does not rot; he seeks out for himself a skillful craftsman to prepare an idol that will not totter. 21 Do you not know? Have you not heard? Has it not been declared to you from the beginning? Have you not understood from the foundations of the earth? 22 It is He who sits above the circle of the earth, and its inhabitants are like grasshoppers, Who stretches out the heavens like a curtain and spreads them out like a tent to dwell in. 23 He *it is* who reduces rulers to nothing, Who makes the judges of the earth meaningless. 24 Scarcely have they been planted; scarcely have they been sown; scarcely has their stock taken root in the earth, but He merely blows on them, and they wither, and the storm carries them away like stubble. 25 To whom then will you liken Me that I would be *his* equal? says the Holy One. 26 Lift up your eyes on high and see who has created these *stars,* the One who leads forth their host by number; He calls them all by name. Because of the greatness of His might and the strength of *His* power, not one *of them* is missing. 27 Why do you say, O Jacob, and assert, O Israel, my way is hidden from the Lord, and the justice due me escapes the notice of my God? 28 Do you not know? Have you not heard? The Everlasting God, the Lord, the Creator of the ends of the earth does not become weary or tired. His understanding is inscrutable. 29 He gives strength to the weary, and to *him who* lacks might He increases power. 30 Though youths grow weary and tired, and vigorous young men stumble badly, 31 yet those who wait for the Lord will gain new strength; they will mount up *with* wings like eagles; they will run and not get tired; they will walk and not become weary" (40:1-31).

Isaiah 40-66 continues the three-fold theme that originated with Moses: (1) Israel was given the promise of blessings for faithfulness (Deut. 28:1-14). (2) Israel broke the covenant and fell under the curses of the covenant (Deut. 28:15-68). (3) The day is coming at the end of the age when God will fulfill the promises of the Abrahamic Covenant (Gen. 12; 13; 15; 17; 21; 22; 26; 35; 49) and restore the nation to a proper covenant relationship (Deut. 30:1-10; cf. Isa. 2:1-4; 4:1-4; 9:1-7; 10:20-23; 11:1-16; 12:1-6; 27:12-13; 40-66; Jer. 30-33; Ezek. 40-48; Dan. 12:1-13; Hos. 1-3; Joel 3:18-21; Amos 9:11-15; Obad. 15-21; Mic. 2:12-13; Zeph. 3:12-20; Hag. 2:20-23; Zech. 8:20-23; 10:9-12; 12-14; Mal. 3:1-4; 4:5-6). When Jesus returns, He will restore Israel, a truth affirmed in the New Testament (Rom. 11:25-36). Hughes reminds us what a great comfort these promises were: "The prophets of Israel, Isaiah in particular, were exhorted to speak words of consolation to God's people in the Babylonian exile."[6]

One major theme that flows through this entire section is the doctrine of the incomparable glory of Yahweh: There is no one like Him, the Creator and Savior of Israel (40:18, 25; 41:4, 26-27; 42:8, 24; 43:1-3, 10-17, 25; 44:1-8, 21-28; 45:5-25; 46:5, 8-11; 47:4; 48:3, 6, 12-17; cf. Exod. 15:11). Israel has a hope, but it is only because of the glorious grace of Yahweh. Chapter 40 may be divided into a series of six messages that reveal the glory and majesty of God as He announces the coming restoration.

First message: A message of restoration (vv. 1-2)

Man's fundamental problem is that he is separated from God and needs restoration from sin (Gen. 3; Rom. 5:12). Israel had the same problem (Isa. 59:1-2). Here in verses 1-2, Isaiah reveals a two-fold promise about this coming restoration.

---

[6] Robert B. Hughes and J. Carl Laney, *Tyndale Concise Bible Commentary*, The Tyndale Reference Library, cited in electronic form with Logos Libronix (Wheaton, IL: Tyndale House Publishers, 2001), 265.

First promise about the coming restoration: Comfort (v. 1-2a)

Three times God gives the command to speak a message of comfort to His people.[7] Interestingly, says Martin, even though the Babylonian exile had not yet even fallen on Judah, "[Isaiah looked] ahead to the Exile, [telling] the covenant nation (My people) to be comforted."[8] Why a message of comfort? Verse 2 tells us the reason why: The Lord has made a victory over evil to give peace to His people Israel.[9]

Second promise about the coming restoration: Peace (v. 2b)

Sin has caused a spiritual war. To use a biblically-based, spiritual, metaphor, when Israel broke the covenant, she plunged herself into long ages of spiritual war. God's promise, however, is that one day He will put an end to this war by His own saving grace—the power of His mighty arm (Isa. 52:10; 59:16; 63:5), for even though they broke the Mosaic Covenant, they are still the chosen people, i.e., "My people" (12 times in 1-39, 9 times in 40-55, and 6 times in 56-66).[10] Never will God break His oath to the people of Abraham (Exod. 6:7; 19:5; Lev. 26:12; Deut. 7:6-9; 26:17-18). Three times in verse 2 God gives a reason why the war is over.[11]

An end is coming to the war. In the end, Israel will turn to the Lord and find forgiveness under a new covenant (Jer. 31:31-34). This means that the iniquity of the nation will be removed through the redeeming grace of God's servant (Isa. 53:5). Biblically speaking, the idea of receiving back "double" is not the idea as receiving back two-times as much, but rather the idea of fair retribution. Unger comments on this idea of receiving double: "[It is not that] God will inflict more than Israel deserves, but she will receive what will be necessary

---

[7] Codex Vaticanus suggests that these commands are given to the priests, but this idea is unpersuasive (Young, *The Book of Isaiah, vol. 3*, 18). God's redeeming grace is universal (cf. Zech. 1:13) as emphasized by the doubling of this command (cf. Isa. 51:9, 17; 52:1, 11; 57:14; 62:10). No longer is the address given with contempt as "this people" as earlier (cf. 6:9; 8:6).

[8] Ludwig Koehler, Walter Baumgartner, et al., *The Hebrew and Aramaic Lexicon of the Old Testament*, cited in electronic form with Logos Libronix (Leiden: E.J. Brill, 1994–2000), 689. "Speak kindly" ("to the heart") conveys tenderness (Gen. 34:3; 50:21; Judg. 19:3; Ruth 2:13; 2 Sam. 19:7; 2 Chron. 30:22; Hos. 2:14).

[9] Isaiah 12:1 tells us that this comfort cannot come until Israel has turned from its sin so that the anger of God might turn away (cf. 5:25; 9:12, 17, 21; 10:4, 25).

[10] Young, *The Book of Isaiah, vol. 3*, 19.

[11] Each of these three reasons is introduced by the word "that," clauses introduced by the Hebrew word *kiy*.

for the purging out of apostates and for the salvation and refinement of the remnant."[12]

The end of the war is not going to be for a long time. The promise in verse 2 is certain, but the timing has not been revealed. The truth of the matter is that Israel will endure subjugation and oppression not only from Babylon (605-539 B.C.), but also from Persia (539-334 B.C.), Greece (334-146 B.C.), and Rome (146 B.C. to the present day). Judah's "hardship and misery" will one day come to an end, but not for a long, long time.

Second message: A message of preparation (vv. 3-5)

Isaiah's second message is one of preparation, hence the voice that calls out for all to hear. If Israel wants the blessings of the kingdom, she must prepare herself by repenting of her sin now.[13] Isaiah gives the call to repentance (vv. 3-4) along with the promise of glory (v. 5).

The call to repentance (vv. 3-4)

For Israel to have God's blessings, she must first deal with her sin. Six times in verses 3-4 Isaiah uses geographical imagery to communicate the message that Israel must repent to enter the kingdom.

First and second calls to repentance (v. 3). The first and second calls to repentance speak about clearing the way in the wilderness to make a smooth path for the Lord.[14] Ancient dirt roads were typically filled with potholes, rocks, and other obstacles, and all of these needed to be cleared to

---

[12] Merrill F. Unger, *Unger's Commentary on the Old Testament, Vol. II: Isaiah-Malachi* (Chicago: Moody, 1981), 1248.

[13] For Christians living in the church, the doctrine of "imminence" teaches the idea that men should prepare themselves right now for the return of Christ who will bring in the messianic kingdom at any time (cf. e.g., Rev. 16:15; 22:12, 14, 20). The same concept of imminence was also at work during the OT.

[14] "Wilderness" (*midbar*) often refers to the desert areas of Judea, while "desert" (*'arabah*) usually speaks about the Jordan Rift where the Dead Sea is found. Some writers suggest this wilderness imagery is like the Exodus with the Lord coming from His distant residence at Sinai to save His people (cf. Deut. 33:2; Hab. 3:3; Ps. 68:7) (Young, *The Book of Isaiah, vol. 3*, 28). Indeed, the desert is a fitting description for our spiritual condition—one that is waterless (41:18; 43:19, 20; 48:1), unfertile (41:19; 51:3; 55:13; 60:13), without smooth paths or living inhabitants (43:19; 64:10), and spiritually dry (Isa. 53:1ff.) (ibid., 29, n. 15).

prepare the way.¹⁵ The King (God) must have a smooth path, and that means the people needed to deal with their sins. Smith explains,

> Since God is holy, all who meet him must be holy or they will be judged (6:1–5). Therefore, 40:3 encourages God's people to make appropriate preparation for the time when all flesh will meet God (40:5; a similar theme is found in 62:10–11).¹⁶

It was sin that sent Israel into Babylon. If she wants a restoration, she must deal with her sin.¹⁷ By His grace, God did release Israel from the Babylonian exile after 70 years (Jer. 25:11-14; 27:5-7; 29:10-14),¹⁸ but how does this passage relate to Jesus Christ in His first advent? According to Isaiah 40, God sent a forerunner (a voice) to call the nation to repentance. Kidner reminds us that his name was John: "John the Baptist, with prophetic symbolism, used the literal wilderness for this very work (*cf.* Mt. 3:1–3)."¹⁹ The Baptist filled the role of a forerunner to call the nation to repentance at the first coming (Mk. 1:1-4; cf. Matt. 11:14; Luke 1:76; John 1:23).

Israel had a responsibility to embrace Christ at His first coming, but they refused to believe (Luke 19:41-44; John 1:11). Israel sinned by rejecting Christ,

---

[15] This idea is comparable to the modern expression "roll out the red carpet."

[16] Gary Smith, *Isaiah 40-66*, vol. 15B, The New American Commentary, cited in electronic form with Logos Libronix (Nashville, TN: Broadman & Holman Publishers, 2009), 95.

[17] Wolf reminds us that the fulfillment of these promises/warnings comes potentially in one of three ways: (1) It is the call to repent and be ready for the kingdom of God through a restoration from the Babylonian captivity. (2) It is the call to repent and be ready for the kingdom of God at the first advent of Christ. (3) It is the call to repent and be ready for the kingdom of God at the second advent of Christ (Herbert M. Wolf, *Interpreting Isaiah* [Grand Rapids: Zondervan, 1985], 184). It is not as though God's eternal plan was contingent upon human deeds, but it does convey the way that God commands men (men with human responsibility) to line up with His plan and purposes.

[18] According to the Law of Moses, Israel was supposed to observe a Sabbatical Year every seventh year in which the people would not till their lands (Lev. 26:34). For 490 years, apparently, Israel failed to keep the Sabbatical Year, and by this they missed 70 such years. The Babylonian captivity gave the land its 70 years of rest from 605 B.C. to roughly 537 B.C. (2 Chron. 36:21-21; Ezra 1:1).

[19] F. Derek Kidner, "Isaiah," in *New Bible Commentary: 21st Century Edition*, ed. D. A. Carson et al., 4th ed., cited in electronic form with Logos Libronix (Leicester, England; Downers Grove, IL: Inter-Varsity Press, 1994), 655.

but all these events were within the eternal plan of God (Isa. 52:13-53:12; Acts 2:23; 4:27-28; 1 Pet. 1:20). Because Israel did not embrace Christ, the Scripture shows us that God will send another forerunner at the end of the age to announce the return of Messiah with His kingdom (Mal. 3:1; 4:5-6; Matt. 17:10-13).

Four more calls to repentance (v. 4). Isaiah gives four more commands using nature imagery to symbolically make a call to repentance: "Let every valley be lifted up, and every mountain and hill be made low; and let the rough ground become a plain, and the rugged terrain a broad valley." Spiritually speaking, Pfeiffer reminds us, "it is apparent that these geographical features symbolize the arid lifelessness of the unconverted soul."[20] Isaiah's command was to make the path smooth by repenting (cf. Hos. 5:15; 6:1-3). This is the highway that God wanted.[21]

The glory of the God in the messianic kingdom (v. 5)

The need is repentance. Verse 5 forms the result clause (i.e., the apodosis) to the conditions found in 3-4 (i.e., the protasis).[22] For Israel to enter the kingdom (v. 5), she must turn to the Lord (vv. 3-4; cf. Dan. 12:7, 10; Hos. 3:5; Zech. 12:10; 13:9; Mal. 3:3).

All flesh will see the glory of God. For Israel, the blessings of restoration will include the fact that they will see the glory of God in His kingdom (Isa. 6:3 [cf. John 12:37-41]; 35:2; 44:23; 49:3; 52:12; 58:8; 60:1-3; 61:3).[23] This glory will be manifested in the person of Jesus Christ in the midst of His restored people. They will realize that Jesus Himself is the Lord of glory, their warrior King (Isa. 12:6; 25:9; 35:2-4; 40:9; 49:26; 52:10; 60:16; cf. Mic. 2:12-13; Zeph. 3:15-17; Zech. 2:5, 10-11).

The glory will come again in full display. Two-thousand years ago eternal God took on flesh and His glory dwelt in the presence of His people under

---

[20] Charles F. Pfeiffer, *The Wycliffe Bible Commentary: Old Testament*, cited in electronic form with Logos Libronix (Chicago: Moody Press, 1962), Is 40:1.

[21] "Highway" (*messilah*) is one of Isaiah's favorite expressions (11:16; 19:23; 33:8; 45:2; 49:11; 57:14; 59:7; 62:10).

[22] Oswalt, *The Book of Isaiah: Chapters 40-66*, 52, n. 24.

[23] In context, the remnant of Israel may be the best understanding, but from other passages we know that the remnant of all the Gentiles will share in this blessing (Isa. 11:10; 49:26; 66:16; cf. Dan. 7:13; Rev. 1:7). The revelation of this glory is not only the deeds of God (Isa. 24:15; 25:3; 41:16; 42:12), but a full manifestation of God's physical glory in the presence of His people (Mark 8:38; 9:1-3).

the veil of frail humanity (John 1:14), but when He returns, He will come in the fulness of His divine glory (Mark 9:1-3; John 17:5, 22-24; Rev. 1:14-15; 19:11-21). Isaiah has spoken this word, so the promise is true and certain (Isa. 1:20; 21:17; 22:25; 24:3; 25:8; 55:8-11; 58:14).[24]

Third message: A message of humiliation (vv. 6-8)

Another voice cries out (v. 6a)

A voice once again cries out with a message of humiliation—not a humiliation that belongs only to Israel because of her sin, but a humiliation that belongs to the entire human race because of its weak and transitory fabric. Mankind's estimation of itself is typically very lofty, but God says we are very weak and transitory: "You are *just* a vapor that appears for a little while and then vanishes away" (Jas. 4:14).

Transient man will not stand, but God's truth will (vv. 6b-8)

Flesh is as grass (vv. 6b-8a). Human flesh is no more permanent than the grass and flowers of the field (Num. 17:23; Ps. 103:15; Isa. 42:7; Jas. 1:10-11; 1 Pet. 2:24).[25] The imagery would be immediately impressive for residents of the land since in the early spring, tender grass and beautiful flowers begin to cover the hills, but by April or May the scorching "Hamsin" winds from the eastern deserts blow over the land and shrivel it up. So it is with man (v. 7; cf. 51:12).

Man will not stand, but God will (v. 8b). Judah need not fear mighty Assyria (nor Babylon). Assyria will come and go like grass and flowers and so too will Babylon,[26] but God's truth will remain forever. Whatever God has said, it will happen (Isa. 55:11; 59:21; Matt. 5:18; Mark 13:31).[27] Martin explains, "This fact would greatly comfort and encourage the people in exile who read

---

[24] Young, *The Book of Isaiah, vol. 3*, 31.

[25] Zemek explains that the word "flesh" (*sarks*) can refer (1) to physical flesh such as meat (Gen. 2:21; Exod. 21:28; Num. 11:4; Deut. 12:15; Ezek. 4:14), (2) to the whole body (Lev. 16:4; 2 Kings 9:36; Job 7:5), (3) to a blood or marital relationship (Gen. 2:24; 37:27), (4) to the "whole person" (Pss. 63:1; 84:2), (5) to all mankind and humanity (Gen. 6:12-13), or as here (6) to mankind as he who is weak and lacking in strength (George Zemek, *A Biblical Theology of the Doctrines of Sovereign Grace* [Little Rock: B.T.D.S.G., 2002], 11-12).

[26] In Daniel 2 we have the reminder that Babylon, Persia, Greece, and Rome will all come and go, but the kingdom of God will never pass away.

[27] Wolf, *Interpreting Isaiah*, 184-185.

these words. Because God's Word stands, His prophecy that the people would be restored to their land was sure to be fulfilled."[28]

Fourth message: A message of exultation (vv. 9-11)

One day the suffering will come to an end, and Zion will have joy and exultation (v. 9). Jerusalem will be the "evangelist" (*mebassereth*) to proclaim this good news (cf. 52:7; 61:1). Kidner explains,

> *You who bring good tidings* is a single Hebrew word, of which 'evangelist' is the Greek equivalent (not as a specialized term). It is feminine here, agreeing with *Zion*, and hence Zion is probably the messenger. In 41:27; 52:7 she is the hearer.[29]

Three times in verses 9-11 Isaiah uses three different names of God to declare why Israel will once again be filled with joy and exultation.

First declaration: God has come (v. 9)

The first reason for rejoicing is that Israel's God (*'Eloah*) has come to His people (cf. 25:9; 35:2; 52:10) to give them a victory over their enemies.[30] Later in chapter 52 we read a similar call to rejoice:

> Therefore, My people shall know My name; therefore in that day I am the one who is speaking, Here I am. How lovely on the mountains are the feet of him who brings good news, who announces peace and brings good news of happiness, who announces salvation, *and* says to Zion, Your God reigns! (52:6-7).

This day is coming, and God's people should live in hope because of it.

Second declaration: Sovereign Yahweh has come (v. 10)

Israel needs to know that the sovereign God of Israel (*'Adonay Yahweh*) is going to come in great power (his arm; cf. 50:2; 51:5, 9; 52:10; 53:1; 59:16, 18; 63:5), and when He does, He will make right every wrong.[31] He will give to

---

[28] Martin, "Isaiah," 1092.
[29] Kidner, "Isaiah," 656.
[30] It is curious to trace the way that the prophets made repeated calls for supreme exultation and celebration over the coming of God in the person of Messiah (Isa. 12:6; Zeph. 3:5, 14-17; Zech. 2:10; 9:9; Rev. 19:1-10).
[31] Smith explains, "One day he will reign as Lord and Master over his people and over

Israel the "wages" from which they were cheated (61:6; 66:12), and He will give judgment to the enemies who brought harm to His people (Isa. 59:18; 65:6; 66:6; cf. Joel 3:7; 2 Thess. 1:6-9; Rev. 16:4-7; 18:20; 19:2).

Third declaration: Israel's Shepherd has come (v. 11)

Isaiah saw the coming Shepherd. The third term for God is the tender term "shepherd" (cf. Ps. 23:1; John 10:11-16). The Messiah will tenderly care for his afflicted people just as a shepherd tenderly cares for his flock, especially the young and tender.[32]

Other prophets saw the coming Shepherd. Micah, a contemporary of Isaiah, made the same promise concerning Messiah that He will come as a Shepherd to gather and care for His flock (2:12-13), but Micah is not alone in the use of this imagery (cf. Jer. 31:10; Ezek. 34:23-24; 37:23-24; Rev. 7:17). The Good Shepherd (Jesus) is going to return, and when He does, He will care for His afflicted flock, both Jews and Gentiles (John 10:16).

Peace and blessing are what the Shepherd will bring. Our sin-ravaged world longs for something better. For those who are willing to trust in the Son, that day is coming, and it will be paradise. Zechariah gives a brief description of what the kingdom will look like for Israel: "Once again men and women of ripe old age will sit in the streets of Jerusalem, each with cane in hand because of his age. The city streets will be filled with boys and girls playing" (Zech. 8:4-5).

Fifth message: A message of exaltation (vv. 12-26)

The tone shifts in verses 12-26 to highlight the incomparable glory of God. Isaiah shows six pictures that magnify the incomparable glory of the living God. There is no one like Him, so Israel can rest in peace.

One: He knows His creation (v. 12)

The first way we see the incomparable glory of God is in the inscrutable knowledge God has of His creation. Unlike the idols, God knows it all since He

---

the whole earth. His strength will assure his victory. This picture of God's power should give the audience confidence that no earthly power will be able to resist his will. These images are suggestive of a Divine Warrior whose power defeats his enemy and rescues his own people" (Smith, *Isaiah 40-66*, 100).

[32] "Lamb" means a young, tender lamb (Isa. 65:25) and was also used of "youths" (1 Sam. 7:9; in fem. form it is Talitha in Mark 5:41). It was common in the ANE for the king to be called shepherd (Oswalt, *The Book of Isaiah: Chapters 40-66*, 55).

made it all (Gen. 1; Exod. 20:11; John 1:1-3; Col. 1:15-17; Heb. 1:1-3). Pfeiffer explains that,

> According to pagan mythology the gods of the heathen were spawned by pre-existent matter. But this God of revelation was eternally pre-existent before creation, and remains transcendent above his creation, utterly unapproachable in wisdom and profundity of thought.[33]

The Living God made it all, and therefore He knows it intimately. If He is so big, He knows the quantity of waters and sands of the earth and the weight of the mountains, He certainly is One we can trust.

Two: He needs no teacher (vv. 13-14)

The God who created the heavens and earth has no need for men to give Him counsel.[34] He knows what He is doing, and His ways are always right despite what we might think (cf. Dan. 4:34-37). Job understood this and wrote, "Can anyone teach God knowledge?" (Job 21:22; cf. 28:1).[35]

Three: He is infinitely higher than His creation (vv. 15-17)

Isaiah's third picture of the incomparability of God revolves around the fact that the true God is infinitely higher than His creation, i.e., He is transcendent above it all (cf. Isa. 57:15; 66:1-2).[36] Therefore, when He looks down upon creation, it is miniscule (vv. 15-16).[37] Babylon may be great in comparison to other nations, but in comparison to God, "All the nations are as nothing before Him; they are regarded by Him as less than nothing and meaningless" (v. 17).[38]

---

[33] Pfeiffer, *The Wycliffe Bible Commentary: Old Testament*, Is 40:9.

[34] The LXX translated the term for "spirit" by the word "mind" (as seen in passages like 1 Chron. 28:12; Ezek. 20:32). Grogan suggests that in view of the context of creative activity, the idea of "Spirit" may in fact be correct (as in Isa. 34:16; cf. Gen. 1:2; Job 33:4) (Grogan, "Isaiah," 245). Paul cites this verse twice in his letters to remind all of us that He is God, and we are not (Rom. 11:34; 1 Cor. 2:16).

[35] He Himself is the "One Who counsels wonder" (Isa. 9:6-7; 11:1ff.; 28:29).

[36] Young, *The Book of Isaiah, vol. 3*, 44.

[37] Isaiah makes numerous references to these "islands" (v. 15), the Mediterranean world to the west of Israel (41:1, 5; 42:4, 10, 12; 49:1; 60:9; 66:19). Lebanon (v. 16) was known for its mighty forests, but they are not too much for God to burn (2:13; 10:34; 14:8; 29:17; 33:9; 35:2; 37:24; 60:13). It was also known for its abundance of animal life in the forests (Ps. 104:16-18).

[38] The strength of Isaiah's statement comes out with three negative words: "nothing" (*'ayin*), "less than nothing" (*me 'ephes*), and "meaningless" (*tohu*).

Four: He is nothing like the idols of the nations (vv. 18-20)

God's message is clear: There is no one like Him. Idols are folly.

No one like Him (v. 18). Since Yahweh is the true God (*'El*), the powerful Creator,[39] it is ridiculous that anyone would turn to an idol. Knowing this, God asks how anyone could compare Him to an idol (46:5: "To whom would you liken Me, and make Me equal, and compare Me, that we would be alike?").

The folly of idolatry (vv. 19-20). Isaiah exposes the folly of idolatry by sarcastically explaining the process of making idols (cf. Isa. 41:7; 44:9-20; 45:16, 20; 46:1-2, 6-7; Pss. 115:4-7; 135:15-18; Jer. 10:8-16; Hab. 2:19). The rich man can afford idols made out of gold or silver (v. 19), but the poor man has to settle for one made out of a wood like cedar that does not easily rot (v. 20). In either case they are a god that has been carved, formed, and sculpted by human hands, but such is not the case with Yahweh.[40]

Five: He is the sovereign Lord of all history (vv. 21-24)

Not only is Yahweh the Creator of the heavens and earth, but He is also the Lord of history, and nothing happens outside of His purpose. Yahweh has "control over the rulers" of the world, and His people can trust Him in His promises for restoration.[41]

The fact of God's sovereignty (vv. 21-22). In this section, Isaiah asks four questions to remind Israel that Yahweh is the transcendent Creator, and therefore stands outside of creation and time. He is the One who "sits about the circle [*chug*; cf. Job 22:14; Prov. 8:27] of the earth." He is the One who, "stretches out the heavens like a curtain and spreads them out like a tent to dwell in" (cf. 42:5; 44:24; 45:12; 51:12; Pss. 19:4; 104:2; Jer. 10:12; 51:15; Zech. 12:1).[42]

The implications of God's sovereignty (vv. 23-24). Isaiah brings out

---

[39] In view of these first two points, the waw of v. 18 should be seen as functioning with an inferential force with conclusions following in vv. 18-20 that no one should seek idols (Oswalt, *The Book of Isaiah: Chapters 40-66*, 62).

[40] Isaiah mockingly reminds them that they would have to secure the idol to a wooden base so that it would never totter and fall on its face, for that would be a terrible thing to happen to your god (Isa. 41:7; 46:7; cf. 1 Sam. 5:2-5).

[41] Wolf, *Interpreting Isaiah*, 186.

[42] He made them and spread them out, but one day He will rip them apart (Isa. 51:6; 2 Pet. 3:10; Rev. 19:11; 20:11).

the implications by showing that the activity of all the nations is under His control. Yahweh is the One who, "reduces rulers to nothing, who makes the judges of the earth meaningless" (v. 23; cf. Job 12:17-21; Jer. 25:17). World leaders come on the scene, but barely do they begin to exercise their God-granted dominion (barely planted and sown), that He, "blows on them,[43] and they wither, and the storm carries them away like stubble" (v. 24; cf. Isa. 46:8-11). Israel needs to understand His sovereignty and trust Him in all things (cf. Matt. 10:29).

Six: He is the Creator and Sustainer of the whole universe (vv. 25-26)

Not only is God the Creator of all things, but He is also the Sustainer of all things. Therefore, says God, "To whom then will you liken Me that I would be *his* equal?" (v. 25).[44] Apparently, as the context suggests, in her newfound captivity Israel was beginning to think that Yahweh was just another god. Such is not the case. Yahweh is the One who not only created the stars (Gen. 1:16; Job 38:2),[45] but also leads forth their host by number,[46] and gives each one of them their names and sustains them: "Because of the greatness of His might and the strength of *His* power, not one *of them* is missing" (v. 26; cf. 34:16). There is no one like Him.

Sixth message: A message of invitation (vv. 27-31)

The implication is that Israel must not think that somehow her captivity was outside of God's power. For this reason, God extends an invitation to Israel to find rest in Him. God does this in these closing verses with three reminders about who He is and why we can rest in Him.

First reminder why we can rest in Him (v. 27)

God gives a rebuke for those might think that He might not see what is happening to them. With the coming of the Babylonian exile, Israel had begun to think that God did not see what was happening and that they were not getting

---

[43] The term for "blow" in v. 24 (*nashaph*) is a close synonym to the one used in v. 7 (*nashab*). God blows and they blow away like stubble (Isa. 41:2; 47:14; cf. Ps. 1:4).

[44] Oswalt, *The Book of Isaiah: Chapters 40-66*, 68, n. 79.

[45] Isaiah utilizes the distinctive word "create" (*bara'*) that is found sixteen times in chs. 40-55, five times in the rest of Isaiah, and twenty-seven times in the rest of the OT with eleven in Genesis, six in the Psalms, and three in Ezekiel (ibid., 69).

[46] As Grogan explains it, with God leading them, "none dares fail to be on parade" (Grogan, "Isaiah," 247, n. 26).

a fair deal.[47] Another accusation that comes later is that God did see these events, but He was not treating His people fairly or with compassion (cf. Isa. 49:14-15).[48] In any case, here in verse 27, the people "expected, based on their covenant relationship with God, that God would deal with them mercifully, but this was not happening."[49]

Second reminder why we can rest in Him (v. 28)

How wrong they were for thinking that something might happen that could be outside of God's knowledge and purposes. Mere men may suffer from such weakness, but not the Lord, for He never tires, and His understanding is inscrutable.

Third reminder why we can rest in Him (vv. 29-31)

He is a God who gives strength and power (v. 29). Isaiah reminds the people that because God is infinite in His resources and we, as finite creatures, are totally dependent upon Him, we need to rely upon Him for the strength we need. If we seek Him, He will give us the strength we need.

He is a God who empowers beyond expectation (vv. 30-31). One expects that people in their youth will have great strength and endurance, but even these grow weary and stumble (v. 30).[50] What about those who are not young? Do they have any hope? The answer is "Yes," says Isaiah: "Yet those who wait for the Lord will gain new strength; they will mount up *with* wings like eagles; they will run and not get tired; they will walk and not become weary" (v. 31).[51] Pfeiffer summarizes: "To his children, who lack both stamina and strength, he liberally grants all they need for their constant progress and spiritual attainment, provided they trustingly wait upon him in expectation and prayer."[52]

---

[47] That is impossible, since Yahweh is the God of justice (11:3-4; 16:5; 42:1-4; 51:4; 61:8). The only fact that is missing is that all attacks against Israel are punishable, a problem that God will rectify (Zech. 1:14-15; 2:6ff.; Hab. 2:4ff.; Rev. 18).

[48] God's answer to the accusation that He was lacking compassion was to have Israel examine the reason why He sent them away in divorce (Isa. 50:1-2). It was their fault, a message that Isaiah repeats elsewhere (1:18; 59:1).

[49] Smith, *Isaiah 40-66*, 120.

[50] The connotation here is that of young men "specifically selected and trained for military service" (Judg. 20:15; 1 Sam. 24:2; Jer. 51:3; Ezek. 23;6, 12) (Oswalt, *The Book of Isaiah: Chapters 40-66*, 71, n. 91).

[51] The one who waits on Yahweh will soar (cf. Prov. 23:5; 30:19; Job 39:27).

[52] Pfeiffer, *The Wycliffe Bible Commentary: Old Testament*, Is 40:27.

ISAIAH 40:1-48:22

Summary and application

Judah went into the Babylonian exile in 605 B.C., an exile that still has not come to a final restoration. God's promise is that one day He will restore them. Israel needed hope, and that is why God spoke these words. The same principle holds true for believers today. One day God is going to bring this world a final restoration. We don't have it yet, but the best thing we can do is to fix our eyes on Jesus and find strength in Him.

OUR STRONG GOD WILL SAVE US (41:1-29)

Chapter 41 continues God's message of comfort and encouragement by telling us the means by which God would set His people free from Babylon. God has an agent who is going to set Israel free from Babylon, and His name was Cyrus.[53]

Chapter 41 reads as follows: "1 Coastlands, listen to Me in silence, and let the peoples gain new strength; let them come forward, then let them speak; let us come together for judgment. 2 Who has aroused one from the east whom He calls in righteousness to His feet? He delivers up nations before him and subdues kings. He makes them like dust with his sword, as the wind-driven chaff with his bow. 3 He pursues them, passing on in safety, by a way he had not been traversing with his feet. 4 Who has performed and accomplished *it*, calling forth the generations from the beginning? I, the Lord, am the first, and with the last. I am He. 5 The coastlands have seen and are afraid; the ends of the earth tremble; they have drawn near and have come. 6 Each one helps his neighbor and says to his brother, Be strong! 7 So the craftsman encourages the smelter, *and* he who smooths *metal* with the hammer *encourages* him who beats the anvil, saying of the soldering, It is good; and he fastens it with nails, *so that* it will not totter. 8 But you, Israel, My servant, Jacob whom I have chosen, descendant of Abraham My friend, 9 you whom I have taken from the ends of the earth, and called from its remotest parts and said to you, You are My servant; I have chosen you and not rejected you. 10 Do not fear, for I am with you; do not anxiously look about you, for I am your God. I will strengthen you; surely I will help you; surely I will uphold you with My righteous right hand. 11 Behold, all those who are angered at you will be shamed and dishonored. Those who contend with you will be as nothing and will perish. 12 You will seek those who quarrel with you, but will not find them; those who war with you will be as nothing and non-existent. 13 For I am the Lord your God, Who upholds your right hand, Who says to you, Do not fear; I will help you; 14 do not fear, you worm Jacob, you men of Israel; I will help you, declares the Lord, and your Redeemer is the Holy One of Israel. 15 Behold, I have made you a new, sharp

---

[53] Wolf, *Interpreting Isaiah*, 187.

threshing sledge with double edges; you will thresh the mountains and pulverize *them,* and will make the hills like chaff. 16 You will winnow them, and the wind will carry them away, and the storm will scatter them. But you will rejoice in the Lord; you will glory in the Holy One of Israel. 17 The afflicted and needy are seeking water, but there is none, and their tongue is parched with thirst. I, the Lord, will answer them Myself; *as* the God of Israel, I will not forsake them. 18 I will open rivers on the bare heights and springs in the midst of the valleys; I will make the wilderness a pool of water and the dry land fountains of water. 19 I will put the cedar in the wilderness, the acacia and the myrtle and the olive tree; I will place the juniper in the desert together with the box tree and the cypress, 20 that they may see and recognize, and consider and gain insight as well, that the hand of the Lord has done this, and the Holy One of Israel has created it. 21 Present your case, the Lord says. Bring forward your strong *arguments,* the King of Jacob says. 22 Let them bring forth and declare to us what is going to take place. As for the former *events,* declare what they *were,* that we may consider them and know their outcome, or announce to us what is coming. 23 Declare the things that are going to come afterward, that we may know that you are gods. Indeed, do good or evil, that we may anxiously look about us and fear together. 24 Behold, you are of no account, and your work amounts to nothing. He who chooses you is an abomination. 25 I have aroused one from the north, and he has come; from the rising of the sun he will call on My name, and he will come upon rulers as *upon* mortar, even as the potter treads clay. 26 Who has declared *this* from the beginning, that we might know, or from former times, that we may say, *He is* right!? Surely there was no one who declared; surely there was no one who proclaimed; surely there was no one who heard your words. 27 Formerly *I said* to Zion, Behold, here they are, and to Jerusalem, I will give a messenger of good news. 28 But when I look, there is no one, and there is no counselor among them. Who, if I ask, can give an answer? 29 Behold, all of them are false; their works are worthless; their molten images are wind and emptiness" (41:1-29).

Chapter 41 reminds God's people that more often than not, His plan gets fulfilled through natural means.[54] Theologians call this aspect of God's work the providence of God, which in this case revolves around God's use of a Persian king named Cyrus.

Chapter 41 breaks down to three major sections: (1) the introduction of Cyrus, (vv. 1-7), (2) the encouragement to Israel to not fear (vv. 8-20), and (3) the reminder that dumb idols cannot do what the Lord does (vv. 21-29).

---

[54] Sometimes His work is directly supernatural and miraculous (e.g., the flood, Sodom and Gomorrah, the Red Sea, the feeding of the 5,000, etc.), but more often He works His plan by His providence as we see with Cyrus.

The introduction of powerful Cyrus (vv. 1-7)

The Lord of the universe has a message for the world. It is the message for His people Israel, and it is also a message for the nations, that He alone is sovereign God. This message begins with a summons to the Gentiles.

The summons by the sovereign God (v. 1)

Chapter 41 opens with a challenge to the nations of the Mediterranean world, i.e., the "coastlands" (cf. 13:22; 34:14; 40:15; 41:1, 5; 42:4, 10; 49:1; 51:5; 60:9). This challenge, explains Martin, "stemmed from His special relationship with Israel. He would sovereignly protect Israel, but the other nations would not enjoy that protection."[55] The nations need to come forward (*nagash*) in silence (cf. Hag. 2:20; Zech. 2:13) and recognize Him as the true God who will give protection to His people.[56] He will do so by raising up a king from the East who will set His people free from Babylon. He is the Living God who will save His own people (no idol can do this). It is folly to trust in anything else, and verses 1-7 serve as a call to court to all the idolaters of the world to see if they can answer God's charges.[57]

The interrogations of a sovereign God (vv. 2-4)

God interrogates the nations to reveal that He is the One at work to set His people free. Isaiah gives a series of seven descriptions about this one who will come as God's chosen servant to set Israel free from Babylon.

First two descriptions of God's servant (v. 2a). First, God's servant is one whom the Lord Himself will *arouse* (*'ur*) to do His will (cf. 41:25; 45:1-3; 46:11). Second, God will do a work in this man's heart to "rouse" ("awaken," "excite," "incite") this man to fulfill His eternal purposes.[58] God is not merely omniscient (He is), but He is also the One who is sovereign over all history. He purposes, plans, and accomplishes, and none can frustrate His plans. This work of God will be fulfilled by God's chosen servant whom He has aroused from the East, the one "He calls in righteousness to His feet" to fulfill His purposes.

The person Isaiah is speaking about was Cyrus the Great, the first king of

---

[55] Martin, "Isaiah," 1093–1094.
[56] If they will turn to the Lord, they will gain new strength (cf. 40:30-31).
[57] This Bible often uses courtroom imagery (41:21-29; 42:18-25; 43:8-13; 44:6-20; 45:20-25), courtroom imagery where God may be the injured party, plaintiff, lawgiver, or judge (Grogan, "Isaiah," 249; Young, *The Book of Isaiah, vol. 3*, 70).
[58] Carl Schultz, "*'ur*," ed. R. Laird Harris, Gleason L. Archer Jr., and Bruce K. Waltke, *Theological Wordbook of the Old Testament*, cited in electronic form with Logos Libronix (Chicago: Moody Press, 1999), 655–656.

the Medo-Persian Empire, the king who overthrew Babylon in 539 B.C., and gave the Jews permission to return to their land. Isaiah makes several references to this king, and even names him by name although he would not come on the scene for some one hundred and fifty years (cf. 41:25; 44:28ff.; 45:1ff.; 46:8-11; 48:14-15). Mitchell provides an excellent background to who Cyrus was and how God used him:

> Cyrus (the Great) assumed the throne about 559 b.c. . . . As an adult, Cyrus organized the Persians into an army and revolted against his grandfather and father (Cambyses I). He defeated them and claimed their throne. One of his first acts as king of Medio-Persia was to launch an attack against Lydia, capital of Sardis and storehouse for the riches of its king, Croesus. Turning eastward, Cyrus continued his campaign until he had carved out a vast empire, stretching from the Aegean Sea to India. The Babylonian Empire next stood in his path, an obstacle that appeared to be insurmountable. Engaging the Babylonian army at Opis, Cyrus' troops routed them and moved on Babylon. The people in the capital welcomed Cyrus with open arms, seeing him as a liberator rather than a conqueror [cf. Dan. 5]. . . . However, he is best remembered for his policies of peace. His famous decree in 539 b.c. (2 Chron. 36:22–23; Ezra 1:1–4) set free the captives Babylon had taken during its harsh rule. Among these prisoners were the Jews taken from Jerusalem in 586 b.c. They were allowed to return to rebuild the temple and city. Along with this freedom Cyrus restored the valuable treasures of the temple taken during the exile.[59]

Four more descriptions of God's servant (v. 2b). God predicts that Cyrus is the one who will (1) deliver up nations, (2) subdue kings, and (3/4) make them like dust and chaff. In his second vision, Daniel described Cyrus and the armies of Persia as a ram, "butting westward, northward, and southward, and no *other* beasts could stand before him nor was there anyone to rescue from his power, but he did as he pleased and magnified *himself*" (Dan. 8:4). All of it was by the purpose of God.[60]

Seventh description of God's servant (vv. 3-4). Cyrus would pursue the kings passing by in safety without any who could oppose (v. 3). Cyrus ruled and conquered virtually without opposition from 550-530.[61] Cyrus was the human

---

[59] Mike Mitchell, "Cyrus," ed. Chad Brand et al., *Holman Illustrated Bible Dictionary*, cited in electronic form with Logos Libronix (Nashville, TN: Holman Bible Publishers, 2003), 377–378.

[60] Daniel prophesied that once Persia fulfilled God's purposes, He would raise up the Greeks to overthrow Persia (Dan. 2:32, 39; 7:6; 8:5-8, 21; 11:3-4).

[61] Grogan, "Isaiah," 250.

actor, but all of this was by the hand of God (v. 4). Who has accomplished this? God answers, "I, the Lord, am the first, and with the last. I am He" (cf. 46:8-11).[62]

The implications of a sovereign God (vv. 5-7)

The coastlands have seen the Persians coming and they are terrified (v. 5a). Their thought is that perhaps they might come together with some kind strategy to stop the eastern hoards (vv. 5b-6). Maybe the answer lies in more idols, so they quickly go to work to make more gods (v. 7).[63] Isaiah wants them to recognize the folly of idols, the sin that sent them into exile:

> In order to show the Israelite audience how ridiculous this worldview is, the prophet describes their deluded trust in idols made by skilled craftsmen, goldsmiths, and other workers (41:7). . . . In order to show how precarious the strength of their faith in the idol was, the prophet explains that it all depends on the nail or peg that will keep the idol standing up securely on a pedestal. If that gives away the idol is in danger of falling over. Can salvation and strength come from this source?[64]

The answer is "No, there is no salvation anywhere except in Yahweh."

Israel need not fear the work of Cyrus (vv. 8-20)

With the opening statement "But you," verse 8 introduces a sharp contrast from the preceding discussion. Israel is not like the nations. Therefore, she must not act like them. Isaiah unfolds four crucial truths that Israel needed to believe.

Israel still has a special covenant relationship (vv. 8-10)

The first truth God wants Israel (cf. Gen. 32:28) to remember is the special covenant relationship that they have with God (v. 8). Israel alone has the privilege of being known as God's "servant" (*'ebed*).[65] Israel alone has the privilege

---

[62] The piling up of these descriptions and titles make the emphatic point that Yahweh is the one true God who is both eternal and sovereign over all the affairs of life (Isa. 43:10; 44:6; 48:12; John 8:58; 18:5; Rev. 1:8, 17; 22:13).

[63] Wolf, *Interpreting Isaiah*, 188.

[64] Smith, *Isaiah 40-66*, 131.

[65] To modern ears, the idea of servant (i.e., slave) carries little value, but in the ANE this was a rich expression when used in relation to a king or deity (cf. Exod. 14:31; Num. 12:7; 2 Sam. 3:18; 7:5; 2 Kings 17:13). This is the first of multiple uses of this

of having been "chosen" by God (*bachar*).⁶⁶ Israel alone has the privilege of being the seed of God's friend Abraham (2 Chron. 20:7; Jas. 2:23).⁶⁷ God took Abraham all the way from Mesopotamia to be His people, a choice God will never revoke (v. 9; Amos 3:2; Rom. 11:1-2, 29). Therefore, they need not fear like the pagans. With this in mind, Oswalt gives us this reminder: "We must experience the wonder that sin cannot change God's love for us, and realize that he will do everything necessary to redeem us, even before we decide how to respond to Him."⁶⁸

God tells them, "Do not fear, for I am with you; do not anxiously look about you, for I am your God. I will strengthen you, surely I will help you; surely I will uphold you with My righteous right hand" (v. 10). God will forever be faithful and true to His own promises (i.e., His righteousness). Martin explains,

> Even though Israel was exiled because of sin and unbelief, she still was not rejected by God. Since the covenant the Lord made with Abraham was unconditional (Gen. 15), his descendants need not fear. The Lord remains their God (cf. Isa. 43:3) so He will continue to be with them (cf. 43:5) and strengthen (cf. 40:31), help (cf. 41:13–14), and uphold them.⁶⁹

Because God is faithful, Israel need not fear, the same admonition that applies to us today (Matt. 28:10, 20; John 14:27; 2 Tim. 2:11-13; Heb. 13:5).

Israel need not fear for God will fight for her (vv. 11-14)

The second reason Israel need not fear is because the Lord will fight for her. Israel is going to have many painful days in the ages ahead, but God will not let the enemies bring her to ruin.

---

expression in chs. 40-66. The term is found twenty-one times in 40-55 and ten times in 56-66 (often parallel with "chosen"; cf. 41:8, 9; 42:1; 43:10; 44:1, 2; 45:4; 65:9, 15). Several uses, such as here, refer to the nation as a whole (cf. Isa. 41:8; 42:19; 43:10; 44:1, 21), but other sections refer to one promised Servant who will save the nation from its sin, Jesus Christ (42:1-9; 49:1-13; 50:4-11; 52:13-53:12).

⁶⁶ God loved/chose Abraham with an eternal promise (Gen. 12:1-3; Neh. 9:7) that his family would be His chosen nation forever (Deut. 4:37; 7:6-9; Amos 3:2). Young explains that "not of its own volition did the nation become the Lord's servant, but only through sovereign grace. The choice was on God's part, and in that He chose Israel, He did not choose other nations but passed them by. By a calling of grace God chose Israel and set her apart to be His servant" (Young, *The Book of Isaiah, vol. 3*, 81).

⁶⁷ The term friend (*'oheb*) is not the common word for friend, but comes from the root "to love" (ibid., 82).

⁶⁸ Oswalt, *The Book of Isaiah: Chapters 40-66*, 91.

⁶⁹ Martin, "Isaiah," 1094.

No enemy will destroy Israel (vv. 11-12). Many nations (past, present, and future) have sought to destroy Israel. God's promise is that He will bring them to ruin (v. 11). This promise is part of the Abrahamic covenant: "I will bless those who bless you and I will curse those who curse you" (Gen. 12:1-3; cf. Zech. 2:8). God repeats this promise so that they might truly believe (v. 12; cf. Isa. 60:12; Zech. 12:1-9; 14:3, 12).

Israel need not fear (vv. 13-14). Because of God's promise that no enemy will prevail, Israel should not live in fear (v. 13).[70] Therefore, says God, "Do not fear, you worm Jacob, you men of Israel; I will help you, declares the Lord, and your Redeemer is the Holy One of Israel" (v. 14).[71] This is the first of thirteen uses of the term Redeemer (*Go'el*; cf. 43:1, 14; 44:6, 22-24; 47:4; 48:17, 20; 49:7, 26; 52:9; 54:5, 8; 59:20; 60:16; 63:9). Elsewhere, the term often speaks about a close relative who steps in to help their family member in crisis,[72] but here, it is the Lord Himself. The key truth Israel needs to understand is that God is faithful to His Word.

Israel will find strength from God to stand (vv. 15-16)

The third reason Israel need not fear is because God will give her strength to endure. He will empower His people so that they will be able to defeat their foes. He will make His people "like a sharp threshing sledge with double edges" (v. 15). Smith explains, "The threshing sled was a wooden platform with sharp stones or metal embedded on the underside. It was used in the threshing process in order to separate the grain from the stalk."[73] God will strengthen His people to stand, fight, and endure, a truth that will see its ultimate outworking during the Great Tribulation Period (cf. Zech. 12:1-9; Mic. 4:10-13).

The enemies will seek her destruction, but by God's enabling grace, Israel will not fall. Rather, the Lord will bring the nations to such ruin that Israel "will winnow them, and the wind will carry them away, and the storm will scatter

---

[70] Because the Lord holds their hand, they will never stumble (cf. 42:6; 45:1; 51:18).
[71] God calls them "You worm," an expression carrying the idea of mortal and insignificant (cf. Job 25:6; Ps. 22:6) (Young, *The Book of Isaiah, vol. 3*, 87).
[72] There are a variety of ways they might do this, e.g., (1) saving them from financial ruin (Lev. 25:25; Ruth 4), or (2) avenging murder (Num. 35:21-27; Deut. 19:6). Isaiah often uses this expression in association with other titles, too: Lord of Hosts, Holy One of Israel, Mighty One of Jacob, King of Israel, First and Last, The One who formed You from the Womb, The One who made everything, God of the whole earth, Our Father (Oswalt, *The Book of Isaiah: Chapters 40-66*, 93).
[73] Smith, *Isaiah 40-66*, 137.

them" (v. 16; cf. Dan. 2:35; Ps. 1:4). Israel will suffer greatly during the Great Tribulation Period, but God will bring her through it (Isa. 40:2; 48:10; cf. Jer. 30:7, 11; 46:28; Dan. 12:7, 10; Amos 9:8-10), and in the end, says God, "you will rejoice in the Lord; You will glory in the Holy One of Israel" (v. 16b; cf. Isa. 12:1-6; Zeph. 3:14-17). Israel should not fear.

Israel will see a day of restoration (vv. 17-20)

Isaiah gives a fourth reason why Israel must not fear. This is God's promise that one day He will satisfy the empty longings of His people and give them a day of restoration. Isaiah does this by painting a beautiful agricultural picture of a land that was desolate and parched (v. 17) getting restored by an abundant outpouring of mighty waters (vv. 18-20).

The present miseries of a parched nation (v. 17). Isaiah often portrays the spiritual character of Israel with agricultural imagery. Spiritually speaking, Israel has been a parched and barren wasteland. These expressions "afflicted and needy" are found elsewhere, oftentimes referring to the afflicted believing remnant (Deut. 15:11; 24:14; Pss. 35:10; 37:14; 40:17; 70:5; 86:10; 109:22; Prov. 31:20; Jer. 20:13; 22:16; Zech. 11:11; Matt. 5:3). These "afflicted" ones are the people who hunger and thirst for righteousness (Matt. 5:6). He will fill them.

God's outpouring will restore the barren nation (vv. 18-20). One day the people will cry out (Zech. 12:10), and God's promise is that He will answer with a mighty outpouring of grace—spiritual waters poured out by the Holy Spirit to refresh, regenerate, and transform a desert wasteland into a spiritual garden (v. 28; cf. Isa. 30:25; 32:15; 35:6-7; 43:18ff.; 44:3-5; 48:21). The barren deserts that had no life will become a place for fruitful vegetation (v. 19).[74] This, dear friends, is what God will do for Israel (and the whole earth) in the Millennial Kingdom. God's purpose is to teach His people about His faithful love (v. 20; cf. Isa. 48:7; 57:19; 65:17-18).

Dumb idols cannot do what the Lord does (vv. 21-29)

God has made His case, the case that He began to lay out in 41:1. Can the idols tell the future and make it come to fulfillment like the God of Israel? The answer is "No." Here in verses 21-29, God rebukes the idol and anyone who would be so foolish to trust in one. God does this with a three-fold challenge to the idol to demonstrate that they are false, weak, impotent and worthless.

---

[74] Cedar, acacia, myrtle, olive, and juniper trees are not found in parched deserts, but God will make it happen in the Millennial Kingdom. This is a message to the Amillennial interpreter that they should not deny what God says He will do.

First challenge to prove the folly of idols (vv. 21-23)

Isaiah's Spirit-inspired argument is that a true god can predict the future and fulfill it. Based on this supposition, the King of Jacob, a title found only here (cf. King of Israel in 44:6), invites the idols to present their evidence (*rîyb*, their case; cf. Hos. 4:1; Mic. 6:1). Surely a god can predict the future (v. 22).[75] The idols cannot predict or explain the "former" things nor the future things (v. 23). True prophets can do both (Deut. 18:15-22; 1 Sam. 3:19-21), but the idols can do neither. One feels the sense of frustration when God says, "Indeed, do good or evil, that we may anxiously look about us and fear together." In other words, "Do something!" God gave them their day in court, but not surprisingly, "none of these gods said anything when God asked for predictions."[76] Idols are supreme folly!

Second challenge to prove the folly of idols (vv. 24-25)

Idols are folly (v. 24). With the complete lack of evidence, God gives His full condemnation of the idol. We see the anger and frustration when Isaiah says, "Behold, you are of no account [*'ayin*, nothing], and your work amounts to nothing [*'epha'*, worthless]. He who chooses you is an abomination [*to'ebah*, detestable, loathsome]" (v. 24; cf. 44:9).

God can tell the future (v. 25). Once again God announces the coming of Cyrus who will fulfill His purpose,[77] and once again, we see it is the work of Yahweh to stir up his chosen vessel who will tread the nations under foot. When Isaiah says that Cyrus will call on the name of the Lord, this should not be understood that he was saved, for Isaiah 45:4-5 seem to make it clear that he was not. Nevertheless, even though Cyrus was not saved, he did recognize that the God of Israel was the One who gave him victories over the nations (Ezra 1:1-4; Isa. 43:1; 44:5; 45:3, 4).[78]

Third challenge to prove the folly of idols (vv. 26-29)

It is time for one more challenge. Will the idols produce any evidence that they are gods?
The idols fail once again (v. 26). Has any idol ever predicted the future as God does? God says, "Surely there was no one who declared; surely there was no one who proclaimed; surely there was no one who heard your words."

---

[75] It seems that this idea of "former" things is referring to past events, and that God is challenging the idols to declare their meaning and significance (cf. Isa. 42:9; 43:9, 18; 46:9; 48:3).
[76] Ibid., 145.
[77] The armies of Persia descended southward to invade Babylon (Jer. 50:3, 9; 51:11).
[78] Young, *The Book of Isaiah, vol. 3*, 102.

God gave Israel her prophets (vv. 27-29). The idols cannot tell the future, but God gave Israel true prophets who could predict the future (v. 27).[79] Sadly, Israel did not listen, but turned aside to lifeless idols (v. 28). The final verdict is that "all of them are false; their works are worthless; their molten images are wind and emptiness" (v. 29; cf. 41:12).

Summary and application

The contemporary church has been overrun with false prophets since the rise of the Pentecostal/Charismatic movement beginning in 1901. Sadly, the spread of the Charismatic movement has created an environment where huge portions of Christianity give heed to false prophets, much in the same way that the people of Israel fell prey to false prophets. Christians need to stick to inspired Scripture and reject the empty claims of the modern-day idols (Matt. 7:15; 2 Tim. 3:16; 2 Pet. 1:21; 2:1-3; 1 John 4:1; Rev. 22:18-19).

THE CHOSEN SERVANT (42:1-25)

Back in 41:8, God called Israel "My servant." Here in chapter 42 Isaiah introduces us to another one of God's servants. This Servant, however, is not one who needed to be told not to fear because of her own sins. Rather, this Servant is One who will accomplish great deeds in the name of Yahweh.

Chapter 42 reads as follows: "1 Behold, My Servant, whom I uphold; My chosen one *in whom* My soul delights. I have put My Spirit upon Him; He will bring forth justice to the nations. 2 He will not cry out or raise *His voice,* nor make His voice heard in the street. 3 A bruised reed He will not break and a dimly burning wick He will not extinguish; He will faithfully bring forth justice. 4 He will not be disheartened or crushed until He has established justice in the earth; and the coastlands will wait expectantly for His law. 5 Thus says God the Lord, Who created the heavens and stretched them out, Who spread out the earth and its offspring, Who gives breath to the people on it, and spirit to those who walk in it, 6 I am the Lord; I have called You in righteousness; I will also hold You by the hand and watch over You; and I will appoint You as a covenant to the people, as a light to the nations, 7 to open blind eyes, to bring out prisoners from the dungeon and those who dwell in darkness from the prison. 8 I am the Lord; that is My name, I will not give My glory to another, nor My praise to graven images. 9 Behold, the former things have come to pass; now I declare new things; before they spring forth I proclaim *them* to you. 10 Sing to the Lord a new song; *sing* His praise from the end of the earth, you who go down to the sea, and all that is in it, you islands, and those who dwell on them. 11 Let the wilderness and its cities lift up *their voices,* the settlements where Kedar inhabits.

---

[79] Some see Cyrus as this "messenger of good news."

Let the inhabitants of Sela sing aloud; let them shout for joy from the tops of the mountains; 12 let them give glory to the Lord and declare His praise in the coastlands. 13 The Lord will go forth like a warrior; He will arouse *His* zeal like a man of war; He will utter a shout; yes, He will raise a war cry; He will prevail against His enemies. 14 I have kept silent for a long time; I have kept still and restrained Myself. *Now* like a woman in labor I will groan; I will both gasp and pant. 15 I will lay waste the mountains and hills and wither all their vegetation; I will make the rivers into coastlands and dry up the ponds. 16 I will lead the blind by a way they do not know; in paths they do not know I will guide them; I will make darkness into light before them and rugged places into plains. These are the things I will do, and I will not leave them undone. 17 They will be turned back *and* be utterly put to shame, who trust in idols, who say to molten images, You are our gods. 18 Hear, you deaf, and look, you blind, that you may see. 19 Who is blind but My servant, or so deaf as My messenger whom I send? Who is so blind as he that is at peace *with Me*, or so blind as the servant of the Lord? 20 You have seen many things, but you do not observe *them; your* ears are open, but none hears. 21 The Lord was pleased for His righteousness' sake to make the law great and glorious. 22 But this is a people plundered and despoiled; all of them are trapped in caves, or are hidden away in prisons; they have become a prey with none to deliver *them,* and a spoil, with none to say, Give *them* back! 23 Who among you will give ear to this? Who will give heed and listen hereafter? 24 Who gave Jacob up for spoil, and Israel to plunderers? Was it not the Lord, against whom we have sinned, and in whose ways they were not willing to walk, and whose law they did not obey? 25 So He poured out on him the heat of His anger and the fierceness of battle; and it set him aflame all around, yet he did not recognize *it;* and it burned him, but he paid no attention" (42:1-25).

Back in chapter 41, we saw how God used the term servant to refer to the corporate nation of Israel. We also saw how God was at work to raise up one special servant (Cyrus) who would accomplish God's purposes by overthrowing Babylon and setting Israel free from Babylon.[80] This chapter tells us about a different Servant (Messiah). This chapter can be broken down into two sections: (1) the chosen Servant who brings justice (vv. 1-9), (2) the Servant's new song (vv. 10-25).

The chosen Servant who brings justice (vv. 1-9)

This passage introduces one special Servant, namely Jesus Christ. Isaiah

---

[80] Even though I have used the term "servant" here to refer to Cyrus' role in God's plan, Isaiah does not actually use this word for Cyrus. Interestingly, though, Isaiah does use the term *mashiyach* for him (45:1). From ch. 41 through ch. 48, Cyrus is a central figure for accomplishing God's purposes in the near term, but from ch. 49 through ch. 53 that central figure is Christ (Wolf, *Interpreting Isaiah*, 190).

immediately indicates the importance of the message by use of the word "behold" (*hen*). This passage is believed to be the first of four particular passages in Isaiah that are sometimes called *The Servant Songs* (a label coined by the commentator Bernhard Duhm). These Servant Songs are prophetic units that speak very directly about Jesus Christ (THE Servant), and what He would one day accomplish for God.[81] Contextual exegesis and New-Testament usage give us a clear connection that these passages are rightly to be taken as direct prophecies of Jesus Christ (Matt. 8:17; 12:18-21; Luke 22:37; 23:33-34; John 12:38; Rev. 7:16-17, etc.).[82]

The divine equipping of the Servant (v. 1a)

The first observation we make is how He has been equipped by God for the task of redemption. This Servant is the chosen one whom God upholds (*tamak*, i.e., supports), and in whom He takes great delight (*ratsah*). This Servant is no ordinary human being. Indeed, Peter tells us that He was "foreknown" from the foundation of the world to come and accomplish God's redemption (1 Pet. 1:20).

This Servant is the One who will come in the full power of God, for God will pour His Spirit out on the Servant in full measure, a promise repeated several times (11:1-2; 48:16; 61:1). This is the anointing that took place at the beginning of Christ's ministry (Matt. 3:13-17; Mark 1:10; Luke 3:22; John 1:32-34; 3:34) when the Father spoke from heaven and declared that Jesus was His beloved Son in whom He was well pleased (cf. Luke 9:35). This Servant comes in the fulness of God's power to accomplish God's saving purposes.[83] Isaiah tells us what these purposes are in verses 1b-7 where we learn about the Servant's mission.

The righteous mission of the Servant (vv. 1b-7)

When Christ came into this world, He came with the knowledge that He had a plan to fulfill, and that plan was to perfectly fulfill God's will in all that He did. In John 5:17 Jesus said, "My Father is working until now, and I Myself

---

[81] Oswalt explains that "there is an atmospheric change at these four places in the text (here; 49:1-6; 50:4-9; 52:13-53:12) (Oswalt, *The Book of Isaiah: Chapters 40-66*, 107). As already noted, in various passages "servant" refers to corporate Israel (Isa. 41:8-9; 42:19; 43:10; 44:1, 2, 21; 45:4; 48:20). Furthermore, we also see numerous uses of "servant" for individual believers (20:3; 22:20; 37:35; 44:26; 54:17; 56:6; 60:12; 63:17; 65:8, 9, 13, 14, 15; 66:14). Commentators make different breaks on which verses they include in the Servant Songs.

[82] Ibid., 108.

[83] The B.C. Targums saw this as Messiah (Young, *The Book of Isaiah, vol. 3*, 108).

am working." In 5:30 Jesus said, "I can do nothing on My own initiative. As I hear, I judge; and My judgment is just, because I do not seek My own will, but the will of Him who sent Me" (cf. John 4:34; 6:38).

He makes right all the wrongs (v. 1b). The Servant will "bring forth justice (*mishpat*) to the nations." His calling is to make things right, something this world has desperately needed ever since Adam introduced the curse. By God's common grace, many human rulers have sought to implement justice for their people,[84] but in the end their efforts have always been flawed, and they have never erased the ubiquitous presence of injustice (Isa. 1:4, 21-23; Mic. 3:1-4, 9-12; 7:1-4). God's Servant will bring perfect, never-ending justice to man (Isa. 9:7; 11:3-5; 16:5; 32:1; cf. Ps. 72).

He brings tender grace to a needy world (vv. 2-4). Human rulers often exercise their rule with brute power. God's Servant, however, will exercise His rule with tender grace—tender grace for those who humble themselves to fear the Lord and receive His forgiveness (v. 2).[85]

Isaiah uses three negations to remind us that the Servant will come in meekness, not with loud fanfare. There is no better picture of this tender grace than the statement "a bruised reed He will not break and a dimly burning wick He will not extinguish;[86] He will faithfully bring forth justice" (v. 3; cf. Matt. 12:13-21). Oswalt explains,

> Whereas all the other royal figures who have claimed to set up justice on the earth have done so through a gleeful use of their power to smash and rebuild, this One will be radically different. He is so far from smashing the mighty that he will not even break off the reed that is bent over and cracked. Rather, He will support it and straighten it. . . . He will not even puff out the most dimly guttering lamp wick (smoldering wick). Rather, He will trim it and rest it more deeply in the oil.[87]

---

[84] Oswalt cites the law code of King Hammurabi as an illustration (Oswalt, *The Book of Isaiah: Chapters 40-66*, 109, n. 12).
[85] King David explains, "The Lord has compassion on those who fear Him" (Ps. 103:13). Tender grace does not obviate the reality that this Servant is the One who comes with vengeance on all sinners to bring in a righteous kingdom (Isa. 2:12; 13:6; 34:2, 8; 35:4; 61:2b; 63:1-6; cf. Rev. 19:11-21).
[86] Sennacherib, on the other hand, bragged about the way he destroyed: "With my many chariots I came up to the heights of the mountains, to the remotest parts of Lebanon; and I cut down its tall cedars *and* its choice cypresses, and I will go to its highest peak, its thickest forest" (Isa. 37:24).
[87] Ibid., 111.

Isaiah tells us that the Servant's mission is not to crush broken sinners, but to gently restore them (cf. 11:4). Later in the third Servant Song we see a similar idea: "The Lord God has given Me the tongue of disciples, that I may know how to sustain the weary one with a word" (Isa. 50:4). He sustains those who are weary and come to Him for grace. The giving of tender grace is the mission of the Servant—saving grace that comes at the cost of the dear Servant's own life.

Despite a world of opposition, He will not be disheartened or crushed until He has established justice in the earth; and the coastlands will wait expectantly for His law (v. 4; cf. 51:5).[88] Like no one else ever could, the Servant will succeed in bringing tender grace to a needy world: "As God's [special] Servant, Jesus did what Israel could never do. He perfectly carried out the will of the father so that people everywhere may believe in the Holy One of Israel."[89]

He restores sinners to God (vv. 5-7). At the heart of the Servant's mission is His calling to save sinners: "For the Son of Man has come to seek and to save that which was lost" (Luke 19:10). Paul wrote, "It is a trustworthy statement, deserving full acceptance, that Christ Jesus came into the world to save sinners" (1 Tim. 1:15).

Here in verses 5-7, God tells us that the heart of the Servant's mission is to save sinners. This declaration begins with God identifying Himself as the Creator and Lord of the whole universe (v. 5; cf. 37:16; 40:22; 44:24; 45:12, 18; 48:13; 51:13; Pss. 102:25; 104:2).[90] He is "the incomparable One who has exclusive right to the cosmos and who maintains an exclusive care for it and its inhabitants."[91] He is the One who has sent His Servant to fulfill these saving purposes for both the Jews and the Gentiles.

The first aspect of the Servant's work is to restore apostate Israel, for God has appointed Him to be a "Covenant to the people" (cf. Isa. 49:8; Acts 26:17-18).[92] That is, the Servant is the One who will bring Israel back to God under a New Covenant (Jer. 31:31-34). The blood has been shed for this covenant to be established (Luke 22:20), but we await the day when Israel will enter that

---

[88] English translations do not convey the wordplay of the Hebrew text in that the word for "disheartened" (*kahah*) is same word for "dimly burning above," i.e., "He will not burn dimly" (absolute dedication to the mission).

[89] Martin, "Isaiah," 1095.

[90] He is "the God" (*Ha'El*), the Lord (*Yahweh*), the Creator (*Bore'*), the Stretcher (*Roqa'*), the Spreader (*Noteh*), and the Giver (*Nothen*).

[91] Oswalt, *The Book of Isaiah: Chapters 40-66*, 117.

[92] The Servant is not the covenant, but He represents and establishes it.

covenant at the second coming (Matt. 25:31-46). He will accomplish what no other man ever could. Grogan explains: "It was, in fact, to be only through the Servant of the Lord (Is. 52:13-53:12), not through Israel's suffering without him, that salvation would be brought to the earth."[93]

Second, the Servant is also said to be "a Light to the nations" (v. 6b; cf. Isa. 2:2-4; 11:10; 19:18-25; 42:1-4; 49:6-8; 60:1-14; John 4:42; 8:12; 9:5; 1 John 4:14). God gave His Son so that whoever believes in Him (no distinction between Jews or Gentiles) will receive the forgiveness He accomplished when He gave Himself to satisfy God's wrath (cf. Rom. 3:21-31). Isaiah vividly describes this spiritual salvation with physical imagery that He will come, "to open blind eyes, to bring out prisoners from the dungeon and those who dwell in darkness from the prison."[94] Smith summarizes it well:

> The specific purposes of the servant (42:7) go far beyond anything that the sinful people of Israel or the pagan nations could do for themselves. Israel is repeatedly seen as sinful and blind (6:10; 29:18; 42:18; 43:8), and the idol worshippers among the nations need to have their eyes opened so that they will reject idolatry (44:18). In earlier messages Isaiah announced that God (35:5) or a righteous king (the Messiah) would accomplish the task of removing the blindness from the eyes of people so that they can see (35:3). Then they will see the light in all of its many meanings.... These promises of freedom and the opening of eyes do not apply just to Israel; they apply to all the nations and most of them were not in Babylonian exile. Therefore, the best approach is to interpret these phrases as metaphors of God's deliverance of people from the prison of spiritual darkness (blindness) and ignorance (9:2; 42:19–20; 43:8; 44:18–19) through the work of the servant.[95]

Israel will receive deliverance from long ages of physical oppression (i.e., prison), but for all who believe (Jew and Gentile), the heart of this deliverance is spiritual redemption from sin.

The doxological calling of the Servant (vv. 8-9)

Philippians 2:5-11 tells us that the redeeming work of Christ exalts and glorifies God (cf. Eph. 1:6, 12, 14). Jesus looked ahead to the cross and the

---

[93] Grogan, "Isaiah," 255.

[94] This kingdom imagery certainly will include a literal fulfilling, but clearly there is a spiritual aspect that stands behind it all that refers to the freedom from curse that will come to all kingdom citizens (cf. Isa. 6:9-10; 29:18; 32:3; 35:5; 42:18-20; 49:6; 61:1-2; John 8:31-32; 9:40-41; Acts 26:17-18; Col. 1:13).

[95] Smith, *Isaiah 40-66*, 168–169.

resurrection and He prayed these words, "Father, the hour has come; glorify Your Son, that the Son may glorify You" (John 17:1, 24). The mission of God's Servant was doxological. This is the message in verses 8-9.

All glory belongs to God alone (v. 8). God declares, "I am the Lord, that is My name; I will not give My glory to another, nor My praise to graven images." Yahweh is a holy God of glory (Isa. 6:3; 24:23; 61:1-3; 66:19),[96] and all the glory belongs to Him and not idols (cf. Isa. 45:20-25).[97] Oswalt explains,

> God's glory lies in his capacity to do all the things the idols cannot. Because he alone transcends the cosmos, he alone can explain the course of history; he alone can turn that course in a whole new direction and tell the world in advance that he is going to do it.[98]

God's glory will be magnified by the Servant (v. 9). God is going to glorify His name once again by telling the world about the yet-to-come redeeming work of His Servant. The "former things" which He predicted already come to pass (e.g., the exodus and Babylonian exile and release by Cyrus), but now it is time to declare the new things (cf. 41:26-27; 43:18-19; 44:3-5) that are about to "spring forth" (i.e., complete redemption and restoration by the work of the Servant).[99] Pfeiffer explains, "All the glory for accurately predicting coming events is to be kept by God alone."[100]

The Servant's new song (vv. 10-25)

The idea of a "new song" refers to fresh praise for a new work of salvation. Isaiah says that a New Song shall be sung, for God is the One, who has established justice and delivered from oppression (cf. Pss. 33:3; 40:3 [MT 4]; 96:1; 98:1; 144:9; Rev. 14:3).[101]

---

[96] Sometimes glory (*kabod*) refers to a physical manifestation of glory, but many times (as here) it speaks about reputation, renown, and all that is worthy of praise.
[97] God will not tolerate men giving glory to idols that belongs to Him alone. This would not preclude human celebrations such as graduation ceremonies, etc.
[98] Oswalt, *The Book of Isaiah: Chapters 40-66*, 119.
[99] Isaiah's use of this word "spring forth" (Heb. *tsamach*) would catch the ear of the keen Bible student since this is the root word that stands behind the messianic title "Branch" (*tsemech*; cf. Isa. 4:2; Jer. 23:5; 33:15; Zech. 3:8; 6:12; 2 Sam. 23:5 uses the verb form where David celebrated the promise that would "spring forth").
[100] Pfeiffer, *The Wycliffe Bible Commentary: Old Testament*, Is 42:5.
[101] Allen C. Myers, *The Eerdmans Bible Dictionary*, cited in electronic form with Logos Libronix (Grand Rapids, MI: Eerdmans, 1987), 761. Young explains that these "new songs" are particularly tied with "the wonders of the new age when the Servant of the

The call for believers to sing a new song (vv. 10-13)

This new song must not be sung merely within the boundaries of Israel, but it must be sung to the ends of the earth.[102]

The call to sing a new song (vv. 10-11). This call to sing goes out not only to the western world, the sea and the islands (v. 10), but also to every part of the world, e.g., to Kedar and the Arab world to the south and to Sela and the nomads in the east (v. 11). Indeed, "people everywhere should sing and shout to the Lord because of His victory over His enemies."[103]

The reason for the new song (vv. 12-13). God needs to be praised because of His great deeds (v. 12). He has defeated all His enemies (v. 13). Two thousand years ago the Servant defeated the curse of sin and death by dying on the cross to pay for our sins (Isa. 52:13-53:15), but for this defeat to become complete and final He must come again to wage war on evil and purge it from His creation.[104] This is exactly what is going to happen when Christ returns: "The Lord will go forth like a warrior; He will arouse *His* zeal like a man of war; He will utter a shout, yes, He will raise a war cry; He will prevail against His enemies" (cf. Isa. 59:16-18; Exod. 15:3; Pss. 2; 110; Zech. 14:3). God has sworn that He will purge this world of all evil, and God's people should rejoice that one day He will make right all wrongs (cf. Rev. 15:1-4; 16:4-7).

The inability of the blind to sing the new song (vv. 14-25)

Israel should have been the first to see these great deeds of God so that she might be the first to sing this new song, but sadly she will be the last, for when God made them these promises they did not believe, and when God sent them their Savior King they still did not believe (Isa. 53:1-3; cf. John 1:11; 12:37-41).[105] Isaiah once again reminds us of the hard-hearted, blinded condition of Israel with a series of three messages about the setting and context that would characterize Israel and the nations before the sending of the Servant.

First message about the setting (vv. 14-15). Verse 14 is interesting where God says, "I have kept silent for a long time; I have kept still and

---

Lord performs his matchless work of redemption" (Young, *The Book of Isaiah, vol. 3*, 125).

[102] As noted earlier, Isaiah's references to the "islands" look westward to the entire Gentile world (cf. 11:11; 24:15; 42:4, 10, 12; 49:1; 51:5; 60:9; 66:19).

[103] Martin, "Isaiah," 1096.

[104] Christians should rejoice in the righteousness and justice of God that assures He will destroy evil as a Man of War (Exod. 15; Isa. 63:3-4; Rev. 19:11-21).

[105] And to this very day they still sit in this state of disbelief.

restrained Myself. *Now* like a woman in labor I will groan; I will both gasp and pant." Verse 14 show us a picture how by the time of Christ's return, God will have allowed His wrath against sin to build up year after year, especially the evils done against His people Israel (cf. Zech. 2:8). Now, however, it is time to bring forth a judgment on such sin. Thus, the "long time" Isaiah speaks about refers to that extended period of persecution and affliction that began with the Babylonians and ends in the Great Tribulation. Wolf explains, "The Lord suffered when His people suffered, and He had to restrain Himself until the time of punishment was over."[106]

The day of restraint is coming to a close, and God says that His wrath will come pouring down upon the earth (v. 15).[107] This wrath will directed against a Christ-hating world, especially against those who have sought the destruction of Israel. Pfeiffer explains,

> Having restrained himself during their disciplinary sufferings, he would now burst forth in judgment upon the heathen powers symbolized by these mountains and hills, and the various water barriers of Babylonia that would keep the Jewish exiles in captivity (v. 15).[108]

Second message about the setting (vv. 16-17). God's eschatological work will also include the work of dealing with spiritual blindness. Verse 16 conveys the idea of both restoration and salvation to those whom He saves (v. 16; cf. 29:18; 35:5; 42:7),[109] but also shame and judgment to those who refuse to turn from idols (v. 17),[110] for the one who chooses an idol is an abomination (41:24). Idolatry was a huge problem in ancient times, and it is going to continue to be a problem until the return of Christ (Rev. 21:8).

Third message about the setting (vv. 18-25). Having declared His plans, God once again expresses His dismay at the hardness of His own people. Up to the time of the Babylonian captivity, the pride of the nation kept them from seeing their own sin. Israel always had its remnant, but most were unregenerate and blinded to their sin. Here in the closing verses of chapter 42 God expresses His dismay at the hardness of Israel.

---

[106] Wolf, *Interpreting Isaiah*, 192.

[107] The imagery of waste and devastation is all for symbolically picturing the outpouring of wrath, the very opposite of the kingdom restoration we see in ch. 35.

[108] Pfeiffer, *The Wycliffe Bible Commentary: Old Testament*, Is 42:5.

[109] God's salvation is likened to a bright and clear path.

[110] Eternal shame will be the heritage of the wicked (Isa. 1:29; 44:9, 11; 45:16). The intensity of the shame is magnified by the use of both the verb and cognate noun (Young, *The Book of Isaiah, vol. 3*, 130, n. 46).

How ironic it is that God commands Israel to hear and see, but they are deaf and blind (v. 18).[111] The servant God speaks to here is not the messianic Servant of 1-9, but the collective nation (v. 19; cf. 41:8; 43:10; 44:1, 2, 21).[112] This is the people of Yahweh who had been entrusted with the message of God (Isa. 53:1; Rom. 3:2; 9:4), but refused to believe. This is why they have now been cast out. It was because, says God, "You have seen many things, but you do not observe *them; your* ears are open, but none hears" (v. 20). Martin gives the following explanation:

> Later when Jews in the Babylonian Exile would read this chapter in Isaiah, they might wonder why they were experiencing such difficulties. . . . They *should* have been a light to the Gentiles (v. 6), helping others come to know God. But they failed. Though they saw and heard certain events they disregarded them (cf. 43:8; 48:8).[113]

God continues His rebuke by declaring that the purpose of His instruction (*torah*) is that it should be a great and glorious revelation for all of mankind (v. 21; cf. 2:3; 42:4; 51:4). God laments the results: "This is a people plundered and despoiled; all of them are trapped in caves, or are hidden away in prisons; they have become a prey with none to deliver *them,* and a spoil, with none to say, "Give *them* back!" (v. 22).[114] God's people are being taken away like cheap leftovers, and all they can do is hide for their lives. Israel's sin has plunged them into a long spiritual war, and God will not deliver them until the appointed time at the end of the age. In light of this disaster, God asks who it is that has done this to the nation. Isaiah answers, "Was it not the Lord, against whom we have sinned, and in whose ways they were not willing to walk, and whose law they did not obey?" (vv. 23-24). "In other words," says Isaiah, "we have no one to blame but ourselves" (cf. Isa. 49:14-15; 50:1; Dan. 9:1-19).

The final result was that God poured out on him "the heat of His anger [*chemah*, burning anger; cf. 44:15; 63:3; 66:15] and the fierceness of battle ['*ezuz*, fierce war violence]; and it set him aflame all around, yet he did not recognize *it;* and it burned him, but he paid no attention" (v. 25). Even while in exile in

---

[111] Terms like "see," "obey" and "hear" bring to mind Mosaic commands (cf. Deut. 28:15; 29:2-4) (Oswalt, *The Book of Isaiah: Chapters 40-66*, 131).
[112] The expression "at peace with Me" may mean "the one committed to me" (Grogan, "Isaiah," 258, n. 19). That is, here is this nation in a covenant relationship with the Living God, and yet there is no one else as blind as them.
[113] Martin, "Isaiah," 1096.
[114] Isaiah uses two different terms to describe the way that they have become spoil to the Gentiles: (1) "plundered/prey" (*bazaz*, plunder, spoil, the leftovers taken away in battle), and (2) "despoiled/spoil" (*shasah*, ransacked).

Babylon, they still did not deal with their sins has they needed to.[115] Smith summarizes:

> The paragraph ends with a dire reminder of what happens when people are not willing to listen to God's *tôrâ*, do not confess their sins, and do not repent. Unfortunately, the people did not understand why they were being consumed. The people did not "connect the dots."[116]

Summary and application

For over 2,600 years (since the beginning of the Assyrian and Babylonian invasions and exile), Israel has been paying a very high price for its refusal to listen to God. By this example, every one of us has an illustration about the danger of hardening our heart to the Word of God. Each one of us should be very quick to apply this lesson to our own lives lest we become hardened by the deceitfulness of sin and find ourselves under the chastising hand of God. Sin has a huge price tag, and we do well to learn from God's work with Israel that it is much better to repent quickly.

THE GREATNESS OF GOD ASSURES A FUTURE (43:1-28)

Chapter 43 continues the ideas found in 42:18-25. However, chapter 43 does this with a transition from the theme of rebuke to the theme of encouragement.[117]

Chapter 43 reads as follows: "1 But now, thus says the Lord, your Creator, O Jacob, and He who formed you, O Israel, do not fear, for I have redeemed you; I have called you by name; you are Mine! 2 When you pass through the waters, I will be with you; and through the rivers, they will not overflow you. When you walk through the fire, you will not be scorched, nor will the flame burn you. 3 For I am the Lord your God, the Holy One of Israel, your Savior. I have given Egypt as your ransom, Cush and Seba in your place. 4 Since you are precious in My sight, *since* you are honored and I love you, I will give *other* men in your place and *other* peoples in exchange for your life. 5 Do not fear, for I am with you; I will bring your offspring from the east, and gather you from the west. 6 I will say to the north, Give *them* up! And to the south, Do not hold *them* back. Bring My sons from afar and My daughters from the ends of the earth, 7 everyone who is called by My name, and whom I have created for My

---

[115] The books of Jeremiah and Ezekiel provide lots of proof for this problem. This is why the anger of the Lord has not turned away (5:25; 9:12, 17; 21; 10:4, 25; 12:1).
[116] Smith, *Isaiah 40-66*, 189.
[117] Oswalt, *The Book of Isaiah: Chapters 40-66*, 136.

glory, whom I have formed, even whom I have made. 8 Bring out the people who are blind, even though they have eyes, and the deaf, even though they have ears. 9 All the nations have gathered together so that the peoples may be assembled. Who among them can declare this and proclaim to us the former things? Let them present their witnesses that they may be justified, or let them hear and say, It is true. 10 You are My witnesses, declares the Lord, and My servant whom I have chosen, so that you may know and believe Me and understand that I am He. Before Me there was no God formed, and there will be none after Me. 11 I, even I, am the Lord, and there is no savior besides Me. 12 It is I who have declared and saved and proclaimed, and there was no strange *god* among you. So you are My witnesses, declares the Lord, and I am God. 13 Even from eternity I am He, and there is none who can deliver out of My hand; I act and who can reverse it? 14 Thus says the Lord your Redeemer, the Holy One of Israel, for your sake I have sent to Babylon, and will bring them all down as fugitives, even the Chaldeans, into the ships in which they rejoice. 15 I am the Lord, your Holy One, the Creator of Israel, your King. 16 Thus says the Lord, Who makes a way through the sea and a path through the mighty waters, 17 Who brings forth the chariot and the horse, the army and the mighty man (they will lie down together *and* not rise again; they have been quenched *and* extinguished like a wick): 18 Do not call to mind the former things, or ponder things of the past. 19 Behold, I will do something new; now it will spring forth; will you not be aware of it? I will even make a roadway in the wilderness, rivers in the desert. 20 The beasts of the field will glorify Me, the jackals and the ostriches, because I have given waters in the wilderness and rivers in the desert, to give drink to My chosen people. 21 The people whom I formed for Myself will declare My praise. 22 Yet you have not called on Me, O Jacob, but you have become weary of Me, O Israel. 23 You have not brought to Me the sheep of your burnt offerings, nor have you honored Me with your sacrifices. I have not burdened you with offerings, nor wearied you with incense. 24 You have bought Me not sweet cane with money, nor have you filled Me with the fat of your sacrifices. Rather, you have burdened Me with your sins; you have wearied Me with your iniquities. 25 I, even I, am the one who wipes out your transgressions for My own sake, and I will not remember your sins. 26 Put Me in remembrance; let us argue our case together; state your *cause,* that you may be proved right. 27 Your first forefather sinned, and your spokesmen have transgressed against Me. 28 So I will pollute the princes of the sanctuary, and I will consign Jacob to the ban and Israel to revilement" (43:1-28).

Throughout his ministry, Isaiah made it clear that Israel's sin is what would plunge the nation into ages of judgment (cf. 8:22), but he also made clear (as here) the good news that "a new day is at hand" and "God will soon act on behalf of his chosen people out of the purest grace" (cf. 9:1-7).[118] The great news is that God will never forsake His promises to His chosen people Israel.

---

[118] Ibid.

These promises highlight five precious attributes of God that should be a comfort to every believer.

By His faithfulness, God commands an end to all fear (vv. 1-7)

The first attribute of God we think of in chapter 43 is that of God's unchanging faithfulness. For that reason, Israel need not fear the future no matter how badly she might suffer for her transgressions.[119] Let us make three observations about this faithfulness that give us hope and not fear.

First observation: The declarations of God's faithfulness (v. 1)

The faithfulness of God is a comfort to every believer, for we know that even if we are faithless to Him, He always remains faithful to His promises (2 Tim. 2:13). If you truly belong to Christ, you can be assured that God will never reject you even if you have stumbled in your sinful weakness (John 5:24; 10:28-29). Here in verse 1 God makes five declarations about His own work to encourage the nation during its exile.

First declaration. The first thing God does is to declare Himself as the Creator (*Bore'*) of Jacob. He is Creator of the universe (42:5; 45:18), but He also is the sovereign Lord who made Jacob to become a people (Isa. 43:15; cf. Gen. 12:1-3; 35:9-12; Pss. 95:6; 100:3). Thus, if God is the One who made Jacob into a people and God says that they need not fear, they need not fear.

Second declaration. In parallel structure, God also says that He is the One who "formed" (*Yotser*) Israel to be a people. Thus, explains Smith,

> Although it may have appeared to some that Israel's life and livelihood was heavily determined by the nation's relationships to its political allies and dreadful rivals (42:22, 24), in reality a nation's past and future is primarily dependent on its relationship to God's acts of blessing or cursing.[120]

Thus, for Jacob/Israel, its destiny hinges ultimately upon the reality that

---

[119] Even though Judah was in exile, many Jews found that it was not as bad as it could have been. Most people were able to settle in appointed regions where they were able to build houses, operate businesses and prosper, a freedom and prosperity that is attested in the Babylonian document called "The Business Documents of Murashu Sons of Nippur" (Young, *The Book of Isaiah, vol. 3*, 141, n. 7). Sadly, when it came time to return after the fall of Babylon, many Jews did not want to leave (Isa. 52:11; Zech. 2:6; cf. Rev. 18:4 for an eschatological application).

[120] Smith, *Isaiah, 40-66*, 192.

Yahweh has created Israel to be His own people (Deut. 4:37; 7:6-9), and for this reason, she need not fear the future.[121]

Third declaration. Yahweh is the One who has redeemed Israel (*ga'al*). Isaiah makes repeated use of this theme (vv. 1, 3, 14; 44:6, 22, 23, 24), which here in verse 1 is probably best understood as God's work to bring Israel out of bondage to Egypt by placing His judgments on Egypt (cf. Exod. chs. 7-15; 34:20; Num. 3:45; 18:16).[122] By His choice of the patriarchs and redemption from Egypt, God has already made Israel His own people. Therefore, they need not fear the trials of exile.

Fourth and fifth declarations. God finishes His affirmation by telling them "I have called you by name; you are mine" (34:7; 43:21; 45:3-4). No doubt these words of assurance have been a tremendous comfort to the nation throughout the ages. Yes, their sin has sent them into exile, but even now He is still their God, and they are still His people (cf. Rom. 11:1-2).

Second observation: The implications of God's faithfulness (vv. 2-4)

The implication of God's gracious work is that no matter how badly they may suffer in exile, He will be with them to preserve them from utter ruin. God reaffirms the promise of safety (v. 2) and follows this with a reaffirmation of the reasons why (vv. 3-4).

The promise of safety (v. 2). God's promise is that whether the nation should pass through deep waters or scorching fires, He will be there with them, and they will not be overcome. History validates these faithful promises, for the people of Israel have gone through more trials than any other people group in the history of mankind, but God has never let them come to complete ruin. Thus, explains Martin,

> Because of God's past work in creating, redeeming, and caring for Israel, He would continue to protect her. Therefore in difficult times, pictured as floodwaters and fire, Israel should not give up and fear, for God would be with her and protect her.[123]

The reason for their safety (vv. 3-4). God has already told Israel why

---

[121] Young, *The Book of Isaiah, vol. 3*, 139.

[122] It could be possible to take the Hebrew perfect stem verb as being a prophetic perfect that is looking to the eschaton, but its placement in between several historical statements makes a past tense idea the better understanding.

[123] Martin, "Isaiah," 1097.

she need not fear, but He reaffirms these reasons once again (as in v. 1) by reminding them that He is their God and Savior who has redeemed them from ruin (v. 3).[124] It is all by grace, notes Pfeiffer,

> The ground for these promises of companionship and deliverance through suffering and trial was not any superiority or merit on the part of the Jews, but God's unmerited favor and grace, and his self-commitment as Father to his covenant people. He had granted to the Persians, beforehand, as a reward for their releasing captive Israel from Babylon, the country of Egypt and a portion of Ethiopia as additions to their empire (these being added in the reign of Cambyses, son of Cyrus).[125]

Furthermore, says God, "Since you are precious in My sight, *since* you are honored and I love you, I will give *other* men in your place and *other* peoples in exchange for your life" (v. 4). Other nations may experience an irreparable judgment as part of God's work, but none of it will ever mean the ruin of Israel. This is not because Israel has earned it, but God has graciously chosen to place His covenant love on Israel.[126] Israel need not fear because God has chosen to make them His people (cf. Jer. 30:1-11; 33:14-26).

Third observation: The results of God's faithfulness (vv. 5-7)

Because of His promises, God again tells His people not to fear, but in these verses, He also gives them the explicit promise that He will regather them from their dispersion and restore them as a nation. No matter where they have been scattered, He will bring back every one of His elect saints and restore them

---

[124] The concept of save/salvation is repeated many times in Isaiah with various forms of the term *yasha'*. The present use is a Hiphil participle translated as "Savior" (19:20; 43:3, 11; 45:15, 21; 47:15; 49:26; cf. Deut. 22:27; 28:29, 31; Judg. 3:9, 15; 6:36; 12:3). God again identifies Himself as the Holy One, another one of Isaiah's favorite titles (Oswalt, *The Book of Isaiah: Chapters 40-66*, 139, n. 16).

[125] Pfeiffer, *The Wycliffe Bible Commentary: Old Testament*, Is 43:1. Cush was just south of Upper Egypt; Seba was lower Sudan. Both were within Egypt's sphere of influence over history and would suffer the same fate as Egypt one day (Grogan, "Isaiah," 262, n. 3). Some think that the idea here is that Cyrus is being promised the prize of the Nile Valley in return for the Jews. Wolf explains, "Under the leadership of Cambyses, the Persians were able to conquer these lands, and this may be viewed as their reward for giving Israel its freedom (cf. Ezek. 29:18-19)" (Wolf, *Interpreting Isaiah*, 194).

[126] They are "precious" (*yaqar*) to God, "honored" (*kabad*) by God, and "loved" (*'ahab*) by God (stated emphatically by the use of the pronoun "I"), all marks of undeserved covenant favor (Mal. 1:2; Rom. 9:13).

in the messianic kingdom (vv. 5-6).[127] God says, that these are the ones who "are called by My name, and whom I have created for My glory, whom I have formed, even whom I have made" (v. 7; cf. Rom. 9:23). God never breaks His promises (Rom. 8:31-39; 11:25-36);[128] therefore, His people should not fear.

By His sovereignty, God will fulfill His Word (vv. 8-13)

In verses 1-7, we saw an emphasis on the faithfulness of God as the first of five divine attributes that should comfort our hearts. In this next section, we see an emphasis on a second attribute of God, His sovereignty. The promises God has made are staggering, so here in verses 8-13 God makes statements that remind us that His sovereignty assures His ability to fulfill them.[129] The broad call is for both Israel (the blind people) as well as the nations to recognize that no idol can predict and fulfill like He can.

The call to court (vv. 8-9)

Paul cites this verse twice in his letters to remind all of us that He is God, and we are not (Rom. 11:34; 1 Cor. 2:16). As we saw earlier, Isaiah often uses courtroom language to confront sinners. The purpose of this gathering is so that all men (Jews and Gentiles) might recognize that there is only one God who is capable of predicting the future and fulfilling it (v. 9).[130] If there is

---

[127] Many texts make it clear that God will save an elect remnant who will enjoy the blessings of the kingdom, but unbelieving Jews (and Gentiles) will be excluded (e.g., Isa. 10:20-23; 11:10-16; 27:12-13; 49:12; 59:20-21; 60:4; cf. Ezek. 20:36-38; 37:21-28; 39:25-29; Zech. 8:23; 10:9-12; 13:8-9; Mal. 3:3; Rom. 9:27-30). Some have sought to see these promises as fulfilled in the release from Babylon, but this explanation is not convincing for a number of reasons. This restoration is the same eschatological restoration that Moses spoke of in Deuteronomy 30:1-10, the restoration that accompanies a final regeneration to the corporate nation and a final settling in the promised land with a destruction to all her enemies.

[128] Hosea 11:9 reminds us that it is God's own nature as God that assures His faithfulness: "I will not execute my fierce anger; I will not destroy Ephraim again, for I am God and not man, the Holy One of Israel in your midst" (cf. Mal. 3:6).

[129] Wolf notes how Isaiah resumes his use of legal courtroom language such as was prominent in ch. 41, a style of language that also reminds us of The Song of Moses in Deuteronomy 32 (Wolf, *Interpreting Isaiah*, 194-195).

[130] The "former things" probably signify anything from the past that have been predicted and fulfilled. God already predicted and fulfilled former things, but He was also in the process of predicting new things that He would fulfill. His track record of doing this for the former things is evidence He can also do it with the things that are new and future (Oswalt, *The Book of Isaiah: Chapters 40-66*, 145-146).

someone who thinks that one of their idols can do the same, God challenges them to, "present their witnesses that they may be justified, or let them hear and say, It is true." God presents His evidence.

God presents incontrovertible evidence of His sovereignty (vv. 10-13)

Israel is called to the witness stand (vv. 10-11). God presents His case directly to Israel since they are the nation whom He chose (Gen. 12:1-3; 18:19; Exod. 19:5-6; Lev. 19:2; Deut. 4:32-40; 7:6-9; Amos 3:2).[131] Because Israel was the chosen servant nation (41:8, 9; 42:19; 43:10; 44:1, 2, 21; 48:20), God reminds them that *they* are the ones who should be witness to the fact that He alone is God (cf. 44:8). They should be able to testify that He alone is God, that before Him there was no God formed, that there will be none after Him, and that He is Lord, and there is no Savior beside Him (vv. 10-11; cf. 17:10; 43:3; 45:15, 21; 49:26; 60:16; 62:11; 63:8).

More testimony (vv. 12-13). God makes it clear that He alone is capable of predicting, fulfilling, and saving. There never should have been a "strange god" among them (v. 12),[132] but sadly there often was. The need of the moment was to know and believe that even from eternity Yahweh is God,[133] and that there is none who can deliver out of His hand, for He acts, and none can reverse it (v. 13). All the other gods are lies.

By His providence, God is using Babylon (vv. 14-17)

This section reintroduces us by name to Babylon who has not been mentioned by name since chapter 39. Here in verses 14-17, Isaiah reminds us about a third attribute of God that should turn every believer away from fear, and that is what we call providence. What is providence? One source explains that providence is,

> God's benevolent and wise superintendence of His creation.... In so doing He attends not only to apparently momentous events and people but also to those that seem both mundane and trivial. Thus, while He holds the lives of both kings and nations in His hand (cp. Isa. 40:21–26; Jer. 18:1–6), God also concerns Himself with the welfare of the lowly and meek (cp. Pss. 104:10–30; 107:39–43). Indeed, so all encompassing is God's attention to events within creation that nothing—not even the

---

[131] Because Israel broke the Mosaic Covenant, the church now occupies the place of being "the people of God" (cf. 1 Pet. 2:9) until the day when God once again restores Israel under a New Covenant (Rom. 11:1-2, 12, 15, 23-24, 25-36).

[132] I.e., idols.

[133] Smith notes that a more literal translation would be "even from today" (Smith, *Isaiah 40-66*, 204.

casting of lots—happens by chance (cp. Prov. 16:33).... To be true to the biblical witness, one's account of providence must provide both for the very active role which God plays in directing events toward ends which He chooses and for the responsibility which humans have for the way in which they contribute toward those ends.[134]

Providence is the work of God by which He employs natural means and processes to accomplish His purpose. This section highlights the providence of God by once again telling us that God is going to fulfill His purposes through the use Babylon. At a human level, Babylon was nothing more than another pagan nation that cared only for its own self-advancement, but the Bible shows us that God had a special purpose for using Babylon to fulfill His purposes. The message for Israel is that God is always in control, even in the midst of invasion and exile, and for this reason Israel must not fear. Isaiah reveals two needs that God will fulfill by His providence.

First need: Israel must be chastised (vv. 14-15)

From one perspective invasion and exile was not something God desired for His people,[135] but their transgression called for it, and God was going to use it for ultimate good.[136] This ultimate good will eventually include not only the restoration of a redeemed Israel, but also the worldwide spread of the gospel through the church.

God affirms His purpose (v. 14). Using three of His favorite names,[137] God pointedly explains that it was for their sake that He sent them to exile in Babylon, but it would not be permanent. The abrupt shift in this verse has led to several ways of explaining what Isaiah is saying. It is probably best to see Isaiah saying that not only was the exile for Israel's good, but also that Babylon herself will fall,[138] fleeing in the very ships they used to use for building riches (cf. Jer. 51:13-14). Keil explains,

> Herodotus (i. 194) describes the freight ships discharging in Babylon; and we know from other sources that the Chaldeans not only navigated the

---

[134] Douglas Blount, "Providence," *Holman Illustrated Bible Dictionary*, ed. Chad Brand et al., cited in electronic form with Logos Libronix (Nashville, TN: Holman Bible Publishers, 2003), 1340–1341.

[135] In Lamentation 3:33 we read, "[The Lord] does not afflict willingly."

[136] Daniel 12:7 says that in the Great Tribulation, God will, "[shatter] the power of the holy people."

[137] Redemption is a major theme in Isaiah (41:14; 43:14; 44:6, 24; 47:4; 48:17; 49:7, 26; 54:5, 8; 59:20; 60:16; 63:16; cf. 1:27 which uses the *padah* root).

[138] Thus, the waw attached to "bring down" is better rendered "but."

Euphrates, but the Persian Gulf as well, and employed vessels built by Phoenicians for warlike purposes also.[139]

The good news for Israel is that mighty Babylon will fall, and Israel need not fear. Smith reminds us that, "the destruction of Babylon was announced earlier in chaps. 13–14 and 21:1–10; so, this news of the fall of Babylon should not have surprised those who knew Isaiah's past preaching."[140]

God affirms His person (v. 15). God assures the certainty of this promise based on His own person: He is the living God. God will change the Babylonians from being the conquerors to the conquered, and Babylon's ships will now be used for refuge.[141] Nevertheless, Israel must first be chastised.

Second need: Israel's enemies must be overthrown (vv. 16-17)

Babylon will fulfill a purpose to judge God's people, but in the end no enemy of God can remain, much less the power that attacked His own people. Babylon must fall, and the Lord is mighty enough to make it happen, for He can make a path through mighty waters just as He did once before at the Exodus (v. 16).[142] Building on the Exodus imagery, God is the One who also "brings forth the chariot and the horse, the army and the mighty man (They will lie down together *and* not rise again; they have been quenched *and* extinguished like a wick" (v. 17). Israel has stumbled badly and an exile is the judgment, but God will redeem His people once again.

By His grace, God will restore (vv. 18-24)

Isaiah shows us a fourth attribute of God that reminds Israel why she need not fear the future, His grace. The grace of God has always been there for Israel, but sadly she did not respond to this grace with submissive faith. God once again announces a work of grace (vv. 18-21), but sadly they still were not willing to listen (vv. 22-24).

God declares a new work for His people Israel (vv. 18-21)

God begins to unfold the promise of something new and big. He has already spoken of this future grace (cf. e.g., 2:1-4; 4:2-6; 9:1-7, etc.), but now He is going to announce a work of grace that will eclipse anything He has ever done in the past.

---

[139] Carl Friedrich Keil and Franz Delitzsch, *Commentary on the Old Testament*, vol. 7, cited in electronic form with Logos Libronix (Peabody, MA: Hendrickson, 1996), 428.

[140] Smith, *Isaiah 40-66*, 205.

[141] Martin, "Isaiah," 1097.

[142] The Bible often uses Exodus imagery (cf. Exod. 14:16-28; Josh. 3:13; Neh. 9:11).

The future is going to eclipse the past (v. 18). Twice God tells His people to stop reflecting on the past. Yes, God's great work in the past is something to marvel over (e.g., the Exodus, the Conquest, Cyrus), but all of it pales in comparison with what He is going to do in the future.[143]

A marvelous new work (v. 19-21). God's new work is going to "spring forth" (*tsamach*; cf. 42:9), and it is something that Israel will not be able to miss. This work of God is one that will bring a complete transformation to the nation. This transformation will include physical transformations (vv. 19-21; cf. 11:6-9, 16; 19:23; 35:6-8; 40:3; 41:18; 44:3-4; 65:19-20, 25; 62:10), but these physical transformations are outward manifestations of the spiritual regeneration that underlies the outward.

The reason for this transformation is that God is pouring out rivers in the desert and waters in the wilderness. All of it, says God, is "to give drink to My chosen people." The imagery of a mighty outpouring of water is really symbolizing the outpouring of grace that will bring Israel to faith in the Son of God. God's purpose is to save His people, the people He formed for Himself, so that they might know Him and declare His praise. Kidner reminds us that we are still waiting for this final restoration of Israel.

> For its real fulfilment we must look beyond the modest homecomings from Babylon of the sixth and fifth centuries bc, although these are certainly in view, to the exodus which the Son of God accomplished at Jerusalem (Luke 9:31; *cf.* 1 Cor. 10:4, 11), which alone justifies the language of this and kindred passages.[144]

The invitation stands: "Ho! Everyone who thirsts, come to the waters; and you who have no money come, buy and eat. Come, buy wine and milk without money and without cost" (55:1). The invitation was there, but Israel's uncircumcised heart hindered her from coming to the waters she so desperately needed (Deut. 10:16; Jer. 4:4; 9:25-26; cf. Rom. 2:28-29; 9:6). Isaiah assures us that one day she will respond with faith in God's Son.

Israel still will not turn to Him (vv. 22-24)

The promise is that one day Israel will respond, but sadly that day still has

---

[143] Former things are not where they are to focus (cf. 41:22; 42:9; 43:9; 46:9; 48:3). Oswalt explains, "We humans are inveterate idolaters. We turn everything into a fetish if we are allowed to do so. So, for Israel, the glorious, saving events of the past with all their details had become a straightjacket into which every other act of God was forced" (Oswalt, *The Book of Isaiah: Chapters 40-66*, 154-55).

[144] Kidner, "Isaiah," 658.

not yet come. Instead of calling on the Lord in faith, they have gotten "weary" of the Lord (*yaga'*; cf. Mic. 6:3; Mal. 1:13).[145] How tragic that the Lord loved them, but they are weary of Him (v. 22). They were not bringing God the thankful sacrifices that should have been given to honor Him (vv. 23-24), for those that were given came from empty hearts (cf. Isa. 1:11-14; 29:13; 66:3; Jer. 7:5-10; Hos. 6:6; Amos 4:4-6; Mic. 6:3-8). Smith explains, "Apparently they did what was technically required by the sacrificial system, even when it did not mean much to them."[146] The Lord wanted honor, but instead of honor, they made God weary by their sins (v. 24).

By His righteousness, God will save Israel (vv. 25-28)

Chapter 43 reminds us of a fifth and final attribute of God that should be a reason for Israel to not fear the future. This attribute was the righteousness of God. In particular, we are talking here about God's faithfulness to His own covenant promises.

The declaration of God's righteousness (v. 25)

One can sense God's passion and frustration when He says, "I, even I, am the one who wipes out your transgressions for My own sake, and I will not remember your sins." Israel does not have it within herself to change her ways or cleanse herself (Jer. 13:23), so God must be the One to make it happen.[147] Thus, writes Keil, the good news is that, "the sustaining power of divine love is greater than the gravitating force of divine wrath. V. 25."[148]

Thus, Yahweh will be the One to wipe out Israel's transgressions (*machah*, wipe clean, blot out),[149] a forgiveness so great so that they will be gone forever and He will not even remember them (Isa. 38:17; Jer. 31:14; Mic. 7:18-19; cf. Ps. 103:12-14). God alone is capable of saving Israel, and the reason why He does so is because of His own righteousness and for His own glory (Isa. 37:35; 48:9, 11; cf. Ezek. 36:22-23).

The challenge to respond to God's righteousness (vv. 26-28)

---

[145] Zechariah uses a different term for "weary" in 11:8 (*bachal*), one that connotes the idea that Israel would loathe/be nauseated over the Messiah.

[146] Smith, *Isaiah 40-66*, 213.

[147] The twice-repeated pronoun "I, I" (*'anokiy, 'anokiy*) emphatically makes the point that God alone can forgive and restore Israel from its filth and guilt. He accomplishes this by sending His Servant to die in their place (Isa. 52:13-53:12).

[148] Keil, *Commentary on the Old Testament*, 431.

[149] In 44:22 God tells them, "I have wiped out your transgressions like a thick cloud and your sins like a heavy mist" (cf. David's use of the term in Ps. 51:1, 9).

Using courtroom language (cf. 41:21-22), God calls His people to testify who has been the cause of their problems (cf. 1:18ff.). The problem certainly has not been due to a failure of God's grace. Rather, the problem continues to be their own sin (v. 26; cf. Isa. 59:1-2).

The "first forefather" could potentially be speaking about Adam, Abraham, or Jacob, but is probably best understood as referring to Abraham, a righteous man, but a sinner nonetheless (Gen. 12:18; 20:9, 11-13). Abraham was a sinner and so too have been their "spokesmen" (*meliyts*, go-betweens, envoys), an expression best understood as their leaders such as their priests, prophets, and princes (v. 27; cf. Mic. 3:1-11).

Because of their unrepentant sin, God tells them, "So I will pollute the princes of the sanctuary, and I will consign Jacob to the ban and Israel to revilement" (v. 28). The judgment cannot be averted: "Ungrateful Israel must first suffer national disaster before these promised blessings could be bestowed."[150] Therefore, because of her refusal to repent, Babylon will overthrow the entire nation and its princes, i.e., its priests (cf. 1 Chron. 24:45), and Israel will be given over to complete "desolation" ("the ban," *cherem*; cf. Isa. 34:2; Deut. 13:12-15) and "revilement" (*gidduph*, defamation and abuse) until the time of restoration. She who had been called to be holy (*qadosh*, Exod. 19:6; Lev. 10:3; 19:2; 20:7) will now be polluted since she did not care to walk in the holiness of God (cf. Isa. 65:1-7).[151]

Summary and application

In this past section, we have seen how Isaiah magnified five attributes of God (His faithfulness, sovereignty, providence, grace, and righteousness). These precious attributions should have been motivators to thankful and obedient faith. Sadly, Israel failed to respond. Let us not follow in the same example of disobedience.

THE SAVING PROMISES OF YAHWEH (44:1-28)

As is common in Isaiah, he quickly shifts the discussion about immediate judgments to that of future blessings. In the flowing context, however, it is better to recognize the first five verses as being more-directly connected with the theme of the preceding section.[152] All of chapter 44 continues the same theme

---

[150] Pfeiffer, *The Wycliffe Bible Commentary: Old Testament*, Is 43:22.
[151] Israel did not want God's holiness, God would cause the entire nation to become profane (Piel stem of *chalal*, to pollute or make profane).
[152] Oswalt, *The Book of Isaiah: Chapters 40-66*, 164.

that Yahweh alone is God; He alone can prophesy the future; He alone can save His people; dumb idols can neither predict nor save. Only Yahweh can save His people.

Chapter 44 reads as follows: "1 But now listen, O Jacob, My servant, and Israel, whom I have chosen: 2 Thus says the Lord who made you and formed you from the womb, Who will help you, Do not fear, O Jacob My servant, and you Jeshurun whom I have chosen. 3 For I will pour out water on the thirsty *land* and streams on the dry ground; I will pour out My Spirit on your offspring and My blessing on your descendants, 4 and they will spring up among the grass like poplars by streams of water. 5 This one will say, I am the Lord's; and that one will call on the name of Jacob; and another will write *on* his hand, belonging to the Lord, and will name Israel's name with honor. 6 Thus says the Lord, the King of Israel and his Redeemer, the Lord of hosts: I am the first and I am the last, and there is no God besides Me. 7 Who is like Me? Let him proclaim and declare it; yes, let him recount it to Me in order, from the time that I established the ancient nation., and let them declare to them the things that are coming, and the events that are going to take place. 8 Do not tremble and do not be afraid. Have I not long since announced *it* to you and declared *it?* And you are My witnesses. Is there any God besides Me, or is there any *other* Rock? I know of none. 9 Those who fashion a graven image are all of them futile, and their precious things are of no profit; even their own witnesses fail to see or know, so that they will be put to shame. 10 Who has fashioned a god or cast an idol to no profit? 11 Behold, all his companions will be put to shame, for the craftsmen themselves are mere men. Let them all assemble themselves; let them stand up; let them tremble; let them together be put to shame. 12 The man shapes iron into a cutting tool and does his work over the coals, fashioning it with hammers and working it with his strong arm. He also gets hungry and his strength fails; he drinks no water and becomes weary. 13 *Another* shapes wood; he extends a measuring line; he outlines it with red chalk; he works it with planes and outlines it with a compass, and makes it like the form of a man, like the beauty of man, so that it may sit in a house. 14 Surely he cuts cedars for himself, and takes a cypress or an oak and raises *it* for himself among the trees of the forest. He plants a fir, and the rain makes it grow. 15 Then it becomes *something* for a man to burn, so he takes one of them and warms himself; he also makes a fire to bake bread. He also makes a god and worships it; he makes it a graven image and falls down before it. 16 Half of it he burns in the fire; over *this* half he eats meat as he roasts a roast and is satisfied; he also warms himself and says, Aha! I am warm; I have seen the fire. 17 But the rest of it he makes into a god, his graven image. He falls down before it and worships; he also prays to it and says, Deliver me, for you are my god. 18 They do not know, nor do they understand, for He has smeared over their eyes so that they cannot see and their hearts so that they cannot comprehend. 19 No one recalls, nor is there knowledge or understanding to say, I have burned half of it in the fire and also have baked bread over its coals; I roast meat and eat *it;* then I make the rest of it into an abomination; I fall down before a block of wood! 20 He feeds on ashes. A deceived heart has turned him aside, and he cannot deliver himself, nor say, Is there not a lie in my right hand? 21 Remember these things, O Jacob, and Israel, for you are My servant; I have formed you. You are My servant, O Israel; you will not be forgotten by Me. 22 I have wiped out your transgressions like a thick cloud and your sins like a heavy mist. Return to Me, for I have redeemed you. 23 Shout for joy, O heavens, for the Lord has done *it!* Shout joyfully, you lower parts of the earth; break forth into a shout of joy, you mountains, O forest, and every tree in it, for the Lord has redeemed Jacob, and in Israel He shows forth His glory. 24 Thus says the Lord, your Redeemer, and the One who formed you from the womb, I, the Lord, am the Maker of all things, stretching out the heavens by Myself, and spreading out the earth all alone, 25 causing the omens of boasters to fail, making fools out of diviners, causing wise men to draw back, and turning their knowledge into foolishness, 26 confirming the word of His servant, and performing the purpose of His messengers. *It is I* who says of Jerusalem, she shall be inhabited, and of the cities of Judah, they shall be built, and I will raise up her ruins *again.* 27 *It is I* who says to the depth of the sea, Be dried up! And I will make your rivers dry. 28 *It is I* who says of Cyrus, *He is* My shepherd! And he will perform all My desire, and he declares of Jerusalem, she will be built, and of the temple, your foundation will be laid" (44:1-28).

God's message has always been, "Trust in Me and do not be afraid," a dominant theme in chapter 44.[153] Chapter 44 may be broken down as consisting of five prophetic promises whose purpose is to give us hope and soothe our fears in the midst of a turbulent world.

A mighty outpouring is coming (vv. 1-5)

God's first promise is a mighty outpouring of grace to restore His fallen people (a continuation of chapter 43).[154] God will save His people and bring them safely into His kingdom. The reason we need not fear is because of God's unchanging faithful character (Mal. 3:6; Jer. 33:14-26; Titus 2:13). God gives the command to not fear (vv. 1-2) and follows this up with the reason to not fear (vv. 3-5).

The command to not fear (vv. 1-2)

God reaffirms Israel's position (v. 1). In this present section, God once again reminds Israel that He has not rejected them. They have sinned badly and

---

[153] Jesus encouraged His timid disciples by telling them, "Do not be afraid, little flock, for your Father has chosen gladly to give you the kingdom" (Luke 12:32).
[154] Wolf, *Interpreting Isaiah,* 196.

are suffering the consequences of covenant disobedience, but Israel is still His servant nation whom He chose for His own glory (cf. 41:8; 42:19; 43:10; 44:1, 2, 21; 45:4; 65:9, 15; Rom. 11:1-2).[155]

Israel's position should mean no fear (v. 2). God reminds them that He is the one who formed them to be His people (cf. 43:7; 44:21, 24),[156] and for this reason He will help them. God even uses the unique name Jeshurun to assure Israel that they do not need to fear—Jeshurun, a poetic name God gave to Israel in the Song of Moses where He tells Israel that even though they would one day turn away from Him, He will never reject them (cf. Deut. 32:15; 33:5, 26).[157] But how can a nation that sinned so badly ever hope to have restoration? The answer is grace, a mighty outpouring of grace God will pour upon Israel at the end of the age.

The reason to not fear (vv. 3-5)

The opening word "for" (*kiy*) gives the reason why Israel should not fear. It is because of His promise to restore them with a mighty outpouring of grace. Isaiah first makes the promise of a mighty outpouring (v. 3) and then shows what the impact will be (vv. 4-5).

The promise of an outpouring of grace (v. 3). As we have seen elsewhere, God once again uses the imagery of a great pouring (*yatsaq*) out of water to symbolize His restoring grace on a spiritually parched nation (cf. Isa. 12:3; 30:25; 32:2, 15; 33:21; 35:1-7; 41:17-18; 43:18-21; 49:10; 51:3; 55:1; 66:12).[158] The heart of this promise is an outpouring of God's Holy Spirit.

Isaiah is not the only prophet who makes such predictions, for the repeated message of the Old Testament is that one day God will restore His people by this kind of outpouring (cf. Joel 2:28-32; Ezek. 36:25-27; Zech. 12:10; 13:1). Moses described this gracious work as God bringing circumcision of the heart (Deut. 30:6), the kind of inner circumcision (i.e., inner cleansing) that the unregenerate do not possess (Deut. 10:16; Jer. 4:4; 9:25-26). This is the

---

[155] We must not forget the tremendous honor and privilege of being a servant to the king (56:6). Other noted servants include Moses (Exod. 14:31; Num. 12:7), David (2 Sam. 3:18; 7:5, 8), and the prophets (2 Kings 17:13; Jer. 7:25). "Choose" always brings up reminders of God's gracious work Torah (Deut. 4:37; 7:6).

[156] The parallel of the creative verbs "make" and "form" occurs only here in Isaiah (cf. 22:11; 27:11; 44:2; 45:18) (Oswalt, *The Book of Isaiah: Chapters 40-66*, 165, n. 8).

[157] The root comes from the verb *yashar* (to be upright). How ironic that God would call His rebellious and sinful people "O upright one."

[158] The fourth servant song emphasizes the spiritually parched character of Israel in which the Servant would minister (Isa. 53:1-3).

regeneration that belongs to all believers whether they are Jew or Gentile (Rom. 2:29; Phil. 3:3; Col. 2:11). Salvation always has been a work of God's grace by His Holy Spirit. This water-driven theological language and imagery is that which stood behind Jesus' words to Nicodemus: "unless one is born of water and the Spirit he cannot enter into the kingdom of God" (John 3:5; cf. 4:10-14; 7:37).

This discussion calls for some brief comment on how these promises relate to the Day of Pentecost. First, we need to note that exegetically speaking, all of the Old Testament restoration passages we have just cited speak in context about God's eschatological work to restore Israel during the Great Tribulation period at the end of the age.[159] These prophecies will, in fact, be fulfilled at the end of the age just as God has spoken. The question arises about how to understand Peter's use of Joel 2:28-32 (cf. Acts 2:16-17). The answer is that *all* the disciples (Peter included) were expecting an imminent restoration of the kingdom to Israel (cf. Acts 1:6-7). When Christ poured out His Spirit at Pentecost, it was natural for Peter to assume that this was part of Israel's restoration promises spoken of in the Old Testament. However, at that point in salvation history, neither Peter, nor anyone else, understood that these events were in fact the birth of the church. It would take several decades of salvation history (cf. e.g., Peter's experience in Acts 10) and the giving of the New Testament (cf. e.g., Eph. 2:11-4:16) before these truths would become clear to the early church.

The point of this text, explains Martin, is that this outpouring of Spirit, "will occur when the people have returned in belief to the land (cf. Ezek. 36:24, 27; 39:25-29; Joel 2:25–29) at the time of the Messiah's second coming to establish the Millennium."[160] God's blessing on Israel will bring a mighty regeneration to every one of God's elect Jews, and they will respond in faith in the Messiah and enter into the New Covenant (Jer. 31:31-34; Zech. 13:8-9).[161]

---

[159] It is beyond the scope of this commentary to defend the exegesis and hermeneutics of this statement, but the author firmly holds to the view that a consistent use of Literal, Grammatical, Historical hermeneutics produces a Premillennial theology that shows a future restoration of the nation of Israel. Furthermore, the NT clearly states that the church is a NT mystery that was not seen or predicted by the prophets of the OT (Eph. 3:1-10; Rom. 16:25-27; Col. 1:26). Therefore, it is illegitimate to see these OT passages referring to the church.

[160] Martin, "Isaiah," 1098.

[161] At His first coming, Messiah gave His life to restore the nation, i.e., on the cross the blood of the New Covenant was shed. However, the shedding of Christ's blood did not automatically produce a ratification of the New Covenant, for this cannot happen apart from a confession of faith and submission to the covenant. This ratification (establishing) of the New Covenant comes at the end of the age when Israel turns to

The impact of an outpouring of grace (vv. 4-5). Isaiah first describes the impact of this regeneration with rich botanical imagery (v. 4),[162] but very quickly brings it down to a personal level that shows the vibrant love of God's people for the Lord their God. The nation that once was weary of God, will now rejoice in Him: "This one will say, I am the Lord's, and that one will call on the name of Jacob, and another will write *on* his hand, Belonging to the Lord, and will name Israel's name with honor" (v. 5).[163]

One day Israel will rejoice exceedingly in the Lord. Smith reminds us that contextually, this is best understood as a restoration to the elect remnant of Israel and not a reference to the Gentiles whom God will save also: "The fact that the Spirit is to be poured out on 'your descendants' (44:3) supports the view that this refers to changes in the Hebrew people."[164] God is going to save a mighty remnant from among the Gentiles (Isa. 2:3-4; 11:10; 56:3-8; 60:10; 61:5), but this passage is about Israel's New Covenant restoration (Jer. 31:31-34).

No one like Him (vv. 6-8)

Having made the promise of a mighty outpouring (vv. 1-5), God gives Israel a second promise to soothe their fearful hearts, the assurance that there is no one like Him. Chapter 44 brings a climax to God's case against idols which began in chapter 41.[165] He alone is God, and it is utter folly to trust in dead idols who can neither speak nor act. God once again reminds Israel that there is no one like Him; therefore, Israel need not fear (cf. John 14:27; 16:33; 20:19; Phil. 4:6-7; 2 Tim. 1:7; 1 Pet. 5:6-7)! Isaiah reveals the character of Israel's God (vv. 6-7) and follows this the implications (v. 8).

Christ in faith (Isa. 44:4-5; cf. Isa. 12:3; Deut. 30:1-3; Jer. 30:19; Ezek. 37:24-28; Dan. 12:7; Hos. 1:10-11; 3:5; Joel 2:32; Amos 9:11-15; Mic. 2:12-13; Zech. 12:10; 13:8-9). The NT affirms this truth (cf. e.g., Matt. 19:28; 21:43-44; 23:39; 24:9, 22, 31; 25:31-46; 26:29, 64; Rom. 11:12, 15, 23-36).

[162] The previously parched land will become rich and fruitful with God's people Israel springing up (*tsamach*) like poplars, a very green tree that may be the one called "the ben tree" (Grogan, "Isaiah," 266, n. 4; Young, *The Book of Isaiah, vol. 3*, 167). In context, these statements contain promises about the restoration of apostate Israel. Many passages also speak about the restoration of the Gentiles.

[163] Three times Isaiah uses the expression "this" one (suggesting a particular person), but the three-fold repetition shows that this is something in mass (ibid., 168). Perhaps the writing may not be permanent in that permanent markings were forbidden in the Law (Lev. 19:28; Isa. 49:16) (Grogan, "Isaiah," 264).

[164] Smith, *Isaiah 40-66*, 220.

[165] Wolf, *Interpreting Isaiah*, 197.

The character of Israel's God (vv. 6-7)

Who is the God of Israel? He is Yahweh (cf. Exod. 3:1-14), the King of Israel (cf. Isa. 6:1ff.), the One who redeems Israel from disaster (cf. Isa. 41:14; 43:1, 14). Israel's God is the Captain and Lord of the armies—the Lord of Hosts (47:4; 48:2; 51:15).[166] He is the first and the last (Isa. 41:4; 43:10; 48:12; cf. Rev. 1:8, 17; 2:8; 21:6; 22:13), and there is no God besides Him (43:10-13). Yahweh, the God who chose Israel, is the only God (v. 6). Having identified Himself, God again issues courtroom language to challenge anyone to bring evidence that an idol has made prophetic prediction and fulfilled it (v. 7; cf. 41:21-24, 26-27; 43:8-13; 45:21; 46:9-11). Kidner explains,

> These verses give the very essence of these chapters, with their emphasis on God as Israel's champion (*Redeemer*, 6; *cf.* 41:14), their explicit monotheism (6b, 8b), their stress on prediction (7b) and their reassuring tone towards a diffident Israel (8).[167]

The implications of Israel's God (v. 8)

The significance of verses 6-7 cannot be overstated. The true God can predict the future. Pfeiffer explains,

> Again he points to the testimony of fulfilled predictions (a phenomenon peculiar to the Hebrew Scriptures) as a type of evidence of divine authority no man-invented religion can ever produce. To this fulfillment of prophecy, the Jewish nation stands as witness, furnishing verification to all the world that only Jehovah is God.[168]

What are the implications of God's ability to predict and fulfill? God answers that question: "Do not tremble and do not be afraid; have I not long since announced *it* to you and declared *it*? And you are My witnesses.[169] Is there any God besides Me,[170] or is there any *other* Rock?[171] I know of none" (v. 8).

---

[166] Although the word "hosts" (*tseba'oth*) does get used for stars and planets (Gen. 2:1; Ps. 33:6), for angels (2 Kings 6:15-18; Pss. 103:21; 148:2), and for armies (Ps. 27:3), this usage (Lord of Hosts) is best understood as referring to the host of Israel as a nation and people (Isa. 1:9, 24) (Oswalt, *The Book of Isaiah: Chapters 40-66*, 171).
[167] Kidner, "Isaiah," 658.
[168] Pfeiffer, *The Wycliffe Bible Commentary: Old Testament*, Is 44:1.
[169] Cf. Isa. 43:10.
[170] Cf. Isa. 45:5; Deut. 6:4.
[171] Cf. Isa. 17:10; 26:4; 30:29; Deut. 32:4, 18, 30, 31, 37.

Therefore, because He is who He is, God tells us, "Do not tremble [*phachad*] and do not be afraid [*yarah*]!"[172]

The folly of idolatry (vv. 9-20)

God gives a third promise to soothe our fears. Yahweh alone is God, and it is folly to trust in idols who are not gods.[173] Isaiah exposes the folly of trusting idols with a detailed rebuke of idols.

The folly of idols (vv. 9-11)

Isaiah begins with a series of four statements about idols: Idols are futile (*tohu*),[174] of no profit (*ya'al*), incapable of life (can't see or hear),[175] and lead only to shame (*bosh*). Therefore, warns Isaiah, "Behold, all his companions will be put to shame, for the craftsmen themselves are mere men. Let them all assemble themselves; let them stand up; let them tremble; let them together be put to shame" (v. 11). The main point is that "idols are man-made, and they are worthless,"[176] and those who follow this path will be put to shame (cf. Hos. 4:17; 6:9).

The construction of idols (vv. 12-17)

The focus shifts slightly in verses 12-17 to all the detailed steps of constructing an idol. Isaiah speaks about two steps involving two kinds of craftsmen, all of which highlight the sad reality that men are at work to make a god whom they will proceed to worship.

First step: The toolmaker (v. 12). One needs tools to make an idol. First, a blacksmith is going to have to labor over fires to make the iron tools. Isaiah mockingly makes the point how weary (cf. 40:28-31) the man gets in all this toil.

Second step: The carpenter (vv. 13-17). Once the blacksmith has made a tool, the carpenter can go to work. Verses 13-17 delineate a series of steps

---

[172] The latter term is not the usual word for fear, but is a hapax synonym that carries the idea of being paralyzed with fear. Young points out, however, that the DSS has a different reading like the usual spelling and suggests that it should be preferred (Young, *The Book of Isaiah, vol. 3*, 171, n. 10).

[173] As Oswalt notes, "The Bible insists that the supreme power in the universe is utterly other than the universe, and even more to the point, cannot be manipulated through any of those forms" (Oswalt, *The Book of Isaiah: Chapters 40-66*, 175).

[174] They are no better than the elemental chaos that characterized the unformed earth (Gen. 1:2; cf. Isa. 24:10; ; 29:21; 34:11; 40:17, 23; 41:29; 44:9; 45:18, 19; 49:4; 59:4).

[175] Those who worship idols are deaf, dumb and blind just like their gods.

[176] Wolf, *Interpreting Isaiah*, 198.

how the carpenter takes the raw wood and shapes it into a god. The end result is a man-made god made in the image of man to sit in the house of a man (v. 13). The True God needs none of this (Isa. 57:15; 66:2; cf. 1 Kings 8:27).

Wooden idols require good wood, so verse 14 emphasizes the importance of planting and harvesting the best kinds of trees (more man-made toil).[177] Martin observes the implication that, "The gods themselves have no life for they are made from metals or from trees which ironically the true God made."[178] Then with the same wood that is used for making a god to worship, part of the wood is used for making a fire with which you can cook food and stay warm (vv. 15-17). Thus, says Martin, people who pray that an idol made of mere wood would save them (v. 17) "are ignorant and have no spiritual sight or comprehension (v. 18; cf. 6:10)."[179]

The self-deception of idols (vv. 18-20)

Isaiah finishes his mockery of idols with the reminder that all of it is self-deception.

Spiritual inability (v. 18). Why is it that idolaters do not understand how foolish they are? It is spiritual inability: "They do not know, nor do they understand, for He has smeared over their eyes so that they cannot see and their hearts so that they cannot comprehend."[180] What we see here is God's progressive judgment on those who have rejected Him and refuse to repent.

---

[177] The most-desirable woods were cedar, cypress, and oak, woods which were hard and durable and did not easily rot (ibid.).
[178] Martin, "Isaiah," 1098–1099.
[179] Ibid., 1099. Young notes that Horace, the ancient Greek poet, even though he himself was a pagan, commented on the stupidity of the whole thing: "Once I was a trunk of a fig tree, a useless piece of wood, when a carpenter, uncertain whether to make a bench or a Priapus, preferred that I should be a god; and so, I became a god. So now I am god, a major terror to birds and thieves" (Young, *The Book of Isaiah, vol. 3*, 177-178; Oswalt, *The Book of Isaiah: Chapters 40-66*, 182, n. 59). Oswalt writes about the folly of the god Priapus: "Priapus was a god of fertility whose identify was marked in the most obvious way, stands as a protector in a graveyard for the indigent . . . greatly troubled by his inability to prevent witches from coming at night to collect bones. . . . But he does fulfill his function after all, for suddenly his idol buttocks split open with a sound of escaping gas and the witches are so terrified they rush away" (ibid.).
[180] In judgment, God has besmeared (*tachach*, hapax) their eyes because of their refusal to turn from sin and give Him the glory (cf. Rom. 1:18-32). They wouldn't listen to God to begin with, so God brought more judgment upon them, an oft-repeated theme in Isaiah (6:10; 29:10; 42:18-19; 43:8).

The utter folly of idolatry (vv. 19-20). Isaiah finishes his sarcastic rebuke by once again exposing their folly. Half the wood is used for making fires, and half is used for making an idol to worship—an abomination.[181] Oswalt explains, "We would rather believe that we can capture the divine in the stuff of this world, with all the contradictions it involves, than to admit that God is utterly beyond our control and manipulation."[182]

Do not forget the Lord's promises (vv. 21-23)

Having exposed the folly of idolatry, Isaiah gives a fourth promise to soothe the fears of God's people. This reassurance consists of three promises: the promise of covenant faithfulness (v. 21), the promise of forgiveness (v. 22), and the promise of complete redemption (v. 23).

The promise of covenant faithfulness (v. 21)

Using a word that is so important in Deuteronomy, "to remember" (*zakar*; cf. Deut. 8:2, 11, 18; 9:7), Isaiah urges the people to reflect upon the truths of God's faithfulness. God comforts His people by telling them, "Remember these things, O Jacob, and Israel, for you are My servant; I have formed you; you are My servant, O Israel; you will not be forgotten by Me" (cf. 41:8-9; 43:10; 44:1-9). Thus, explains Pfeiffer, even though the nation had sinned and was now in exile, by His own faithfulness, "The many and grievous sins of the Jews would be canceled out, and they might come to God for forgiveness, since he would act for their redemption."[183]

The promise of forgiveness (v. 22)

The heart of God's faithfulness is His willingness to forgive the sins of His people. As promised earlier, He tells them that He will "wipe out" (*machah*, 43:25; cf. Ps. 53:1, 9; Exod. 32:32) their transgressions like a thick cloud and their sins like a heavy mist (cf. Mic. 7:18-19).[184] With this promise, God says,

---

[181] This word abomination (*to'ebah*) is regularly used to speak about the detestable nature of idols in the mind of God (Deut. 7:26; 27:15; 32:16; 1 Kings 11:5-7; 2 Kings 23:13-14; Jer. 16:18; Ezek. 5:9; 7:20; 11:18, 21; 16:36; cf. Isa. 1:13; 41:24: "he who chooses you is an abomination").

[182] Ibid., 186.

[183] Pfeiffer, *The Wycliffe Bible Commentary: Old Testament*, Is 44:21.

[184] I.e., one minute you look and see the clouds and mist, but you look again, and they are gone forever.

"Return to Me, for I have redeemed you."[185] The promise of forgiveness is there, but at a human level, the only way Israel can receive it is by responding to God's call in faith.[186]

The promise of complete redemption (v. 23)

God is going to forgive His people, so three times there is the call to heaven and earth that they would shout for joy (*ranan*; cf. Isa. 35:1; 49:13; Joel 2:23; Zeph. 3:14; Zech. 9:9).[187] The reason, says Isaiah, is because, "the Lord has redeemed Jacob and in Israel He shows forth His glory."[188] The day is coming when God will bring a complete and final redemption; therefore, Israel should not fear, for the Lord will do it. How could God ever forgive such unworthy sinners? That answer is because He Himself paid the price when He sent Christ to take away our sins by giving His own life (Isa. 52:13-53:12; cf. Matt. 20:28). What a precious truth this is!

God has His man (vv. 24-28)

The fifth and last promise to soothe the fears of the people is the promise that God has a chosen man who is going to set them free from the captivity to Babylon.[189] God will set them free from Babylon (see earlier comments on 40:3), and He will do so by raising up His chosen man. This final section reiterates God's restoration with three main messages.[190]

First message: The power to accomplish restoration (vv. 24-25)

God identifies Himself as the One who both created the universe and

---

[185] In this futuristic context, the perfect stem verbs of both v. 22 and v. 23 are better translated as "will redeem" and not "have redeemed" (Oswalt, *The Book of Isaiah: Chapters 40-66*, 191).

[186] Ibid., 188. Oswalt rightly recognizes the aspect of human responsibility, but also that if dead Israel is to respond to this call "God alone must do that" (i.e., divine grace in regeneration). Jeremiah pleaded for God to turn the nation that they might turn to Him (Lam. 5:21).

[187] Paul reminds us that even though the whole creation is groaning under the agonies of the curse, one day the Lord will lift this curse forever (Rom. 8:18-27).

[188] Cf. Isa. 6:1ff.; 35:2; 40:5; Ezek. 36:19-26.

[189] This is the same man God introduced in 41:2, but now in chapters 44-46 God will expand on this theme.

[190] The expression "Thus says the Lord" is characteristic for introducing God's oracles in this portion of Isaiah (41:14; 42:5; 43:1, 14, 16; 44:2, 6, 24; 45:1, 11, 14, 18; 48:17; 49:7; 51:22; cf. 1:24; 30:15; 37:21).

made Israel into His own special people (v. 24; cf. 40:22; 42:5; 43:1, 7, 15, 21; 44:2, 21, 24; 45:18; 48:12-13). The idols, however, are nothing and neither are the false prophets who speak for them. The true God is the One who has the sovereignty to frustrate the false prophets by "causing the omens of boasters [the *baddïym*, i.e., chatterers] to fail, making fools out of diviners [*qasam*, soothsayers and witches], causing wise men to draw back, and turning their knowledge into foolishness" (v. 25).[191] Because He is the Creator, He is the One who has the power to predict Israel's restoration.

Second message: The promise of restoration (vv. 26-27)

Idols cannot predict the future, but God can—the proof that He is God (cf. 41:4, 26-29; 42:9; 43:19; 44:7-8, 25-26). Whatever He says will happen. With this in view, we see two clear promises that God's Word will stand.

First promise: The general promise (v. 26a). Stated in general terms, God will confirm His word (cf. Isa. 40:8; 55:11; 59:21; Matt. 5:18) and He will perform His purpose (*'etsah*).[192] Whatever He says, He will do.

Second promise: The specific promise (vv. 26b-27). The specific promise is that God is not only going to set His people free from Babylon, but also that He will say, "*It is I* who says of Jerusalem, she shall be inhabited, and of the cities of Judah, they shall be built, and I will raise up her ruins *again*" (v. 26b). Pfeiffer comments on this great prophecy:

> Worldlings would never have believed that Jerusalem and its holy Temple would be completely rebuilt seventy years after the Chaldeans had demolished them; yet the city and the Temple were restored exactly as God had foretold. Worldlings, too, would have scornfully rejected the possibility that a repopulated Judah would be rebuilt by descendants of Nebuchadnezzar's deportees; yet Jehovah was to bring even that to pass. Least likely of fulfillment, to the mind of an unbeliever, was the prediction that the Jews would be liberated by a non-Israelite pagan like Cyrus; and yet so it was, 150 years after the Lord predicted it.[193]

All of these prophecies were fulfilled just as the pre-exilic prophets said they would take place (Jer. 25:11-12; 27:6-9; 29:10-13; 32:15). Babylon fell to the

---

[191] Young, *The Book of Isaiah*, vol. 3, 188.
[192] This term "purpose" speaks about God's determined plan, a term that frequently is used where God declares how His eternal plan will have its outworking (Isa. 14:24, 26; 25:1; 40:8; 46:8-11, esp. vv. 10-11; cf. Eph. 1:11).
[193] Pfeiffer, *The Wycliffe Bible Commentary: Old Testament*, Is 44:24.

Persians on October 12, 539 B.C. (as seen in Dan. 5), and within a year King Cyrus gave the decree that Israel would be free to return to her homeland and rebuild the temple (2 Chron. 36:20-23; Ezra 1:1-4). The work of God was so great Isaiah uses language to compare it to the Exodus from Egypt: "*It is I* who says to the depth of the sea, be dried up, and I will make your rivers dry" (v. 27; cf. Isa. 11:15; 37:25; 43:16-17; 50:2; 51:10).[194]

Third message: The agent of restoration (v. 28)

How will God fulfill these prophecies? Here in verse 28, God names out for the first time, the name of this man whom God will use for the release of His captive people, King Cyrus of Persia. This is one of the most amazing passages of the Bible, for God foretold by name the exact identity of the individual who would eventually set His people free from captivity in Babylon. We need to remember that Isaiah wrote these words in approximately 700 B.C., but Cyrus did not overthrow Babylon until 539 B.C., over 150 years later. Oswalt confirms the importance of these words:

> The centerpiece of the whole argument against the idols is that they cannot declare the future. Nothing they have said in the past can explain the present, and nothing they say now is anything but a vague rehash of what has already happened. But God not only has done so in the past, he does so now, and evidence clearly supports both claims (41:21-24, 26-29; 43:8-13; 44:6-9, 24-26; 45:20-21; 46:9-11; 48:3-5, 14-16). Three of the four references to Cyrus (41:25; 44:28; 46:11) are directly connected to this argument, and the other (41:2) is connected by implication. . . . [the whole passage is] the very fulcrum on which the whole argument for God's uniqueness turns.[195]

No one can do what God does! What is just as staggering is the way that God describes Cyrus. Here in verse 28, we read, "*It is I* who says of Cyrus, *He is* My shepherd! And he will perform all My desire, and he declares of Jerusalem, she will be built, and of the temple, your foundation will be laid." Here is an interesting question to ponder: Just how is it that God could call a Gentile king "My Shepherd"?[196] The answer lies in the sovereignty of God who, by His providence, is going to use a Gentile king to accomplish His eternal purposes. Smith explains,

---

[194] The armies of Persia diverted the Euphrates River that ran under the walls of Babylon, making an open path for the armies to invade.

[195] Oswalt, *The Book of Isaiah: Chapters 40-66*, 196.

[196] If the reader is shocked by God calling this pagan king "My shepherd," how much more when God calls the antichrist a shepherd to Israel (cf. Zech. 11:15)?

As God's shepherd (a symbol of a king), Cyrus (Hb. Koresh) will be obedient and do everything God pleases. Specifically, he will give the instructions (*lēʾmōr* "by saying") that Jerusalem and the temple should be rebuilt. The passive verbs ("let it be rebuilt" and "let its foundations be laid") indicate that Cyrus will not do the building but give permission so that others may do this work.[197]

This is how Cyrus will function as God's shepherd: He will be the human agent to fulfill God's purpose. Martin tells us a little additional background about this great Persian king called Cyrus (cf. Isa. 13:17; Jer. 51:11):

> Cyrus, founder of the Persian Empire, first came to the throne of Anshan in Eastern Elam in 559. In 549 he conquered the Medes and became the ruler of the combined Persian and Median Empire. In 539 he conquered Babylon (Dan. 5:30) and the very next year issued a decree that the Jews could return to Jerusalem and rebuild the temple (2 Chron. 36:22–23; Ezra 1:1–4). In doing this Cyrus was serving God's purposes as if he were God's shepherd.[198]

At a human level, Cyrus was just another Gentile ruler, but by God's design He would perform all God's "desire" (*chephets*), i.e., God's determined plan and purpose:

> The noun *ḥēpeṣ* is used more frequently, thirty-nine times, and in varying contexts. . . . Isaiah writes that the "delight" of God will prosper in the hand of Christ (53:10). The word is also used in reference to that in which God finds delight. The Persian king, Cyrus, would perform that in which God had "delight" (Isa 44:28).[199]

God's "desire" was His plan that He would raise up Cyrus to become the sovereign ruler of the Middle East, and that Cyrus would fulfill His purpose to set His people free to return home and rebuild their ruined temple.[200] These amazing deeds of Cyrus—deeds that were 150 years in the future—call for even further explanation:

> Babylon, the next goal for Cyrus' ambitions, was ripe for change.

---

[197] Smith, *Isaiah 40-66*, 250.

[198] Martin, "Isaiah," 1099.

[199] Leon J. Wood, "*chapats*," ed. R. Laird Harris, Gleason L. Archer Jr., and Bruce K. Waltke, *Theological Wordbook of the Old Testament*, cited in electronic form with Logos Libronix (Chicago: Moody Press, 1999), 311.

[200] Cf. Isa. 46:8-11 where the term shows a determinative force behind it.

Nabonidus, the last of the Neo-Babylonian kings, had absented himself from the capital for fourteen years to pursue his own antiquarian and religious hobbies at Teimā in northern Arabia. His continued failure to take part in the New Year festival at Babylon, the chief religious ceremony of the Babylonian cult, had alienated the powerful priesthood of the city-god Marduk, as had also his bestowal of favors upon the worship of Sin, the moon deity of Haran. The government of Babylon and of the empire was in the hands of his son Belshazzar, undoubtedly one of the less capable Neo-Babylonian rulers. Nabonidus, sensing no doubt that Cyrus' success spelled severe danger for his own empire, returned to Babylon in the spring of 539 b.c. and began to bring into the city the statues of other Babylonian city-gods in order to afford greater protection to Babylon. Though New Year's day was celebrated in proper form on Apr. 4, 539 b.c., by late summer it was clear that nothing could hold back Cyrus. In early October Cyrus defeated a Babylonian force at Opis on the Tigris, and on Oct. 10 Sippar fell without a battle. Nabonidus hastily left Babylon, and on Oct. 12 Cyrus' troops under Gobryas (Ugbaru) governor of Gutium, a former general of Nebuchadrezzar who had defected to the Persians, entered the city. That night, according to Dnl. 5:30, Belshazzar king of the Chaldeans (Neo-Babylonians) was slain. When Nabonidus returned to Babylon he was made prisoner. Cyrus himself entered the city on Oct. 29, and presented himself to the citizens as its liberator. According to Herodotus, the Persians used the following stratagem to enter the city: "drawing off the river by a canal into the lake, which was till now a marsh, he [Cyrus] made the stream to sink till its former channel could be forded. When this happened, the Persians who were posted with this intent made their way into Babylon by the channel of the Euphrates, which had now sunk to about the height of the middle of a man's thigh" (i.191). A similar story is told by Xenophon (*Cyropaedeia* vii.5.7–34), though no cuneiform evidence supports this course of events. Although the chief evidence for Cyrus' reception comes from sources obviously very favorable to Cyrus, there is little reason to doubt that his presence was welcomed. According to the "Nabonidus Chronicle," "in the month of Arahshamnu, the 3rd day, Cyrus entered Babylon, green twigs were spread in front of him—the state of 'Peace' was imposed upon the city. Cyrus sent greetings to all Babylon" (ANET, p. 306). The Cyrus Cylinder, apparently composed by a Babylonian temple official, reports that "all the inhabitants of Babylon as well as of the entire country of Sumer and Akkad, princes and governors (included), bowed to him (Cyrus) and kissed his feet, jubilant that he (had received) the kingship, and with shining faces (ANET, p. 316)."[201]

---

[201] D. J. A. Clines, "Cyrus," ed. Geoffrey W. Bromiley, *The International Standard Bible*

What we have here is one more illustration of the supreme sovereignty of Yahweh to predict and fulfill. He is the true God, so Israel need not fear.

The process of restoration began with Cyrus' decree (ca. 538; cf. Ezra 1:1-4), and the first wave of Jewish immigration probably started around 537 B.C. The initial founding of the temple began in 536 B.C. (Ezra 3), but opposition and indifference led to a twenty-year delay in finishing it, a delay that led to the rise of Haggai and Zechariah (520 B.C.). Four years later they finally finished the second temple (516 B.C.). Smith explains,

> Cyrus permitted the laying of the foundations for the temple and Ezra's record indicates that did happen during his reign (Ezra 3:10). As events worked out over the years, opposition by local inhabitants led to delays and the stopping of construction (Ezra 4:1–5); so the temple was not completed until the sixth year of Darius (516 BC, Ezra 6:14), about twenty years after the original decree. The complete rebuilding of the cities of Judah and the city of Jerusalem was not completed under Cyrus, for Nehemiah was still working on this in 445 BC during the reign of Artaxerxes. Cyrus's decree in the Cyrus Cylinder (ANET, 315–16) indicates that he not only authorized the return of exiled people to their native lands, but also the building of their cities and sanctuaries.[202]

God said He would do it, and He did it!

Summary and application

No matter how big the odds might seem against you, if God promised it, you can trust Him. Do not live your life in fear, but keep your eyes on the Lord and keep trusting in Him no matter what!

GOD CAN CHOOSE (45:1-25)

It would have been better for no break to come between chapters 44 and 45 since the subject matter is all part of one flowing theme, God's work to raise up Cyrus.[203] Since the beginning of chapter 40, God has made it clear that He has a plan to save Israel, and that plan is going to include the use of a pagan king named Cyrus. Thus far, God has made four declarations about Cyrus. One, he is the Lord's shepherd. Two, he will perform all God's desire. Three, he will

---

Encyclopedia, Revised, cited in electronic form with Logos Libronix (Wm. B. Eerdmans, 1979–1988), 847.

[202] Smith, *Isaiah 40-66*, 252.

[203] We do recognize, however, that the formula "Thus says the Lord" does create a new sub section at the very least.

release Israel from captivity. Four, he will command the temple to be rebuilt. All of it is working out the eternal plan of God. Chapter 45 continues this same theme.

Chapter 45 reads as follows: "1 Thus says the Lord to Cyrus His anointed, whom I have taken by the right hand, to subdue nations before him and to loose the loins of kings, to open doors before him so that gates will not be shut: 2 I will go before you and make the rough places smooth. I will shatter the doors of bronze and cut through their iron bars. 3 I will give you the treasures of darkness and hidden wealth of secret places, so that you may know that it is I, the Lord, the God of Israel, who calls you by your name. 4 For the sake of Jacob My servant, and Israel My chosen *one*, I have also called you by your name; I have given you a title of honor though you have not known Me. 5 I am the Lord, and there is no other; besides Me there is no God. I will gird you, though you have not known Me, 6 that men may know from the rising to the setting of the sun that there is no one besides Me. I am the Lord, and there is no other, 7 the One forming light and creating darkness, causing well-being and creating calamity; I am the Lord who does all these. 8 Drip down, O heavens, from above, and let the clouds pour down righteousness. Let the earth open up and salvation bear fruit, and righteousness spring up with it. I, the Lord, have created it. 9 Woe to *the one* who quarrels with his Maker—an earthenware vessel among the vessels of earth! Will the clay say to the potter, What are you doing? Or the thing you are making *say,* He has no hands? 10 Woe to him who says to a father, What are you begetting? Or to a woman, To what are you giving birth? 11 Thus says the Lord, the Holy One of Israel, and his Maker: Ask Me about the things to come concerning My sons, and you shall commit to Me the work of My hands. 12 It is I who made the earth and created man upon it. I stretched out the heavens with My hands and I ordained all their host. 13 I have aroused him in righteousness and I will make all his ways smooth; he will build My city and will let My exiles go free, without any payment or reward, says the Lord of hosts. 14 Thus says the Lord, The products of Egypt and the merchandise of Cush and the Sabeans, men of stature, will come over to you and will be yours; they will walk behind you; they will come over in chains, and will bow down to you; they will make supplication to you: Surely, God is with you, and there is none else, no other God. 15 Truly, You are a God who hides Himself, O God of Israel, Savior! 16 They will be put to shame and even humiliated, all of them. The manufacturers of idols will go away together in humiliation. 17 Israel has been saved by the Lord with an everlasting salvation. You will not be put to shame or humiliated to all eternity. 18 For thus says the Lord, Who created the heavens. He is the God who formed the earth and made it; He established it *and* did not create it a waste place, *but* formed it to be inhabited, I am the Lord, and there is none else. 19 I have not spoken in secret, in some dark land; I did not say to the offspring of Jacob, Seek Me in a waste place. I, the Lord, speak righteousness, declaring things that are upright. 20 Gather yourselves and come;

draw near together, you fugitives of the nations. They have no knowledge, who carry about their wooden idol and pray to a god who cannot save. 21 Declare and set forth *your case;* indeed, let them consult together. Who has announced this from of old? Who has long since declared it? Is it not I, the Lord? And there is no other God besides Me, a righteous God and a Savior. There is none except Me. 22 Turn to Me and be saved, all the ends of the earth, for I am God, and there is no other. 23 I have sworn by Myself; the word has gone forth from My mouth in righteousness and will not turn back, that to Me every knee will bow, every tongue will swear *allegiance*. 24 They will say of Me, Only in the Lord are righteousness and strength. Men will come to Him, and all who were angry at Him will be put to shame. 25 In the Lord all the offspring of Israel will be justified and will glory" (45:1-25).

One of the main themes that flows throughout chapter 45 is the idea that God is the One who has raised up Cyrus. Chapter 45 may be broken down as follows: (1) God's choice of Cyrus (vv. 1-8), (2) God's choice is His sovereign right (vv. 9-13), (3) God's choice can follow any path He wills (vv. 14-17), and (4) God's choice has redemptive purposes (vv. 18-25).[204]

God's choice is to use Cyrus (vv. 1-8)

God always has purpose in what He does, and this also holds true for Cyrus. Here in verses 1-8, we see three specific purposes behind God's choice to raise up Cyrus.

God's purpose will give Cyrus overwhelming victory (vv. 1-3)

This section continues with the amazing kind of language that we saw in 44:28 where God called Cyrus "My shepherd." Here God calls him His "anointed one" (*mashiyach*).[205] Cyrus is the king God has chosen to fulfill His purpose.[206] Young explains, "The term, rather, suggests that there is a specific task that he is to accomplish and that for this he has been anointed by the sovereign God of Israel."[207] How is God going to give him victory?

A message about Cyrus (v. 1). Speaking in the third person, God says that He will take Cyrus by the right hand to empower Him. Three infinitive

---

[204] Oswalt reminds us that "above all, the oracle is not really addressed to Cyrus, but to the despairing Israelites who cannot see how the glowing promises of restoration can possibly be kept (Oswalt, *The Book of Isaiah: Chapters 40-66*, 200).
[205] This is the Hebrew term that means "messiah," the same term used of Jesus Christ (1 Sam. 2:10; Ps. 2:2; Dan. 9:25-26; John 1:41; 4:25; cf. Isa. 61:1).
[206] In a similar way God called Nebuchadnezzar His servant (Jer. 25:9; 27:6; 43:10).
[207] Young, *The Book of Isaiah, vol. 3*, 195.

clauses follow, the promise to subdue (*radad*),[208] to loose (*pathach*), and to open (*pathach*), all showing how God's empowering will give victory.

A message to Cyrus (vv. 2-3). God addresses Cyrus directly with three promises of how He will be with Cyrus to give him these victories, all introduced with the promise "I will."[209] No nation would be able to withstand the brute power of Persia,[210] not even mighty Babylon.[211] The riches of Babylon (and others) will belong to Persia (v. 3a).[212]

All of this is so that Cyrus might know that, "it is I, the Lord, the God of Israel, who calls you by your name" (v. 3b). Cyrus recognized that the God of Israel was showing him this favor.[213] This does not mean that Cyrus was a believer in Yahweh, but only the reality of Yahweh's existence and power (cf. Exod. 6:7).[214] Josephus wrote that after Cyrus overthrew Babylon, the prophecy of Isaiah was shown to Cyrus and actually did have an influence on the king.[215] Furthermore, we cannot ignore the impact that Daniel must have had on Cyrus. Daniel would likely have had opportunity to show Cyrus the prophecies about him in Isaiah, Jeremiah, and even his own prophetic writings.

God's purpose will work for Israel's good (v. 4)

---

[208] I.e., to beat down so as to conquer (cf. Ps. 144:2).
[209] The language clearly has echoes of 40:3-5.
[210] Daniel 8:3-4 conveys the same truth when it pictures Persia as a powerful ram pushing westward, northward and southward, before whom no one could stand.
[211] If the descriptions given by Herodotus are accurate, Babylon had over 100 gates to the city, "all of bronze with bronze uprights and lintels" (Grogan, "Isaiah," 270). Although Babylon was well-fortified, God's promise to Cyrus is that He (God) would "shatter" (*shabar*) the bronze gates and "cut through" (*gada'*) the iron bars to give him the victory. Herodotus also reported that the openness of the city (because of their anger at their present kings) was so great that the Persians were taking prisoners as they moved to the palace in the center.
[212] Both Xenophon and Herodotus wrote about endless fortunes that Cyrus had captured from Croesus in Lydia and also in Babylon (Oswalt, *The Book of Isaiah: Chapters 40-66*, 201). One day, however, all the wealth will revert back to the King of Israel as declared by the post-exilic prophets (Hag. 2:7-9; Zech. 6:9-15).
[213] The Bible records the words of Cyrus who recognized the work of Yahweh to give him these victories (2 Chron. 36:22-23; Ezra 1:1-4).
[214] In the Cyrus Cylinder, Cyrus actually attributes his victory to the Babylonian God Marduk—probably to gain favor of the people of Babylon who did not like their former king and to persuade them to accept him (Grogan, "Isaiah," 270).
[215] Young, *The Book of Isaiah, vol. 3*, 197-98.

God's purpose for Cyrus was not simply to give him lordship over the nations, but to show favor to God's people Israel. Thus, "For the sake of Jacob My servant, and Israel My chosen one,[216] I have also called you by your name; I have given you a title of honor though you have not known Me" (v. 4). Smith explains,

> This suggests that God desired that this king would honor him and that he gave him every opportunity to recognize Israel's God and the Hebrew people as God's chosen ones, but somehow Koresh never did come to a full acknowledgment of Israel's God. Why was this? If this Koresh was Cyrus, a Persian king, he grew up accepting the Zoroastrian religion that honored Ahura-mazda as their good god and Angra-Mainyu as his great adversary.[217]

Israel's greatest need was to recognize the truth of who her God was, and not let herself fear, since God has made it clear that He is in control.

God's purpose reveals God's glory to a dark world (vv. 5-8)

Isaiah reveals a third purpose in raising up Cyrus, that of revealing the glory of God.[218] Isaiah records three of these purposes.

God will reveal Himself to Cyrus (v. 5). Speaking directly to Cyrus, God declares, "I am the Lord, and there is no other; besides Me there is no God.[219] I will gird you, though you have not known Me." For the second time, the Lord makes it clear that He will use Cyrus even though he does not know Him. Oswalt explains, "Everything that happens is a result of the plans and purposes of the one divine, transcendent being."[220]

God will reveal Himself to the world (vv. 6-7). The significance of God's work with Cyrus is that it will extend beyond him to the entire world so that all men might know that Yahweh is God and there is no other (v. 6), "the One forming light and creating darkness, causing well-being and creating calamity; I am the Lord who does all these" (v. 7; cf. Amos 3:6).[221] God will raise

---

[216] Israel was in a state of apostasy for breaking the Mosaic Covenant, but God assures them that they are still the chosen people (cf. e.g., Isa. 42:1; 43:20).

[217] Smith, *Isaiah 40-66*, 256.

[218] The very fact that we Gentiles (scattered across the world) are reading about God's work in Cyrus is a proof how God has revealed His glory.

[219] Once again, God identifies Himself as being the only God (cf. 43:10-11; 44:6, 8; 45:6, 14, 18, 21; 46:9).

[220] Oswalt, *The Book of Isaiah: Chapters 40-66*, 202.

[221] God makes it clear that He is sovereign over all things, even the things we might

up Cyrus to use Him towards this end, and from the Scripture, we see that this will be fully and finally realized in the messianic kingdom (Isa. 11:9; 45:21-24; Jer. 31:34; Hab. 2:13-14; Mal. 1:11; Rev. 7:9-17).

God will reveal Himself for His own glory (v. 8). God commands the heavens above and the earth below to break forth with an outpouring of waters and growth (cf. 32:15; 44:3; Hos. 10:12; 14:5; Joel 3:18). His purposes will be fulfilled just as He has promised so that the world might see His faithfulness.[222] God made the promises, and He will fulfill them.

God's choice is His sovereign right (vv. 9-13)

In verses 1-8, Isaiah emphasized that it was God's choice to use Cyrus. However, notes Kidner, here in verses 9-13, "the focus turns from Cyrus to a rather querulous Israel."[223] God must once again rebuke His rebellious people for not trusting Him, a lack of faith that was even willing to challenge the ways of the Lord (cf. 46:8-11).[224] Because of Israel's challenge to God, the dominant theme of this section revolves around the sovereignty of God and His right to work according to His own purpose. This section includes both an illustration of God's right to choose (vv. 9-10) as well as an example (vv. 11-13).

The illustration of God's right to choose (vv. 9-10)

The basic principle comes out as God pronounces "woe" (*hoy*) on one who would quarrel (*riyb*) with his Maker (*Yotser*, to form; cf. Gen. 2:7).[225] God uses two illustrations to demonstrate the folly of Israel to argue.

---

call the bad things like darkness and calamity (Gen. 45:1-5; 50:20; Exod. 4:11; Rom. 8:28). Oswalt explains that even though God is not the direct cause of any kind of evil, "what Isaiah asserts is that God, as creator, is ultimately responsible for everything in nature, from light to dark, and for everything in history, from good fortune to misfortune. No other beings or forces are responsible for anything" (ibid., 204). Thus, nothing is outside of God's sovereignty and plan (cf. Ps. 33:11; Isa. 14:24; 46:8-11; Dan. 4:35; Acts 2:23; Eph. 1:11; Rev. 17:17).

[222] When God fulfills His promise, it is a manifestation of His righteousness (41:2; 42:6; 61:11). Oswalt explains, "As is frequent in this part of the book, *tsedeq/tsedeqah* here describes the character of God's dealings" (ibid., 206).

[223] Kidner, "Isaiah," 659 (querulous: complaining in a petulant or whining manner).

[224] Their complaint was that God should not use pagan Cyrus to bring His people out of captivity to Babylon (Grogan, "Isaiah," 271). This sounds similar to Habakkuk when he objected that God was unjust for using Babylon (Hab. 1).

[225] The imagery reminds us of Isaiah's woes elsewhere (cf. 5:8-23; 6:5; 28-35).

First illustration: Pottery arguing with a potter (v. 9).[226] Isaiah boldly introduces his first example by describing the reality of what Israel is like to God, "an earthenware vessel among the vessels of earth!" Isaiah asks, "Will the clay say to the potter, What are you doing? Or the thing you are making *say*, He has no hands?"[227] Pfeiffer explains,

> It is the part of folly to subject God's dealing to man's criticism or condemnation. All human understanding of the issues of right and wrong has originated in him as Creator, and therefore can never surpass him in excellence or validity.[228]

Second illustration: Children arguing with parents (v. 10). Isaiah supplies a second example, this one a child rebuking his parent, not just a child, but a baby during the birth process. Pfeiffer once again provides a helpful summary: "A child may not properly call his parents to an accounting, as if he possessed judicial authority over them. How much less may a man be critical of God!"[229] The point, says Martin, is that, "When someone who is created voices disapproval of the Creator's work he risks receiving a pronouncement of impending doom."[230]

The example of God's sovereign right to choose (vv. 11-13)

The significance of both of these illustrations comes out in this section where God asserts His absolute sovereignty as the Creator to use any means He chooses to work His plan, including His choice to use Cyrus. God states His sovereignty as Creator (vv. 11-12) and follows this with a restatement of His plan to raise up Cyrus (v. 13).

The sovereignty of God (vv. 11-12). Once again, we have another one of God's declarations about His absolute sovereignty as the Creator of all (vv. 11-12; cf. e.g., 40:22, 26; 42:5; 43:10-15; 44:1-2, 6, 21, 24; 45:18; Ps. 147:4-6). Based on this sovereignty, God challenges His people to ask Him about His plans for Israel. Smith explains how the grammar of this verse allows for two potentially different understandings:

> As a statement God would be encouraging the people to "ask me concerning the things to come for my sons," but it seems more likely that this is a question, "Should you ask me about the things to come for my sons?" The

---

[226] There are significant textual variants in v. 9 between the MT, LXX, and Targum. The MT is preferable (Oswalt, *The Book of Isaiah: Chapters 40-66*, 206, n. 30).
[227] The Bible uses this illustration often (Isa. 29:15-16; 64:8; Jer. 18:6; Rom. 9:20-24).
[228] Pfeiffer, *The Wycliffe Bible Commentary: Old Testament*, Is 45:7.
[229] Ibid.
[230] Martin, "Isaiah," 1100.

area of the people's concern relates to things that will happen in the future, presumably the hard and fearful times that are coming before the future rebuilding of the nation.[231]

This much is clear: All men need to trust God and not question His ways.

The purpose of God (v. 13). God's purpose is to use Cyrus: "I have aroused him in righteousness and I will make all his ways smooth; he will build My city and will let My exiles go free, without any payment or reward, says the Lord of hosts." Israel need not fear, for God's plan is to use Cyrus who "would build up Jerusalem again, and set the captivity free (*gâlûth*, as in Isa. 20:4), and all this without redemption with money (Isa. 52:3)."[232] God will "arouse" (*'ur*, awake, stir up; cf. 13:17; 41:2, 25; 45:1-3; 46:8-11) him in righteousness, and guide His path to carry out His will.[233] Not only will Cyrus not demand a payment (*mechiyr*, a wage) or reward (*shochad*, gift or bribe) from Yahweh for setting His people free, he will even make financial provision for the temple to be rebuilt (Ezra 6:3-4). God is at work in everything, and we can trust Him without fear.

God's choice can follow any path He wills (vv. 14-17)

God's choice can follow any path He wills to make happen. Isaiah makes two points on how this will work itself out.

First point: Israel will have a payday (vv. 14-15)

Israel was the chosen nation, but this also required obedience. Isaiah describes both the nature (v. 14) and marvel of Israel's payday (v. 15).

The nature of Israel's payday (v. 14). Cyrus is not going to ask for payment or reward (v. 13), but God is going to use Cyrus to give His people a

---

[231] Smith, *Isaiah 40-66*, 264.

[232] Keil, *Commentary on the Old Testament*, 446–447.

[233] This emphasis is clearly discernible in the OT passages which use this verb in the causative form with God as subject. God stirred up Tiglath-pileser against the tribes in the Transjordan area (1 Chron. 5:26). He also aroused the Babylonians against Jerusalem (Ezek. 23:22), and then He stirred up the Medes against Babylon (cf. 2 Chron. 36:22; Ezra 1:1; Jer. 50:9, 11; 51:11).

reward.²³⁴ Cyrus will conquer them and lead them in full subjugation (v. 14),²³⁵ but in the end when Israel's King comes to reign, the riches of these nations will all pass over to Israel (cf. 62:10; 66:18).²³⁶ This is the age when all the nations show submission to the King of Kings, and give their gifts and prayers to Him in recognition that God is with Israel and there is no other (cf. Isa. 19:23-25; 45:6, 18-22; 49:23; 54:3; 60:14; cf. Jer. 16:19; Zech. 8:20-23; 14:16-21; Mal. 1:11).

The marvel of Israel's payday (v. 15). To a nation that has just been destroyed and taken into exile, these promises were beyond imagination. For this reason, Isaiah says, "Truly, You are a God who hides Himself, O God of Israel, Savior!"²³⁷

Second point: Grace is the only salvation (vv. 16-17)

Isaiah again brings a condemning message for the idolator. Eternal shame will be their lot (v. 16; cf. 41:24; 42:17; 44:9-20; 45:24). In ages past, Israel chose idols, but by the grace of God that will not be her future. Rather, she will be, "saved by the Lord with an everlasting salvation," and she "will not be put to shame or humiliated to all eternity" (v. 17; cf. 49:23; 54:4). Smith explains,

> The encouraging conclusion to this paragraph is that the Israelites will never suffer shame or disgrace throughout all eternity. The details of all these events are not spelled out. The reader is not told when the nation will turn to God, what will happen to cause the nations to change course and trust in God for their salvation, or exactly what this "everlasting salvation" involves.²³⁸

God will save Israel, and all of this will be by the redeeming grace of Jesus Christ (Isa. 10:20-23; 59:20-21; Rom. 11:25-36).

---

²³⁴ As seen earlier (cf. 43:3), it is true that Cyrus' payment will be Egypt, Cush, and Seba, i.e., the Sabeans, a people group connected with the Ethiopians who dwelt in Upper Egypt, a race known for its tall stature (cf. Isa. 18:2; Num. 13:32).

²³⁵ Though this may suggest slavery or unwilling submission, it seems best in the whole context to see this as voluntary submission to the God of Israel.

²³⁶ The pronouns and suffixes are all feminine suggesting that Jerusalem, and not Cyrus, is the referent (Oswalt, *The Book of Isaiah: Chapters 40-66*, 214).

²³⁷ The idea that God hides Himself reflects the marvel of how God works His eternal purposes—purposes hidden in God's eternal counsel, but made known through the prophets and fulfilled in history (Young, *The Book of Isaiah, vol. 3*, 208).

²³⁸ Smith, *Isaiah 40-66*, 272.

God's choice has redemptive purposes behind it (vv. 18-25)

God's redemptive purposes for Israel continue to unfold in this final section. Isaiah highlights four particular redemptive purposes of the Lord.

God's redemptive purposes have design (v. 18)

God's work has purpose behind it. With reference to the earth, Isaiah says that God is the One who created and formed it so that it would not be "a waste place" (*tohu*, formless in Gen. 1:2). God's design was that the earth not remain "formless" (*tohu*) and "empty" (*bohu*).[239]

God's redemptive purposes are meant to be known (v. 19)

God's works are a cause for praise. Thus, God declares, "I have not spoken in secret in some dark land; I did not say to the offspring of Jacob, Seek Me in a waste place'; I, the Lord, speak righteousness, declaring things that are upright." Martin explains that what we have is another proof of, "the very nature of God's word. He speaks only what is true. In captivity the Jews could count on the fact that the Lord would deliver them from exile by Cyrus."[240] Whatever God does is perfect.

God's redemptive purposes are to bring men to truth (vv. 20-21)

Sinners have a hard time in recognizing that there is only one God. For this reason, God once again calls everyone to His courtroom.

The call to court (v. 20). Isaiah uses legal terminology to call sinners to a time of disputation. Oswalt explains that this time He is summoning the nations, "to dispute the true identity of deity."[241] Just who is the true God? Those who carry their gods around, and pray to gods who cannot save, have no knowledge. They are as dumb as their gods (v. 20).

The evidence says that there is only one God (v. 21). God continues calling on the Gentiles to present their evidence:

> Declare and set forth *your case;* indeed, let them consult together. Who has announced this from of old? Who has long since declared it? Is it not I, the Lord? And there is no other God besides Me, a righteous God and a

---

[239] Thus, the same principle holds true for God's own people and land.
[240] Martin, "Isaiah," 1100.
[241] Oswalt, *The Book of Isaiah: Chapters 40-66*, 221.

Savior. There is none except Me (v. 21; cf. Isa. 43:10; 44:6; 45:6; Deut. 4:35; Rev. 1:8, 17-18; 21:6; 22:13).

This is a truth God wants all men to know and believe.

God's redemptive purposes are universal (vv. 22-25)

God has always made His call to salvation open and universal (cf. e.g., Gen. 3:15; Ezek. 18:23, 30, 32; Ps. 19:1-6; Matt. 11:28-30; Luke 7:29; Acts 10:34-35; Rom. 1:18-32; 10:13; 2 Pet. 3:9). Isaiah makes a call for universal salvation (v. 22), and follows this with the promise of universal salvation (vv. 23-25).[242]

The call for universal salvation (v. 22). God calls out, "Turn to Me and be saved, all the ends of the earth, for I am God, and there is no other." All men have to do is to turn to Him and believe (cf. 1 Thess. 1:9; Acts 14:15; 15:19). God makes the call, but what will be the end result?

The promise of universal salvation (vv. 23-25). The day is coming when His grace will bring a mighty redemption that touches an elect remnant across the face of the whole earth. Isaiah writes, "I have sworn by Myself; the word has gone forth from My mouth in righteousness and will not turn back, that to Me every knee will bow, every tongue will swear *allegiance*" (v. 23). Many will make this confession from the agonies of hell because of their refusal to believe, but by His grace God is going to save a massive remnant of sinners from every corner of the world (Isa. 2:2-4; 11:10; 56:7; cf. Rev. 7:9-17).[243] These will be the ones who put their trust in God's victorious Servant (cf. Phil. 2:5-11) and say, "Only in the Lord are righteousness and strength" (v. 24). These are the ones who enter into His kingdom (Matt. 25:34). However, for those who refuse to believe, Isaiah says, "all who were angry at Him will be put to shame" (v. 24; cf. Isa. 41:11; 66:24; Ps. 2:5, 12; Matt. 25:41). What about the nation of Israel?

God's final promise is that, "In the Lord all the offspring of Israel will be justified and will glory," i.e., the remnant whom God has chosen and called and drawn to faith (v. 25; cf. Isa. 59:20; Zech. 12:10; 13:8-9; Rom. 11:25). Through faith in God's Servant who died for them (Isa. 53:4-6), they will be justified, and their sins will be forgiven forever (Isa. 53:11; cf. Rom. 3:21-26). At long last, Israel will glory in Yahweh as she should have done from the very beginning (cf. 41:16). As Wolf explains, "The Lord has the power to vindicate His people and to judge His enemies."[244]

---

[242] The idea is not that of "universalism" which asserts that all get saved, but that God's invitation to the world to repent is always given to all men universally.
[243] Pfeiffer, *The Wycliffe Bible Commentary: Old Testament*, Is 45:20.
[244] Wolf, *Interpreting Isaiah*, 200.

Summary and application

The true God is a holy God who judges sins. The great news is that this God of perfect righteousness is also a gracious God who delights in saving and forgiving repentant sinners (Luke 15:7, 10, 32; 19:10). This great mercy should fill every one of us with praise for His grace.

THE LORD IS THE TRUE GOD (46:1-13)

Chapter 46 continues many of the same themes that began in chapter 40, e.g., the Lord will save Israel; the Lord is greater than all the idols; those who worship idols are fools; only God can predict and fulfill.[245]

Chapter 46 reads as follows: "1 Bel has bowed down; Nebo stoops over; their images are *consigned* to the beasts and the cattle. The things that you carry are burdensome, a load for the weary *beast*. 2 They stooped over, they have bowed down together; they could not rescue the burden, but have themselves gone into captivity. 3 Listen to Me, O house of Jacob, and all the remnant of the house of Israel, you who have been borne by Me from birth, and have been carried from the womb, 4 even to *your* old age I will be the same, and even to *your* graying years I will bear *you!* I have done *it,* and I will carry *you;* and I will bear *you* and I will deliver *you.* 5 To whom would you liken Me and make Me equal and compare Me, that we would be alike? 6 Those who lavish gold from the purse and weigh silver on the scale hire a goldsmith, and he makes it *into* a god; they bow down; indeed they worship it; 7 they lift it upon the shoulder *and* carry it; they set it in its place and it stands *there*. It does not move from its place. Though one may cry to it, it cannot answer; it cannot deliver him from his distress. 8 Remember this, and be assured; recall it to mind, you transgressors. 9 Remember the former things long past, for I am God, and there is no other; *I am* God, and there is no one like Me, 10 declaring the end from the beginning, and from ancient times things which have not been done, saying, My purpose will be established, and I will accomplish all My good pleasure, 11 calling a bird of prey from the east, the man of My purpose from a far country. Truly I have spoken; truly I will bring it to pass. I have planned *it, surely* I will do it. 12 Listen to Me, you stubborn-minded, who are far from righteousness. 13 I bring near My righteousness, it is not far off, and My salvation will not delay, and I will grant salvation in Zion, *and* My glory for Israel" (46:1-13).

Israel had two basic problems. One was worshipping idols, and the other was not she was not trusting the Lord. Israel had become like the Babylonians, but the idols could not help Israel nor Babylon. Martin explains,

---

[245] Oswalt sees it as the third section of the unit that began at 45:14 (Oswalt, *The Book of Isaiah: Chapters 40-66*, 227).

Babylon would be used by God to judge Judah, but she in turn would be destroyed by God. Her gods, mere idols, would not be able to save her from defeat (chap. 46), and Babylon would fall in spite of her sorceries and wisdom (chap. 47).[246]

God wants His people to know Him and to trust Him. Smith explains,

> These messages continue the prophet's attempt to persuade his hard-hearted Hebrew audience (not the Babylonians) that Yahweh, Israel's God, is the sovereign ruler who will accomplish all his plans to save his people. He is not like the silent and motionless images of Bel or Nebo that can do nothing (46:1–13).[247]

The Lord makes four declarations to remind Israel that He alone is God, the God who can save, the One they needed to trust (45:17-21; 46:2-13).

The Lord mocks idols (vv. 1-2)

Babylon, like virtually every other nation in the ANE, practiced idolatry. Bel and Nebo were two of the chief gods of Babylon. Bel represents another spelling for the name "Baal" (lit. lord), the Phoenician chief god of Babylon. Bel was also another name for the chief god of Babylon, "Marduk." Bel was originally a title given to Enlil, the so-called "father of the gods" whose center was at Nippur, but over time the name Marduk began to overtake the use of the name Bel (cf. Jer. 50:2; 51:44).[248] Marduk, explains Smith, was the god who, "saved the younger gods of Mesopotamia from annihilation by defeating Tiamat in the Babylonian creation myth (the Enuma Elish), so Marduk was named the king of the gods (ANET, 60–72)."[249] Nebo, the son of Marduk, was considered the god of learning whose seat was at Borsippa, a city some 10 miles south of Babylon.[250] Nebo also was,

> the god of wisdom, writing, and in charge of the "Tablets of Destiny," which described what would happen in the coming year. Ironically, in this

---

[246] Martin, "Isaiah," 1100.

[247] Smith, *Isaiah 40-66*, 282.

[248] Wolf, *Interpreting Isaiah*, 201; Oswalt, *The Book of Isaiah: Chapters 40-66*, 228.

[249] Smith, *Isaiah 40-66*, 287.

[250] Young notes that a twelfth-century B.C. boundary stone of the Kassite period shows the crowned Marduk with a horned mythical animal at his feet. At Calah, a statue of Nebo from the time of Adad-nirari III (810-782) was excavated, bearing the inscription: "Trust in Nebo; do not trust in any other god" (Young, *The Book of Isaiah*, vol. 3, 220, n. 2).

message God announces that he himself will determine the destiny of these two gods.[251]

These are the gods of Babylon, but the Lord mocks these false gods as created things which weary their owners because they must be carried around. Because they are not real, they will not be able to deliver Babylon from Yahweh. Instead, they will bow down and stoop over when Babylon falls by the hand of Yahweh. Thus, just like those who worship them; they too will go into captivity by the Persians (cf. Jer. 48:7; 49:3).[252]

The Lord is unique (vv. 3-7)

Yahweh makes a second declaration to remind His people that there is no one like Him (cf. 43:10-13). Israel really needs to know this truth.

Israel needs to recognize the uniqueness of Yahweh (vv. 3-4)

God reminds His people that contrary to idols which must be carried, He is the One who carries them,[253] a work of grace that began while they were still in the womb and will continue into their "graying years." He will "deliver" them (*malat*, delivering out of mortal danger).[254]

No one like Him (vv. 5-7)

God wants His people to know and trust Him. For this reason, God once again tells His people that He cannot be compared to idols.

A God without equal (v. 5). God asks, "To whom would you liken Me and make Me equal and compare Me, that we would be alike?" After 1,400 years, the answer should be apparent: No one can be compared to God (cf. 40:18-20; 41:7, 10, 20; 43:7; 44:9-20; 45:16, 20; 46:1-2).

---

[251] Smith, *Isaiah 40-66*, 287.

[252] Grogan, "Isaiah," 274. It seems that Cyrus did not actually dishonor or take away these gods out of respect to the people. Rather, they simply have been brought down as conquered.

[253] In Deuteronomy Moses writes, "The LORD your God who goes before you will Himself fight on your behalf, just as He did for you in Egypt before your eyes, and in the wilderness where *you saw how the LORD your God carried you, just as a man carries his son*, in all the way which you have walked until you came to this place" (Deut. 1:30-31).

[254] Francis Brown, Samuel Rolles Driver, and Charles Augustus Briggs, *Enhanced Brown-Driver-Briggs Hebrew and English Lexicon*, cited in electronic form with Logos Libronix (Oxford: Clarendon Press, 1977), 572.

Idols cannot save (vv. 6-7). Idols can be carried around and worshipped, but they cannot save. God illustrates the folly of thinking that a man-made god can save by showing five steps of the life cycle of an idol.

First of all, since it takes money to make a god, you need to dig into your purse and pull out some gold or silver. Secondly, you need to find a skilled "craftsman" who can shape it into a god (the *tsoreph* is a smith who knows how to smelt and mold; cf. 40:19). Third, now it is your turn to bow down in worship (*sagad*, a rare term for bowing in worship; v. 6; cf. Isa. 44:15, 17, 19; 46:6).[255] Fourth, you need to pick it up and carry it around. Fifth (not stated here), you must nail it down so that it does not totter (cf. 40:20; 41:7).

Now that you have made your god, it is time to worship it,[256] but sadly, "though one may cry to it, it cannot answer; it cannot deliver him from his distress" (v. 7; cf. 41:28; 45:20). Why? The answer, says Paul, is because the powers behind them are from demons and not God (1 Cor. 10:20; cf. 1 Cor. 8:4). Israel needs to trust and worship Yahweh alone.[257]

The Lord can predict and fulfill (vv. 8-11)

Isaiah makes a third declaration that Yahweh alone is God whom Israel needs to trust. God reveals that the unfolding of future events is without condition, and the reason why is because all of these events are nothing less than the outworking of God's eternal plan of God.

God is the One Israel needs to know and trust (vv. 8-9)

Three times God commands His covenant transgressing people, the *poshe'iym* (Isa. 1:20, 23, 28; 30:1; 43:27; 48:8; 50:1; 57:4; 59:13; 66:24; cf. esp. Dan. 8:12, 13, 23; 9:24), that they need to study their own history that Yahweh has been the One to care for them (vv. 8-9a; cf. 41:22; 42:9).[258] He is God, and there is no one like Him (v. 9b; cf. 41:26-27; 45:5, 21). But how can Israel know this?

---

[255] Ludwig Koehler et al., *The Hebrew and Aramaic Lexicon of the Old Testament*, cited in electronic form with Logos Libronix, 741–742.

[256] In 44:17, God says that he falls down before this stick and says, "You are my god. Deliver me!"

[257] Keil, *Commentary on the Old Testament*, 453.

[258] As seen earlier (cf. e.g., 43:18), the former things could include God's great works like creation, the flood, the patriarchs, and most immediately the Exodus. With reference to these former things, God reminds Israel that He spoke the word and fulfilled the word (Isa. 48:3), something the idols cannot do (48:4).

God is the One who possesses all power and sovereignty (v. 10)

The answer is that He alone is capable of predicting the end of time from the very beginning of time. In other words, the unfolding of these prophesied events is nothing less than the work of God to fulfill His eternal plan: "My purpose [*'etsah*] will be established,[259] and I will accomplish all My good pleasure [*chephets*]."[260] As the usage of "purpose" and "good pleasure" demonstrate, both of them accentuate the truth that Yahweh is a sovereign God whose eternal purpose encompasses every event in history.

God is the One raising up Cyrus (v. 11)

Isaiah moves from the general (v. 10) to the specific (v. 11) by explaining how He will demonstrate His sovereignty. He will raise up King Cyrus to save His people from Babylon. God describes His purpose and good pleasure as the act of calling a bird of prey (cf. 18:6; 41:2; Jer. 49:22) from the east. To be more specific, God calls him "the man of My purpose" from a far country. Cyrus from Persia the east (cf. 41:2) is the man whom God will use to save His people. This is a truth Israel needs to know and believe: "Truly I have spoken; truly I will bring it to pass; I have planned *it, surely* I will do it."[261] Thus, explains Pfeiffer,

> As Jehovah had predicted the fall of Jerusalem, the seventy years' exile, and the return to the homeland, so all should come to pass, fulfilling the forecast to the letter, and demonstrating that the Scripture speaks the truth of the one true and omnipotent God.[262]

Israel needs to know the Lord, for "neither Assyria, nor Babylon, nor Persia acted independently. God superintends all the nations (cf. 40:15-17)."[263]

The Lord will act quickly (vv. 12-13)

Isaiah makes a fourth and final declaration to remind Israel that Yahweh alone is God whom they need to trust. Clearly God is not happy with His people when He calls them "stubborn-minded" (v. 12; cf. Isa. 48:4; Num. 14:1-10) and "far from righteousness" (cf. 41:2; 45:8). Nevertheless, He still extends an

---

[259] I.e., his determined plan (cf. 5:19; 14:24, 26; 25:1; 44:26; 46:11; Eph. 1:11).
[260] I.e., what God has determined is good and best (cf. 44:28; 48:14; 53:10; Eph. 1:11).
[261] The particle *'aph* ("surely") stresses the emphatic truth that if God has said He is going to do something, He will do it.
[262] Pfeiffer, *The Wycliffe Bible Commentary: Old Testament*, Is 46:1.
[263] Wolf, *Interpreting Isaiah*, 201.

invitation to trust Him: "I bring near My righteousness; it is not far off, and My salvation will not delay, and I will grant salvation in Zion, *and* My glory for Israel" (v. 13; cf. Isa. 4:2-6; 44:23; 62:3; Ezek. 43:1-5; 44:4). This promise of God bringing His righteousness near, explains Oswalt, "refers to God's righteous actions in regard to his covenant with Israel. That is, He will be faithful to the promises He made to be their God and to deliver them from all their enemies."[264] God has promised this restoration, and this is the promise Israel needs to believe.

Summary and application

God's promise to restore Israel is staggering, but it is true (cf. Isa. 55:8-11; Jer. 33:14-26; Rom. 11:25-32). For the present writer, it is disappointing when Bible scholars choose to follow their own (non-premillennial) theological systems that deny these promises. The Lord has spoken over and over that He will restore Israel. This should be a cause of rejoicing for every Christian, for if God has promised something, He will do it (Rom. 5:1-11; 8:23; 2 Cor. 1:21-22; 5:5; Eph. 1:13-14; 4:30).

A LAMENT FOR FALLEN BABYLON (47:1-15)

In the previous chapters, God demonstrated His infinite superiority to idols. Because He is God and the idols are nothing, He is the One who is able to predict and fulfill, something no idol can do. In the flowing context, the future He has already predicted is that Persia is going to rise up under Cyrus, and Persia will overthrow Babylon. Babylon is going to die, and every death calls for a funeral. The basic theme of Isaiah 47 is that it is a funeral dirge (a lament) for Babylon.

Chapter 47 reads as follows: "1 Come down and sit in the dust, O virgin daughter of Babylon; sit on the ground without a throne, O daughter of the Chaldeans! For you shall no longer be called tender and delicate. 2 Take the millstones and grind meal. Remove your veil; strip off the skirt; uncover the leg; cross the rivers. 3 Your nakedness will be uncovered; your shame also will be exposed. I will take vengeance and will not spare a man. 4 Our Redeemer, the Lord of hosts is His name, the Holy One of Israel. 5 Sit silently, and go into darkness, O daughter of the Chaldeans, for you will no longer be called the queen of kingdoms. 6 I was angry with My people; I profaned My heritage and gave them into your hand. You did not show mercy to them. On the aged you made your yoke very heavy. 7 Yet you said, I will be a queen forever. These things you did not consider, nor remember the outcome of them. 8 Now, then, hear this, you sensual one, who dwells securely, who says in your heart, I am,

---

[264] Oswalt, *The Book of Isaiah: Chapters 40-66*, 238.

and there is no one besides me. I will not sit as a widow, nor know loss of children. 9 But these two things will come on you suddenly in one day: Loss of children and widowhood. They will come on you in full measure in spite of your many sorceries, in spite of the great power of your spells. 10 You felt secure in your wickedness and said, No one sees me. Your wisdom and your knowledge, they have deluded you, for you have said in your heart, I am, and there is no one besides me. 11 But evil will come on you which you will not know how to charm away; and disaster will fall on you for which you cannot atone; and destruction about which you do not know will come on you suddenly. 12 Stand *fast* now in your spells and in your many sorceries with which you have labored from your youth; perhaps you will be able to profit; perhaps you may cause trembling. 13 You are wearied with your many counsels. Let now the astrologers, those who prophesy by the stars, those who predict by the new moons, stand up and save you from what will come upon you. 14 Behold, they have become like stubble; fire burns them; they cannot deliver themselves from the power of the flame. There will be no coal to warm by *nor* a fire to sit before! 15 So have those become to you with whom you have labored, who have trafficked with you from your youth; each has wandered in his own way; there is none to save you" (47:1-15).

Chapter 47 is a lament over the fall of Babylon, but the larger purpose is to comfort Israel and assure her that God's promises are certain. Chapter 47 gives us a four-fold explanation of Babylon's coming ruin.

Babylon's ruin will be catastrophic (vv. 1-5)

Babylon's ruin will be catastrophic. The empire that had enjoyed universal supremacy for a brief period will suddenly see it all taken away.

Babylon will lose all her elegance (vv. 1-3)

God commands the virgin daughter of Babylon to come down from her throne and sit in the dust. Smith explains the humiliations to come:

> The imperative verbs "go down" (*rĕdî*) and "sit" (*šĕbî*) picture the queen's movement from the glorious throne in the luxurious royal court to the filthy dust of the earth, a place where a highly privileged queen would never sit.[265]

Calling Babylon a "virgin daughter" utilizes the imagery of "a young woman of fastidious and luxurious tastes, who has never had to face the harsh side of life," especially that of a complete violation of all her intimacy (cf. Isa. 3:26; 23:12;

---

[265] Smith, *Isaiah 40-66*, 300.

37:22; Ps. 137:8; Jer. 50:42; 51:33; Zech. 2:7).[266] No longer will she be a delicate queen lounging in her palace,[267] but she will be forced into a life of humiliating servitude like a slave girl who cannot even keep her own body covered.[268] All this ruin will be the work of Yahweh to bring "vengeance" (*naqam*) on the one who brought the same kind of ruin to His own people Israel, i.e., equal retribution for her evil deeds (cf. 34:8; 35:4; 59:17; 61:2; 63:4; Deut. 32:35; Mic. 5:14).[269]

Babylon will realize that Yahweh is the true King (vv. 4-5)

When Babylon invaded Judah, she was following suit in the way that world empires operate (i.e., get powerful, conquer, make them pay tribute). What Babylon did not know is that there is a true God, The Lord of Hosts,[270] and that He is the Redeemer of Israel (41:14; 43:14; 44:6, 22-24),[271] the Holy One of Israel (v. 4).[272] The Living God, the Holy One of Israel, will not allow Babylon to go unpunished (cf. Zech. 2:8).[273] Therefore, He tells her, "Sit silently, and go into darkness, O daughter of the Chaldeans, for you will no longer be called the queen of kingdoms" (v. 5). For Babylon, it is going to be a "lights-out" kind of existence. The party and gaiety are all coming to an end very soon. Smith explains,

> The lights, excitement, and noise of this busy capital city will end, but it is not clear that this symbolism should be carried even further to include aspects of imprisonment in a dark dungeon or consignment to death and the netherworld.[274]

---

[266] Oswalt, *The Book of Isaiah: Chapters 40-66*, 241. There were seasons in ancient Babylon in past ages when she had fallen to enemy powers, but the work of Cyrus would bring a first for Neo-Babylon (Young, *The Book of Isaiah, vol. 3*, 231-232).

[267] The term "tender" (*rak*) carries the idea of soft, spoiled, and coddled (Deut. 28:54, 56), and the synonym "delicate" (*'anog*) the idea of pampered (Deut. 28:54, 56).

[268] She used to think that her feminine beauty was too excellent for anyone to see, but now her body will be exposed for all to see. God's judgment will force her to go out in the streets like a common slave or beggar (Grogan, "Isaiah," 277).

[269] Ludwig Koehler et al., *The Hebrew and Aramaic Lexicon of the Old Testament*, cited in electronic form with Logos Libronix, 721.

[270] God identifies Himself as "the Lord of Hosts" some 61 times in Isaiah, an epithet that identifies Yahweh as God of all the armies (cf. 44:6 for explanation).

[271] See comments at 43:14 for further explanation.

[272] Isaiah uses the expression Holy One or Holy One of Israel some 26 times. See comments at 6:3 for further explanation.

[273] Just as it had been with Assyria who invaded the northern kingdom (cf. Isa. 10), Babylon also was an agent of God's judgment who would now have to give an account for sinning against God (Isa. 39:5-7; 43:14; cf. Hab. 1:6-11).

[274] Smith, *Isaiah 40-66*, 303.

Babylon's ruin was due to her own sin (vv. 6-7)

Isaiah's second explanation of Babylon's explains that her ruin is due to her own evil. Yes, God was angry at Israel (Isa. 54:9; 57:16), and God did use Babylon to judge them (Jer. 25:8-11; 27:6; Dan. 1:1-2),[275] but Babylon was still the one in sin (v. 6).[276]

Isaiah magnifies the sin of Babylon: "You did not show mercy to them; on the aged you made your yoke very heavy.[277] Yet you said, I will be a queen forever. These things you did not consider, nor remember the outcome of them" (v. 7). Babylon was a tool in God's hand, but she will pay dearly. Zechariah 1:15 explains, "I am very angry with the nations who are at ease; for while I was only a little angry, they furthered the disaster." The Abrahamic Covenant says that God will curse the one who curses Israel (Gen. 12:3). Jeremiah declares a similar message a generation later:

> Israel is a scattered flock; the lions have driven *them* away. The first one *who* devoured him was the king of Assyria, and this last one *who* has broken his bones is Nebuchadnezzar king of Babylon. Therefore, thus says the Lord of hosts, the God of Israel, Behold, I am going to punish the king of Babylon and his land, just as I punished the king of Assyria (Jer. 50:17-18; cf. 51:30-33).

Babylon did great evil against Israel, and for this reason God will judge her for her own sin. Thus, explains Kidner,

> It is Babylon's proper fate: there can be no mercy, for she has shown none (6; *cf.* Jas. 2:13). Yet the description is not without pity. We are watching the triumph of justice, but equally the tragedy of the sinner. Dust and toil, nakedness and shame, silence and darkness (1–5).[278]

Babylon's ruin will catch her unprepared (vv. 8-11)

Isaiah's third explanation of Babylon's ruin focuses on the fact that Persia's overthrow will catch Babylon unprepared. One of Babylon's main errors was that she had a very "lofty opinion of herself."[279]

---

[275] The outpouring of wrath caused the holy land of Yahweh to be profaned (*chalal*, polluted, defiled) by pagan invaders (Isa. 43:28; cf. Ezek. 24:21; 36:19-23).

[276] God calls His people Israel "My heritage" (*nachalah*, a permanent inheritance; cf. Deut. 4:20; 1 Sam. 10:1; 1 Kings 8:51, 53; Jer. 12:7).

[277] Oswalt notes, however, that we have no reason to believe that Babylon treated Judah in a way that was unusually cruel in comparison to other nations of the ANE (Oswalt, *The Book of Isaiah: Chapters 40-66*, 247).

[278] Kidner, "Isaiah," 659.

[279] Wolf, *Interpreting Isaiah*, 202.

Babylon's view of herself (vv. 8-10)

Babylon had a high view of herself. This pride would be her downfall.

A false sense of immunity (v. 8). God confronts arrogant Babylon by calling her, "you sensual one [*'adin*],[280] who dwells securely." Babylon thought, "I am, and there is no one besides me. I will not sit as a widow, nor know loss of children" (v. 8). No nation—no matter how wealthy and powerful they might be—should ever think that they are invincible, but Babylon saw herself as immune from calamity.[281]

God's correction (v. 9). God's warning is that she would soon be suffering a complete loss. The arrogant queen would suddenly lose both her husband and her children,[282] and all of this despite her great magical resources.[283] No spell, charm, or enchantment (cf. 12; Deut. 18:11; Ps. 58:6) will save her from the vengeance of Yahweh.

Babylon's staggering sense of security (v. 10). It is amazing how secure Babylon felt: "You felt secure in your wickedness and said, No one sees me." God replies, "Your wisdom and your knowledge, they have deluded you, for you have said in your heart, I am, and there is no one besides me." Smith explains, "Babylon thought she was divine (47:8, 10b) and acted like no one would see her."[284] How wrong she was!

God's plan for Babylon (v. 11)

God announces His plan: "But evil will come on you which you will not

---

[280] One lexical source explains that this word "sensual" connotes the idea of "voluptuous, i.e., pertaining to being beautiful and desirable, implying a sensuality and desirability of a woman" (James Swanson, *Dictionary of Biblical Languages with Semantic Domains: Hebrew (Old Testament)* [Oak Harbor: Logos Research Systems, Inc.], cited in electronic form with Logos Libronix, 1997).

[281] They should have known better from Daniel's prophecies, including the one that came to Nebuchadnezzar himself. In her pride, though, she felt "secure" (*sha'anan*; cf. Isa. 32:9, 11 where it refers to the women of Judah and Zech. 1:15 where it refers to the pagan nations).

[282] The expression "one day" simply means suddenly (cf. Isa. 9:13; 10:17; 66:8; Zech. 3:9; Rev. 18:8, 17, 19).

[283] Sorceries (vv. 9, 12) translates *keseph* (here, 2 Kings 9:22; Mic. 5:12; Nah. 3:4), a word that conveys the idea of seeking information about the future by means of demonic forces (cf. Dan. 2:2 where several witchcraft terms occur).

[284] Smith, *Isaiah 40-66*, 307.

know how to charm away, and disaster will fall on you for which you cannot atone, and destruction about which you do not know will come on you suddenly."

Babylon did have tremendous exposure to God's truth through the prophet Daniel, but she chose to ignore this light (Dan. 5:18-23). The consequences would be disastrous. Pfeiffer explains, "The only fitting judgment for these moral and intellectual degenerates was sudden and appalling destruction, the slaughter of Babylon's armies (v. 9a), and the abrupt termination of her political power."[285]

Babylon's ruin cannot be averted by sorcery (vv. 12-15)

Isaiah gives a fourth explanation of Babylon's ruin. This one emphasizes the impotence of Babylon's gods and satanic rituals.

God taunts Babylon for her witchcraft (vv. 12-13)

God makes a mockery of the idols, this time by taunting Babylon to keep seeking her worthless sorcery (cf. v. 9 for same terms). Babylon was overrun with sorcery (cf. Ezek. 21:21; Dan. 2:2; 5:7-8), but none of it ever brought profit (v. 13). God taunts Babylon, telling her to seek help through her satanic rites.[286]

Babylon's witchcraft will not save her (vv. 14-15)

Babylon's astrologers will not save her, but they will all become like "stubble" and fire will burn them up. They have no power, so they will not even be able to deliver themselves when God's judgment comes. These last statements in verse 14 ("there will be no coal to warm by *nor* a fire to sit before") seem to be saying that the overwhelming fire of God's judgment will leave the land with nothing in which it will be able to find hope or comfort (cf. Isa. 30:30; 31:9; 33:14; 66:16, 24; Obad. 18; Nah. 1:10; Mal. 4:1), not even a nice little charcoal fire for warmth.[287] The sorcerers they trusted have failed to save, and that now leaves Babylon with no one (v. 15; cf. 46:1-2). Smith gives a helpful summary of Babylon's end:

---

[285] Pfeiffer, *The Wycliffe Bible Commentary: Old Testament*, Is 47:1.
[286] Oswalt notes that there is a catalog of astrological phenomena called Enuma Anu Enlil that was formulated during the old Babylonian Period of the 18th century B.C., copies of which have been found in the library of Ashurbanipal dating to 650 B.C. This collection includes more than 70 clay tablets from which the priests would make predictions based upon different kinds of astronomical signs (Oswalt, *The Book of Isaiah: Chapters 40-66*, 254, n. 56).
[287] Ibid., 255.

The final point that illustrates the uselessness of the advice of the sorcerers and magicians is that each of them go off in their own direction, following a different theory with a different means of influencing the gods. Their wandering around for an answer only demonstrates their lack of knowledge of the real truth. One enchanter may recommend examining the liver of a chicken, another will advise watching the stars, and a third will want to interpret a dream, but none of these spiritual advisors will actually be able to offer any help.[288]

Summary and application

God is not going to let the course of this world continue on forever. The day is coming when He will judge all evil, and the only hope anyone has is refuge in the Lord.

TRUST GOD AND DO NOT BE STUBBORN (48:1-22)

The focus of chapter 48 turns back to Israel, but not in a good way. Kidner notes that, "the shift of attention from Babylon back to Israel is far from flattering."[289] The reason why is because God is now going to readdress the sin of Israel. One of the recurring sub-themes we find in 40-48 is the stubbornness of Israel. After 1,400 years of the Lord's faithfulness to the people of Israel, they should have known that she could trust the Lord. God confronts Israel for being unwilling to trust His Word.

Chapter 48 reads as follows: "1 Hear this, O house of Jacob, who are named Israel and who came forth from the loins of Judah, who swear by the name of the Lord and invoke the God of Israel, *but* not in truth nor in righteousness. 2 For they call themselves after the holy city, and lean on the God of Israel; the Lord of hosts is His name. 3 I declared the former things long ago and they went forth from My mouth, and I proclaimed them. Suddenly I acted, and they came to pass. 4 Because I know that you are obstinate, and your neck is an iron sinew and your forehead bronze, 5 therefore I declared *them* to you long ago; before they took place I proclaimed *them* to you, so that you would not say, My idol has done them, and my graven image and my molten image have commanded them. 6 You have heard; look at all this. And you, will you not declare it? I proclaim to you new things from this time, even hidden things which you have not known. 7 They are created now and not long ago; and before today you have not heard them, so that you will not say, Behold, I knew them. 8 You have not heard, you have not known. Even from long ago your

---

[288] Smith, *Isaiah 40-66*, 311.
[289] Kidner, "Isaiah," 659.

ear has not been open, because I knew that you would deal very treacherously, and you have been called a rebel from birth. 9 For the sake of My name I delay My wrath, and *for* My praise I restrain *it* for you, in order not to cut you off. 10 Behold, I have refined you, but not as silver; I have tested you in the furnace of affliction. 11 For My own sake, for My own sake, I will act, for how can *My name* be profaned? And My glory I will not give to another. 12 Listen to Me, O Jacob, even Israel whom I called. I am He, I am the first, I am also the last. 13 Surely My hand founded the earth, and My right hand spread out the heavens; when I call to them, they stand together. 14 Assemble, all of you, and listen! Who among them has declared these things? The Lord loves him; he will carry out His good pleasure on Babylon, and His arm *will be against* the Chaldeans. 15 I, even I, have spoken; indeed I have called him; I have brought him, and He will make his ways successful. 16 Come near to Me, listen to this: From the first I have not spoken in secret; from the time it took place, I was there, and now the Lord God has sent Me, and His Spirit. 17 Thus says the Lord, your Redeemer, the Holy One of Israel, I am the Lord your God, who teaches you to profit, Who leads you in the way you should go. 18 If only you had paid attention to My commandments! Then your well-being would have been like a river, and your righteousness like the waves of the sea. 19 Your descendants would have been like the sand, and your offspring like its grains; their name would never be cut off or destroyed from My presence. 20 Go forth from Babylon! Flee from the Chaldeans! Declare with the sound of joyful shouting, proclaim this, Send it out to the end of the earth. Say, The Lord has redeemed His servant Jacob. 21 They did not thirst when He led them through the deserts. He made the water flow out of the rock for them; He split the rock and the water gushed forth. 22 There is no peace for the wicked, says the Lord" (48:1-22).

Many commentators recognize that chapter 48 appears to be bringing a close to a larger unit (a unit that embraces chapters 40-48). Here in this closing section, God again turns His attention to stubborn Israel (cf. Neh. 9:26-30). One way of outlining this chapter is to see it as consisting of a series of four messages from Israel's history about the danger of not heeding the voice of God.

First message: A failure to listen to God's messengers (vv. 1-8)

From the time of the Exodus (1446 B.C.) until the time of the Babylonian exile (605 B.C.), Israel had over 800 years of God's prophetic word. In this section, Isaiah brings a focus upon prophecies of past events, and how Israel refused to believe these prior prophecies that have now been fulfilled though their exile to Babylon. Isaiah highlights two broad areas of sin that Israel has been guilty of.

First area of sin (vv. 1-2)

God's people have been dishonest and hypocritical when it comes to God's word. For this reason, God gives Israel a call to listen to His passionate rebuke.

The claim of Israel. The house of Jacob are the people of Israel (cf. Gen. 32:28; 35:10).[290] This is the nation who would look to Yahweh as the ultimate power by whom oaths would be taken. This is the nation who claims Jerusalem as their capital (Isa. 52:10; 64:10; Pss. 48:2; 132:13-18; Matt. 5:35). This is the nation who claims they lean on Yahweh.

The hypocrisy of the nation. Israel's problem was not that she claimed allegiance to the Lord, but that it was not in truth or righteousness. God's purpose, explains Young, is not simply to complain about His disobedient people but, "to bring home to the people their sinful and unworthy condition" that they might listen and turn back to Him in faith.[291]

Second area of sin (vv. 3-8)

The second area of Israel's sin was that God had to give them predictive prophecy ahead of time so that they would not attribute the work of Yahweh an idol. This section is quite interesting in that it exposes the inclination of sinners to pervert God's truth no matter how much or how little God may give. Isaiah highlights two ways this sin shows itself.

The first way Israel's perversion showed itself (vv. 3-5). The first kind of sin Isaiah rebukes is Israel's failure to believe past prophecies of a coming exile. We have already seen Isaiah speak several times about the "former things" (41:22; 42:9; 43:9; 44:7-8; 45:21; 46:10). Some think that the "former" things are still future but are the near future events, like the release by Cyrus.[292] Others think that it may be referring to other former prophecies that have already been fulfilled, e.g., the Exodus or the downfall of Jerusalem. It may be best to understand that it is referring to the fall of Jerusalem as promised by all the prophets

---

[290] It is both curious and unusual that Isaiah should mark the lineage of Israel as being from Judah and not Jacob (Num. 24:7; Deut. 33:28; Ps. 68:26). The MT literally reads "[Those who gone forth] from the *waters* of Judah." This difficult reading has led to several variations in the translations, e.g., LXX: from Judah, Syr.: loins (Oswalt, *The Book of Isaiah: Chapters 40-66*, 256, n. 1). One view is that "waters" could be a reference to semen but it seems better that the reference is that of a "fountain or source" (cf. Num. 24:7; Deut. 33:28; Ps. 68:26) (ibid., 260).
[291] Young, *The Book of Isaiah, vol. 3*, 245.
[292] Ibid., 247.

of old (cf. Deut. 28:15-68 and numerous prophecies by the pre-exilic prophets). God made the warnings and "suddenly" (after 800 years) He acted (v. 3).

Interestingly, God tells them that the reason why He openly predicted these things for them is because He knew that they were so sinful that if He had not given them these prophecies, they would have claimed that their idols were the ones who accomplished these events (vv. 4-5).[293] Idols, however, never predicted the Babylonian exile, but God did. Thus, explains Martin, "one reason God made those predictions was to point up His superiority to idols."[294]

The second way Israel's perversion showed itself (vv. 6-8). In the last section God told Israel that He had given them prophetic truth concerning the former things, otherwise they would have acted perversely. These are the things that He has already fulfilled, the things He is now calling them to look at and declare (v. 6a).[295] Now, however, God does just the opposite and tells them that there are other messages about the new things He plans to do that he did *not* tell them up until now otherwise they would have acted perversely with that truth.

The "new" and "hidden" things Isaiah speaks about (v. 6; cf. 42:9) seem to be things that were not revealed in previous ages, or at least not in the clarity that they would now be revealed. This would be looking at those prophecies which God is making known concerning things to come in the future that were not previously revealed. This would include something like the release from Babylon by Cyrus (13:17; 41:25; 44:28-45:8; 46:11),[296] but also fresh revelation about the Messiah and how He will bring a complete redemption by His death, resurrection, and victory over all enemies (cf. e.g., Isa. 49:1-7; 50:4-11; 52:13-53:12). Israel's Savior King will come, and He will bring a complete victory to the world with a restoration of Israel in the kingdom of God (Isa. 2:1-4; 4:2-6; 9:1-7; 11:1ff.; 25:6-12; 26:19-21; 35; 54; 63:1-6; 65:17; 66:22). God will do it (v. 7), but Israel needs to believe it (55:6-13). These are the "new things" they need to know and believe.

The plans are eternal, but God has not revealed them until now, for He knows how perverse His people are: "You have not heard, you have not known. Even from long ago your ear has not been open, because I knew that you would

---

[293] Clearly, God recognizes the stubborn character of His largely unregenerate people: you are obstinate (Exod. 32:9; Deut. 31:27; Ezek. 2:4; 3:7), your neck is an iron sinew (2 Chron. 36:13; Acts 7:51), and your forehead bronze (Ezek. 3:7-9).
[294] Martin, "Isaiah," 1102.
[295] In other words, take action on it and believe in the Lord.
[296] Wolf, *Interpreting Isaiah*, 202.

deal very treacherously; and you have been called a rebel from birth" (v. 8).[297] If God had made these things known before, they would have twisted them.[298] Oswalt makes a keen observation: "[Predictive prophecy] is given ... as confirmatory evidence that we can and should trust God. To use it for the purpose of knowing the future and making ourselves secure is only another form of idolatry."[299] Martin reminds us that in the outworking of God's redeeming grace, God wants them to recognize that, "their physical and spiritual deliverance would come not from their goodness or their own plans, but from God's grace."[300]

Second message: It is only by grace Israel stands (vv. 9-11)

God's people were defiant idolaters, but because of God's unchanging faithfulness, they still have a future (cf. Mal. 3:6). Here in verses 9-11, Isaiah gives his people three reminders that the only reason they remained was the grace of God (cf. Mal. 3:6).

First reason it is only grace that they stand (v. 9)

God is patiently restraining His wrath (*'aph*), but it is not because the people of Israel do not deserve judgment. Rather, it is for the sake of His own name and praise,[301] for if He gave them what they deserved, they would be "cut off" (*karath*).[302] God's saving grace always serves to bring glory to God.

Second reason it is only grace that they stand (v. 10)

Isaiah further clarifies that the reason why Israel continues to stand is because in the end God's chastening is going to involve an eschatological purification that will purge all rebellion from Israel and bring an elect remnant to

---

[297] The expression "deal very treacherously" employs the verb *bagad* that carries the idea of unfaithful, disloyal or treacherous (cf. e.g., Exod. 21:8; Hos. 5:7; Mal. 2:14). The present construction combines an infinitive form followed by the finite verb, a construction which intensifies the action very strongly (Young, *The Book of Isaiah, vol. 3*, 252). Sadly, says Isaiah, God's people have been "a rebel" (*poshe'a*) from birth (cf. Dan. 8:12, 13, 23; Isa. 57:4).

[298] Perhaps we might call it a "need to know" basis.

[299] Oswalt, *The Book of Isaiah: Chapters 40-66*, 268.

[300] Martin, "Isaiah," 1102.

[301] We see this idea very clearly in Ezekiel 36:16-32 and 39:25-29 (cf. Isa. 37:35; 43:25; 60:21; 61:3; Eph. 1:6, 12, 14; 2:7; 3:8-10).

[302] God's purpose is not to destroy Israel, but to save and restore, even if this requires chastening (Isa. 10:25; 12:1; 26:20; 40:2; Jer. 4:27; 5:10, 18; 30:7, 11; 46:28; Dan. 8:19; 9:27; 11:36; Amos 9:8-10).

faith. God explains this purification process with the metallurgical language of refining (*tsaraph*) and testing (*bachar*).[303] During the seven-year tribulation period, Israel is going to go through the most-severe time of testing it has ever experienced (Matt. 24:21). All rebellious disbelief will be purged (Isa. 65:11-15; cf. Ezek. 20:36-38; Zech. 5:1-4; Mal. 3:3) and God will purify and save His elect remnant (one third) so that they might know Him and enter the blessings of His kingdom (Isa. 1:25; 4:4; Dan. 12:10; Zech. 13:8-9; Rom. 11:25-36).

Third reason it is only grace that they stand (v. 11)

Isaiah reminds Israel that they do not deserve this grace: "For My own sake, for My own sake, I will act, for how can *My name* be profaned? And My glory I will not give to another." Smith explains,

> Although God does interact and respond to the sinful acts or repentance of people, in the final analysis God's actions are not determined by the behavior of people. He will act for his own sake to accomplish his purposes and to carry out his plans.[304]

Ultimately God's purpose revolves around His own glory. Martin explains:

> The Exile was to refine them so they would return to the land in belief.... The Captivity was like being in a furnace, to test them, not destroy them. If God would go back on His word about the return, His reputation would be defamed.[305]

Third message: Accept God's choice of Cyrus (vv. 12-16)

Verses 12-16 give us the third message about the danger of not listening to God. This involves an exhortation to Israel to accept God's sovereign choice of Cyrus (vv. 12-13), that He has the right to work according to His own purpose (vv. 14-15), and that His eternal purposes will stand (v. 16).

---

[303] The former term consists of melting down ore to separate the metals and the second term the idea of pulling out the metals that have been purified ("to choose). In this present, future context the perfect stem verbs should be rendered with a future force ("will refine" and "will test"). The second term *bachar* ("to choose") does not make a particularly good parallel with the verb *tsaraph*. It has been suggested that *bachar* is a textual variant from an original reading *bachan*, another metallurgical term that means "to test," a Hebrew verb that differs from *bachar* only by a slight variation in the third consonant. Both 1QIs[a] and the Targ. support the reading *bachan* (Oswalt, *The Book of Isaiah: Chapters 40-66*, 265).
[304] Smith, *Isaiah 40-66*, 323–324.
[305] Martin, "Isaiah," 1102.

God asserts His sovereign authority (vv. 12-13)

As He has done many times in 40-48, God again asserts His sovereignty as the true God and Creator of all things, even Israel whom He called to Himself (cf. 40:21-26; 41:4; 42:5; 43:1-13; 44:6, 24; 46:4; 45:12, 18; 51:13, 16).[306] The main point is this: Israel needs to listen to the Lord and His word (cf. 46:3).[307]

God declares His choice of Cyrus (vv. 14-15)

Chapters 40-48 have repeatedly spoken about God's choice of Cyrus as one proof of His ability to predict and fulfill (cf. 13:17; 41:2; 44:28-45:8; 46:8-11). This is the final time where God speaks about His choice of Cyrus: "Assemble, all of you, and listen! Who among them has declared these things? The Lord loves him; he will carry out His good pleasure on Babylon, and His arm *will be against* the Chaldeans" (v. 14). How curious it is what language God uses when talking about Cyrus! In 44:28 God called him His "shepherd." In 45:1 He called him his anointed one whom He takes by the right hand. In 45:5 He gave the promise that He would gird him for action, and in 46:10-11 he is the man of God's purpose who accomplishes all of God's good pleasure.

Here in 48:14 we read that the Lord "loves him" (*'ahab*),[308] that Cyrus is the one who will accomplish all of God's good pleasure (*chephets*), that God is the One who calls him and brings him, and that God is the One who will make his way successful. God has spoken that Cyrus is the one who shall bring down Babylon—the message Israel needs to hear and believe. Pfeiffer explains how it is that all of this marvelous prediction could ever take place. It is only because of who Yahweh is:

> As eternal Creator, God is the Lord of human history and brings to pass amazing providences beyond all human surmise or ability to predict. It was indeed a marvel that God should call Israel's deliverer, Cyrus, by name 150 years before he was even born, and love him as His chosen instrument to smite Babylon and destroy her power.[309]

---

[306] Young, *The Book of Isaiah, vol. 3*, 255.

[307] Oswalt explains that God is challenging them to prove Him wrong in His choice to use Cyrus (Oswalt, *The Book of Isaiah: Chapters 40-66*, 276).

[308] The concept behind "loved" is the idea of choice, cf. e.g., Deut. 4:37 where we see that God, in His sovereignty, loved and chose Israel and no other nation (Isa. 43:4; Mal. 1:2; Rom. 9:10-13; cf. Pss. 87:2 [He has loved Zion]; 132:13 [He has chosen Zion]).

[309] Pfeiffer, *The Wycliffe Bible Commentary: Old Testament*, Is 48:12.

God affirms the certainty of His eternal purposes (v. 16)

Verse 16 makes an interesting statement, one that in context appears to be affirming the certainty of God's eternal purposes. If God has planned it and spoken it, He will fulfill it. The interesting theological question is whether or not this passage contains a trinitarian statement. Even though it is possible that Isaiah is the one speaking, it is better to see this as the preincarnate Son of God speaking. Christ is the One calling Israel to listen to Him. Christ is the One who has not spoken in secret from the very beginning (cf. 45:19). Christ is the One who has been there from the time anything took place (John 8:58; 12:37-41), and Christ and His Spirit are the Ones the Lord have sent (Isa. 42:1; 61:1-2; 63:9-11, 16).[310]

Fourth message: God laments their past disbelief (vv. 17-22)

God laments the past disbelief of Israel. Had they been willing to listen, they could have averted the exile. Isaiah reminds Israel of three final truths to encourage them to not disobey in the future.

First truth: He is the God who wants their blessing (v. 17)

The Lord, Israel's Redeemer and Holy One, is the One who leads His people in the way they should go that they might profit with His blessings.[311] God's moral will for man is that he would believe and obey.

Second truth: Obedience would have brought blessings (vv. 18-19)

Although it can be interesting to ask hypothetical questions, we know that they are speculative and unfruitful since they are not reality.[312] Nevertheless, Scripture itself makes statements in certain places about what could have been if men had chosen differently (cf. e.g., 1 Sam. 23:11; Luke 19:41-44). God here

---

[310] Oswalt writes, "I see no way in which the subject of the first part of the verse could be the prophet. The things said there can be said only of God" (Oswalt, *The Book of Isaiah: Chapters 40-66*, 278). Grogan explains that the Spirit is in all likelihood not a second subject who is doing the sending along with "Sovereign Yahweh," for "in the Old Testament, the Spirit never sends but is always sent" (Grogan, "Isaiah," 281).

[311] Oswalt explains, "The relationship between [YHWH] and His people is not one of power manipulation" (Ibid., 281). In truth, He is their guide and teacher (cf. Isa. 2:3; 28:26; 30:20-21; Jer. 32:33).

[312] For example, "What if Adam had never sinned?" or "What if Israel had not rejected Christ at His first coming?"

tells Israel how they could have had His blessings:

> If only you had paid attention to My commandments![313] Then your well-being would have been like a river, and your righteousness like the waves of the sea. Your descendants would have been like the sand, and your offspring like its grains. Their name would never be cut off or destroyed from My presence (vv. 18-19; cf. 32:16-17; 35:7; 49:10; 54:13-14; 60:17; Gen. 22:17; 32:12).

God wanted His chosen people the nation of Israel to be blessed, and He gave them exhortation after exhortation to be faithful so that they might have His blessings, but in their sin they would not respond. Smith explains how this unfolded in history:

> Although God tried again and again to communicate his will, the Israelites seldom ever listened to his commandments. God communicated to them the wonderful promises that the people could have received in order to enjoy God's blessing of peace and righteousness (key characteristics of God's rule), but they never did.[314]

It is so sad to see that the people of Israel did not listen in the past (and it cost them greatly), but here we see God's plea to them now that they would begin to listen to Him.

Third truth: Future grace will take them out of Babylon (vv. 20-22)

God's final point to encourage obedience is another reminder that He will deliver them from Babylon. They do not deserve it, but according to His own faithfulness, He will favor them with His grace and set them free.

The command to flee Babylon (v. 20). With this assurance, God gives Israel the command to flee from Babylon, a command that many were not so eager to obey, hence the need for such exhortation (cf. Jer. 50:8; 51:6, 45; Zech. 2:6-7; Rev. 18:4).[315] Israel's need is to recognize that they must flee Babylon and return to their land.[316]

---

[313] This conditional structure gets created through the particle *lu'* ("oh that," "if only that").
[314] Smith, *Isaiah 40-66*, 330.
[315] The Babylonians had allowed the Jews to freely live and develop their lives, and after 70 years in a rich culture many were hesitant to leave.
[316] God makes it clear that this departure from Babylon should be a joyful and peaceful departure (cf. Isa. 52:6-12).

The promise of provision for the faithful (v. 21). Israel knew that it would be a difficult path to leave the comforts of Babylon, but God assures them that He can provide for their needs. Using imagery from the Exodus, God tells them, "They did not thirst when He led them through the deserts. He made the water flow out of the rock for them; He split the rock and the water gushed forth." Here is the message: God provided for Israel at the first Exodus (cf. Exod. 16; 17:1-7; Num. 20:11), so He certainly can provide for them in a second Exodus.

The warning of ongoing judgment for disbelievers (v. 22). The promises are there, and all Israel needs to do is believe the Lord and follow His will. But what about those who will not believe? The answer comes in 48:22: "There is no peace for the wicked, says the Lord" (cf. 57:21).[317] Once again, we are reminded of what God said in 48:18: "If only you would pay attention to My commandments." The promise of blessing is there, but no one can have God's blessings unless they are willing to obey.

Summary and application

Every man needs God's grace, and the wonderful truth we find in the Bible is that this grace is freely available to anyone who is willing to ask God for it (Isa. 55:1-3; cf. Matt. 11:28-30; Rev. 22:14, 17). The price has been paid (Isa. 53:4-6; 59:16; Matt. 20:28), and the invitation is there.

---

[317] The repetition of this expression in 57:21 (an inclusio) suggests that chs. 49-57 work together as a literary unit wherein Isaiah lays a heavy emphasis on the redeeming work of God's heaven-sent Servant, the Lord Jesus Christ.

9
SALVATION BY THE SERVANT OF GOD
(49:1-57:21)

Chapter 49 introduces us to a new section that runs from 49:1 through 57:21 and focuses heavily upon Israel's greatest Deliverer, God's heaven-sent Servant, the Lord Jesus Christ.[1] Cyrus of Persia was a significant figure in 40-48, but he is largely out of the picture in 49-57.[2] Martin explains,

> The previous nine-chapter section (chaps. 40–48) dealt mainly with Cyrus and his mission in the Jews' restoration. These nine chapters (49–57) deal primarily with the Servant-Messiah fulfilling His ministry of restoring the covenant people to the land just before the Millennium will begin. Neither person would fail in his mission. Because of the similarity of their missions, several of the same expressions and figures of speech are used in the two nine-chapter sections.[3]

---

[1] Herbert M. Wolf, *Interpreting Isaiah* (Grand Rapids: Zondervan, 1985), 205. In terms of big-picture themes, these chapters may be labeled as follows: 49: The Servant of Yahweh who restores Jews and Gentiles; 50: The disobedient servant nation versus the obedient Servant; 51: Trust in God and depart from evil; 52: Be alert and turn to the Lord; 53: The suffering Servant; 54: Israel's glorious and fruitful future; 55: The invitation to share in grace; 56: Universal blessings through faith; 57: Condemnation upon the wicked.

[2] Oswalt notes that while the language of captivity and deliverance continues, neither Cyrus nor Babylon are mentioned by name throughout the rest of the book (John N. Oswalt, *The Book of Isaiah: Chapters 40-66*, The New International Commentary On The Old Testament, R. K. Harrison, Gen. Ed. [Grand Rapids: Eerdmans, 1998], 286).

[3] John A. Martin, "Isaiah," in *The Bible Knowledge Commentary: An Exposition of the*

This section opens with an immediate focus on God's supreme Servant. His mission is to save God's people and a restore a sin-cursed world.

THE MISSION OF GOD'S SUPREME SERVANT (49:1-26)

Chapter 49 brings us the second Servant Song. The Servant Songs are four particular literary units of messianic prophecy that give us important information about who the Messiah will be and what He will accomplish.

Chapter 49 reads as follows: "1 Listen to Me, O islands, and pay attention, you peoples from afar. The Lord called Me from the womb; from the body of My mother He named Me. 2 He has made My mouth like a sharp sword; in the shadow of His hand He has concealed Me; and He has also made Me a select arrow; He has hidden Me in His quiver. 3 He said to Me, You are My Servant, Israel, in Whom I will show My glory. 4 But I said, I have toiled in vain, I have spent My strength for nothing and vanity. Yet surely the justice *due* to Me is with the Lord, and My reward with My God. 5 And now says the Lord, who formed Me from the womb to be His Servant, to bring Jacob back to Him, so that Israel might be gathered to Him (For I am honored in the sight of the Lord, and My God is My strength). 6 He says, It is too small a thing that You should be My Servant to raise up the tribes of Jacob and to restore the preserved ones of Israel; I will also make You a light of the nations so that My salvation may reach to the end of the earth. 7 Thus says the Lord, the Redeemer of Israel *and its* Holy One, to the despised One, to the One abhorred by the nation, to the Servant of rulers, Kings will see and arise; princes will also bow down, because of the Lord who is faithful, the Holy One of Israel who has chosen You. 8 Thus says the Lord, In a favorable time I have answered You, and in a day of salvation I have helped You; and I will keep You and give You for a covenant of the people, to restore the land, to make *them* inherit the desolate heritages, 9 saying to those who are bound, Go forth, to those who are in darkness, Show yourselves. Along the roads they will feed, and their pasture *will be* on all bare heights. 10 They will not hunger or thirst, nor will the scorching heat or sun strike them down, for He who has compassion on them will lead them, and will guide them to springs of water. 11 I will make all My mountains a road, and My highways will be raised up. 12 Behold, these will come from afar, and lo, these *will come* from the north and from the west, and these from the land of Sinim. 13 Shout for joy, O heavens! And rejoice, O earth! Break forth into joyful shouting, O mountains! For the Lord has comforted His people, and will have compassion on His afflicted. 14 But Zion said, The Lord has forsaken me, and the Lord has forgotten me. 15 Can a woman forget her nursing child and have no compassion

---

Scriptures, ed. J. F. Walvoord and R. B. Zuck, vol. 1, cited in electronic form with Logos Libronix (Wheaton, IL: Victor Books, 1985), 1103.

on the son of her womb? Even these may forget, but I will not forget you. 16 Behold, I have inscribed you on the palms *of My hands*. Your walls are continually before Me. 17 Your builders hurry; your destroyers and devastators will depart from you. 18 Lift up your eyes and look around. All of them gather together, they come to you. As I live, declares the Lord, you will surely put on all of them as jewels and bind them on as a bride. 19 For your waste and desolate places and your destroyed land—surely now you will be too cramped for the inhabitants, and those who swallowed you will be far away. 20 The children of whom you were bereaved will yet say in your ears, The place is too cramped for me; make room for me that I may live *here*. 21 Then you will say in your heart, Who has begotten these for me, since I have been bereaved of my children and am barren, an exile and a wanderer? And who has reared these? Behold, I was left alone. From where did these come? 22 Thus says the Lord God, Behold, I will lift up My hand to the nations and set up My standard to the peoples, and they will bring your sons in *their* bosom, and your daughters will be carried on *their* shoulders. 23 Kings will be your guardians, and their princesses your nurses. They will bow down to you with their faces to the earth and lick the dust of your feet, and *you* will know that I am the Lord. Those who hopefully wait for Me will not be put to shame. 24 Can the prey be taken from the mighty man, or the captives of a tyrant be rescued? 25 Surely, thus says the Lord, Even the captives of the mighty man will be taken away, and the prey of the tyrant will be rescued, for I will contend with the one who contends with you, and I will save your sons. 26 I will feed your oppressors with their own flesh, and they will become drunk with their own blood as with sweet wine; and all flesh will know that I, the Lord, am your Savior and your Redeemer, the Mighty One of Jacob" (49:1-26).

Once again God commands men to listen to His word (cf. 34:1; 41:1; 46:3, 12; 48:1, 12, 16). This time, however, God is sending this invitation not directly to Israel, but to the "the islands" (*'iyim*, the islands and coastlands of the western Mediterranean Gentile world; cf. 11:11; 20:6; 23:2; 24:15; 40:15; 41:1; 42:4, 10, 12; 49:1; 51:5; 59:18; 60:9; 66:19).[4]

We see two main ideas in chapter 49: (1) God's Servant will not fail (vv. 1-13), and (2) God's promises to Israel will not fail (vv. 14-26). Through these messages we are again reminded that there is only one way for redemption to be accomplished, and that is through the work of the Servant.

---

[4] These people from the islands are further described as "peoples from afar." This would extend as far as Tarshish and the British Isles and beyond (the same principle would apply to the Gentile world in every direction).

ISAIAH 49:1-57:21

God's Servant will not fail (vv. 1-13)

Throughout chapters 40-48 God assured His people that His promises will never fail. This certainly holds true for the Servant. These first thirteen verses might be broken down as emphasizing the Servant's determination (vv. 1-4), the Servant's redemptive calling (vv. 5-6), the Servant's promised exaltation (v. 7), and lastly the Servant's liberating victory (vv. 8-13).

The Servant's determination (vv. 1-4)

The path of God's Servant will be difficult, but His determination will bring success, a determination that He recognized was always His calling.

God's Servant recognized His eternal calling (v. 1). Because the Servant recognized God's calling on His life, He calls out to the Gentile world, "Listen to Me, O islands, and pay attention, you peoples from afar. The Lord called Me from the womb; from the body of My mother, He named Me." The Servant is calling on the nations to recognize that He is the Savior of the world who has been chosen and sent from God.[5]

God gave special equipping to His Servant (v. 2). When Isaiah says that God made the Servant's mouth like a sharp sword, this conveys the idea that the Servant will speak and accomplish God's plan exactly as God has purposed (Isa. 11:4; cf. Ps. 2:9; Rev. 1:16; 2:12, 16; 19:15). Young explains, "Through the Servant's mouth, the truth of redemption will be proclaimed to the poor and needy."[6] Furthermore, God has made His Servant into a "select" (sharp) arrow hidden in His quiver to go out and fulfill all His purposes in judging sinners (cf. Deut. 32:23, 42).[7]

God's Servant has the calling to glorify of God (v. 3). God's calling for the Servant is that He is the One in whom God will show His glory (cf. 4:2; 42:12; 44:23; 49:3; 60:21; 61:3; John 1:14; Phil. 2:11). Despite the addition of "Israel," we have good reason for saying that these words are not being spoken to the nation as in certain other passages (41:8, 9; 42:19; 43:10; 44:1, 2, 21; 48:20), but to the One man who comes out of the corporate nation. He is the

---

[5] Grogan notes that the Servant recognized that God's calling on His life was the beginning (cf. Jer. 1:5; Gal. 1:15), but in reality this, too, is part of God's eternal purposes (cf. 1 Pet. 1:20). See G. W. Grogan, "Isaiah," in *The Expositor's Bible Commentary*, ed. Frank E. Gaebelein, vol. 6 (Grand Rapids: Zondervan, 1986), 285.

[6] Edward J. Young, *The Book of Isaiah, vol. 3* (Grand Rapids: Eerdmans, 1972), 269.

[7] Messiah is the instrument of God, but He will not be revealed until the time that has been appointed by the Lord (Oswalt, *The Book of Isaiah: Chapters 40-66*, 290).

ideal and perfect Israel who does not fail like the nation failed (cf. Isa. 26:16-18).[8] Keil's explanation is helpful:

> Although the speaker is called Israel in v. 3*b*, he must not be regarded as either a collective person representing all Israel, or as the collective personality of the kernel of Israel, which answered to its true idea. It is not the former, because in v. 5 he is expressly distinguished from the nation itself, which is the immediate object of his special work as restorer and (according to v. 8 and Isa. 42:6) covenant-mediator also; not the latter, because the nation, whose restoration he effects, according to v. 5, was not something distinct from the collective personality of the "servant of Jehovah" in a national sense, but rather the entire body of the "servants of Jehovah" or remnant of Israel (see, for example, Isa. 65:8–16). Moreover, it cannot be either of these, because what he affirms of himself is expressed in such terms of individuality, that they cannot be understood as employed in a collective sense at all, more especially where he speaks of his mother's womb.[9]

Isaiah is unmistakably clear: Corporate Israel, a nation that was blind, deaf, and rebellious (Isa. 1:1-15; 5:5-7; 26:18; 41:8-10; 42:19, 24; 44:1; 54:17) was completely overtaken by sin and she was in no position to glorify God, for her righteousness was like that of a filthy rag (64:6).[10] This Servant, however, will prevail and save His people by His own perfect righteousness (Isa. 52:10; 53:11; 59:16; 63:5).

---

[8] We see this concept of corporate solidarity with a relationship between corporate Israel and the One Savior in many ways: (1) the nation is the seed of Abraham (Gen. 15:5; 22:17; 26:4), but Jesus is "the" Seed (Gal. 3:16); (2) Israel is God's vineyard (Isa. 5), but Jesus is the True Vine (John 15); (3) Israel is God's unique firstborn son (Gen. 22:16; Exod. 4:222-23), but Jesus is God's unique only Son (John 3:16); (4) God gave His nation prophets (Deut. 18:18-22), but Jesus is "the" Prophet (John 6:14; 7:40); (5) God gave His nation faithful high priests (1 Sam. 2:35), but Jesus is "the" faithful High Priest (Heb. 3:1).

[9] Carl Friedrich Keil and Franz Delitzsch, *Commentary on the Old Testament*, vol. 7, cited in electronic form with Logos Libronix (Peabody, MA: Hendrickson, 1996), 468. The importance of this point lies in the fact that many Jews hold the view that the Servant Songs refer not to Jesus but to the nation and how the nation will bring redemption to both itself and all the world.

[10] Oswalt, *The Book of Isaiah: Chapters 40-66*, 290-291; Young, *The Book of Isaiah, vol. 3*, 270. Oswalt adds, "Jacob cannot restore Jacob to a right relationship with God any more than Israel can restore itself to Judah from Babylon" (Oswalt, *The Book of Isaiah: Chapters 40-66*, 293).

God's Servant will not be overcome by the great task (v. 4). Judging by worldly standards, the Servant might be tempted to regard His own mission as a failure, that His work was in vain (*rîyq*) and that He labored for nothing (*tohu*) and vanity (*hebel*).[11] After all, He was rejected by His own people (Isa. 53:1-3; John 1:9-11). Nothing, however, could be further from the truth, for the Servant's justice (cf. 53:9) and reward (cf. 53:10-12) would come from the Lord Himself (Matt. 28:6; Rom. 1:4).[12] In His earthly ministry, Jesus knew that He would achieve a crushing victory over sin and death, and it was this hope that gave Him strength to persevere to the very end (Isa. 50:7; John 4:34; 5:30; 6:38; 17:24; Heb. 12:2).

The Servant's redemptive calling (vv. 5-6)

The topic of the Servant's calling becomes the prominent theme here in verses 5-6. Smith explains how the statement "and now,"

> introduces this segment and points to something new, just as it introduces a change in the situation in other subparagraphs (43:1, 19; 44:1; 47:8; 48:7, 16b). The servant reminds everyone that it was God, Yahweh, who speaks, and he has authority over what the Servant does.[13]

This new revelation focuses on the special calling of the Servant. Isaiah singles out two particular purposes in the Servant's calling.

First purpose: Save Israel (vv. 5-6a). The Servant declares that God's purpose for Him is to save Israel from its apostasy, i.e., "to bring Jacob back to Him, so that Israel might be gathered to Him (For I am honored in the sight of the Lord, and My God is My strength)." The Servant is not the nation, for the mission of the Servant is to restore the nation to God, a task that was also His special focus at His first advent (Isa. 9:1-2; Matt. 4:16; 10:5-6; 15:24). Israel had the opportunity to receive her King at His first coming (Luke 19:41-44), but sadly she rejected Him and has suffered terribly for this disbelief over the last 2,000 years.

---

[11] The concepts of toil and weariness are common themes in Isaiah (40:28, 40:30-31; 43:22, 43:23-24, 47:12, 15, 49:4, 57:10, 62:8, 65:23).

[12] The entire redeemed creation will be the Servant's reward (Isa. 53:10-12; Col. 1:16; Heb. 1:2), especially His own glorified saints (Isa. 53:10; 54:3; 61:9; 66:22; Pss. 22:30; 110:3; Matt. 16:18; John 17:24; Heb. 2:11-13).

[13] Gary Smith, *Isaiah 40-66*, vol. 15B, The New American Commentary, cited in electronic form with Logos Libronix (Nashville, TN: Broadman & Holman Publishers, 2009), 347.

By His unfailing grace Jesus Christ will fulfill this purpose at His second advent. God will save the remnant of Israel and bring them into the messianic kingdom (Isa. 2:1ff.; 4:1ff.; 9:6-7; 10:20-23; 11:11-16; 27:12-13; 35:1ff.; 59:15-21; Ezek. 20:36-38; 39:25-29; Zech. 10:8-12; 12:10; 13:8-9; Matt. 24:31; Luke 1:67-79; Rom. 9:27; 11:25-32; Rev. 7:1-8; 12:6, 11-17). This is the elect remnant whom Isaiah calls "the preserved ones of Israel" (*natsar*, cf. e.g., Deut. 32:10; Pss. 25:20; 37:28), i.e., those that have been preserved through the eschatological fires of the Great Tribulation (Isa. 4:2; 10:20; Joel 2:32; Obad. 17).[14]

Second purpose: Save the Gentiles (v. 6b). God chose corporate Israel as a vessel through whom He would work to bring blessings to the whole world (Gen. 12:3; 22:18; 26:4; 28:14; Acts 3:25; Gal. 3:8), a calling the corporate nation failed to uphold (Isa. 26:16-18). Nevertheless, He is not only the God of Israel, but He is also the God of all mankind (Deut. 32:43; Isa. 2:1-4; 11:10; 42:6; 51:4; 60:3; Mal. 1:11; Matt. 28:19; Luke 24:47; John 4:42; Acts 1:8; 13:47; 1 John 4:14; Rom. 1:5; 3:23-24, 29; 9:24; 10:12; 11:30; 15:9-12, 18-19; 16:25-27; Rev. 7:9-17). The Servant fully understood that His calling was to not only restore Israel, for this would be much too small. No, He must also bring salvation to the Gentiles. Jesus declared, "I am the Light of the world; he who follows Me will not walk in the darkness, but will have the Light of life" (John 8:12; cf. 1:4; 9:5; 10:16; 12:35).

The Servant's promised exaltation (v. 7)

Peter tells us that the prophets foresaw both the sufferings and glory of the Christ. Verse 7 contains both within one single verse.

A promised suffering (v. 7a). Verse 7 makes clear the sad reality that even though God's Servant had come to love and save His people, He would be rejected by them (cf. John 1:9-11). He, the chosen King, the Redeemer, the Holy One of Israel will also be known as, "the despised One," i.e., disdained, held in contempt (cf. Isa. 50:4-11; 53:3; Ps. 22:6),[15] the One "abhorred by the nation," i.e., detested and seen as abominable (cf. Job 9:31; 19:19; 30:10; Ps. 107:18).[16]

---

[14] Walter C. Kaiser, "*ntsr*," ed. R. Laird Harris, Gleason L. Archer Jr., and Bruce K. Waltke, *Theological Wordbook of the Old Testament*, cited in electronic form with Logos Libronix (Chicago: Moody Press, 1999), 595.

[15] Bruce K. Waltke, "*bzh*," ed. R. Laird Harris, Gleason L. Archer Jr., and Bruce K. Waltke, *Theological Wordbook of the Old Testament*, cited in electronic form with Logos Libronix (Chicago: Moody Press, 1999), 98–99.

[16] Ronald F. Youngblood, "*t‘b*," ed. R. Laird Harris, Gleason L. Archer Jr., and Bruce

A promised glory (v. 7b). God's Servant is going to experience supreme hatred and rejection (cf. David in Ps. 22:1-21), but Isaiah also makes it clear that one day God will reverse this so that the whole world (Jews and Gentiles) might recognize Him and bow down in worship (45:21-25; 52:13-15; Ps. 22:22-31; Zech. 14:9). For this reason, Isaiah adds these words: "Kings will see and arise; princes will also bow down, because of the Lord who is faithful, the Holy One of Israel who has chosen You." Thus, the hatred and rejection of Jesus by His own people does not *disprove* Him as being the Messiah, but rather it shows that He is the promised One.[17] Pfeiffer's comments are helpful: "In his humiliation he would be despised and rejected, even by his own nation, the Jews. But in his exaltation, after the resurrection victory, he would eventually be worshiped as Lord, even by the kings of the heathen."[18]

The Servant's liberating victory (vv. 8-13)

The Servant's war against sin and curse will be the hardest task ever undertaken, but God's Word assured Him that He would have the victory (cf. John 16:33).[19] For Israel, this will mean a national restoration to God under a "New Covenant."[20] Here in verse 8 God makes the promise that He will answer the Servant "in a favorable time" (*ratson*, i.e., a time that is according to God's perfect purpose; cf. Isa. 60:10; 61:2; Lev. 25:1-10; Cor. 6:1-2),[21] and use Him to restore His apostate nation in a new covenant relationship.[22] Verses 8-13 lay out five promises God will fulfill.

K. Waltke, *Theological Wordbook of the Old Testament*, cited in electronic form with Logos Libronix (Chicago: Moody Press, 1999), 976–977. By this expression "Servant of rulers" we are reminded of the fact that in ancient culture, the king never was obliged to arise from his throne when someone entered the palace, but not so with this King.

[17] Even though He allowed Himself to become "a slave of tyrants," one day God will reverse this supreme humiliation and He will receive supreme glorification and worship (cf. Isa. 49:23; 60:12-16; 66:23) (Oswalt, *The Book of Isaiah: Chapters 40-66*, 295).

[18] Charles F. Pfeiffer, *The Wycliffe Bible Commentary: Old Testament*, cited in electronic form with Logos Libronix (Chicago: Moody Press, 1962), Is 49:1.

[19] The string of perfect stem verbs should be viewed as "prophetic perfects" which will be fulfilled in the eschaton (Young, *The Book of Isaiah, vol. 3*, 278).

[20] The expression "new covenant" is found only in Jeremiah 31:31, but the concept is embodied in every promise God has made about the eschatological restoration of Israel in the messianic kingdom.

[21] Ludwig Koehler et al., *The Hebrew and Aramaic Lexicon of the Old Testament*, cited in electronic form with Logos Libronix, 1282–1283. The language and imagery echo promises about complete redemption in the Year of Jubilee (Lev. 25; Isa. 61:1-2).

[22] The redeeming work of the Servant becomes the basis for restoring Israel under a New Covenant as seen in 42:6 (Oswalt, *The Book of Isaiah: Chapters 40-66*, 297).

First promise: Israel's land will be restored (v. 8). The Abrahamic land promises (Gen. 12:1-3) get repeated many times throughout the Scripture.[23] The promise is explicit that not only will God save Israel, but He will also give them their land forever,[24] a promise that cannot rightly be understood as getting fulfilled at the return from the Babylonian exile. God's promise is that He will, "restore the land, to make *them* inherit the desolate heritages." Due to the exile, the Land of Israel will suffer great desolations (*shomemoth*), but it will not be permanent (Isa. 58:12; 61:4; 62:4; Jer. 30:18; 31:4-6, 27-28, 38-40; 32:15, 26-27; 33:7, 12; Ezek. 36:10, 33).

Second promise: Prisoners will be set free (v. 9). Israel's covenant apostasy made her a prisoner to sin. God's promise is that one day He will set all prisoners free. God commands those who had been in bondage, "Go forth," and those who were in spiritual darkness, "Show yourselves." The King has won the victory, and now they are safe to return to God (Isa. 52:11; 61:1-2; Zech. 2:7; Rev. 18:4). The path may be frightening, but the Lord will meet their needs, and they "will feed, and their pasture *will be* on all bare heights" (cf. 17:2; 40:10-11; 41:18; 43:19; 63:11). This is not a mere return from Babylon for, as Kidner explains, "The *captives* flocking home in vs 8–13 are visualized as the dispersed of Israel throughout the world."[25]

Third promise: Grace will shelter and protect (v. 10). Hunger, thirst, and scorching sun had been their lot for long ages, but by His compassion (*racham*), their Shepherd (cf. Ps. 23) will put an end to such misery. The Millennium will see a huge fulfilling of these promises to the whole world, but one day in the heavenly presence of God they will find their ultimate and final fulfillment (cf. Rev. 7:16-17; 21:1-4; 22:1-5).

Fourth promise: All the elect will be regathered (vv. 11-12). God promises to make a smooth path for the restoration of the remnant (cf. comments under vv. 5-6). God will make "highways" for His people to return from their diaspora (v. 11; cf. Isa. 11:16; 19:23 [Gentiles]; 27:12-13; 35:8; 40:4-5; 42:16; 43:5-7; 62:10). His elect Jews will return from every corner of the earth

---

[23] These land promises were first made to Abraham and the patriarchs (Gen. 12:1-3; 13:14-15; 17:7-8; 28:13; 35:11-12; 48:4), but got repeated through many prophets over the ages (Deut. 30:1-10; 2 Sam. 7:10; Jer. 30:10, 17-18; 31:38-40; 32:15, 37-44; Ezek. 37:25; 39:25-29; Joel 3:17-21; Amos 9:14-15; Zech. 14:11; Mic. 4:4-7).

[24] Grogan, "Isaiah," 286.

[25] F. Derek Kidner, "Isaiah," in *New Bible Commentary: 21st Century Edition*, ed. D. A. Carson et al., 4th ed., cited in electronic form with Logos Libronix (Leicester, England; Downers Grove, IL: Inter-Varsity Press, 1994), 661.

to live in the land sworn to Abraham, Isaac, and Jacob (v. 12). There is some debate about the identity of "the land of Sinim." Some older commentators sought to identify this as China, but it is best to see it as referring to "Syene" or "Aswan," the southern edge of Egypt.[26]

Fifth promise: Joy will purge out lamentation (v. 13). Apostasy plunged Israel into ages of misery, but God's comfort will purge all such misery; hence, Isaiah gives this call for extreme rejoicing.[27] Smith reminds us that the return from Babylon brought joy, but the limited joy of that return will be nothing like their eschatological joy.

Although Jesus fits the roles and experiences of this Servant, it is clear that the complete and final fulfillment of Isaiah's prophecy in 49:1–13 awaits a future day when God will transform nature and the hearts of people from the four corners of the earth at the second coming of Christ.[28] The Word of God is clear, though: The Servant will not fail. Jesus Christ will accomplish the victory, and this is what He did by His victorious cross (John 16:33; 19:30).

God's promises to Israel will not fail (vv. 14-26)

The discussion in the rest of the chapter shifts from directly dealing with God's Servant, but still the overall theme focuses on the restoration of Israel. God's promises to Israel will not fail, but sadly Israel had begun to make accusations against God that the Babylonian exile was actually His fault. Nothing could be further from the truth. God reminds Israel of two particular promises that He will never fail to fulfill.

First promise: God's people will be restored (vv. 14-23)

God first cites the accusation the people were making (v. 14) before making His reply (vv. 15-23): "But Zion said, The Lord has forsaken me, and the Lord has forgotten me" (v. 14; cf. 40:27). Now, for anyone who knows the faithful character of God, Israel's allegations were absurd and blasphemous. These, however, were the indictments Israel was making. The truth is that it was their own sins. Hughes reminds us,

---

[26] Oswalt, *The Book of Isaiah: Chapters 40-66*, 296-297, n. 45, 299-300. We know from the so-called "Elaphantine Letters" that there was a large colony of Jews there as early as the fifth century B.C. and that from a biblical perspective this was the southernmost edge of Egypt and thus the civilized world (cf. Ezek. 29:10; 30:6).
[27] Cf. Isa. 12:1-6; 16:10; 24:14; 26:19; 35:2, 6; 42:11; 44:23; 49:13; 52:8, 9; 54:1; 55:12-13; 61:7; 65:14, 17; Zech. 8:7-23.
[28] Smith, *Isaiah 40-66*, 357.

Because of her sins, God divorced and sold Israel to her enemies (50:1). But those terms are descriptive of Israel's discipline only. God never broke his commitment to the relationship he had with Israel. The nation was temporarily rejected because of sin (cf. Jer. 31:35–37).[29]

God had not abandoned His people, so here in verses 15-23 He gives a series of four replies to assure Israel that they were still His people and that one day He would restore them.

First reply: His love is greater than all (vv. 15-16). Israel was unfaithful to God, but they do not understand that His love and His faithfulness is greater than anything they have ever known in any earthly relationships.[30] Even though it is unfathomable that a nursing mother would ever abandon her baby, the sad truth is that it can happen. God's faithful love, however, is infinitely greater (v. 15).[31] To illustrate God says, "Behold, I have inscribed you on the palms *of My hands*; your walls are continually before Me" (v. 16; cf. Ps. 27:10).[32] They still belong to Him, and one day He will restore them (cf. Hos. 1:10-11; 2:14-23; 3:5).[33]

Second reply: God will restore His ruined nation (vv. 17-18). Yes, Judah has been destroyed, but God will reverse this and restore His ruined nation, and the builders will hasten, and the destroyers will depart (v. 17).[34] Israel's sons/builders will return, so God tells the nation, "Lift up your eyes and look around; all of them gather together, they come to you. As I live, declares the Lord, you will surely put on all of them as jewels and bind them on as a bride" (v. 18). Restoration is on the way (Isa. 11:11; 27:13; 43:5-7; 66:20), and those

---

[29] Robert B. Hughes and J. Carl Laney, *Tyndale Concise Bible Commentary*, cited in electronic form with Logos Libronix (Wheaton, IL: Tyndale House Publishers, 2001), 266.

[30] His promise is unbreakable (cf. Jer. 33:14-26; Rom. 11:29).

[31] Our relationship with God is secure because of His own grace and covenant loyalty (Mal. 3:6; John 6:37, 44; 10:27-30; 2 Tim. 2:13; Titus 1:2).

[32] In other words, His people are never out of His thoughts.

[33] The Holy Spirit expresses this same truth through Jeremiah: "Is Ephraim My dear son? Is he a delightful child? Indeed, as often as I have spoken against him, I certainly *still* remember him; therefore, My heart yearns for him; I will surely have mercy on him, declares the Lord" (Jer. 31:20).

[34] The textual sources give us a choice between two very similar readings, "builders" (*bwnyk*, 1 QIs^a. LXX, Targ., Aquila, Vg., NASB, NRSV, ESV) and "sons" (*banayik*, MT, Syr., KJV, NIV). "Sons" seems to match up better with the sense of v. 18, but either reading produces the idea that a speedy restoration to ruined Judah is on the way (Oswalt, *The Book of Isaiah: Chapters 40-66*, 301, n. 57).

who will make this restoration a reality will be as beautiful as the jewels adorning a new bride (*'adiy*; cf. Exod. 33:4, 5, 6; 2 Sam. 1:24; Jer. 2:32; 4:30; Ezek. 7:20; 16:7, 11; 23:40).

Third reply: The future will be more fruitful (vv. 19-21). Even though Judah's past sins produced desolation (cf. 3:24-:4:1; 8:22; Lam. 1:5),[35] her future will be rich and fruitful (cf. 9:1-7; Jer. 32:40). Israel will experience so much fruitful explosion they will cry out for more space to accommodate the bulging population.[36]

Fourth reply: The Gentiles will assist in restoration (vv. 22-23). Israel's restoration will come due to a providential work of God's grace, and part of His work will be to use the redeemed Gentiles to make it happen (v. 22; cf. Isa. 11:11-12; 43:6; 60:4; 66:20).[37] Martin explains,

> When Israel returns to the land in the future the Gentiles will worship before the Lord and will be friendly toward Israel. In fact the Gentiles will even help transport Israelites to Palestine. Gentile leaders will be subservient to Israel, which will cause her to realize that the Lord really is in control of the world" (v. 23; cf. Isa. 2:1-4; 4:2-6; 45:14; 60:3, 10-11; 14; Zech. 8:20-23).[38]

The world's submission to Israel's King finds no stronger affirmation than Isaiah's promise to Israel: "You will also suck the milk of nations and suck the breast of kings; then you will know that I, the Lord, am your Savior and your Redeemer, the Mighty One of Jacob" (Isa. 60:16).[39] God wants Israel to understand is that He will restore them (Jer. 32:17).

Second promise: God's enemies will be destroyed (vv. 24-26)

Restoration is going to require a purging of all evil and a destruction of those enemies who were seeking her destruction (Luke 1:67-79). In

---

[35] An elliptical idea must be supplied which says that even though Israel suffered past desolations, a future restoration is on the way.

[36] This promise gets repeated in various places (Isa. 9:3; 26:15; 27:6; 43:5; 54:1-3; cf. Zech. 8:3-5).

[37] The idea of raising a "standard" (*nes*) is that of making a rallying point for the nations (Isa. 5:26; 11:10, 12; 13:2; 18:3; 30:17; 62:10).

[38] Martin, "Isaiah," 1104.

[39] The Gentiles will know the Lord, but at long last so, too, will Israel (Ezek. 20:41; 23:49; 25:7-17; 28:22; 29:21; 34:31; 35:4-15; 36:23; 37:14, 28; 38:14-23; 39:25) and those who have hoped in the Lord will never be shamed (Isa. 28:16; 40:28-31).

Deuteronomy God told Israel that one day there would be an eschatological restoration (Deut. 30:1-10). This is going to include a destruction of all of Israel's enemies (cf. Deut. 30:7), a promise that gets repeated many times in the prophets (Jer. 30:11; 46:28; Joel 3:1-17; Amos 9:8; Zech. 12:1-9; 14:1-4; Rev. 19:11-21).[40] Israel will be rescued (vv. 24-25), and her enemies will be destroyed (v. 26).

Israel will be rescued (vv. 24-25). Isaiah uses an earthly analogy to illustrate that even though nations like Babylon are powerful tyrants,[41] God Himself is stronger, and He will overthrow the tyrants (cf. Matt. 12:29; Luke 11:21). God will save His people Israel.[42]

The oppressors will be destroyed (v. 26). Smith notes that this chapter ends, "with concluding statements about what will happen to the strong tyrants God fights with in 49:25."[43] Just as it was for Egypt at the Exodus, Israel's eschatological salvation will mean the destruction of her enemies. The language reminds us that the Great Tribulation will be a bloodbath: "I will feed your oppressors with their own flesh, and they will become drunk with their own blood as with sweet wine" (Isa. 49:26; cf. 63:1-6).[44] The result is that, "all flesh will know that I, the Lord, am your Savior And your Redeemer, the Mighty One

---

[40] It is curiously sad how non-premillennial, replacement theologians, especially those who embrace Preterism, assert that God's overthrow of Israel in A.D. 70 is a sign that God is finished with Israel. Biblical exegesis tells us that God will bring an end to Gentile oppression and restore Israel.

[41] The first term "mighty man" (*gibbor*) often refers to mighty warriors. The second term "tyrant" includes a textual variant with one reading being "righteous" (*tsadiyq*, MT, Tagum, LXX) and the other reading being either "giant" Syr.), "mighty one" (Vg.) or "fierce warrior/violent terrorist" (*'arits*, 1QIs^a and v. 25; cf. 2:19; 11:4; 13:11; 25:3; 29:5, 20; 47:12; 8:12, 13; 49:25; Ezek. 28:7; Jer. 15:21; 20:11). The similarity of *'arits* with *tsadiyq* suggests that *'arits* is the original and preferred reading (Oswalt, *The Book of Isaiah: Chapters 40-66*, 312, n. 88).

[42] The use of the Hebrew pronoun "I" (*'anokiy*) makes the statement very emphatic: "I myself will save your sons" (cf. 35:4).

[43] Smith, *Isaiah 40-66*, 373.

[44] This statement affirms how God will cause the nations to turn on one another in a way that brings self-destruction, an idea repeated elsewhere (Ezek. 38:21; Joel 3:11; Zech. 14:13; Matt. 24:7; Rev. 6:8; 16:14; 17:16-17). The intense conflict against one another will be like a man who has become drunk with tasty, sweet wine (*'asiys*, sweet fresh juice) (Young, *The Book of Isaiah, vol. 3*, 294). Given Islam's unified hatred of Israel, it is curious to wonder what place Islam will have in fulfilling these prophecies. Isaiah is not alone in telling us what a bloodbath this will look like (Ezek. 39:1-6, 17-20; Zech. 14:12; Rev. 16:4-7; 19:17-18).

of Jacob" (*'abîyr*; cf. Isa. 1:24; 60:16; Gen. 49:24; Ps. 132:2, 5; Ezek. 36:22-23; Zech. 14:9; Matt. 6:9-10).

Summary and application

God's work to restore this fallen world is going to involve unthinkable human carnage. For those who have lived in a time of relative peace it might be easy to overlook the reality of how devastating evil really is. Isaiah's words should stir us to love the truths of God's Word even more.

THE DISOBEDIENT AND OBEDIENT SERVANTS (50:1-11)

In chapter 50 God contrasts the unresponsiveness of the servant nation (vv. 1-3) with the perfect responsiveness of His messianic Servant (vv. 4-11).[45]

Chapter 50 reads as follows: "1 Thus says the Lord, Where is the certificate of divorce by which I have sent your mother away, or to whom of My creditors did I sell you? Behold, you were sold for your iniquities, and for your transgressions your mother was sent away. 2 Why was there no man when I came? When I called, *why* was there none to answer? Is My hand so short that it cannot ransom, or have I no power to deliver? Behold, I dry up the sea with My rebuke; I make the rivers a wilderness; their fish stink for lack of water and die of thirst. 3 I clothe the heavens with blackness and make sackcloth their covering. 4 The Lord God has given Me the tongue of disciples, that I may know how to sustain the weary one with a word. He awakens *Me* morning by morning; He awakens My ear to listen as a disciple. 5 The Lord God has opened My ear, and I was not disobedient, nor did I turn back. 6 I gave My back to those who strike *Me*, and My cheeks to those who pluck out the beard. I did not cover My face from humiliation and spitting. 7 For the Lord God helps Me; therefore, I am not disgraced; therefore, I have set My face like flint, and I know that I will not be ashamed. 8 He who vindicates Me is near. Who will contend with Me? Let us stand up to each other. Who has a case against Me? Let him draw near to Me. 9 Behold, the Lord God helps Me; who is he who condemns Me? Behold, they will all wear out like a garment; the moth will eat them. 10 Who is among you that fears the Lord, that obeys the voice of His servant, that walks in darkness and has no light? Let him trust in the name of the Lord and rely on his God. 11 Behold, all you who kindle a fire, who encircle yourselves with firebrands, walk in the light of your fire and among the brands you have set ablaze. This you will have from My hand: you will lie down in torment" (50:1-11).

Chapter 50 has two messages: (1) The tragic disobedience of the servant nation (vv. 1-3) and the wonderful obedience of the chosen Savior Servant (vv. 4-11).

---

[45] Wolf, *Interpreting Isaiah*, 209.

ISAIAH: THE LORD SAVES

The servant nation's disobedience (vv. 1-3)

Back in 49:14 we saw that Israel blamed God for their woes (cf. 40:27). God already answered that accusation back in chapter 49, but there is still more to say. The first part of this reply uses the metaphor of marriage and divorce for Him and Israel to make it clear that Israel is the cause of failure.[46]

Israel ruined the marriage (v. 1)

To get to the heart of the problem, we need to look at the historical circumstances that led to the exile. God asks where the divorce certificate is (*sepher keriythuth*) that explained the cause of the ruined marriage.[47] God did not divorce his wife to pay off His creditors (cf. 2 Kings 4:1; Matt. 18:25) or for any other superficial reason. No, the cause of the divorce was that Israel got sold for its own iniquities (*'awon*). Israel's transgressions (*pesha'*) sent them into exile.[48] In 52:3, God tells them, "For thus says the Lord, You were sold for nothing and you will be redeemed without money." The divorce certificate is clear: The divorce was Israel's fault (Isa. 54:6-7; 62:4; Jer. 31:31).[49] The only good news is that the divorce is not going to be permanent. Martin explains, "The Lord declared that He was temporarily 'divorcing' Zion because she had rejected Him without cause. He temporarily sent away their mother because she sinned."[50]

Only God can fix Israel's failure (vv. 2-3)

Israel cannot fix its problems, for it is a nation that has been overtaken by evil. Israel can fix its own problem, but God can. Verses 2-3 show how God will reverse their hopeless dilemma.

Israel is in a state of helplessness (v. 2a). If the relationship is to ever get restored, God is the One who must make it happen.[51] God exposes Israel's helpless condition by asking, "Why was there no man when I came? When I

---

[46] Jeremiah uses the marriage metaphor to illustrate God's relationship with Israel (cf. Jer. 31:31) and Hosea uses it heavily. Due to her unrepentant sin, God was forced to give Israel a divorce, but biblically we never see Israel remarry anyone else (cf. Hos. 1-2). Thus, according to Deut. 24:1-4 she can remarry her husband.

[47] From limited OT evidence we see that a husband was required to give a certificate when divorcing his wife (Deut. 24:1-4; Jer. 3:18; Matt. 19:7).

[48] The term *'awon* speaks about guilty deeds that cause trouble, and the term *pesha'* speaks about rebellious deeds against one's authority (cf. Isa. 1:28; 48:8).

[49] Young, *The Book of Isaiah, vol. 3*, 296.

[50] Martin, "Isaiah," 1104.

[51] From a human perspective, Israel must repent and turn to Christ in faith.

called, *why* was there none to answer?" Smith explains,

> God asks two additional probing questions that get to the heart of the problem in order to cause the audience to reflect more deeply on the real reason for past trials and difficulties. God asks why none of them answered him when he came and called them? This line of questioning lays the real blame at the feet of the people, for God was present. . . . They were not willing to come to talk to God about it in order to restore their relationship.[52]

Only God can fix their problem (vv. 2b-3). God corrects any mistaken notion that He was incapable of keeping Israel from disaster. It certainly is not that God's hand cannot save, i.e., that He is not powerful enough (59:1; cf. similar use of arm in 40:10; 51:5, 9; 52:10; 53:1; 59:16; 63:5; Exod. 7:18; 10:21; 15:16; Deut. 26:8; Josh. 3:16; 4:23; Ps. 77:15). Yahweh is the God who dried up the Red Sea and Jordan River so that His people could receive redemption, and He is the One who can do it again (v. 2). The next Exodus will even include mighty works that bring disturbances in the stellar realms as well (v. 3; Isa. 13:10; Rev. 6:12). Smith explains, "God's negative power to destroy is illustrated by additional examples."[53] God is strong enough to bring salvation, but the truth is that Israel was the problem.

The chosen Servant's obedience (vv. 4-11)

Since the nation was in no position to save itself, it will be up to the Lord. Isaiah 50:4-11 brings us the third Servant Song that tells us how God will send His people a special Servant, a man of perfect obedience to God. Jesus, aware of His own sinless perfection, told His disciples of this perfect submission. On one occasion He said, "My food is to do the will of Him who sent Me and to accomplish His work" (John 4:34). On another occasion, He said, "Truly, truly, I say to you, the Son can do nothing of Himself, unless *it is* something He sees the Father doing, for whatever the Father does, these things the Son also does in like manner" (John 5:19; cf. John 3:11; 5:30; 6:38; 8:28, 46; 12:49; 14:10). Jesus was fully aware of His own sinlessness and perfect submission to God.

Isaiah describes the perfect submission of the Servant by explaining how His entire body was a vessel submitted for service to God. In this, we see the perfect obedience of God's Servant, but we also see that this perfect obedience

---

[52] Smith, *Isaiah 40-66*, 376; Young, *The Book of Isaiah, vol. 3*, 296. It was because they would not listen that God sent them invaders who spoke in foreign languages (Isa. 28:11; cf. Jer. 25:4-7).

[53] Smith, *Isaiah 40-66*, 376.

is because of the divine help that made it possible. Four times the Servant affirms that His help comes from the Sovereign Lord.[54]

First affirmation of God's help (v. 4)

The first affirmation speaks about the equipping God has given Him in His speech (tongue) so that He can fulfill the task of sustaining His own weary people (cf. 8:16; 54:13). The Lord God is also the One who wakens Him daily with attentive ears so He can perfectly fulfill the calling God has given Him to restore broken lives (vv. 4b-5a; cf. 42:1-4; Matt. 11:28).[55]

Second affirmation of God's help (vv. 5-6)

The divinely-opened ear also enabled the Servant to stay faithful in the midst of the worst opposition.[56] In other words, no matter how badly sinners treated the Servant, He stayed faithful to God and never turned from the mission God sent Him to accomplish. Martin reminds us, "In extremely difficult circumstances, more difficult than what Isaiah's original readers were facing, the Servant was obedient and submissive."[57] This is exactly what we saw in the Lord Jesus Christ.

Third affirmation of God's help (vv. 7-8)

The Servant again affirms that it is only by God's grace that He can live with a face like flint (Jer. 1:15; Ezek. 3:8-9; Luke 9:51) and not be overwhelmed by the shame (v. 7). Because He knows He is doing the will of God and that God is on His side, He knows that it will result in glory and not shame. Pfeiffer explains, "Unlike national Israel, the Servant would present to God perfect obedience, and willingness to endure humiliation and persecution for the Father's sake."[58]

Fourth affirmation of God's help (vv. 9-11)

In this final section, we see how the Servant has been strengthened by God to know that in the end He will have a perfect vindication when all those who tried to destroy Him see that He is God's righteous Servant.

---

[54] Each of these four statements are tied with the use of the expression "The Lord God" (*'Adonay Yahweh*), an expression that highlights the sovereignty of God.
[55] Unlike the rebellious nation (cf. 48:18), the Servant does listen to God.
[56] David's messianic Psalms show us the same picture of divinely-enabled obedience from God's chosen King (Pss. 22:2-21; 40:6-10; 41:9; 69:4, 7-12; 109:4-5, 25).
[57] Martin, "Isaiah," 1104–1105.
[58] Pfeiffer, *The Wycliffe Bible Commentary: Old Testament*, Is 50:4.

The Servant will not be condemned (v. 9a). God's Servant is going to face intense opposition, but He knows that He is the One who will be vindicated with none to condemn.[59] A godless world condemned Him to death, but they were wrong, and for this reason God did not condemn Him (cf. Isa. 53:7-9; Ps. 22:22-31). When He returns the world will see how wrong they were.

The Servant's enemies will be condemned (vv. 9b-11). None who oppose God will stand in the day of judgment (Ps. 1:4-6). Isaiah describes their ruin by saying, "they will all wear out like a garment; the moth will eat them" (v. 9b). For anyone to reject God, their destiny will be like an old, raggy piece of clothing that has worn out, or like a piece of cloth that has been consumed by the moths, i.e., total ruin (cf. 51:8; Job 13:28; Hos. 5:12).

With this certainty of His own calling, the Servant calls out, "Who is among you that fears the Lord, that obeys the voice of His servant, that walks in darkness and has no light? Let him trust in the name of the Lord and rely on his God" (v. 10). The Servant is pleading with His people to trust Him that they might have His blessing. Why is it crucial to believe the Servant? Kidner says it is because, "commitment to God is clearly allegiance at the same time to his Servant."[60] Jesus said that all should, "honor the Son even as they honor the Father. He who does not honor the Son does not honor the Father" (John 5:23).

The Servant utters these final words: "Behold, all you who kindle a fire, who encircle yourselves with firebrands, walk in the light of your fire and among the brands you have set ablaze.[61] This you will have from My hand: you will lie down in torment" (v. 11). Those who reject the Servant will pay the infinite price in eternal torment (*ma'atsebah*) for their refusal to believe in Him (cf. 66:24). This is the "terror," "pain" and "sorrow" that belongs to those who refuse God's chosen Servant (cf. Dan. 12:1-3; Rev. 14:9-11; 20:11-15).[62] The choice is set before all men, explains, Hughes: "The followers of the Servant [v. 9] were called upon to trust in God, who would bring judgment upon the

---

[59] It is not unlikely that Paul had these OT passages in his mind when he asked the four questions of Romans 8:31-39. The principle is the same in both passages: Those who belong to the Lord will never be condemned (cf. Rom. 8:1).

[60] Kidner, "Isaiah," 661.

[61] They thought that they had light with their firebrands, but the truth is that they were rejecting the Light of the Word (John 8:12) and walking blindly in total darkness (John 9:40-41).

[62] Ronald B. Allen, "*'atsab*," ed. R. Laird Harris, Gleason L. Archer Jr., and Bruce K. Waltke, *Theological Wordbook of the Old Testament*, cited in electronic form with Logos Libronix (Chicago: Moody Press, 1999), 687–688.

disobedient (50:10–11)."⁶³ All they have to do, says Wolf, is "follow the lead of the Servant."⁶⁴ Those who do trust will find the blessing of never facing shame.

Summary and application

Jesus extended many invitations for men to believe in Him. For example, Jesus said, "I am the Light of the world; he who follows Me will not walk in the darkness, but will have the Light of life" (John 8:12). Follow Him, and you will have the light of life. What a wonderful promise.

TRUST IN GOD AND DEPART FROM EVIL (51:1-23)

A dominant theme in chapter 51 is the oft-repeated idea that Israel needs to trust God and depart from all evil. This is the basic truth that the remnant of Israel needs to realize, that even though the nation went into exile for its sin, the exile will not last forever. God will save and restore them just as He has sworn.

Chapter 51 reads as follows: "1 Listen to me, you who pursue righteousness, who seek the Lord: Look to the rock from which you were hewn and to the quarry from which you were dug. 2 Look to Abraham your father and to Sarah who gave birth to you in pain. When *he was but* one, I called him; then I blessed him and multiplied him. 3 Indeed, the Lord will comfort Zion; He will comfort all her waste places, and her wilderness He will make like Eden, and her desert like the garden of the Lord. Joy and gladness will be found in her, thanksgiving and sound of a melody. 4 Pay attention to Me, O My people, and give ear to Me, O My nation, for a law will go forth from Me, and I will set My justice for a light of the peoples. 5 My righteousness is near; My salvation has gone forth, and My arms will judge the peoples; the coastlands will wait for Me, and for My arm they will wait expectantly. 6 Lift up your eyes to the sky; then look to the earth beneath, for the sky will vanish like smoke, and the earth will wear out like a garment and its inhabitants will die in like manner, but My salvation will be forever, and My righteousness will not wane. 7 Listen to Me, you who know righteousness, a people in whose heart is My law. Do not fear the reproach of man, nor be dismayed at their revilings, 8 for the moth will eat them like a garment, and the grub will eat them like wool, but My righteousness will be forever, and My salvation to all generations. 9 Awake, awake, put on strength, O arm of the Lord; awake as in the days of old, the generations of long ago. Was it not You who cut Rahab in pieces, Who pierced the dragon? 10 Was it not You who dried up the sea, the waters of the great deep, Who made the depths of the sea a pathway for the redeemed to cross over? 11 So the ransomed

---

⁶³ Hughes, *Tyndale Concise Bible Commentary*, 266.
⁶⁴ Wolf, *Interpreting Isaiah*, 210.

of the Lord will return and come with joyful shouting to Zion, and everlasting joy *will be* on their heads. They will obtain gladness and joy, and sorrow and sighing will flee away. 12 I, even I, am He who comforts you. Who are you that you are afraid of man who dies and of the son of man who is made like grass, 13 that you have forgotten the Lord your Maker, Who stretched out the heavens and laid the foundations of the earth, that you fear continually all day long because of the fury of the oppressor as he makes ready to destroy? But where is the fury of the oppressor? 14 The exile will soon be set free, and will not die in the dungeon, nor will his bread be lacking. 15 For I am the Lord your God, who stirs up the sea and its waves roar (the Lord of hosts is His name). 16 I have put My words in your mouth and have covered you with the shadow of My hand, to establish the heavens, to found the earth, and to say to Zion, You are My people. 17 Rouse yourself! Rouse yourself! Arise, O Jerusalem, you who have drunk from the Lord's hand the cup of His anger; the chalice of reeling you have drained to the dregs. 18 There is none to guide her among all the sons she has borne, nor is there one to take her by the hand among all the sons she has reared. 19 These two things have befallen you; who will mourn for you? The devastation and destruction, famine and sword; how shall I comfort you? 20 Your sons have fainted, they lie *helpless* at the head of every street, like an antelope in a net, full of the wrath of the Lord—the rebuke of your God. 21 Therefore, please hear this, you afflicted, who are drunk, but not with wine: 22 Thus says your Lord, the Lord, even your God Who contends for His people, Behold, I have taken out of your hand the cup of reeling, the chalice of My anger; you will never drink it again. 23 I will put it into the hand of your tormentors, who have said to you, Lie down that we may walk over *you*. You have even made your back like the ground and like the street for those who walk over *it*" (51:1-23).

One of the main ideas in chapter 51 is that Israel needs to believe God and His Word. Chapter 51 can be broken down into four main sections: One, Israel needs to trust the Lord (vv. 1-8); two, God will bring a second Exodus (vv. 9-11); three, Israel should not fear (vv. 12-16); four, the cup of wrath brings ruin (vv. 17-23).

Israel needs to trust the Lord (vv. 1-8)

Here in verses 1-8, God reminds His people Israel of their need to trust Him no matter what.[65] Isaiah gives four exhortations to Israel about trusting the Lord.

---

[65] Faith in God and His word has been necessary since God placed man in the Garden, and it will continue to be necessary until the day when all of His people are in His presence in glorious resurrection (1 Cor. 13:13).

Israel needs to follow in the footsteps of Abraham (vv. 1-2)

For Israel, no one carried greater honor than the patriarch Abraham. Abraham is the man to whom God swore that He would bring blessings, not only to Israel, but also to the whole world (Gen. 12:1-3; 17:5; 22:18; 26:4; 35:9-12). The defining characteristic of Abraham is that he was a man who believed God's word despite all odds.[66] God is calling Israel to look back to the promises He made to Abraham and to remember that they, too, needed to be people of faith. Keil explains, "The prophecy is addressed to those who are striving after the right kind of life and seeking Jehovah, and not turning from Him."[67] The bottom line is that Israel needs to trust Yahweh, for Yahweh is always faithful to His Word.

With Abraham as the object in view, Isaiah exhorts those who pursue righteousness, i.e., the godly remnant (cf. 50:10), to look to the rock/quarry from which they originated. Abraham and Sarah are both brought into the picture, but it may be best to see this as going beyond Abraham and Sarah to God Himself who swore the covenant promises to them.[68] In other words, the real issue here is probably best seen as emphasizing the unchanging nature of God and His unfailing grace. They believed the promises even when Abraham was one solitary man, but in the end, it was God who gave the promises by His grace. He fulfilled His promises when Abraham was one, and He will do it again now that they are many.

Israel needs to believe God's promises for Israel (v. 3)

Just as God fulfilled promises to Abraham and Sarah, He will also fulfill His promises to the nation in the days to come.[69] Thus, explains Grogan, "The Lord had brought this nation into being from such small beginnings, in fulfillment of His promises; and so, it is implied, He is able still to translate His Word into events."[70] Isaiah highlights three ways these promises will see fulfillment.

The promise of comfort. Isaiah says, "Indeed, the Lord will comfort Zion" (*nacham*).[71] This promise of comfort is that which formed the opening

---

[66] Paul calls him "the father of all who believe" (Rom. 4:11).
[67] Keil, *Commentary on the Old Testament*, 485.
[68] Young, *The Book of Isaiah, vol. 3*, 307.
[69] Smith, *Isaiah 40-66*, 392. Smith explains "Now the prophet reassures his audience (*ki*, "surely, it is indisputable," omitted in NIV) that these are God's words of comfort or compassion for the people of Zion because God is going to act on their behalf."
[70] Grogan, "Isaiah," 294.
[71] When Joab captured the city of Jebus, David renamed it The City of David with

words of 40-66 (40:1; cf. 49:13; 51:3, 12, 19; 52:9; 54:11; 57:6; 61:2; 66:13). Wilson explains the significance of this word in Jewish eschatology:

> This Hebrew word was well known to every pious Jew living in exile as he recalled the opening words of Isaiah's "Book of Consolation," *naḥămû naḥămû 'ammî*: "Comfort ye, comfort ye my people" (Isa 40:1). The same word occurs in Ps 23:4, where David says of his heavenly Shepherd, "Thy rod and thy staff, they comfort me."[72]

Israel's spiritual war has been very long and very painful, but at long last it will come to an end, and the day of comfort will finally arrive (cf. 52:7-12).

The promise of fruitfulness. God "will comfort all her waste places, and her wilderness He will make like Eden, and her desert like the garden of the Lord." This is but one of many passages in Isaiah (cf. e.g., 27:10; 30:25; 35:1; 41:18; 55:12), and other prophets (Deut. 30:9; Joel 3:18-21; Amos 9:13), where God promises great fruitfulness for the restored nation (and for the whole world).

The promise of joy. "Joy [*sason*] and gladness [*simchah*] will be in her, thanksgiving [*todah*] and sound of a melody [*zimrah*]." God's anger has finally turned away (Isa. 12:1), and He commands the restored elect, "Cry aloud and shout for joy, O inhabitant of Zion, for great in your midst is the Holy One of Israel" (Isa. 12:6; cf. Zech. 8:1-6). Israel needs to believe God's promises.

Israel needs to believe He is Savior of the world (vv. 4-5)

God calls on Israel to believe that a law (*torah*) will go forth from Him into the world,[73] a law that brings instruction not only for Israel, but also for the whole world (Isa. 2:3; Mic. 4:2).[74] God's instruction that flows from Messiah

---

Zion being a secondary name (2 Sam. 5). The name Zion eventually came to embrace the entire temple mount and the entire city of Jerusalem, as seen here. God's promise is that He will comfort Zion when the Messiah establishes the kingdom and restores Israel from its apostasy (Isa. 12:1; 40:1; 49:13).

[72] Marvin R. Wilson, "*nchm*," ed. R. Laird Harris, Gleason L. Archer Jr., and Bruce K. Waltke, *Theological Wordbook of the Old Testament*, cited in electronic form with Logos Libronix (Chicago: Moody Press, 1999), 571.

[73] The root idea behind *torah* is that of instruction.

[74] Once again, Isaiah refers to the western, Gentile world using the term "coastlands" (Isa. 11:11; 13:22; 20:6; 23:2, 6; 24:15; 34:14; 40:15; 41:1, 5; 42:4, 10, 12, 15; 49:1; 50:1; 51:5; 59:18; 60:5; 66:1, 19).

the King will bring justice, light, righteousness, and perfect salvation from the ravages of sin (Isa. 42:4).[75]

Israel needs to believe that God will fulfill His Word (vv. 6-8)

Isaiah gives a fourth truth that Israel needed to know and believe. They need to know that God will fulfill His Word.

God's promises will never fail (v. 6). Because of its consistency, we often look at the physical creation as being eternal and immutable, but the truth is that it is neither. The progressive revelation that comes in the New Testament shows us that at the end of the Millennium this present universe will be destroyed and recreated (2 Pet. 3:7-11; Rev. 20:11-15; 21:1). This passage alludes to the mutability and weakness of the physical creation (Isa. 13:13; 24:4; 34:4; Ps. 102:25-26), but the point is that powerful nations (like Babylon) will not last forever. The nations will fall, but God's salvation will be forever, and His righteousness will never wane. Smith explains,

> The fading destiny of this world (the heaven and the earth) is contrasted with the permanent salvation God will provide his people in order to encourage the audience to maintain their faith in God. . . . These promises give every believer a solid foundation for their faith in God; they can live in hope as they face the future even though the events of life may be difficult and appear quite hopeless.[76]

There is no need to fear (vv. 7-8). Because God will fulfill His word, Isaiah says, "Do not fear the reproach of man, nor be dismayed at their revilings" (v. 7; cf. 7:8; 20:5; 30:31; 31:4, 9; 37:27; 51:7). No matter how powerful the nations might be, they are still nothing but mere men. Thus, God tells His people not to be afraid, "for the moth will eat them like a garment, and the grub will eat them like wool,[77] but My righteousness will be forever, and My salvation to all generations" (v. 8). Oswalt explains,

> God is not some local deity who is but a projection from creation; rather, He is the Creator, whose promises of salvation will outlast the cosmos (vv. 4-6), and they should know that those who reproach and revile them, like all that has not partaken of the permanence of God, are doomed to slow

---

[75] We once again see a close parallel that exists between God's "salvation" and His "righteousness" (51:5, 6, 8). The exercise of God's faithful promises to save His people is an outworking of His own righteousness (cf. 46:13; 58:8; 59:16; 61:11).
[76] Smith, *Isaiah 40-66*, 396–397.
[77] Cf. 14:11; 50:9; 66:24.

destruction from which none whom have made this world their God can ever escape.[78]

The main point is that Israel needed to believe God's salvation promises.

God will bring a second Exodus (vv. 9-11)

The salvation God wants them to trust in gets likened to that of a second Exodus. God was faithful to bring salvation at the first Exodus, and He will be faithful to accomplish His second Exodus, too.

God crushed His enemies at the first Exodus (vv. 9-10)

In the sixth century B.C. God went to work to "arouse" (*'ur*, awake, stir up) Cyrus to free Israel from Babylon (41:2, 25; 44:28; 46:8-11; Jer. 51:11), and with this divine arousing, Cyrus went forth to fulfill God's purposes.

The call to crush future enemies (v. 9a). Isaiah again uses the term *'ur* to arouse God's redeeming grace to save Israel: "Awake, awake, put on strength, O arm of the Lord. Awake as in the days of old, the generations of long ago."[79] The reason for this call is because the past faithfulness of God is a certain indicator for His future faithfulness. Isaiah goes back to the Exodus (vv. 9b-10) before telling about God's future work.

The history of crushing past enemies (vv. 9b-10). With reference to Pharaoh and Egypt (cf. Isa. 30:7), Isaiah employs mythological terms that were familiar to Isaiah's historical setting and asks who it was that cut Rahab in pieces (*rahab*; cf. Job 9:13; 26:12; Pss. 87:4; 89:10) and pierced the dragon (*tanniyn*; cf. Isa. 27:1; Ps. 74:13; Ezek. 29:3 [prob. a crocodile]; 32:2 [prob. a crocodile]).[80] Both expressions as used here are being applied to Pharaoh/Egypt as a reminder of the way that God crushed His enemies at the Exodus long ago in the days of Moses (v. 9).[81]

---

[78] Oswalt, *The Book of Isaiah: Chapters 40-66*, 338.

[79] As has been noted, Isaiah often uses either the term "arm" (Isa. 30:30; 48:14; 51:5, 9; 52:10; 53:1; 59:16; 62:8; 63:5) or "hand" (Isa. 40:2; 41:20; 45:11; 50:2; 51:17; 53:10; 59:1; 62:3; 64:8; 66:14) to symbolize God's active work.

[80] The author recalls a National Geographic story about the discovery of a forty foot long crocodile skeleton found in the middle of the Sarah Desert (coming out of the Nile River).

[81] Young, *The Book of Isaiah, vol. 3*, 313. In Isaiah 30:7 Isaiah calls Pharaoh/Egypt "Rahab-the-do-nothing" (NIV) because Judah was hoping for a military alliance with

Not only did God crush Egypt with plagues, but Isaiah also asks, "Was it not You who dried up the sea [Exod. 14:21-31; Isa. 11:15-16; 50:2; 63:11-12], the waters of the great deep, Who made the depths of the sea a pathway for the redeemed to cross over" (v. 10)? God's mighty arm saved His people once at the Exodus, and the day is coming for God to do it again. Martin explains, "In the same way the Lord by His strength will allow Israel to return in a new 'Exodus' (cf. Isa. 51:3)."[82]

God will crush His enemies at the second Exodus (v. 11)

God's promise to His exiled people is that, "the ransomed of the Lord will return and come with joyful shouting to Zion,[83] and everlasting joy *will be* on their heads. They will obtain gladness and joy, and sorrow and sighing will flee away." There will be a second Exodus, and God will bring His people back (cf. Ezek. 36:19ff.; 37; 39:21-29). Thus, explains Smith,

> Just as the people rejoiced and sang God's praise in the Song of Moses after the exodus (Exod. 15), so God's people will desire to sing his praise when He redeems them in the future. One day we will see the removal of all sorrow (25:8; 30:19; 60:20; 61:3; 65:19).[84]

Thus, Israel should not fear the future.

Israel should not fear (vv. 12-16)

God is faithful and omnipotent, and God has made the promise that He will restore fallen Israel. Israel should not be afraid of the future, an idea Isaiah communicates through three simple promises.

First promise: There is only One whom they should fear (vv. 12-13)

God has already promised His people comfort and restoration (12:1; 40:1;

Egypt to withstand Babylon, but God was telling Judah that they would be of no help. This name *tanniyn* was also applied at times, as we see in certain Ugaritic writings, to "the twisting monster" in the struggles between Baal with the Yam, the god of the sea (Oswalt, *The Book of Isaiah: Chapters 40-66*, 341). In none of this is God ascribing existence to mythical figures like a monster called Rahab or Tannin the dragon, although it is true that there were real animals that become the basis for dragon stories.

[82] Martin, "Isaiah," 1105.

[83] The idea of "ransomed" (*padah*) carries the idea of being purchased out of slavery (Isa. 1:27; 29:22; 35:10; 51:11) and often stands parallel to "redeemed" (*ga'al*).

[84] Smith, *Isaiah 40-66*, 406.

49:13; 51:3; 52:9; 61:2; 66:13; cf. Jer. 31:10-14; Zeph. 3:14-17). God repeats His promise,[85] reminding them that they should not fear mere men who are no more enduring than grass (v. 12; cf. 40:6-7).[86] Israel should know that He will restore them, and no human power will stop Him. Their need is to turn to Yahweh their Maker and remember that He, the Creator (cf. 40:22; 45:12, 18; 48:13), is the One who has promised restoration with no oppressor to stop Him (*tsiyq*, v. 13; cf. Deut. 28:53, 55, 57; Isa. 29:2, 7; Jer. 19:9).[87] Oswalt explains, "to live in fear of humans is to have effectively forgotten God."[88] Israel must stop fearing.

Second promise: Liberation is coming (vv. 14-15)

God reinforces His promise by telling them that "the exile" (*tso'eh*, i.e., fettered and cast down) will soon be set free (v. 14). Yahweh is the God of all creation who has the power to do this (Job 26:12; Ps. 107:25; Jer. 31:35), and He has promised He will do it (cf. 61:1ff.).

Third promise: God's gracious election still stands (v. 16)

The fundamental reason why Israel's future is assured is the unchanging character of God (Mal. 3:6). Thus, God's promise will be fulfilled,[89] and God's election of Israel will stand. Therefore, God declares, "You are My people" (cf. Isa. 65:17-19; Hos. 1:10-11; 2:1, 23; 3:5).

The cup of wrath brings ruin (vv. 17-23)

Israel's future restoration is assured, but that did not change the fact that she was suffering at the present time because of her covenant rebellion (cf.

---

[85] Twice God uses the first-person pronoun "I" (*'anokiy*).

[86] The term Isaiah uses for man is the noun *'enosh* which signifies man as one that is weak and mortal, especially as one who is weak in contrast with God. See Thomas E. Mccomiskey, "*'nsh*," ed. R. Laird Harris, Gleason L. Archer Jr., and Bruce K. Waltke, *Theological Wordbook of the Old Testament*, cited in electronic form with Logos Libronix (Chicago: Moody Press, 1999), 59.

[87] Speaking on this same subject, Jeremiah cries out, "Ah Lord God! Behold, You have made the heavens and the earth by your great power and by your outstretched arm! Nothing is too difficult for You" (Jer. 32:17; cf. 32:27; Num. 11:23; Zech. 8:6; Luke 1:37).

[88] Oswalt, *The Book of Isaiah: Chapters 40-66*, 346.

[89] The Lord is apparently speaking to His Servant the Messiah and tells Him that He has put His Words into His mouth (ibid., 348). This passage (like 48:16) indicates that there are certain references to the Servant outside of the four Servant Songs (Grogan, "Isaiah," 295).

Amos 3:2). God's punishment is being figuratively described as a cup that contains God's anger (Isa. 29:9; 51:17, 21, 22; 63:6; cf. Job 21:20; Jer. 25:15, 26; 51:7; Rev. 14:8, 10; 16:19; 17:4; 18:6). Yes, Israel must drink from the cup of God's wrath (vv. 17-20), but soon enough this cup will be given to the Gentiles then they will drink from it (vv. 21-23).

God's cup of wrath for Israel (vv. 17-20)

God's cup of wrath has left Israel in a state of spiritual reeling, but God's command to Jerusalem is that she rouse (*'ur*) herself (cf. 41:2; 51:9, 21; 52:1),[90] for the cup of wrath is ruinous. The future does hold hope, but at the moment it is nothing but misery. Smith explains,

> The reasons why some of Jerusalem's children could not comfort her was because many of them were overcome, dazed, had fainted in streets throughout the city. Being powerless to continue, they would lie down in the streets to await their inevitable fate, just like a helpless and exhausted antelope/oryx caught in a v-shaped trap or in a net.[91]

The wrath of God left Israel in a devastated condition with no one to comfort (vv. 17-20; cf. Lam. 2:11-22), but soon enough the cup would pass into the hand of her enemies (vv. 21-23).

God's cup of wrath for Israel's enemies (vv. 21-23)

God turns their attention away from their own miserable condition to the certainty of His promises. Israel was drunk, but the cause was the chastising wrath of God (v. 21). Because He is a faithful God,[92] that wrath will soon turn away and fall upon their enemies,[93] a promise we have seen numerous times throughout Isaiah (vv. 22-23; cf. Isa. 10:25; 33:22; 35:4; 49:26; Jer. 30:7, 11; Amos 9:8-10). God will reverse her fortunes.[94]

Summary and application

God's promises to Israel are certain, and His promises to you and me are

---

[90] The Hithpolel form of imperative stresses the aspect of human responsibility to listen to God and repent.

[91] Smith, *Isaiah 40-66*, 413–414.

[92] This is the promise of The Lord (*'Adonay*), The LORD (*Yahweh*), "Your God," He says to Israel, the "One who contends" for His people (cf. 45:9; 49:25; 50:8).

[93] Israel had become like one on whom the enemy could trample at will. Assyrian monuments show the conquered nations were placed on the ground and trampled underfoot (Young, *The Book of Isaiah, vol. 3*, 323).

[94] Wolf, *Interpreting Isaiah*, 213.

certain, too. God's promises are to encourage us to keep trusting Him. Jesus Himself said, "Behold, I am coming quickly, and My reward *is* with Me, to render to every man according to what he has done" (Rev. 22:12).

THE GOOD NEWS (52:1-12)

Chapter 52 brings good news. Spiritually speaking, Israel's sin plunged the nation into ages of spiritual war and an extended spiritual drunkenness from which she needed to wake up. That day has finally arrived, and it is now time for her to wake up. Hughes explains that here in chapter 52,

> Zion (God's people) was called upon to throw off the stupor of God's judgment ("Wake up") in preparation for the blessings of God's future kingdom reign (52:1). The "good news" for the exiles was that they could return to their homeland (52:7).[95]

Good news is coming, and that means Israel needs to be responsive to the Lord so that they can have their promised restoration.

Chapter 52 reads as follows: "1 Awake, awake, clothe yourself in your strength, O Zion; clothe yourself in your beautiful garments, O Jerusalem, the holy city, for the uncircumcised and the unclean will no longer come into you. 2 Shake yourself from the dust, rise up, O captive Jerusalem; loose yourself from the chains around your neck, O captive daughter of Zion. 3 For thus says the Lord, You were sold for nothing and you will be redeemed without money. 4 For thus says the Lord God, My people went down at the first into Egypt to reside there; then the Assyrian oppressed them without cause. 5 Now therefore, what do I have here, declares the Lord, seeing that My people have been taken away without cause? *Again* the Lord declares, those who rule over them howl, and My name is continually blasphemed all day long. 6 Therefore My people shall know My name, therefore in that day I am the one who is speaking, Here I am. 7 How lovely on the mountains are the feet of him who brings good news, Who announces peace and brings good news of happiness, Who announces salvation, *and* says to Zion, Your God reigns! 8 Listen! Your watchmen lift up *their* voices; they shout joyfully together, for they will see with their own eyes when the Lord restores Zion. 9 Break forth, shout joyfully together, you waste places of Jerusalem, for the Lord has comforted His people. He has redeemed Jerusalem. 10 The Lord has bared His holy arm in the sight of all the nations, that all the ends of the earth may see the salvation of our God. 11 Depart, depart, go out from there. Touch nothing unclean. Go out of the midst of her; purify yourselves, you who carry the vessels of the Lord. 12 But you will not go

---

[95] Hughes, *Tyndale Concise Bible Commentary*, 267.

out in haste, nor will you go as fugitives, for the Lord will go before you, and the God of Israel *will be* your rear guard" (52:1-12).

Chapter 52 reveals that the ages of mourning have now come to an end (vv. 1-6), and this calls for Israel to take action (vv. 7-12).

The ages of mourning have now come to an end (vv. 1-6)

Chapter 40 opened with a call to comfort the people of God. Here in 52:1 the Lord speaks directly to Jerusalem with the urgent call to awake. Verses 1-2 give the call to take action, and verses 3-6 tell Jerusalem the reason why she needs to take action.

The call to take action (vv. 1-2)

God's saving grace never obviates human responsibility. God does have a sovereign plan, but He works His plan in association with the moral choices of His creatures. Here in verses 1-2, Isaiah issues two urgent commands for Jerusalem to take action.

The call to get up and get dressed (v. 1). Once again Isaiah employs a call to awake (*'ur*, arouse, stir up; cf. Isa. 13:17; 41:2, 25; 42:13; 45:13; 50:4; 51:9, 17; 2 Chron. 36:22; Ezra 1:1). Keil explains that in the most-recent context, this same call which "was addressed in Isa. 51:9 to the arm of Jehovah that was then represented as sleeping, is here addressed to Jerusalem, which is represented as a sleeping woman."[96] Jerusalem needs to wake up and get clothed, but this time it will not be in the rags of slavery, but in garments of beauty (cf. Isa. 49:18; 61:3, 10; Zech. 3:4). How could this be? The answer is that Jerusalem has been liberated from her invaders and, "the uncircumcised and the unclean will no longer come into you" (cf. Zech. 14:21).[97] Martin explains that this promise, "no doubt refers to the time when the Messiah will establish God's kingdom on earth, for only then will pagans never again trample the city."[98]

The call to rise up and cast away chains (v. 2). For long ages Jerusalem has been like a young girl cast down in chains of slavery. At the end of this age, Jesus Christ will return and bring an end to this spiritual war, and the slaves will

---

[96] Keil, *Commentary on the Old Testament*, 494.
[97] The only ones allowed entrance into the messianic kingdom are those who have repented of their sins and trusted in Jesus Christ (Isa. 1:25; 4:3; 19:23-25; 35:8; 42:6; 49:6; Ezek. 20:36-38; Dan. 12:10; Zech. 13:8-9; Mal. 3:3; Matt. 25:31-46).
[98] Martin, "Isaiah," 1106.

finally go free.⁹⁹ When this happens, He will restore His people and usher in an age of joy such as this world has never seen.

The reasons to take action (vv. 3-6)

God is the One who not only sent them into exile, but He also is the One who will free them. Redemption will come by the working of grace, but it will also be through Israel turning to the Lord in repentant, saving faith.

Redemption without money (v. 3). When God says, "You were sold for nothing and you will be redeemed without money," He is reminding them that *He* is not the One who sold them into exile; it was their own sins (cf. 50:1).¹⁰⁰ Smith explains, "there is no external power that can prevent God from fulfilling his plan to redeem his people."¹⁰¹

A history of past oppression (v. 4). Israel has a long history of oppression from foreign nations, oppression that has always angered God.¹⁰² Verse 4 speaks about two of these powerful nations that oppressed Israel in ages past, Egypt, the place where Israel lived as an alien (*gur*), and Assyria the empire who invaded without cause (*be'ephes*). These nations had no reason to oppress Israel, and all of it made God angry.

A present experience of Babylonian oppression (v. 5). The present oppression is the one now coming from Babylon. God explains, "Now therefore, what do I have here, declares the Lord, seeing that My people have been taken away without cause?"¹⁰³ God says, "Those who rule over them howl, and

---

⁹⁹ It is inadequate and un-biblical to see these promises as being fulfilled with the return from Babylon after the Persian victories. Biblical prophecy tells us that the final restoration will include many elements: (1) the Messiah will rule on the throne of David from a restored Jerusalem (e.g., Isa. 2:1-4; 4:2-6; 9:1-7, et al.). This has not yet been fulfilled; (2) the messianic kingdom will include a removal of all hostile nations (Isa. 10:25; 33:22; 35:4; 49:26; 51:23; cf. Jer. 30:7, 11; Amos 9:8-10). This has not been fulfilled; (3) Daniel's prophecies explicitly tell us about Israel being in subjection to the Persians, the Greeks, and the Romans; (4) not only did Israel never again have a king, but they were always under Gentile dominion (cf. Neh. 9:36-37); (5) Daniel's Seventy-Week prophecy demands a prophetic gap that has never seen its fulfillment (Dan. 9:24-27).

¹⁰⁰ The redemption price was the life of God's own Servant (Isa. 52:13-53:12).

¹⁰¹ Smith, *Isaiah 40-66*, 419.

¹⁰² Young, *The Book of Isaiah, vol. 3*, 327.

¹⁰³ This statement "without cause" is parallel to v. 4, but here uses the adverb *chinnam*

My name is continually blasphemed all day long." Babylon had no reason for attacking Judah, and all of it angered God greatly. Liberation is on the way, but only if Israel will turn to the Lord in faith.

A future liberation that comes only by faith in the Lord (v. 6). Israel needs to trust in God's Servant, and this is exactly what is going to happen in the closing days of this age during the Great Tribulation. God says, "Therefore My people shall know My name, therefore, in that day I am the one who is speaking, Here I am" (cf. Isa. 9:6; 10:20-23; 41:20; 43:10; 49:23, 26; 60:16; Zech. 12:10-14). One day Israel will trust the One they rejected the first time He came, and that faith is what will restore them in a New Covenant (Jer. 31:31-34).

This good news calls for action (vv. 7-12)

Wolf explains, "The news that Israel would be released is good news indeed, and verses 7-12 celebrate this great event."[104] This good news first gets announced (v. 7), but then it calls for a proper response (vv. 8-12).

God's victory is good news (v. 7)

The messengers of the ancient world brought their messages by horse or swift foot messengers who could tirelessly run to deliver important war-time messages (cf. 1 Sam. 4:17; 2 Sam. 18:26). This message is the most special one that could ever be delivered, for it is the message that Israel's spiritual war is finally over!

One can just picture the precious vision of the army messenger coming over the top of the hill with the good news (*mebasser*, gospel messenger; cf. 40:9; 41:27; 60:6; 61:1) that your warrior King has won the victory, and the war is over.[105] The heart of this good news is that God's Servant has paid the price of sin by giving His own sinless life to satisfy the wrath of God (Isa. 53:4-6; cf. Rom. 3:21-26; 10:15; Eph. 6:15; 1 Pet. 2:24; 3:18). Wrath has been satisfied, and sinners can now have peace without condemnation (Isa. 12:1; Rom. 5:1; 8:1).

God's victory calls for a response from Israel (vv. 8-12)

Salvation can come without limitation to anyone who is willing to believe. Isaiah expresses this with three calls to respond to the good news.

(without cause, without reason, freely, for no reason). The end result is terrible blasphemy against the name of the Lord (cf. Ezek. 36:19-23).
[104] Wolf, *Interpreting Isaiah*, 214.
[105] The feet represent the whole messenger (synechdoche).

First call: The call to listen (v. 8). Good news is worthless if no one listens. Isaiah writes, "Listen, your watchmen lift up *their* voices; they shout joyfully together, for they will see with their own eyes when the Lord restores Zion."[106] The watchmen of the city have heard the news (cf. Isa. 56:10; Jer. 6:17; Ezek. 3:17; 33:2), and now there is a jubilant cry of joy. The good news is there. All you have to do is listen.

Second call: The call to break forth (vv. 9-10). Isaiah gives a call to the "waste places" (*chorboth*) of Jerusalem to break forth and shout joyfully (v. 9).[107] The city that was in desolation will now be rebuilt, for the day of comfort (*nacham*)[108] and redemption (*ga'al*),[109] have finally arrived. All of this is a cause for great celebration.[110]

The reason for this restoration is nothing less than the powerful grace of God. Isaiah explains, "The Lord has bared His holy arm in the sight of all the nations, that all the ends of the earth may see the salvation of our God" (v. 10).[111] God's saving acts at the first Exodus were a great sight to reveal the glory of the Lord, but as great as the Exodus was, it will pale in comparison to God's saving acts in Christ when "the glory of the Lord will be revealed, and all flesh will see *it* together" (cf. 40:5; 45:22-25).

Third call: The call to flee (vv. 11-12). This section ends with a call to flee Babylon. This call includes both a command and a promise. The command calls out, "Depart, depart, go out from there; touch nothing unclean; go out of the midst of her, purify yourselves, you who carry the vessels of the Lord" (v. 11). Exile brought great defilement, but now it is time to leave the exile and get cleansed from all ritual uncleanliness and defilement (1:10-16; 64:6; 65:1-7).[112]

---

[106] Although the expression can mean "when the Lord restores Zion" this infinitive construct and other passages suggest that it is speaking about the way that He Himself will return (cf. Isa. 59:20; 61:1ff.; 63:1ff.; Ezek. 43:1-3; 44:1-3).

[107] Both terms "break forth" (*patsach*; cf. Isa. 14:7; 44:23; 49:13; 54:1) and "shout joyfully" (*ranan*; cf. Isa. 12:6; 24:14; 35:6; 42:11; 44:23; 49:13; 54:1; 61:7; 65:14) convey the idea of extreme jubilation.

[108] Cf. Isa 12:1; 40:1; 49:13; 51:3, 12; 52:9; 54:11; 66:13; Luke 2:25.

[109] Cf. Isa. 41:14; 43:1, 12, 14; 44:6, 23, 24; 47:4; 48:17; 49:7, 26; 54:5, 8; 59:20; 60:16; 63:16; Luke 2:38.

[110] God offered this day of comfort and redemption when Christ came to His people 2,000 years ago, but they would not believer (cf. Luke 19:41-44).

[111] See comments at 51:9 for the meaning of the Lord's "arm."

[112] Special attention to purity would be necessary for the priests and Levites who would bring back stolen temple vessels (Ezra 1:7-11; Num. 3:6-8; 2 Chron. 5:4-7).

God commanded His people to flee, but many had become comfortable and complacent in Babylon.[113]

Unlike the first Exodus, God's promise is that they will not depart in haste or fear (v. 12). She will not return as a frightened fugitive (*menusah*), for the Lord will go before them to lead the way, and the God of Israel will be their rear guard to protect them from behind (Isa. 42:16; 49:10; cf. Exod. 13:21; 14:19-20). In other words, says God, I will be with you, I will protect you, and you do not need to be afraid of anything. Smith gives us a wonderful summary of the issue:

> God's people need to wake up to God's plans, to cleanse themselves from uncleanness, and trust in God's promises. Life in this sinful earth is often very difficult, but God's reign will bring an end to these problems and usher the glorious era when he will rule as King.[114]

Summary and application

Experience shows us that the longer we remain in this sin-cursed world, the more we are going to grow weary of the misery that sin brings. The Bible tells us that when Jesus Christ died on the cross, He made a perfect sacrifice that paid the price of all sin for all time (Isa. 53:4-6; Matt. 20:28; 1 Pet. 2:24; 3:18). His promise is perfect and eternal forgiveness if we believe. One day He is coming back, and when He does, He will bring us to Himself forever (John 14:1-3).

THE VICTORIOUS SUFFERING SERVANT (52:13-53:12)

The fourth Servant Song (52:13-53:15),[115] this passage that emphasizes the suffering Servant, could arguably be called the most important passage of the whole Bible because of its detailed prophecies about the rejection, death and resurrection of Christ. The victorious suffering Servant is the One who will suffer and die to take away our sins, but by His self-sacrifice He will conquer death and rise again to receive His infinite reward.

Some within the Jewish community have tried to argue that chapter 53 is not about one particular man who will die for sins, but that it is telling how

---

[113] This command to depart from exile and return to God and His land had application after the fall of Babylon to Persia (Zech. 2:6-7), but it also has application to Israel's restoration at the end of the age (Rev. 18:4).
[114] Smith, *Isaiah 40-66*, 428–429.
[115] Isa. 42:1-9; 49:1-13; 50:4-11; 52:13-53:12.

Israel the nation will suffer on behalf of others. Hughes explains that this is not the oldest understand of the passage,

> Early Jewish interpretation of this passage understood the "servant" (52:13) to refer to the Messiah. This also was the interpretation by the early church (cf. Acts 8:30–35). Not until the twelfth century was it suggested that the "servant" of Isaiah 53 was the nation of Israel.[116]

Smith describes why this passage cannot be interpreted as meaning that the nation will suffer to bring atonement for the world:

> Those who identify the suffering servant with the nation of Israel suggest that the historical setting of this message reflects the suffering of the people of God in Babylonian exile and their deliverance from it [or some other idea that denies one future man to fulfill the prophecies]. . . . Most of these interpretations are not very convincing if one takes the view that all of these Servant poems are prophetic of a future figure in an eschatological setting when God will bring salvation to his people and the nations. . . . The examination of these earlier poems [42:1-9; 49:1-13; 50:4-11; cf. 9:1-7; 11:1-5] led to the conclusion that this Servant was a messianic royal figure who would establish justice for all the nations but suffer opposition and physical abuse before his eventual vindication and exaltation. The present poem explains these issues in more detail.[117]

No, this passage is not about the nation, but it is a messianic prophecy telling how the sinless Savior of the world would take away sin by giving Himself as a perfect sacrifice to satisfy the wrath of God.

Chapter 53 reads as follows: "13 Behold, My Servant will prosper, He will be high and lifted up and greatly exalted. 14 Just as many were astonished at you, *My people,* so His appearance was marred more than any man and His form more than the sons of men. 15 Thus He will sprinkle many nations. Kings will shut their mouths on account of Him, for what had not been told them they will see, and what they had not heard they will understand. 1 Who has believed our message, and to whom has the arm of the Lord been revealed? 2 For He grew up before Him like a tender shoot, and like a root out of parched ground. He has no *stately* form or majesty that we should look upon Him, nor appearance that we should be attracted to Him. 3 He was despised and forsaken of men, a man of sorrows and acquainted with grief; and like one from whom men hide their face He was despised, and we did not esteem Him. 4 Surely our griefs He

---

[116] Hughes, *Tyndale Concise Bible Commentary*, 267.
[117] Smith, *Isaiah 40-66*, 430–432.

Himself bore, and our sorrows He carried, yet we ourselves esteemed Him stricken, smitten of God, and afflicted. 5 But He was pierced through for our transgressions. He was crushed for our iniquities. The chastening for our well-being *fell* upon Him, and by His scourging we are healed. 6 All of us like sheep have gone astray, each of us has turned to his own way, but the Lord has caused the iniquity of us all to fall on Him. 7 He was oppressed and He was afflicted, yet He did not open His mouth. Like a lamb that is led to slaughter, and like a sheep that is silent before its shearers, so He did not open His mouth. 8 By oppression and judgment He was taken away; and as for His generation, who considered that He was cut off out of the land of the living for the transgression of my people, to whom the stroke *was due?* 9 His grave was assigned with wicked men, yet He was with a rich man in His death, because He had done no violence, nor was there any deceit in His mouth. 10 But the Lord was pleased to crush Him, putting *Him* to grief. If He would render Himself *as* a guilt offering, He will see *His* offspring; He will prolong *His* days, and the good pleasure of the Lord will prosper in His hand. 11 As a result of the anguish of His soul, He will see *it and* be satisfied. By His knowledge the Righteous One, My Servant, will justify the many, as He will bear their iniquities. 12 Therefore, I will allot Him a portion with the great, and He will divide the booty with the strong, because He poured out Himself to death, and was numbered with the transgressors; yet He Himself bore the sin of many, and interceded for the transgressors" (52:13-53:12).

Despite the chapter division, this pericope is best seen as starting at 52:13 rather than 53:1. For the sake simplicity, however, we will simply refer to the entire unit as Isaiah 53. Isaiah 53 is one of the passages of the Old Testament that combines together in one tight package both the sufferings and the glories of the Messiah (cf. 1 Pet. 1:10-12). In the end, the Servant will save His people from ruin and reign in glory in the messianic kingdom, but the full work of salvation would first have to include a violent death to take away sin. Both glory and suffering come out in this passage, but the sections that emphasize the sufferings are contained largely in the second through fourth stanzas, being bracketed by the first and fifth stanzas which emphasize the victory and glory of the Servant.

Isaiah 53 breaks down into five stanzas of three verses each, with the following dominant themes: the supreme irony of the Servant (52:13-15); the supreme rejection of the Servant (53:1-3); the supreme, substitutionary suffering of the Servant (53:4-6); the supreme injustice against the Servant (53:7-9); the supreme reward of the Servant (53:10-12).[118]

---

[118] Oswalt, *The Book of Isaiah: Chapters 40-66*, 376.

ISAIAH 49:1-57:21

The supreme irony of the Servant (vv. 13-15)

When we say supreme irony, we are talking about the great irony that was at work in the way that God worked through the Servant to bring salvation to the world. We see the irony reflected in the fact that the Servant will experience not only a great and glorious exaltation, but also great humiliation and suffering.

The exaltation and glory of the Servant (v. 13)

Verse 13 tells us how God's Servant will one day experience a glorious exaltation that is higher than anyone has ever experienced or ever will. We see this explained in with a four-fold description of His exaltation.

First description: The Servant will prosper. Isaiah once again introduces his bold declaration with the interjection "behold" (*hinneh*; cf. 42:1).[119] The first declaration is that God's Servant will "prosper." When the NASB says that the Servant will prosper, it translates the Hebrew verb *sakal* which carries the idea of acting with such wisdom (NIV) that you will prosper and succeed (cf. Josh. 1:8; Jer. 10:21).[120] The corporate nation acted foolishly and failed, but God's Servant will prosper and succeed. In His High-Priestly prayer Jesus said, "I glorified You on the earth, having accomplished the work which You have given Me to do" (John 17:4), and on the cross Jesus cried out "it is finished" (John 19:30). He prospered.

Second and third descriptions: The Servant will be high and lifted up. Both terms "high" (*rum*) and "lifted up" (*nasa'*) continue to emphasize supreme exaltation.[121] This intense language could only be speaking about God Himself accomplishing redemption. This Servant is no ordinary man, but He is God in flesh saving His people from their sins (Isa. 4:2; 9:6-7; 10:20-23; 12:6; 43:10-13; 49:26; 60:16).

Fourth description: The Servant will be greatly exalted. The Servant will enjoy the highest exaltation (*gabah me'od*) any man has ever had. Many kings have held positions of tremendous power and glory, but He will be the greatest of all. Paul takes directly from this passage in Philippians and tells us that because God's Servant poured Himself out to death,

> God highly exalted Him, and bestowed on Him the name which is above every name, so that at the name of Jesus every knee will bow, of those who

---

[119] Young, *The Book of Isaiah, vol. 3*, 335.
[120] Oswalt, *The Book of Isaiah: Chapters 40-66*, 373. The ESV has "act wisely."
[121] These two verbs are paired together four times in Isaiah (6:1; 33:10; 52:13; 57:15), but nowhere else in the OT.

are in heaven and on earth and under the earth, and that every tongue will confess that Jesus Christ is Lord, to the glory of God the Father (Phil. 2:9-11).

There is only one Lord, and His name is Jesus. The irony of the whole picture comes in the verses that follow where Isaiah tells us about the supreme humiliation and suffering this exalted One must first endure.

The humiliation and suffering of the Servant (vv. 14-15)

Isaiah's shocking news is that this most-exalted man of God is the same One who will experience the most-horrific humiliation and suffering imaginable. This was a hard message for Israel to accept. They eagerly embraced the promises of a conquering, warrior King, but conveniently paid no heed to those passages that prophesied rejection and death. Jesus rebuked two such disciples after the resurrection by telling them, "O foolish men and slow of heart to believe in all that the prophets have spoken! Was it not necessary for the Christ to suffer these things and to enter into His glory?" (Luke 24:25-26). Verses 14-15 are in the form of a correlation with verse 14 saying "just as" (*ka'asher*) and verse 15 finishing the correlation with the word "thus" (*ken*).[122] All of this emphasizes the way the nations would be shocked to speechlessness when they hear who this Servant is (v. 14). The truth is that this is how God provided atonement for sins (v. 15).

The appalling suffering of the Servant (v. 14). The NASB starts by saying "just as many were astonished at you, *My people*," but two items call for comment. First of all, the word "astonished" (*shamam*) may be better rendered by the English word "appalled," a stronger word that better represents the Hebrew. TWOT explains that this verb conveys ideas like "desolate," or "appalled," or "horrified." Thus,

> Basic to the idea of the root is the desolation caused by some great disaster, usually as a result of divine judgment.... From the above it is not difficult to see how the second major use of the root is derived, the sense of "horror" and "shock" brought about by the vision of desolation. It is the inner response to the outward scene.[123]

---

[122] Smith, *Isaiah 40-66*, 437. Thus, the "just as" correlates with the "so" in v. 15 and not in the middle of v. 14.
[123] Hermann J. Austel, "*shmm*," ed. R. Laird Harris, Gleason L. Archer Jr., and Bruce K. Waltke, *Theological Wordbook of the Old Testament*, cited in electronic form with Logos Libronix (Chicago: Moody Press, 1999), 936–937.

When the world sees the ruin that falls on God's special Servant, it will be appalled. Thus, the NIV reads, "Just as there were many who were appalled at him."

The next observation is that the NIV reads "appalled *at him*" (third person masculine singular), and not "appalled *at you*" (second person masculine singular) as in the NASB. The reason for this difference is based on the internal difficulty in reading "you," and some variation in the textual data.[124] The rendering given by the NIV is based on the effort to have this statement match the third person language that follows,[125] but this is not the preferred understanding. It is better to understand that the address is made directly to the Servant (2ms), but after this Isaiah abruptly, but not in an unusual manner (cf. Zech. 12:10), shifts from the second person to a third person description of the Servant. This happens with two subordinate clauses that tell us, so His appearance was "marred" (*shachath*, i.e., "inhumanly deformed," the same term used in Mal. 1:14 for a disfigured animal) more than any man and His form more than the sons of men. This man is going to suffer such ruin (physical and spiritual) He will be virtually unrecognizable as a human.[126]

The significance of the Servant's suffering (v. 15).[127] The "so" in verse

---

[124] Based on the variant "you," the NASB adds the italicized words "my people" based on the idea that the world was astonished at the people of Israel, and that this is also how they felt about the Servant, but this is better seen as an address directly to the Servant.

[125] Some suggest the need to emend the MT to "him" as we see in the Syriac, BHS, NRSV, and maybe the Targ. (Oswalt, *The Book of Isaiah: Chapters 40-66*, 373, n. 53). However, the DSS support the MT, and the MT is harder reading, and is thus to be preferred.

[126] The physical ruin was so horrible that the Servant did not even look like a human being (Isa. 50:6; Ps. 22:6; Matt. 26:67; 27:30; John 19:3), but the ruin was also at a deeper spiritual level (Young, *The Book of Isaiah, vol. 3*, 338).

[127] As already noted above, Young also thinks that the contrast (the "just as" and "so" contrast) is that which comes between "the many" here in v. 14 and the "nations" and "kings" in v. 15. In other words, "just as many were appalled over 'you,' the Messiah, . . . so kings will shut their mouths" (ibid., 336-337). Young's view would make ". . . so his appearance" and "so shall he sprinkle" as two subordinate clauses which both give further explanation of this horrible condition. Oswalt says that most agree that the first "so" in the middle of v. 14 is not the one that corresponds to the "thus" at the beginning. Oswalt also says that many see this idea to mean that there is a contrast between two shocks: (1) they were shocked at his disfigurement and (2) they were shocked at his exaltation (v. 15 picking up on the theme from v. 13) (Oswalt, *The Book of Isaiah: Chapters 40-66*, 379, n. 80).

15 (*ken*) is what completes the correlation with the "just as" in verse 14. This could be taken in one of two ways, though, depending in part on how one translates the word "sprinkle" (*nazah*).[128] Although some hold that this word should be understood as "startle,"[129] it is preferable to accept the translation "sprinkle," and to understand it as sacrificial sprinkling that brings cleansing from sin.[130] Thus, explains Kidner,

> For *sprinkle*, the rsv's "startle" (supported by the lxx) makes a good opening to the sequence, startled—silenced—convinced. But *sprinkle* (av, rv), which is grammatically suspect but not indefensible, suits the context well with its implications of sacrificial cleansing (*cf.* 1 Pet. 1:2) and perhaps of covenant making (*cf.* Ex. 24:6, 8; a different word).[131]

Thus, the apodosis in verse 15 is showing us that even though the Servant suffered the worst ruin ever (v. 14), this is how God would bring forgiveness (v. 15). The impact on those who understand is that "kings will shut their mouths on account of Him, for what had not been told them they will see, and what they had not heard they will understand." Paul cites this verse as his motivation for taking the gospel into the entire world:

> and thus I aspired to preach the gospel, not where Christ was *already* named, so that I would not build on another man's foundation, but as it is written, They who had no news of Him shall see, and they who have not heard shall understand (Rom. 15:20-21).

---

[128] Note: Oswalt takes it that the "just as" finds its correlation with the "thus" in v. 15, and he also sees the verb "sprinkle" to be from a similar Semitic root (*yazzeh*) that means "to startle" (ibid.). The translation "startle" is found in the NLT, but "sprinkle" is found in the KJV, NKJV, NIV, ESV, and NASB and has the best textual and lexical evidence to support it.

[129] There is an Arabic cognate term from the same consonants that means "to leap" (in Heb. it would be found in the Hiphil stem) and this could produce the idea of "to startle" or "to cause marvel" (Grogan, "Isaiah," 306, n. 15). This meaning seems to also be supported by the LXX, but it is not to be preferred.

[130] The verb *nazah* has a primary meaning of a light sprinkle of blood such as would happen when the priest would sprinkle (i.e., spatter) blood for cleansing according to OT sacrificial law (Lev. 4:6; 5:9; 8:11; 14:7, 51; 16:14; Num. 8:7; 19:4, 18-19; cf. 1 Pet. 1:2; Heb. 9:13-14). In other words, it is in this horrible, marred condition that God's own Servant will carry out this work of purification, and He will sprinkle people in many nations.

[131] Kidner, "Isaiah," 663.

Having revealed the supreme irony of the Servant's work, Isaiah now tells us about the supreme rejection He would suffer.[132]

The supreme rejection of the Servant (vv. 1-3)

It is not uncommon in Jewish circles to assert that the reason Jesus could not have been the promised Messiah was because the nation rejected Him (cf. John 1:11). Ironically, the very opposite is the truth. The rejection of Christ by His own people Israel is not a proof against Him being the Messiah, but rather it is a proof that He is the Messiah according to the prophecies we see in Isaiah 53 (and elsewhere).

The people had all the evidence they needed. They heard His marvelous teaching (Matt. 7:28-29). The witnessed His marvelous miracles (John 3:1-2; 12:37-42). They watched Him live a life of perfect obedience to the Father (John 8:29, 46) as He carried out the will of Him who sent Him (John 4:34; 5:17-19, 30; 6:38). They saw Him conquer death, both that of others (John 11:47-53) and also that of Himself (John 20-21). Israel had all the proof in the world, but they still rejected Him. The reason is because they were carrying out God's eternal purpose by choosing to hate and reject God's Son so that He might die for our sins (Acts 2:22-23; 4:27-28).

Christ had to be rejected, a fact that Isaiah prophesied seven-hundred years before it came to pass. Here in verses 1-3 Isaiah shows us both the marvel over the Servant's rejection (v. 1) as well as the description of the Servant's rejection (vv. 2-3).

The marvel over the Servant's rejection (v. 1)

How ironic it is that the Gentile nations will listen and believe in the Servant (v. 52:15), but His own people will not (vv. 1-3). Isaiah opens this section with two rhetorical questions about the rejection of the Servant.

First question (a question that focuses on human responsibility). Isaiah asks, "Who has believed our message?" That is, how is that there were so few who believed the message that God had entrusted to the nation of Israel, i.e., "our message" (cf. Rom. 3:2; 9:4). Isaiah incredulously asks, "Who has believed" (cf. Rom. 10:16)? Isaiah appears to be speaking from the eschatological perspective of what is going to take place in the future when the Messiah establishes God's kingdom. This is the time when the people will be in dismay over the fact that the One they hated and rejected for so long is actually their promised King. Smith explains,

---

[132] Wolf, *Interpreting Isaiah*, 216.

Thus the "we" statements [i.e., the first-person plural verbs] seem to best fit with the [eschatological] believing people of Israel. They are the ones who observed what God revealed to them. F. Delitzsch also notes that the "we" speeches in 16:6; 24:16a; 42:24; 64:5–6 all refer to Israelites.[133]

Oswalt explains further,

> If the Servant is not Israel, as seems evident, then the 'we' is most likely Israel, who fails to recognize the 'arm of the Lord' when it is revealed to them.... Thus, the prophet is probably identifying himself with his people and speaking for them (see Jer. 14:7-9)."[134]

This author thinks it is best understood as Isaiah writing on behalf of his collective nation without any special distinguishing that it should be understood solely on the basis of the eschatological elect remnant. It is written from an eschatological perspective looking back, but it is looking back in shock over the way that the chosen nation rejected God's Servant.

Second question (a question that focuses on divine sovereignty). Isaiah then asks a second, parallel question, this one containing a distinct emphasis on the saving grace of God: "To whom has the arm of the Lord been revealed?"[135] In other words, who is there who has been touched by God's grace to open their hearts to believe?[136] Isaiah asks these two questions how it is that so many rejected Him, but then in verses 2-3 he continues by giving a description of the Servant's rejection.

The description of the Servant's rejection (vv. 2-3)

Here we see the sad picture about what Israel thought of God's Servant. Isaiah answers the questions of verse 1 with a series of nine descriptions of how Israel loathed and rejected God's precious Servant.

First and second descriptions (v. 2a). Isaiah says that the Servant grew up "before Him" (i.e., before God) "like a tender shoot [*yoneq*],[137] and like a root

---

[133] Smith, *Isaiah 40-66*, 442.
[134] Oswalt, *The Book of Isaiah: Chapters 40-66*, 381.
[135] See comments at 51:9 for the meaning of the Lord's "arm."
[136] This statement reflects the soteriological reality that because of total depravity, God must call and draw a man to Christ if he is to ever respond in faith (Matt. 11:25-27; John 6:37, 44, 65; Rom. 8:28; 1 Cor. 2:14; Eph. 1:3-6; 2 Thess. 2:13; 2 Tim. 1:9; Titus 3:5; 1 Pet. 1:1-2; Rev. 13:8; 17:8).
[137] The root of this term "tender shoot" (*yoneq*) carries a root meaning "to suck," and

[*shoresh*] out of parched ground."[138] In the eyes of the nation, the Servant was a nothing, a nobody, someone of no importance or any spiritual relevance. Oswalt notes that here, as in 52:14, the real issue was that the people totally despised Him:

> The real issue is not whether this person was good looking, but that the way in which He set about delivering His people was just as shocking and as off-putting as it would be to have the ugliest man in a group chosen "best looking."[139]

The sad reality is that they did not want a humble Servant to bear their sins; rather, they all they wanted a victorious warrior to crush their enemies.

Third and fourth descriptions (v. 2b). Isaiah tells us, "He has no *stately* form or majesty that we should look upon Him, nor appearance that we should be attracted to Him" (v. 2b).[140] In other words, God's Servant was not one who would be characterized by astounding physical stature such as that which had been possessed by King Saul (1 Sam. 10:23).

Fifth and sixth descriptions (v. 3a). Following the thoughts of verse 2, Isaiah tells us that the Servant would be despised (*bazah*) and rejected (*chadal*) by men. The former term carries the idea of looking down on something as being worthless (Isa. 49:7; cf. Pss. 22:6-8; 69:7-9; Luke 18:31-33).[141] The latter term also emphasizes the way the nation would reject Him because they saw Him as worthless to them. Here He is—God's glorious, loving, and gracious Savior—and His own people want absolutely nothing to do with Him.

Seventh and Eighth descriptions (v. 3b). The Servant will be a man of sorrow (*mak'oboth*) and acquainted with grief (*choliy*). The former term carries the idea of the miseries and pains of a sin-cursed world (cf. v. 4; Ps. 32:10; Lam.

---

in botany it refers to young sapling (sucker) twigs. Earlier in Isaiah 11:1, Isaiah spoke about a "shoot" (*choter*) that would spring forth from Jesse and a "branch" (*netser*) from his roots, but neither of these words are the same one that is here. A "tender shoot" would be that little shoot that comes out of the side or base of the tree (insignificant and unwanted growth).

[138] One can just envision the insignificance of a tiny root in parched, desert soil.
[139] Ibid., 382.
[140] The term "form" (*to'ar*) speaks about outward shape and form, e.g., Rachel was "beautiful in form" (Gen. 29:17). "Majesty" (*hadar*) speaks about the idea of outward splendor (cf. Isa. 35:2). "Appearance" (*mar'eh*) speaks simply to looks.
[141] Young, *The Book of Isaiah, vol. 3*, 343. Esau, for example, despised his birthright (Gen. 25:34) and Michal despised David (2 Sam. 6:16).

1:12, 18), and the latter term is the word that means "sick" (Isa. 1:5; 38:9; 53:4, 10). Physical sickness is not the issue, though, but the sickness of sin. Earlier, Isaiah described the nation like a man who has been beaten from head to toe so that the whole head is "sick" (Isa. 1:5).

Sin has left the nation in a horrible condition, and the only One who can fix it is God's Servant. The good news is that in the incarnation of the Son of God, eternal God stepped down out of the glories of heaven and plunged himself right in the midst of the agonies of a sin-cursed world, for this was the only way for redemption to take place.[142] In Hebrews we read, "He had to be made like His brethren in all things, so that He might become a merciful and faithful high priest in things pertaining to God, to make propitiation for the sins of the people" (Heb. 2:17).

Ninth description (v. 3c). Isaiah lastly tells us, "like one from whom men hide their face He was despised, and we did not esteem Him." Their contempt and disgust for Jesus Christ was so bad they did not even want to look at Him; thus, they did not esteem (*chashab*) Him. How ironic it is, says Martin, that even though they looked at Him as being utterly worthless, "yet He was and is the most important Person in the world, for He is the Servant of the Lord."[143] The irony of this paradox is great, but this was the good and perfect plan of God for bringing salvation to a sin-cursed world (Luke 19:41-44; Acts 2:23; 4:27-28; Eph. 1:11).

The supreme, substitutionary suffering of the Servant (vv. 4-6)

This third section brings the focus upon the work of the Servant to give His own life as a substitutionary sacrifice, the heart of the Servant's work, and the literary center of the fourth Servant Song. Kidner explains,

> This is the central stanza, in every sense. Here the meaning of the Servant's disgrace breaks through, with the inverted word-order of v 4a to stress the exchange of roles, and the emphatic pronouns *he* and *we* (4a–4b) to expose our misunderstanding.[144]

Isaiah lays out three facts of the Servant's work, prophesying how the Servant would give His life in the place of sinners who deserved the punishment

---

[142] The verb form is used in 53:10 where it literally reads that God "made Him sick," i.e., God poured all the sickness of sin onto the Servant so that He could take it away by His death.
[143] Martin, "Isaiah," 1107.
[144] Kidner, "Isaiah," 663.

that would fall on Him (cf. v. 6; 2 Cor. 5:21; 1 Tim. 2:4-6; 4:10; 1 Pet. 2:24; 3:18).

First fact of the Servant's substitutionary suffering: The judgment deserved by the nation is what He Himself took (v. 4a)

Isaiah first tells us "Surely our griefs He Himself bore." Two key ideas stick out in this statement.

First key idea. The expression "surely" (*'aken*) accentuates the contrast that exists between verses 1-3 and 4-6.[145] The former stanza highlights the utter contempt the nation held against the Servant, but the latter stanza brings out the real truth that He was bearing their "griefs" (same term as v. 3, i.e., the *sickness* of our sin).

Second key idea. The second idea that sticks out is the strong emphasis on substitution. The use of the pronoun "He Himself" (*hu'*) stresses this idea of substitution, and that He Himself was the One who came to take away our "griefs." Pfeiffer reminds us that according to the Hebrew, the word is "more literally, *sickness*. In token of Christ's power to forgive sins, he did heal many of men's physical sicknesses. But since the subject matter here is illness of soul rather than of body, the rendering griefs is justifiable."[146] That is, the Servant came to earth to die as a substitute sacrifice in the place of sinners. Jesus once explained that He had come to give His life as "a ransom [*lutron*] for [*anti*, in place of] many" (Matt. 20:28; cf. 1 Cor. 15:3; 2 Cor. 5:21; Gal. 3:13; 1 Pet. 2:24; 3:18; Heb. 2:9; 9:28; 1 John 2:2; 4:10). This is the clear message: God's Servant would die in the place of sinners (you, me, all men)!

Second fact of the Servant's substitutionary suffering: The nation utterly failed to understand the meaning of His death (v. 4b)

God's Servant is the One who carried our sorrows (same term as v. 3). Once again, Isaiah shows us the tremendous irony of it all, for Isaiah tells us that the Servant carried the load of their sin (v. 4a), but none of the people understood that this was what was happening (v. 4b).

His death was bearing their sin. The Servant is the One, the only One,

---

[145] Oswalt, *The Book of Isaiah: Chapters 40-66*, 385.
[146] Pfeiffer, *The Wycliffe Bible Commentary: Old Testament*, Is 53:4. Matthew applied this passage when Jesus healed physical sicknesses in His first advent (Matt. 8:17). It is true that Christ's final work of restoration in the kingdom will include a removal of all physical impact from the curse of sin, but this is not the import of Isaiah 53:4 which is focused on the Servant's death to take away sin.

who can carry (*sabal*) this heavy burden of sorrow and pain that sin has given to the human race. He can do it, and this is exactly what He did.

The people could not see this truth. The Servant took their sin, but this is not the way the nation looked at it. They thought God was striking Him down for calling Himself the Son of God. An emphatic contrast comes out through the use of the pronoun "we." Isaiah says, "Yet *we ourselves* esteemed Him stricken, smitten of God, and afflicted." In other words, the nation looked at His death as an act of God to strike (*naga'*, to touch violently), to smite (*nakah*, violent blows), and to "afflict" (*'anah*, to bring low) Jesus for having claimed to be the Son of God. In John, the Jewish leaders told Pilate, "We have a law, and by that law He ought to die because He made Himself out *to be* the Son of God" (John 19:7), and in Matthew we read how the Jewish leaders said, "He trusts in God; let God rescue *Him* now, if He delights in Him; for He said, I am the Son of God" (Matt. 27:43). What we see here is that these leaders of Israel fulfilled exactly what Isaiah said they would do. Smith adds one final comment that helps explain the truth:

> The speakers wrongly concluded that he was suffering afflictions that were justly sent by God for the sins he had committed. Their perspective was partially right and partially wrong, for God did smite him (cf. 53:10), but their understanding of why he was smitten was wrong (he was not being punished for his own sins).[147]

Third fact of the Servant's substitutionary suffering: Isaiah says that His death was to be a sacrifice for the sins of the nation (vv. 5-6)

Once again, we see a strong contrast in the flow of Isaiah's description in that the end of verse 4 shows us the false conclusions drawn by the nation, but here in verses 5-6 Isaiah shows us the real truth. Isaiah does so by giving five additional statements about the substitutionary suffering of the Servant, and that He was dying for the sins of the whole nation.

First and second statements that He was dying for the sins of the nation (v. 5a). Isaiah writes, "but He was pierced through for our transgressions;[148] He was crushed for our iniquities." The subject of discussion gets intense and specific, and now makes it clear that this man is dying to pay the price of sin. The word for "pierce" (Poel participle of *chalal*) is not the same term used in Psalm 22:16 (*kur*, bore through), nor is it the same term used in

---

[147] Smith, *Isaiah 40-66*, 450.

[148] The word for transgression (*pesha'*) speaks about rebellion against God and His rightful authority over men.

Zechariah 12:10 (*daqar*, pierce through). This term *chalal* is one that can carry the idea of "to profane" or "to pollute," but here in the intensive Poel stem it carries the idea of "to pierce" or "fatally wound" (cf. 22:2; 51:9; 53:5; 66:16; Ps. 69:26). TWOT explains, "The verb itself is used only eight times" and usually means "a fatal wounding of persons."[149] Keil notes that, "there were no stronger expressions to be found in the language, to denote a violent and painful death."[150]

Moreover, says Isaiah, God's chosen Servant was also "crushed [*daka'*] for our iniquities." That is, God's pulverizing judgment (cf. Isa. 19:10; Job 22:9; Jer. 44:10) brought this man to the greatest depths of the worst ruin imaginable. Ironically, however, this pulverizing judgment was not for anything that He Himself had done, but rather, say Isaiah, it was for "our iniquities" (*'awon*, a strong term for sin that comes from the root idea of twisting).[151] Smith comments on the intensive language that shows the substitutionary force of these words:

> The first half of the verse indicates that the reason for this suffering was "because of our rebellion"[37] and "because of our iniquities." This forthright confession of guilt plainly states that the Servant suffered the consequences for "our" (the Israelite speakers) sinful acts. This act was penal, for it involved a just punishment for rebellious acts. It was also substitutionary because the punishment that should have fallen on the Israelites who sinned were transferred instead to the Servant.[152]

From these statements, God makes it clear that the wrath that would fall on the Servant would be beyond imagination, but Isaiah is not done and there is still more to come.

Third and fourth statements that He was dying for the sins of the nation (v. 5b). Isaiah tells us, "the chastening for our well-being *fell* upon Him, and by His scourging we are healed." Both terms "chastening" (*musar*, discipline to correct; cf. Job 5:17; Prov. 22:15; 23:13),[153] and "scourging" (*chaburah*, wound,

---

[149] Donald J. Wiseman, "*chll*," ed. R. Laird Harris, Gleason L. Archer Jr., and Bruce K. Waltke, *Theological Wordbook of the Old Testament*, cited in electronic form with Logos Libronix (Chicago: Moody Press, 1999), 288.

[150] Keil, *Commentary on the Old Testament*, 509.

[151] Carl Schultz, "*'wh*," ed. R. Laird Harris, Gleason L. Archer Jr., and Bruce K. Waltke, *Theological Wordbook of the Old Testament*, cited in electronic form with Logos Libronix (Chicago: Moody Press, 1999), 650–651.

[152] Smith, *Isaiah 40-66*, 450–451.

[153] Young, *The Book of Isaiah, vol. 3*, 348.

slash; cf. Isa. 1:6), carry the connotation of beatings. For sinners to have "well-being" or "healing" a mighty blow must be inflicted on this righteous Servant. The death was horrific, but Martin reminds us, "His death satisfied the wrath of God against sin and allows Him to 'overlook' the sins of the nation (and of others who believe) because they have been paid for by the Servant's substitutionary death."[154]

Fifth statement that He was dying for the sins of the nation (v. 6). Isaiah writes, "All of us like sheep have gone astray, each of us has turned to his own way, but the Lord has caused the iniquity of us all to fall on Him." Twice Isaiah uses the expression "all of us" (*kullanu*). The first time is to tell us that *all* have gone astray, and the second is to say that the sin of *all* were laid on the Servant. The entire nation is in view, just as it has been throughout the entire passage. These are the same people who failed recognize Him when He came to them (v. 1). These are the same people who despised Him and did not esteem Him (vv. 2-3). These are the same people for whose sins He was brutally killed when they rejected Him and handed Him over to be killed (vv. 4-5). These are the same people who *all* turned away and went their own way. Nevertheless, says Isaiah, the Lord has caused the iniquity of us all to fall on Him (cf. John 1:29; Heb. 2:9; 1 John 2:1-2; 4:10).[155] The point, notes Pfeiffer is that, "the remedy was to have just as universal application (us all) as the need (all we)."[156]

The supreme injustice against the Servant (vv. 7-9)

Verses 7-9 introduce the fourth stanza, one that emphasizes the supreme injustice that fell on the Servant. This man was completely innocent, so He deserved none of this mistreatment. Despite the injustice, though, He quietly submitted Himself to the plan of God and did not rise up in rebellion. In this section, Isaiah highlights six declarations about the injustice of Servant's death and how the Servant stayed completely faithful to God's plan that He suffer such injustice.

First and second declarations about the injustice: He was oppressed and afflicted (v. 7)

In the Old Testament, the Bible prophesied that the Servant would suffer

---

[154] Martin, "Isaiah," 1108.
[155] These words remind us of the way that the "scapegoat" took away the sins of the whole nation on the Day of Atonement (cf. Lev. 16:21).
[156] Pfeiffer, *The Wycliffe Bible Commentary: Old Testament*, Is 53:4. The immediate context has its focus on the nation of Israel, but as we have noted the Bible makes numerous and clear declarations that the Servant's death was for the entire human race.

unjust oppression. Just as the Bible prophesied, this is precisely what happened to Jesus Christ.

The promise of oppression. Both terms "oppressed" (*nagas*; cf. Exod. 3:7; Isa. 3:5, 12; 58:3) and "afflicted" (*'anah*) convey the idea that the Servant was being unjustly accused by the people who held power. The injustice suffered by the Servant was the worst, but in the midst of it all Jesus did not retaliate. It is not that He did not have the power to do so, for at the time of His arrest, Jesus told Peter, "Or do you think that I cannot appeal to My Father, and He will at once put at My disposal more than twelve legions of angels? How then will the Scriptures be fulfilled, *which say* that it must happen this way?" (Matt. 26:53-54). Jesus had the power to destroy those seeking His destruction, but He did not use that power. Instead, says Isaiah, "He did not open His mouth; like a lamb that is led to slaughter, and like a sheep that is silent before its shearers, so He did not open His mouth." It is a mystery that God would allow such a travesty of justice to fall upon the obedient Servant, but this was the only way for sin's debt to be satisfied.

The experience of oppression. It is interesting to see in the gospels just how this unjust condemnation worked itself out in the crucifixion of Jesus Christ. It is beyond the scope of this commentary to cover this in detail, but it is worth noting that from the time Christ was arrested until He was crucified, He went through a series of six sham trials, three of them by the Jewish leaders and three of them by the Roman leaders.[157] Despite the fact that none of these trials found any evidence of crime or sin, they still condemned Jesus to die on the cross. The operative principles to be noted are (1) the supreme injustice experienced by Jesus, and (2) His complete submission to the Father's will to go to the cross (Matt. 27:42; 1 Pet. 2:21-25). Just as Isaiah predicted seven-hundred years before the cross, Jesus Christ let the wicked leaders of the land take Him to slaughter without resistance.

---

[157] The first phase of Jewish trial was at house of Annas immediately after His arrest (John 18:13-24). The second phase of Jewish trial came when Annas sent Jesus off to Caiaphas the High Priest all bound up (Mark 14:53-65; cf. Matt. 26). The third phase of Jewish trial came when Jesus stood before the Sanhedrin early that morning at the break of day (Luke 22:66-71; cf. Matt. 27). The first phase of Roman trial came when Jesus was brought to Pontius Pilate at daybreak (Matt. 27:2; Mark 15:1; Luke 23:1; John 18:28ff.). The second phase of Roman trial came when Pilate sent Jesus to Herod Antipas (Luke 23:5-12). The third phase of Roman trial came when Herod sent Jesus back to Pilate, and Pilate eventually gave in to the Jewish leaders despite the fact that Pilate knew Jesus was fully innocent (Matt. 27:18ff.; Mark 15:6ff.; Luke 23:13ff.; John 19).

Third and fourth declarations of the injustice: He was taken away by a severe abuse of unchecked power (v. 8a)

Isaiah describes this abuse of unchecked power by saying, "by oppression and judgment He was taken away."[158] The idea here is similar to verse 7, but the term for "oppression" is different (*'otser*),[159] and we also have another term "judgment" (*mishpat*).[160] Martin explains: "He died not because of any sins of His own (for He was sinless; cf. 2 Cor. 5:21; Heb. 4:15; 1 John 3:5) but because of the transgressions (*pešaʻ*; cf. Isa. 53:5) of others."[161]

Fifth declaration of the injustice: He was given the death sentence deserved by the nation (v. 8b)

Throughout the whole book, Isaiah has demonstrated the severe guilt of the nation. Isaiah explains that even though the nation itself was the one that deserved to be condemned, no one realized that the Servant's life was being given as a substitute for the whole nation, i.e., "cut off out of the land of the living for the transgression of my people, to whom the stroke *was due*" (cf. John 11:47-53).[162] This one man, God's Servant, became the substitute for the nation,[163] despite the reality that His generation would not (could not) recognize this truth.[164] By God's sovereign grace, though, His death would become the basis for Israel to have forgiveness and restoration under a New Covenant (Isa. 42:6; 49:5-8; 55:3; 61:8; cf. Jer. 31:31-34). The blood has been shed for this New Covenant (Luke 22:20), and all that remains is for Israel to turn in repentance to embrace the Savior and ratify the covenant (cf. Zech. 13:8-9).

Sixth declaration of the injustice: Though completely innocent, He was treated like a common criminal (v. 9)

Verse 9 brings out more irony. The world treated Jesus as a wicked man who deserved death, but opposite is the truth. He was not evil, but righteous, a righteousness that God began to demonstrate from the moment of His death.

---

[158] That is, He was taken away because of these things. "His treatment was unjust from start to finish" (Oswalt, *The Book of Isaiah: Chapters 40-66*, 393).

[159] To press down (cf. e.g., Judg. 18:7).

[160] I.e., using the legal system un-righteously to bring a negative judgment (Grogan, "Isaiah," 303).

[161] Martin, "Isaiah," 1108.

[162] The term "cut off" (*gazar*), not the same one used in Daniel 9:26 (*karath*), conveys the idea of being cut off/separated from life.

[163] We are reminded about the annual Day of Atonement festival in which a sacrifice was made on behalf of the entire nation (Lev. 16-17; cf. Heb. 9:11-28).

[164] Young, *The Book of Isaiah, vol. 3*, 352.

He was treated as a wicked man. God's Servant was treated like a common criminal in that, "His grave was assigned with wicked men." We recall how Jesus was crucified in between two violent criminals who both deserved to die (Luke 23:33-43). Jesus, however, was completely innocent.

The truth is that He was innocent. Even though Jesus was treated like a common criminal, from the moment He died, God began to vindicate His Son. For this reason, says Isaiah, "He was with a rich man in His death, because He had done no violence, nor was there any deceit in His mouth" (cf. 1 Pet. 2:22, 24; 3:18). Jesus was a righteous man with no sin, and that is why God gave Him an honorable burial.[165] In the gospels we see how this played itself out when Nicodemus and Joseph (a rich man) came forward to give Jesus an honorable burial that even included a wrapping with spices, and a burial in Joseph's new tomb (cf. Matt. 27:57-60; Mark 15:42-46; Luke 23:50-53; John 19:38-40).

The supreme reward of the Servant (vv. 10-12)

Throughout the last three stanzas, the reader was inundated with a deluge of misery as Isaiah unfolded the sacrificial suffering that God would heap upon His obedient Servant. In this fifth stanza Isaiah reintroduces the theme of supreme exaltation with which he began in 52:13 by showing five glorious rewards that will come to the victorious Servant.[166]

First reward: Success in carrying out the will of God (v. 10a)

The Servant will succeed, but the victory will be very costly. Nevertheless, the Servant will be willing to take it all upon Himself.

Success will come by a crushing blow from God. When Isaiah tells us, "but the Lord was pleased to crush Him, putting *Him* to grief," this does not mean that God took emotional delight in the death of the Servant, but rather that this was the good and perfect plan of God for making atonement for sin.[167] The Servant's death was not a cosmic accident, but it was the good pleasure of the Lord to pay the price of sin by crushing (*daka'*, crush, pulverize; cf. 3:15; 19:10; 53:5) His obedient Servant.[168]

---

[165] The sinlessness of Jesus is affirmed in a number of passages (John 4:34; 5:19, 30; 6:38; 8:29, 46; 12:49; 14:10; Acts 3:14; 2 Cor. 5:21; Heb. 4:15; 7:26; 1 Pet. 3:18; 1 John 3:5).

[166] Wolf, *Interpreting Isaiah*, 218.

[167] See the noun form at the end of v. 10 (cf. 44:28). The determinative nature of this term is clearly seen in 46:10-11 where it stands parallel with God calling it His purpose that He will accomplish.

[168] Young, *The Book of Isaiah, vol. 3*, 354. Young explains that the Servant's death was the "accomplishing of the divine will."

Success will come by imputed sickness. Even though the NASB treats the next clause as a participle ("putting Him to grief"),[169] it may be grammatically preferable to recognize this finite verb as standing as an independent clause, i.e., "He made Him sick" (cf. ESV). All the sickness of sin that brought ruin to the nation (1:5) was now being heaped on the Servant so that He could take it all away (Acts 2:23; 4:27-28), and it was carried out by the perfect submission of the Servant. Jesus said, "No one has taken it [My life] away from Me, but I lay it down on My own initiative. I have authority to lay it down, and I have authority to take it up again. This commandment I received from My Father" (John 10:18; cf. vv. 11, 15, 17). God was in control of it all and He was using the evil hearts of sinners to fulfill His perfect plan (Rom. 8:28).

Second reward: A spiritual harvest by His perfect obedience (v. 10b)

Spiritually speaking the history of Israel was one of much failure (cf. Isa. 26:16-19). Even though the nation could not deliver spiritual children, the Servant will succeed in bringing forth a mighty harvest of spiritual children. Isaiah first states the condition that must be met, and then gives a three-fold description of what this spiritual reward will look like.

The condition (the protasis). Isaiah begins by stating a condition: "If He would render Himself as a guilt offering." A guilt offering is a sacrifice that makes atonement for sin/guilt, a sacrifice that includes the death of the sacrificial victim (*'asham*; cf. Lev. 5:15; 6:5; 19:21).[170]

The Servant's reward (the apodosis). Isaiah tells us three things that will happen if the Servant does this: (1) He will see His offspring (*zera'*); (2) He will prolong His days; and (3) the good pleasure of the Lord will prosper in His hand. By giving His own sinless life for the sins of His people, the Servant will conquer death and "prolong His days," i.e., this is the promise of an endless resurrection life (cf. Ps. 16:10). In endless resurrection life, He will see His spiritual children ("seed") and be firstborn of many brethren (Isa. 54; Rom. 8:29).

David also predicted that the Messiah would have His own "seed." These are the believers whom Messiah calls "My brethren" (Ps. 22:22), the ones who fear Lord (Ps. 22:23, 25), the seed of Israel (Ps. 22:23), the afflicted ones who

---

[169] Oswalt explains that this finite verb (a Hiphil stem of *chalah*, "to be sick"; cf. 1:5 where it is translated "sick" and 53:3-4 where it is translated "grief") that comes after the infinitive without a conjunction in between could possibly be treated as a hendiadys, i.e., "crush painfully," but this would be unusual (Oswalt, *The Book of Isaiah: Chapters 40-66*, 400, n. 50).

[170] Martin, "Isaiah," 1108–1109.

seek God (Ps. 22:26), the Gentiles who seek the Lord (Ps. 22:27-29; cf. Isa. 52:15), and the future "seed" will who believe in God's chosen King and be with Him in His kingdom (Ps. 22:30-31). David elsewhere describes the people of the Messiah by saying, "Your people will volunteer freely in the day of Your power; in holy array, from the womb of the dawn, Your youth are to You *as* the dew" (Ps. 110:3). Jesus talked about His own people when He said, "I will build My church" (Matt. 16:18). Jesus spoke about this seed when He said, "Father, I desire that they also, whom You have given Me, be with Me where I am, so that they may see My glory which You have given Me, for You loved Me before the foundation of the world" (John 17:24). These are the sheep for whom the Servant would lay down His life (John 10:11, 15, 17, 18). These are the sheep who hear His voice and follow Him (John 10:27; 12:26). This is the good pleasure of the Lord that prospered in the Servant's hand.

Third reward: The joy of a perfect victory over evil (v. 11a)

By giving His own life to accomplish the torturous work of redemption (i.e., "the anguish of soul"), the Servant knew that He would have the perfect satisfaction of destroying sin and evil. Hebrews alludes to this idea by telling us that Jesus endured the cross because He was looking ahead to the joy that was before Him (Heb. 12:2).[171] Yes, the Servant had times of terrible discouragement and sorrow, but He also knew that He would succeed, and this gave Him strength to persevere (cf. 49:4).[172]

Fourth reward: Perfect forgiveness by a perfect sacrifice (v. 11b)

The sacrificial death of the Servant is that which will bring a perfect forgiveness of all sin (i.e., justification) because He has born their iniquities (*'awon*; cf. 53:5). Several theological concepts call for further explanation.

Forgiveness comes by substitution. What Isaiah shows us here is that He, the innocent One, paid the price of sin, giving Him the ability to grant full justification to the ones who are guilty (i.e., the imputation of righteousness to those who are guilty). No one else can accomplish this great work (Rev. 5:3-5) but God's Servant (the *'Ebed*). The Righteous One (the *Tsadiyq*), and the Righteous One alone, has this divine knowledge,[173] i.e., this divine capacity, to

---

[171] Young suggests the possibility of a grammatical hendiadys that could be rendered "he shall see with abundant satisfaction" (Young, *The Book of Isaiah, vol. 3*, 356).

[172] Note: this is why good theology and doctrine are so absolutely crucial to our own sanctification as well.

[173] There is significant debate on whether "His knowledge" should be taken to mean

accomplish this work of justifying guilty sinners (*yatsdiyq*).[174] Smith gives helpful light on the meaning of this passage:

> It is because the "Righteous One" is just that he is able to cause the "many" (functioning as the object) to be right with God. The verb "will justify" has a forensic sense because the context of this chapter mentions bearing the guilt of others, punishment, and court proceedings (53:5, 8, 10).... Since the Servant bears the sins of the unjust and dies as a restitution offering to pay for the guilt of the sinner, the declaration of the "many" as just is possible because they now are without sin or guilt (it was carried away by the Servant). For some unknown reason the author chose not to use atonement or forgiveness terminology that is common in Leviticus, but the context of having "he" (*hû*), the Servant, bearing the sins and iniquities of the many argues not only for a substitutionary role of the Servant, but also the justness of those who now are no longer guilty of iniquity.[175]

The New Testament tells us how Christ accomplished this. For careful scholars, it is unmistakable that the Apostle Paul had this passage in mind when He described the sacrificial work of Jesus Christ in Romans 3:21-26. It is in the work of Christ on the cross that "the righteousness of God" is manifested for the whole world to see (3:21). It is a righteousness that is given to all men, Jew or Gentile, and it is one that comes on the basis of faith alone (3:22). It is a righteousness that all men need (3:23), and it is one that comes as a free gift when God justifies the believer because Christ bought their redemption by His death on the cross (3:24). This justification and righteousness for sinners is possible only because Christ's death accomplished propitiation (satisfaction of divine wrath), thus making it possible for God to freely forgive (3:25). This means that when God "justifies" (*dikaioo*) the guilty believer, He can do so and still

---

knowledge about Him (objective genitive) or knowledge that He possesses (subjective genitive), a knowledge reflected in v. 11a and worked out in His perfect obedience (cf. Isa. 11:2). The main point of the passage does not change in either choice, but the present author favors the idea that this is speaking about the knowledge possessed by the Servant.

[174] One must not overlook the two uses of the root *tsadaq* (to be righteous), the first is the adjectival use which speaks about the Servant being righteous, and the second is the verbal use which shows how He brings and grants righteousness to sinners who believe. The Hiphil stem used here conveys the idea of obtaining rights for another (Isa. 50:8; cf. 1 Sam. 15:24; Ps. 82:3) or treating one as innocent by justifying them (Exod. 23:7; cf. Rom. 8:33-34). Thus, we recognize the concept of "imputed righteousness" at work.

[175] Smith, *Isaiah 40-66*, 462.

uphold Himself as "just" (*dikaios*) and perfectly righteous (3:26). This is precisely what Isaiah predicted in 53:11.[176] Here is what Isaiah told us seven-hundred years before it happened: God's Servant would bring perfect forgiveness to His people by becoming the perfect sacrifice to satisfy the perfect holiness of a perfect God. This is the glorious salvation that Paul came to experience and preached from the day He came to believe.

Fifth reward: The exaltation to be heir of all creation (v. 12)

Isaiah's Servant message now comes to its close and, as noted by Hughes, "the Servant Song concluded with God's promise to exalt his Servant because he did the Father's will in dying as a guilt offering (53:10–12; cf. Phil. 2:9–11)."[177] Peter explained, "Therefore let all the house of Israel know for certain that God has made Him both Lord and Christ—this Jesus whom you crucified" (Acts 2:36).

Thus, the song began with the promise of supreme exaltation, and it ends on that same note. Here, however, God explicitly tells the Servant that this will make Him the heir of all creation (Col. 1:16; Heb. 1:2). Thus, says the Lord, because He has borne their iniquities (v. 11),

> Therefore, I will allot Him a portion with the great, and He will divide the booty with the strong, because He poured out Himself to death, and was numbered with the transgressors; yet He Himself bore the sin of many, and interceded for the transgressors.

Isaiah first tells us about the nature of the Servant's reward (v. 12a) and then explains the basis for it (v. 12b).

The nature of the Servant's reward (v. 12a). The "portion" (*chalaq*) God gives the Servant is that which has now become His earned inheritance which God has apportioned to His obedient Servant (cf. Josh. 13:7, et al. for such usage). This inheritance is further described using the military metaphor of dividing the booty (*shalal*) now that the enemy has been defeated (cf. Deut. 20:14; Josh. 11:14). The One who once came as the suffering Servant is now the Victorious Warrior King, and the time of His reward has finally arrived. Paul explains it by saying,

---

[176] Thus, explains Young, "The Servant bears the iniquities of the many that He may expiate them, and they in turn receive His righteousness (Young, *The Book of Isaiah, vol. 3*, 357-358).

[177] Hughes, *Tyndale Bible Commentary*, 267.

God highly exalted Him, and bestowed on Him the name which is above every name, so that at the name of Jesus every knee will bow, of those who are in heaven and on earth and under the earth, and that every tongue will confess that Jesus Christ is Lord, to the glory of God the Father (Phil. 2:9-11).

The basis of the Servant's reward (v. 12b). Why should all this reward and inheritance belong to this One? Summarizing the dominant theme of the whole chapter, Isaiah gives a four-fold answer why all this reward belongs to the Servant: (1) "He poured out Himself to death"; (2) He "was numbered with the transgressors"; (3) "He Himself bore the sin of many"; and (4) He interceded for the transgressors." In other words, by His own wisdom and righteousness, He alone brought God the victory by conquering sin. Therefore, He alone is the One who shall be the rightful Heir.

Summary and application

Jesus Christ accomplished the work of redemption that no one else was ever capable of accomplishing (Rom. 8:1-3). For those who have trusted in the victorious Suffering Servant, it should be a truth that breaks our heart over our own sin and stirs us to be sold out in loving, following, serving, and worshipping our beautiful Savior (Rom. 8:4).

ISRAEL'S FRUITFUL FUTURE (54:1-17)

In the closing verses of chapter 53, Isaiah told us about the "offspring" (*zera*') that the Servant would look upon in His resurrection (53:10). Chapter 54 tells us what this offspring will look like in Israel's restored kingdom. The land of Israel will be overcome with a massive population explosion of redeemed, elect saints, an explosion so great that it will eclipse all of the prosperity of former ages. For this reason, there is a great call for rejoicing. Hughes notes, "Israel was exhorted to 'break forth into loud and joyful song' (54:1) for her punishment was past. Now the nation could anticipate blessing and prosperity."[178]

Chapter 54 reads as follows: "1 Shout for joy, O barren one, you who have borne no *child;* break forth into joyful shouting and cry aloud, you who have not travailed, for the sons of the desolate one *will be* more numerous than the sons of the married woman, says the Lord. 2 Enlarge the place of your tent; stretch out the curtains of your dwellings; spare not; lengthen your cords, and strengthen your pegs. 3 For you will spread abroad to the right and to the left, and your descendants will possess nations and will resettle the desolate cities. 4 Fear not, for you will not be put to shame, and do not feel humiliated, for you

---

[178] Ibid.

will not be disgraced, but you will forget the shame of your youth, and the reproach of your widowhood you will remember no more. 5 For your husband is your Maker, whose name is the Lord of hosts, and your Redeemer is the Holy One of Israel, Who is called the God of all the earth. 6 For the Lord has called you, like a wife forsaken and grieved in spirit, even like a wife of *one's* youth when she is rejected, says your God. 7 For a brief moment I forsook you, but with great compassion I will gather you. 8 In an outburst of anger I hid My face from you for a moment, but with everlasting lovingkindness I will have compassion on you, says the Lord your Redeemer. 9 For this is like the days of Noah to Me, when I swore that the waters of Noah would not flood the earth again; so I have sworn that I will not be angry with you nor will I rebuke you. 10 For the mountains may be removed and the hills may shake, but My lovingkindness will not be removed from you, and My covenant of peace will not be shaken, says the Lord who has compassion on you. 11 O afflicted one, storm-tossed, *and* not comforted, behold, I will set your stones in antimony, and your foundations I will lay in sapphires. 12 Moreover, I will make your battlements of rubies, and your gates of crystal, and your entire wall of precious stones. 13 All your sons will be taught of the Lord, and the well-being of your sons will be great. 14 In righteousness you will be established; you will be far from oppression, for you will not fear, and from terror, for it will not come near you. 15 If anyone fiercely assails *you*, it will not be from Me. Whoever assails you will fall because of you. 16 Behold, I Myself have created the smith who blows the fire of coals and brings out a weapon for its work, and I have created the destroyer to ruin. 17 No weapon that is formed against you will prosper, and every tongue that accuses you in judgment you will condemn. This is the heritage of the servants of the Lord, and their vindication is from Me, declares the Lord" (54:1-17).

Some commentators, as noted by Grogan, have claimed that there is little relationship between chapters 53 and 54, but this is not true.[179] Indeed, we have left behind the suffering of the Servant, and so the tone lightens up greatly as Isaiah unfolds the blessings that come to the world as a result of the Servant's work.[180] Martin elaborates on this idea:

> These chapters speak of the great salvation which will come to Israel (chap. 54) and proselytes (55:1–56:8) on the basis of the work of the Servant, and of the condemnation which will come on the wicked (56:9–57:21). Ultimately the Servant will establish the millennial kingdom. Unlike Israel, He will not fail in His mission.[181]

---

[179] Grogan, "Isaiah," 308.
[180] Wolf, *Interpreting Isaiah*, 219; Oswalt, *The Book of Isaiah: Chapters 40-66*, 413-414.
[181] Martin, "Isaiah," 1109.

As noted by Martin, what we see here in chapter 54 (and following) is the way that God's redemptive promises to Israel (and to the whole world) get fulfilled in the millennial kingdom (and eternally in a new creation). Non-Premillennialists typically assert that these promises do not get fulfilled in national Israel, but in the church. This author cannot accept such conclusions that disregard the plain exegetical meaning of the text.[182] God's promise is that Zion (i.e., Jerusalem specifically, and all Israel by extension) will be restored in the messianic kingdom. Chapter 54 breaks down into two major units: (1) the promise of a fruitful Zion (vv. 1-10), and (2) the promise of a beautiful Zion (vv. 11-17).

The promise of a fruitful Zion (vv. 1-10)

Chapter 54 brings out the theme that the age of God's judgment and bad news is over, and the age of good news has arrived. Zion will be fruitful beyond anything she has ever seen, and the nation is going to explode in its redeemed population. Armed with this truth, Isaiah announces the joy of Israel's future population explosion (v. 1) as well as the implications of this future population explosion (vv. 2-10).

The joy of Israel's population explosion (v. 1)

With the attention on corporate Zion (as in 51:17-20)—the barren woman (*'aqarah*) who has not been able to bear children—God gives three commands to rejoice exceedingly.[183] In the ancient world, nothing was more heartbreaking and shameful for a woman than the inability to bear children. Spiritually speaking, Zion has been like a wife who was never able to bear children. Now, however, the command is to rejoice exceedingly, for "the sons of the desolate one *will be* more numerous than the sons of the married woman." Zion, who for long ages could not bear children in her youth,[184] is now going to bear a huge number of children.

---

[182] This is but one of many passages which speaks about the kingdom God is bringing (e.g., Isa. 2:1-4; 4:2-6; 9:1-7; 10:20-25; 11:1-16; 12:1-6; 26:1ff.; 27:12-13; 35; 42:10-11; 49:13; 61:10).

[183] The first command, "shout for joy" (*ranan*), speaks about the idea of a loud ringing cry (Isa. 12:6; 24:14; 35:6; 42:11; 44:23; 49:13; 54:1; 61:7; 65:14). The second command, "break forth into joyful shouting" (*patsach rinnah*), repeats the call for great rejoicing (Isa. 14:7; 44:23; 49:13; 54:1; 55:12). The third call, "cry aloud" (*tsahal*), continues to strengthen the command for joyful celebration (Isa. 10:30; 12:6; 24:14; 54:1). All the commands are in a second-person, feminine, singular form as being addressed to Zion.

[184] Paul cites this passage in Galatians 4:27 to make the point that contemporary Jerusalem was still spiritually dead.

Interestingly, we see many such examples among God's people in the Bible who experienced this same phenomenon (Sarah, Rebekah, Rachel, the mother of Sampson, Hannah, and Elizabeth the mother of John the Baptist). Through these women God has given us real-life illustrations of what is going to happen with His people Israel. What will this mean?

The implications of Israel's population explosion (vv. 2-10)

Life in Zion is going to change radically when Zion experiences this fruitful population explosion. Here in verses 2-10 Isaiah lays out three implications of this harvest of spiritual fruit.

First implication: The need for expansion (vv. 2-3). First, God commands to Zion to enlarge the tent and stretch out the curtains, lengthen the cords, and strengthen the pegs.[185] Mother Zion needs to get a much bigger home to accommodate her growing family (v. 2).

The reason, says God is, "you will spread abroad to the right and to the left [cf. Gen. 28:13], and your descendants will possess nations and will resettle the desolate cities" (v. 3; cf. Isa. 14:1; 43:5; 45:14; 49:23; 60:3; Amos 9:11-15; Obad. 15-21).[186] The land that had been stolen by the nations will revert back to Israel, and they will fill it with redeemed saints like never before (Isa. 49:19; Jer. 31:27-28, 38-40; 32:15, 37-44). Smith explains,

> There will be so many children that they will end up taking possession of property in other nations. Although this might suggest to some that there will be wars in which the Israelites will defeat and dispossess people living in other nations, there is no reference to war in this verse. Thus it is probably better to understand this passage to be describing the peaceful settlement of these additional believers in abandoned cities where no one lives.[187]

In 9:3, God repeats the same idea: "You shall multiply the nation; You shall increase their gladness; they will be glad in your presence as with the

---

[185] It was generally the wife who took care of the tent in the life of the nomadic, shepherd family (Gen. 24:67; 31:34) (Young, *The Book of Isaiah, vol. 3*, 362).
[186] This could be the idea of "dispossess" as in taking away from those who had stolen it from them in earlier ages, the same kind of usage we see in Deuteronomy 9:1; 11:23; 12:2; and 31:3 (Grogan, "Isaiah," 308). Thus, God will give Israel back all that was taken away so that she will have everything that God had promised her (Oswalt, *The Book of Isaiah: Chapters 40-66*, 417).
[187] Smith, *Isaiah 40-66*, 479.

gladness of harvest as men rejoice when they divide the spoil." In 26:15 we read, "You have increased the nation, O Lord; You have increased the nation; You are glorified; You have extended all the borders of the land." In 49:19-21 we read,

> For your waste and desolate places and your destroyed land—surely now you will be too cramped for the inhabitants, and those who swallowed you will be far away. The children of whom you were bereaved will yet say in your ears, The place is too cramped for me; make room for me that I may live *here*. Then you will say in your heart, Who has begotten these for me, since I have been bereaved of my children and am barren, an exile and a wanderer? And who has reared these? Behold, I was left alone. From where did these come?

Here is the promise: Israel is going to explode with a redeemed populace when Messiah restores her in the Millennial kingdom (cf. Zech. 8:4-8; 10:9-10).[188]

Second implication: The need to not fear the future (vv. 4-8). The promise certain. For Israel this means that she need not fear the future. Twice God tells Zion not to be afraid, for she will not be put to shame (*bowsh*), humiliated (*kalam*), or disgraced (*chaphar*) (v. 4a). Rather, all the shame of being childless in earlier days, which here is said to include widowhood, will be forgotten when her marital restoration results in great fruitfulness (v. 4b).[189] Young explains that Zion needs to rejoice, for her sins will, "be forgotten and the shame of that former time removed."[190]

Isaiah continues to encourage Israel with the assurance that their past failure to uphold the Mosaic Covenant does not mean that God has abandoned His promises made under the Abrahamic Covenant (Rom. 11:1-2, 29). The Lord

---

[188] Oswalt notes that we should not re-interpret this to refer to the church instead of Israel: "Particularly in the absence of any NT appropriation of the passage in that way (that this refers to the church), such a view does not seem to be warranted" (Oswalt, *The Book of Isaiah: Chapters 40-66*, 418, n. 30).

[189] Both expressions "youth" and "widowhood" are best understood as referring to the lack of spiritual fruitfulness that resulted in the exile, and not that youth refers to Egypt as held by some (Wolf, *Interpreting Isaiah*, 220).

[190] Young, *The Book of Isaiah, vol. 3*, 364.

of Hosts,[191] the Redeemer of Israel,[192] the One who made them into a people,[193] the God of all the earth,[194] is still their God (v. 5).[195] Yes, Israel's unfaithfulness has caused her to become like a rejected wife (v. 6; cf. 50:1); nevertheless, the punishment will run its course in due time,[196] and God will call her back to Himself with great compassion (*rachamiym*) and lovingkindness (*chesed*) (vv. 7-8; cf. Isa. 10:25; 14:1; 26:20; 40:1; 49:10, 13; 51:3; Deut. 30:7; Jer. 30:7, 11; Dan. 12:7; Hos. 2:14-23; 3:1-5; 5:14-6:1).[197] God is "both able and willing to restore them to Himself."[198]

Third implication: The need for hope (vv. 9-10). Not only does Israel need to plan for expansion (vv. 2-3) and not fear the future (vv. 4-8), but she also needs to believe that God will fulfill these promises. To give Israel hope, God compares His restoration promises to the promises He made after the flood (Gen. 9:8-17). God will fulfill His promises (v. 9).[199]

To reinforce the certainty even more, God says, "for the mountains may be removed and the hills may shake, but My lovingkindness (*chesed*) will not be removed from you,[200] and My covenant [*beriyth*] of peace will not be shaken, says the Lord who has compassion on you" (v. 10).[201]

---

[191] Cf. comments at 44:6.

[192] Israel's *Go'el* (cf. 43:1, 14; 44:6, 22-24; 47:4; 48:17, 20; 49:7, 26; 52:9; 54:5, 8; 59:20; 60:16; 63:9).

[193] Cf. 5:1-4; 17:7; 27:11; 29:16; 37:16; 41:4, 20; 42:16; 43:7, 19; 44:2, 24; 45:7, 9, 12, 18; 51:13; 57:16; 62:4-5; 66:2, 22.

[194] Cf. 6:3; 11:9; 65:16.

[195] Both expressions "husband" and "maker" are plural, a grammatical phenomenon which most explain as "an honorific of excellence" (Oswalt, *The Book of Isaiah: Chapters 40-66*, 412, n. 8).

[196] The expression "outburst" of anger renders the term "flood [of anger]," an expression that is only found here (Young, *The Book of Isaiah, vol. 3*, 366, n. 9; cf. 5:25; 9:12, 17, 21; 10:4, 25; 12:1).

[197] Israel has been in this state of apostasy for over 2,600 years, but God calls it a "brief moment" from His eternal perspective. Yahweh the faithful husband will restore His formerly unfaithful wife (Jer. 3:14; 31:32; Hos. 2:16).

[198] Grogan, "Isaiah," 309.

[199] Young, *The Book of Isaiah, vol. 3*, 367. This author finds it curious how Amillennial theologians like Young can recognize the clear force of the text and yet still hold an eschatology that denies the nation its future restoration.

[200] These are the things we typically see as immovable and certain (Gen. 49:26; Deut. 33:15; Hab. 3:6; Ps. 90:2).

[201] See (New) "covenant" promises using this term *beriyth* in Isa. 42:6; 49:8; 55:3; 56:4,

The promise of a beautiful Zion (vv. 11-17)

Restored Zion will not only be fruitful (vv. 1-10), but she will also be very beautiful as described by the numerous beautiful stones that will adorn her. God gives seven descriptions of what this beauty will look like.

First through fifth descriptions: The beauty of the city (vv. 11-12)

God promises His sin-ravaged city (cf. 51:21) that He will set her stones in antimony (*puk*, a black, turquoise or red pigment from liches, used as eye shadow at times) and her foundations in sapphires (*sappiyr*, lapis-lazuli) (v. 11).[202] We see three more descriptions: "Moreover, I will make your battlements (pointed wall extensions) of rubies, and your gates of crystal, and your entire wall of precious stones" (v. 12).[203] Pfeiffer notes, "The Lord describes the purity and glory of the converted Israel of the future. . . . The full glory of this new city of God will be that of New Jerusalem described in Rev 21."[204]

Sixth description: The beauty of the citizens (v. 13)

We move from the physical city to its people. All will be "taught of the Lord" (Isa. 2:3; 11:9) and their well-being will be great.[205] The nation that

---

6; 59:21; 61:8 (cf. Jer. 31:31-34; 32:40; 33:20; 50:5; Ezek. 20:37; 34:25; 37:26; Hos. 2:18). One certainly should not restrict "New Covenant" promises to the only place where the exact expression is used (Jer. 31:31). All of the eschatological restoration promises that God made to national Israel are what comprise the New Covenant. Thus, the "covenant of peace" refers to God's New Covenant with Israel that assures her of peace. The expression itself occurs in Num. 25:12 and Mal. 2:5 with reference to God's covenant with the Levitical priests (Oswalt, *The Book of Isaiah: Chapters 40-66*, 423, n. 42).

[202] Antimony may be continuing the marriage analogy since this powder was used as adornment as an eye shadow of a bride (2 Kings 9:30; Jer. 4:30; cf. 1 Chron. 29:2 where it is apparently a setting for stones). Grogan notes that both are possibilities but thinks that the stone setting idea is more likely (Grogan, "Isaiah," 310, n. 11-12). Sapphires were beautiful blue stones (Exod. 24:10; 28:18; 39:11; Job 28:6, 16; Song 5:14; Lam. 4:7; Ezek. 1:26; 10:1; 28:13). The idea is clearly of great beauty. All of this millennial beauty will be superseded by the perfect beauty of the New Jerusalem in the New Heavens and New Earth (cf. Rev. 21:18-21).

[203] Rubies (*kadkod*) are glowing red stones. Crystal (*'eqdah*) may be a reference to beryl or flint. The reference to other precious (*chephets*) stones serves to tell us that the beauty will include other precious stones as well.

[204] Pfeiffer, *The Wycliffe Bible Commentary: Old Testament*, Is 54:11.

[205] The NT applies this passage twice (John 6:45; 1 Thess. 4:9).

formerly been blind (Isa. 6:9-10; 29:9-10; 30:9) and uncircumcised in heart (Deut. 10:16; Jer. 4:4; 9:25-26) will now be filled with nothing but regenerate saints (Isa. 11:9 35:8-10; cf. Deut. 30:6; Jer. 31:34).

Seventh description: The beauty of the peace (vv. 14-17)

Because of its restored relationship, Israel will have the blessings of prosperity and wholeness (peace and the blessings that flow from it).

The promise of peace (v. 14). Therefore, "In righteousness you will be established; you will be far from oppression, for you will not fear, and from terror, for it will not come near you" (v. 14). God's promise is never-ending peace (Isa. 9:6-7; 11:1ff.; cf. Deut. 30:8-10). Never has this promised been fulfilled, but it will happen in the kingdom. Smith explains,

> It is only God who can bring salvation and righteousness to Zion (46:13). In many ways God's righteousness and his salvation are overlapping concepts (51:6b, 13). When righteousness reigns in Zion, the world of oppression, tyranny, fear, destruction, and terror will be a thing of the past. This will be a new world without war and evil (cf. 2:4). This promises a level of security never known before, for God will be in this transformed city of Zion and his righteousness and peace will impact every area of life.[206]

Just as promised earlier, the one who trusts will never be put to shame (cf. 8:16).

The reassurance of peace (vv. 15-17). God made the promise of peace, and now He gives the reassurance. He will never again be the One to bring wrath against His people, and if anyone should attempt it,[207] they will fail (v. 15).[208] How can Israel be sure? Yahweh is the sovereign God, and He can do anything. To illustrate, God says, "Behold, I Myself have created the smith who blows the fire of coals and brings out a weapon for its work, and I have created the destroyer to ruin" (v. 16). In other words, explains Smith, "His sovereign ability to create or not create enables him to have full control of the future."[209]

---

[206] Smith, *Isaiah 40-66*, 490.

[207] The expression "fiercely assails" combines the infinitive absolute and imperfect forms of the verb *gur* (attack) to stress the idea that Israel will never again experience catastrophic attacks like she had in past ages.

[208] Furthermore, these promises also serve to assure Israel that never again will there be things like invasions, exiles, or the threat of destruction from enemy powers. One final attempt at the end of the Millennium will fail (Rev. 20:7-10).

[209] Ibid., 491.

With this, God makes one final promise to assure Israel that her future is secure: "No weapon that is formed against you will prosper, and every tongue that accuses you in judgment you will condemn. This is the heritage of the servants of the Lord, and their vindication is from Me" (v. 17; cf. 17:12-14). Israel will have never-ending peace and never needs to fear.[210]

Zacharias, the father of John the Baptist, understood that the establishing of the messianic kingdom would bring salvation from all enemies (Luke 1:68-75), but what he did not understand at that point is that God's eternal plan would first require the rejection and death of God's messiah (Luke 19:41-44; Acts 2:23; 4:27-28). God used the rejection of the Messiah to bring us forgiveness (Isa. 53), but when He returns, He will usher in the final salvation of God's people into the messianic kingdom (cf. Heb. 1:14; 2:3, 5; 4:9; 9:28; 10:25; 12:28).

Summary and application

Where does all this promise leave us? Certainly, it should be an encouragement to the people of Israel to put their faith in God's Servant, the Lord Jesus Christ, for none of these promises belong to those who refuse Him. For Christians, we are reminded of the absolute faithfulness of God. If God has promised it, we can know His promise is certain.

THE INVITATION TO SHARE IN GRACE (55:1-13)

Chapter 55 provides another invitation to share in God's redeeming grace.[211] The promises in this chapter are overflowing with grace. Kidner notes that, "this call to the needy is unsurpassed for warmth of welcome."[212] Many see 55 as part of a larger unit extending from 49-57, but Smith suggests that the grammar indicates a certain shift of focus:

> This chapter completes the long section of chaps. 40–55, as well as the shorter section of 53:12–55:13. Following a pattern somewhat similar to the promises and the imperative invitations to a feminine singular audience Zion in chap. 54, this chapter has additional divine promises and imperative exhortations to a masculine plural audience (to "everyone" in 55:1, which goes beyond "the servants of the Lord" in 54:17) to encourage them to respond to God's invitation to enjoy his abundant blessings. The

---

[210] Note that from this point on, the term servant is plural when referring to restored Israel (54:17; 56:6; 63:17; 65:8, 9, 13, 14, 15; 66:14).
[211] Wolf, *Interpreting Isaiah*, 221.
[212] Kidner, "Isaiah," 664.

connections between chaps. 54 and 55 are evident in the common reference to (a) joy and singing at the beginning (54:1) and at the end of these two chapters (55:12–13), (b) the coming of peace in 54:10, 13; 55:12, (c) God's compassion on his people (54:7–8, 10; 55:7), (d) God's love (54:10; 55:3), (e) God's covenant (54:10; 55:3), and (f) a new relationship with the nations (54:3; 55:4–5).[213]

Chapter 55 reads as follows: "1 Ho! Everyone who thirsts, come to the waters; and you who have no money come, buy and eat. Come, buy wine and milk without money and without cost. 2 Why do you spend money for what is not bread, and your wages for what does not satisfy? Listen carefully to Me, and eat what is good, and delight yourself in abundance. 3 Incline your ear and come to Me. Listen, that you may live, and I will make an everlasting covenant with you, *according to* the faithful mercies shown to David. 4 Behold, I have made him a witness to the peoples, a leader and commander for the peoples. 5 Behold, you will call a nation you do not know, and a nation which knows you not will run to you, because of the Lord your God, even the Holy One of Israel, for He has glorified you. 6 Seek the Lord while He may be found; call upon Him while He is near. 7 Let the wicked forsake his way and the unrighteous man his thoughts, and let him return to the Lord, and He will have compassion on him, and to our God, for He will abundantly pardon. 8 For My thoughts are not your thoughts, nor are your ways My ways, declares the Lord. 9 For *as* the heavens are higher than the earth, so are My ways higher than your ways and My thoughts than your thoughts. 10 For as the rain and the snow come down from heaven, and do not return there without watering the earth and making it bear and sprout, and furnishing seed to the sower and bread to the eater, 11 so will My word be which goes forth from My mouth; it will not return to Me empty without accomplishing what I desire, and without succeeding *in the matter* for which I sent it. 12 For you will go out with joy and be led forth with peace. The mountains and the hills will break forth into shouts of joy before you, and all the trees of the field will clap *their* hands. 13 Instead of the thorn bush the cypress will come up, and instead of the nettle the myrtle will come up, and it will be a memorial to the Lord for an everlasting sign which will not be cut off" (55:1-13).

In the Bible, God extends many invitations for men to turn from sin and seek His favor. In Ezekiel 18:32 God says, "For I have no pleasure in the death of anyone who dies, declares the Lord God. Therefore, repent and live." In Matthew 11:28 Jesus said, "Come to Me, all who are weary and heavy-laden, and I will give you rest." Salvation is a work of divine grace and it is freely given,

---

[213] Smith, *Isaiah 40-66*, 493.

but no one can share in that saving grace unless they are willing to believe. Isaiah extends three calls for His people to turn to Him.

First call: The call to eat what is good (vv. 1-2)

God invites His people to come buy (without cost) four different kinds of commodities. The invitation opens with the exclamation "Ho,"[214] signaling that this message of good news is one of great importance.

First invitation: Invitation to come to the waters (v. 1a)

The first invitation reminds us how God has already promised an outpouring of redeeming grace as symbolized by an outpouring of waters (cf. Isa. 32:15; 41:17; 43:18; 44:3-5).[215] Thus, this invitation to come to the waters is not about mere physical water, but saving grace. If someone feels the thirst of needing grace, the invitation is there (cf. John 4:10-14; 7:37-38).

Second and third invitations: Invitations to buy wine, milk (vv. 1b-2)

The next invitations are to buy (*shabar*) wine and milk, and the wonderful news is that there is no cost, so there is no reason to not come (v 1b). Isaiah continues by explaining that it makes no sense why anyone would turn down such a wonderful offer while pursuing other things that can never satisfy (v. 2). The last part of verse 2 magnifies the richness of this wonderful offer (Isa. 25:6; cf. Joel 3:18).[216] The term for "abundance" is the Hebrew term *deshen* which literally is the idea of "fatness" (Isa. 30:23; cf. Judg. 9:9; Jer. 31:14; Pss. 36:9; 63:6; 65:12),[217] and the command "delight yourself" (Hithpael of *'anag*) renders a term that can even convey the sense of pampering oneself with pleasure (Deut. 28:56; cf. Isa. 57:4; 58:14), even like that of a soft breast to nurse on (Isa. 66:11).[218] Martin explains,

---

[214] Elsewhere this interjection carried the force of "woe" or "alas" (Isa. 1:4, 24; 5:8, 11, 18, 20-22; 10:1; 17:12; 28:1; 29:1, 15; 31:1; 33:1; 45:9), but this positive context calls for a positive rendering.

[215] Isaiah is the only one who uses the adjective "thirsty" as a substantive (Oswalt, *The Book of Isaiah: Chapters 40-66*, 432, n. 1; cf. 21:14; 29:8; 32:6; 44:3). The metaphor of thirst and quenching waters is especially relevant for those living in the arid land of Israel

[216] Wolf, *Interpreting Isaiah*, 221.

[217] Ludwig Koehler et al., *The Hebrew and Aramaic Lexicon of the Old Testament*, cited in electronic form with Logos Libronix, 234.

[218] R. Laird Harris, Gleason L. Archer Jr., and Bruce K. Waltke, eds., *Theological*

The Lord asked the people how they could be interested in other things besides Himself as He is the only One who can bring genuine satisfaction. Throughout all history people have tried to find satisfaction through many things other than God.[219]

The lesson is simple, but sadly we are often so slow to learn it. There is nothing that is going to satisfy us except what the Lord Himself gives.

Second call: The call to understand God's promises (vv. 3-5)

God wants His people to understand the certainty of His promises. His promise to Israel is that of "an everlasting covenant" (*beriyth 'olam*),[220] one that is just as certain as the covenant He swore to King David since it is based upon the "faithful mercies" (*chesed*) of God's own character (v. 3; cf. 2 Sam. 7:12-16; Isa. 9:6-7; 11:1ff.; 16:5; 32:1-5; 33:17-22; 39:7).[221] The covenant made to David will see its ultimate realization when Jesus Christ returns and establishes the kingdom (v. 4; cf. Pss. 22:27-31; 89:1-4, 19-29; 110). The covenant to David is certain, and so is the promise God has extended to the whole nation.

Verse 5 may be seen as spoken to the whole nation with the promise that redeemed Gentile nations will turn to them as they seek grace through their Davidic King (Isa. 2:2-4; 45:14).[222] On the other hand, this could be speaking directly to Christ who will call His people to Himself since the Lord has glorified

---

Wordbook of the Old Testament, cited in electronic form with Logos Libronix (Chicago: Moody Press, 1999), 679.

[219] Martin, "Isaiah," 1110.

[220] This is nothing less than the promise of the New Covenant (Jer. 31:31-34; 32:40; 50:5; cf. Isa. 61:8; Ezek. 16:60; 20:37; 34:25; 37:26; Hos. 2:18). This will be a covenant that will never be broken, unlike the Mosaic Covenant, since God's redeeming grace in Christ is what stands behind it.

[221] Grogan explains the significance of David's witness to God's saving grace: "During the reign of David, Israel's kingdom reached its greatest extent. David, as a faithful worshipper of the Lord was therefore a witness to God's truth to all the peoples in his empire, as well as being their leader [Ps. 18:43]. He therefore anticipated in himself the prophetic and kingly functions of the Messiah. In God's future for his people, as here depicted, the empire would be wider still [cf. Acts 3:15; Rev. 1:5]" (Grogan, "Isaiah," 312).

[222] Some passages speak about the nation receiving glory (46:13; 60:7, 19; 62:3). Other passages emphasize the idea of God getting glorified by the work of the Servant (45:21-23; 49:3; 61:3). Still other passages speak about the Servant getting glorified (1:4; 4:2; 41:14; 52:13; 53:10-12; John 17:1, 4-5; Acts 2:36; 3:1-3; Phil. 2:5-11). All are true.

Him. We saw this idea in the second Servant Song:

> Thus says the Lord, the Redeemer of Israel *and* its Holy One, to the despised One, to the One abhorred by the nation, to the Servant of rulers, Kings will see and arise; princes will also bow down, because of the Lord who is faithful, the Holy One of Israel who has chosen You (Isa. 49:7).

This author favors the messianic understanding of verse 5. In either case, explains Pfeiffer, "Verse 5 is a prediction that Gentiles will be converted and will join themselves to redeemed Israel."[223]

Third call: The call to repentance (vv. 6-13)

God has made the promise, and all the people need to do is respond. Here in verses 6-13 Isaiah gives the exhortation to seek restoration (vv. 6-7), and then he follows this is with an assurance about the certainty (vv. 8-13).

The exhortation to seek God (vv. 6-7)

The offer of grace only becomes effective when a man turns to the Lord. Kidner explains, "If man is hungry and needs satisfying (1–5), he is also *wicked* and needs salvation. God's calling and seeking (1–5) must be matched by [a response]."[224] Isaiah gives five exhortations to seek God.

Two exhortations to seek God (v. 6). The first two exhortations come when he says, "*Seek* the Lord while He may be found; *call* upon Him while He is near." The time to seek the Lord is now (Isa. 45:19, 22; 49:7; 58:9; 65:24; cf. Deut. 4:29; Pss. 14:2; 77:2; 78:34; Jer. 29:13; Lam. 3:25; Hos. 10:12; Amos 5:4-6). Paul put it this way, "Behold, now is the acceptable time; behold, now is the day of salvation" (2 Cor. 6:2).

Three more exhortations to seek God (v. 7). The next three exhortations get more specific about the need for repentance.[225] If Israel wants divine favor, she must turn from her evil ways (cf. Deut. 30:1-2, 8-10). A century later, Jeremiah gave the same exhortations and promises.

---

[223] Pfeiffer, *The Wycliffe Bible Commentary: Old Testament*, Is 55:1. The salvation of elect Gentiles is a major theme in Isaiah (2:3; 19:23-25; 42:6, 6; 49:6; 66:18, 21) (Oswalt, *The Book of Isaiah: Chapters 40-66*, 440).

[224] Kidner, "Isaiah," 664.

[225] True faith that saves is a faith that includes repentance from sin (Acts 2:38; 3:19; 20:21; 26:20; Rom. 1:5; 15:18-19; 16:25-27).

You will seek Me and find *Me* when you search for Me with all your heart. I will be found by you, declares the Lord, and I will restore your fortunes and will gather you from all the nations and from all the places where I have driven you, declares the Lord, and I will bring you back to the place from where I sent you into exile (Jer. 29:13-14).

If a man will turn to the Lord, He will restore him, and "have compassion [*racham*] on him" and "abundantly pardon [*salach*]" (cf. Prov. 28:13).[226] But can a people who have fallen so badly ever have any hope that God would restore them? The answer is a resounding "Yes!" as seen in verses 8-13.

The assurance of God's promises (vv. 8-13)

If God says He is going to do something, He will do it, for "God's prophetic 'word' will most certainly be fulfilled, for it rests on the character of his own person (55:11; 40:8)."[227] Here in verses 8-13 Isaiah makes eleven declarations to assure Israel of the certainty of these promises.

First and second assurances (v. 8). First, God says that He can forgive and restore Israel because His thoughts are not our thoughts, and His ways are not our ways. In other words, fallen Israel (and others) may think they are beyond any hope of restoration, but that is not the way God sees it.

Third and fourth assurances (v. 9). God builds on verse 8 by telling them, "For *as* the heavens are higher than the earth, so are My ways higher than your ways and My thoughts than your thoughts." These words are meant to assure all doubters that if God says He is going to restore Israel, we can be absolutely sure that He will do it.[228]

Fifth assurance (vv. 10-11). Isaiah uses an analogy from nature to illustrate. Just as rain and snow go out from heaven to earth with the certainty that they will bring forth a fruitful result (v. 10), so too God's Word goes out from heaven with the absolute certainty that it will bear fruit and accomplish what God wills to accomplish (v. 11; cf. 46:11; 53:10; Jer. 29:11). Thus, explains Smith, "When God swears something, it will certainly happen."[229]

Sixth through ninth assurances (v. 12). Isaiah once again uses the word

---

[226] The former term speaks about the tenderness God will extend to not treat the sinner as he deserves, and the latter term speaks about the way that God will take away and remove all sins to give full forgiveness.
[227] Hughes, *Tyndale Concise Bible Commentary*, 267.
[228] Young, *The Book of Isaiah, vol. 3*, 382-383.
[229] Smith, *Isaiah 40-66*, 511.

"for" (*kiy*) to reemphasize the certainty of the restoration promises.[230] This time he says, "For you will go out with joy and be led forth with peace; the mountains and the hills will break forth into shouts of joy before you, and all the trees of the field will clap *their* hands" (cf. 35:10; 44:23; 52:8-9). When restoration comes, "the effects of sin will be reversed in the Millennium, including the provision of inner joy and peace (see comments on 54:10) and changes in the physical creation."[231]

Tenth and eleventh assurances (v. 13). The assurance of restoration continues: "Instead of the thorn bush the cypress will come up, and instead of the nettle the myrtle will come up." The impact of sin will be purged and the earth will bear good fruit instead of things like cursed thorns (cf. Isa. 5:6; 7:19, 24, 25; 32:13; Gen. 3:17-19).[232] All creation—both animate and inanimate—will become the objects of God's restoring grace, and when it happens Isaiah says, "it will be a *memorial* to the Lord [cf. 63:12, 14], for an everlasting *sign* [cf. Isa. 6:5; 7:11, 14; 8:18; 19:20; 20:3; 37:30; 38:7, 22; 44:25; 54:13; 56:5; 66:19] which will not be cut off."

Summary and application

What we are seeing here is a brief glimpse at the glory that is about to be revealed when Jesus Christ returns (cf. Rom. 8:18ff.). When God's redemption promises are ultimately fulfilled in a new creation, every trace of sin and curse and death will be purged for all time (cf. Rev. 21-22). It is sometimes hard to think that these things could really be true because the promises are so wonderful, but because God says that they are true, He will do it. In this, we find hope.

THE BLESSINGS OF TRUE RIGHTEOUSNESS (56:1-12)

Chapter 56 gives a call for persevering and faithful service in view of God's promises. The offer of saving grace has been given numerous times throughout this book, and it is clear that all men need to do to find God's favor is to turn to Him in genuine faith. Chapter 56 enlarges the promise by making it clear that it does not matter what kind of background one has. If a man will turn to the Lord, he will find the blessings of true righteousness.

Chapter 56 reads as follows: "1 Thus says the Lord, preserve justice and do righteousness, for My salvation is about to come and My righteousness to be revealed. 2 How blessed is the man who does this, and the son of man who

---

[230] Oswalt sees this as an assertive *kiy*, i.e., "indeed" or "surely," with vv. 12-13 serving as a conclusion to vv. 6-13 (Oswalt, *The Book of Isaiah: Chapters 40-66*, 447).
[231] Martin, "Isaiah," 1111.
[232] Grogan, "Isaiah," 313, n. 13.

takes hold of it, who keeps from profaning the sabbath, and keeps his hand from doing any evil. 3 Let not the foreigner who has joined himself to the Lord say, The Lord will surely separate me from His people, nor let the eunuch say, Behold, I am a dry tree. 4 For thus says the Lord, To the eunuchs who keep My sabbaths, and choose what pleases Me, and hold fast My covenant, 5 to them I will give in My house and within My walls a memorial, and a name better than that of sons and daughters; I will give them an everlasting name which will not be cut off. 6 Also the foreigners who join themselves to the Lord to minister to Him, and to love the name of the Lord, to be His servants, everyone who keeps from profaning the sabbath and holds fast My covenant, 7 even those I will bring to My holy mountain and make them joyful in My house of prayer. Their burnt offerings and their sacrifices will be acceptable on My altar, for My house will be called a house of prayer for all the peoples. 8 The Lord God, Who gathers the dispersed of Israel, declares, Yet *others* I will gather to them, to those *already* gathered. 9 All you beasts of the field, all you beasts in the forest, Come to eat. 10 His watchmen are blind; all of them know nothing; all of them are mute dogs unable to bark, dreamers lying down, who love to slumber, 11 and the dogs are greedy; they are not satisfied, and they are shepherds who have no understanding. They have all turned to their own way, each one to his unjust gain, to the last one. 12 Come, *they say,* let us get wine, and let us drink heavily of strong drink; and tomorrow will be like today, only more so" (56:1-12).

Chapter 56 reminds us about the free blessings God offers to sinners. In some ways it is hard to imagine what more could be said, but there still is more to say. Here in chapter 56, we find four main ideas that build upon the promises of chapter 55: the condition for God's blessings (vv. 1-2), the universality of God's blessings (vv. 3-5), the opportunity for God's blessings (vv. 6-8), and Israel's blindness to God's blessings (vv. 9-12).

The condition for God's blessings (vv. 1-2)

There are conditions for God's blessing. That is, the only way to experience God's blessing is by genuine faith. We will call this persevering faith. Isaiah first gives a call to persevering faith, and then he tells what kinds of promises flow from it.

The call to persevering faith (v. 1)

God expresses the call to persevering faith with the concrete commands, "preserve justice and do righteousness."[233] True faith must show itself in a

---

[233] These commands are tantamount to the principle of keeping the commands and

genuine turning from sin toward God. Micah expressed this same principle when he wrote, "He has told you, O man, what is good; and what does the Lord require of you but to do justice, to love kindness, and to walk humbly with your God?" (Mic. 6:8). In other words, explains Smith, Isaiah is encouraging behavior, "that is characteristic of the acts of God and the Messiah (5:16; 9:7; 11:4; 16:5; 32:1, 16-17; 33:5), so it is not surprising to hear that Isaiah earlier admonished his readers to 'learn to do right and seek justice' (1:17)."[234] Without obedient faith, we cannot be in a position to receive blessing (Isa. 51:4-5; Matt. 3:2; 4:17; 7:21-23; Rom. 1:5; 15:18-19; 16:25-27; 1 Pet. 1:14-17; Rev. 16:15). God tells Israel to respond now, for His salvation is about to come and His righteousness be revealed (cf. 41:10; 59:16). Israel needs to respond now in true faith.

The promise for persevering faith (v. 2)

With words that echo Psalm 1, Isaiah declares, "How blessed is the man who does this, and the son of man who takes hold of it, who keeps from profaning the sabbath,[235] and keeps his hand from doing any evil" (cf. Isa. 30:18; 32:20; Ps. 119:1; Prov. 8:32, 34). The idea of blessing (*'ashrey*) conveys the connation of enviable favor. TWOT explains that this word *'ashrey* is a term that, "is reserved for man," a word that connotes the sense of "happiness," "bliss," or "envious desire."[236] In other words, those who believe the Lord and submit to His Word will find supreme blessings. This promise is not restricted to those who come only from the family of Israel.

The universality of God's blessings (vv. 3-5)

The invitation given in 55:1 was open-ended and universal, and this universality gets emphasized again, even to those who would have been considered social outcasts in ancient Israel (e.g., foreigners and eunuchs). The invitation to saving grace is there for anyone who is willing to accept it.

The foreigner (v. 3a)

Isaiah gives an illustration of how God's promises come to anyone who

---

principles of the Torah (cf. Isa. 1:27; 5:7, 16; 28:17; 32:16; 58:2; 59:14) (Young, *The Book of Isaiah*, vol. 3, 388).

[234] Smith, *Isaiah 40-66*, 528.

[235] According to Exodus 31:12-17, the Sabbath was the sign of the Sinaitic Covenant. Refusal to keep the Sabbath was tantamount to Israel saying it did not recognize Yahweh as Lord of Israel.

[236] Victor P. Hamilton, "*'ashr*," ed. R. Laird Harris, Gleason L. Archer Jr., and Bruce K. Waltke, *Theological Wordbook of the Old Testament*, cited in electronic form with Logos Libronix (Chicago: Moody Press, 1999), 80–81.

responds in faith. The "foreigner" (literally, "son of a foreigner," *ben hanekar*; cf. 60:10; 61:5; 62:8), is the true believer who has come from outside of Israel to attach himself to Yahweh and His people.[237] This is the person who wants to be part of God's community.[238] God's promise is that if they come in faith, they will be accepted.

The eunuch (vv. 3b-5)

The second kind of social outcast who is welcome in the kingdom is the one called "the eunuch" (*sariys*), i.e., a male who has been forcibly emasculated for service to a king in overseeing his harem.[239]

The encouragement to the eunuch (v. 3b). According to Deuteronomy 23:1-8, under the Mosaic Law such men were forbidden from entering the assembly of Yahweh, but Isaiah makes it clear that "a new era was dawning" and this particular restriction would no longer apply under the New Covenant.[240] Physically this eunuch may be a "dry tree," but he must not see himself as unfruitful or incapable of having a lasting place in God's community.[241]

The promise to the eunuch (vv. 4-5). To the eunuch who comes in faith (v. 4), God promises that not only will they not be cast out of the assembly, but God also gives them these amazing promises: "To them I will give in My house and within My walls a memorial, and a name better than that of sons and daughters; I will give them an everlasting name which will not be cut off" (v. 5).[242] All they have to do is come in faith, just like the Ethiopian eunuch who put his trust in Jesus (Acts 8:27-39).

The opportunity of God's blessings (vv. 6-8)

---

[237] This would not include the idea of unbelieving Gentiles and pagan foreigners (cf. Isa. 57:3-13; Zech. 14:21). Unbelieving Gentiles would be akin to the people we see in Ezekiel 44:7 ("foreigners, uncircumcised in heart and uncircumcised in flesh"), or in Malachi 2:11 ("daughters of a foreign god") (Oswalt, *The Book of Isaiah: Chapters 40-66*, 457).

[238] Examples would include Rahab, Ruth, and others.

[239] There are many examples where *sariys* simply refers to a court official working for a king, but they have not been emasculated (e.g., Gen. 37:36; 39:1; 40:2, 7; Isa. 39:7; Dan. 1:3). This may be referring to a man who has been forcibly emasculated.

[240] Wolf, *Interpreting Isaiah*, 223.

[241] Grogan, "Isaiah," 315.

[242] These words "memorial" (*yad*) and "name" (*shem*) make the name for the Holocaust museum in Jerusalem, *Yadveshem*. Absalom attempted to do this for himself (2 Sam. 18:18).

All who come in faith are welcome, even those who formerly were social outcasts (v. 6). Amazingly, not only are they welcome to come, but they are even welcome to serve. Martin explains, "Redeemed Gentiles, though not in the covenantal family of Israel, can still receive God's blessings. They show their devotion to the Lord by their service, worship, and obedience."[243] They will not be allowed roles that are reserved for priests and Levites (cf. Jer. 33:14-26; Ezek. 40-48), but they will be allowed to come to Zion's temple to serve (*sharath*, cultic kinds of service) the Lord in various ways even though they are Gentiles (v. 7; cf. Isa. 2:2-3; 60:7, 10; 61:6; 66:20; 1 Kings 8:41-43; Matt. 21:13; Mark 11:17).[244] If one comes in humble faith, he will be exalted by God, and God will accept his praise and sacrifice even though he is not a physical descendent of Abraham (v. 7). Israel needs to understand that Yahweh is the God of the whole earth. Therefore, says God, "Yet *others* I will gather to them, to those *already* gathered" (v. 8; cf. Isa. 60:3-11; 66:18-21; John 10:16).

Israel's blindness to God's blessings (vv. 9-12)

God has made it clear how free and beautiful His redeeming grace is, but sadly the majority of His own people were blind to it. This was especially true among the various leaders of the nation. This last portion of chapter 56 introduces a radical change of tone where God rebukes those evil leaders who kept refusing Him (cf. 5:11; 22:11; 28:1; 29:1).[245]

The call to judge Israel's blindness (vv. 9-10a)

The leaders of a nation typically establish the direction of the nation. Unfortunately, Israel's leaders, i.e., their watchmen (kings, princes, priests, and prophets), were terrible (cf. Jer. 6:17; Ezek. 33:7). For this reason, God extended a call to the nations to come witness how bad it was, and to bring upon them a well-deserved judgment: "All you beasts of the field, all you beasts in the forest, come to eat. His watchmen are blind; all of them know nothing" (cf. Hos. 4:6).[246] As blind leaders, "they do not know the desperate nature of the times, they do not know the nature of their people, they do not know their own failings."[247]

---

[243] Martin, "Isaiah," 1111.

[244] The idea that foreigners could have such blessing so as to serve God with high service was so offensive to some scribes that this statement was omitted in 1QIs[a] (Oswalt, *The Book of Isaiah: Chapters 40-66*, 460).

[245] This rebuke against evil leaders starts in 56:9, but extends through 57:21.

[246] This is not the only place where we see such an idea (Isa. 5:5; Jer. 12:9; Ezek. 34:5, 7-10). We have seen that Isaiah often uses the metaphor of blindness to represent spiritual blindness.

[247] Ibid., 468.

The illustration of Israel's blindness (vv. 10b-12)

To make the point about how bad the leaders were, Isaiah uses two different illustrations to make the point.

First illustration: Dumb dogs (vv. 10b-11a). Just as a dumb dog is worthless as a guardian, Israel's watchmen were also worthless. Kidner reminds us how universal the illustration is: "Our own phrases, dumb dogs, sleeping dogs, greedy dogs, are all, substantially, in vs 10–11a, and they characterize the spiritual leaders (*watchmen; cf.* Ezk. 3:17)."[248] Instead of watching over their domain, they are lazy dogs that do nothing but eat and sleep and fail to watch the flock (cf. Ezek. 34; Job 30:1). They should have been teaching the truth of God (Mal. 2:7-8), but they were dedicated to sin.

Second illustration: Shepherds dedicated to evil (v. 11b-12). Israel's leaders were not even as good as a lazy, greedy, dumb dog. They were actively dedicated to the pursuit of evil. With language reminiscent of 53:6, Isaiah says, "they have all turned to their own way, each one to his unjust gain (*betsa'*, one's cut or gain), to the last one."[249] Their interest was not God and His truth, but money and sinful pleasure.

Their dedication to sinful pleasure is exemplified in the final verse where Isaiah repeats their words: "Come, *they say,* let us get wine [*yayin*],[250] and let us drink heavily of strong drink [*shekar*],[251] and tomorrow will be like today, only more so." Here is their mindset: "Man, we really had a great drunken party tonight, but tomorrow it is even going to be bigger."

Summary and application

We might marvel over how the people could hear about God's saving grace and be so unwilling to believe (cf. John 12:37-41). At the same time, we know that this is still how it works in our own day and age. All of this reminds us of the reality of man's fallen condition and the absolute need for God to work in the heart if anyone is to get saved (John 6:37, 44; Titus 3:5). We must stay committed to evangelizing and praying for God to save.

---

[248] Kidner, "Isaiah," 665.
[249] Shebna the selfish steward serves as a good example (ch. 22).
[250] This is the most common term for wine.
[251] We do not know of distilled liquor in that time, but this is possibly any kind of alcohol coming from various grains or fruits (Num. 28:7; Ps. 69:12; Prov. 31:6).

ISAIAH: THE LORD SAVES

CONDEMNATION UPON THE WICKED (57:1-21)

Chapter 57 continues the theme that began in the last verses of chapter 56 dealing with God's anger against wicked leaders. Hughes explains that in contrast to the blessings for the righteous in the kingdom (56:1-8), "the wicked face certain condemnation."[252]

Chapter 57 reads as follows: "1 The righteous man perishes, and no man takes it to heart, and devout men are taken away, while no one understands. For the righteous man is taken away from evil. 2 He enters into peace; They rest in their beds, *each one* who walked in his upright way. 3 But come here, you sons of a sorceress, offspring of an adulterer and a prostitute. 4 Against whom do you jest? Against whom do you open wide your mouth and stick out your tongue? Are you not children of rebellion, offspring of deceit, 5 *who* inflame yourselves among the oaks, under every luxuriant tree, who slaughter the children in the ravines, under the clefts of the crags? 6 Among the smooth *stones* of the ravine is your portion; they are your lot. Even to them you have poured out a drink offering; you have made a grain offering. Shall I relent concerning these things? 7 Upon a high and lofty mountain you have made your bed; you also went up there to offer sacrifice. 8 Behind the door and the doorpost you have set up your sign; indeed, far removed from Me, you have uncovered yourself, and have gone up and made your bed wide; and you have made an agreement for yourself with them; you have loved their bed; you have looked on *their* manhood; 9 you have journeyed to the king with oil and increased your perfumes; you have sent your envoys a great distance and made *them* go down to *Sheol*; 10 you were tired out by the length of your road, *yet* you did not say, It is hopeless. You found renewed strength; therefore, you did not faint. 11 Of whom were you worried and fearful when you lied, and did not remember Me nor give *Me* a thought? Was I not silent even for a long time so you do not fear Me? 12 I will declare your righteousness and your deeds, but they will not profit you. 13 When you cry out, let your collection *of idols* deliver you. But the wind will carry all of them up, *and* a breath will take *them away*. But he who takes refuge in Me will inherit the land and will possess My holy mountain. 14 And it will be said, Build up, build up; prepare the way; remove *every* obstacle out of the way of My people. 15 For thus says the high and exalted One Who lives forever, whose name is Holy, I dwell *on* a high and holy place, and *also* with the contrite and lowly of spirit in order to revive the spirit of the lowly and to revive the heart of the contrite. 16 For I will not contend forever, nor will I always be angry, for the spirit would grow faint before Me, and the breath *of those whom* I have made. 17 Because of the iniquity of his unjust gain I was angry and struck him; I hid *My face* and was angry, and he went on turning away, in the way of his heart. 18

---

[252] Hughes, *Tyndale Concise Bible Commentary*, 267.

I have seen his ways, but I will heal him; I will lead him and restore comfort to him and to his mourners, 19 creating the praise of the lips. Peace, peace to him who is far and to him who is near, says the Lord, and I will heal him. 20 But the wicked are like the tossing sea, for it cannot be quiet, and its waters toss up refuse and mud. 21 There is no peace, says my God, for the wicked" (57:1-21).

Chapter 57 continues the harsh rebuke against Israel's evil leaders that began in 56:9 by showing us just how badly evil had overtaken the land. Keil explains,

> Whilst watchmen and shepherds, prophets and rulers, without troubling themselves about the flock which they have to watch and feed, are thus indulging their own selfish desires, and living in debauchery, the righteous man is saved by early death from the judgment, which cannot fail to come with such corruption as this.[253]

Chapter 57 highlights three kinds of evil that had were so widespread there was nothing left for God but to bring the curses of the covenant.

First description: Inversion of right and wrong (vv. 1-2)

Isaiah was living in a day when the widespread rejection of God was producing a radical inversion of all moral and spiritual values. Years earlier Isaiah pronounced a woe on such people: "Woe to those who call evil good, and good evil, who substitute darkness for light and light for darkness, who substitute bitter for sweet and sweet for bitter!" (5:20). Decades later things had only gotten worse. Micah was a contemporary to Isaiah, and expressed the same frustrations,

> Woe is me! For I am like the fruit pickers, like the grape gatherers. There is not a cluster of grapes to eat, *or* a first-ripe fig *which* I crave. The godly person has perished from the land, and there is no upright *person* among men. All of them lie in wait for bloodshed; each of them hunts the other with a net. 3 Concerning evil, both hands do it well. The prince asks, also the judge, for a bribe, and a great man speaks the desire of his soul; so they weave it together. The best of them is like a briar; the most upright like a thorn hedge (Mic. 7:1-4).

From both Micah and Isaiah we see that the times were desperate, and tragically for the righteous the only bright side was that an early death was sometimes better than remaining on.

---

[253] Keil, *Commentary on the Old Testament*, 542.

No concern about the death of the righteous (v. 1a)

Isaiah describes an age in which no one had any concern about the death of the righteous.[254] "No one takes it to heart,"[255] and "no one understands" as the righteous are taken down to the grave by evil leaders.

Death was actually a path to peace (vv. 1b-2)

Death (lying on your eternal "bed") might seem to be the ultimate defeat, but Isaiah ironically says that the righteous man is actually "taken away from evil" (v. 1b). Martin explains,

> The society then was so bad that the righteous people in Israel (also called devout and those who walk uprightly) had to die in order to find peace. Observing the evil all around apparently frustrated them. They could do nothing to turn the nation back to the Lord. The only way the righteous could be spared from such frustration was to die.[256]

Those were terrible times, indeed, but as Christians we recognize that in an ultimate sense, "it is better to depart to depart and be with Christ, for *that* is very much better" (Phil. 1:23), especially in a world overtaken by evil. Christians today need to remember that this world is not our home, and we are nothing more than pilgrims.

Second description: Dedication to idolatrous evil (vv. 3-10)

The leaders were leading the nation to become increasingly evil. The Lord issues a series of condemning rebukes against the leaders.

A rebuke for their mockery of God (vv. 3-4)

Using a direct, second-person address, Isaiah speaks to these leaders as "sons of a sorceress,"[257] and "offspring of an adulterer and a prostitute," an

---

[254] Both terms "righteous" (*tsadiyq*) and "devout" (*chesed*) refer to the believer who was dedicated to knowing the Lord and walking in His paths (cf. Ps. 1).

[255] In our own time we often see how society bemoans the death of a famous celebrity despite the depth of their wickedness. When a godly man dies, however, they do not even blink an eye. So it was in Isaiah's time.

[256] Martin, "Isaiah," 1112.

[257] A sorcerer (*'anan*) is one who observes times and attempts to use magic and fortune telling and witchcraft to predict and control the future (Lev. 19:26; Deut. 18:10; 2 Kings 21:6; Isa. 2:6; Mic. 5:12; Jer. 27:9; Mal. 3:5).

extremely strong contrast to the tender language used for believers in verses 1-2.[258] These are very evil people leading the country (v. 3). The evil character of these leaders showed itself in their mockery of God and His Word (v. 4; cf. 29:14). Martin explains,

> In fertility religions "worshipers" engaged in sexual relations with prostitutes, supposedly identifying in that way with gods and goddesses to help guarantee fertility in crops, animals, and families. Such people in Israel were mocking the righteous while they were involved in shameful deeds.[259]

God saw it all, and for this mockery and disregard of His Word—the covenant they had agreed to at Mt. Sinai—He would judge them. For believers today, we recognize the reality that the unsaved world hates Jesus Christ, and because it hates Jesus Christ, it is going to hate us (John 15:18-19; 1 John 3:13).

A rebuke for their blatant idolatry (vv. 5-10)

Virtually all non-Jewish cultures in the ANE were pagan and polytheistic. The Canaanites who possessed the land before Israel were no exception. God's command at the time of the conquest was to utterly annihilate all traces of the Canaanites. Moses wrote,

> You shall utterly destroy them, the Hittite and the Amorite, the Canaanite and the Perizzite, the Hivite and the Jebusite, as the Lord your God has commanded you, so that they may not teach you to do according to all their detestable things which they have done for their gods, so that you would sin against the Lord (Deut. 20:16-18).

The command was to completely purge the land of all the different Canaanite groups, but Israel did not fully carry out these commands (cf. Judg. 2-3). The eventual result, just as God had warned, was that Israel began to embrace Canaanite idolatry. God gives three rebukes for their idolatry.

Baal worship (v. 5a). God condemns them for inflaming themselves under the trees.[260] Historical studies show it was common for Canaanite, sex-cult

---

[258] Oswalt, *The Book of Isaiah: Chapters 40-66*, 476. The language of sexual immorality, "adulterer" (participle of *na'aph*) and "prostitute" (*zanah*) has a literal basis behind it, but points ultimately to the spiritual unfaithfulness of the nation. The latter term, however, is in the form that points to their past deeds.

[259] Martin, "Isaiah," 1112.

[260] The term "inflame" (Niphal Pt of *chamam*) conveys the sense of intense sexual heat as part of Baal worship.

worship to take place on hill tops among oak (or other) groves (Isa. 1:29; 2 Kings 16:4; 17:10; Jer. 2:20; 3:13; Ezek. 6:13; Hos. 4:12-13).[261]

Molech worship (v. 5b). Child sacrifice was found in various Canaanite religions (cf. Jer. 19:5) and was central in the worship of Molech, the god of the Ammonites (cf. 1 Kings 11:5; 2 Chron. 28:3). People believed that the sacrifice of their children would appease their god and he would give them prosperity, so it became somewhat widespread (cf. 2 Kings 3:27; 16:3; 17:17, 31; 23:10; Jer. 7:31; 19:5; 32:35; Ezek. 16:20, 36; 23:37, 39). At Jerusalem, this detestable practice took place on the south-west edge of the city in a valley called *Gey Hinnom*,[262] but it also took place in other places, often in desert wadis and caves (v. 5b).

Cult prostitution (vv. 6-10). Cult prostitution was also a major part of Canaanite worship. The living God should have been their lot and portion (*cheleq*), but sadly they rejected Yahweh for filthy idols whom they worshipped in the deserted wadis. To these non-gods, they freely gave every form of sacrifice with the false belief that these idols would give them prosperity.[263] One hundred years later, Jeremiah tells us the following:

> Then all the men who were aware that their wives were burning sacrifices to other gods, along with all the women who were standing by, *as* a large assembly, including all the people who were living in Pathros in the land of Egypt, responded to Jeremiah, saying, As for the message that you have spoken to us in the name of the Lord, we are not going to listen to you! But rather we will certainly carry out every word that has proceeded from our mouths, by burning sacrifices to the queen of heaven and pouring out drink offerings to her, just as we ourselves, our forefathers, our kings and our princes did in the cities of Judah and in the streets of Jerusalem; for *then* we had plenty of food and were well off and saw no misfortune. But since we stopped burning sacrifices to the queen of heaven and pouring out drink offerings to her, we have lacked everything and have met our end by the sword and by famine. And, *said the women,* when we were burning sacrifices to the queen of heaven and were pouring out drink offerings to her, was it without our husbands that we made for her *sacrificial* cakes in her image and poured out drink offerings to her? (Jer. 44:15-19).

Jeremiah portrays their defiant mindset, and why the only option was to judge without relenting (*nacham*) (v. 6; cf. Jer. 5:9; 9:9). With cult prostitution as the

---

[261] Oswalt, *The Book of Isaiah: Chapters 40-66*, 476.
[262] Young, *The Book of Isaiah, vol. 3*, 402. This name later evolved into Gehenna.
[263] Drink offerings (*nesek*) and grain offerings (*minchah*) were both part of the kinds of offerings that should have been made to Yahweh alone.

backdrop, Isaiah writes, "Upon a high and lofty mountain you have made your bed. You also went up there to offer sacrifice" (v. 7). But it was not only at these high places where they worshipped Baal and Astarte (cf. Jer. 2:20; 3:6; Ezek. 16:6), but also right within their own houses:

> Behind the door and the doorpost you have set up your sign [*zikron*, "memorial"];[264] indeed, far removed from Me, you have uncovered yourself, and have gone up and made your bed wide. And you have made an agreement for yourself with them; you have loved their bed; you have looked on *their* manhood (v. 8).

Here is what we see: The people wanted their perverted worship, but they had to keep trying to rid themselves of the knowledge of Yahweh (a knowledge that they could not escape). Satan had powerfully captivated the land with sexual sin as noted by Smith:

> The phrase "you made your bed wide" may literally mean the temple prostitute opened her bed to many lovers, or it may be a metaphorical reference to people being open to the worship of many gods. The second half of 57:8 is equally difficult to understand. Often interpreters associate the "you cut, cut off" (*kārat*) with cutting a covenant, but the word covenant is not found in this text and the prepositional phrase "from them" (*mēhem*) is used instead of the more usual phraseology of making a covenant "with them" (*'imhem*).... The final charge accuses these people of loving their beds, the places where the immoral sexual activities took place. If there is any doubt about what these people loved to do or what was going on in these beds at their temple, the final two words at the end of the verse clarify that the person involved in this bed was looking at a naked person.[265]

The reference to a journey to the king could be speaking about a journey to a foreign pagan king,[266] but it may be better understood as referring to

---

[264] In Deuteronomy 6:4-9 God told Israel to inscribe a memorial to Him upon their door post so that He would always be in their remembrance, but here we see that they were giving their hearts to other gods (ibid., 404; Grogan, "Isaiah," 319). They were taking the knowledge of God away from their faces and putting in places where they would not be reminded of Him every time they go in and out.

[265] Smith, *Isaiah 40-66*, 554–555. The text literally refers to a "hand" (*yad*), a euphemism for the male genitalia, i.e., the strength of the male (cf. Ezek. 23:20).

[266] We see one such example in 2 Kings 16:7-18 where Ahaz sent to the Tiglath Pileser III, King of Assyria, for help (Young, *The Book of Isaiah, vol. 3*, 406). Isaiah notes how Israel kept seeking alliances with foreign kings and embracing their gods instead of trusting Yahweh (cf. Is. 7-8; 10:20-21; 22:11).

Molech worship since the consonants of Molech come from the word that means "king," and the name Baal literally means "lord" (v. 9). Kidner explains, "the Hebrew text has 'the king', which could be either *Molech* (see the first paragraph, above) or an earthly ally (*cf. e.g.* 30:2–5)."[267] In this context, it is probably best seen as referring to idol worship. All the prosperity that Yahweh had given them was now being poured out for the worship of idols, a terrible violation of the covenant.[268]

In Hosea (a generation before Isaiah) we read, "For their mother has played the harlot; she who conceived them has acted shamefully. For she said, I will go after my lovers, who give *me* my bread and my water, my wool and my flax, my oil and my drink" (Hos. 2:5). God rebukes her for this deception by telling her, "For she does not know that it was I who gave her the grain, the new wine and the oil, and lavished on her silver and gold, *which* they used for Baal" (Hos. 2:8). Yahweh was the One who gave them all their blessings, but they attributed it all to idols. How sad!

The idea of finding blessing and prosperity from false gods was hopeless, but those deceived idolaters simply could not let go of the lies: "You were tired out by the length of your road; *yet* you did not say, It is hopeless. You found renewed strength; therefore, you did not faint" (v. 10). Her pursuit of these demon lovers wore her out, but even then she would not stop (cf. Hos. 7:11; 8:9; 12:1).

Third description: No fear of the living God (vv. 11-21)

Israel's big problem was that it was a nation filled with unregenerate sinners; for this reason, there was no fear of God. In this last portion, Isaiah gives a rebuke to unbelievers (vv. 11-13), a promise of blessing to those who do believe (vv. 14-19), and a final warning of judgment to those who refuse to repent (vv. 20-21).

A rebuke to the unbelievers of the land (vv. 11-13)

Corrupt leadership eventually brings judgment on entire societies, and Israel would be no exception. The entire land turned its back on God.

They lied and broke the covenant (v. 11). For over seven-hundred years

---

[267] Kidner, "Isaiah," 665.

[268] Young, *The Book of Isaiah, vol. 3*, 405. In Ezekiel 23:41 we see how Israelites would gorgeously dress themselves and use rich perfumes when worshipping these idols (Oswalt, *The Book of Isaiah: Chapters 40-66*, 480).

Israel had to deal with evil leaders. Many thought that God would never bring judgment, so God says, "Was I not silent even for a long time so you do not fear Me?" (v. 11; cf. 51:13).

The consequences of breaking the covenant (vv. 12-13). First, God tells them what real justice will look like when their deeds are tested (v. 12). Second, God mocks them by telling them they can turn to their dead idols for help, but none will help, and their lies will be exposed (cf. 58:2-3; 64:6; 66:3). All idols and those who love them will be ruined (cf. 42:17; 44:11). The only hope is in repentance: "But he who takes refuge in Me will inherit the land and will possess My holy mountain" (v. 13; cf. Isa. 11:9; 24:23; 25:6-8; 40:27-31; 49:8; 60:21; 65:9, 25; 66:20; Ps. 37; Matt. 5:5; Rev. 2:28). All who seek refuge in Yahweh will find it in the Rock (17:10; 26:4; 30:29; 44:8; 49:8).

The destiny of those who do believe (vv. 14-19)

Isaiah builds upon this promise of refuge in verses 14-19 by making three promises for the one who is willing to turn to Yahweh.

First promise: God will restore the humble (vv. 14-15). For many, it might seem there could never be any restoration, but God makes it clear that such is not the case. For this reason, God gives the command to make preparations for a return and restoration (v. 14). Every obstacle must be removed for God's restoration highway (cf. Isa. 11:11-12, 15-16; 19:23; 35:8; 40:3; 62:10).[269] The real need is repentance, so God tells them,

> For thus says the high and exalted One who lives forever, whose name is Holy, I dwell *on* a high and holy place, and *also* with the contrite and lowly of spirit in order to revive the spirit of the lowly and to revive the heart of the contrite (v. 15; cf. 42:3; 50:4).[270]

The obstacle to restoration was their own refusal to repent. One day, God's grace will invade their lives and they will repent (cf. Zech. 12:10; 13:1). Martin explains, "In the past He had to be harsh with His people . . . but when they repent He forgives."[271] The promise is there for those who are willing to repent (Matt. 5:3-12).[272] One day it will come to reality, for the One who lives forever has sworn it (Isa. 40:28; cf. Deut. 33:27).

---

[269] The indefinite voice that calls out reminds us of 40:3.

[270] Isaiah uses exaltation language in a number of places (e.g., here; cf. ch. 6; 52:13; 66:1-2).

[271] Martin, "Isaiah," 1113.

[272] I.e., the one who is "contrite" (*daka'*, "crushed") and "lowly of spirit" (*shaphal*, "bowed down"). Because He alone is high and exalted, He accepts no competitors for

God's anger will turn away (vv. 16-17). God's anger was heavy upon His rebellious nation, but God makes two declarations to show that it will not remain forever, otherwise none would remain to live (v. 16).[273] What we see here is another example of the compassion God has for weak and sinful humanity, for if He did not show compassion none would be spared (cf. Pss. 78:38-39; 103:8-14; Matt. 24:22). Israel's sin in past ages was great and caused great anger (v. 17), but none of that will stop God from restoring Israel in the kingdom.

God will bring healing and peace (vv. 18-19). Because of His pity and mercy, He will forgive and restore. God will heal (*raphe'*; cf. Isa. 1:5-6; 6:10; 19:22; 30:26; 53:5; 61:2-3; 66:10; Hos. 6:1-3), lead (*nachah*; cf. e.g., Isa. 58:11; Mic. 2:12-13; Ps. 23:3), and comfort (*nacham*; cf. Isa. 2:1; 40:1; 49:13; 51:3, 12; 52:9; 61:1-3; 66:13) those who mourn and seek Him (v. 18). The result, says God,[274] will be that of the praise of the lips, peace to him who is far and to him who is near, says the Lord, and I will heal him (v. 19).[275]

The destiny of the wicked who refuse to believe (vv. 20-21)

The promise to the believer is precious, "but the wicked will not find rest."[276] Smith explains,

> After dealing with God's grace to the righteous, the paragraph ends with a brief contrasting comparison about what God will do with the wicked.... The wicked leaders fail to take care of God's flock (cf. 56:9–12), persecute the righteous (57:1–2), and worship pagan gods (57:3–10). These people

---

His place as God (cf. Isa. 2:6-22; 14:4-21) (Oswalt, *The Book of Isaiah: Chapters 40-66*, 488).

[273] The first expression "contend" (*riyb*) carries the idea of legal fighting, an idea elsewhere in Isaiah (e.g., Isa. 3:13; 50:8; cf. Hos. 4:1-3), and the second idea of "anger" (*qatsaph* here) is also found many times throughout (Isa. 47:6; 54:9; 57:17; 64:4; cf. 5:25; 9:12, 17, 19, 21; 10:5, 25; 12:1 where the synonym *'aph* is used).

[274] The participle "creating" (v. 19) carries a result force which flows out of the restoration promises in v. 18. Praise from the lips of His people is what God will bring forth—praise for the mercy and grace He has poured on them as He took pity on them (Isa. 12:5-6; 26:1, 19; 42:11-12; 42:23; 52:9; 54:1; cf. Heb. 13:15).

[275] Contextually, the reference to those far off is best understood as referring to the restoration of the elect remnant of Israel (Isa. 11:11-16, et al.), but we know this also will include an elect Gentile remnant as well (Isa. 11:10; 56:1-8; Eph. 2:17).

[276] Wolf, *Interpreting Isaiah*, 227.

have forsaken God (57:8), wearied God (57:10), and have dealt deceitfully with God (57:11), so now God will expose their evil (57:12).[277]

The wicked are as unsettled as the raging sea that never ceases to be in turmoil (v. 20; cf. Isa. 3:9, 11; Job 18:5-14; Jer. 49:23). For the "wicked" (*rasha'*; cf. 3:11; 5:23; 11:4; 13:11; 14:5; 26:10; 48:22; 53:9; 55:7; 57:20), God says, "There is no peace, says my God, for the wicked" (v. 20; cf. 48:22 where we see the same expression). Rather, their destiny will be that of eternal judgment in hell (Isa. 66:24; Rev. 20:11-15).

Summary and application

God's promises continue to stand, both for good and for harm. Each man must make his choice, but the best choice is to repent and believe.

---

[277] Smith, *Isaiah 40-66*, 567.

10
SALVATION TO A GLORIOUS FUTURE
(58:1-66:24)

Chapter 58 brings us to the final major section of Isaiah with a focus on salvation to a glorious future.[1] Hughes notes,

> In 58:1–66:24 Israel is divided into the faithful and the faithless to clarify the conditions for entering into God's future glory. It forms a final invitation and comfort. The heart of this section is the remnant's prayer for deliverance (63:7–64:12) and God's answer (65:1–25). The book ends by showing who will be excluded from the blessings of the new heavens and earth (66:1–24).[2]

Chapter 58 introduces this final section with a reminder to Israel about what God is really seeking from them, true religion.[3] True religion and true worship of Yahweh must flow from a heart of faith and not dead religious

---

[1] In terms of general themes for these last nine chapters, one might see the following: the "true fast," i.e., a contrast between true and false worship (ch. 58); confession that leads to salvation (ch. 59); the future glory and peace of Zion (ch. 60); the Spirit-filled Messiah (ch. 61); Zion's glory by answered prayer (ch. 62); Yahweh the Avenger (ch. 63); prayers for deliverance (ch. 64); God's mercy on true Israel (ch. 65); the restoration of true worship in Zion (ch. 66).

[2] Robert B. Hughes and J. Carl Laney, *Tyndale Concise Bible Commentary*, The Tyndale Reference Library, cited in electronic form with Logos Libronix (Wheaton, IL: Tyndale House Publishers, 2001), 268.

[3] John N. Oswalt, *The Book of Isaiah: Chapters 40-66*, The New International Commentary On The Old Testament, R. K. Harrison, Gen. Ed. (Grand Rapids: Eerdmans, 1998), 493.

rituals. This is the true fast God is seeking. Sadly, this was not what characterized Israel in Isaiah's day. One day God's grace will make it a reality. Thus, explains Martin,

> In this final nine-chapter section of the book, Isaiah looked to the present and the future. In his day most of the people were not righteous (chap. 58). Because of their depravity the restoration of the nation must be God's initiative (chap. 59). Eventually peace and prosperity will come to Israel and the whole world (chap. 60). Isaiah wrote of the coming of the Messiah and of the Father (61:1–63:6) and of the nation's prayer and the Lord's response (63:7–65:25). In conclusion the prophet wrote again that God will fulfill His promises to Israel as well as the entire world (chap. 66).[4]

Israel needed to understand the nature of a true fast, the kind that God Himself will bring to reality one day by pouring out of His saving grace.

THE TRUE FAST (58:1-14)

The people thought that God looked with favor on their religious rituals. Such was not the case. The only fast God will accept is a true fast which flows out of an obedient heart of faith.

Chapter 58 reads as follows: "1 Cry loudly, do not hold back raise your voice like a trumpet, and declare to My people their transgression and to the house of Jacob their sins. 2 Yet they seek Me day by day and delight to know My ways, as a nation that has done righteousness and has not forsaken the ordinance of their God. They ask Me *for* just decisions; they delight in the nearness of God. 3 Why have we fasted and You do not see? *Why* have we humbled ourselves and You do not notice? Behold, on the day of your fast you find *your* desire, and drive hard all your workers. 4 Behold, you fast for contention and strife and to strike with a wicked fist. You do not fast like *you do* today to make your voice heard on high. 5 Is it a fast like this which I choose, a day for a man to humble himself? Is it for bowing one's head like a reed and for spreading out sackcloth and ashes as a bed? Will you call this a fast, even an acceptable day to the Lord? 6 Is this not the fast which I choose, to loosen the bonds of wickedness, to undo the bands of the yoke, and to let the oppressed go free, and break every yoke? 7 Is it not to divide your bread with the hungry and bring the homeless poor into the house, when you see the naked, to cover him, and not to hide yourself from your own flesh? 8 Then your light will break out like the dawn,

---

[4] John A. Martin, "Isaiah," in *The Bible Knowledge Commentary: An Exposition of the Scriptures*, ed. J. F. Walvoord and R. B. Zuck, vol. 1, cited in electronic form with Logos Libronix (Wheaton, IL: Victor Books, 1985), 1113.

and your recovery will speedily spring forth, and your righteousness will go before you; the glory of the Lord will be your rear guard. 9 Then you will call, and the Lord will answer; you will cry, and He will say, Here I am. If you remove the yoke from your midst, the pointing of the finger and speaking wickedness, 10 and if you give yourself to the hungry and satisfy the desire of the afflicted, then your light will rise in darkness and your gloom *will become* like midday. 11 And the Lord will continually guide you, and satisfy your desire in scorched places, and give strength to your bones; and you will be like a watered garden, and like a spring of water whose waters do not fail. 12 Those from among you will rebuild the ancient ruins; you will raise up the age-old foundations, and you will be called the repairer of the breach, the restorer of the streets in which to dwell. 13 If because of the sabbath, you turn your foot from doing your *own* pleasure on My holy day, and call the sabbath a delight, the holy *day* of the Lord honorable, and honor it, desisting from your *own* ways, from seeking your *own* pleasure and speaking *your own* word, 14 then you will take delight in the Lord, and I will make you ride on the heights of the earth, and I will feed you *with* the heritage of Jacob your father, for the mouth of the Lord has spoken" (58:1-14).

Clearly, God is not happy with His people Israel. They are weighed down in sin, but in their hypocrisy, they acted as if nothing was wrong with their dead rituals. God issues a series of four stinging rebukes to let them know how angry He is.

God's rebuke for Israel's hypocrisy (vv. 1-2)

God begins by exposing their hypocrisy (cf. 1:11-15). Their heart was far from God, but they still acted like they could give Him acceptable worship. God commands Isaiah to speak loud about His displeasure.

The intensity of God's rebuke (v. 1)

God commands Isaiah, "Cry loudly; do not hold back; raise your voice like a trumpet."[5] God has a message He wants all to hear, and He wants His people to recognize their "transgression" and "sins."[6] Thus, explains Pfeiffer, to expose their hypocrisy, "the prophet is bidden to denounce unsparingly the spurious faith of the Jews, with its sanctimonious pose at worship services."[7] Verse 2 begins showing us why God is so angry.

---

[5] The Hebrew reads, "Cry out with the throat," i.e., "Make it loud and do not hold back."

[6] The latter term "sins" (*chatta'th*) is the more general term, while the former term "transgressions" (*pesha'*) connotes the idea of rebellion against one's authority.

[7] Charles F. Pfeiffer, *The Wycliffe Bible Commentary: Old Testament*, cited in electronic form with Logos Libronix (Chicago: Moody Press, 1962), Is 58:1.

The reason for God's rebuke (v. 2)

Israel was under the false impression that God looked with favor on their religion even though it did not come out of faith.[8] This was the same problem Paul wrote about in Romans some seven-hundred years later:

> I testify about them that they have a zeal for God, but not in accordance with knowledge, for not knowing about God's righteousness and seeking to establish their own, they did not subject themselves to the righteousness of God (Rom. 10:2-3).

The issue here is that Isaiah was dealing with a mass of unsaved religious people who thought their rituals made them acceptable to God. They were mistaken.[9] Smith explains,

> What this verse is revealing is that people can look, act, talk, and delight in the things of God, yet still not be the people of God (cf. Matt 7:21–23). A good, moral, cultural Israelite knows how to act, talk, and behave in religious circles, but knowing the cultural expectations of an Israelite is not the same as knowing God.[10]

God's rebuke for Israel's meaningless fasts (vv. 3-9a)

Isaiah takes the general problem of hypocrisy found in verses 1-2, and now turns to a specific manifestation of the problem found in Israel's empty fasts.[11] Isaiah first confronts the people for their empty fasts (vv. 3-7), and then he tells them how God will respond to them positively if they truly repent and follow the Lord in truth (vv. 8-9a).

---

[8] Verse 2 is loaded with sarcasm as God describes how Israel would seek God, delight in His ways, do righteousness, not forsake the Lord to ask for just decisions, and delight in being near to God.

[9] Proverbs 15:8 says the sacrifice of the wicked is an abomination to the Lord.

[10] Gary Smith, *Isaiah 40-66*, vol. 15B, The New American Commentary, cited in electronic form with Logos Libronix (Nashville, TN: Broadman & Holman Publishers, 2009), 574.

[11] Even though fasting was a common expression of brokenness in the ANE, the only fast God actually commanded in Scripture was The Day of Atonement (cf. Lev. 16 where the same term "humbled" is used). In Zechariah 7-8, we see how Israel had added four fasts during the Babylonian Captivity to try and appease God for their sins, but God tells them in four answers that all of them were empty and meaningless. Self-inflicted penance is no substitute for true repentance and faith.

Isaiah confronts Israel's empty fasts (vv. 3-7)

The people understood that God was not giving heed to their fasts. The people demanded an answer (v. 3a), so God gave them one (vv. 3b-7).

The demand for an answer (v. 3a). The people demanded, "Why have we fasted and You do not see? *Why* have we humbled ourselves and You do not notice?" They actually had the gall to accuse God.[12] Keil notes, "There follow now the words of the work-righteous themselves, who hold up their fasting before the eyes of God, and complain that He takes no notice of it. And how could He?!"[13] The problem, explains Wolf, is not that Israel had a religious ritual called fasting, but that, "it degenerated into an external display of piety" that was not driven by broken hearts of faith.[14]

God's answer why He would not hear them (vv. 3b-7). Israel had their fasts, plenty of them, but they were still dedicated to their sinful ways: "Behold, on the day of your fast you find *your* desire, and drive hard all your workers" (v. 3b). Instead of delighting in God's ways, they were driven by their own desires (*chephets*) which often involved oppression of their workers.[15] Oswalt believes that their religious experiences were, "primarily for themselves, primarily to serve those covetous instincts that motivate all our lives far more than we care to admit."[16]

Israel had its fasts, but God says that their fasts were for nothing more than for "contention and strife and to strike with a wicked fist" (v. 4).[17] In the blindness of their unsaved condition, the people of Israel "saw no connection between their mistreatment of the poor and the lowly and their religion."[18] Instead of dead rituals, they should have applied the words of Joel: "Rend your heart and not your garments. Now return to the Lord your God" (Joel 2:13).

God tells them in verses 5-7 the kind of fasts He was really seeking. It is

---

[12] Just as we see right here, the Book of Malachi is filled with examples of Israel rebuking God as though He were the problem.

[13] Carl Friedrich Keil and Franz Delitzsch, *Commentary on the Old Testament*, vol. 7, cited in electronic form with Logos Libronix (Peabody, MA: Hendrickson, 1996), 553.

[14] Herbert M. Wolf, *Interpreting Isaiah* (Grand Rapids: Zondervan, 1985), 229.

[15] The expression "drive hard" (*nagas*) is found Exodus 3:7 where it speaks about the harsh taskmasters who afflicted the Children of Israel in Egypt. Messiah will purge this kind of evil when He brings His kingdom (Isa. 9:4; Zech. 9:8).

[16] Oswalt, *The Book of Isaiah: Chapters 40-66*, 498.

[17] Edward J. Young, *The Book of Isaiah, vol. 3* (Grand Rapids: Eerdmans, 1972), 418.

[18] Oswalt, *The Book of Isaiah: Chapters 40-66*, 498.

the kind of fast that is characterized by humility (*'anah*), the kind of fast where outward things like sackcloth and ashes (cf. 1 Kings 21:27; Jonah 3:5-8) really represented a broken heart on the inside (v. 5; cf. Ps. 51:16-17). A broken heart of this nature would show itself in compassion for their fellow countrymen by easing the yoke of oppression on those who were struggling to survive harsh servitude, for this is what real love would look like (v. 6; cf. Isa. 1:17; Jer. 34:8-11; Lev. 19:18; Matt. 22:27-39).[19] True righteousness would show itself in mercy and compassion, and it would include the positive side of helping the afflicted: "Is it not to divide your bread with the hungry and bring the homeless poor into the house, when you see the naked, to cover him, and not to hide yourself from your own flesh?" (v. 7). That is what a true fast should look (cf. Matt. 25:35-36). Martin explains,

> The Israelites were to consider themselves members of one family who at one time had been slaves in Egypt. Therefore they were not to neglect each other. When someone shared with one in need, it was a reminder that everything he owned belonged to the Lord.[20]

For those who would listen, there is also the promise of great blessing.

The promise of blessing for true repentance (vv. 8-9a)

Isaiah declared the conditions for blessing in verses 3-7, and now verses 8-9a he tells them what these blessings will look like.[21]

The promise of God's restoring favor (v. 8). It is probably best to understand both expressions "light" (*'ur*) and "recovery" (*'arukah*, healing or repair) as including the idea of "the joy of salvation and prosperity,"[22] the same kind of blessing as found in the Aaronic prayer (Num. 6:24-27).[23] If Israel will turn to God in faith, *then* their light will break forth (*baqa'*, burst forth) like the dawn, and their recovery will speedily spring forth (*tsamach*, to branch), and never again will darkness overtake them (Isa. 8:23/9:1; 60:1-3).

The promise of "righteousness" does not exclude personal righteousness,

---

[19] Young notes, "According to the law, slaves of Israelitish descent were to be emancipated every three years" (Young, *The Book of Isaiah, vol. 3*, 419).

[20] Martin, "Isaiah," 1113.

[21] Both verses 8 and 9 begin with the Hebrew particle *'az* ("then") which indicates a promised result for obedience to God's commands (unlike what we see in 58:3).

[22] Wolf, *Interpreting Isaiah*, 230.

[23] The root word for "light" (*'ur*) is the same term in Numbers 6:25 where it says, "make His face shine."

but in context the expression is best seen as referring to the righteousness of God that has brought Israel salvation when "the glory of the Lord will be [their] rear guard," i.e., it is the exercise of God's faithful promises to save (cf. Isa. 11:5; 51:5-8; 46:13; 56:2; 59:16; 61:11).

The promise of God's restoring presence (v. 9a). Verse 8 promised that God's glory would be their rear guard just as at the Exodus (Exod. 13:21-22; 14:19; Isa. 52:12), and verse 9 continues this theme: "Then you will call, and the Lord will answer; you will cry, and He will say, Here I am." The Lord will be there just as He promised (Isa. 41:10; 43:2; 55:6; 65:24; cf. Hag. 1:13; 2:4-5).

God's rebuke for Israel's lack of true righteousness (vv. 9b-12)

Isaiah rebukes the nation for their lack of true righteousness. The blessings He has spoken about can be theirs, but only if they turn to the Lord. Isaiah lays out the conditions for blessings (vv. 9b-10a) and then tells them what those blessings will be if they will truly listen (vv. 10b-12).

The conditions for blessings (vv. 9b-10a)

Blessing comes to those who honor God with faith that shows itself in obedience. Isaiah highlights two areas where they needed to change.

First area the people needed to change (v. 9b). As we have already seen, "removing the yoke" is the idea of ending oppressive slave practices against their own people (cf. 58:6). The idea of "pointing the finger and speaking wickedness" speak about "a gesture of contempt" against one's fellow man (Isa. 57:4; 66:5; cf. Prov. 6:13).[24] In other words, God is telling them to get rid of all forms of wicked thinking and conduct towards others, and practice the love of God toward their neighbor in every area (cf. Lev. 19:18; Rom. 13:10).

Second area the people needed to change (v. 10a). God commands a righteousness that is active in practice, so He also tells them, "give yourself to the hungry and satisfy the desire of the afflicted." They needed to be willing to take of their own personal resources and help their fellow Israelites, for this is what genuine love looks like. John writes, "But whoever has the world's goods, and sees his brother in need and closes his heart against him, how does the love of God abide in him? Little children, let us not love with word or with tongue, but in deed and truth" (1 John 3:17-18). If His people will repent of their greed, the Lord will bless them.

---

[24] Ibid., 231. Young points out, "Among the Arabs, this gesture was a means of bringing misfortune upon others" (cf. Young, *The Book of Isaiah, vol. 3*, 422, n. 10).

The promised blessings (vv. 10b-12)

The promise of blessing is there if they respond. Isaiah outlines eight promises how God will bless Israel if they do.

First and second promised blessings (v. 10b). In a promise similar to verse 8, God tells them that if they obey from the heart, "your light will rise in darkness and your gloom [*'aphelah*; cf. 8:22; 59:9] *will become* like midday." Here is the issue: The darkness of judgment will vanish if they turn to the Lord.

Five more promised blessings (v. 11). Isaiah names five more blessings: "The Lord will continually guide you, and satisfy your desire in scorched places, and give strength to your bones, and you will be like a watered garden, and like a spring of water whose waters do not fail." The Shepherd of Israel will guide His weary flock (cf. Isa. 57:18; Mic. 2:12-13). He will take away all lack (cf. Isa. 1:30), and prosperity will overtake them (cf. Isa. 35; 43:18-21; 44:3-5; Jer. 31:12; Joel 3:18-21). All they need to do is repent and obey.

Final promised blessing (v. 12). The whole land of Israel will experience a rebuilding and restoration after its ages of ruin and desolation: "Those from among you will rebuild the ancient ruins; you will raise up the age-old foundations; and you will be called the repairer of the breach, the restorer of the streets in which to dwell." This wonderful promise is one that originated with Moses (Deut. 30:1-10), but gets repeated numerous times in the prophets (Jer. 30:18-24; 31:38-40; 32:15-25; 33:14-26; Amos 9:11-15; Zech. 8). All Israel needs to do is turn to the Lord.

God's rebuke for Israel's rejection of the Sabbath (vv. 13-14)

Verses 3-12 focused largely on social sins, but in these last two verses the focus shifts to sins that were directly against God, in particular its sin of failing to observe the Sabbath. Kidner explains,

> But lest it should seem that philanthropy is all, these verses describe the strictness and the gladness of the Sabbath-keeping God desires. If fasting is to be an opportunity to show love to our neighbour, the Sabbath should express, first of all, our love of God.[25]

Once again, God presents an if/then kind of proposition to the people. If they will respond (v. 13), God will bless (v. 14).

---

[25] F. Derek Kidner, "Isaiah," in *New Bible Commentary: 21st Century Edition*, ed. D. A. Carson et al., 4th ed., cited in electronic form with Logos Libronix (Leicester, England; Downers Grove, IL: Inter-Varsity Press, 1994), 666.

The proposition (v. 13)

God wants Israel to honor Him as their God. This includes keeping the Sabbath (56:2). The original basis for Israel's Sabbath was based on the creation pattern found in Genesis 1-2 where God created in six days and ceased creating on the seventh. On this basis, God gave the command that Israel was not to labor on the seventh day (Exod. 20:8-11). Later in Exodus, God says that the Sabbath also functioned as the special "sign" of the Sinaitic covenant (Exod. 31:12-17). For Israel, the Sabbath was like a wedding ring that commemorated God's covenant (and a reminder of the Exodus as seen in Deut. 5).

Yahweh wanted His people to honor Him by keeping the Sabbath, but Israel did not want to be troubled with it because they had other pursuits they preferred to chase down, e.g., pleasure activities and money-making activities.[26] Therefore, God tells them they needed to repent and turn from their own selfish pleasure (*chephets*) to keep the Sabbath. They needed to love and honor the Lord enough where this special day would be a delight (*'oneg*; cf. 13:22 and see the verb form in 47:1; 55:2; 57:4; 58:14; 66:11). How will God respond to this kind of faith?

The promise (v. 14)

Isaiah highlights three promises of what God will fulfill if they turn to Him in obedient faith.

First promise. A turn from self to the Lord will also give them a change of heart so that they might delight (*'oneg*; cf. 58:13) in the Lord.[27] In other words, obedience to God will bring with it a change of affections.

Second promise. If they truly turn to Him, He will make them ride on the heights of the earth. By this unique expression, God is effectively saying, "to people of this spirit God can safely give great things."[28]

---

[26] They had too many things to do that kept them from "going to church" you might say. Young suggests that the reference to speech "probably refers to idle and vain talk, in which God is forgotten" (Young, *The Book of Isaiah, vol. 3*, 427).

[27] R. Laird Harris, Gleason L. Archer Jr., and Bruce K. Waltke, eds., "*'anag*," *Theological Wordbook of the Old Testament*, cited in electronic form with Logos Libronix (Chicago: Moody Press, 1999), 679.

[28] Kidner, "Isaiah," 666. It is also possible that the reference to "high places" is even a veiled jab at the Baal worship, but this is questionable (Young, *The Book of Isaiah, vol. 3*, 427).

Third promise. Lastly, God tells them, "And I will feed you *with* the heritage of Jacob your father." All the promises made to Abraham, Isaac, and Jacob will be theirs in full measure if they will only turn to Him. The promises are both wonderful and certain, for they have been spoken by the mouth of the Lord, "and that mouth cannot lie" (cf. 1:20; 40:5).[29]

Summary and application

Oswalt gives an apt summary of God's wonderful promises: "Here is the golden key of all biblical revelation: those who give themselves away find themselves; those who relinquish the throne receive the crown."[30] These truths are not simply for the nation of Israel, but for each and every man. For those who respond, God will give them the greatest blessings.

CONFESSION THAT LEADS TO SALVATION (59:1-21)

Chapters 57-58 were filled with strong messages of condemnation, especially for the leaders of Israel. The solution to all their problems was simple. All they had to do was turn from their sin to trust and obey the Lord. Chapter 59 reminds us that our greatest need is to confess our sin that we might be restored to God.

Chapter 59 reads as follows: "1 Behold, the Lord's hand is not so short that it cannot save, nor is His ear so dull that it cannot hear. 2 But your iniquities have made a separation between you and your God, and your sins have hidden *His* face from you so that He does not hear. 3 For your hands are defiled with blood and your fingers with iniquity; your lips have spoken falsehood; your tongue mutters wickedness. 4 No one sues righteously, and no one pleads honestly. They trust in confusion and speak lies; they conceive mischief and bring forth iniquity. 5 They hatch adders' eggs and weave the spider's web; he who eats of their eggs dies, and *from* that which is crushed a snake breaks forth. 6 Their webs will not become clothing, nor will they cover themselves with their works; their works are works of iniquity, and an act of violence is in their hands. 7 Their feet run to evil, and they hasten to shed innocent blood. Their thoughts are thoughts of iniquity. Devastation and destruction are in their highways. 8 They do not know the way of peace, and there is no justice in their tracks; they have made their paths crooked; whoever treads on them does not know peace. 9 Therefore justice is far from us, and righteousness does not overtake us. We hope for light, but behold, darkness, for brightness, but we walk in gloom. 10 We grope along the wall like blind men; we grope like those who have no eyes; we stumble at midday as in the twilight, among those who are vigorous *we are*

---

[29] Wolf, *Interpreting Isaiah*, 231.
[30] Oswalt, *The Book of Isaiah: Chapters 40-66*, 509.

like dead men. 11 All of us growl like bears, and moan sadly like doves. We hope for justice, but there is none, for salvation, *but* it is far from us, 12 for our transgressions are multiplied before You, and our sins testify against us, for our transgressions are with us, and we know our iniquities: 13 Transgressing and denying the Lord, and turning away from our God, speaking oppression and revolt, conceiving *in* and uttering from the heart lying words. 14 Justice is turned back, and righteousness stands far away, for truth has stumbled in the street, and uprightness cannot enter. 15 Yes, truth is lacking, and he who turns aside from evil makes himself a prey. Now the Lord saw, and it was displeasing in His sight that there was no justice. 16 And He saw that there was no man, and was astonished that there was no one to intercede. Then His own arm brought salvation to Him, and His righteousness upheld Him. 17 He put on righteousness like a breastplate, and a helmet of salvation on His head; and He put on garments of vengeance for clothing and wrapped Himself with zeal as a mantle. 18 According to *their* deeds, so He will repay, wrath to His adversaries, recompense to His enemies; to the coastlands He will make recompense, 19 so they will fear the name of the Lord from the west, and His glory from the rising of the sun, for He will come like a rushing stream which the wind of the Lord drives. 20 A Redeemer will come to Zion, and to those who turn from transgression in Jacob, declares the Lord. 21 As for Me, this is My covenant with them, says the Lord: My Spirit which is upon you, and My words which I have put in your mouth shall not depart from your mouth, nor from the mouth of your offspring, nor from the mouth of your offspring's offspring, says the Lord, from now and forever" (59:1-21).

Chapter 59 brings the message that Israel has only one hope, and that hope comes by turning to the Lord, a message Israel was not heeding. Wolf explains, "Why had the Lord delayed this great deliverance? The problem was not with God."[31] No, salvation cannot come until they deal with their sins by turning to the Lord. The chapter may be broken down as follows: no salvation for unrepentant sinners (vv. 1-8); no salvation while still in sin (vv. 9-15a); no salvation without God's Redeemer (vv. 15b-21).

No salvation for unrepentant sinners (vv. 1-8)

Israel habitually made the mistake of blaming God for its woes instead of recognizing that the problem was their own sin. Isaiah makes it clear that God is not the problem (v. 1), but they are (vv. 2-8).

God is not the problem (v. 1)

The opening exclamation is meant to grab the attention of the people.

---

[31] Wolf, *Interpreting Isaiah*, 231-232.

Smith explains, "The introductory 'behold' (*hēn*, NIV "surely") draws attention to a new literary segment in the argumentation against the idea that God has not responded to the people."[32] They thought God was too weak to save, so Isaiah uses two bodily metaphors (God's hand and ear) to illustrate that Israel's exile is not because God is incapable of saving.[33] Ancient pagan nations like Assyria, Babylon, Persia, Greece, and Rome were powerful nations, but never would they be too strong for God.

Israel is the problem (vv. 2-8)

God is not the problem, but Israel is with its unrepentant heart (v. 2; cf. Isa. 50:1-2).[34] Israel's iniquities (*'awon*, twisted, perverted; cf. 1:15; 50:1) have separated her from God, and her sins (*chatta'th*, missing the mark) have caused God's face to be hidden so that He does not hear (1:10-15; 58:4; cf. Ps. 66:18; Prov. 15:8, 29; 28:9; 1 Pet. 3:7).[35] Isaiah illustrates in verses 3-8.

Illustrations with four body parts (v. 3). Isaiah illustrates Israel's sin by using four body parts to make the point that their entire lives have been given over to sin.[36] All four terms convey the depth of their depravity.[37] How tragic it is that the people whom God saved for the purpose of being holy (Exod. 19:6; Lev. 19:2; 20:7) would be so completely overcome by the worst kinds of evils (Isa. 1:21-23).

Illustrations of greedy oppression (v. 4). This second set of illustrations exposes the problems of rampant corruption, dishonesty, and oppression (cf. 5:20-23). The legal process God gave to protect the innocent and promote justice was being twisted by powerful people so that "lying and oppression

---

[32] Smith, *Isaiah 40-66*, 588.
[33] The "hand" often symbolizes God's power to save (40:10; 50:2; 51:9; 59:1, 16; 62:8).
[34] Grogan notes that God was not about to hear their salvation petitions as long as they were rebels against His rule (G. W. Grogan, "Isaiah," in *The Expositor's Bible Commentary*, ed. Frank E. Gaebelein, vol. 6 [Grand Rapids: Zondervan, 1986], 325).
[35] "Separation" is a participle, conveying the idea of ongoing verbal activity (Young, *The Book of Isaiah, vol. 3*, 430). His ear will listen if they will not repent (58:9; 65:24).
[36] Oswalt, *The Book of Isaiah: Chapters 40-66*, 514.
[37] Blood (*dam*) speaks of bloodshed that can be literal, but often conveys the idea of social violence through oppression of the weak (Isa. 1:15, 21; Jer. 2:30, 34; Hos. 4:2). Iniquity (*'awon*) is a somewhat broad sin term that relates to the idea of deviation (1:15; 50:1). Falsehood (*sheqer*) speaks of lies and deceit (Isa. 28:15; 30:9; 59:13). Wickedness (*'awlah*) speaks of malice and injustice based on the root idea of deviation (Isa. 61:8; Mal. 3:10).

universally prevail."[38] Isaiah's contemporary Micah decried the same sad state of affairs:

> The godly person has perished from the land, and there is no upright *person* among men. All of them lie in wait for bloodshed; each of them hunts the other with a net. Concerning evil, both hands do it well. The prince asks, also the judge, for a bribe, and a great man speaks the desire of his soul; so they weave it together. The best of them is like a briar, the most upright like a thorn hedge (Mic. 7:2-4).

Illustrations of nature (vv. 5-6). This third set of illustrations show that even though there was considerable outward religious activity, it was only activity that lead to ruin. The imagery of adder's eggs (*tsiph'oniy*; cf. 11:8) conveys the idea that, "the apostate people were like poisonous serpents that produce evil influences calculated to destroy the unwary who trust them,"[39] and the imagery of a spider web reinforces the idea that they had become a people who produce nothing but poison and death. Instead of the kind of weaving that could produce a blessing like warm clothing, their weaving produced nothing but iniquity (*'awen*, i.e., trouble and sorrow; cf. Isa. 31:2; 58:9; Mic. 2:1) and violence (*chamas*, both physical social; cf. Gen. 6:11; Isa. 53:9; 60:18; Jer. 6:7; Ezek. 7:11; Mal. 2:16). Their whole society was crumbling before their eyes, a sad picture that looks like present-day Western/American culture.

Illustrations of social violence (vv. 7-8). Sins of social violence continue, shifting from the hand (v. 6b) to their feet and thoughts (v. 7). Israel was on a path that would take them to utter ruin.[40] Twice God declared that there is no peace for the wicked (48:22; 57:21), and once again He says, "They do not know the way of peace, and there is no justice in their tracks. They have made their paths crooked; whoever treads on them does not know peace" (v. 8). Israel was coming apart at the seams from its own internal corruption.

No salvation while still in sin (vv. 9-15a)

As long as Israel was committed to sin, salvation would be far from them. Oswalt explains that all of us remain in our sin until we come to a point where,

---

[38] Keil, *Commentary on the Old Testament*, 560. The people of God had become masters of confusion (*tohu*, formless, without order; cf. Gen. 1:2; Isa. 24:10; 34:11; 44:9; 45:18, 19). That is, they were experts at evading truth by the use of lies and confusion, just as we often see in our own modern-day legal system.

[39] Pfeiffer, *The Wycliffe Bible Commentary: Old Testament*, Is 59:1.

[40] God's highway is one of salvation (Isa. 11:16; 19:23; 35:8; 40:3; 49:11; 62:10), but their highways are highways of devastation and destruction (cf. 7:3; 33:8; 36:2).

"we admit the heinousness of our crimes and own our helplessness to clear their guilt or their power from our lives."[41] Israel would not do this, and for this reason her situation was most desperate. Here in verses 9-15a we see the description of Israel's desperation (vv. 9-11), and the reason for Israel's desperation (vv. 12-15a).

The description of Israel's desperation (vv. 9-11)

Isaiah continues to expose the failure of the nation by giving three descriptions of the sin of his people.

Darkness (v. 9). Israel wanted God to come down and save them from their oppressors, i.e., to bring them justice and righteousness,[42] but because of their sin they were consigned to the "darkness" (*choshek*; cf. 5:30; 8:22; 29:18; 42:7; 49:9; 58:10) and "gloom" (*'aphelah*) of exile and captivity (Isa. 8:22; 58:18; Zeph. 1:15).[43]

Blindness (v. 10). Not only is the nation consigned to darkness, but to blindness as well (Isa. 29:18; 35:5; 42:7, 16, 18, 19; 43:8; 56:10).[44] The best they would be able to do is to grope around (*gashah*) like a blind man in the dark. Young notes, "As blind men feel the wall with their hands seeking a way of escape from prison, so men in their sins grope about seeking for deliverance and never finding it"[45] (cf. Acts 17:27). Even in mid-day, they stumble because of their alienation from God. The blindness was so great they could not even perceive the Light of God when He stood in their presence (John 1:4-5; 8:12). Kidner explains, "The groping in broad daylight is the judgment that Jesus' contemporaries [both] courted (*cf.* Jn. 3:19) and suffered (*cf.* Jn. 12:35–40)."[46]

---

[41] Oswalt, *The Book of Isaiah: Chapters 40-66*, 518-519.
[42] Oswalt notes that in 1-39 these terms generally refer to the ethical conduct God demands from His people, but in 40-66 these terms, especially "righteousness, often become a synonym for salvation (ibid., 519). Grogan describes such righteousness as God's faithfulness to His covenant people (Grogan, "Isaiah," 326).
[43] Moses used this term *'aphelah* in Deuteronomy 28:29 to tell the people that this is what would befall them for rebellion against the covenant.
[44] Once again, we see Isaiah drawing directly from the curses of the covenant: "The Lord will smite you with madness and with blindness and with bewilderment of heart; and you will grope at noon, as the blind man gropes in darkness, and you will not prosper in your ways; but you shall only be oppressed and robbed continually, with none to save you" (Deut. 28:28-29).
[45] Young, *The Book of Isaiah, vol. 3*, 434. There is debate about the statement "among those who are vigorous, we are like dead men," but the idea seems to mean that in the place where there should be life and vitality, there is weakness and death.
[46] Kidner, "Isaiah," 666.

Agonizing groans (v. 11). Hopeless desperation has left the nation making sad sounds like growling bears or moaning doves (Isa. 38:14; Ezek. 7:16; Nah. 2:7) as they hope for deliverance, but it never comes, all because of the ravages of enemy invasion due to their unrepentant hearts.[47]

The reason for Israel's desperation (vv. 12-15a)

The problem is the multiplied transgressions (cf. 58:1), sins (cf. 59:2), and iniquities (cf. 59:2) of Israel (v. 12). The six sins that follow all take the form of Hebrew infinitive absolutes emphasizing the never-ending nature of Israel's sin (v. 13; cf. Ezra 9:6-7). Because there is no truth or uprightness, salvation remains far away (v. 14; cf. 59:9). Even if someone wanted to escape, they could not (v. 15). Pfeiffer explains, "Anyone who attempted to lead an honest life made himself a victim of the ruthless cutthroats who dominated Israelite society."[48] Amos agonized over this societal decay: "They hate him who reproves in the gate, and they abhor him who speaks *with* integrity," and "Therefore at such a time the prudent person keeps silent, for it is an evil time" (Amos 5:10, 13).

No salvation without God's Redeemer (vv. 15b-21)

Israel needed to recognize the truth that there could be no salvation without God's Redeemer. Here in these last seven verses, Isaiah gives his people two basic reminders about the need for a Redeemer.

First reminder: The need for a Redeemer (vv. 15b-16)

Israel desperately needed a Redeemer, but tragically there was no one. This was a sad situation, but one that God was ready to fix:

> Now the Lord saw, and it was displeasing in His sight that there was no justice. And He saw that there was no man, and was astonished that there was no one to intercede. Then His own arm brought salvation to Him, and His righteousness upheld Him (vv. 15b-16).

God describes Israel's situation as one that was hopeless according to its own resources. Throughout their history, Israel had some great leaders who led them in various temporal victories (e.g., Moses, Joshua, Samson, David), but sadly they had no one who could deliver them from their sin. Because Israel had no one to get the job done, God Himself would have to step in with His mighty arm (50:2; 51:9; 52:10; 53:1, 9; 59:1; 63:5; 66:18) and saving righteousness to save His people from ruin (cf. 11:5; 45:8; 51:6; 56:1; 59:9; 61:10). God would give them the Redeemer they needed.

---

[47] Wolf, *Interpreting Isaiah*, 233.
[48] Pfeiffer, *The Wycliffe Bible Commentary: Old Testament*, Is 59:9.

Second reminder: God's promise of a Redeemer (vv. 17-21)

Isaiah describes this promised Redeemer as One who would not only save and restore His people, but also bring judgment upon those who were seeking the destruction of the nation. Isaiah gives us three descriptions of the Redeemer: the Redeemer's motivation (v. 17), the Redeemer's wrath (vv. 18-19), and the Redeemer's salvation (vv. 20-11).

The description of the Redeemer's motivation (v. 17). Isaiah describes the coming Redeemer with four kinds of battle equipping images (cf. Eph. 6:13-17). The breastplate of righteousness (*tsedeqah*) stresses the faithfulness of God to His people. The helmet of salvation (*yeshuah*) emphasizes God's activity to save "on behalf of those unjustly treated" (cf. 49:24-26).[49] The garments of vengeance (*naqam*) remind us God hates evil, especially when it is being unjustly perpetrated against His own people (cf. Isa. 34:8; 63:1ff.; 2 Thess. 1:6-9; Rev. 19:11ff.), and the mantle of zeal (*qin'ah*) reminds us of the passion that God has for His own people (Isa. 9:7; 11:13; 26:11; 37:32; 42:13; 63:15; Zech. 1:14; 8:2).[50]

The description of the Redeemer's wrath (vv. 18-19). The holy character of God and His faithfulness to His people are going to come to full expression when He pours out His wrath on those nations seeking the destruction of Israel in the Day of the Lord. Four times God tells how He will bring a wrathful judgment on the nations, all according to the evil of those nations.[51] Full recompense will come to those nations, even those in the western edges of the known world—the oft-cited "coastlands" (*'iy*) who, as we see many times, will also be the objects of saving grace (v. 18; cf. 11:11; 13:22; 20:6; 23:2, 6; 24:15; 34:14; 40:15; 41:1, 5; 42:4; 42:10, 12, 15; 49:1; 50:1; 51:5; 59:18; 60:9; 66:1, 19).

The result of God's eschatological judgments will be that the whole world will know that the God of Israel is the true and living God. Isaiah says, "So they will fear the name of the Lord from the west and His glory from the rising of the sun, for He will come like a rushing stream which the wind of the Lord drives" (v. 19; cf. Isa. 5:16; 30:7; 35:2; 40:5; 42:12; 45:6, 22-25; 52:10; Ezek. 20:41; 38:23; 39:7, 25). Ezekiel reveals that this worldwide recognition of Yahweh will take place at the end of the age when God brings a final restoration of Israel:

---

[49] Grogan, "Isaiah," 326.

[50] Wolf, *Interpreting Isaiah*, 234.

[51] To repay (*shalam*) means to make full and whole repayment. The idea of recompense (*gemul*) is that of requital and retribution (35:4; 66:6). In the end, every man will be perfectly judged according to his deeds (Ecc. 12:13-14; Rev. 20:11-15).

I will vindicate the holiness of My great name which has been profaned among the nations,[52] which you have profaned in their midst. Then the nations will know that I am the Lord, declares the Lord God when I prove Myself holy among you in their sight. For I will take you from the nations, gather you from all the lands and bring you into your own land. Then I will sprinkle clean water on you, and you will be clean; I will cleanse you from all your filthiness and from all your idols" (Ezek. 36:23-25; cf. Matt. 6:9-10).

Here is a precious truth we must not forget: Jesus Christ is returning very soon to establish the kingdom of God on this earth, and He will rule it in perfect righteousness. When that day comes, the whole earth will recognize that He alone is Lord (Zech. 14:9).

The description of the Redeemer's salvation (vv. 20-21). In verses 18-19, the emphasis on Christ's return was on the negative aspect of wrath, but in verses 20-21 the focus shifts to the positive aspect of God's saving grace. Israel had no one who could save them (v. 16), so God Himself had to become their Redeemer (*Go'el*).[53] This prophecy is fulfilled in none other than Jesus Christ. For this reason, Paul quotes Isaiah 59 in Romans 11:26 telling us that it is Jesus who will fulfill this prophecy when He returns to this world to bring redemption to every one of God's saints (v. 20). The promise of covenant restoration continues:

As for Me, this is My covenant with them, says the Lord: My Spirit which is upon you, and My words which I have put in your mouth shall not depart from your mouth, nor from the mouth of your offspring, nor from the mouth of your offspring's offspring, says the Lord, from now and forever (v. 21; cf. 11:9; 45:6; 54:13; Jer. 24:7; 31:34; Hab. 2:14).

In ages past, Israel fell into terrible apostasy, but the good news is that her apostasy is not too great for the redeeming grace of Yahweh, energized by the powerful work of the Spirit in His elect saints (cf. Isa. 32:15-19; 43:18; 44:3-5; Zech. 12:10; 13:1). The Lord will restore His fallen nation under a New

---

[52] This is precisely what Jesus told us we should pray for when He told the disciples, "Pray, then, in this way: Our Father who is in heaven, hallowed be Your name, Your kingdom come, Your will be done on earth as it is in heaven" (Matt. 6:9-10).
[53] As noted earlier, the idea of God being Israel's "Redeemer" (participle *Go'el*) flows out of the idea of the near relative who steps in to rescue His close relative from ruin, an oft-used term in Isaiah (Isa. 41:14; 43:1, 14; 44:6, 22-24; 47:4; 48:17, 20; 49:7, 26; 52:3, 9 [verbal form]; 54:5, 8; 60:16; 63:9, 16; cf. Exod. 6:6; 15:13; Ruth 2:2; 3:9, 12; 4:1, 3, 4, 6, 8, 14).

Covenant that will never get broken as did the first covenant (cf. Isa. 55:1-3; 61:8; Jer. 31:31-34; Ezek. 16:60; 34:25; 37:26; Hos. 2:14-23). The covenant is unbreakable, for it is assured by the redeeming grace of Yahweh in the lives of His redeemed saints.

Summary and application

Is there any hope at all for this mess that we call home (the world)? Is there any hope for deliverance from the wars, the fighting, the killing, the sickness and the death that we call a natural part of life? The answer is Yes, there is hope. That hope, however, does not come from our own abilities. The only hope we have lies in God's Redeemer, the Lord Jesus Christ.

THE FUTURE GLORY AND PEACE OF ZION (60:1-22)

Chapter 59 showed us that a Redeemer is coming for those who turn from their transgression, but what will their future look like? Chapter 60 continues to unfold the future glory and peace that will belong to Zion and all who dwell in her. Smith notes:

> The themes in 60:1–63:6 continue and expand ideas already introduced in 1–59, creating continuity with and the expansion of earlier visions of the eschatological situation in Zion. Some of the earlier themes that are picked up in this section include (a) the gathering of the sons of Israel in 60:4 is connected to the same idea in 11:11–12; 43:5–6; 49:18, 22; 54:7b; (b) the gates being open and never shut is found in both 60:11 and 45:1; (c) the knowledge that God is Savior, Redeemer, the Mighty One of Jacob is used in 60:16 and 41:14; 48:17; 49:7, 26; (d) the work of the Anointed One in 61:1–3 is similar to the work of the Servant in 49:8–9; (f) the preparation of the way in 62:10 appears to be based on imagery similar to what was used in 40:3; (g) God's coming with his recompense with him is found in 62:11 and 40:10; 59:18; and (h) God's wrath is poured out on the evil nations in 63:1–6 and 34:1–15; 59:15–18.[54]

Chapter 60 is continuing the same redemptive themes found throughout the whole prophecy, but clearly this chapter also introduces an "unparalleled glory and splendor" that God will bring to His city Zion.[55]

Chapter 60 reads as follows: "1 Arise, shine; for your light has come, and the glory of the Lord has risen upon you. 2 For behold, darkness will cover the earth and deep darkness the peoples, but the Lord will rise upon you and His

---

[54] Smith, *Isaiah 40-66*, 607–608.
[55] Wolf, *Interpreting Isaiah*, 235.

glory will appear upon you. 3 Nations will come to your light, and kings to the brightness of your rising. 4 Lift up your eyes round about and see; they all gather together, they come to you. Your sons will come from afar, and your daughters will be carried in the arms. 5 Then you will see and be radiant, and your heart will thrill and rejoice, because the abundance of the sea will be turned to you; the wealth of the nations will come to you. 6 A multitude of camels will cover you, the young camels of Midian and Ephah; all those from Sheba will come; they will bring gold and frankincense, and will bear good news of the praises of the Lord. 7 All the flocks of Kedar will be gathered together to you; the rams of Nebaioth will minister to you; they will go up with acceptance on My altar, and I shall glorify My glorious house. 8 Who are these who fly like a cloud and like the doves to their lattices? 9 Surely the coastlands will wait for Me, and the ships of Tarshish *will come* first to bring your sons from afar, their silver and their gold with them, for the name of the Lord your God, and for the Holy One of Israel because He has glorified you. 10 Foreigners will build up your walls, and their kings will minister to you, for in My wrath I struck you, and in My favor I have had compassion on you. 11 Your gates will be open continually; they will not be closed day or night, so that *men* may bring to you the wealth of the nations, with their kings led in procession. 12 For the nation and the kingdom which will not serve you will perish, and the nations will be utterly ruined. 13 The glory of Lebanon will come to you, the juniper, the box tree and the cypress together, to beautify the place of My sanctuary; and I shall make the place of My feet glorious. 14 The sons of those who afflicted you will come bowing to you, and all those who despised you will bow themselves at the soles of your feet; and they will call you the city of the Lord, the Zion of the Holy One of Israel. 15 Whereas you have been forsaken and hated with no one passing through, I will make you an everlasting pride, a joy from generation to generation. 16 You will also suck the milk of nations and suck the breast of kings. Then you will know that I, the Lord, am your Savior and your Redeemer, the Mighty One of Jacob. 17 Instead of bronze I will bring gold, and instead of iron I will bring silver, and instead of wood, bronze, and instead of stones, iron; and I will make peace your administrators and righteousness your overseers. 18 Violence will not be heard again in your land, nor devastation or destruction within your borders, but you will call your walls salvation, and your gates praise. 19 No longer will you have the sun for light by day, nor for brightness will the moon give you light, but you will have the Lord for an everlasting light, and your God for your glory. 20 Your sun will no longer set, nor will your moon wane, for you will have the Lord for an everlasting light, and the days of your mourning will be over. 21 Then all your people *will be* righteous. They will possess the land forever, the branch of My planting, the work of My hands, that I may be glorified. 22 The smallest one will become a clan, and the least one a mighty nation. I, the Lord, will hasten it in its time" (60:1-22).

In ancient times, the glory days of Zion would have been the days of David (ca. 1010-970 B.C.) and Solomon (ca. 970-931 B.C.). Those days were great, but they will be nothing in comparison to the millennial kingdom. God's promise to restored Zion is unprecedented favor that will make her greater than any time in ages past. We can break that greatness down into three particular promises to Zion: unprecedented glory (vv. 1-3), unprecedented growth (vv. 4-9), and unprecedented greatness (vv. 10-22).

First promise to Zion: Unprecedented glory (vv. 1-3)

Themes of restoration and glory dominate these last chapters of Isaiah.[56] The kingdom will bring a complete restoration that calls for great rejoicing, and for this reason God gives the command to Jerusalem, "Arise, shine; for your light has come, and the glory of the Lord has risen upon you" (v. 1; cf. 2:1-4; 4:2-6; 9:1-7; 24:23; 35; 40:1ff.).[57] At long last, the glory of the Lord has returned to Zion,[58] a restoration of glory that has been accomplished by God's sovereign grace through the return of Jesus Christ (Isa. 6:3; Mal. 4:2; John 12:37-41; Acts 1:11; Rev. 19:11ff.).

Darkness on the unsaved (v. 2a)

The return of Jesus Christ will bring blessings to the whole world, but not for those who were unwilling to turn to Christ. On these, "darkness will cover the earth, and deep darkness the peoples." Smith notes,

> Another motivation for shining [v. 1] is "because" (*kî*) there is a great need in this world for light and for the impact of God's salvation. At the time of God's brilliant appearing, the earth and all the people in it will be covered with darkness, doom, and hopelessness (cf. 9:1). . . . [T]he author is speaking of undefined circumstances in a distant eschatological era. The severity of that dark time is emphasized by its grip on the whole earth.[59]

Numerous prophetic passages tell us that during the Great Tribulation a

---

[56] Oswalt sees at least eight major themes: God saves His people; He gives light; He shares His glory with them; He draws the nations to Israel; He restores her children by the hands of the Gentiles; His grace stirs the Gentiles to bring their wealth; all who oppressed will now come in service Yahweh; Israel will both experience and exemplify the righteousness of YHWH (Oswalt, *The Book of Isaiah: Chapters 40-66*, 553).
[57] Both commands are feminine and directed to Zion.
[58] Ezekiel recorded the departure of the shekinah glory shortly before Solomon's temple was destroyed by Babylon in 586 B.C. (cf. Ezek. 10:1-3; 11:1-3), but he also prophesied that this glory would return in the kingdom (Ezek. 43:1ff.; 44:1ff.).
[59] Smith, *Isaiah 40-66*, 614.

massive portion of the world is going to seek Israel's destruction, but be brought to ruin by the direct intervention of the Messiah (Isa. 9:2-5; 10:25; 26:20-21; 63:1-6; Jer. 30:5; Ezek. 38-39; Dan. 7:23-28; 9:27; Joel 3:1-17; Zech. 12:1-9; 14:1ff.; Rev. 19:11-21).[60] Darkness will overtake the nations in the worst way possible.

Glory on Zion (vv. 2b-3)

In contrast to the darkness that will overwhelm the nations, Isaiah says, "but the Lord will rise upon you and His glory will appear upon you. Nations will come to your light, and kings to the brightness of your rising."[61] Malachi described this glorious coming of the Messiah by saying, "but for you who fear My name, the sun of righteousness will rise with healing in its wings" (Mal. 4:2). The glory of the Lord is coming to Israel in the person of Jesus Christ, and His presence will draw all the nations to come and worship the King (v. 3; cf. 45:22-25; 52:15; Phil. 2:9-11).

Second promise to Zion: Unprecedented growth (vv. 4-9)

Israel's restoration will also include a time of unprecedent growth within the nation that will impact all the families of the earth (Gen. 12:1-3). Isaiah highlights three kinds of such growth and its impact.

Unprecedented growth in the population (v. 4)

God tells Zion to look all around at the restoration of her scattered children from all over the earth (Isa. 9:3; 10:20-23; 11:11-16; 27:12-13; 37:4, 31; 46:3; 49:18-23; 54:1ff.; cf. Jer. 33:7; Ezek. 20:36-38; 36:19-25; 37:21; 39:25-29; Zech. 10:8-12; Matt. 24:31). Some have found it hard to believe that this restoration could take place, but we know it will, for God has spoken and God never lies, and nothing is impossible for Him (Jer. 32:17, 27; Rom. 11:23-36).

Unprecedented growth in material wealth (vv. 5-7)

Israel had times of great prosperity in the days of David and Solomon (cf. 1 Kings 4; 10:1-9). However, none of that prosperity will compare with the great wealth that will come to Israel in the kingdom of God.

---

[60] Great numbers of unsaved Gentiles will fall during the tribulation period, but we know that God has a massive remnant of Gentiles whom He will save out of that darkness (cf. e.g., Isa. 2:2-4; 11:10; Zech. 8:20-23; Matt. 8:11; 25:31-46; Rev. 7:9-17).

[61] We see this term "brightness" (*nogah*) numerous times in Isaiah (4:5; 50:10; 60:3, 19; 62:1) (Oswalt, *The Book of Isaiah: Chapters 40-66*, 536, n. 19).

Wealth from the wider Gentile world (v. 5). Israel will see an unprecedented growth in wealth that comes not only from her own productivity, but also from an influx of wealth that flows to her from all the nations (Isa. 18:7; 45:14; 60:11; 61:6; 66:12; cf. Ps. 72; Hag. 2:7; Zech. 6:9ff.; 14:14). Zion will be radiant and rejoice over these blessings.

Wealth from the Arab world (vv. 6-7). Isaiah continues to describe this great influx of wealth, but all the places named in these two verses speak about the Arab world to the east and south of Israel, nations that have historically been hostile to Israel (v. 6; cf. ch. 21). Martin explains,

> Examples of the kinds of wealth to be brought are gold ... incense flocks ... rams and silver (Isa. 60:6–7, 9). Examples of the nations that will bring those riches are: (a) Midian, south of the Dead Sea; (b) Ephah, a branch of the Midianites as Midian was Ephah's father (Gen. 25:4; 1 Chron. 1:33); (c) Sheba, probably the Sabeans in southwest Arabia (see comments on Seba in Isa. 43:3); (d) Kedar in northern Arabia; (e) Nebaioth, apparently an Arabian tribe (Nebaioth was Ishmael's eldest son, Gen. 25:13).[62]

Not only will the grateful nations come with gifts, but God also says, "they will go up with acceptance on My altar, and I shall glorify My glorious house," i.e., the millennial temple (v. 7; cf. Ezek. 40-42).[63]

Unprecedented growth in worldwide spiritual influence (vv. 8-9)

Turning from those of the east, Isaiah now turns to the west and describes the vision of these incoming ships like a huge covey of doves on the horizon flying into Israel (v. 8). These are none other than the well-known ships of Tarshish (Spain),[64] commercial ships from ancient times that will one day be coming to Israel from the coastlands (*'iyyim*) to bring the wealth of the nation (v. 9; cf. Isa. 11:11; 13:22; 20:6; 23:2, 6; 24:15; 34:14; 40:15; 41:1, 5; 42:4, 10, 12, 15;

---

[62] Martin, "Isaiah," 1115.

[63] Hughes, *Tyndale Concise Bible Commentary*, 268.

[64] Tarshish, also known as Tartessus, was located "in southwest Spain, at the mouth of the Guadalquivir, near Gibraltar. It includes the adjoining region: a Phoenician colony; hence its connection with Palestine and the Bible (2 Ch 9:21). The name was also used in a wide sense for *the farthest west*, as our West Indies (Is 66:19; Ps 48:7; 72:10). 'Ships of Tarshish' became the phrase for *richly laden* and *far-voyaging* vessels" (Robert Jamieson, A. R. Fausset, and David Brown, *Commentary Critical and Explanatory on the Whole Bible*, vol. 1, cited in electronic form with Logos Libronix [Oak Harbor, WA: Logos Research Systems, Inc., 1997], 431).

49:1; 50:1; 51:5; 59:18; ; 60:9; 66:1, 19). These so-called "ships of Tarshish" were so prominent in the ancient world that they call for some additional explanation (Isa. 2:16; 23:1, 14; 60:9; 1 Kings 10:22; Ps. 48:7). ISBE suggests that their home base and origin might have been in the east and not in Spain (as held by many):

> Tarshish was a descendant of Javan (Gen. 10:4; 1 Ch. 1:7), grouped with Elishah, Kittim, and Dodanim (Rodanim in 1 Ch. 1:7). These have been identified with peoples and places in the Mediterreanean [sic] area near Greece, including a portion of North Africa, Crete, Cyprus, and Rhodes. Jonah attempted to flee to Tarshish, taking a ship from Joppa (Jonah 1:3; 4:2), hence Tarshish was on a Mediterranean ship lane. The juxtaposition of Put, Lud, Tubal, and Javan (Isa. 66:19) again suggests that Tarshish was somewhere in the eastern Mediterranean region. Products of Tarshish included silver (Jer. 10:6), iron, and tin, which were imported by Tyre (Ezk. 27:12)—minerals that came from Asia Minor and the islands of Cyprus and Crete. Various places have been suggested: Tartessos in Spain, Tyrseni (Etruscans) in Italy, Carthage in North Africa, and Tarsus in Cilicia—to name just four. Tarshish is also mentioned in connection with Sheba, Seba, and Dedan (Ps. 72:10; Isa. 60:9; Ezk. 38:13). Ships were constructed in Ezion-geber to go to Tarshish (2 Ch. 20:30). It is, of course, possible to understand the term "ships of Tarshish" as describing a *kind* of ship, e.g., an ore ship or refinery ship (cf. W. F. Albright, BASOR, 83 [Oct. 1941], 14ff), and thus to agree that, even if Tarshish was in the Mediterranean, such a ship could be built on the Gulf of Aqabah for service in Arabia and east Africa. But this ignores the clear statement in 2 Ch. 20:36, "ships to go to Tarshish," and the implications of passages that connected Tarshish with Sheba and other locations in south Arabia. Furthermore, Solomon's fleet, stationed at Ezion-geber, saw service on the Red Sea and brought back products of Arabia and east Africa: gold, silver, ivory, apes, and peacocks (or baboons) (1 K. 10:22). It seems reasonable to conclude that there was a place, or a descriptive word for such a place, located in Arabia or east Africa, probably on the Red Sea.[65]

The point to note is that any statement about Ships of Tarshish bringing both Israelites and Gentile wealth to Israel tells us that Israel's eschatological restoration will be of a magnitude such as the world has never seen. Dockery explains that,

> The Lord's glorious return would begin a bright new era for Jerusalem (60:1–22). The city's exiled population would return, and nations would

---

[65] W. S. Lasor, "Tarshish," ed. Geoffrey W. Bromiley, *The International Standard Bible Encyclopedia, Revised*, cited in electronic form with Logos Libronix (Wm. B. Eerdmans, 1979–1988), 734.

bring their wealth as tribute to the Lord. Signs of the Lord's renewed blessing would be everywhere.[66]

In view of the widespread hatred of Israel today, it is hard for many to believe that these prophecies will ever be fulfilled, but God has spoken them, so we can be certain He will fulfill them. All these promises were meant to encourage Israel to not give up hope (cf. Zech. 8:13-23).

Third promise: Unprecedented greatness (vv. 10-22)

The kingdom of God is going to bring radical changes to this world, and for Israel it will include the fulfillment of a multitude of restoration promises. Pfeiffer explains, "Here the Scripture gives us a picture of the glory and peace of Millennial Zion, as Gentile believers join hands with Jewish believers to establish the new theocracy."[67] These promises continue in verse 10.

Great help from the Gentiles (v. 10)

We have already seen a number of statements that the Gentiles are going to be gracious to Israel in the Millennium. This idea continues with the promise that they will help restore the fallen nation (cf. Isa. 14:1; 49:23; 61:5).[68] Zechariah repeated this promise: "Those who are far off will come and build the temple of the Lord. Then you will know that the Lord of hosts has sent me to you [perhaps the Spirit of Messiah speaking through Zechariah], and it will take place if you completely obey the Lord your God" (Zech. 6:15). The age of wrath (*qetseph*) was hard on Israel (cf. 54:8), but the age of compassion (*rechem*) will eclipse it when God's grace turns Israel to Christ.

Great riches to restore a fallen nation (vv. 11-13)

Human history shows that rich and powerful nations last for a time, but eventually get overthrown by other nations. God's promise to Israel is that this will not happen to her (cf. Dan. 2:44-45; 7:14, 27).

The promise of peace (v. 11). In the ancient world, strong walls and gates were essential elements of defense. One historical source explains,

> The gates of walled cities were shut at sundown, or shortly thereafter, but always before dark. Travelers nearing cities would hurry as they saw the

---

[66] David S. Dockery, ed., *Holman Bible Handbook*, cited in electronic form with Logos Libronix (Nashville, TN: Holman Bible Publishers, 1992), 406.
[67] Pfeiffer, *The Wycliffe Bible Commentary: Old Testament*, Is 60:10.
[68] The term "to minister" (*sharath*) is often used in cultic contexts (e.g., Exod. 28:35), but it can also be used in a secular sense as here (cf. e.g., Gen. 39:4, et al.).

shadows lengthening so that they would reach the city before the gates closed.[69]

God's promise to Israel is that her peace and prosperity will last forever, and she will not even need to close her gates at nighttime in such a way that would interrupt the flow of goods coming in from the Gentile nations.[70]

The promise of protection (vv. 12-13). Lest Israel doubt these promises, God assures her that never again will any nation rise up against her, for the Lord would destroy them should they attempt it (v. 12).[71] Rather, these Gentile nations who have come to Jesus Christ will come in service by bringing those supplies that are needed for restoration of the land, especially the temple: "The glory of Lebanon will come to you, the juniper, the box tree and the cypress together to beautify the place of My sanctuary, and I shall make the place of My feet glorious" (v. 13; cf. 1 Chron. 28:2; Pss. 99:5; 132:7; Ezek. 43:6-7).[72]

Great gratitude from a redeemed world (vv. 14-16)

God's promise is that the ages of persecution for bearing the name of Yahweh will come to an end, and Israel will worship without fear.[73]

The promise of preeminence (v. 14). In the Millennium, Israel will have a central position, but this should not be understood to mean that the Gentiles will have an inferior spiritual status. Properly understood, verse 14 is showing us that all mankind will recognize the special place that Israel has had in being a mediator of blessing to the human race (Isa. 19:18-25; 41:11; 45:14, 24; cf. Gen. 12:3; 22:18; 26:4; 28:14). Those who used to hate and curse the Jews, will now have gratitude, and when they look at Jerusalem, they will call it the city of the Lord, the Zion of the Holy One of Israel (Pss. 48:2; 132:13-18; Matt. 5:35).[74]

---

[69] James M. Freeman and Harold J. Chadwick, *Manners & Customs of the Bible*, cited in electronic form with Logos Libronix (North Brunswick, NJ: Bridge-Logos Publishers, 1998), 365–366.

[70] Grogan, "Isaiah," 330. The idea of Gentile nations coming into Jerusalem carries no connotation of having been conquered, but that of willing service. John pulls from this imagery to show the absolute and perfect peace that will come in the New Heavens and New Earth (Rev. 21:25-26).

[71] The promise of utter ruin (*charab*, ruin, desolation) utilizes a forceful combination of the infinitive absolute followed by the finite verb.

[72] Lebanon was very rich in timber, but interestingly this verse mentions pines, the box tree (fir), and cypress, but not cedars for which it was particularly famous (cf. 1 Kings 5:10, 18).

[73] Zacharias, the father of John the Baptist, understood these promises of peace and removal of persecution (cf. Luke 1:67-79).

[74] Isaiah uses a favorite expression "Holy One of Israel" (cf. 1:4; 5:19, 24; 10:20; 12:6; 17:7; 30:11, 12, 15; 31:1; 37:23; 41:14; 43:3, 14; 45:11; 47:4; 48:17; 54:5; 60:14).

The promise of pride (vv. 15-16). God's promise is that the redeemed remnant of the Gentiles will no longer look with hatred on Zion,[75] but Zion will become a source of pride for the whole world (v. 15; cf. Zech. 8:13-23). From exile and captivity, these words must have been hard to believe, but God's promise is that Zion will become, "a source of joy for all the generations," a joy and exalted status that "characterizes the marvelous way God will transform his people and his holy city."[76]

The blessings become especially rich in verse 16 where God tells Zion, "You will also suck the milk of nations and suck the breast of kings; then you will know that I, the Lord, am your Savior and your Redeemer, the Mighty One of Jacob" (v. 16; cf. 49:23).[77] Martin notes,

> Much as a nursing child gets sustenance from its mother, so Israel will be sustained by the wealth of the nations (v. 16; cf. vv. 5, 11; 61:6). This blessing will cause Israel to recognize all the more that the Lord really is the unique God of the world, her Savior (see comments on 43:11), Redeemer (see comments on 41:14), and her Mighty One (cf. 49:26).[78]

The imagery is meant to assure Israel that even though she was previously at the lowest status, one day God will reverse it all.

Great restoration from ages of desolation (v. 17a)

God's promise is that one day He will reverse Israel's fortunes and bring them a restoration from ages of desolation (Jer. 30:3, 18; 31:23). Whatever they had previously lost will be replaced with something more precious. Oswalt gives the helpful reminder that even though we believe these promises to have a literal meaning behind them, we also recognize that these descriptions are pointing to something that is more than physical metals, but to the realm of spiritual blessings.[79]

Great peace (vv. 17b-18)

Israel's history has always been a struggle for survival. Oftentimes troubles

---

[75] The sad condition was caused by Israel's sin (Isa. 5:1-7; 6:11; 62:4; Jer. 29:18-20).

[76] Smith, *Isaiah 40-66*, 622.

[77] The language is very graphic and shows extreme privilege (cf. Deut. 33:19) (Young, *The Book of Isaiah, vol. 3*, 453). Many in the ancient world believed that a mark of greatness and exaltation was the privilege of suckling at the breast of a goddess (Oswalt, *The Book of Isaiah: Chapters 40-66*, 552).

[78] Martin, "Isaiah," 1115.

[79] Oswalt, *The Book of Isaiah: Chapters 40-66*, 556.

came from outside enemies, but the greatest threat always came from her own sins. God assures His people that one day He will purge every form of oppression, both from the outside as well as the inside.

Peace and righteousness will rule the land (v. 17b). One of the biggest problems Israel had was that of leaders who both tolerated and practiced evil ways (Isa. 5:20ff.; cf. Micah 7:1ff.). When the Messiah comes, this will never happen again (cf. Isa. 9:7; 11:1-5; 16:5; 32:1).

Righteous leaders will assure a righteous society (v. 18). With Christ ruling in righteousness, God's promise to Zion is, "violence will not be heard again in your land, nor devastation or destruction within your borders, but you will call your walls salvation, and your gates praise" (cf. 26:1-4; 33:20-22). All of the evil that had overtaken her in former ages will be gone forever, all by the redeeming grace of Christ (cf. 35:8-10).

Great grace (vv. 19-20)

God's promise is a perpetual glory through the presence of the Lord that is so bright that Zion will not even have need of the sun or moon (v. 19; cf. 2:5; 9:2; 30:26; 41:16; 45:25; Zech. 2:5).[80] The presence of the Lord will assure Israel that never again will they experience the darkness and sorrow of sin and curse (v. 20). Smith observes,

> The text now returns to the theme of God's glory as the light that will remove all darkness. This moves the topic back to the initial theme in 60:1–3, creating something of an inclusio in this chapter. The glory of God's presence will be so bright that the sun and moon will not be needed "again, any longer" (*'ôd*).... Isaiah 60:19 does not say that God will destroy or remove the sun and moon, just that they will be redundant and rather unnecessary in light of the wonderful light that proceeds from the glory of God.[81]

Great righteousness (vv. 21-22)

In these last two verses, Isaiah gives the assurance that great righteousness will come upon Zion and never again leave it. Her righteousness will be there from the very beginning (v. 21), and it will continue all throughout the ages (v. 22).

---

[80] The present cosmos will remain intact during the Millennium, but in the New Heavens and New Earth it will be recreated (Rev. 21:23; 22:5).

[81] Smith, *Isaiah 40-66*, 626.

A righteous beginning (v. 21). God's promise to Zion is, "Then all your people *will be* righteous; they will possess the land forever, the branch of My planting, the work of My hands that I may be glorified."[82] When Jesus restores Israel, the entire nation will experience restoration, but we must remember that it is only the saved remnant that enters the kingdom (Isa. 10:20-23; 35:8-10; Ezek. 20:36-38; Zech. 13:8-9; Rom. 9:27-28). God promises that this redeeming grace in the New Covenant will never be lost, for it is based on His gracious forgiveness (Isa. 55:3; 61:8; cf. Jer. 31:31-34).

A righteous continuation (v. 22). Because of God's sustaining grace, Israel has the assurance that they will prosper forever in their land. Isaiah says, "the smallest one will become a clan, and the least one a mighty nation. I, the Lord, will hasten it in its time." All of this is part of the precious promises to the patriarch Abraham (Gen. 12:1-3; 13:15; 15:18-21; 17:7-8; Isa. 49:8; 57:13; 61:7; Ps. 37; Matt. 5:5). Oswalt reminds us of the certainty: "Although it may take a long time for all things to be ready, nevertheless, when they are ready, God will suddenly bring it to pass."[83]

Summary and application

The Word of God is here to tell us how we can know the Lord and be saved from our sins. At a very practical level, prophetic Scripture is also here to encourage us to not grow weary in this sin-cursed world that often beats us down to the ground. Each one of us needs to believe the truth of God's promises and remember that no matter how bad this world might beat us down, His saving promises will never fail us.

THE SPIRIT-FILLED MESSIAH (61:1-11)

If there is one thing all men need, it is hope. Hope is what strengthens us, and hope is what enables us to continue on when life is hard and we feel like giving up (Heb. 6:19-20). Israel was a nation that desperately needed hope. Both Scripture and life show us that sometimes the things that people hope in fail them.[84] On the other hand, those who hope in the Lord and His promises will never be disappointed (Isa. 8:13-14; 26:3-4; 28:16; 40:31; cf. Rom. 9:33; 10:11; 1 Pet. 2:6). The only true hope is God's Spirit-filled Messiah, the One who is the major focus on chapter 61.

---

[82] This is God's plant that will never die (cf. 4:1; 6:13), the work of God's hands (cf. 29:23; 43:7; 45:11; 64:8), a work of grace that never fails (Grogan, "Isaiah," 331).

[83] Oswalt, *The Book of Isaiah: Chapters 40-66*, 561.

[84] False sources of trust could include things like political leaders, military might, personal strength, good looks, sharp intellect, or accumulated wealth, etc.

Chapter 61 reads as follows: "1 The Spirit of the Lord God is upon me, because the Lord has anointed me to bring good news to the afflicted. He has sent me to bind up the brokenhearted, to proclaim liberty to captives and freedom to prisoners, 2 to proclaim the favorable year of the Lord, and the day of vengeance of our God, to comfort all who mourn, 3 to grant those who mourn *in* Zion, giving them a garland instead of ashes, the oil of gladness instead of mourning, the mantle of praise instead of a spirit of fainting. So, they will be called oaks of righteousness, the planting of the Lord, that He may be glorified. 4 Then they will rebuild the ancient ruins; they will raise up the former devastations, and they will repair the ruined cities, the desolations of many generations. 5 Strangers will stand and pasture your flocks, and foreigners will be your farmers and your vinedressers. 6 But you will be called the priests of the Lord. You will be spoken of *as* ministers of our God. You will eat the wealth of nations, and in their riches you will boast. 7 Instead of your shame *you will have a* double *portion,* and *instead of* humiliation they will shout for joy over their portion. Therefore, they will possess a double *portion* in their land; everlasting joy will be theirs. 8 For I, the Lord, love justice; I hate robbery in the burnt offering. And I will faithfully give them their recompense and make an everlasting covenant with them. 9 Then their offspring will be known among the nations, and their descendants in the midst of the peoples. All who see them will recognize them because they are the offspring *whom* the Lord has blessed. 10 I will rejoice greatly in the Lord; My soul will exult in my God, for He has clothed me with garments of salvation; He has wrapped me with a robe of righteousness, as a bridegroom decks himself with a garland, and as a bride adorns herself with her jewels. 11 For as the earth brings forth its sprouts, and as a garden causes the things sown in it to spring up, so the Lord God will cause righteousness and praise to spring up before all the nations" (61:1-11).

Isaiah 61 reminds us that the one thing that will never disappoint us is God's Spirit-anointed and Spirit-filled Servant. With a prophetic focus on Jesus Christ who fulfills this prophecy, Isaiah 61 shows us three reasons why we can find hope in the promises of God and never be put to shame.

First reason for hope: The ministry of God's anointed One (vv. 1-3)

The first section of this chapter opens up with the Spirit of Christ declaring, "The Spirit of the Lord God is upon me, because the Lord has anointed me."[85] One source explains that the process of anointing consisted of the custom of,

---

[85] Jesus identifies Himself as the One who fulfills this prophecy (Luke 4:18-19). It was "the Lord God" (*'Adonay Yahweh*) who placed His Spirit onto Him (Isa. 50:4-5, 7-9), an anointing we that came upon Jesus at His baptism (Matt. 3:16-17; Mark 1:10; Luke 3:22; John 1:31-34).

smearing or pouring oil on a person or object. . . . Dignitaries, especially priests, were anointed before they assumed office (40:13–15); this rite symbolized their consecration (e.g., Lev. 8:12). Some of the prophets were anointed as well (Elisha, 1 Kgs. 19:16). . . . It was important that Israel's kings be anointed, thus signifying royal competence—e.g., Saul (1 Sam. 10:1), David (16:3, 12–13), Solomon (1 Kgs. 1:39). In the Old Testament they were called the Lord's anointed (Heb. *māšîah*), a title applied specifically to Saul (1 Sam. 24:6; 26:9–11; 2 Sam. 1:14, 16), David (1 Sam. 16:6; 2 Sam. 23:1), and Solomon (2 Chr. 6:42). Isaiah uses it for Cyrus (Isa. 45:1), as does perhaps the author of Daniel (Dan. 9:25). In the Psalms it is a general title for the king (e.g., Ps. 18:50). As such the Old Testament kings may be said to prefigure the great Anointed One, Jesus Christ.[86]

As noted by Myers above, it is only several particular passages in the Old Testament that use the verb "to anoint" (*mashach*) or the adjective "anointed" (*mashiyach*) to speak about the promised Son of God (1 Sam. 2:10; Isa. 61:1; Dan. 9:25, 26; cf. John 1:41, 49; 4:25; Matt. 16:16, 20; 26:63-64; John 11:27; Isa. 11:2; 42:1; 59:21).[87] This passage is one of the ones that tells us that God anointed and sent His Servant to come and accomplish God's saving purposes. Seven of these purposes can be seen in verses 1-3.

First purpose (v. 1a)

Here in verse 1, the Messiah says that the first purpose of His coming is to bring good news to the afflicted. The afflicted (*'anaw*; cf. Isa. 11:4; 29:19; 32:7) refers to the people of Israel who have been invaded by enemy armies, trampled down, and taken into captivity. Oftentimes, this term focuses especially on the believing remnant—the down-trodden believers who always seem to receive the brunt of harsh treatment from an unsaved world (Zeph. 3:12; Zech. 11:7; Matt. 5:3). This passage has application to the way that God brings good news to the afflicted at both the first coming and second coming of Jesus Christ. Hughes explains, "Isaiah 61 revealed that the Messiah, who ministered salvation at his first coming, will minister comfort for redeemed Israel at his second coming."[88]

Good news at His first coming. The Messiah's ministry is to bring good

---

[86] Allen C. Myers, *The Eerdmans Bible Dictionary*, cited in electronic form with Logos Libronix (Grand Rapids, MI: Eerdmans, 1987), 58.
[87] Even *Mashiyach* is commonly used to refer to Jesus (usually with the Greek translation *Christos* in the NT), it is not often used in this sense in the OT.
[88] Hughes, *Tyndale Bible Commentary*, 268.

news,[89] the good news that the day of deliverance has finally arrived (cf. Matt. 4:12-17; 11:2-6; Luke 1:67-79; 4:18-19; 7:22). Earlier in the second Servant Song we read, "Shout for joy, O heavens! And rejoice, O earth! Break forth into joyful shouting, O mountains! For the Lord has comforted His people *and will have compassion on His afflicted*" (Isa. 49:13; cf. 57:18). These promises will see final realization when Christ returns, but they had an element of fulfillment at the first coming in that Christ was the promised One who had come to announce good news.

Good news at His second coming. Jesus read this passage in the synagogue and applied it to Himself (Luke 4:18-19), for He is the One who fulfills the prophecy. However, a proper understanding of the meaning of Isaiah 61 must take into account the reality that God's plan for Christ first had to include His rejection and crucifixion at His first coming (cf. Isa. 52:13-53:12) so that according to the plan of God the ultimate fulfillment of this passage would not take place until His second coming (cf. Luke 24:25-26; Acts 2:23; 4:27-28).[90]

Second purpose (v. 1b)

Secondly, God sent His anointed Servant to bind up (*chabash*) the brokenhearted. The Servant is on a mission to bandage up broken lives (cf. 57:15). In the first Servant Song God said, "a bruised reed He will not break, and a dimly burning wick He will not extinguish" (Isa. 42:3). That is, His mission is to bandage up lives ravaged by sin (Isa. 1:5-6; 30:26).[91]

Third purpose (v. 1c)

God's people were in bondage and needed to be set free. The Messiah's third purpose is to proclaim *liberty* (*deror*, release) to captives and freedom to prisoners, the kind of release one sees in the Year of Jubilee (Lev. 25:10; cf. Isa. 49:8; 63:4).[92] Once again, we see that a literal fulfilling of these words has significance in at least two levels.

---

[89] This expression good news is a favorite term for Isaiah (Piel inf. of *basar*, to bring good news; cf. Isaiah's numerous uses of this term, the term translated by *euaggelizomai* in Greek: 9:19; 10:18; 17:4; 22:13; ; 31:3; 40:5, 6, 9; 41:27; 44:16, 19; 49:26; 52:7; 58:7; 60:6; 61:1; 65:4; 66:16, 17, 23, 24).

[90] Smith, *Isaiah 40-66*, 634.

[91] Grogan, "Isaiah," 333.

[92] Back in Isaiah 42:7 in the first Servant Song, Isaiah promised that the anointed One would "open blind eyes…[and] bring out prisoners from the dungeon and those who dwell in darkness from the prison."

A literal fulfilling in the original setting. The literal aspect of this prophecy revolves around the role of Messiah in setting His people free from bondage to invading powers, the most-immediate way this passage would be understood by the nation (Isa. 42:22; 49:9; 51:14). Kidner explains, "The setting continues to be the captivity, viewed in turn from Babylon (1b) and the ruined Jerusalem (3). To its first hearers the promise would be as literal as the earlier threat of exile (*cf.* 39:6)."[93]

A literal fulfilling at a universal level. The final fulfilling of these words awaits the second coming of Christ, but again, the Word of God also makes it clear that we should recognize a wider, spiritual principle in these promises as well (cf. John 8:31-36).

Fourth purpose (v. 2a)

The Messiah is to proclaim the favorable year of the Lord. The language reminds us of the Year of Jubilee command to release all debts and set all prisoners and slaves free (Isa. 49:8; 63:4; cf. Lev. 25:10; 27:24; Jer. 34:8-10; Ezek. 46:17). This Old Testament command had a literal meaning for the nation of Israel, but as we see it also has an ultimate and final fulfilling in the redeeming work of Jesus Christ.

Fifth purpose (v. 2b)

The Son of God has a ministry that is not only to save His own people, but also to judge sinners. This passage reminds us of both truths.

A fulfillment that came with the incarnation. When Jesus read from the Isaiah scroll in Luke 4, He read up to 61:2a, but then He stopped, returned the scroll, sat down, and then told all the people in the synagogue that this portion of Isaiah that He had just read was fulfilled that day in their hearing. Interestingly, He did not read from the next clause which says that He has come to proclaim, "the day of vengeance of our God."[94]

A fulfillment that awaits the second coming. The Son of God has a ministry to not only save His people,[95] but also to bring vengeance [*naqam*] on all who refuse to repent, especially those who had tried to harm His people (Isa.

---

[93] Kidner, "Isaiah," 667.

[94] The context makes it clear that the terms "year" and "day" stand parallel to each other (Young, *The Book of Isaiah, vol. 3*, 460).

[95] I.e., to gather His wheat into His barn (Matt. 3:11-12).

34:8; 35:4; 47:3; 63:4; cf. Mic. 5:14, 15).[96] Vengeance may seem harsh to some, but it reminds us that God is holy and must judge sin, especially of those who persecute His people (2 Thess. 1:6-9; Rev. 16:4-7; 19:11-21). TWOT explains,

> The concept of divine vengeance must be understood in the light of OT teaching about the holiness and justice of God and its effect on man as a sinner. . . . God cannot be true to his character of holiness and justice if he allows sin and rebellion to go unpunished. . . . The Bible balances the fury of God's vengeance against the sinner with greatness of his mercy on those whom he redeems from sin. God's vengeance must never be viewed apart from his purpose to show mercy.[97]

The return of Christ is going to bring horrific judgment to all unsaved sinners. Men do well to turn to God before that day comes and it is too late.

Sixth and seventh purposes (vv. 2c-3)

Isaiah speaks of two final purposes for the coming Messiah. Both of them encourage us with the promise of restoration in the kingdom of God.

A God who comforts (v. 2c). Once again, Isaiah uses this precious term "to comfort" (*nacham*).[98] To the reader of the Hebrew text, Isaiah's word play jumps out in that the word "vengeance" comes from *naqam* and the word "comfort" comes from the homonym *nacham*. Our God is a God who delights in comforting His hurting people. Jesus once said,

> Come to Me, all who are weary and heavy-laden, and I will give you rest. Take My yoke upon you and learn from Me, for I am gentle and humble in heart, and you will find rest for your souls, for My yoke is easy and My burden is light (Matt. 11:28-30).

God's promise is comfort in the kingdom. Jesus Himself said, "Blessed are those who mourn, for they shall be comforted" (Matt. 5:4).

A God who replaces mourning with joy (v. 3). Agony and sorrow overtook Israel in the Babylonian exile, an agony and sorrow that has never been fully rectified. The promise here is that of a colorful and poetic illustration of

---

[96] I.e., to burn up the chaff with unquenchable fire (cf. Matt. 3:11-12).
[97] Elmer B. Smick, "*nqm*," ed. R. Laird Harris, Gleason L. Archer Jr., and Bruce K. Waltke, *Theological Wordbook of the Old Testament*, cited in electronic form with Logos Libronix (Chicago: Moody Press, 1999), 598–599.
[98] Cf. Isa 12:1; 40:1; 49:13; 51:3, 12; 52:9; 54:11; 66:13; Luke 2:25.

the full reversal of all such miseries.[99] At long last, God will receive the glory He deserves from Israel, all because of the redeeming work of Christ (Isa. 45:24-25; Phil. 2:5-11). Here is a precious truth: Israel does have a hope.

Second reason for hope: The impact of God's anointed One (vv. 4-9)

God promised Israel a total restoration of all that had been lost, but the truth is that God's grace is going to transform the whole world (Rom. 8:18ff.).

The impact on the Gentile world (vv. 4-5)

Isaiah tells us that a redeemed Gentile world is going to help restore devastated Israel. Two declarations make this truth clear.

First declaration of Gentile assistance (v. 4). In context, the "they" is best understood as being the people of Israel who are setting out to restore their devastated nation (Isa. 10:23; Dan. 9:27). As we see in other passages, the Gentile world is going to be active in providing wealth to help make restoration a reality (Isa. 60:3-14; Hag. 2:6-9; Zech. 6:9-15; 14:14).

The promises of Israel's restoration (both physically and spiritually) are literal and true, and no one should make the error of spiritualizing these promises by saying that they are fulfilled in the church. One such illustration comes from Young who says that this speaks about, "the building up of the Church from the ravages sin has made throughout the ages."[100] God's Word says otherwise: "They will resettle the desolate cities" (Isa. 54:3). "Those from among you will rebuild the ancient ruins. You will raise up the age-old foundations, and you will be called the repairer of the breach, the restorer of the streets in which to dwell" (Isa. 58:12; cf. Jer. 30:3, 18; 31:23). To the doubter, God says, "Behold, I am the Lord, the God of all flesh; is anything too difficult for Me?" (Jer. 32:27).

Second declaration of Gentile assistance (v. 5). The Gentile nations are mentioned in verse 5 where it says, "Strangers will stand and pasture your flocks, and foreigners will be your farmers and your vinedressers." This verse is not teaching that the world becomes a slave to Israel, but that believing Gentiles will come into the covenant nation to both help restore it, and also to become

---

[99] A garland (*pe'er*) is an ornamental headdress (61:10), and they will put it on instead of ashes (*epher*), the kind of thing you throw on your head when mourning. Each promise points to the great reversal God will bring: oil of gladness (Pss. 23:5; 45:7; 104:15), mantle of praise (Isa. 42:8, 10; 43:21; 48:9; 60:18; 61:11; 62:7), oaks of righteousness planted by the Lord (Isa. 1:29-31; 60:21).
[100] Young, *The Book of Isaiah, vol. 3*, 462.

a part of that nation (cf. 56:3; 60:10; 66:18-20). Redeemed Gentiles will long to be part of the covenant nation (Isa. 14:1; cf. Zech. 8:20-23), and when they come, they will serve in whatever way they are able. Smith comments, "There is no indication that this involves any kind of forced labor or revenge against the nation; rather, one should assume that this service will be done out of gratitude, thankfulness, and cooperation."[101]

The impact on Israel (vv. 6-9)

The impact of the Messiah's grace on Israel will be something like never seen.[102] Isaiah singles out three ways that grace will impact Israel.

First impact on Israel: Acceptable service to God (v. 6a). God's call to Abraham always carried with it the idea that they were to be a light to the world (Gen. 12:1-3; 17:9; 18:19). The nation failed badly, but in the day of restoration God says, "But you will be called the priests of the Lord [*kohen*; cf. 66:21]; you will be spoken of *as* ministers [*mesharath*; cf. Ezek. 44:11] of our God." Martin writes,

> As a nation of priests each one will know the Lord, and have access to Him, and mediate on behalf of others, as did the Levitical priests. This was to be one of Israel's functions in the world (Ex. 19:6), but unfortunately she will not fully carry out that responsibility till in the Millennium.[103]

Second impact on Israel: Overflowing prosperity (vv. 6b-7). Invasion and exile brought Israel into a state of immense poverty, but in the kingdom, they will be flooded with prosperity, much of it coming from Gentile contributions to help them restore (v. 6b; cf. 60:5, 11).[104]

Grace will bring a radical reversal from ages of lack, and Israel will now have a double portion—the kind of blessing that characteristically went to the firstborn. Going along with the great physical blessings is the promise that curse and shame will be taken away forever (cf. Zech. 8:12-13), and in its place they will have everlasting joy (v. 7; cf. 35:10; 51:11-13).

Third impact on Israel: The purging of all wickedness (vv. 8-9). God assures Israel that because He loves what is good and holy and true, He will

---

[101] Smith, *Isaiah 40-66*, 637.

[102] See how Paul describes it in Romans 11:12, 15.

[103] Martin, "Isaiah," 1116.

[104] Young once again errs by saying, "the church will thrive on the goods of those who are converted to her" (Young, *The Book of Isaiah, vol. 3*, 463).

remove all forms of evil from them forever. This will be God's gracious recompense (*phelluah*, wage, payment; cf. 40:10; 49:4; 62:11) to His undeserving people. All of this will be part of the everlasting New Covenant (v. 8; Isa. 42:6-7; 49:6-8; 54:10; 55:3; 59:21; Jer. 31:31-34; 32:40; Ezek. 37:25-26; Hos. 2:14-18). In this restoration, the whole earth will recognize them as the nation that has been blessed by Yahweh (v. 9; cf. 65:23). These promises were to give hope.

Third reason for hope: The calling of God's anointed One (vv. 10-11)

Isaiah gives a third and final reason for Israel to hope. This one centers around God's calling for His anointed Servant, and the righteousness and praise that He will produce in Zion at His second advent.

The equipping of the anointed One (v. 10)

It is easy for those who live in America to lose focus of just how miserable this world can be. Americans certainly are impacted by the curse, but in some ways our physical blessings camouflage the ugliness of the curse. It was not so for captive Israel. Here in verse 10, we see a cry of joy to assure Israel that one day the Lord is going to purge all sorrow and replace it with joy. Scholars offer different opinions about who is speaking here, but this does not hinder us from understanding the main point.[105] Perhaps the best interpretation is that this is restored Zion. Keil notes that the common view in past days was to see it as Zion: "The Targum precedes this last turn with 'Thus saith Jerusalem.'"[106] Zion has now become the object of Yahweh's restoring salvation/righteousness,[107] and it is a beautiful salvation (58:8; 62:1). Earlier we saw similar words: "Awake, awake, clothe yourself in your strength, O Zion; clothe yourself in your beautiful garments, O Jerusalem, the holy city, for the uncircumcised and the unclean will no longer come into you" (Isa. 52:1; cf. 49:18; 62:1).

The victories of the anointed One (v. 11)

The promises are amazing, and once again we are reminded that they are certain, for they are God's Word. God conveys the certainty of this restoration with these words: "For as the earth brings forth its sprouts, and as a garden causes the things sown in it to spring up, so the Lord God will cause righteousness and praise to spring up before all the nations." Just as the earth makes

---

[105] Possibilities include Isaiah, the church (Young, 465), the penitent sinner (Pfeiffer, 61:10), or perhaps Zion (Grogan, 334; Oswalt, 574). One can make a reasonable case for saying that this is Christ Himself speaking, but the best option is probably that it is Zion speaking.

[106] Keil, *Commentary on the Old Testament*, 584.

[107] Note the emphatic "He" (God) has done it (v. 10), the Lord God (v. 11).

vegetation, so it is as certain that if God says He will do, He will certainly make it "spring up" (*tsamach*; cf. 4:2; Jer. 23:5; 33:15; Zech. 3:8; 6:12; 2 Sam. 23:5) and be fulfilled (cf. Isa. 55:8-13).[108] For this reason, Israel needs to put away all fear, and keep hoping and trusting in the Lord.

Summary and application

God's promises to Israel have direct application to every believer today. God has sworn a restoration to this world, so we can be sure He will do it. Furthermore, God has sworn that if we trust His Son, He will give us eternal forgiveness. This truth should give great peace and hope.

ZION'S GLORY BY ANSWERED PRAYER (62:1-12)

Chapter 62 continues many of the themes of chapters 60 and 61.[109] Here in chapter 62 we see an emphasis on the need for ongoing prayers.

Chapter 62 reads as follows: "1 For Zion's sake I will not keep silent, and for Jerusalem's sake I will not keep quiet, until her righteousness goes forth like brightness, and her salvation like a torch that is burning. 2 The nations will see your righteousness, and all kings your glory, and you will be called by a new name which the mouth of the Lord will designate. 3 You will also be a crown of beauty in the hand of the Lord, and a royal diadem in the hand of your God. 4 It will no longer be said to you, Forsaken, nor to your land will it any longer be said, Desolate, but you will be called, my delight is in her, and your land, Married," for the Lord delights in you, and *to Him* your land will be married. 5 For *as* a young man marries a virgin, *so* your sons will marry you, and *as* the bridegroom rejoices over the bride, *so* your God will rejoice over you. 6 On your walls, O Jerusalem, I have appointed watchmen; all day and all night they will never keep silent. You who remind the Lord, take no rest for yourselves, 7 and give Him no rest until He establishes and makes Jerusalem a praise in the earth. 8 The Lord has sworn by His right hand and by His strong arm, I will never again give your grain *as* food for your enemies, nor will foreigners drink your new wine for which you have labored. 9 But those who garner it will eat it and praise the Lord, and those who gather it will drink it in the courts of My sanctuary. 10 Go through, go through the gates; clear the way for the people; build up, build up the highway; remove the stones; lift up a standard over the peoples. 11 Behold, the Lord has proclaimed to the end of the earth, Say to the daughter of Zion, Lo, your salvation comes. Behold His reward is with Him, and His

---

[108] Young, *The Book of Isaiah, vol. 3*, 466.
[109] E.g., light, righteousness, salvation, marriage joy, deliverance from oppression, restoration of the land (Oswalt, *The Book of Isaiah: Chapters 40-66*, 577). Wolf sees ch. 62 as bringing a climax to all these themes (Wolf, *Interpreting Isaiah*, 240).

recompense before Him, 12 and they will call them, the holy people, the redeemed of the Lord, and you will be called, Sought out, a city not forsaken" (62:1-12).

Zion's future is one of great glory. Chapter 62 presents four major themes related to this future glory: the prayer for Zion's glory (v. 1), the metaphorical illustrations of Zion's glory (vv. 2-5), the intercession for Zion's glory (vv. 6-9), and the preparation for Zion's glory (vv. 10-12).

The prayer for Zion's glory (v. 1)

The Babylonian invasion brought the fall of Judah, an interruption to the Davidic dynasty, the destruction of Jerusalem, and the destruction of God's temple.[110] God had to judge the sin of His people, but exile and desolation are not the end of the story. Hughes explains, "While Israel experienced separation from God because of her sin (Isa. 50:1), a day is coming when the believing nation will be fully restored as Yahweh's bride (cf. 54:4–10)."[111] By His design, Israel did repopulate the land after the fall of Babylon, but they were again sent into dispersion by the Romans in A.D. 70. For over 1800 years Israel was driven from Zion and the city lay in ruins. The need is prayer for restoration.

The intensity of the prayer (v. 1a)

Here in verse 1, we see a two-fold, parallel prayer for the restoration of Zion's glory: "For Zion's sake I will not keep silent, and for Jerusalem's sake I will not keep quiet." Commentators have questioned who is speaking this prayer. Some believe this is Isaiah,[112] but many have seen it as being God Himself.[113] Martin notes, "Since 'I' in verse 6 seems to be the Father, verses 1–5 may also be spoken by Him."[114] The idea is clear: God Himself will never rest, and He will never take a passive place of rest until everything that He has promised is fully accomplished.[115]

---

[110] Three major dates are associated with these events: (1) the initial invasion and overthrow of Judah and the Davidic dynasty (605 B.C.), (2) the second wave of exile when Jehoiachin was taken captive (597 B.C.), the destruction of Jerusalem and Solomon's temple (586 B.C.).

[111] Hughes, *Tyndale Concise Bible Commentary*, 268.

[112] Grogan, "Isaiah," 336.

[113] Oswalt, *The Book of Isaiah: Chapters 40-66*, 578.

[114] Martin, "Isaiah," 1116.

[115] At different points in Isaiah, Israel has accused God of being silent or uncaring (e.g., 40:27; 42:20, 25; 49:14; 50:1), but despite His judgment on their sin, this accusation is not true (42:14; 45:15-19; 50:1; 57:11; 64:12; 65:6).

God's people should also be committed to praying for the coming of the kingdom and the restoration of Zion. Jesus exemplified this priority when He told the disciples that the first thing they should pray is, "Our Father who is in heaven, hallowed be Your name. Your kingdom come. Your will be done on earth as it is in heaven" (Matt. 6:9-10).[116]

The object of the prayer (v. 1b)

The goal, writes Isaiah, is that Zion's righteousness would go forth like brightness (*nogah*),[117] and her salvation would go forth like a burning torch. Once again, we see the pairing of the ideas "righteousness" and "salvation" in such a way that they represent God's faithfulness to His promises (cf. 58:8; 60:1, 3). His salvation will bring ethical righteousness to Zion, but it comes because of the operation of God's faithful saving grace.

The metaphorical illustrations of Zion's glory (vv. 2-5)

Throughout history kings have bragged about the glory of their kingdoms (cf. e.g., Dan. 4:30). Isaiah uses two illustrations to show that the restoration of Zion is going to eclipse anything this world has ever seen.

First metaphor: A crown metaphor (vv. 2-3)

Based on the intensity of the language, one can only imagine how beautiful this restoration will be. We are reminded of God's word to Daniel: "How blessed is he who keeps waiting and attains to the 1,335 days!" (Dan. 12:12; cf. Isa. 30:18). The world will marvel over the glory of Zion (v. 2), a glory that can be compared to a beautiful crown (v. 3).

A glory for the world to marvel at (v. 2). The future glory of Zion will be so great that all the nations will see and take note (cf. 2:3; 45:14, 22-25; 49:23; 60:3).[118] God tells Zion, "You will be called by a new name which the mouth of the Lord will designate." From the Old Testament we see that this expression "new name" typically conveys the idea of a fresh start and new beginning (cf. e.g., Gen. 17:5, 15; 32:8). Since one's name often signifies one's character, it is probably best to understand that Zion's new name will be something related to

---

[116] This passage shows a strong relationship with Ezekiel 36:19-23 where Ezekiel spoke about a worldwide recognition of God's holiness in the messianic kingdom.

[117] We see this term "brightness" (*nogah*) numerous times in Isaiah (4:5; 50:10; 60:3, 19; 62:1) (Oswalt, *The Book of Isaiah: Chapters 40-66*, 536, n. 19).

[118] Here we see the pairing of righteousness (cf. 58:8; 61:10) and glory (cf. 40:5; 44:23) instead of the pairing of righteousness and salvation that we often see elsewhere.

the righteousness that Zion will experience when Christ brings her restoration.[119] Jeremiah writes,

> In those days and at that time I will cause a righteous Branch of David to spring forth; and He shall execute justice and righteousness on the earth. In those days Judah will be saved and Jerusalem will dwell in safety; and this is *the name* by which she will be called: the Lord is our righteousness (Jer. 33:15-16).

An appeal to the immediate context comes in verse 4 where God says, "But you will be called, My delight is in her, and your land, Married, for the Lord delights in you, and *to Him* your land will be married." God's grace will restore Zion, and it will be a glory over which the world will marvel.

A glory comparable to a beautiful crown (v. 3). Isaiah goes on to compare future Zion to a beautiful crown using two different Hebrew terms for crown. The "crown of beauty," perhaps "beautiful crown,"[120] comes from the Hebrew *'atarah* (Isa. 28:1, 3, 5; 2 Sam. 12:30; 1 Chron. 20:2; Song 3:11; Zech. 6:11-14), a general word for crown, but one that can be used for nobility (Esth. 8:15) or royalty (Jer. 3:18). The key point is beauty and glory. The second term "royal diadem" comes from *tsenuph*, the idea of a royal turban wrapped around the head (Isa. 3:23; 62:3; Zech. 3:5). Despite Zion's past sin, God's grace will make her an object of supreme glory (Isa. 46:13; 60:9). Pfeiffer explains, "God will not be permanently thwarted in his plan to create a holy nation, despite Israel's sorry record of failure."[121]

Second metaphor: A marriage metaphor (vv. 4-5)

The metaphor shifts to that of marriage and a bride. The point is that in her youth, Zion was a complete failure in being a bride, wife, and mother. All that will change when God restores her.

The dreadful past (v. 4a). Because of her sin and exile, Zion's past could be described by the terms "forsaken" (*'azubah*) and "desolate" (*shemamah*). Both of these expressions reflect the shame and reproach of the former punishments that made Zion forsaken and desolate and without children (cf. 54:1).[122] This will change one day.

---

[119] Grogan, "Isaiah," 336.
[120] Young, *The Book of Isaiah, vol. 3*, 468.
[121] Pfeiffer, *The Wycliffe Bible Commentary: Old Testament*, Is 62:1.
[122] The latter term (*shamam*) often speaks about the desolation and pollution that brought defilement and ruin upon all Zion, and especially the temple (Isa. 49:8, 19; 54:1; 61:4; Dan. 8:13; 9:26, 27; 12:11; Matt. 23:38).

A glorious future (vv. 4b-5). When Christ restores Israel in the kingdom God, He will take away the shame and reproach of Zion's past, and she will become a beautiful, fruitful bride. God says, "you will be called, My delight is in her [*chephtsiy-bah*],[123] and your land, "Married" [*be'ulah*], for "the Lord delights in you" [*chaphats*], and *to Him* "your land will be married" [*tibba'el*]" (v. 4b; cf. Hos. 2:19-20).

Isaiah explains, "For *as* a young man marries a virgin, *so* your sons will marry you; and *as* the bridegroom rejoices over the bride, *so* your God will rejoice [*sus*] over you" (v. 5). When Jesus returns, Israel will be permanently reunited with her land. And, as we saw in chapter 54, when this marriage is restored, the land will explode with a huge growth of spiritual seed. Thus, explains Smith, these new names,

> accurately describe the new state of the nation in the future when God has marvelously transformed his people and their land. The old way of life will be over, and this new reality will involve a complete transformation of God's people.[124]

This is the glory that God has promised to His city Zion.

The intercession for Zion's glory (vv. 6-9)

All of these great promises are something to pray for. Here in verses 6-9 the theme turns back to prayer for the restoration of Zion. Isaiah explains this as watchmen who remind the Lord of these promises (vv. 6-7), and then follows this with the solemn promise that Zion will never again fall to enemy invasions (vv. 8-9).

Watchmen who always remind the Lord (vv. 6-7)

Watchmen were soldiers posted on the tops of the city walls. Their job was to keep constant watch at night and sound the alarm if an enemy should attack (21:11ff.; cf. 52:8 where a synonym is used).[125] Constant attention and vigilance are key ideas. God uses this imagery to convey the idea that His watchmen are there to constantly remind Him about His promise to restore Zion (v. 6). It is not that God needs anyone to keep Him awake, but Isaiah uses this metaphor to say that these watchmen will give God no rest, "until He establishes and makes Jerusalem a praise in the earth" (v. 7; cf. Jer. 33:9-11; Zeph. 3:20).

---

[123] This was the name of Hezekiah's wife (2 Kings 21:1).
[124] Smith, *Isaiah 40-66*, 648.
[125] In the OT, this term was sometimes applied to the prophets (Ezek. 3:17; 33:7).

Zion's future security (vv. 8-9)

Back in 54:17, God told Zion, "No weapon that is formed against you will prosper, and every tongue that accuses you in judgment, you will condemn." Zion will be secure in the messianic kingdom, the same idea we see again here in verses 8-9. With a most-solemn oath (45:23; 54:9; cf. 22:14; Heb. 6:13-20), God assures Zion that never again will enemy powers plunder them as in past ages (v. 8; cf. Isa. 52:1). From now on, the fruit of one's labor will stay with the one who labored for it: "But those who garner it will eat it and praise the Lord, and those who gather it will drink it in the courts of My sanctuary" (v. 9; cf. Isa. 65:21-23).[126] God's promise is that Zion will be saved and forever secure forever:

> So I have sworn that I will not be angry with you nor will I rebuke you. For the mountains may be removed and the hills may shake, but My lovingkindness will not be removed from you, and My covenant of peace will not be shaken, says the Lord who has compassion on you (Isa. 54:9-10; cf. 12:1).

God's promises are great, and God's promises are certain. All of this gives Israel great reason for joy and hope no matter what life might bring.

The preparation for Zion's glory (vv. 10-12)

These great promises call for preparation, the final idea we find in the closing verses of chapter 62. Isaiah shows us the need for a smooth path (v. 10), and the need for a loud proclamation (vv. 11-12).

The need for a smooth path (v. 10)

Isaiah cries out, "Go through, go through the gates, clear the way for the people; build up, build up the highway, remove the stones, lift up a standard over the peoples" (11:16; 19:23; 35:8; 49:11, 22; 52:11; 57:14). The King is coming, and it is urgent that the path is smooth (cf. Isa. 40:3-5).[127] Israel needs to

---

[126] According to the OT, when Israel would come to the temple, the people would eat of the tithe in the courtyards, the place where they would give corporate praise in the name of Yahweh (Lev. 23:39-40; Deut. 14:22-26) (Young, *The Book of Isaiah, vol. 3*, 472).

[127] This expression "standard" (*nes*) also is another favorite (Isa. 5:26; 11:12; 13:2; 18:3; 33:23; 62:10). The idea is that of a flag, banner, or pole that signals the coming of the King.

prepare for the King by turning to the Lord.[128] Smith explains, "This road that the people in Zion are to prepare is a spiritual way of life that smooths the relationship between God and man . . . [so that] all offensive stumbling stones are removed."[129]

It was the Baptist who first cried out, "Repent, for the kingdom of heaven is at hand. For this is the one referred to by Isaiah the prophet when he said, the voice of one crying in the wilderness, make ready the way of the Lord; make His paths straight!" (Matt. 3:2-3). Jesus gave the same command: "Repent, for the kingdom of heaven is at hand" (Matt. 4:17).

The need for a loud proclamation (vv. 11-12)

The message of the King is urgent, and for this reason there needs to be a loud proclamation that goes out to the whole earth.

God's own proclamation (v. 11). God makes His own proclamation by crying out, "Say to the daughter of Zion, Lo, your salvation comes. Behold His reward is with Him, and His recompense before Him." The King is coming and He will deal righteously with every man according to his deeds. For those who respond, the "reward" (*sakar*, wage; cf. Isa. 40:10; 65:7) and "recompense" (*phelullah*, wage, punishment; cf. 40:10; 49:4; 61:8; 65:7) will be entrance into the kingdom, but to those who disregard God's Word it will be eternal judgment according to deeds (cf. 66:24).

The proclamation by the Gentiles (v. 12). Verse 12 shows us the proclamation that will come from the Gentiles: "And they will call them, the holy people, the redeemed of the Lord, and you will be called, sought out, a city not forsaken" (cf. 62:4). The redemption (*ga'al*; cf. 35:9-10; 51:10-11) of Israel has come because of the cleansing of her sins, so from now on she will be the holy people whom God has always desired (Exod. 19:6; Lev. 19:2; 20:7; Zech. 14:20-21; 1 Pet. 1:15-16).

Summary and application

God's promises are great, and God's promises are certain. For Israel, this means that she can live with hope for a future and not let fear overcome her. The same principle applies to every Christian who walks by faith during the present age. Among the most precious of these promises is the promise that Jesus made when He told us that He would come again and bring us to Himself forever (John 14:1-3).

---

[128] Grogan, "Isaiah," 337.
[129] Smith, *Isaiah 40-66*, 653.

ISAIAH 58:1-66:24

YAHWEH THE AVENGER (63:1-19)

All the blessings we have read about in the preceding chapters are not going to come without a cost. Now, on the one hand we know that the ultimate cost was that which Christ Himself paid on Calvary 2,000 years ago (Isa. 53:4-6; Matt. 20:28; 1 Pet. 2:24-25). However, at another level there is the metaphorical price that God Himself is going to have to pay when He comes to deliver Israel from annihilation in the Day of the Lord. In the Bible we read in multiple prophets that there is going to be a massive, multi-nation attempt to destroy Israel at the end of this age (e.g., Joel 3:1-17; Ezek. 38-39; Zech. 14:1ff.; Matt. 24:4-31; Rev. 19:11-21). The nations of the world are going to rise up against Israel, but Yahweh the Avenger will save His people.

Chapter 63 reads as follows: "1 Who is this who comes from Edom, with garments of glowing colors from Bozrah, this One who is majestic in His apparel, marching in the greatness of His strength? It is I who speak in righteousness, mighty to save. 2 Why is Your apparel red, and Your garments like the one who treads in the wine press? 3 I have trodden the wine trough alone, and from the peoples there was no man with Me. I also trod them in My anger and trampled them in My wrath; and their lifeblood is sprinkled on My garments, and I stained all My raiment, 4 for the day of vengeance was in My heart, and My year of redemption has come. 5 I looked, and there was no one to help, and I was astonished and there was no one to uphold, so My own arm brought salvation to Me, and My wrath upheld Me. 6 I trod down the peoples in My anger and made them drunk in My wrath, and I poured out their lifeblood on the earth. 7 I shall make mention of the lovingkindnesses of the Lord, the praises of the Lord, according to all that the Lord has granted us, and the great goodness toward the house of Israel, which He has granted them according to His compassion and according to the abundance of His lovingkindnesses. 8 For He said, Surely, they are My people, sons who will not deal falsely. So He became their Savior. 9 In all their affliction He was afflicted, and the angel of His presence saved them. In His love and in His mercy He redeemed them, and He lifted them and carried them all the days of old. 10 But they rebelled and grieved His Holy Spirit. Therefore He turned Himself to become their enemy; He fought against them. 11 Then His people remembered the days of old, of Moses. Where is He who brought them up out of the sea with the shepherds of His flock? Where is He who put His Holy Spirit in the midst of them, 12 who caused His glorious arm to go at the right hand of Moses, who divided the waters before them to make for Himself an everlasting name, 13 who led them through the depths? Like the horse in the wilderness, they did not stumble; 14 as the cattle which go down into the valley, the Spirit of the Lord gave them rest. So You led Your people to make for Yourself a glorious name. 15 Look down from heaven and see from Your holy and glorious habitation. Where are Your zeal and Your mighty deeds? The stirrings of Your heart and Your compassion are restrained toward me. 16 For You are our Father, though Abraham does not know us and Israel does not recognize us. You, O Lord, are our Father; our Redeemer from of old is Your name. 17 Why, O Lord, do You cause us to stray from Your ways and harden our heart from fearing You? Return for the sake of Your servants, the tribes of Your heritage. 18 Your holy people possessed Your sanctuary for a little while; our adversaries have trodden *it* down. 19 We have become *like* those over whom You have never ruled, *like* those who were not called by Your name" (63:1-19).

Chapter 63 centers around the theme of vengeance against those seeking the destruction of Israel. It has been over 4,000 years since God first told Abraham, "I will curse those who *curse* you" (Gen. 12:3).[130] This warning stands as part of the unconditional promises God made to the people of Abraham, the promises commonly called The Abrahamic Covenant (Gen. 12:3; 22:18; 26:4; 28:14; Acts 3:25; Gal. 3:8). The Abrahamic Covenant originated with God's call to Abraham when he was still living in Ur, but finds repeated confirmation throughout the life of Abraham. One source explains, "The relationship between God and Abraham should be understood as a Covenant relationship— the most solemn form of arrangement between individuals in the ancient world."[131] Here in chapter 63 we see three ways that the Abrahamic Covenant will bring these blessings to fulfillment.

The Abrahamic covenant brings vengeance (vv. 1-6)

One element of the Abrahamic covenant is that God will bring curse (here the idea of vengeance) on those who harm His people. Back in 62:6 we saw that God has His watchmen guarding over His city, but here in 63:1-6 we see that the time has finally come for vengeance to be poured out by the hand of God's Servant. Not only does Isaiah show us the marks of vengeance (vv. 1-2), but also the reasons for such vengeance (vv. 3-6).

---

[130] Leonard J. Coppes, "*qll*," ed. R. Laird Harris, Gleason L. Archer Jr., and Bruce K. Waltke, *Theological Wordbook of the Old Testament*, cited in electronic form with Logos Libronix (Chicago: Moody Press, 1999), 800. "The basic meaning of this root (*qll*, "to curse") sets forth the quality of 'slightness' as to provision, speed (where it means swift), or circumstance. In the latter instance the condition described is less than that deserved by or divinely intended for the object. So, this root is used (especially in the intensive stems) of intending a lowered position, technically, to curse. . . . As God said to Abraham: 'he who curses (*qālal*) you' (pronounces a formula), 'I will curse (*'ārar*) him' (put him in the state). To curse God's prophet was to attack God and to bring on one's head divine judgment."

[131] Ronald F. Youngblood, F. F. Bruce, and R. K. Harrison, Thomas Nelson Publishers, eds., *Nelson's New Illustrated Bible Dictionary*, cited in electronic form with Logos Libronix (Nashville, TN: Thomas Nelson, Inc., 1995).

The marks of vengeance (vv. 1-2)

The colors of vengeance. The marks of vengeance show themselves in bright, crimson red (*chamuts*) clothing on One who is valiantly approaching Zion from Bozrah/Edom (Isa. 34:5; Jer. 49:13; Ezek. 25:12-14; 35:1-15; Amos 1:12; Obad. 1:14; Mal. 1:2-5; Ps. 137:7). Isaiah asks, "Who is this?" The Messiah Himself answers, "It is I who speak in righteousness, mighty to save."

The reasons for vengeance. A second question sounds out, "Why is your apparel red, and your garments like the one who treads in the wine press?" (cf. Rev. 19:13-15). This One is so covered in red that it looks like He has been treading grapes in a wine press. However, the red stains are not from grapes, but from the blood of his enemies. Vengeance against the wicked must come, and it will be a blood bath. Every enemy of God must receive recompense, especially those who have sought the destruction of His people Israel.[132]

The objects of vengeance. All of this raises the question who Edom is. Edom is an ancient people whose origin goes back to the days of the patriarchs (Gen. 25).[133] Edom descended from the older twin Esau who had been born to Isaac and Rebekah. Before the twins were even born, God had prophetically informed Rebekah that the younger son (Jacob) would be the one to have preeminence (Gen. 25:23), and thus be the line of the Abrahamic Covenant. Esau freely validated this prophecy by rejecting his own firstborn status by selling it for a bowl of stew (Gen. 25:32-34). Years later God confirmed it would indeed be Jacob, and not Esau, through whom He would fulfill the Abrahamic Covenant:

> I am the Lord, the God of your father Abraham and the God of Isaac; the land on which you lie, I will give it to you and to your descendants. Your descendants will also be like the dust of the earth, and you will spread out to the west and to the east and to the north and to the south; and in you and in your descendants shall all the families of the earth be blessed (Gen. 28:13-14).

---

[132] Young explains, "How can Zion safely endure as long as enemies as hostile and vicious as Edom are at hand?" (Young, *The Book of Isaiah, vol. 3*, 475).

[133] Geographically, Edom lay to southeast of the Jordan Valley in an area that formerly had been called Seir. Esau showed further contempt to his parents and the Abrahamic promises when he married Canaanite women (Gen. 26:34-35). "[Bozrah], called *Bostra* by the Romans, &c., assigned in Je 48:24 to Moab, so that it seems to have been at one time in the dominion of Edom, and at another in that of Moab (Is 63:1; Je 49:13, 20, 22); it was strictly not in Edom, but the capital of Auranitis (the *Houran*). Edom seems to have extended its dominion so as to include it (compare La 4:21)" (Jamieson, *Commentary Critical and Explanatory on the Whole Bible*, 467).

Throughout history, Edom was quite antagonistic against Israel,[134] and the Bible indicates that at the end of the age they are once again going to show much hostility, a hostility that will cost them greatly.[135] It is for this reason that God will send His Servant to bring vengeance on Edom (cf. ch. 34).[136] All of this must come as part of the process for Christ to establish His kingdom. Oswalt explains, "To be sure, the enemies of God must be destroyed if the people of God are to know His blessing."[137]

The reasons for vengeance (vv. 3-6)

Isaiah continues to explain the reasons for vengeance in verses 3-6. Isaiah names three reasons why the Servant must bring vengeance.

The Servant was the only one was qualified to avenge (v. 3). The first reason is because He is the only One qualified to bring such vengeance. Isaiah writes, "I have trodden the wine trough alone,[138] and from the peoples there was no man with Me" (cf. 59:16-20).[139] The time for God's righteous judgment has come, and no one was there to help, neither from inside the nation nor from outside:

> The Lord indicates that he did this work alone; no other nations were employed to carry out his destructive plans. Earlier God used the nation of Assyria as the rod of his punishment to judge Judah in 10:5, but this time he did not use another nation. . . . He alone is the only one who is truly able to destroy evil from this world.[140]

Christ is the only One who can bring Israel salvation (cf. 43:10-13), and Christ is the One who says, "I also trod them in My anger and trampled them in My

---

[134] Cf. Gen. 36:12; Exod. 17:8-16; Num. 14:45; 20:14-22; Isa. 34:5-8; Ezek. 35:1ff.; Amos 1:11-12; Mal. 1:2-4.

[135] At the present time this area is the country called Jordan.

[136] Many see a strong parallel between this present passage and former passages that speak about God's Servant (Grogan, "Isaiah," 338; cf. 42:1-9; 49:1-13; 50:4-11; 52:13-53:12). This is the One to execute the faithful righteousness of Yahweh to save His covenant people (cf. 45:8; 46:13; 59:16).

[137] Oswalt, *The Book of Isaiah: Chapters 40-66*, 595.

[138] Wine troughs (a *purah*) were carved out of a large rock outcropping with an upper and lower trough, each about four to six inches deep with a channel to connect them. Grapes were trampled in the upper trough allowing the juice to flow into the lower trough. Tel-Avdat in the Negev provides an excellent example.

[139] Wolf observes a parallel between this and 59:16-20 (Wolf, *Interpreting Isaiah*, 242).

[140] Smith, *Isaiah 40-66*, 659.

wrath; and their lifeblood is sprinkled on My garments, and I stained all My raiment." It will be a literal blood bath (cf. Rev. 19:13-15).

The Servant had a heart to avenge (v. 4). The second reason why the Servant is the One to bring wrath is because He is the One who has a heart to avenge the evils done against His name and His people. Thus, we read, "For the day of vengeance [*naqam*; cf. 34:8; 35:4; 61:2] was in My heart,[141] and My year of redemption has come [*ge'eliym*; cf. verb in 41:14; 43:1, 14; 44:6, 22-24; 47:4; 48:17, 20; 49:7, 26; 54:5, 8; 60:16; 63:9, 16]."[142] This is Jesus Christ establishing His kingdom at the close of the seven-year tribulation (cf. 2 Thess. 1:6-9; Rev. 16:4-7).

The Servant's faithfulness required Him to avenge (vv. 5-6). No one else can accomplish the task, so the covenant faithfulness of the Servant requires Him to avenge His people. God Himself will do it by the great power of His own arm (Isa. 40:10; 52:10; 59:16, 18; 63:12; cf. hand in 50:2; 51:9; 53:1, 9; 59:1). Christ will fully satiate the wrath of God as He repays hatred and contempt to those who hate Him. The imagery of making them drunk relates to the idea that God has given them so much wine that they are drunk and incapable of self-defense (cf. Isa. 51:17-23; Jer. 51:7; Rev. 14:8; 18:3). Pfeiffer explains, "A Christ-rejecting, Gospel-spurning world leaves the Lord no other alternative but to send fearful and terrible destruction when the time of his long-suffering is past."[143]

The Abrahamic covenant brings faithfulness (vv. 7-14)

Israel needed faithfulness, but it was not going to come from within. Only God could exercise the faithfulness that could save them. Here in verses 7ff. it is best to see the speaker as being Isaiah making intercession on behalf of the remnant of his needy people. We see both God's faithfulness to Israel (vv. 7-9) and Israel's unfaithfulness to God (vv. 10-14).

God's faithfulness to Israel (vv. 7-9)

If there is one truth we can learn from the Bible, it is the fact that our God is always faithful (2 Tim. 2:13). God's faithfulness is based upon His own character (v. 7), and it is also a faithfulness that God has demonstrated throughout the history of the nation (vv. 8-9).

---

[141] As noted previously, vengeance is deserved retribution for evil deeds.
[142] As noted previously, in the OT the Redeemer was typically the close relative who intervened to make wrongs right.
[143] Pfeiffer, *The Wycliffe Bible Commentary: Old Testament*, Is 63:1.

God's faithfulness is grounded God's character (v. 7). Isaiah celebrates the faithful character of God when he writes,

> I shall make mention of the lovingkindnesses of the Lord, the praises of the Lord, according to all that the Lord has granted us, and the great goodness toward the house of Israel, which He has granted them according to His compassion and according to the abundance of His lovingkindnesses.

The idea of "lovingkindnesses" (plural of *chesed* reflecting the intensity of God's faithfulness; cf. Rom. 12:1) concerns the faithfulness of God to His own character and promises (54:10; 55:3).[144] In other words, Israel's only hope for restoration is based on the faithful character of God.

God's faithfulness is shown in Israel's history (vv. 8-9). If Israel needed proof, all they had to do was look to the past. God breaks in with a prophetic oracle and says, "For He said, Surely, they are My people, sons who will not deal falsely. So He became their Savior" (v. 8; cf. 19:20; 43:3, 11; 45:15, 21; 60:16).[145] Even though God knew the future faithlessness of His own people (cf. Deut. 32), He still gave them the opportunity to show themselves to be faithful sons.

God's faithfulness showed itself in the way that He came down to rescue them from the consequences of their own sin: "In all their affliction He was afflicted, and the angel of His presence saved them [cf. Exod. 23:20-23; 33:14-15].[146] In His love, He redeemed them, and lifted them and carried them all the days of old" (v. 9). God was always there for them.

Israel's unfaithfulness to God (vv. 10-14)

Despite God's faithfulness, the people were not faithful sons to Him. Isaiah says, "But they rebelled" (*marah*; cf. 1:20; 3:8; 50:5; Jer. 5:23) and "grieved His Holy Spirit" (v. 10a; cf. 1:2-3; Eph. 4:30).[147] The history of Israel was that

---

[144] Wolf, *Interpreting Isaiah*, 244.

[145] God's election of Israel inevitably resulted in Him stepping down to save them from ruin (Oswalt, *The Book of Isaiah: Chapters 40-66*, 606).

[146] The "Angel of His presence" would be none other than The Angel of the Lord, the preincarnate Christ (cf. e.g., Gen. 3:8, 10; 16; 7-16; 17-18; 22:11ff.; 32:24-32; Exod. 3:1-5; 14:19; 23:20-22; 33:14; Josh. 5:13-15; Judg. 6:11-25; Mal. 3:1). Young explains, this is "the Messenger who brings God's presence" (Young, *The Book of Isaiah, vol. 3*, 482).

[147] It is only here and v. 11 and Psalm 51:11 where we find this precise expression "Holy Spirit."

of perpetual faithlessness (cf. Neh. 9:26-31). Two results flowed from Israel's disobedience.

First result: God become their adversary (v. 10b). Because they rebelled, God "turned Himself to become their enemy" and "fought against them" (Ps. 54:5; Prov. 13:21). As we saw in 59:2, their iniquities separated them from God, so that He became their opponent who got angry, hid His face, and struck them (Isa. 57:17; cf. Deut. 31:18; 32:18-20; Mal. 3:4).

Second result: Israel longed for a second Exodus (vv. 11-14). Israel's founding as a people began with Abraham, but her founding as a nation was grounded with her redemption at the Exodus. The coming of the Babylonian exile made Israel long for a second Exodus (cf. Jer. 2:1ff.; Hos. 2:15ff.). Isaiah says that they looked back to the Exodus and wondered where God was, the God who brought them through the Red Sea (v. 11; 51:10; Exod. 13:21; 14:16; 15:5, 8; Pss. 77:16; 106:9),[148] and came to dwell in their very presence (Exod. 23:20-21; Num. 11:17, 25, 29).

A second Exodus would be like when God extended His great power through Moses (i.e., His arm) to part the sea and guide His people to safety (vv. 12-13), a second Exodus like when God's Spirit guided the people to rest (v. 14).[149] One day God will once again show this kind of saving grace, but it will not be realized until they turn to God's Servant in faith.

The Abrahamic covenant brings triumph (vv. 15-19)

Isaiah reminds us that Yahweh will bring a final triumph for His people Israel. This, however, is something that calls for intercessory prayer. Verses 15-19 show us both the plea for victory (vv. 15-16) as well as the delay of victory (vv. 17-19).

The plea for God to bring victory (vv. 15-16)

In light of the historical reminder of God's saving grace in ages past, Isaiah lifts up a plea for God to once again bring victory to Israel.[150] This plea for grace begins in verse 15, but extends all the way through 64:12.

---

[148] Some have suggested this might include the drying up of the Jordan, but it is preferable to see it only referring to the Red Sea (Grogan, "Isaiah," 342).

[149] The imagery is that of cattle being led to a place of "abundant pasture" (cf. Deut. 3:20; 12:9; Josh. 1:13; 22:4; Ps. 95:11) (Young, *The Book of Isaiah, vol. 3*, 486).

[150] Wolf, *Interpreting Isaiah*, 245.

The call for God to look down (v. 15). Isaiah pleads for God to look down on His desperate people (57:15; 66:1-2) from His glorious habitation in heaven.[151] God's zeal and great deeds have been there in ages past, but where are they now? The context does not suggest the idea of accusation, but wonder for why there is such silence. Smith explains, "The lamenter does not accuse God of some wrong but simply calls for God to 'look, take notice' from his distant heavenly abode (as in Ps 80:1–2) in order to find out what is really happening on earth."[152] Isaiah's actions remind us that no matter why we are suffering, the best thing we can do is to seek the Lord in prayer and ask Him to help us.

The call for God to stop withholding grace (v. 16). Isaiah is well aware that his people have turned aside from the Lord. In light of this apostasy, he declares, "For You are our Father, though Abraham does not know us and Israel does not recognize us. You, O Lord, are our Father, our Redeemer from of old is Your name." In other words, if Abraham were to look at them now, he would not even recognize them; nevertheless, Yahweh is still the Father of Israel (we see "Father" twice here and once again in 64:8; cf. 52:2-7). Israel needs God's favor, and this is what Isaiah is pleading for (cf. similar prayers in Ezra 9; Neh. 9; Dan. 9).

The delay in God bringing victory (vv. 17-19)

The prayers for restoration are there, but the grace is not. Unfortunately, without such grace, Israel is spiritually incapable of turning to God. To be clear, it is always true that men are fully responsible to obey God, but the problem is that Adam's sin has rendered all men spiritually dead (Rom. 5:12; Eph. 2:1-3), and thus incapable of turning to God unless God works in the heart (cf. Lam. 5:21; 1 Cor. 2:14).[153] Oswalt explains,

> Isaiah is obviously at one with the rest of Scripture, which insists that a person's relationship with God is not a matter of human initiative with an essentially passive deity. If persons turn to God, it is because God in his grace has enabled them to do so.[154]

---

[151] This term rendered "habitation" (*zebul*) is a less-used term that connotes the idea of a realm over which one rules (cf. 1 Kings 8:13; Ps. 49:16; Hab. 3:11) (Oswalt, *The Book of Isaiah: Chapters 40-66*, 609, n. 67).

[152] Smith, *Isaiah 40-66*, 680.

[153] Young explains, "The prayer is a confession or acknowledgment that God has forsaken, but that the fault lies with the people themselves, so that God's vengeance and actions against them are righteous" (Young, *The Book of Isaiah, vol. 3*, 489).

[154] Oswalt, *The Book of Isaiah: Chapters 40-66*, 613.

If Israel is to have any hope for restoration, God must work, so Isaiah raises the plea for grace.

The desperate need is for grace (v. 17). Isaiah's plea begins with the question, "Why, O Lord, do You cause us to stray from Your way and harden our heart from fearing You" (v. 17a; cf. Job 39:16)? It was Israel's choice to turn away from God, and Isaiah recognizes that Israel's only hope lies in an outpouring of grace.[155] With this, Isaiah cries out, "Return for the sake of Your servants, the tribes of Your heritage" (*shub*; cf. Lam. 5:21).[156]

The desperate need is for restoration like days of old (vv. 18-19). Isaiah reminds God of what it was like in the former days before the exile. Those were the few days (800 years) when Israel possessed the sanctuary (*miqdash*) and lived in the land (v. 18a). Those days ended, however, with the Babylonian exile when God poured out covenant curses on Israel and spewed them out of the land (cf. Deut. 28:15-68; Ps. 74:3-7). The desolation of Israel was so bad, one could not even tell that Israel had possessed the land for 800 years: "We have become *like* those over whom You have never ruled, *like* those who were not called by Your name" (v. 19). Martin reminds us of the powerful nature of God's prophetic Word:

> This is one of many places in chaps. 40–66 which shows that Isaiah, living more than 100 years before the Babylonian Captivity, wrote prophetically to prepare that future generation of exiles for it. Though the nation had belonged to God for centuries (from of old), it had been a long time since the people were in a proper relationship.[157]

Summary and application

Chapter 63 reminds us of three major theological truths. The first is that all men are always responsible to believe and obey God. Second, we must never forget that Adam's sin has rendered every one of us as fallen and sinful creatures. Third, because we are responsible to believe and serve God, and because we are fallen, we must always recognize our desperate need to depend on God and His sustaining grace.

---

[155] Grogan, "Isaiah," 343.

[156] The master cannot abandon his servants (singular referring to the corporate nation in 41:9; 42:19; 43:10; 44:1; 45:4 and plural referring to individual believers in 54:17; 56:6; 63:17; 65:8, 9, 13, 14, 15; 66:14) nor can the owner abandon his heritage (Deut. 4:20; 32:9).

[157] Martin, "Isaiah," 1118.

ISAIAH: THE LORD SAVES

PRAYERS FOR DELIVERANCE (64:1-12)

Chapter 64 continues the same theme as 63 by showing Israel's need for intercessory prayer. The theme continues, but Wolf notes that in chapter 64, Isaiah's prayer "increased in intensity and in emotional fervor."[158]

Chapter 64 reads as follows: "1 Oh, that You would rend the heavens *and* come down, that the mountains might quake at Your presence—2 as fire kindles the brushwood, *as* fire causes water to boil—to make Your name known to Your adversaries, *that* the nations may tremble at Your presence! 3 When You did awesome things which we did not expect, You came down; the mountains quaked at Your presence. 4 For from days of old they have not heard or perceived by ear, nor has the eye seen a God besides You, who acts on behalf of the one who waits for Him. 5 You meet him who rejoices in doing righteousness, who remembers You in Your ways. Behold, You were angry, for we sinned; *we continued* in them a long time; and shall we be saved? 6 For all of us have become like one who is unclean, and all our righteous deeds are like a filthy garment; and all of us wither like a leaf, and our iniquities, like the wind, take us away. 7 There is no one who calls on Your name, who arouses himself to take hold of You, for You have hidden Your face from us and have delivered us into the power of our iniquities. 8 But now, O Lord, You are our Father. We are the clay, and You our potter; and all of us are the work of Your hand. 9 Do not be angry beyond measure, O Lord, nor remember iniquity forever; behold, look now, all of us are Your people. 10 Your holy cities have become a wilderness; Zion has become a wilderness, Jerusalem a desolation. 11 Our holy and beautiful house where our fathers praised You has been burned *by* fire, and all our precious things have become a ruin. 12 Will You restrain Yourself at these things, O Lord? Will You keep silent and afflict us beyond measure?" (64:1-12).

Pfeiffer observes, "Isaiah represents the people of Israel as entreating Jehovah to intervene in the world scene and enforce the claims of his holiness and sovereignty."[159] Isaiah offers up four kinds of prayers.

The prayer for a powerful descent (vv. 1-2)

Isaiah's passionate prayer is for God to come down to shake mountains (Exod. 19:18), ignite fires,[160] boil water, and make His name known to all those who would dare to try and oppose Him (cf. Ezek. 36:23; 38:16, 23; 39:6-23). This world is going to think differently about God when Christ brings God's kingdom to this world. Smith explains, "One thing is certain: if God had only

---

[158] Wolf, *Interpreting Isaiah*, 246.
[159] Pfeiffer, *The Wycliffe Bible Commentary: Old Testament*, Is 64:1.
[160] Fire is frequently seen in association with the presence of God (Gen. 3:21; Exod. 3:1; Isa. 4:5; 6:6; 9:5; 10:16; 29:6; 30:27, 30; 31:9; 33:12, 14; 66:15, 16, 24).

appeared in all his glory and power as he had in the past, things would be totally different now."[161]

The prayer for a second Exodus (vv. 3-4)

Isaiah again uses second Exodus imagery to describe the future salvation of Israel. After 400 years of life in Egypt, everyone was surprised when God came down to save His people from slavery with "awesome" deeds that made the mountains quake (v. 3; cf. Exod. 15:11; 34:10; Deut. 10:21; 2 Sam. 7:23; Ps. 106:22). These are the kinds of awesome deeds that the world does not understand. For this reason, Isaiah says, "For from days of old they have not heard or perceived by ear, nor has the eye seen a God besides You, who acts on behalf of the one who waits for Him" (v. 4; cf. 1 Cor. 2:9). Smith notes that the main point is that Israel can trust the Lord since He showed Himself faithful in the past (Hab. 3:3-7; Hag. 2:6, 22; Heb. 12:18-20). Smith writes,

> When God revealed himself through the plagues in Egypt and by dividing the Red Sea, his action also proved that he can be trusted to assist his people. Thus, from experience the Israelites know that God is one who acts on behalf of those who trustingly wait for him.[162]

The prayer for God to forgive past sins (vv. 5-7)

Salvation is there to be had, but it cannot happen until Israel repents and finds restoration by the redeeming grace of the Servant (59:1-2). Isaiah shows us three key principles in obtaining forgiveness and restoration.

Forgiveness is for those rejoice in God's truth (v. 5a)

To put it quite simply, sinners reject the ways of God because they love the ways of sin (John 3:19-21). On the other hand, says Isaiah, "You meet him who rejoices in doing righteousness, who remembers You in Your ways" (v. 5a). That is, God will come and meet the one who turns to Him.

Forgiveness is for those who confess their sins (vv. 5b-6)

Isaiah further describes the person who obtains forgiveness as the one who recognizes and confesses his sin.

---

[161] Smith, *Isaiah 40-66*, 686.

[162] Ibid., 687.

Israel needs to see its sin (v. 5b). Thus, on behalf of the nation Isaiah declares, "Behold, You were angry, for we sinned, *we continued* in them a long time; and shall we be saved" (v. 5b; cf. 5:25; 9:12, 17, 19, 21; 10:4, 25; 12:1)? Without confession of sin, there can be no forgiveness. Thankfully, the day is coming for Israel when this is what they will do.

Israel needs to see its sin for what it really is (v. 6). It is not enough for sinners to simply know they are imperfect people. Sinners also need to see sin for what it really is, a horrible offense against a holy God. For this reason, Isaiah describes the sin of the nation in these words: "For all of us have become like one who is unclean, and all our righteous deeds are like a filthy garment, and all of us wither like a leaf, and our iniquities, like the wind, take us away."

These powerful words call for additional comment. For Isaiah to say that they have all become unclean (*tame'*; cf. 6:5), not just a few, but "all of us" (*kullanu*; cf. 53:6; Lev. 13:45), is to recognize that their sin has made them ceremonially impure and unacceptable to God. TWOT explains,

> Animals and foods were considered clean or unclean by their nature. Persons and objects could become ritually unclean. Personal uncleanness could be incurred through birth, menstruation, bodily emissions, "leprosy," sexual relations and misdeeds and contact with death. Priests and Levites were especially concerned with the issues of cleanness and uncleanness. The greatest uncleanness was idolatry which defiled the temple and the land. The prophets, in denouncing moral uncleanness, used ritual uncleanness as a metaphor for the wickedness which only God can cleanse.[163]

A second graphic description of their sin takes it a step further when Isaiah says, "and all our righteous deeds are like a filthy garment." Wolf holds that Isaiah may be comparing the righteousness of the nation "to the menstrual cloths used by a woman during her period, a time when she was ceremonially unclean" (cf. Ezek. 36:17).[164] Furthermore, says Isaiah, "all of us wither like a leaf, and our iniquities, like the wind, take us away." The bottom line is that there is no spiritual life or spiritual power (cf. 1:30; 17:13; 28:1; 40:24).

Forgiveness is for those who call on the Lord for grace (v. 7)

Lastly, Isaiah emphasizes the need to turn to the Lord, i.e., to call on the name of the Lord (Jer. 33:3; Joel 2:32; Acts 2:21; Rom. 10:13). Israel needed to

---

[163] Edwin Yamauchi, "*tm'*," ed. R. Laird Harris, Gleason L. Archer Jr., and Bruce K. Waltke, *Theological Wordbook of the Old Testament*, cited in electronic form with Logos Libronix (Chicago: Moody Press, 1999), 349.
[164] Wolf, *Interpreting Isaiah*, 246.

ask God for mercy, but sadly no one wanted to do so. Thus, says Isaiah, "There is no one who calls on Your name, who arouses himself to take hold of You; for You have hidden Your face from us and have delivered us into the power of our iniquities."

The prayer for God to act according to His fatherhood (vv. 8-12)

Knowing that the situation is hopeless from a human perspective, Isaiah does the only thing one can: He turns to the Lord to ask for mercy.

A prayer for God to remember His fatherhood (v. 8)

Isaiah reminds God of the unique relationship He has with Israel. Israel alone has this Father/son relationship with God (Isa. 63:16; cf. Exod. 4:22-23; Deut. 4:32-37; 7:6; Amos 3:2), so Isaiah pleads with God to remember and take action, for Israel is the work of His hands (43:7; 60:21).

A prayer for God to relent of His anger (v. 9a)

Because of this special relationship, Isaiah pleads with God to relent of the anger that brought them into exile: "Do not be angry beyond measure, O Lord, nor remember iniquity forever." God's anger was upon them, but Isaiah's prayer is that God would be quick to relent (43:25; 54:8).

A prayer for God to take pity on the ravaged nation (vv. 9b-12)

Because the situation was hopeless at a human level, Isaiah again appeals to the special covenant relationship God had with the nation: "Behold, look now, all of us are Your people" (v. 9b; cf. 63:16). Because they are His people and known by His name, Isaiah makes two special pleas.

First plea: A plea based on the desolate cities (v. 10). Isaiah brings to the mind of Yahweh that all of His cities, especially Zion, have become desolate ruins, a wilderness (*midbar*) and a desolation (*shemamah*).[165] Tragically, by virtue of Israel's sin, God's name was profaned (Ezek. 36:20), and Zion had become a spiritual wasteland (Isa. 1:7-9; 6:11; cf. Jer. 12:11).

Second plea: A plea based on the desolate temple (vv. 11-12). Isaiah makes a special plea based on the desolation of God's glorious temple—the house of God that later got burned to the ground with all of its precious things (v. 11). Isaiah wrote these prophetic words sometime early in the seventh-

---

[165] Jesus declared that this desolation would be perpetuated because of their rejection of Him (Matt. 23:37).

century B.C. (ca. 680 B.C.), and within 100 years they all came to fulfillment in 586 B.C. (cf. 2 Kings 25:8-17). Humanly speaking the situation was hopeless, so Isaiah's appeal is only based on the faithful character of God: "Will You restrain Yourself at these things, O Lord [cf. 42:14; 63:15]?[166] Will You keep silent and afflict us beyond measure" (v. 12)? Israel needed mercy, so Isaiah casts himself on the mercy of God. As Oswalt puts it,

> The only question is whether God's pity for the condition of His children and His concern for His name, which is inextricably linked with Israel, might prompt Him to intervene in the hearts and lives of His people, doing in them what they cannot do for themselves.[167]

Summary and application

Israel was in a desperate situation and the only hope was God's undeserved grace. The fact of the matter is that this is the desperate situation that faces every man. Every man needs God's undeserved grace. The Apostle Paul reminds us that undeserved grace is exactly what God has given us in the cross of Christ (Rom. 3:21-26). Jesus paid the price of restoration by giving His own life to take the punishment that each one of us deserves. God's promise is that He will freely give it if we believe.

GOD'S MERCY ON TRUE ISRAEL (65:1-25)

Chapters 63-64 were dominated by restoration prayers for Israel. Chapter 65 shows us that this restoration is coming, but it will not include every Jew. Only a remnant is going to be saved to inherit the messianic kingdom (cf. e.g., 10:20-23). The believing remnant will inherit these promises, but all unbelievers will be cut off. Chapter 65 deals with this by presenting numerous contrasts between the destinies of these two groups—those we call God's servants, and those we call God's rebels.[168]

Chapter 65 reads as follows: "1 I permitted Myself to be sought by those who did not ask *for Me;* I permitted Myself to be found by those who did not seek Me. I said, Here am I, here am I, to a nation which did not call on My name. 2 I have spread out My hands all day long to a rebellious people, who walk *in* the way which is not good, following their own thoughts, 3 a people who continually provoke Me to My face, offering sacrifices in gardens and

---

[166] This verb (Hithpael of *'aphaq;* cf. Gen. 43:31; 45:1; Esth. 5:10; Isa. 42:14; 64:11) is used in Genesis to show how Joseph could no longer restrain his emotions.
[167] Oswalt, *The Book of Isaiah: Chapters 40-66*, 631.
[168] Ibid., 632.

burning incense on bricks, 4 who sit among graves and spend the night in secret places, who eat swine's flesh, and the broth of unclean meat is *in* their pots, 5 who say, Keep to yourself, do not come near me, for I am holier than you! These are smoke in My nostrils, a fire that burns all the day. 6 Behold, it is written before Me, I will not keep silent, but I will repay; I will even repay into their bosom, 7 both their own iniquities and the iniquities of their fathers together, says the Lord. Because they have burned incense on the mountains and scorned Me on the hills, therefore I will measure their former work into their bosom. 8 Thus says the Lord, As the new wine is found in the cluster, and one says, Do not destroy it, for there is benefit in it, so I will act on behalf of My servants in order not to destroy all of them. 9 I will bring forth offspring from Jacob, and an heir of My mountains from Judah; even My chosen ones shall inherit it, and My servants will dwell there. 10 Sharon will be a pasture land for flocks, and the valley of Achor a resting place for herds for My people who seek Me. 11 But you who forsake the Lord, who forget My holy mountain, who set a table for Fortune, and who fill *cups* with mixed wine for Destiny, 12 I will destine you for the sword, and all of you will bow down to the slaughter, because I called, but you did not answer; I spoke, but you did not hear, and you did evil in My sight, and chose that in which I did not delight. 13 Therefore, thus says the Lord God, Behold, My servants will eat, but you will be hungry. Behold, My servants will drink, but you will be thirsty. Behold, My servants will rejoice, but you will be put to shame. 14 Behold, My servants will shout joyfully with a glad heart, but you will cry out with a heavy heart, and you will wail with a broken spirit. 15 You will leave your name for a curse to My chosen ones, and the Lord God will slay you. But My servants will be called by another name, 16 because he who is blessed in the earth will be blessed by the God of truth, and he who swears in the earth will swear by the God of truth, because the former troubles are forgotten, and because they are hidden from My sight! 17 For behold, I create new heavens and a new earth, and the former things will not be remembered or come to mind. 18 But be glad and rejoice forever in what I create, for behold, I create Jerusalem *for* rejoicing and her people *for* gladness. 19 I will also rejoice in Jerusalem and be glad in My people, and there will no longer be heard in her the voice of weeping and the sound of crying. 20 No longer will there be in it an infant *who lives but a few* days, or an old man who does not live out his days, for the youth will die at the age of one hundred, and the one who does not reach the age of one hundred will be *thought* accursed. 21 They will build houses and inhabit *them;* they will also plant vineyards and eat their fruit; 22 they will not build and another inhabit; they will not plant and another eat, for as the lifetime of a tree, *so will be* the days of My people, and My chosen ones will wear out the work of their hands; 23 they will not labor in vain, or bear *children* for calamity, for they are the offspring of those blessed by the Lord, and their descendants with them. 24 It will also come to pass that before they call, I will answer; and while they are still speaking, I will hear. 25 The wolf and the lamb will graze together, and the lion will eat straw like the ox; and dust will be the serpent's food. They will do no evil or harm in all My holy mountain, says the Lord" (65:1-25).

Chapter 65 tells us about the destinies of the saved and the unsaved, a message that also serves as an evangelistic invitation. Chapter 65 may be broken down as follows: rebuke for the rebels (vv. 1-7), restoration for the remnant (vv. 8-10), ruin for the recalcitrant (vv. 11-12), riches for the righteous (vv. 13-16), and renewal for the regenerate (vv. 17-25).

Rebuke for the rebels (vv. 1-7)

The way to God has always been by grace through faith, regardless of ethnicity. Being Jewish provided no special salvific privilege, but Jews often thought that they were spiritually superior to the Gentiles because of God's choice of the nation. This was an attitude that was highly offensive to God. Thus, explains Kidner, "Far from ending in a general radiance, these chapters unsparingly sharpen the contrast of light and darkness and strip away all cover of privilege."[169] Here in verses 1-7, Isaiah gives three explanations of God's offer of grace and Israel's response to this offer.

First explanation: God's open invitation to grace (vv. 1-2)

The Old Testament shows a long history of God reaching out to His people. Verses 1-2 show us three ways that God kept making His grace available to Israel even though they would not respond.

First two ways God offered free grace (v. 1). Here in verse 1, the first two statements read, "I permitted Myself to be sought by those who did not ask *for Me;* I permitted Myself to be found by those who did not seek Me. I said, 'Here am I, here am I,' to a nation which did not call on My name."[170] Clearly, God's offer of grace was always there for Israel.

These statements in verses 1-2 raise interpretive questions on how we are to understand Isaiah's authorial intent. We have one of four possibilities. The first possibility is that Isaiah is speaking about the Gentiles who had never sought God in the past, but will respond in faith at the end of the age and enter the millennial kingdom. A second possibility is that Isaiah is referring to

---

[169] Kidner, "Isaiah," 669.
[170] The Niphal verb stem of "sought" (*darash*) and "found" (*matsa*) allows for this "tolerative" permissive verbal force such as seen in the Greek "permissive middle voice" (Bruce Waltke and M. O'Connor, *An Introduction to Biblical Hebrew Syntax* [Winona Lake: Eisenbrauns, 1990], 379).

Gentiles who are responding in faith now in the church age. A third possibility is that Isaiah is referring the eschatological Jewish remnant who will respond to Christ during the tribulation period. A fourth possibility is that verses 1-2 convey nothing about a positive response, but are speaking strictly about Israel's lack of responsiveness in past ages. This fourth interpretation may have the best contextual support and be the preferred view.

With reference to the first view, it is true that God's saving grace will draw a huge remnant of elect Gentiles to Himself during the Great Tribulation, and that these saved Gentiles will enter the messianic kingdom (cf. Isa. 2:1-4; 4:2-6; 11:10; 19:23-25; 42:6; 49:6; 53:15; 56:6-8; 60:1ff.; 61:5; 66:18-24; Rev. 7:9-19). This, however, is not best contextual understanding.

Neither should this passage be understood to be Gentiles getting saved into the church. For one thing, the New Testament teaches us that the church is a "mystery" that was never seen or predicted by the Old Testament prophets (Rom. 16:25-27; Eph. 3:1-10; Col. 1:26). Now, it is true that Paul quotes this passage in Romans 10:20 when he describes Gentiles coming to faith in the Body of Christ. What we have in Romans 10:20, though, is the application of a principle, i.e., people coming to faith who previously were not seeking God. This, however, is no more than an application of a spiritual principle,[171] the gracious salvation of those who were dead in sin but drawn to faith by God's grace.[172] Kidner, however, favors this view:

> The Hebrew as it stands supports Rom. 10:20–21 in referring v 1 to the Gentiles and v 2 to Israel. In the niv the Hebrew phrase 'a nation ... not called by my name', (*i.e.* the Gentiles) has been adjusted to read *a nation that did not call on my name* (which could still be Israel).[173]

It is true that in the church God is saving Gentiles who had never sought Him, but this is not the proper understanding of Isaiah 65:1-2.

Third way God offered free grace (v. 2). For the third time we see Isaiah talk about the offer of God's free grace when he writes, "I said, Here am I, here

---

[171] Paul is perfectly correct when he *applies* this principle to those Gentiles and Jews whom God is saving in the church today (Rom. 9:24-26; 10:19-20; cf. Hos. 1:10-11; 2:23; 1 Pet. 2:10). It is not a prophecy of the church, but the application is true.

[172] The Bible shows us that Adam's sin plunged the human race into a state of spiritual death (Rom. 5:12-21; Eph. 2:1-3; 4:17-19), a condition from which it is incapable to escape apart from the intervention of God's regenerating grace (Matt. 11:25-27; John 6:37, 44; Rom. 9:22-23; Eph. 1:3-6; 2 Tim. 1:9; Titus 3:5).

[173] Kidner, "Isaiah," 669.

am I, to a nation which did not call on My name."[174] Some see verses 1-2 as referring to Gentile inclusion in the millennial kingdom. This is possible, but still it is not the best view.[175]

It must be noted that verses 1-2 may not be referring to either future Gentile conversions nor to future Jewish conversions, but simply to present-day Israel. Thus, it is best understood as God showing His contempt for Israel's lack of responsiveness. Smith writes,

> To this sinful Israelite "nation" (*gôy*), a derogatory term for foreign nations that is used instead of the covenant term "people" (*'am*), God says, "Here I am; here I am!" This repetition could indicate something of God's frustration with this obstinate nation that did not call and the urgent need for them to wake up and turn to him. One can almost imagine in modern terminology, God waving his hand and screaming out this exclamation, "Wake up, over here, I'm right beside you!" The failure to call on the name of God indicates just how far these people are from God.[176]

Smith's view would be consistent with the way that Israel's disbelief eventually culminated with God rejecting the generation of Jews who rejected Jesus two thousand years ago. That generation of unbelieving Jews got rejected, but God also made it clear that one day His grace would bring the nation a restoration (Matt. 21:33-46, esp. v. 43; cf. 10:23; 12:39-45; 23:35-39). This is the restoration of the remnant Isaiah speaks about numerous times (Isa. 1:9; 4:2; 6:13; 7:3; 10:20-23; 11:11-16; 37:31-32; 41:17; 46:3; 49:6; 65-66). Here is a key point: No one can share in the kingdom apart from faith.[177]

Israel had that special privilege of being the custodians of God's special revelation (Isa. 53:1; Rom. 3:2; 9:1-5), but sadly this rebellious people (*sorer*)

---

[174] The MT conveys a passive idea with the Pual stem ("to a nation which was not called by His name"), but 1QIs[a] and all the versions read an active idea like, "a nation which did not call on His name" (Oswalt, *The Book of Isaiah: Chapters 40-66*, 632, n. 3).

[175] The context could embrace the idea of Gentile inclusion in the kingdom, but this would not obviate all the other promises about Israel's restoration such as seen in other passages (Young, *The Book of Isaiah, vol. 3*, 501; Grogan, "Isaiah," 349).

[176] Smith, *Isaiah 40-66*, 701. In summary, in the view of the present writer, it is best to see vv. 1-7 as God's rebuke for their lack of responsiveness and that positive response is not part of Isaiah's point. This much is clear, explains Young, God's free grace reached to those who did not know Him and who made no effort to find Him (Young, *The Book of Isaiah, vol. 3*, 501).

[177] Matthew's Gospel repeatedly emphasizes the warning that no unbelieving Jews will enter the kingdom (e.g., Matt. 3:10; 8:11-12; 21:33-46; 23:36-39; cf. Acts 2:40).

trusted in their own righteousness, and this self-righteousness kept them from salvation despite God's desire for them to seek Him (Ezek. 18:23; 30-32; Matt. 23:37; Rom. 9:30-10:3). Thus, explains Keil, "That which led them, and which they followed, was not the will of God, but selfish views and purposes, according to their own hearts' lusts."[178]

Israel's self-righteous rejection of grace (vv. 3-5)

Verses 3-5 continue to magnify Israel's self-righteous rebellion of God's saving grace. Isaiah highlights two aspects of this rebellion.

Israel's dedication to idolatry (vv. 3-4). Israel continually chose paths of idolatry which provoked God to anger.[179] These acts included pagan sacrifices in the gardens (1:29; 66:17),[180] burning incense on bricks (Jer. 44:17-19),[181] detestable nighttime acts in hidden places like graveyards,[182] and the eating of pig meat (Isa. 66:3, 17; cf. Lev. 11:7-8).

Israel's dedication to self-righteous (v. 5). Isaiah further describes Israel as being self-righteous hypocrites in that they are completely immersed in sin, but shun others as unworthy to even approach them, an attitude that God finds disgusting: "These are smoke in My nostrils, a fire that burns all the day."

The consequences of rejecting grace (vv. 6-7)

When God says "It is written before Me," the idea would appear to mean that all the sins of the nation have been written down and recorded so that God can judge them according to their deeds (v. 6; cf. Rev. 20:11-15).[183] The people wondered why God has been silent (63:15ff.; 64:12), but soon He will no longer keep His silence, but not in the way that they thought. The Day of the Lord is coming, but contrary to what they expect, it will not be good for them when God pays them back (*shalam*) in full for all their idolatry (v. 7; cf. 57:7; Amos 5:18; Mal. 3:1-7).

---

[178] Keil, *Commentary on the Old Testament*, 614.

[179] The articular participle (a Hiphil stem of *ka'as*, to provoke) emphasizes the durative force of the action. This list of idolatrous sins reminds us of unrepentant sins that keep men out of the New Jerusalem as seen in Rev 21:8; 22:15 (Grogan, "Isaiah," 349-350).

[180] Canaanite rituals were often held in luxuriant gardens.

[181] The exact meaning is not clear (Young, *The Book of Isaiah, vol. 3*, 503).

[182] This probably involved necromancy—communication with the dead (cf. Isa. 8:19; Deut. 18:11). Historical sources, like Jerome and Horace, show that such practices were common in the ancient world (ibid., 503, n. 4).

[183] Ibid., 505.

Martin notes that, "the Assyrian threat (Isa. 1–37) and the Babylonian Exile (chaps. 38–66) were two of the ways the Lord disciplined His people,"[184] but in reality, we need to recognize that the covenant curses that brought exile in Babylon (cf. Deut. 28:15-68) are still at work against Israel today. It will not be until the Tribulation Period has run its course that these judgments that God is measuring out (*madad*) will come to their final end (Isa. 10:25; 26:20-21; Dan. 9:27; 11:36; Matt. 24:3-31).

Restoration for the remnant (vv. 8-10)

Having discussed those who will not be heirs of the kingdom (vv. 1-7), Isaiah now turns his attention to that elect remnant who will come to faith in Messiah and be part of His kingdom. Yahweh has His people, and by His grace He will save them.

The illustration of the remnant (v. 8)

Isaiah uses a viticultural analogy to illustrate the idea that God has a remnant He will save out of Israel, and that He will not let the failure of the nation stop Him from fulfilling His redemptive promises (cf. Rom. 11:29). Back in chapter 5 God used a vineyard metaphor to illustrate the principle that Israel failed horribly to be a fruitful nation (cf. Jer. 2:21). Nevertheless, even though the nation failed badly, God knows that good can come out of it, those whom He calls "My servants," and for this reason He will not completely destroy the nation (cf. Isa. 27:1-6).

The descriptions of the remnant (v. 9)

Isaiah uses four terms to describe this eschatological remnant. He first calls them "offspring" (*zera'*, seed) from Jacob. We saw earlier that the victorious Servant will conquer death and see His seed (53:10; cf. 45:25; 54:3; 61:9; 66:22; Jer. 31:36). This "seed" consists of the huge number of Jewish believers who come to faith by the redeeming grace poured out on Israel by the Servant at the end of the age (Isa. 32:15; 43:18; 44:3-5; 59:21; Zech. 12:10).[185] Paul describes this restoration of Israel most vividly as being as though it is "life from the dead" (Rom. 11:15, 25-36).

Second, Isaiah describes the redeemed remnant as being "an heir [*yoresh*] of My mountains from Judah." The contemporary prophet Micah described One particular man who was to come out of Judah as being the eternal One who will come out of Bethlehem to be King forever (Mic. 5:2). Here, however,

---

[184] Martin, "Isaiah," 1119.
[185] David described the beauty of the Messiah's people in Psalm 110:3.

the context is speaking about the collective nation (v. 9; cf. Ezek. 36:8; 38:8; Ps. 37).

Third, Isaiah describes this redeemed remnant as God's "chosen ones" (*bachiyr*; cf. 65:15, 22) who will inherit (*yarash*) the land so as to possess it. Contrary to the mistaken views of replacement theologians, it is not the church who fulfills these prophecies, but a restored Israel in the messianic kingdom, thus bringing a final fulfillment to the land promises sworn to Abraham, Isaac, and Jacob (Gen. 12:1-3, et al.).

Fourth, God describes this redeemed remnant as His "servants" (the plural of *'ebed*; cf. 54:17 et al.) who will dwell in the land forever (Isa. 49:8; 60:21).[186] At long last, the redeemed remnant will dwell in their own land in peace, and dwelling with them will be the Lord Himself in the person of God's Servant, the Lord Jesus Christ (cf. Ezek. 48:35).

The response of the remnant (v. 10)

Having described the divine reason why these people are heirs of the kingdom,[187] Isaiah now shows the human reason. It is because these are the people who "seek" (*darash*) the Lord. These are the ones who have turned in faith, and for this reason these are the ones who will see Sharon become a rich pastureland, and the valley of Achor a resting place for herds. Sharon was historically a rich plain along the Mediterranean coast north of Joppa on the western edge of the land, but Achor, an ancient city on the eastern edge of the land near Jericho (cf. Josh. 7:24-26; cf. Hos. 2:15), was quite barren.[188] Those who trust the Lord will see the entire land transformed just as promised, for God has chosen Israel (cf. 41:8-9).

Ruin for the recalcitrant (vv. 11-12)

The offer of blessings has been there all along, but sadly there would still be those who refuse to turn to the Lord in faith. In the end, those who refuse to believe the Lord will be banned from the kingdom. Isaiah gives two broad explanations of the sins of these people: (1) they are dedicated to idolatry (v. 11), and (2) they refuse to repent (v. 12).

---

[186] Isaiah used the term servant at times to refer to the collective nation (e.g., 41:8), other times to Christ (e.g., 42:1), but other times as here in a plural sense as referring to the redeemed remnant.

[187] We say "divine reason" because all four expressions in v. 9 point back to the work of God.

[188] They will have great productivity (Oswalt, *The Book of Isaiah: Chapters 40-66*, 647).

First explanation: They are dedicated to idolatry (v. 11)

Idolatry has plagued the human race ever since the Tower of Babel, a sin that also dominated most of the ANE over the ages of Old Testament history. Israel fell to the lies of idolatry, and this is one of the major reasons God cast them out of the land. Isaiah gives a four-fold description of these apostates.

First description: They have forsaken the Lord. Isaiah's use of the second person plural pronoun (i.e., "But you" [(*we'attem*)]) emphasizes a contrast between the blessed believers of verses 8-10 and those who refused to listen (i.e., "you who forsake the Lord"). These are the people who lived in the land as descendants of Abraham under the Law—the covenant they swore to uphold (Exod. 19:5-6; 24:7-8), but who chose to reject it (Deut. 28:20; 29:24; 31:16; Judg. 10:10; 1 Kings 19:10; 2 Chron. 24:18; Jer. 1:16; 2:11-19; Dan. 11:28-32).

Second description: They forgot God's holy mountain. In context, the term "mountain" is best understood as speaking about Mount Zion, i.e., the temple mount in Jerusalem (Isa. 2:2-3), but perhaps the reference could also be understood in the wider sense of kingdom, as the term mountain sometimes connotes (Isa. 2:2-3; 11:9; 66:20; Dan. 2:35; Mic. 4:1). The point is that God is talking about His own people who have rejected Him.[189]

Third description: They set a table for Fortune. The idea of setting a table for "Fortune" (*Gad*) refers to a sacrificial feast for the demon god Gad, a well-known god in Syria that was connected with place names like Baal-Gad (Josh. 11:17; 12:7; 13:5) and Migdal-Gad (Josh. 15:37).[190]

Fourth description: They fill wine cups for Destiny. "Destiny" (*Meniy*) is not found elsewhere in Scripture, but was another one of the demon-gods Israelites had begun to worship. Archeologists have found inscriptions where both the names *Gad* and *Meniy* are used together.[191] By forsaking the Lord to worship these other gods, Israel had turned from the true and living God to serve demons (1 Cor. 10:21-22).

Second explanation: They would not repent (v. 12)

In itself, idolatry is not an unforgivable sin, but a refusal to repent is. Enemy invasion and slaughter will be their lot because God repeatedly called out

---

[189] In Isaiah 8:6 such apostates are described as those who "have rejected the gently flowing waters of *Shiloah*," i.e., the spring waters which originate at the Gihon Spring which was located in the City of David.

[190] Oswalt, *The Book of Isaiah: Chapters 40-66*, 648.

[191] Ibid.

to them through His prophets (cf. 65:2; 66:4), but they refused to respond. Therefore, God will "destine" (*manah*) them for the sword.[192]

Riches for the righteous (vv. 13-16)

Isaiah presents the stark contrast between the destinies of those who refuse the Lord and those who do listen.[193] Isaiah lays out three kinds of blessings that will belong to such believers (i.e., God's servants).

The physical blessings of the kingdom (v. 13a)

God's servants will eat and drink in plenty, but those who disbelieve will hunger and thirst. What we see here is a most-basic kind of life provision, the kind of provision that will be forfeited due to disbelief (cf. 5:13; 8:21 41:17; 49:10). In other words, those who refuse the Lord lose everything.[194]

The emotional blessings of the kingdom (vv. 13b-14)

Isaiah continues the contrast by telling us that God's servants will rejoice, but the rebels will be put to shame. The blessings of forgiveness will overtake believers with joy (Isa. 35:10; 51:11; 54:1; 61:7; 66:14), but eternal misery will be the lot of those who refuse to heed the Lord (Isa. 66:24; cf. Dan. 12:2; Matt. 8:12; 13:42, 50; 22:13; 25:30).

The restoration blessings of the kingdom (vv. 15-16)

All these blessings can be summed up as the restoration blessings of the kingdom. Verse 15, however, goes on to remind us of the terrifying reality that disbelief will only lead to everlasting judgments: "You will leave your name for a curse to My chosen ones, and the Lord God will slay you, but My servants will be called by another name" (v. 15). Keil explains,

> The former, perishing in the land of captivity, leave their name to the latter as *sh^ebhū'âh*, i.e., to serve as a formula by which to swear, or rather to execrate or curse (Num. 5:21), so that men will say, "Jehovah slay thee, as He slew them."[195]

---

[192] Isaiah creates a word play in that their worship of the "god" destiny (*Meniy*) will lead to God giving them a "destiny" (*manah*) of ruin.

[193] We see the solemnity of this by virtue of the name that God uses, *'Adonay Yahweh*, i.e., the sovereign Lord (cf. Isa. 48:16; 50:4-5, 7, 9).

[194] Grogan, "Isaiah," 350.

[195] Keil, *Commentary on the Old Testament*, 620.

Here is the idea: Those who called themselves Jews but were not saved will for all eternity become the kind of name that is used for a curse, but those who do believe will be called by a new name (Isa. 62:2-4; cf. Rev. 2:17; 3:12).

The destiny of the believer, however, will be radically different, for they will be blessed (*barak*) by the God of truth (cf. Ps. 31:15), and their former troubles will be gone forever (v. 16). The only reason why is because of their willingness to respond to God's grace and believe.[196]

Renewal for the regenerate (vv. 17-25)

The previous descriptions of joy and restoration now lead Isaiah to describe the "ultimate happiness and peace" that God will one day bring to His restored creation.[197] Sin has made our present world crooked, corrupt, and perverse, but God's promise is that one day He is going to perfectly restore it. All of this should cause us to long for the blessings of God's kingdom. Peter explained it this way, "Therefore, prepare your minds for action, keep sober *in spirit*, fix your hope completely on the grace to be brought to you at the revelation of Jesus Christ" (1 Pet. 1:13). Isaiah reveals six ways that God will make a radical transformation through the restoration of six lost blessings.

A restoration of a lost paradise (v. 17)

The declaration about God creating (*bara'*) a new heavens and earth raises the question of whether or not Isaiah understood this as fully as what gets revealed in the New Testament (2 Pet. 3:7-11; Rev. 21:1ff.). Martin does not think Isaiah saw a new creation such as seen in the New Testament,

> The Lord described the millennial kingdom, which is seemingly identified here with the eternal state (new heavens and a new earth). In Revelation, however, the new heavens and new earth (Rev. 21:1) *follow* the Millennium (Rev. 20:4). Most likely Isaiah did not distinguish between these two aspects of God's rule; he saw them together as one. After all, the Millennium, though 1,000 years in duration, will be a mere pinpoint of time compared with the eternal state.[198]

Thus, there appears to be reason to doubt that God gave Isaiah the extent of prophetic revelation that He gave to Peter and John in the New Testament.

---

[196] Because of their faith in Yahweh, they swore by His name and not the names of the Baals (cf. Jer. 12:16).
[197] Wolf, *Interpreting Isaiah*, 250.
[198] Martin, "Isaiah," 1120.

Nevertheless, God is going to make a total restoration of all that was lost through the entrance of sin and curse—a restoration in which all the former troubles are taken away and forgotten forever (Isa. 65:16; cf. Rev. 21:4).[199] Thus, explains Young, at the very least what we see here is the truth that one day God is going to bring in a full renewal of His creation.[200] Therefore, we can live with the hope that the woes of this life will one day pass and be replaced with the restoration of paradise lost.

A restoration of a lost joy (vv. 18-19)

God's restoration of His sin-cursed creation will eventually bring a recovery of all the joys that had been lost due to sin. For this reason,[201] God gives the command, "But be glad [*sus*; cf. Isa. 35:1; 61:10; 62:5; 64:4; 65:18, 19; 66:10, 14; Zeph. 3:17] and rejoice [*giyl*; cf. Isa. 9:2; 16:10; 25:9; 29:19; 35:1-2; 41:16; 49:13; 61:10; 66:10; Joel 2:23; Zeph. 3:17] forever in what I create, for behold, I create Jerusalem *for* rejoicing [*giylah*] and her people *for* gladness [*masos*]" (v. 18). The command is for extreme and unrestrained joy. Jerusalem, which for much of its history has been a cause of misery and pain, will one day become a source of great joy, and never again be the cause of weeping (*bekiy*) and crying (*ze'aqah*), for everlasting joy will replace the age of sorrow (Isa. 25:8; 30:19; 35:10; 51:11; 61:2-3; cf. Rev. 7:17; 21:4). This much is clear: God is going to restore the joy that was lost due to sin.

A restoration of a lost vitality (v. 20)

God warned Adam that disobedience would bring death (Gen. 2:17), and this is exactly what happened (Rom. 5:12). Adam's sin made death the king of the whole earth (Rom. 5:14, 17), but God's promise is that one day He will restore the life He had appointed from the beginning. For this reason, says Isaiah,

> No longer will there be in it an infant *who lives but a few* days, or an old man who does not live out his days, for the youth will die at the age of one

---

[199] Yahweh is the One who not only brought the creation into existence (Isa. 42:5), but will one day cause it to vanish (Isa. 51:6) and one day be completely recreated (65:16). The idea of "creating" (*bara'*) could mean a literal recreation of all the elements (cf. Gen. 1:1, 21, 27; 2:3), or perhaps that of bringing into existence without an ex-nihilo idea standing behind it (Isa. 43:1; cf. Ezek. 21:30; 28:13, 15). In this context, the latter is the best understanding.

[200] Young, *The Book of Isaiah, vol. 3*, 513.

[201] The Hebrew "But" (*kiy 'im*) accents a strong contrast ("But rather") between the former sorrows of the past age (v. 17) and the blessings of the future (vv. 18-25).

hundred and the one who does not reach the age of one hundred will be *thought* accursed.

This verse calls for several observations. First, we recognize that even though the Millennium is going to include a radical restraining of sin and death (Rev. 20:1-3), there will still be mortal human beings living in a state of sinfulness. For this reason, because sin still exists, death will still be part of human existence although greatly restrained.[202]

In the Millennium, lifespans will be very long, but death will still be a reality. Kidner explains, "The point of *a hundred* years old (20) is that in this new setting a mere century is shamefully brief."[203] The reality of death will be largely restrained during the Millennium so that death at age 100 is viewed as an anomaly. However, in the New Heavens and New Earth, these things will be completely purged forever (Rev. 21-22).

A restoration of a lost peace (vv. 21-23)

Throughout history, all civilizations have had to deal with the threat of foreign invasion that would bring a loss to all of life's labors. God's promise is that this will never happen again. Work and procreation will continue to be part of God's order during the Millennium, but it will not get frustrated by sin (cf. Lev. 26:16; Deut. 28:15-46; Isa. 13:16; Hos. 5:14; 7:12; ; 9:15; 10:10; 13:7, 16; Amos 5:11; Mic. 6:15; Zeph. 1:13).

A restoration of a lost intimacy (v. 24)

Israel's sin caused a separation from God so that He would not hear them (49:14; 59:1-2; 63:17; 64:12). One day this will change, for in the kingdom, God will restore the lost intimacy. They will pray, and He will respond (Isa. 30:19; 58:9; cf. Ps. 145:18-19).

A restoration of a lost harmony (v. 25)

Lastly, God will restore the harmony between all living creatures that was lost due to the entrance of sin: "The wolf and the lamb will graze together, and the lion will eat straw like the ox, and dust will be the serpent's food. They will

---

[202] It is only the regenerate (believers) who are allowed into the kingdom, but these people are still mortal sinners. Furthermore, the children born to them will be mortal sinners who need to make a choice to trust in Jesus Christ. Because these kingdom citizens are sinners, death will be a reality until the time when God purges all sin and death in an absolute sense (Rev. 21-22).

[203] Kidner, "Isaiah," 669.

do no evil or harm in all My holy mountain, says the Lord" (cf. Isa. 11:6-9). Sin brought enmity and death into the creation (Gen. 3:15; Rom. 8:20), but when He returns Christ will bring an end to all such enmity and death so that animals will never again bring harm to other animals, or even human beings (Isa. 35:9; cf. Hos. 2:18; Rom. 8:21-22). Kidner gives us an apt summary:

> The wicked will no longer flourish, nor the strong prey on the weak, nor the tempter escape his sentence (*cf.* v 25 with Gn. 3:14–15), in the perfect world to come. But all this is expressed freely, locally and pictorially, to kindle hope rather than feed curiosity.[204]

Summary and application

If you want life, and you want it abundantly, God is offering it to you right now. This was true for Israel twenty-seven centuries ago, and it is still true today. The only condition is that you must be willing to believe the word of the Lord and turn to Him for the cleansing and forgiveness.

THE RESTORATION OF TRUE WORSHIP IN ZION (66:1-24)

Isaiah's prophetic ministry spanned some 60 years from roughly 740 B.C. to at least 687 B.C. (prob. about 680). Here we come to the final chapter that highlights the restoration of true worship in Zion.

Chapter 66 reads as follows: "1 Thus says the Lord, Heaven is My throne and the earth is My footstool. Where then is a house you could build for Me? And where is a place that I may rest? 2 For My hand made all these things; thus all these things came into being, declares the Lord. But to this one I will look, to him who is humble and contrite of spirit, and who trembles at My word. 3 But he who kills an ox is *like* one who slays a man; he who sacrifices a lamb is *like* the one who breaks a dog's neck; he who offers a grain offering *is like one who offers* swine's blood; he who burns incense is *like* the one who blesses an idol. As they have chosen their *own* ways, and their soul delights in their abominations, 4 so I will choose their punishments, and will bring on them what they dread, because I called, but no one answered, I spoke, but they did not listen and they did evil in My sight and chose that in which I did not delight. 5 Hear the word of the Lord, you who tremble at His word: Your brothers who hate you, who exclude you for My name's sake, have said, Let the Lord be glorified, that we may see your joy. But they will be put to shame. 6 A voice of uproar from the city, a voice from the temple, the voice of the Lord who is rendering recompense to His enemies. 7 Before she travailed, she brought forth; before her pain came, she gave birth to a boy. 8 Who has heard such a thing? Who has

---

[204] Ibid.

seen such things? Can a land be born in one day? Can a nation be brought forth all at once? As soon as Zion travailed, she also brought forth her sons. 9 Shall I bring to the point of birth and not give delivery? says the Lord. Or shall I who gives delivery shut *the womb?* says your God. 10 Be joyful with Jerusalem and rejoice for her, all you who love her; be exceedingly glad with her, all you who mourn over her, 11 that you may nurse and be satisfied with her comforting breasts, that you may suck and be delighted with her bountiful bosom. 12 For thus says the Lord, Behold, I extend peace to her like a river, and the glory of the nations like an overflowing stream; and you will be nursed, you will be carried on the hip and fondled on the knees. 13 As one whom his mother comforts, so I will comfort you, and you will be comforted in Jerusalem. 14 Then you will see *this,* and your heart will be glad, and your bones will flourish like the new grass, and the hand of the Lord will be made known to His servants, but He will be indignant toward His enemies. 15 For behold, the Lord will come in fire and His chariots like the whirlwind, to render His anger with fury, and His rebuke with flames of fire. 16 For the Lord will execute judgment by fire and by His sword on all flesh, and those slain by the Lord will be many. 17 Those who sanctify and purify themselves *to go* to the gardens, following one in the center, who eat swine's flesh, detestable things and mice, will come to an end altogether, declares the Lord. 18 For I know their works and their thoughts. The time is coming to gather all nations and tongues, and they shall come and see My glory. 19 I will set a sign among them and will send survivors from them to the nations: Tarshish, Put, Lud, Meshech, Tubal and Javan, to the distant coastlands that have neither heard My fame nor seen My glory, and they will declare My glory among the nations. 20 Then they shall bring all your brethren from all the nations as a grain offering to the Lord, on horses, in chariots, in litters, on mules and on camels, to My holy mountain Jerusalem, says the Lord, just as the sons of Israel bring their grain offering in a clean vessel to the house of the Lord. 21 I will also take some of them for priests *and* for Levites, says the Lord. 22 For just as the new heavens and the new earth which I make will endure before Me, declares the Lord, so your offspring and your name will endure. 23 And it shall be from new moon to new moon and from sabbath to sabbath, all mankind will come to bow down before Me, says the Lord. 24 Then they will go forth and look on the corpses of the men who have transgressed against Me, for their worm will not die and their fire will not be quenched, and they will be an abhorrence to all mankind" (66:1-24).

The Bible indicates that God's work includes the (ultimate?) purpose of bringing glory to His own name (Isa. 6:3; 22:23; 40:5; 42:8, 12; 43:7; 44:23; 45:25; 46:13; 48:11; 49:3; 58:8; 59:19; 60:1, 19; 66:18; Eph. 1:6, 12, 14).[205] Here in this

---

[205] To assert that God's ultimate purpose is to glorify His own name does not

final chapter, Isaiah shows us six ways that the sovereign Lord will glorify Himself when He sends Jesus to bring the kingdom of God to this earth.

Sovereign Yahweh accepts the humble (vv. 1-2)

Theological discussions about the attributes of God show us two complementary truths. One is that God is infinite in His transcendence, and the other is that He is also infinite in His immanence. These truths remind us that God is completely set apart from all sinners, but He is also willing to embrace and receive those who love Him and believe His Word (praise God).

The Lord is infinite in His transcendence (vv. 1-2a)

Mere religion will never satisfy the demands of a God who is perfectly holy and righteous, for God's requirement is that of perfect righteousness (cf. Rom. 3:19-20). Verses 1-2 remind us of the infinite transcendence of Yahweh and why it is that no amount of self-righteous effort by fallen man will ever make him acceptable to God.

Yahweh needs no one (v. 1). First of all, says God, "Heaven is My throne and the earth is My footstool [1 Chron. 28:2; Pss. 99:5; 110:1; 132:7]. Where then is a house you could build for Me? And where is a place that I may rest?" (v. 1). Some have wrongly supposed that God is commanding those in Babylon not to rebuild a temple, but such is not the case. Rather, this is a rebuke to sinners that God needs nothing from them.[206]

Yahweh is Creator of all (v. 2a). God is always there, but He cannot be reached by fallen men who trust in dead religion or, as Keil expresses it, "The prophecy is addressed to the entire body now ready to return, and says to the whole without exception, that Jehovah, the Creator of heaven and earth, does not stand in need of any house erected by human hands."[207] Isaiah reaffirms this truth by once again reminding His people that He is the One who made everything: "For My hand made all these things; thus all these things came into being, declares the Lord." Here is the point: God needs nothing from man.

---

preclude everything the Scripture says about God's love for humanity and His desire to save and bless sinners, for both concepts have biblical support.

[206] Both David (2 Sam. 7:4-14) and Solomon (1 Kings 8:27) expressed this truth with reference to the building of a temple for Yahweh (cf. Ps. 11:4; Matt. 5:34, 35).

[207] Keil, *Commentary on the Old Testament*, 627.

The Lord is infinite in His immanence (v. 2b)

Despite the transcendence and holiness of God, we also see that the Lord is still willing to accept sinners who come to Him in faith: "But to this one I will look, to him who is humble and contrite of spirit, and who trembles at My word" (Isa. 57:15; 66:5).[208] God saves sinners who humble themselves and believe (Ps. 138:6; Prov. 3:34; Matt. 5:3; 11:28; James 4:6).

Sovereign Yahweh rejects the proud (vv. 3-4)

God's invitation to the humble stands, but for the proud sinner who delights in dead religion over the way of the Lord, there will be nothing but judgment. The reason, explains Hughes, is because, "God is never pleased with hand ritual apart from heart righteousness."[209] Isaiah shows us both the deeds of dead religion (v. 3) and the destiny of dead religion (v. 4).

The deeds of dead religion (v. 3)

God hates dead religion (i.e., religious rituals done by unsaved men). Isaiah gives a four-fold description of Israel's dead religion, telling us how God felt about their empty rituals.

First two descriptions of Israel's dead religion. Isaiah says, "But he who kills an ox is *like* one who slays a man; he who sacrifices a lamb is *like* the one who breaks a dog's neck" (cf. Exod. 13:13; Deut. 21:4). Because of their separation from God, their sacrifices were no better than the most-wicked of deeds, and completely unacceptable to God (Isa. 1:10-15; 59:1-2; cf. Amos 5:21-23; Prov. 15:8). Israel would have much done better by applying the words of King David: "The sacrifices of God are a broken spirit; a broken and a contrite heart, O God, You will not despise" (Ps. 51:17). God's real desire was a heart of faith that delights in genuine righteousness (Amos. 5:23; Mic. 6:8).

Two more descriptions of Israel's dead religion. Isaiah continues to explain God's view of Israel's dead religion: "He who offers a grain offering *is like one who offers* swine's blood; he who burns incense is *like* the one who blesses an idol. As they have chosen their *own* ways, and their soul delights in their abominations" (cf. 65:2, 12). The daily offering of incense was a standard part of Israel's temple worship (Isa. 1:13; cf. Lev. 24:7; Num. 5:26; Ps. 38:1), but God says that it is no more acceptable than pig's blood (Lev. 11:7-8). We must understand that the problem did not lie in the offering itself, but that Israel's

---

[208] This verse uses three different expressions to indicate repentant, saving faith.
[209] Hughes, *Tyndale Concise Bible Commentary*, 269.

sin made its worship unacceptable, i.e., no better than the blessing of an idol.[210]

The destiny of dead religion (v. 4)

Because they chose their own ways, God will bring upon them the punishments they dreaded most. The term for punishments (*ta'aluliym*) is an interesting one that is found elsewhere only in 3:4 with the translation "capricious children," but here with the sense of being wanton, or making sport of, or causing mockery, or mistreating (cf. Judg. 19:25).[211] Here is the idea: Those who refuse the Lord will never experience peace (48:22; 57:21), but only unrelenting wrath.

Sovereign Yahweh cares about the pains of His people (vv. 5-6)

Despite the widespread disbelief, there was still a believing remnant in the land. Isaiah describes the believers as those who tremble (*charad*; cf. 66:5) at His Word. These are the ones who, simply because they believe in Yahweh, are hated by their Jewish brethren (cf. Amos 5:10), the ones who get shunned and excluded because of their faith in Yahweh.[212] The New Testament reminds us that the unsaved world hates those who belong to the Lord (cf. John 9:34; 15:18-19; 1 John 3:13).

These unsaved people are the ones who make all kinds of mocking statements about believers, taunting them for their faith in the Lord with words like, "Let the Lord be glorified, that we may see your joy," i.e., Let's see God come save them according to their claim to trust in His salvation (cf. Isa. 5:19; Zeph. 1:12). The key points to note are that (1) the world is always going to hate those who have true faith, and (2) God certainly will judge those unbelievers and they will be put to shame. The Lord cares for His people. He sees the pain of being hated for His name's sake, and He wants them to know that He will judge those who persecute His people: "A voice of uproar from the city, a voice from the temple, the voice of the Lord who is rendering recompense to His enemies" (v. 6). Thus, explains Smith, "Knowing this, all the humble and contrite can rest assured that eventually God will justly deal with those who hate them and repay all those who are involved with syncretistic worship."[213] Scripture is clear that God will judge all who hate Him and reject His Word.

---

[210] Literally, the blessing of "iniquity" (*'awen*; cf. Isa. 41:29; Hos. 4:15).
[211] Carl Schultz, "*'ll*," ed. R. Laird Harris, Gleason L. Archer Jr., and Bruce K. Waltke, *Theological Wordbook of the Old Testament*, cited in electronic form with Logos Libronix (Chicago: Moody Press, 1999), 670–671.
[212] Young explains, "The apostates cannot tolerate the righteous and want nothing to do with them" (Young, *The Book of Isaiah, vol. 3*, 522).
[213] Smith, *Isaiah 40-66*, 738.

Sovereign Yahweh will fulfill His promises (vv. 7-9)

Verses 7-9 remind us once again of the glorious return of Christ when Israel will experience a marvelous spiritual rebirth at a national level (Isa. 54; cf. Zech. 12:10-13:1; Rom. 11:25-36).[214] Actually, though, here in verses 7-9 Isaiah speaks about two interrelated promises of birth that mother Jerusalem will experience. Even though there is scholarly debate about how to interpret some of the statements in this section, in the opinion of the present writer Isaiah is telling us first about the promised birth of the Messiah (vv. 7-8a), and then about the spiritual rebirth of the entire nation because of the redeeming work of the Messiah (vv. 8b-9).

The interrelationship comes out by virtue of the solidarity that exists between the corporate nation and the One Savior whom God will bring forth out of that corporate nation. Thus, explains Unger, in these following verses, "the figure of the male child comprehends the spiritually regenerated nation, the many sons being viewed as one under the returning Messiah, who will be manifested as their representative head."[215] This writer concurs with Unger on how we should see verses 7-9 speaking first about the physical birth of the Messiah (vv. 7-8a), and then secondly about the spiritual birth of the entire nation (vv. 8b-9).

First promise: A child to rule as King (vv. 7-8a)

The promise of Messiah's birth. Virtually all conservative scholars recognize that the promise of redemption begins in Genesis 3:15 and runs throughout the entire Bible. This promised Messiah will be a male child who comes as a descendent of Eve (Gen. 3:15),[216] who comes from the nation of Israel (Gen. 12:1-3; 35:9-12; Num. 24:17), who comes from the tribe of Judah (Gen. 49:10), who comes from the royal line of David (2 Sam. 7:12-16; Isa. 9:6-7), who is born in Bethlehem (Mic. 5:2), and who is killed before the destruction of Israel's second temple (Dan. 9:24-27).

The marvel of the Messiah's birth. The marvel of the Messiah's birth is that it came to Israel before (*beterem*) Israel's travail (*chiyl*) and before (*beterem*)

---

[214] Hughes, *Tyndale Concise Bible Commentary*, 269.
[215] Merrill F. Unger, *Unger's Commentary on the Old Testament, Volume II Isaiah-Malachi* (Chicago: Moody, 1981), 1337.
[216] In Genesis 3:15 both lexical (*'ish*) and grammatical evidence show us the Savior will be a male, a fact confirmed here by Isaiah's use of the distinctive term for "boy" (*zakar*, literally, "male"; cf. Gen. 1:27), and Revelation's description of the birth of the male (*arsen*) Christ child (Rev. 12:2, 4, 5).

Israel's labor pain (*chebel*), i.e., before the future seven-year tribulation period.[217] It is a marvel that a child could be brought forth before travail, but that is why Isaiah asks, "Who has heard such a thing? Who has seen such things?" (v. 8a). This passage is best understood as referring to the birth of Messiah. The words are obscure, but it is interesting that this messianic interpretation was held in ancient Israel, as noted by Oswalt: The significance of *zakar*, "male," here is unclear. The Targ. paraphrases "her king will be revealed," which is plainly a messianic reference. Rev. 12:5 uses similar terminology in what is apparently a messianic setting.[218] The present writer believes that this is the best interpretation.[219]

Thus, the birth of this male child is also the same one spoken of in Isaiah 9:6-7, the child who comes to the nation after long ages of darkness, but before the horrors of the Tribulation Period. A careful study of the Hebrew text shows us that this child, the One who is called "Mighty God" (*'El Gibbor*), is the same One who will restore the remnant of Israel at the end of the age (cf. Isa. 10:20-23).[220] As other Scripture and salvation history show us, the salvation of the nation would not coincide immediately with the birth of the Promised One, for we know that the Promised One would first be despised, and rejected and killed for the sins of His people before conquering death in resurrection (Isa. 52:13-53:12), all fulfilled by Jesus.

Second promise: The birth of a nation (vv. 8b-9)

Verses 8b-9 continue the birth promises by shifting the focus away from the Messiah to the corporate nation of Israel and the spiritual birth she will experience during the Tribulation Period, in particular in the last half of this period.[221]

---

[217] Twice Isaiah uses *beterem* to tell us that this special birth comes before the agonies of labor.

[218] Oswalt, *The Book of Isaiah: Chapters 40-66*, 674, n. 42.

[219] One of the other common ways of interpreting this passage is to say that Israel's spiritual birth in the seven-year tribulation period will be so quick that it will be virtually like she did not go through labor. Given the horrors of the tribulation period (Jer. 30:6-7; Matt. 24:8, 21-22; 1 Thess. 2:16; 5:1-3; Rev. 12:13-17), we cannot accept the plausibility of this explanation.

[220] In Isa. 10:20-23 we are told that the remnant of Jacob will turn to "the Mighty God" (*'El Gibbor*), the One who was born as a child in 9:6 and destined to reign eternally as King over Israel (9:7).

[221] The redemption and sealing of the 144,000 would represent a small portion of this remnant (Rev. 7:1-8; cf. 12:17; 14:1).

The suddenness of Israel's spiritual birth (v. 8b). Those seven years, especially the last three-and-a-half, will be horrific for Israel, but God will use it to bring regeneration to the nation. Isaiah likens it to a land being born in one day and a nation being brought forth all at once (v. 8b). This spiritual birth is the same one Isaiah described back in chapter 54. God's desire had always been to see such spiritual fruit from Israel, but she never produced it in ages past (cf. 26:17-18; 33:11).

The certainty of Israel's spiritual birth (v. 9). Lest anyone doubt the certainty of these promises, the Lord asks, "Shall I bring to the point of birth and not give delivery? says the Lord. Or shall I who gives delivery shut *the womb?* says your God" (v. 9). In other words, God certainly will bring spiritual birth to His people Israel (cf. Isa. 49:15-26; 54:1-17).

Sovereign Yahweh will satisfy the longings of the saints (vv. 10-14a)

In light of God's promise to bring spiritual birth, the Lord now issues a call to rejoice. This includes the call for rejoicing (v. 10), the cause for rejoicing (vv. 11-13), and the consequence of rejoicing (v. 14a).

The call for rejoicing (v. 10)

As we survey world history. We see that few nations have suffered as much as Israel,[222] but here the call here is for supreme rejoicing (60:20; 61:2-3; 65:18-19). God gives the three-fold command, "Be joyful [*samach*] with Jerusalem, and rejoice [*giyl*] for her, all you who love her; be exceedingly glad with her, all you who mourn over her [*sus*, an imperative combined with noun to intensify of "be glad"]."[223]

The cause for rejoicing (vv. 11-13)

The reason for this rejoicing is on account of the fact (*lema'an*, here with the sense "on account of"[224]) that all kingdom citizens will have the privilege of being blessed in the messianic kingdom. Oswalt explains, "The direct cause of the rejoicing that Isaiah promises to the new Jerusalem's inhabitants is that their

---

[222] Her suffering was from her own rebellion (Isa. 5:5-6; 49:19; cf. Deut. 28:15-68).

[223] It is interesting to trace the repeated use of commands to rejoice in contexts where the call for supreme rejoicing is because of the restoration blessing of having the messianic King in their very presence (Isa. 12:6; Zeph. 3:14-20; Zech. 2:10; 9:9).

[224] Ludwig Koehler et al., *The Hebrew and Aramaic Lexicon of the Old Testament*, cited in electronic form with Logos Libronix (Leiden: E.J. Brill, 1994–2000), 614.

city will provide for all their needs."[225] These nourishing and comforting blessings are described in the tenderest terms using the image of Jerusalem nursing (*yanaq*) her little babies (i.e., those who inhabit the city). The language is very tender and intimate,[226] and there could be no greater illustration of the beauty of the Lord's blessings that will come to His redeemed saints in the Kingdom (cf. 49:23; 60:4-16).

Gone forever will be the age of sin, conflict and war, and in its place, says God, "Behold, I extend peace to her like a river, and the glory of the nations like an overflowing stream" (v. 12). Years earlier (8:6-8) Isaiah used similar imagery (i.e., "overflowing stream"), but for a much different reason. In its earlier use, the overflowing stream was used to describe the furious power of the King of Assyria invading Judah, but now the overflowing stream will be the eternal peace and glory (i.e., wealth) of the nations.[227]

The consequence of such rejoicing (v. 14a)

God says, when this day comes, "Then you will see *this,* and your heart will be glad, and your bones will flourish like the new grass [cf. 58:11];[228] and the hand of the Lord will be made known to His servants." Gladness and joy will replace sadness and sorrow, and never again will the sorrows and pains of sin and curse be their lot. God's promise is there to encourage us to keep our hope vibrant and to not grow weary.

---

[225] Oswalt, *The Book of Isaiah: Chapters 40-66*, 676.

[226] For example, (1) the *satiation* (*saba'*, "eat one's fill") that a baby receives while nursing (*yanaq*, "nurse, suckle"), (2) the *comfort* (*tanchum*) a baby experiences while nursing at the breast (*shad*), (3) the sucking (*matsats*, "to slurp or lap" or "to drain every drop") and delighting (*'anag*, "to take pleasure in"; cf. 58:14) in a bountiful bosom (*ziyz kabod*, prob. best as "full breast," but *ziyz* can refer more narrowly to the nipple or tit), and (4) the great comfort (*nacham*) that comes to a baby who is being nursed, carried on the hip, and fondled on the knees (Palpal of *sha'a'*, "played with" or "rocked to and fro" or "fondled"). As we have seen, starting in 40:1 this idea of comfort (*nacham*) is a major theme in the latter portion of Isaiah (cf. 40:1 (bis); 49:13; 51:3 (bis), 11, 12, 19; 52:9; 54:11; 57:6; 61:2; 66:13) (ibid., 679, n. 52).

[227] Grogan, "Isaiah," 352. The "glory of the nations" is not only the idea that the nations will come to Jerusalem to worship the King (cf. 2:2-4; 11:10; 48:18; 52:7; 54:13; 57:19; 60:17), but also that they will freely worship with gifts from their wealth (40:1-11; 41:17-20; 49:13-18; 51:3-12; 60:5, 13; 61:6; 66:12-13).

[228] The expression "flourish (*parach*) is common in growing objects in nature.

Sovereign Yahweh will judge the sins of the wicked (vv. 14b-24)

For those who refuse, God "will be indignant (*za'am*) to His enemies" (v. 14b).[229] Smith sees this as potentially including Jews and Gentiles:

> The final paragraph begins with a description of the glorious coming of God in a theophany, accompanied by fire, his sword, and his chariot (66:15–16). He will come in wrath to bring destruction on all those who worship pagan gods, including any Hebrews who are involved with syncretistic worship (66:17). It is at this time that God will reveal the majesty of his presence on earth so that all people, even the foreign nations around the world who have not known him, will see his glory (66:18; 60:1–3).[230]

Isaiah makes it clear that no unsaved man will enter the Messiah's kingdom or escape His fiery judgment. Here in this final section, we see the Agent of God's judgments (v. 15), the objects of God's judgments (vv. 16-17), and the goal of God's judgments (vv. 18-24).

The Agent of God's judgments (v. 15)

This verse opens with the expression "for behold" (*kiy hinneh*), an expression that signals an important message: God is coming to judge sinners. The coming of God to judge is portrayed as a theophany in which Yahweh comes to judge the wicked (Deut. 33:26; Isa. 5:28; 10:17; 29:6; 30:27; 33:14; 57:18; 59:18; 65:6; 66:6; cf. Pss. 18:19; 68:17; 104:3; Hab. 3:8).

The Scripture leaves no doubt that this Judge is Jesus Christ (Zech. 2:5; 9:14-15; 14:3-4; Matt. 25:31; Rev. 19:11-21; 22:12). Jesus Himself said, "The Son of Man is going to come in the glory of His Father with His angels, and will then repay every man according to his deeds" (Matt. 16:27). Paul describes the coming of Christ to judge sinners:

> For after all it is *only* just for God to repay with affliction those who afflict you, and *to give* relief to you who are afflicted and to us as well when the Lord Jesus will be revealed from heaven with His mighty angels in flaming fire, dealing out retribution to those who do not know God and to those who do not obey the gospel of our Lord Jesus. These will pay the penalty of eternal destruction, away from the presence of the Lord and from the glory of His power (2 Thess. 1:6-9).

---

[229] God's "indignation" that previously had been against His rebellious nation (Isa. 10:5, 25; Dan. 8:19; 11:36) will now be poured out against all who refuse Him (Isa. 10:25; 26:20; 34:2).

[230] Smith, *Isaiah 40-66*, 744.

Who are these objects of judgment?

The objects of God's judgments (vv. 16-18a)

Eschatological wrath to the nations. Numerous passages show us the eschatological wrath of God on unsaved Gentiles (Deut. 30:7; Isa. 9:1-7; 10:25-34; 26:20-21; 34:1-17; Ezek. 38-39; Dan. 7:23-28; 9:27; 11:36-45; Joel 3:1-17; Zech. 14:1-15; Rev. 17:11-18; 19:11-21). These verses include such people.

Eschatological wrath to unsaved Israel. God will destroy the unsaved nations who are seeking Israel's destruction, but in the present context Isaiah appears to be focusing on unsaved Jews. Isaiah describes this judgment by saying, "For the Lord will execute judgment by fire and by His sword on all flesh,[231] and those slain by the Lord will be many" (v. 16). God hated the empty religious pride of Israel in the days of Isaiah (cf. 29:13), and He is still going to hate it in its final form at the end of the age. These were the idolaters of Israel, those who, "sanctify and purify themselves *to go* to the gardens [cf. 1:29; 65:3],[232] following one in the center, who eat swine's flesh [*chaziyr*; cf. Lev. 11:7; Isa. 65:4], detestable things [*sheqets*] and mice [*'akbar*]" (v. 17a; cf. Lev. 11:11-43; 20:25). God never condemned Gentiles for eating any kinds of foods that had been declared unclean for Israel, but He did condemn Israel for such rebellion. For this reason, God says they will "come to an end altogether" (*suph*) (v. 17b; cf. Zeph. 1:1-3).

Here is what we see from Isaiah's prophecy: When the Messiah comes, He will purge His people of all filth and rebellion, many of which will fall by means of the sword through enemy invasion (v. 16b). Ezekiel reminds us of the truth that being a physical Jew does not assure entrance into the messianic kingdom, for God will purge all the rebels (Ezek. 20:36-38; cf. Zech. 13:8-9). Malachi affirmed this truth:

> He will sit as a smelter and purifier of silver, and He will purify the sons of Levi and refine them like gold and silver, so that they may present to the Lord offerings in righteousness. Then the offering of Judah and Jerusalem will be pleasing to the Lord as in the days of old and as in former years (Mal. 1:1-4).

---

[231] The expression "all flesh" certainly could be speaking universally about all the nations, but the context appears to be limiting this to all the nation of Israel (cf. e.g., Joel 2:28). Grogan is probably correct that though the "all" is capable of embracing Gentiles, is best seen as unsaved Jews (Grogan, "Isaiah," 352).

[232] These same kinds of terms (e.g., to sanctify and purify) were used in the Law of Moses to describe priestly rituals of worship (Gen. 35:2; Exod. 19:22; Num. 8:7; 11:18; 2 Chron. 30:17) (Young, *The Book of Isaiah, vol. 3*, 530).

The hypocrites may think that they will escape judgment, but God tells them, "I know their works and their thoughts" (v. 18a).[233]

The goal of God's judgments (vv. 18b-24)

Isaiah indicates that the goal of God's judgments is to glorify His name among all men so that He might receive the honor and praise that is due His name. This work to glorify His name will include two kinds of gatherings: (1) the gathering of elect Gentiles to see His glory (vv. 18b-19), and (2) the gathering of elect Jews to see His glory (vv. 20-24).

The gathering of elect Gentiles (vv. 18b-19). Once again, we return to a theme we have seen many times: Yahweh is a holy God who deserves praise from all men. One of the ways God will do this is by causing His grace to redeem His elect saints from every corner of the earth. Isaiah says, "[The time] is coming to gather [*qabats*] all nations and tongues, and they shall come and see My glory" (v 18b).[234] In the eschaton, the nations of the world are going to make the choice to invade Israel, but God Himself is really the One drawing these nations to fulfill His purposes (Ezek. 38:4-8; 39:1-2; Joel 3:1-2; Mic. 4:12; Zech. 14:2; Rev. 16:14; 17:13-18). The nations want to destroy Israel, but God is using their evil for the purpose of saving a remnant of Israel for His glory. Isaiah says,

> I will set a sign among them and will send survivors from them to the nations: Tarshish,[235] Put,[236] Lud,[237] Meshech,[238] Tubal,[239] Javan,[240] and to the distant coastlands[241] that have neither heard My fame nor seen My glory, and they will declare My glory among the nations" (v. 19).

---

[233] Young explains that as for the things that they think are secret, God says He knows all about them (ibid., 531).

[234] The subject "the time" is not found in the Heb. text, but the NASB is justified in supplying it.

[235] Most identify Tarshish with Spain at the far west edge of the Mediterranean world (2:16; 60:9).

[236] Codex B in LXX reads *Phoud*, i.e., Put, i.e., Libya while the MT reads *pul* (cf. Gen. 10:6; Ezek. 27:10; 30:5; 38:5) (ibid., 533).

[237] Unknown (cf. Ezek. 27:10).

[238] Ancient Asia, i.e., modern Turkey, perhaps in the Caucasus region (Ezek. 27:13; 38:2, 3; 39:1).

[239] Caucasus region (Gen. 10:2; Ezek. 27:13; 38:2, 3; 39:1).

[240] Basically, the area of Greece or perhaps the Ionian coast of Asia (Gen. 10:2, 4; Ezek. 27:13).

[241] The Mediterranean world (Isa. 11:11; 13:22; 20:6; 23:2, 6; 24:15; 34:14; 40:15; 41:1, 5; 42:4, 10, 12, 15; 49:1; 50:1; 51:5; 59:18; 60:9; 66:1).

The way that God saves them is that He will set a sign (*'oth*) among them that He uses to save His elect Gentiles, i.e., those whom God has gathered together against Israel, but who saw His saving grace and came to faith.[242] The text does not explain exactly what this sign is (see *'oth* in Isa. 7:11, 14; 8:18; 19:20; 20:3; 37:30; 38:22; 55:13; cf. Exod. 10:2; Ps. 78:43.). Smith writes,

> It might be the miraculous defeat of Gog and Magog (Ezek 38:18–23; Joel 3:9–16), God's personal appearance on the Mount of Olives to save his people with a great earthquake (Zech 14:1–5) or some completely new divine act unparalleled in previous history."[243]

Probably the best understanding is that Isaiah is speaking in general about the miraculous work of Christ to save Israel from annihilation, and the way that God's Spirit uses this to draw God's remnant of all nations to faith.[244] Then, once the battles of Armageddon have ended, these Gentile survivors (the *peleytiym*),[245] i.e., those from the invading armies who came to faith, will now be ready to serve the Lord and do His bidding. They will go back to their home countries as living witnesses to the mighty deeds of Yahweh. Kidner explains, "The Lord's coming will be followed by the further evangelizing of the world."[246] Thus, the Gentiles who once sought Israel's destruction will become missionaries who go back to their home countries and take the gospel into the world (cf. Isa. 19:18-25; 42:12).[247] This is such great news. Even at this final stage of human history, God is still at work to save sinners by His grace.

The gathering of elect Jews (vv. 20-24). The last statement in verse 19 tells about God's glory going out to the nations, but here in verses 20-24 we see that these Gentiles are going to respond to God's grace by helping regather to God's holy mountain, i.e., Jerusalem (cf. 2:2-3; 11:9; 56:7; 65:11; Zech. 14:16-21), the remnant of the Jews scattered all over the world (v. 20; cf. 11:12; 14:2; 27:12-13; 43:6; 49:22; 60:1-22; Matt. 24:31). God likens this willing ministry of the

---

[242] Some commentators, like Unger and Young and others, understand this to be saying that God sets a sign among the remnant of the Jews to save them, but the connection between 18b and 19 suggests that it is a sign to the Gentiles who have come against Israel and gotten saved by seeing God's miraculous work in Christ (Unger, *Unger's Commentary on the Old Testament, Volume II Isaiah-Malachi*, 1338; Young, *The Book of Isaiah, vol. 3*, 531-532).

[243] Smith, *Isaiah 40-66*, 749.

[244] Oswalt, *The Book of Isaiah: Chapters 40-66*, 688.

[245] Scripture also speaks of Jewish *peleytiym* (Isa. 4:2; 10:20; Joel 2:32; Obad. 17).

[246] Kidner, "Isaiah," 669.

[247] These names all seem to center around the Mediterranean world to the west of Israel.

Gentiles to regather saved Jews to that of a grain offering that comes out of gratitude and thankfulness to the Lord (cf. Lev. 2:2, 9, 16). Isaiah saw the means of restoration coming through animals, but this will be fulfilled by any modern means of transportation.

Then, from among these regathered Jews, God will take some of them to serve as Levites and priests (v. 21).[248] In other words, not only will God restore a Son of David to rule as King over Israel, but He will also restore the priesthood (Isa. 61:6; cf. Jer. 33:14-26), the priestly line that comes through Levi (Num. 3:12-13), Aaron (Exod. 28:1-3), Phineas (Num. 25:10-13), and Zadok (1 Kings 1:32-35; 2:26-27, 35; Ezek. 44:15-16). God once again gives absolute assurance that He will fulfill these promises: "For just as the new heavens and the new earth which I make will endure before Me, declares the Lord, so your offspring and your name will endure" (v. 22).[249] God said He will restore Israel, and He will do it (Isa. 55:6-13; Jer. 33:14-26).

Not only will the elect remnant of Israel have its eternal restoration, but so will the remnant of the Gentiles as well. Hence, we read, "and it shall be from new moon to new moon and from sabbath to sabbath, all mankind will come to bow down before Me, says the Lord" (v. 23). It is not only Jews who receive the blessings of the messianic kingdom, but finally at long last all the nations of the earth, i.e., "all flesh" (*kal basar*) will get blessed and worship the Lord in Zion (Gen. 12:3; Isa. 56:2-5; Ezek. 45:18-25; Zech. 14:16-21).[250]

Isaiah's final word comes with the sober reminder that no matter what God does to show sinners that they need His grace, there will also be many who still refuse to believe. When the battles of Armageddon have come to a close at the end of the seven-year tribulation period and masses of unsaved human beings lay slaughtered on the ground, Isaiah tells us that the believers, "will go forth and look on the corpses [*peger*] of the men who have transgressed against Me" (v. 24a). Huge numbers of corpses will call for an extended time period before they can all be buried, a most-horrific site to behold (Isa. 26:20-21; 34:1-8; 63:1-6; cf. Jer. 25:33; Ezek. 39:9-16; Rev. 16:13-21; 19:11-21). All these unrepentant sinners who died in disbelief will experience an eternal judgment in the never-ending flames of hell (Dan. 12:2). Isaiah describes this by saying, "their

---

[248] It is incorrect to assert that God is taking Gentiles and turning them into Levites and priests (Grogan, "Isaiah," 353).

[249] For discussion about the New Heavens and Earth, see comments on 65:17.

[250] Oswalt notes that the point here is not that the worship is only on certain days of times, but that of continuity and duration (Oswalt, *The Book of Isaiah: Chapters 40-66*, 692, n. 87).

worm will not die and their fire will not be quenched,"[251] and "they will be an abhorrence to all mankind" (v. 24b). Progressive revelation speaks about the reality of eternal punishment (Rev. 14:9-11; 20:11-15), but as we see, even the Old Testament makes this truth clear.

Summary and application

Isaiah is a book of good news and bad news. For those who are willing to humble themselves and turn to the Lord, it is a book of good news. On the other hand, for those who refuse to believe, it is the worst message imaginable. Isaiah's prophecies encourage us to keep trusting the Lord no matter what. Our God is a saving God, and His salvation is there for any who are willing to believe, but Isaiah's prophecies also show us that there was a huge cost for this salvation—the life of God's Servant, Jesus Christ. May this commentary be a blessing to you in helping you to know and love the Lord with all of your heart, soul, and strength, and through this relationship, to serve Christ until the day when He returns to take us home to Himself (Rev. 22:20-21).

---

[251] The Greek word Gehenna developed out of the place called "the valley of the sons of Hinnom" (Isa. 30:33; cf. Josh. 15:8; 2 Kings 23:10; Jer. 7:32; Matt. 3:12; 5:22; Mark 9:43; Luke 12:25, et al.), the valley on the southern edge of Jerusalem where child sacrifice took place that was eventually turned into a perpetually burning garbage dump (Wolf, *Interpreting Isaiah*, 254).

11
APPENDIX ONE: A CONCISE CHART OF DISPENSATIONAL PREMILLENNIALISM

This chart represents Dispensational Premillennialism, the eschatological view in this commentary. Two of the key doctrines are (1) Jesus Christ will return at the end of the age to bring a kingdom to this earth, and (2) the church is not a spiritual Israel which fulfills God's promise made to the nation of Israel.

Old Testament: Creation, Fall, Flood, Babel, Patriarchs, Egypt, Exodus, Judges, Monarchy, Exile, Return, Birth and Ministry of Christ (Genesis-Gospels).	The Church: Begins at Pentecost and is resurrected before the seven-year Tribulation Period with a "Pre-Trib" rapture Tribulation Period Acts-Revelation).	Seven-Year Tribulation: Wrath poured out in Seals, Trumpets, Bowls. God's elect saved, some martyred, others enter kingdom. Christ's return at the end (Rev. 6-19).	Millennial Kingdom: Christ rules restored Israel and nations from Jerusalem. Demons bound for 1,000 years. Restoration to world. Final judgment at end (Rev. 20).	Eternal State: New Heavens and Earth. All trace of sin, curse and death purged forever. All resurrected saints dwell with God forever in New Jerusalem (Rev. 21-22).

12
APPENDIX TWO: TOPICAL INDEX

ABRAHAM 17, 64, 105, 106, 109, 117, 120, 130, 139, 141, 151, 177, 179, 202, 218, 220, 237, 243, 244, 270, 291, 313-14, 325, 330-331, 355, 389, 406, 410-11, 420, 422, 460, 474, 495, 513, 520, 530-33, 536, 549, 550
ALLEGORICAL 19, 196 interpretation (figurative)
AMMON 112, 141-42, 151, 252, 480
ANGELS 61-62, 206-07, 209, 292, 361, 449, 564
ANTICHRIST 29, 45, 107, 167, (man of 206, 213, 220-21, lawlessness, the 367 beast)
APOCALYPTIC 125-26 genre
ARK OF THE 116, 292
COVENANT
ARMAGEDDON 567-68
ASHERAH 154
ASIA 508, 566
ASSYRIA 5-11, 14-16, 18, 34, 54, 56-58, 66-69, 71-74, 78-80, 82-84, 88, 90, 92, 96, 100-11, 116, 119, 123, 125, 127-28, 133-38, 139-40, 142-44, 148, 151-56, 158-61, 168-71, 173, 177-78, 180-85, 188, 190, 192-96, 222, 226, 230, 232-35, 239-40, 242-43, 246-47, 251-57, 261-68, 280-300, 302, 307-08, 318, 344, 385, 388-89, 428, 429, 431, 481, 497, 532, 548, 563
ATONEMENT 46, 73, 435, 438, 448, 450-54, 489
BAAL 134, 154, 192, 230, 382, 426, 479-82, 494, 550, 552

BABYLON 3, 6, 8-11, 16, 18, 30, 38, 54, 56-57, 80, 90-92, 103, 105-06, 116-17, 119, 121-24, 126-29, 131-35, 136-37, 171-78, 180, 182-85, 190-91, 195-96, 209, 215, 220, 262-225-26, 256, 262-63, 273-74, 280, 296, 298-99, 306-11, 313-16, 318, 321, 323, 325, 327-28, 333, 335, 339-340, 342-46, 348-53, 355, 365-69, 373, 375, 377, 381-383, 385-93, 395, 398, 400-02, 406, 410-411, 414, 424-26, 431-35, 489, 497, 505, 517-18, 523, 535, 537, 548, 557
BAN (the) 345, 355
BEL 381-82
BONDAGE 99, 178, 244, 278, 335, 347, 410, 516-17
CANAANITES 192, 235, 479
CHURCH 25, 29-30, 46, 94, 106, 199, 206-07, 211, 259, 279, 315, 334, 350-51, 359, 435, 453, 458, 460, 494, 519-21, 545, 549, 570
COASTLANDS/ 112, 116, 171,
ISLANDS 191-92, 200, 204, 312, 321, 325, 327, 329, 334-35, 338, 341, 403-405, 420, 423, 475, 496, 501, 504, 507, 556, 566
COSMIC 24, 34, 126, 451
DISTURBANCES
COVENANT (Abrahamic) 109, 120, 177, 202, 313, 331, 389, 460, 530-31, 533, 535
COVENANT 74, 94, 112 (Davidic)
COVENANT 41, 46, 116-17, (New) 224, 263, 314, 338, 350, 359-60, 409, 432, 450, 462, 467, 473, 504, 513, 521

COVENANT (Sinaitic) 90, 106, 224, 472, 494

CYRUS 3-4, 124, 127-28, 173-74, 325-29, 333-35, 340, 348, 353, 357, 366-79, 383, 385-86, 388, 394-95, 397-98, 402, 425, 515

CREATION 17, 29, 46, 61, 76, 96, 114, 123, 127, 196, 207-08, 212, 251, 272, 274, 276, 279, 292, 320-22, 341, 350, 365, 382, 384, 407, 424, 427, 455, 458, 470, 494, 552-55, 570

DAVID 4, 7, 10, 14, 43-44, 53, 57, 60, 63, 67-69, 71, 72, 74, 77-79, 83-84, 89, 94, 108, 111-13, 117-18, 127, 139, 142, 145-47, 149, 151-53, 173, 181-82, 186-88, 192, 215, 218, 235-36, 238, 281, 284, 289, 296, 298, 302, 305, 337, 340, 354, 358, 409, 418, 422-23, 431, 443, 452-53, 465, 467, 500, 505-06, 515, 525, 548, 550, 557-58, 560, 568

DAY OF THE LORD 34, 56, 79, 121, 125-26, 145, 198-204, 488, 501, 529, 547

DEATH (eternal) 91, 132, 186, 208, 545

DEATH (physical) 5, 6, 14, 19, 29, 42-43, 47, 54, 59-60, 62, 69, 71, 79, 87, 93, 105-06, 118, 120, 131-33, 139-40, 162, 173, 183, 194, 196-97, 202, 211-12, 216, 218-20, 228, 233-34, 256, 275, 279, 290, 292, 297, 299-305, 341, 386, 388, 395, 407, 419, 434, 436-38, 441, 444-48, 450-56, 464-65, 470, 477-78, 498-99, 503, 540, 548, 553-55, 561, 570

DEMONS 87, 115, 206-07, 384, 550, 570

DISPERSION 161, 348, 523

DRAGONS 45, 222, 223, 420, 425

EDOM 10, 11, 18, 57, 112, 141, 144-46, 170, 176-78, 180, 213, 227, 271-74, 529, 531-32

EGYPT 10-11, 17-18, 35, 63, 68, 72, 80, 101, 109, 112, 116-17, 128, 130, 138-39, 157-71, 177, 187-88, 190, 193-94, 222-23, 226-27, 234, 240, 242, 244-45, 247-49, 253-54, 257, 281-85, 289-91, 294, 297, 344, 347-48, 367, 371, 378, 383, 411, 414, 425-26, 429, 431, 460, 480, 490-91, 539, 570

ELECT 45, 51, 57, 70, 92, 105-07, 109, 115-18, 165-68, 182, 204, 221, 225-26, 262, 296, 311, 348-49, 359-60, 380, 396-97, 408, 410, 423, 427, 442, 456, 468, 484, 502, 534, 545, 548, 566-68, 570

EUPHRATES 68, 81, 89, 103, 117, 123, 151, 175-76, 223, 226, 291, 352, 367, 369

EVIL 12-13, 17-18, 22-24, 37, 39-40, 48, 52, 55, 67, 74, 77-79, 85, 89, 99, 122, 129, 135-36, 154, 172, 176, 192, 196, 199, 201, 204, 207, 209, 212-13, 215-16, 223, 224, 227, 243, 253, 255, 257, 259-60, 263-64, 268, 272, 277-78, 294, 311, 314, 326, 333, 341-42, 346, 356, 375, 387-90, 392, 402, 413, 415-16, 420, 450, 452-53, 463, 468, 471-72, 474-79, 483, 485, 490, 495-98, 500-01, 503, 512, 521, 532-33, 543-44, 555

EXILE 5, 10-11, 22, 48, 53-54, 70-71, 88, 90-91, 106, 117-18, 131, 135, 169, 188, 195, 209, 215, 220, 225-26, 280, 286, 291, 310, 313-14, 316, 318, 323, 325, 328-30, 339-40, 342-44, 346-47, 351-52, 364, 370-71, 377-78, 389, 385, 393-95, 397, 399, 404, 410-11, 416, 420-21, 423, 426-27, 429, 431, 433-35, 460, 463, 469, 497, 499,

TOPICAL INDEX

508, 511, 517-18, 520, 523, 525, 535, 537, 541, 548, 570
EXODUS 46, 116, 119, 130, 147, 167, 221, 248, 315, 340, 352-53, 367, 384, 393-94, 401, 414, 417, 421, 425-26, 433-34, 472, 490, 492, 494, 535, 539, 570
FALL (the) 31, 43, 133-34, 155, 197, 200, 206, 209, 213, 217, 233, 241, 243, 269-70, 276, 279, 303, 357, 475, 502, 509, 537, 557, 570
FALSE 38, 231, 240,
PROPHETS 248, 334, 366
FASTING 489-90, 493
FEAR 6, 67-68, 70-71, 80-82, 85-86, 101, 109-112, 114, 119, 143, 157-59, 163, 165-66, 174, 177, 215-16, 223-24, 230, 244, 259-60, 264, 275, 277, 281, 283, 289-90, 295, 301, 304, 312, 318, 325-26, 329-34, 337, 344, 346-52, 354, 356-58, 360, 362, 364-65, 370, 374, 377, 415, 419-21, 424, 426-27, 434, 452, 456-57, 460-61, 463-64, 476, 482-83, 496, 501, 506, 510, 522, 528, 530, 533, 537
FORGIVENESS 27, 32, 36, 62, 108, 117, 120, 196, 314, 337, 339, 354, 364-65, 434, 440, 450, 453-55, 464, 469, 513, 522, 539-40, 551, 555
GENTILES 29, 44, 89-92, 94, 116, 169, 173, 189, 219-20, 311, 317, 320, 327, 338-39, 343, 349, 360, 374, 379, 402, 408-10, 412, 413, 428, 453, 468, 473-74, 505-06, 509-11, 519-20, 528, 544-45, 564-68
GOD (as Creator) 211, 222, 242, 313, 322-23, 338, 344-46, 366, 375-76, 398, 424, 427, 557
GOD (incomparable) 313, 320, 338
HAND/ARM 97, 257, 329,
OF GOD 344, 530

HOLY(ness) 9, 17, 54, 59, 61-62, 111, 114, 275, 278, 355, 455, 502, 518, 524, 538, 558
HOLY SPIRIT 3, 73, 76, 97, 114, 119, 251, 262, 332, 358-59, 412, 529, 534
HOPE 6, 18-19, 21, 31-32, 36, 40, 43-44, 47, 63, 86, 88, 92, 106-07, 110-13, 118, 140, 145-47, 155-56, 159, 162-65, 169, 171, 178, 182, 185-86, 188-89, 200, 204, 219, 229, 231, 233-35, 239, 249, 252, 258, 265, 266, 277, 281, 283-84, 290-91, 299, 311, 313, 319, 324-25, 346, 357-58, 391-92, 404, 407, 413, 416, 424, 428, 461, 469-70, 476, 482-83, 495-96, 500, 503, 505, 509, 513-14, 519, 521-22, 527-28, 534, 537, 541-42, 552-53, 555, 563
HORSE(s) 8, 11, 27, 33, 58, 174, 228, 246, 249, 253-54, 281, 285, 345, 352, 432, 529, 556
IDOL(atry) 2, 7, 9, 24, 26-28, 32-33, 36, 39, 52-53, 100-01, 103-104, 149, 154, 160, 163-64, 166, 169, 225, 229, 244, 250, 253, 255, 287, 293, 301, 311-12, 320, 322, 326-27, 329, 332-35, 339-40, 342, 349-50, 353, 356, 360-64, 366-67, 371-72, 378, 381-84, 386, 391-92, 394-96, 476, 478-80, 482-83, 502, 540, 547, 549-50, 555, 558-59, 565
IMMANUEL 4, 67, 74, 76-78, 81-82, 84, 87
IMMINENCE 201, 221, 315
IMMORALITY 479
INCARNATION 444, 517
INCENSE 5, 13-14, 20, 60, 62, 150, 154, 222, 345, 504, 507, 543, 547, 555, 558
INDIGNATION 43, 56-57, 96, 100-01, 103, 109, 119, 121, 124, 173, 214, 220-21, 224, 246, 271-72, 564

INIQUITY 12-13, 17, 21, 48, 55, 59, 122, 126, 129, 181, 186, 214, 221-22, 245, 253, 265, 311, 314, 436, 448, 454, 476, 495, 497-98, 538, 541, 559

INJUSTICE 7, 20, 24, 46, 337, 436, 448-50, 497

INVITATION 21, 51, 323, 353, 380, 386, 401-02, 404, 420, 464-67, 472, 486, 544, 558

ISRAEL 2, 5-7, 9-19, 21-33, 35-36, 39, 42-58, 60-64, 67-75, 77-98, 100-113, 116-21, 125, 128, 130-131, 135, 137, 139, 141-48, 150-55, 158-59, 161-62, 166-69, 171-73, 175-80, 184, 187, 191, 193-94, 200, 204, 206, 211, 214-27, 229-32, 235-37, 239-40, 243-48, 250-55, 257, 260, 262-63, 266, 269-71, 273, 276, 285, 287-88, 291-94, 307, 311-27, 329-36, 338-39, 341-61, 364-67, 370-89, 392-414, 416-18, 420-32, 434-35, 438-39, 441-42, 446-48, 450, 452, 455-69, 471-74, 477-79, 481-84, 486-513, 515, 517-23, 525-42, 544-50, 554-56, 558, 560-62, 565-68, 570

JERUSALEM 3, 6, 8, 10-12, 14-16, 19, 23, 25-28, 30-31, 37, 42, 45, 47-48, 50, 57, 60, 67, 69-71, 77, 79, 82, 85, 94, 100-01, 103, 106, 110, 117, 133, 154, 156, 159, 181-85, 207, 209, 215, 222, 225, 228, 230, 233, 238-39, 244, 246, 250, 252-53, 261-62, 264, 270, 281-86, 288-89, 291-92, 294-97, 302, 307-08, 311-12, 319-20, 326, 328, 353, 357, 366-68, 370, 377-78, 385, 394, 421, 423, 428-31, 433, 458, 462, 473, 480, 505, 508, 510, 517, 521-23, 525, 526, 538, 543, 547, 550, 553, 556, 560, 562-63, 565, 567, 569-70

JESUS 30-32, 45, 47, 58, 61-63, 73, 75-77, 85, 95, 107, 109, 111-13, 115, 118, 120, 126, 128, 140, 147, 156, 167, 169, 176, 189, 196, 199, 204, 206-07, 210-12, 216, 220, 224, 236, 244-45, 249, 253, 262-63, 270, 275, 293, 310, 313, 316-17, 320, 325, 330, 335-39, 357, 359, 372, 378, 401-02, 406-09, 411, 416, 417-20, 429-430, 434, 437-38, 441, 444-46, 449-56, 464, 465, 467, 470, 473, 479, 499, 502-03, 505-06, 510, 513-18, 524, 526, 528, 533, 541-42, 546, 549, 552, 554, 557, 561, 564, 569-70

JUSTICE 11, 13, 20, 23-25, 46-47, 51, 55, 89, 95, 99, 145, 147, 189, 228, 231, 234, 246, 251-52, 258, 264, 266, 295, 312-13, 324, 334-35, 337-38, 340-41, 389, 403, 407, 420, 424, 435-36, 449, 470-72, 483, 495-500, 514, 518, 525

KINGDOM 5, 9-10, 22, 25-32, 43-46, 53, 58, 69, 79, 83, 85, 89-90, 92-97, 99-100, 104, 106-08, 110, 113, 115-16, 121-27, 124, 128-30, 150, 52-54, 156, 160, 167-68, 173, 189-90, 195-97, 206-08, 210-13, 215, 217-21, 227, 229, 233, 242-44, 250-51, 256, 258-60, 261-63, 269-70, 274-79, 288, 306, 310, 315-18, 320, 322, 337, 339, 342, 349, 357, 375, 380, 386, 388, 395, 397, 408-09, 423, 429-31, 436, 441, 445, 453, 456-58, 460, 463-64, 467, 473, 476, 484, 490, 502, 504-06, 509, 513, 518, 520, 524, 527-28, 532-33, 538, 542, 544-46, 548-52, 554, 570, 575, 527-30, 531-35, 540, 544, 546-48, 550-54, 557, 562-65, 568, 570

LAND 2, 8, 13, 15, 18, 24-25, 27, 33, 38-39, 44, 47-48, 52, 54, 59, 64, 67-68, 71, 74, 78-82, 84, 88-97, 97-98, 101, 112, 116-18, 121-27, 125-26, 129-31, 134-36,

138, 141-45, 149-52, 157-58, 159, 162, 165-66, 169, 171-73, 177-79, 184, 186, 188-93, 199-200, 202, 204, 213-14, 218, 222, 225-26, 230-31, 234, 243-45, 248, 251, 257-61, 263-67, 269-71, 274-77, 280, 281-83, 285, 288-90, 297, 299, 304, 307, 316, 318-19, 326, 328, 332, 348-49, 356, 359-60, 370-71, 379, 389, 391, 397, 400, 402-04, 410-11, 413, 429, 434, 436, 449-50, 456, 459-60, 466, 476-77, 479-83, 493, 498, 502, 504, 510, 512, 514, 522-23, 525, 531, 537, 540, 543, 549-51, 556, 559, 562

LIFE 4, 6, 16, 18, 21, 28, 30, 36, 38, 42, 45, 53, 66, 86, 98, 102, 111, 113, 120, 132, 138, 162-63, 173, 201, 203, 211, 236, 244, 259, 269-70, 274, 280, 292, 295, 298-306, 309, 321, 329, 332, 338, 344, 346, 348, 359, 362-63, 365, 370, 384, 387-88, 405, 408, 420, 422, 424, 431-32, 434, 441, 444-45, 450, 452-53, 459, 463, 499-500, 503, 513, 526-28, 530, 539-40, 542, 548, 551, 553-55, 569

LION 48, 58, 112, 141, 144, 175, 238, 245, 248, 253, 255, 275, 299, 304, 389, 543, 554

LOVE 13, 24, 52, 83, 94, 109, 187, 232, 241, 248, 305, 330, 332, 344, 348, 354, 360, 393, 398, 408, 412, 415, 453, 465, 471-72, 476, 481-83, 491-94, 514, 520, 529, 534, 539, 556-57, 562, 569

MESSIAH
(see Christ)

MIDIAN 41, 89, 92, 101, 109, 504, 507

MILLENNIAL/ism 25, 29-30, (Pre,Post, A, Preterism) 46, 94, 115, 119, 167-68, 175, 225, 279, 332, 359, 386, 414, 457-58, 460-62, 505, 507, 509, 544, 546, 552, 570

MOAB 10, 112, 140-49, 153, 170, 176, 201, 208, 212-13, 273, 531

MONOTHEISM 361

MOON 13, 20, 41, 122, 200, 207, 246, 251, 369, 387, 504, 512, 556, 568

MOURNING 42, 51, 142-43, 193, 201-02, 204, 207, 236, 260-61, 430, 504, 514, 518-19

NATIONS
(see Gentiles)

NEBUCHADNEZZAR
9, 53, 71, 123, 131, 141, 143, 173, 192, 195, 308, 366, 372, 389-90

NEW TESTAMENT 1, 4, 21, 45, 72-73, 87, 119, 136, 205, 313, 359, 424, 454, 545, 552, 559

OBEDIENCE 17, 54, 85, 182, 232, 241, 248, 250-51, 269, 275, 355, 377, 399-400, 415, 417-18, 441, 452, 454, 474, 491-92, 494

OLIVET 45
DISCOURSE

OPPRESSION 7, 40, 78, 92, 99, 106, 108-09,117, 130-31, 147-48, 245-46, 259-60, 263, 268, 315, 341, 415, 433, 437, 450-51, 458, 464, 491-92, 492-99, 513, 523

PAGAN(ism) 24, 26, 103-04, 106-07, 109, 142, 163, 166, 189, 221, 285, 301, 303, 321, 330, 339, 351, 363, 366-67, 370, 375, 389-90, 430, 473, 479, 481, 484, 497, 547, 564

PAUL 3, 30, 52, 63, 108, 145, 217, 232, 236, 242, 254, 276, 321, 338, 349, 365, 384, 419, 422, 437, 440, 454-55, 458, 468, 489, 502, 520, 542, 545, 548, 564

PEACE 31, 79, 89, 92, 94, 138, 211-12, 214-18, 222, 224, 244, 251, 258, 263-64, 266-67, 269, 270, 282, 307, 311, 314, 319-20,

328, 335, 343, 369, 393, 400-01, 415, 429, 432, 457, 459, 461-65, 470, 476-78, 484-87, 495, 498, 503-04, 509-12, 522, 527, 549, 552, 554, 556, 559, 563
PERSECUTION 45, 56, 90, 128-29, 257, 342, 418, 510
PERSIA 3, 41, 92, 116, 124, 127-28, 135-36, 172-75, 179, 195-96, 315, 318, 326, 328-29, 333, 348, 352, 367-69, 373-74, 383-85, 386, 389, 402, 431, 434, 497
PHILISTINES 7, 27, 33, 89, 96, 112, 138-39, 235
PHOENICIANS 352
PLAGUES 426, 539
POLYTHEISM 180
POOR 37, 40, 52, 89, 99, 112, 140, 154, 157, 210, 243, 285, 322, 405, 487, 490-91
PRAISE 1, 34, 61, 118-20 204, 208-10, 213, 293, 299, 305-06, 311, 334-35, 340-41, 345, 353, 379, 381, 393, 396, 426, 474, 477, 484, 504, 512, 514, 519, 521-22, 526-27, 529, 534, 538, 557, 566
PRAYER 11, 13, 20, 60, 64, 214, 216-18, 265-67, 288, 290, 292-93, 298, 300-04, 306, 309, 311, 324, 378, 437, 471, 486-87, 491, 522-24, 535-36, 538-39, 541-542
PRIDE 5, 9, 14, 16, 18, 22, 28, 34-36, 41-43, 55, 60, 89, 96, 102, 104-05, 109, 122, 126, 133-34, 136, 145, 148-49, 154, 190, 194, 208, 213, 229-31, 233, 238, 251, 263, 300, 306-09, 342, 390, 504, 511, 565
PRIESTHOOD 25, 117, 369, 568
PROPHECY/PROPHETS
1, 10, 21, 24, 28-30, 38, 44, 51, 59, 62-63, 66, 97, 100, 117, 147, 165, 175, 176, 219, 230-32, 237, 240, 245, 248, 250, 268, 272, 254, 302, 313, 319-20, 333-34, 355, 358, 359, 361, 366, 373, 378, 388, 394-96, 406, 408, 401, 403, 411, 414, 422-23, 431, 435, 438, 446, 451, 474, 477, 493, 502-03, 514-17, 526, 529, 531, 540, 545, 551, 557, 565
PROVIDENCE 326, 350-51, 355, 367, 398
PUNISHMENT 4, 14, 18, 34, 40, 54, 89, 102, 104-05, 130, 135, 206-07, 218, 225, 246, 249, 279, 342, 428, 444, 447, 454, 456, 461, 525, 528, 532, 542, 555, 559, 569
PURITY 17, 55, 433, 462
RAPTURE 29, 106, 116, 199, 206, 220, 279, 570
REBELLION 8, 12, 16-18, 31, 38, 53, 56, 63-64, 109, 139-40, 158, 170, 173, 212, 217, 230-31, 243, 245, 263, 284, 296, 396, 427, 446-48, 476, 488, 499, 518, 547, 562, 565
REDEEM/REDEMPTION
13, 25, 31, 36, 40, 45, 85, 97, 115, 118, 166, 168, 196, 208-10, 215-16, 226, 237, 244-45, 270, 276, 278-79, 311, 314, 325, 330-31, 336, 339-41, 344-45, 347-48, 351-52, 356-57, 361, 364-65, 377-78, 380, 386, 388, 393, 395-96, 399, 401, 403-09, 413-14, 416-17, 420, 425-26, 429, 431, 433, 437, 444, 453-54, 456-61, 464, 466-68, 470, 474, 496, 500-04, 510-13, 515, 517-20, 523, 528-30, 533-34, 535-36, 539, 548-49, 560-61, 563, 566
RESTORATION
22, 24-25, 28, 31, 42-43, 45-46, 51, 54, 64, 76, 90-92, 95, 100, 105-08, 111, 114-18, 120, 130-31, 135, 165, 182, 196, 223-24, 226-27, 235-36, 243-44, 250, 255, 262, 263, 270, 275-78, 280, 296, 305, 311,

313-14, 316-17, 322, 325, 332, 340, 342, 349, 351, 353, 355, 358-60, 365-67, 370, 372, 386, 395, 402, 406, 409, 410-14, 426-27, 429, 431, 433-34, 445, 450, 460-62, 468-70, 483-84, 486-87, 493, 501-02, 505-06, 508-11, 513, 518-26, 534, 536-37, 539, 542, 544, 546, 548, 551-55, 562, 568, 570

REMNANT 4, 19, 25, 29, 31, 45, 56-57, 64, 70, 75, 87, 92, 101, 105-09, 112, 115-16, 118, 131, 135, 141-42, 145, 150-51, 175, 204, 210, 221, 226, 228, 230-31, 244-45, 262, 288-90, 295-96, 315, 317, 332, 342, 349, 360, 380-81, 396-97, 406, 408, 410, 420, 422, 442, 484, 486, 506, 511, 513, 515, 533, 542, 544-46, 548-49, 559, 561, 566-68

REPENT 20, 22, 25-27, 36, 63, 90, 98, 107-08, 148, 186, 218, 224, 235, 245, 256, 260, 315-17, 344, 355, 363, 380-81, 397, 416, 428, 430-31, 465, 482-83, 485, 489, 492-94, 517, 528, 539, 549-50

RETRIBUTION/REVENGE 131, 140, 209, 252, 265, 273-74, 314, 388, 501, 520-21, 533, 564

REWARDS 13, 24, 451

RIGHTEOUS(ness) 13-14, 19, 23, 25-26, 47-48, 51, 54, 95, 101, 108, 112-13, 145, 147, 214, 217, 228, 231, 243, 257-58, 260, 263-64, 266, 268, 278, 300, 325, 327, 330, 332, 334-37, 339, 341, 354-55, 371-72, 375, 377, 379-81, 385-86, 392-94, 400, 406, 414, 418, 420, 422, 424, 436, 448, 450-51, 453-57, 463, 470-72, 476-79, 484, 487-92, 495-96, 499-502, 504-06, 512-14, 519, 521-22, 524-25, 529, 531-32, 536, 538-40, 544, 547, 551, 557-59, 565

RITUALS 20, 391, 487-90, 547, 558, 565

ROME 128, 230, 315, 318, 497

SABBATH 13, 20, 471-72, 488, 493-94, 556, 568

SACRIFICE 13, 19-20, 25, 47, 73, 142, 167, 230, 238, 252, 271, 273, 284, 345, 354, 434-35, 444-46, 450, 452-53, 455, 471, 474, 476, 480-81, 489, 542, 547, 555, 558, 569

SALVATION 1-2, 10-11, 45, 58, 66, 68, 70, 73, 87, 93, 106, 108-10, 118-21, 150, 155, 165-68, 178, 187, 198, 204, 208, 212, 214-16, 219, 222, 235, 242, 247, 249, 253, 264-67, 296-97, 302, 310-11, 315, 319, 329, 339-40, 342, 348, 359, 371, 378, 380-81, 386, 402-03, 408, 414, 417, 420, 424-25, 429, 432-33, 435-37, 444, 455, 457, 463-65, 468, 470, 472, 486, 491-92, 495-502, 504-05, 512, 514-15, 521-22, 524, 528-29, 532, 539, 545, 547, 559, 561, 569

SAMARIA 6-8, 15, 67, 69, 71-72, 78, 81, 83, 98, 100, 103, 110, 152-53, 203, 229-31, 282, 287, 291

SATAN 31, 45, 90, 106, 132-34, 199, 206, 211, 223, 391, 481

SAVIOR 2, 44, 113, 118, 140, 160, 167, 270, 275, 277, 313, 341, 344-45, 348, 350, 371-72, 378, 380, 395, 404-06, 413-15, 423, 435, 443, 450, 456, 503-04, 511, 529, 534, 560

SEA 3, 7, 14, 35, 48, 58, 89-90, 101, 109, 112, 115, 117, 123, 138, 141, 143-45, 150, 152, 156-58, 160, 163, 171-73, 177, 179, 184, 189-93, 200, 202, 204, 222-23, 230, 267, 273, 303, 315, 326, 328, 334, 341, 345, 357, 367, 393, 400, 415, 417, 420-21, 426, 477, 485, 504, 507-08, 529, 535, 539

SEALS 202, 570

SENNACHERIB 5-6, 8, 11, 15, 78, 110, 133, 137, 139-40, 149, 156, 159, 173, 182-84, 192, 195, 240, 247, 256, 261, 265-66, 281, 283-84, 288-91, 294-299, 307, 337

SERVANT (Christ) 311, 334-41, 343, 354, 358, 380, 401-09, 411, 415, 417-20, 427, 431-32, 434-57, 464, 467-68, 503, 514-16, 521, 530, 532-33, 535, 539, 548, 569

SERVANT(s) 129-30, 282, 284, 288, 290, 296, 314, 325, 327-30, 334-36, 343, 345, 350, 356-58, 364, 371-72, 374, 393, 406-07, 415-16, 457, 464, 471, 537, 542-43, 549, 551, 556, 563

SEVEN-YEAR COVENANT/ SEVENTIETH WEEK 29, 34, 43, 164, 211, 279, 296

SHEOL 48, 67, 129, 132, 228, 233-34, 299, 304, 476

SIGN 67-68, 72-74, 76 81-82, 86, 160, 167, 169-71, 230, 233, 289-90, 295, 298-99, 301-02, 306, 309, 311, 391, 414, 465, 470, 472, 476, 481, 494, 509, 556, 566-67

SIN 7, 10, 11, 12, 15, 18, 20, 22-26, 28, 33-34, 36-43, 45-46, 46-48, 51-56, 58-60, 62-63, 65, 76, 84-86, 91, 93, 95-96, 98-100, 102-04, 106, 113, 118, 120-21, 124, 126-27, 133, 135-36, 139-40, 148-49, 152, 154, 159, 163, 169, 171, 178, 180-81, 186, 196-97, 200-03, 205, 210-12, 216, 220, 222-23, 231, 234, 241-42, 245, 249, 253, 255, 260, 262-63, 265-66, 267, 272-73, 275, 277, 279, 299, 301, 305-06, 308-09, 312-16, 318, 320, 329-30, 334, 339, 341-42, 344-45, 347, 354-55, 357, 363-65, 380-81, 389, 392-94, 400, 403, 406-07, 409-13, 416, 420, 424, 429-32, 434-38, 440-41, 443-56, 460, 462, 465, 468-69, 470, 472, 475, 479, 481, 484, 487-89, 493, 495-500, 511-13, 516, 518-19, 523, 525, 528, 534, 536-37, 539-41, 545, 547, 549-50, 552, 553-55, 559, 561, 563-64, 570

SONG 11, 16, 40, 42, 47, 49, 51, 53, 55, 75, 118-19, 126, 131, 143, 148-49, 180, 190, 196, 200, 203, 208, 213-15, 246, 294, 299, 303, 305, 334-36, 338, 340-41, 349, 358, 403, 406, 417, 426-27, 434, 444, 455-56, 462, 468, 516-17, 525

SORROW 117, 146, 184, 202, 222, 250, 276, 419, 421, 426, 435-36, 443, 445-46, 453, 498, 512, 518, 521, 553, 563

SOVEREIGNTY 9, 57, 60, 96, 102, 137-38, 150, 208, 223, 235-36, 241-42, 294, 322-23, 349-50, 355, 366-67, 370, 375-76, 385, 398, 418, 442, 538

SYMBOLISM 2, 18, 169, 316, 388

TABERNACLE 46

TEMPLE 6, 15, 30, 34, 46, 59-62, 69, 77, 79, 85, 106, 116-17, 123, 141, 143, 152, 183, 192, 194, 238, 262, 290, 301, 305-06, 308, 328, 357, 366-71, 377, 423, 433, 474, 481, 505, 507, 509-10, 523, 525, 527, 540-41, 550, 555, 557-60

TEXTUAL VARIANT 92, 106, 126, 166, 376, 397, 414

THRONE 15, 44, 59-60, 68-69, 89, 94, 108, 117-18, 129, 134, 145, 147, 173, 182, 288, 292, 301, 328, 368, 386-87, 409, 431, 495, 555, 557

TORAH 31-32, 343, 358, 423, 472

TOPICAL INDEX

TRANSGRESSION 43, 50, 57, 130, 200, 205, 220, 345-46, 351, 354, 357, 364, 415-16, 436, 446, 450, 487-88, 496, 500, 503

TRIBULATION PERIOD 29, 34-35, 43-45, 56-57, 96, 106-07, 109, 119, 126, 167, 200, 202, 204-06, 211, 213, 243, 259, 272, 279, 296, 331-32, 359, 397, 506, 545, 548, 561, 568, 570

TRUST 6, 8, 11, 15, 26, 32-36, 38, 45, 47, 66, 68-72, 74, 81, 84-86, 88, 102, 106-07, 109-10, 115, 118-19, 128, 138, 140, 145, 154-56, 166, 169-71, 181-87, 184-86, 189-90, 194, 197, 207, 211-12, 215-16, 227, 229, 231-34, 236, 239-40, 241-42, 245-49, 251, 253-59, 263, 265-70, 279-82, 284-93, 298, 301-03, 306, 309, 311, 320-24, 327, 329, 332, 335, 357, 360, 362, 370, 375, 377-78, 380-86, 392, 396, 402, 415, 419-22, 425, 429-30, 432, 434, 441, 446, 456, 463, 473, 481, 495, 498, 513, 522, 539, 547, 549, 554, 557, 559, 569

WAITING on the LORD 30, 199, 212, 353, 524

WAR 6-8, 10-11, 13, 16-17, 21-22, 24-27, 31-34, 37, 56-57, 67, 70, 97-98, 142, 154, 174, 175, 177, 183, 212, 218, 237, 253-55, 265, 281, 291, 314-15, 325, 335, 341, 343, 409, 423, 429, 430, 432, 459, 463, 503, 563

WARNINGS 11, 33, 51, 79, 153, 155, 230, 316, 395

WATERS 81, 83-84, 112, 115, 119, 141, 144, 150, 156-58, 160, 176, 181, 185, 189, 195, 227-28, 231, 251, 258, 275, 277, 282, 288, 312, 321, 332, 344, 347, 352-53, 375, 394, 420, 426, 457, 465-66, 477, 488, 493, 529, 550

WICKED(ness) 35, 40, 60, 89, 98, 210, 257, 259, 293, 311, 342, 387, 390, 393, 401-02, 436, 449-51, 457, 465, 468, 476-78, 484-85, 487-90, 492, 495, 497-98, 520, 531, 540, 555, 558, 564

WISDOM 31-32, 39, 63, 74, 93, 100, 104, 111, 113-14, 131, 164, 228, 233, 236-37, 241, 254, 259, 264, 321, 382, 387, 390, 437, 456

WOES 49, 51, 85, 95, 98, 141, 149, 229, 233, 238, 254, 258, 264-65, 375, 416, 496, 553

WOMEN 37-38, 40-42, 75, 146, 160, 165, 222, 257-58, 260-61, 320, 390, 459, 480, 531

WORD of GOD 59, 88, 233, 253, 344, 411, 513, 517

WORSHIP 8, 20, 26-28, 30, 33-34, 36, 41, 49, 61, 74, 79, 143, 154-55, 159-61, 166-67, 192, 210, 222, 226, 230, 238, 281, 285, 297, 301, 303, 306, 311, 339, 356, 362-64, 369, 381, 383-84, 409, 413, 456, 467, 474, 479-82, 484, 486, 488, 494, 506, 510, 550-51, 555, 558-59, 563-65, 568

WRATH of GOD 51, 55, 56, 95, 117, 144, 185, 201-02, 206, 428, 432, 435, 448, 533, 565

ZION 4, 11, 13, 19, 25, 27, 30, 37, 41-43, 45, 70, 75, 82-83, 94, 100-01, 104, 109, 116, 118, 120, 138, 140, 145, 147, 157, 195, 200, 212-13, 215, 218, 226, 228, 234, 36, 237, 246, 250-52, 255, 264, 270-71, 273, 276, 279, 288-89, 295, 311-12, 319, 326, 381, 386, 398, 403, 411, 416, 420-23, 426, 429, 433, 458-60, 462-64, 474, 486, 496, 503-14, 521-28, 531, 538, 541, 550, 555-56, 568

13
SCRIPTURE INDEX

GENESIS
1 321
1:2 .... 274, 379
1:14-19 126
1:16 323
2:7 .... 36, 375
2:13 157
2:17 .... 77, 211, 269, 275, 553
3 313
3:1 223
3:1-3 130
3:13-14 553
3:15 .... 93, 275, 380, 560
3:17-19 .... 210, 470
3:18 .... 50, 98, 261
4:1 93
6 231
6:9 55
7:11 205
9:6-7 77
9:8-17 202
9:17 93
9:25 191
10:4 508
10:6 161
10:6-8 157
10:8-10 135
10:10 122
10:20-23 77
10:24 151
10:25 .... 122, 152, 161
11 231
11:1 .... 122, 135, 152, 161
12 .... 130, 313
12:1-3 .... 19, 23, 120, 182, 265, 330, 346, 350, 410, 422, 506, 513, 520, 549, 560
12:3 .... 273, 389, 408, 510, 530
12:4 152
12:8 166
12:18 355
13 313
13:3 168
13:10 144
13:14-17 130
13:15 513
14:2 144
14:15 152
15 .... 313, 330
15:2 152
15:5 108
15:18-21 513
16:2 179
17 313
17:5 .... 422, 524
17:7 202
17:7-8 513
17:9 520
17:13 202
17:15 524
17:15-21 179
17:19 202
18:19 .... 350, 520
18:20 40
19 231
19:1-11 40

SCRIPTURE INDEX

19:22 144
19:24-28 274
19:24-29 19
19:30-38 141
20:9 355
20:11-13 355
20:16 21
21 313
21:12 179
21:32 139
22 313
22:5 220
22:17 .... 108, 400
22:18 .... 408, 422, 510, 530
24:4 152
24:20 41
24:43 75
25 531
25:1-4 179
25:4 507
25:12-18 179
25:13 507
25:23 .... 177, 273, 531
25:27-34 177
26 313
26:4 .... 108, 408, 422, 510, 530
26:34-35 177
27:46 177
28:8-9 179
28:13 459
28:13-14 531
28:14 .... 408, 510, 530
28:22 166
32:3 177
32:8 524
32:12 .... 108, 400
32:28 .... 329, 394

35 313
35:4 41
35:9-10 19
35:9-12 .... 106, 347, 422, 560
35:10 394
35:11-12 130
36:8 273
36:20-30 177
36:40-43 .... 177, 274
37:29 287
39:1 283
43:9 304
45:1-8 .... 102, 294
45:5-9 208
49 313
49:10 .... 270, 560
49:24 415
50:20 .... 102, 208, 294

EXODUS
2:8 75
3:1-4 361
3:7 449
3:20 24
4:21-22 17
4:22-23 .... 265, 540
6:7 .... 314, 373
7:3 .... 30, 302
7:18 417
10:2 567
10:21 417
13:7 245
13:13 558
13:21 .... 434, 535
13:21-22 .... 46, 47, 492
14:16 535

581

14:19	492
14:19-20	434
14:20	47
14:23-31	426
15:3	341
15:5	535
15:6	24
15:8	535
15:11	209, 313, 539
15:16	417
15:20	83, 252
16	401
17:1-7	401
18:25	39
19:5	314
19:5-6	159, 350, 550
19:5-8	17
19:6	497, 528
19:16-19	239
19:18	61, 538
20:8-11	20, 494
20:11	321
20:18-19	61
22:22	99
23:6	99
23:8	24
23:20-21	535
23:24	166
24:6	440
24:7-8	550
24:8	440
24:10	151
24:11	14
24:16	46
28:1-3	568
29:16	267
31:12-17	494
31:12-18	20
32:3	41
32:7-14	302
32:20	250
32:32	45, 364
33:2	191
33:4, 5, 6	413
33:9	61
33:14-15	534
33:17-23	62
34:6-7	62
34:10	539
34:20	347
35:22	41
40:34	47, 292

LEVITICUS

2:2, 9, 16	568
5:15	452
6:5	452
8:12	515
10:3	355
11:7-8	547, 558
11:11-43	565
13:45	540
18:25-27	64
19:2	355, 497, 528
19:4	33
19:6	356
19:18	491, 492
19:21	452
19:31	87
20:6	87
20:7	355, 497, 528
20:25	565
20:27	87
24:7	559
25:10	516, 517
25:1-10	409
25:23-25	52
26:1	33
26:12	314
26:14	202
26:16	554

26:21 166
27:24 519

NUMBERS
3:12-13 568
3:45 347
5:21 551
5:26 558
6:24-27 491
6:25-26 86
7:89 292
9:15-23 46
10:10 20
11:17, 25, 29 535
13:22 164
14:1-10 385
14:21 61
17:23 318
18:16 347
19:2 350
20:11 402
20:14-21 273
21:10-13 141
21:21-30 144
21:25 143
21:30 143
24:2 28
24:17 ..... 93, 560
24:18 177
25:10-13 568
27:7-11 52
28:11 20
32:3 ..... 143, 144
32:34 143
32:36 144
32:37 143
33:45-46 143
35:30 82

DEUTERONOMY
1:34 186
1:39 77
2:25 166
4:29 468
4:32-37 541
4:32-40 350
4:34 302
4:35 380
5:15 155
5:26 292
6:4 159
6:16 73
6:22 302
7:5 ..... 26, 166
7:6 541
7:6-9 ..... 314, 347, 350
7:18 155
7:19 302
7:25 250
8:2 ..... 155, 364
8:10-14 155
8:11 364
8:18 364
9:7 364
10:16 ..... 353, 358, 463
10:17 94
10:21 539
12 270
12:5 285
13:1 170
13:12-15 355
14:1 42
15:7-8 99
15:11 332
16:21 26
17:6 82
17:16 245
17:16-17 33
18:10 38
18:11 87
18:15-22 333
20:14 455
20:16-18 ..... 191, 479
23:4 151
23:7-8 177

24:14 332
25:17-18 99
25:24 73
26:8 .... 302, 417
26:17-18 314
27:25 24
28:1-14 .... 182, 278, 313
28:1-68 .... 17, 22, 56, 88
28:6 295
28:15 202
28:15-46 554
28:15-68 .... 106, 173, 182, 217, 220, 251, 263, 269, 280, 313, 395, 537
28:20 550
28:21 64
28:25-36 22
28:26 .... 22, 64
28:27 205
28:30 127
28:36 54
28:45 .... 22, 232
28:46 170
28:49 270
28:53 426
28:55 426
28:57 426
28:64 .... 22, 54, 225
29:3 170
29:23 .... 18, 274
29:24 550
29:28 64
30:1-2 468
30:1-10 .... 51, 106, 117, 215, 263, 296, 313, 413, 493
30:6 .... 358, 463
30:7 .... 221, 414
30:8-10 .... 463, 468
30:9 423
31:4 155
31:16 550
31:18 535
31:30 273
32 .... 16, 534
32-33 248
32:4 .... 85, 216
32:9 168
32:11 255
32:13 224
32:15 .... 85, 358
32:18 85
32:18-20 535
32:23 405
32:33 125
32:35 388
32:41-42 223
32:42 .... 22, 405
32:43 408
33:5 358
33:21 270
33:26 .... 163, 359, 564
33:27 483
34:1 143
34:11 170

JOSHUA
1:8 437
3:10 292
3:16 417
4:3 166
4:20-21 166
4:23 417
6:21 272
7:2 110
7:6 287
7:24-26 549
7:26 166
8:11 230
8:29 166
10:11 235

10:27	166
10:29	291
10:30	291
11:14	455
11:17	550
12:7	550
12:15	291
13:3-4	192
13:5	550
13:7	455
13:9	143
13:17	143
13:37	144
15:8	154
15:37	550
15:42	291
18:16	154

JUDGES

2:3	479
3:7	26
3:8	151
4:4	83
4:5	239
5:4	177
5:13-14	270
6:2	34
6:7	302
6:22-23	62
7:25	109
8:26	41
9:9	466
10:10	550
13:22	62
14:12	41
18:11	139
18:21	41
18:26	41
18:29	139
19:25	559

RUTH

3:15	41

I SAMUEL

2:2	216
2:5	201
2:10	515
3:19-21	333
4:4	292
4:17	432
6:17	139
7:5-11	139
8:12	39
10:1	515
10:23	443
13:6	34
14:11	34
14:47	142
15:3	272
15:22	238, 241
16:6	515
16:23	139
17:26	292
17:26-30	290
17:36	292
18:6	252
23:11	399
24:6	515
26:9-11	515
28:7-8	87
28:13	88
28:38	38

II SAMUEL

1:14	515
1:16	515
1:24	413
4:1	125
5	270
5:11	192
5:17-25	139
5:18-25	154
5:20	235
6:2	292
6:19	148
7:1-17	43
7:12-16	71, 94, 112, 296, 467, 560
7:23	539
8:14	177

10:4	170
10:4-5	80
12:30	525
15:12	85
18:26	432
22:2	216
22:32	216
23:1	515
23:1-5	43
23:5	113, 522

I KINGS

1:32-35	568
1:33	70
1:39	515
2:26-27	568
3:7	295
3:9	77
4	506
4:25	286
4:30	164
7:2-6	185
8	62, 270, 290
8:1	46
8:10	285
8:10-13	292
8:18	285
8:27	362
8:41-43	474
10:1-9	506
10:17	185
10:22	193
10:27-29	285
10:28-29	254
11:5	481
11:13-36	296
11:15	177
11:32	285
12:25	229
13:30	51
14:9	305
14:23	166
14:30	98

16:18	261
18:25-29	149
19:10	550
19:16	515
19:35	183
20:31	290
21:17-24	52
21:27	289, 491
22:48	193
25	123

II KINGS

1:9	39
2:3-6	58
3.	141
3:4	146
3:27	480
4:1	416
6:25	286
8:12	127
8:19	296
11:12	41
11:14	85, 287
13:14	283
13:20	142
14:7	146, 177
14:17	230
15:3-5	14
15:25	261
15:29	79, 91
15:34	15, 69
15:36-38	68
16:1-11	68, 69, 79
16:3	480
16:4	480
16:7-8	152
16:7-9	71, 72, 79, 80, 106
16:7-16	16, 69
16:10-16	152
16:23-24	230
17	230

17:4..72, 158
17:10 ....16, 26, 480
17:17 ....38, 266, 480
17:24..72
17:31..480
18-20..280
18:1..283
18:3..296
18:4..16, 285
18:7..242
18:9-10......................................15, 283
18:13..15, 133
18:19-20..104
18:22-23..104
18:29-35..104
19:1..287
19:8-13..266
19:9..16
19:28..295
19:35..156
19:35-37..111
19:36..133
19:37..133
20:1..16
20:1-11..300
20:7..306
21:6..87
22:2..16
22:11..287
22:14..83
23:4-14..250
23:10..252, 480
24:1-5..123
24:6-12..123
24:12-16..309
24:14..39
25:4-7..184
25:8-17..542
25:19..283
29-35..104

I CHRONICLES
1:7..508
1:8-10..157
1:33..507
10:13..87
15:20..75
15:32..184
16:15-17..202
19:6..151
19:7..143
20:2..525
24:45..355
28:2..510, 557

II CHRONICLES
6:42..515
7:14..98
14:1..235
20..177
20:7..330
20:30..508
21:8-10..273
23:13..85
24:18..550
25:11..273
26-33..16
26:3-5..14
26:16-21..14
26:16-23..60
27:1-2..15, 17
28:1-24..69
28:3..15, 480
28:5-18..18
28:16..71
28:17..273
28:18..140
29:25-30..305
29:30..303
30:1..16, 285
32:21..111, 266
32:23..159
32:24-26..300
32:27-29..308

32:30	70
32:31	303
33	295
33:6	87
33:11	72, 309
36:20-23	367
36:22-23	328, 368

EZRA

1:1	430
1:1-4	328, 367, 368, 370
1:4	333
3	370
3:10	370
4:1-5	370
4:2	69, 71, 72
4:9-19	230
6:3-4	377
6:14	370
9	536
9:6-7	500

NEHEMIAH

1:4	156
1:11	283
2:15	70
2:19	128
3:25-27	262
4:7	128
6:1	128
6:14	83
9	536
9:1	290
9:10	302
9:26-30	394
9:26-31	217, 535
9:36	117
11:31	110

ESTHER

8:15	525

JOB

1:3	75

1:19	172
1:20	287
2:12	287
3:23-26	304
4:3	125
5:6	113
5:17	447
6:7	18
9:13	425
9:26	158
10:21-22	305
12:17-21	323
13:4	33
13:28	419
14:2	113
14:8	113
14:16	242
18:5-14	485
18:11	156
18:13	140
18:25-27	220
19:2	40
19:26-27	14, 40
21:20	428
21:22	321
22:9	447
22:14	322
23:7	21
26:12	427
27:18	19
27:20	156
28:1	321
29:14	42
30:1	475
30:21	125
30:29	128
31:4	242
34:14	36
38:2	323
38:17	304
39:16	537
40:24	113
41:2	125

PSALMS

Reference	Page
1:1	233
1:1-4	420
1:4	26, 156, 332
2	71, 272, 342
2:1	294
2:1-3	31
2:5	380
2:7	94
2:8	196
2:9	114, 205, 405
2:12	380
6:5	305
9:6	156
9:13	304
11:6	274
11:7	14
14:2	468
14:4	96
15:24	268
16:10	452
17:15	14
18:2	85
18:7-15	239, 252
18:10	163
18:19	261, 564
19:4	322
19:14	216
22:1-21	409
22:6	408
22:6-8	443
22:16	446
22:22	452
22:22-31	409
22:23	452
22:25	452
22:26	453
22:27-29	453
22:27-31	467
22:28	196
22:30	251
22:30-31	453
23	410
23:3	484
23:4	423
23:6	305
24:3-4	215
24:4	20
27:10	412
30:2	292
30:4	164
30:5	250
30:9	305
30:10	410
31:3	86, 341
31:7	86
31:15	552
31:16, 19	86
32:6	20
32:10	443
32:15	231
33:6-11	137
35:10	332
36:9	466
37	513
37:9	215
37:11	215
37:14	332
37:18, 27, 29	215
38:1	558
39:9	304
40:3	340
40:5	209
40:7	175
40:17	332
42:2	292
45:5-6	58
46:1	75
46:1-7	140
46:9-10	92
48	207, 210
48:1	30, 296

48:2 .... 94, 394, 510	77:16 535
48:3 203	78:12 .... 164, 209
48:7 193	78:34 468
48:8 140	78:38-39 484
50:3 252	78:43 567
50:3-23 16	78:68 296
51:12-15 62	80:1-2 536
51:15-19 186	80:8-16 40
51:16-17 491	84:2 292
51:17 557	87:1-5 140
51:19 305	87:4 425
53:1 364	87:5 140
53:9 364	88:10 .... 132, 209, 332
54:5 535	88:10-12 305
54:8 209	88:12 209
55:23 305	88:13 156
58:6 390	89:1-4 467
61:2 216	89 .... 71, 112
62:7 140	89:5 209
63:6 466	89:10 425
65:12 466	89:11 40
66:18 497	89:13-37 147
68:17 564	89:19-29 467
68:25 75	90:3-8 36
68:31 158	91:1 146
68:33 163	91:2 140
69:7-8 443	91:9 140
69:23 241	92:15 251
69:26 447	93:2 61
70:5 332	93:4 111
71:3 85	96 252
72 .... 94, 337	96:1 340
72:10 508	96:5 33
72:10-11 196	98:1 340
73:19 23	99:5 .... 510, 557
74:1 130	102:25 338
74:3-7 537	102:25-26 424
74:13 425	103:8-14 484
75:9 55	103:12 305
76:5 111	103:12-14 354
77:2 468	103:15 318
77:11, 14 209	
77:15 417	

SCRIPTURE INDEX

103:19 61
104:2 .... 322, 338
104:3 .... 163, 564
104:10-30 350
104:29 36
105:10 202
106:9 .... 156, 535
106:15 105
106:22 539
107:18 .... 304, 408
107:25 427
107:39-43 350
108:12 69
109:22 332
110 .... 272, 342, 467
110:1 557
110:3 .... 220, 244, 453
111:5, 9 202
112:7-8 216
115:4-7 322
115:17 305
118:6-9 154
118:8 .... 69, 86
118:8-9 .... 171, 254
118:15-16 24
118:28 209
119:1 472
119:73 168
119:105 32
121:8 295
122:7 261
126:1-6 250
131:2 304
132 .... 71, 112, 270
132:2, 5 415
132:7 .... 510, 557
132:11 94
132:11-12 296
132:13-18 .... 296, 394, 510
132:17 113
132:17-18 .... 44, 94
135:9 170
135:15-18 322
137:7 .... 178, 273, 531
138:6 558
138:8 .... 168, 388
139 242
139:2 295
139:16 275
142:5 140
144:9 340
145:1 209
145:13 61
145:18-19 554
146:3 154
147:4-6 376

PROVERBS

1:7 278
1:22 233
3:14 193
3:34 558
5:19 273
5:22 54
6:13 492
6:16-17 .... 96, 104, 309
6:23 32
6:35 24
7:18 273
7:23 86
8:27 322
8:32 472
8:34 472
10:3 54
10:8 278
10:10 278

11:22	41
12:15	249
13:21	535
14:23	113
15:8	497, 558
15:29	496
16:33	351
19:21	137
21:4	96, 104
22:15	447
23:13	447
23:30	55
27:22	278
28:9	497
28:13	470
28:26	249
29:1	85, 240, 246
29:9	278
29:15	249
30:13	96
30:19	75
31:18	193
31:20	332
31:24	42

ECCLESIASTES

5:10	52
9:7-9	53
9:10	305
10:16	53

SONG OF SONGS

2:5	148
3:11	525
5:7	42
6:8	75
7:4	143
8:2	55

ISAIAH

1:1-15	406
1:2-3	534
1:3	54, 167
1:4	56, 254, 337, 408
1:5-6	63, 97, 484, 516
1:7	99, 261
1:7-9	541
1:8	19
1:9	57, 64, 546
1:9-10	40
1:10-12	496
1:10-16	433
1:11	238
1:11-14	354, 488
1:13	558
1:15	497
1:16-17	268
1:17	491
1:18	255, 355
1:18-20	235
1:20	318, 384, 495, 534
1:21	184
1:21-23	259, 497
1:22-23	337
1:23	184, 268, 384
1:24	415
1:25	397
1:26	93
1:28	384
1:29	259, 354, 480, 547, 565
1:29-31	105
1:30	201, 493, 540
2:1	408
2:1-4	29, 92, 94, 95, 296, 313, 353, 395, 413, 505, 545
2:2	140
2:2-3	474, 552, 567

SCRIPTURE INDEX

2:2-4 .... 147, 168, 210, 212, 226, 339, 381, 467
2:3 .... 58, 344, 423, 462, 524
2:3-4 .... 147, 360
2:4 .... 263, 270
2:5 512
2:5-21 .... 32, 95
2:6-22 154
2:8 .... 33, 256
2:11 .... 106, 126
2:11-17 104
2:12 125
2:12-13 320
2:13 .... 105, 267
2:15 34
2:16 193
2:17 .... 106, 126
2:18 33
2:20 .... 33, 106, 256
3:1 .... 32, 88, 95, 147
3:1-4:1 .... 32, 95
3:2 184
3:3 93
3:5 449
3:8 534
3:8-4:1 104
3:9 485
3:11 485
3:12 449
3:14-15 268
3:15 451
3:16-17 146
3:23 .... 82, 525
3:24-26 261
3:24-4:1 413
3:26 .... 201, 387
4:1 .... 231, 408
4:1-2 106
4:1-4 .... 296, 313
4:2 .... 44, 57, 64, 107, 113, 196, 206, 405, 408, 437, 522, 546
4:2-6 .... 353, 386, 395, 413, 505, 545
4:4 .... 25, 398
4:5 277
4:6 146
4:10-18 359
5:1-7 .... 80, 98
5:2 224
5:3 203
5:4 224
5:5 234
5:5-7 406
5:6 .... 224, 261, 470
5:8 254
5:11 .... 254, 474
5:12 235
5:13 .... 184, 551
5:15 .... 34, 104
5:16 .... 471, 501
5:17 261
5:18 254
5:18-23 232
5:19 .... 209, 232, 248
5:20 .... 78, 97, 512
5:20-22 254
5:20-23 497
5:21 93
5:23 .... 98, 485
5:24 42

5:25 .... 96, 195, 236	148, 217, 278
5:26 .... 57, 115, 124, 158	7:18 57
	7:19 471
5:27-28 140	7:22 203
5:28 564	7:23-25 .... 50, 88, 98, 224, 261
5:29 144	
5:30 499	7:24 471
6:1 .... 240, 267, 361	7:25 .... 234, 471
6:1-3 269	7:37-39 359
6:1-5 316	8:1 111
6:3 .... 317, 340, 505, 556	8:1-4 55
	8:1-16 248
	8:3 194
6:5 .... 297, 470, 540	8:5-8 .... 72, 217
	8:6 70
6:9-10 .... 240, 259, 277, 463	8:6-8 .... 294, 465
6:10 .... 243, 339, 363, 484	8:9 205
	8:12 85
6:11 541	8:13-14 513
6:11-13 111	8:16 .... 418, 464
6:12 203	
6:13 .... 45, 57, 64, 105, 113, 546	8:17 .... 32, 234
	8:18 .... 170, 471, 567
6:16 238	
6:17 54	8:19 .... 87, 234
6:18 277	8:19-20 163
6:25 203	8:21 .... 235, 550
7 58	
7:2 .... 184, 296	8:21-22 .... 217, 250, 278
7:3 .... 45, 64, 108, 266, 546	8:22 .... 58, 93, 345, 413, 499
7:4 290	8:23 491
7:8 424	9 88
7:11 .... 302, 567	9:1-10:4 90
	9:1 .... 58, 93
7:12 64	9:1-2 407
7:13 292	9:1-3 252
7:14 .... 76, 87, 111, 113, 194, 302, 567	9:1-5 .... 108, 118
7:17 292	9:1-7 .... 176, 250, 276, 278, 296, 313, 345,
7:17-25 72,	

SCRIPTURE INDEX

395, 413, 505, 565
9:2 .... 339, 512, 553
9:2-5 506
9:3 .... 87, 506
9:4 .... 109, 137
9:5 408
9:6 .... 31, 194, 209, 241, 269, 432
9:6-7 .... 39, 87, 108, 111, 113, 118, 147, 218, 296, 400, 437, 463, 467, 560
9:7 .... 25, 147, 263, 337, 501, 512
9:8 213
9:10 34
9:11-12 .... 57, 96, 100
9:12 .... 56, 236, 540
9:16 268
9:17 .... 56, 57, 96, 100, 236, 540
9:18 .... 50, 105
9:19 540
9:21 .... 56, 57, 96, 100, 163, 236, 540
9:22 64
10:1 254
10:3 125
10:4 .... 57, 96, 100, 195, 540
10:5 .... 56, 109, 125, 173, 256
10:5-6 .... 252, 285
10:5-15 294
10:5-34 137
10:6 .... 234, 268
10:6-7 124
10:10 33
10:12 .... 34, 125, 159, 252, 256
10:12-19 265
10:12-34 286
10:15 .... 252, 272
10:15-19 284
10:16 408
10:17 .... 50, 98, 107, 224, 564
10:20 .... 106, 249, 407
10:20-21 .... 32, 45, 94, 269
10:20-22 .... 57, 64, 87
10:20-23 .... 19, 32, 109, 111, 113, 118, 218, 221, 296, 313, 378, 408, 430, 437, 507, 513, 542, 546, 561
10:22 108
10:23 .... 108, 203, 519
10:24 168
10:24-25 265
10:25 .... 56, 159, 173, 221, 236, 272, 428, 461, 506, 540, 548
10:25-34 565
10:27 .... 92, 137
10:32 159
10:33-34 111
11:1 .... 39, 224, 270, 296, 395, 463, 467
11:1-2 336
11:1-5 .... 231, 258, 435, 512
11:1-10 .... 87, 93, 118
11:1-16 313
11:2 515
11:3-4 243
11:3-5 .... 31, 337
11:4 .... 147, 210, 252, 263, 270, 406, 473, 485,

515
11:4-5 260
11:5 .... 492, 500
11:6-9 .... 31, 212, 278, 353, 555
11:9 .... 215, 375. 462, 483, 502, 550, 567
11:10 .... 57, 106, 159, 206, 262, 339, 360, 381, 408, 545
11:11 .... 57, 157, 296, 404, 412, 501, 507
11:11-12 .... 226, 413, 483, 503
11:11-16 .... 46, 107, 118, 262, 408, 506, 507, 545
11:12 .... 57, 106, 124, 567
11:13 501
11:15 367
11:15-16 .... 426, 485
11:16 .... 106, 168, 266, 278, 353, 410, 527
12:1 .... 56, 96, 209, 426, 484, 527, 540
12:1-6 .... 118, 236, 296, 313, 332
12:2 304
12:3 358
12:4 .... 106, 209
12:4-6 131
12:6 .... 269, 317, 423, 437
12:35 408
13:2 .... 57, 159, 203
13:4 26
13:5 .... 56, 173, 272
13:6 .... 34, 140
13:8 174
13:9 125
13:11 .... 210, 213, 485
13:13 .... 272, 424
13:16 554
13:17 .... 368, 377, 395, 398, 430
13:17-19 135
13:20-22 274
13:22 .... 327, 494, 501, 507
14:1 .... 32, 459, 461, 5109, 520
14:1-2 .... 117, 140, 176
14:2 567
14:5 485
14:9 .... 113, 206
14:11 174
14:23 136
14:24 .... 164, 166, 187, 194
14:24-27 .... 265, 286
14:24-28 256
14:24-37 209
14:25 252
14:26 194
14:27 194
14:28 72
14:28-32 138
14:32 147
14:47 176
15:2 .... 42, 140
15:6 201
16:1-14 144
16:5 .... 94, 140, 263, 296, 337, 467, 472, 512
16:6 213
16:7 140
16:8 .... 201, 202

SCRIPTURE INDEX

16:9 273
16:10 553
16:18 55
17 72
17:1-2 194
17:2 410
17:7 .... 34, 206
17:7-9 209
17:8 256
17:10 .... 350, 483
17:12 254
17:12-14
17:13 540
18:1 254
18:3 .... 57, 115, 124
18:6 385
18:7 .... 140, 167, 507
18:22 233
18:23-29 233
19:1 .... 33, 125
19:3 93
19:5 158
19:6 106
19:8 .... 201, 202
19:10 .... 447, 451
19:11-15 93
19:12 166
19:14-16 284
19:17 140
19:18, 19 106
19:18-25 .... 339, 510, 567
19:19-20 210
19:20 .... 470, 534, 567
19:21 106
19:22 484
19:23 .... 106, 194, 206, 266, 278, 353, 410, 483, 527
19:23-25 .... 226, 378, 545
19:24 .... 106, 203
19:29 194
20:1-6 139
20:3 .... 302, 470, 567
20:3-5 158
20:4 377
20:5 424
20:6 .... 404, 501, 507
21:1-10 .... 172, 352
21:3 125
21:9 209
21:11 526
21:11-12 177
21:13-17 179
21:17 318
22:1 261
22:1-5 182
22:1-20 258
22:2 203
22:9 70
22:11 474
22:14 527
22:20 107
22:20-23 284
22:22 296
22:23 556
22:25 .... 107, 318
23 270
23:1 140
23:2 .... 405, 501, 507
23:3 .... 193, 295, 318
23:6 .... 501, 507
23:7 203

23:12 387
23:13 261
23:14 193
23:18 .... 193, 210
24:4 .... 202, 272, 424
24:7 202
24:8 203
24:9 .... 201, 224
24:10 215
24:11 203
24:15 .... 210, 404, 501, 507
24:16 .... 57, 442
24:17-18 86
24:19 205
24:21 .... 107, 256
24:23 .... 47, 226, 277, 340, 483, 505
24:35   506
25:1 .... 209, 241
25:2 .... 215, 261
25:3-11 210
25:5 224
25:6 226
25:6-8 483
25:6-9 279
25:6-12 395
25:7-8 219
25:8 .... 250, 318, 426, 553
25:9 .... 107, 206, 234, 317, 319, 553
25:10 .... 117, 226, 273
25:10-11 148
25:11 213
25:12 216
26:1 .... 107, 206, 224
26:1-4 512
26:3-4 513
26:4 .... 304, 483
26:7 174
26:8 234
26:10 485
26:11 501
26:14 132
26:15 269
26:16 238
26:16-18 .... 194, 406, 408
26:16-19 452
26:17 125
26:17-18 .... 120, 218, 562
26:18 406
26:19 .... 199, 224
26:19-21 395
26:20 .... 96, 109, 173, 223, 236, 461
26:20-21 .... 272, 272, 506, 565, 568
27:1 .... 107, 223, 256, 425
27:2 107
27:2-6 222
27:3 224
27:4 .... 50, 98, 272
27:5 224
27:7-11 223
27:9 26
27:10 .... 261, 423
27:11 54
27:12 .... 46, 56, 107, 168
27:12-13 .... 223, 262. 296, 313, 408, 410, 506, 567
27:13 .... 46, 56,

107, 116, 168, 221, 412
28:1 .... 201, 254, 258, 264, 474, 525, 540
28:1-29 229
28:2 252
28:3 525
28:4 201
28:5 .... 45, 210, 525
28:6 147
28:7 184
28:7-10 93
28:11 270
28:12 .... 233, 249
28:14 184
28:14-15 187
28:14-17 233
28:16 .... 39, 140, 234, 249, 513
28:17 25
28:17-28 175
28:20 235
28:23-29 235
28:28-29 221
28:29 .... 209, 236, 241
28:40-66 236
29:1 .... 254, 264, 474
29:2, 7 427
29:5 156
29:6 .... 252, 564
29:8 54
29:9 .... 63, 205, 259, 428
29:9-10 463
29:9-14 93
29:10 259
29:13 .... 354, 565
29:14 .... 259, 479
29:15 .... 184, 254, 258, 264
29:17-21 24
29:18 .... 339, 342, 499
29:19 .... 515, 553
29:20 210
29:20-21 259
29:22 32
29:23 168
30:1 .... 17, 136, 249, 254, 258, 264, 384
30:1-2 .... 93, 259
30:1-3 233
30:1-5 .... 171, 187
30:1-33 247
30:2-3 146
30:2-5 482
30:3-7 284
30:5-7 254
30:7 .... 425, 501
30:8-9 290
30:8-11 55
30:9 .... 17, 463
30:18 .... 86, 234, 472, 524
30:19 .... 426, 553, 554
30:20-21 277
30:23 .... 107, 466
30:25 .... 332, 358, 423
30:26 .... 485, 512, 516
30:27 .... 56, 564
30:27-33 297
30:29 .... 216, 279, 483
30:30 391
30:30-33 265

30:31	424
30:32	256
30:33	207
31:1	258, 259, 264
31:1-3	93
31:1-13	171
31:1-15	233
31:2	498
31:3	195
31:4	424
31:5	296
31:7	33
31:8	252
31:8-9	265, 286, 297
31:9	391, 424
32:1	207, 231, 269, 270, 337, 472, 512
32:1-5	467
32:2	358
32:3	146, 243
32:3-4	277
32:7	515
32:11-13	186
32:13	203, 470
32:14	261
32:15	45, 119, 251, 277, 332, 358, 375, 466, 548
32:15-19	502
32:16	25, 147
32:16-17	400, 472
32:17	276
32:17-19	212
33:1	254, 258, 264, 297
33:1-24	265
33:2	234
33:5	25, 26, 147, 260, 263, 267, 472
33:7	263
33:8	168
33:9	201, 202
33:11	562
33:12-14	26
33:13-17	238
33:14	391, 561
33:14-26	263
33:17	207, 269, 297
33:17-21	286
33:17-22	467
33:18-19	297
33:20	14
33:20-22	512
33:21	111, 358
33:22	207, 257, 269, 428
33:23	124
34	178
34:1	404
34:1-8	568
34:1-17	272, 565
34:2	56, 125, 173, 355
34:3	256
34:4	201, 424
34:5	117, 213, 243, 531
34:5-17	213
34:7	347
34:8	125, 277, 388, 500, 518, 533
34:8-12	26
34:11	135
34:13	128, 261
34:14	327,

501, 507
34:16 323
35 493
35:1 .... 262, 365, 408, 423, 553
35:1-2 553
35:1-7 358
35:1-10 276
35:2 .... 266, 319, 501
35:2-4 317
35:3 .... 125, 340
35:4 .... 273, 290, 388, 428, 518, 533
35:5 .... 339, 342
35:5-6 259
35:6-7 .... 119, 251, 332
35:7 400
35:8 .... 168, 178, 410, 485, 523
35:8-10 .... 45, 115, 206, 215, 46, 512, 5133
35:9 555
35:10 .... 211, 239, 470, 520, 551 553
36 183
36:2 70
36:6 248
36:11 270
36:19 103
37 183
37:1 287
37:3 194
37:4 .... 64, 506
37:9 16
37:16 338
37:21-38 156
37:22 388
37:24 .... 105, 111
37:25 .... 64, 367

37:27 424
37:29 252
37:30 .... 302, 470, 565
37:31 .... 224, 506
37:31-32 .... 57, 64, 545
37:32 501
37:35 354
37:36-37 137
37:36-38 111
37:37 .... 184, 266
38 16
38:6 296
38:7 470
38:9-20 280
38:14 500
38:17 354
38:18 209
38:22 567
39:1-9 307
39:2 185
39:7 467
40-66 .... 236, 313
40:1 .... 423, 426, 505
40:1-2 .... 31, 221
40:1-4 217
40:2 266
40:3 .... 278, 483
40:3-5 527
40:4-5 410
40:5 .... 277, 316, 433, 495, 501, 556
40:6-7 427
40:7-8 201
40:8 .... 366, 469
40:9 .... 317, 432

40:10 .... 417, 503, 520, 528, 533
40:10-11 410
40:12 218
40:15 .... 156, 327, 404, 501, 507
40:15-17 386
40:18 313
40:18-20 384
40:19 .... 113, 384
40:20 384
40:21-26 .... 351, 398
40:22 .... 338, 365, 376, 427
40:24 540
40:25 313
40:26 .... 292, 376
40:27 .... 413, 416
40:27-31 483
40:28 .... 57, 292, 485
40:28-31 362
40:31 .... 86, 330, 513
41:1 .... 327, 404, 501, 507
41:2 .... 367, 377, 385, 398, 425, 428, 430
41:4 .... 313, 361, 366, 398
41:5 .... 57, 327, 501, 507
41:7 .... 322, 329, 384, 384
41:8 .... 343, 358
41:8-9 .... 23, 350, 364, 406, 549
41:8-10 406
41:9 57

41:10 .... 384, 472, 492
41:11 .... 380, 510
41:12 334
41:13-14 330
41:14 .... 361, 361, 388, 503, 533
41:15-16 175
41:16 .... 512, 553
41:17 .... 466, 545, 551
41:17-18 .... 251, 358
41:18 .... 262, 353, 410, 423
41:19-20 277
41:20 .... 384, 432
41:21 207
41:21-22 355
41:21-24 .... 361, 367
41:22 .... 384, 394
41:23-24 218
41:24 .... 26, 342, 378
41:25 .... 327, 328, 377, 395, 425, 430
41:26-27 .... 313, 340, 361, 384
41:26-29 366
41:27 .... 319, 432
41:28 384
41:29 362
42:1 .... 399, 515
42:1-4 .... 147, 339, 418
42:1-9 434
42:3 483,

515
42:4 .... 327, 343, 404, 423, 424, 501, 507
42:5 .... 292, 292, 322, 346, 366, 376, 398
42:6 .... 105, 131, 168, 262, 296, 406, 409, 450, 545
42:6-7 521
42:7 .... 58, 259, 277, 318, 339, 342, 499
42:8 .... 313, 556
42:9 .... 353, 366, 384, 395
42:10 .... 57, 327, 405, 501, 507
42:12 .... 405, 406, 501, 507, 556, 567
42:13 .... 430, 501
42:14 542
42:15 .... 501, 507
42:16 .... 277, 410, 434, 499
42:17 .... 378, 483
42:18 .... 339, 499
42:19 .... 63, 350, 358, 405, 406, 537
42:19-20 340
42:22 .... 346, 517
42:24 .... 313, 346, 406
42:25 272
43:1 .... 296, 331, 333, 361, 366, 407, 533
43:1-3 313
43:1-13 398
43:1-2:16 47
43:2 492

43:3 .... 330, 350, 534
43:5 .... 330, 459
43:5-6 .... 57, 503
43:5-7 .... 131, 226, 410, 412
43:6 .... 413, 567
43:6-7 168
43:7 .... 358, 366, 384, 541, 556
43:8 .... 63, 292, 339, 340, 343
43:8-13 .... 361, 367
43:9 394
43:10 .... 343, 350, 358, 361, 364, 380, 405, 432, 532
43:10-13 .... 384, 437
43:10-15 376
43:10-17 313
43:11 534
43:13 137
43:14 .... 331, 361, 388, 533
43:15 .... 207, 269, 346, 366
43:16-17 367
43:17 174
43:18 .... 119, 332, 466, 502, 548
43:18-19 .... 277, 340
43:18-21 .... 251, 262, 358, 493
43:19 .... 366, 407, 410
43:20 128
43:21 .... 296, 347, 366
43:25 305,

313, 364, 541
43:27 384
44:1 .... 405, 406
44:1-2 .... 343, 350, 358, 365, 376
44:1-5 225
44:1-8 313
44:2 366
44:3 .... 262, 361, 375
44:3-4 353
44:3-5 .... 45, 119, 194, 251, 262, 277, 332, 340, 466, 493, 502, 548
44:5 333
44:6 .... 207, 331, 333, 347, 376, 388, 398, 533
44:6-9 367
44:7-8 .... 366, 394
44:8 .... 350, 483
44:8-9 365
44:9 .... 26, 149, 333
44:9-18 154
44:9-20 .... 322, 378, 384
44:11 .... 39, 483
44:15 .... 344, 384
44:17 384
44:17-19 549
44:18 339
44:18-19 340
44:19 384
44:21 .... 343, 350, 358, 366, 376, 405
44:21-28 313
44:22 305
44:22-24 .... 331, 347, 389, 533
44:23 .... 317, 386, 405, 470, 556
44:24 .... 322, 338, 358, 366, 376, 398
44:24-25 .... 165, 241
44:24-26 367
44:25 471
44:25-26 366
44:26 209
44:28 .... 328, 368, 395, 398, 425
45:1 .... 328, 503, 556
45:1-3 .... 327, 377
45:3-4 .... 333, 347
45:4 358
45:4-5 333
45:4-6 124
45:5 .... 384, 398
45:5-25 313
45:6 .... 378, 380, 501, 502
45:7 218
45:8 .... 385, 396, 398, 500
45:9 254
45:10-11 194
45:12 .... 292, 322, 338, 398, 427
45:13 430
45:14 .... 58, 130, 193, 413, 459, 467, 507, 510, 524
45:15 .... 350, 534
45:16 .... 39, 322, 384
45:17 244
45:18 .... 338, 346, 366, 376, 398, 428
45:18-22 378

SCRIPTURE INDEX

45:19 .... 399, 468
45:20 .... 322, 384
45:20-21 367
45:20-25 340
45:21 .... 350, 362, 384, 394
45:21-24 375
45:22 468
45:22-23 .... 35, 57
45:22-25 .... 58, 433, 506
45:23 .... 137, 527
45:24 .... 378, 510
45:24-25 519
45:25 .... 512, 548, 556
46:1-2 .... 322, 384, 391
46:3 .... 32, 45, 57, 64, 296, 445, 506, 545
46:5 .... 313, 322
46:5-13 24
46:6 384
46:6-7 322
46:8-11 .... 124, 208, 209, 241, 294, 313, 323, 328, 329, 375, 377, 398, 425
46:9-11 367
46:10 394
46:10-11 398
46:11 .... 327, 395, 469
46:12 404
46:13 .... 464, 492, 525, 556
47:1 .... 174, 494
47:3 518
47:4 .... 313, 331, 361, 533
47:8 .... 174, 194, 390, 407
47:9 135
47:10 390
47:10-13 93
48:1 .... 32, 404
48:2 361
48:3 313
48:3-5 367
48:4 385
48:6 313
48:7 .... 332, 407
48:8 .... 343, 384
48:9 .... 354, 519
48:10 .... 25, 332
48:11 .... 355, 556
48:12 361
48:12-13 366
48:12-17 313
48:13 .... 338, 427
48:14 398
48:14-15 328
48:14-16 366
48:16 .... 336, 407
48:17 .... 24, 331, 503, 533
48:18 401
48:20 .... 57, 331, 350, 405, 533
48:21 332
48:22 .... 401, 484, 498, 559
49:1 .... 268, 327, 404, 501, 508
49:1-7 395
49:1-13 .... 434, 435

49:2 146
49:3 .... 317, 405, 556
49:4 .... 453, 521, 528
49:5-8 450
49:6 .... 57, 64, 105, 131, 168, 262, 296, 545, 546
49:6-8 .... 339, 521
49:7 .... 331, 443, 468, 503, 533
49:8 .... 338, 468, 483, 513, 516, 517, 549
49:8-9 503
49:9 517
49:10 .... 269, 358, 400, 434, 461, 551
49:11 .... 168, 266, 278, 527
49:13 .... 119, 366, 423, 427, 461, 516, 553
49:14 554
49:14-15 .... 324, 343
49:14-16 226
49:15-26 562
49:18 .... 430, 503, 521
49:18-23 506
49:19 459
49:20-21 244
49:21 194
49:22 .... 57, 116, 262, 503, 527, 567
49:22-23 .... 117, 131
49:23 .... 58, 117, 130, 244, 378, 432, 459, 509, 511, 524, 563
49:24-26 500
49:25 210
49:26 .... 317, 331, 350, 414, 428, 431, 437, 503, 511, 533
50:1 .... 343, 384, 412, 431, 461, 496, 501, 508, 523
50:1-2 497
50:1-11 415
50:2 .... 319, 367, 426, 500, 533
50:4 .... 277, 338, 430
50:4-11 .... 395, 408, 435
50:5 534
50:7 407
50:10 .... 249, 422
50:10-11 420
51:3 .... 119, 277, 358, 423, 423, 427, 461, 484
51:4 .... 262, 270, 344, 408
51:4-5 472
51:5 .... 147, 319, 327, 338, 404, 417, 501, 508
51:5-8 492
51:6 .... 272, 463, 500
51:7 424
51:8 419
51:9 .... 266, 319, 417, 428, 430, 447, 500, 533
51:10 .... 215, 319, 367, 535
51:10-11 528
51:11 .... 225, 239, 279, 551, 553
51:11-13 520
51:12 .... 119, 318, 423
51:13 .... 338, 398, 463, 483
51:14 517
51:15 361
51:16 398

SCRIPTURE INDEX

51:17 .... 240, 428, 430
51:17-20 458
51:17-23 533
51:19 423
51:21 .... 428, 461
51:21-22 240
51:22 428
52:1 .... 428, 429, 521, 526
52:2-7 536
52:3 377
52:4 217
52:6 107
52:6-7 319
52:7 .... 175, 207, 319, 429
52:7-12 423
52:8 .... 26, 526
52:8-9 470
52:9 .... 119, 331, 423, 427, 484
52:10 .... 57, 266, 277, 314, 317, 319, 394, 406, 417, 500, 501, 533
52:11 .... 410, 527
52:12 .... 317, 492
52:13 .... 44, 279, 316, 339, 395
52:13-15 .... 268, 436
52:13-53:12 .... 91, 515, 561
52:13-53:15 341
52:14 443
52:15 .... 441, 506
53:1 .... 266, 319, 343, 417, 500, 502, 533, 548
53:1-3 .... 342, 407, 436

53:2 113
53:3 408
53:4 444
53:4-6 .... 26, 118, 119, 381, 401, 432, 434, 438, 529
53:5 .... 18, 314, 447, 451, 453, 484
53:6 .... 120, 250, 540
53:7-9 419
53:9 .... 407, 484, 498, 500, 533
53:10 .... 40, 219, 244, 296, 369, 444, 447, 455, 469, 548
53:10-12 .... 119, 407, 436, 454
53:11 .... 380, 406, 454
53:12 .... 279, 316, 339, 395
53:15 545
54 .... 218, 453, 560
54:1 .... 194, 269, 296, 466, 506, 525, 551
54:1-2 244
54:1-17 562
54:3 .... 378, 419, 465, 519, 548
54:4 378
54:4-10 523
54:5 .... 331, 533
54:6-7 416
54:6-8 225
54:7 503
54:7-8 .... 236, 465
54:8 .... 331, 509, 533, 541
54:9 .... 389, 527

54:9-10 527
54:10 .... 94, 465, 521, 534
54:11 423
54:13 .... 115, 465, 470, 502
54:13-14 400
54:14 94
54:17 .... 406, 464, 549
54:23 130
55:1 .... 119, 254, 354, 358, 466
55:1-3 .... 270, 401
55:1-13 466
55:2 494
55:3 .... 211, 296, 450, 465, 513, 520, 534
55:4-5 465
55:6 492
55:6-13 .... 395, 568
55:7 .... 465, 485
55:8-11 .... 318, 386, 523
55:11 .... 318, 366, 469
55:12 .... 423, 465
55:12-14 465
55:13 567
56:1 500
56:1-8 .... 262, 476
56:1-12 471
56:2 .... 492, 494
56:2-5 568
56:3 520
56:3-8 360
56:6-8 545
56:7 .... 290, 380, 567
56:8 .... 116, 262
56:9-12 484
56:9-57 24
56:10 .... 433, 499
57:1-2 484
57:3-10 484
57:4 .... 384, 466, 492, 494
57:5 .... 14, 24, 26
57:6 423
57:7 547
57:8, 10 485
57:13 513
57:14 .... 118, 527
57:15 .... 238, 321, 363, 515, 536, 558
57:16 389
57:17 535
57:17-19 226
57:18 .... 493, 516, 564
57:18-19 270
57:19 .... 268, 332
57:20 485
57:21 .... 402, 498, 559
58:1 500
58:1-4 489
58:2-3 483
58:3 449
58:4 497
58:6 491
58:6-9 238
58:6-12 268
58:8 .... 270, 317, 521, 556
58:9 .... 468, 498, 500, 554

SCRIPTURE INDEX

58:10 .... 58, 499
58:11 .... 484, 563
58:12 .... 410, 519
58:13 494
58:14 .... 318, 466, 494
58:18 499
59:1 .... 417, 500, 533
59:1-2 .... 218, 313, 355, 539, 554, 558
59:2 .... 20, 500
59:7 266
59:9 .... 493, 500
59:13 384
59:15-20 226
59:15-21 408
59:16 .... 266, 314, 319, 401, 406, 417, 472, 492, 533
59:16-18 341
59:16-20 532
59:17 388
59:18 .... 272, 319, 320, 404, 501, 503, 507, 533, 564
59:19 556
59:20 .... 331, 380
59:20-21 378
59:21 .... 262, 318, 366, 515, 520, 548
60 296
60:1 .... 524, 545, 556
60:1-2 .... 47, 88, 277
60:1-3 .... 131, 317, 491, 564
60:1-14 .... 196, 339

60:1-22 .... 44, 567
60:3 .... 408, 413, 460, 524
60:3-11 474
60:3-12 31
60:3-14 519
60:4 .... 131, 413, 503
60:4-16 563
60:5 520
60:6 432
60:6-7 507
60:7 .... 167, 474
60:9 .... 193, 327, 404, 501, 507, 508, 525
60:10 .... 360, 409, 473, 474, 520
60:10-11 413
60:10-14 168
60:11 .... 503, 507, 520
60:12 .... 117, 331
60:13 277
60:14 .... 26, 378, 413
60:15 203
60:16 .... 167, 317, 331, 350, 413, 415, 432, 437, 503, 533, 534
60:17 400
60:18 498
60:19 .... 207, 556
60:19-22 251
60:20 .... 426, 562
60:21 .... 113, 168, 215, 405, 483, 541, 549
61:1 .... 319, 336, 427, 432, 515
61:2 .... 388, 422, 427

61:1-2 .... 175, 399, 410
61:1-3 .... 340, 484, 503
61:2 .... 119, 125, 273, 409
61:2-3 .... 250, 484, 553, 562
61:3 .... 405, 426, 430
61:4 410
61:5 .... 31, 360, 473, 509, 545
61:6 .... 320, 474, 507, 511, 568
61:6-7 196
61:7 .... 513, 551
61:8 .... 450, 503, 528
61:9 548
61:10 .... 458, 500, 553
61:11 492
61:19 .... 14, 88
62 296
62:1 521
62:2-4 552
62:3 .... 42, 58, 386, 525
62:4 .... 410, 416, 528
62:5 553
62:8 .... 137, 473
62:10 .... 57, 116, 117, 118, 124, 168, 266, 278, 316, 353, 378, 410, 483
62:11 .... 57, 316, 350, 503, 521
63:1 .... 117, 273, 500
63:1-6 .... 213, 274, 395, 414, 506, 568

63:3 343
63:4 .... 273, 388, 516, 517
63:5 .... 266, 314, 319, 406, 417, 500
63:6 428
63:8 350
63:9 .... 240, 297, 331, 533
63:9-11 399
63:11 410
63:11-12 426
63:12 .... 471, 533
63:15 .... 501, 542, 547
63:16 .... 399, 533, 541
63:17 554
64 178
64:1-12 538
64:4 553
64:5 201
64:6 .... 406, 433, 482
64:8 .... 168, 536
64:10 .... 26, 394
64:11 26
64:12 .... 547, 554
65-66 546
65:1-2 545
65:1-7 .... 355, 433
65:2 .... 551, 558
65:3 .... 26, 565
65:4 565
65:6 .... 320, 564
65:7 528
65:8-16 406
65:9 358,

SCRIPTURE INDEX

483
65:11 567
65:11-12 26
65:11-15 397
65:12 558
65:15 .... 358, 549
65:16 553
65:17 395
65:17-18 332
65:17-19 427
65:18 .... 203, 553
65:18-19 562
65:19 426
65:19-20 .... 279, 353
65:21-23 527
65:20 212
65:22 549
65:24 .... 468, 493
65:25 .... 115, 353, 483
66:1 .... 501, 508
66:1-2 .... 321, 536
66:1-12 238
66:1-23 196
66:2 .... 116, 363
66:3 .... 26, 354, 547
66:4 551
66:5 .... 492, 558
66:6 .... 26, 320, 482, 564
66:7-9 219
66:9 194
66:10 .... 203, 484, 553
66:11 .... 466, 494
66:12 .... 320, 358, 507
66:13 .... 119, 423, 427, 484
66:14 .... 173, 551, 553
66:14-15 272
66:15 .... 58, 343
66:15-16 566
66:16 .... 21, 391, 447
66:17 .... 26, 547, 564
66:18 .... 277, 378, 556
66:18-20 520
66:18-21 474
66:18-24 545
66:19 .... 340, 404, 470, 501, 508
66:20 .... 131, 226, 412, 474, 483, 550
66:21 520
66:22 .... 396, 548
66:23 .... 31, 168
66:24 .... 26, 380, 384, 391, 419, 485, 528

JEREMIAH
1:9 62
1:15 418
1:16 550
2:1 535
2:11-13 155
2:11-19 550
2:13-19 234
2:16 164
2:17-19 155
2:20 .... 23, 480
2:21 548
2:32 .... 41, 413
3:1 23
3:2 127

3:6 481	13:23 354
3:13 480	13:34 172
3:17 25	14:7-9 442
3:18 525	14:14 .... 33, 97
4:4 .... 353, 358, 463	15:2 205
4:11 172	15:9 201
4:13 58	17:5 154
4:22 17	17:5-6 .... 33, 69
4:23 274	17:5-9 254
4:26 115	17:6 26
4:30 413	17:12 26
4:31 .... 19, 125	17:27 261
5:9 480	18:1-6 350
5:15 .... 232, 270	19:5 480
6:5 261	19:6 252
6:7 498	19:9 427
6:13-14 97	20:3 256
6:17 .... 433, 474	20:13 332
6:24 125	22:6 186
6:25 256	22:7 124
7:1-8 84	22:16 332
7:5-10 354	22:23 125
7:31 480	23:5 .... 113, 258, 269, 522
7:31-32 252	23:5-6 .... 44, 77
8:9 241	23:9-22 38
8:10-11 87	23:13 24
8:17 39	23:36 292
8:18 18	24:1 39
9:9 480	24:7 502
9:20 261	25:8-11 389
9:25-26 .... 353, 358, 463	25:11-12 .... 175, 366
10:8-16 322	25:11-14 316
10:10 292	25:15 428
10:12 322	25:17 323
10:21 437	25:33 568
11:4 168	27:5-7 316
12:10 .... 40, 97	27:6 389
12:11 541	27:6-9 366
13 169	28:1-17 97
13:21 125	29:1 39
	29:11 469
	25:10-14 175

SCRIPTURE INDEX

29:10-13................................366
29:10-14................................316
29:13-14................................469
30-33......................................313
30:1-3....................................349
30:3..511, 519
30:5..506
30:5-7....................................108
30:6..125
30:7..25, 332, 428, 461
30:8-9....................................109
30:8-11..................................349
30:11......................................167, 221, 332, 414, 428
30:17......................................167
30:18......................................261, 263, 410, 511, 519
30:18-24................................493
31:4-6....................................410
31:10......................................320
31:10-14................................427
31:12......................................493
31:14......................................354, 466
31:23......................................263, 510, 519
31:27-28................................410, 459
31:31......................................225, 314, 416
31:31-34................................25, 116, 224, 263, 270, 296, 339, 359, 361, 432, 450, 503, 513, 521
31:34......................................115, 215, 305, 376, 463, 502
31:35......................................427
31:35-37................................410
31:36......................................548
31:38-40................................410, 459, 493
32:14......................................86, 460
32:15......................................366, 410
32:15-25................................493
32:17......................................413
32:18......................................94
32:20-21................................170
32:26-27................................410
32:27......................................519
32:35......................................480
32:37-44................................263, 460
32:40......................................413, 521
33:3..540
33:6-8....................................270
33:7..411, 506
33:9-11..................................526
33:11-16................................349
33:12......................................410
33:14-26................................250, 357, 386, 474, 493, 568
33:15......................................44, 77, 113, 269, 522
33:15-16................................525
34:7..283
34:8-10..................................517
34:8-11..................................491
36:3..270
39:3..283
39:13......................................283
44:1..164
44:10......................................447
44:15-19................................480
45..402
46:9..174
46:10......................................273, 273
46:14......................................164
46:19......................................164
46:28......................................332, 414
47:4..138
48:7..383
48:24......................................144

48:29	148
48:35	143
48:40	117
48:41	125
49	178
49:3	383
49:7	241
49:18	274
49:20	209
49:22	117, 125, 385
49:23	485
49:24	125
49:25	203
49:27	261
50-51	136
50:1-5	176, 176
50:2	115, 382
50:8	400
50:17-18	389
50:17-20	176
50:19	267
50:20	270
50:23	103
50:37	165
50:38-39	135
50:38-40	176
50:42	388
50:43	125
50:45	209
51:1	173
51:6	173, 400
51:7	533
51:8	176
51:11	368, 425
51:13-14	351
51:15	322
51:20	103, 173
51:24-26	176
51:25	173
51:30	165
51:30-33	389
51:33	388
51:37	135, 209
51:40	273
51:44	382
51:48	173, 204
51:53	173
51:53-56	135
51:55	173
51:56	173
51:59-64	176
52:1	291

LAMENTATIONS

1:5	413
1:6	19
1:12	444
1:18	444
1:22	18, 239
1:25	239
2:6	50
2:13	19
2:15	203
2:22	256
3:21	236
3:25	468
4:3	125
4:9	183
4:21	273
4:21-22	178
5:15	203
5:21	536, 537

EZEKIEL

1:22	61
3:8-9	418
3:17	435, 475
4	169
5:5	25
5:13	25

SCRIPTURE INDEX

6:2 41
6:13 .... 26, 480
7:11 498
7:16 500
7:17 125
7:19-24 250
7:20 413
9:4 290
9:4-10 130
9:14 172
16 23
16:6 481
16:7 413
16:11 413
16:16 504
16:20 480
16:36 480
16:47-52 24
15:55-57 146
17:20-24 110
18:5-9 40
18:23 .... 14, 22, 36, 380, 547
18:30 .... 14, 22, 36, 380
18:32 .... 14, 22, 36, 380
20:27 103
20:36-38 .... 45, 107, 221, 245, 397, 408, 506, 513, 565
20:41 501
20:47-48 239
21:7, 12 125
21:21 391
21:27 64
22:19 25
23:35 305
23:37 480
23:39 480
23:40 413
24:25 203
25:12-14 531
26:21 156

27:6 267
27:12 508
27:12-21 193
27:25 193
27:36 156
28:2 191
28:7 210
28:12-19 133
28:19 156
29:3 425
29:6-7 284
29:21 44
30-32 547
30:3 125
30:11 210
30:13, 14 164
31:12 210
32:2 425
32:7 272
32:12 210
33:2 433
33:7 474
34 474
34:14 251
34:16 .... 164, 251
34:23-24 320
34:25 503
34:25-29 115
35 178
35:1-15 .... 273, 531
36:8 549
36:10 410
36:16-28 221
36:17 540
36:19 426
36:19-23 244
36:19-25 506
36:20 .... 25, 541
36:22-23 .... 354, 415
36:22-32 296
36:23 210,

538
36:23-25 502
36:24 359
36:25 119
36:25-27 358
36:27 359
36:30 224
36:33 410
36:38 210
37 427
37:1-14 220
37:15-28 117
37:16 82
37:21 506
37:21-28 221
37:23-24 320
37:24-26 216
37:24-28 269
37:25-26 521
37:26 503
38&39 206,
272, 506, 529, 565
38:4 252
38:4-8 566
38:8 549
38:13 508
38:16 210,
538
38:18-23 567
38:23 501,
538
39:1-2 566
39:6-23 538
39:7 501
39:7-8 210
39:9-10 .... 93, 105
39:9-16 568
39:18-20 272,
273
39:20-21 426
39:21-23 210
39:25 501
39:25-29 107,
118, 226, 408, 506

39:25-39 221
39:27-29 210
39:29 262
40-42 507
40-48 313,
474
40:1-47:12 30
43:1-5 386
43:6-7 510
44:4 386
44:15-16 568
45:18-25 568
46:7-17 517
48:35 269,
549

DANIEL
1:1-2 389
1:1-3 309
2:2 391
2:35 332,
550
2:44-45 509
3:17-18 293
4 111
4:28-33 241
4:30 524
4:34-37 .... 61, 321
5 328
5:7-8 391
5:18-23 391
5:30-31 173
6:20 292
6:26 292
7:10 .... 61, 275
7:12 206
7:13 163
7:13-14 95
7:15-28 206
7:23-28 272,
506, 565
8:9 109
8:15-19 61
8:19 173
8:17 57

SCRIPTURE INDEX

9:1-19 343
9:3 290
9:7 505
9:15-19 292
9:20-27 61
9:24 .... 57, 73
9:24-27 560
9:25 515
9:26 515
9:27 .... 35, 57, 64, 107, 108, 519, 548, 565
10:10 61
11:28-32 550
11:36 .... 35, 57, 64, 108, 109, 173, 546
11:36-45 565
11:41 .... 213, 274
12:1 45
12:1-3 419
12:1-13 313
12:2 .... 551, 563
12:2-3 .... 115, 212, 220
12:7 .... 35, 46, 57, 64, 108, 167, 317, 332, 461
12:10 .... 317, 332, 397
12:12 524
12:12-13 115

HOSEA
1:2 23
1:10 .... 168, 292
1:10-11 .... 412, 427
1:10-12 107
2:1 427
2:2 23
2:5 .... 23, 482
2:8 482
2:13 .... 155, 203
2:14-18 521
2:14-23 .... 412, 461
2:15 .... 41, 535, 549
2:18 555
2:19-20 526
2:23 .... 168, 427
3:1 .... 23, 148
3:1-5 .... 25, 296, 461
3:4 38
3:4-5 .... 147, 225
3:5 .... 107, 317, 412, 427
4:1 333
4:1-14 .... 24, 26
4:6 .... 54, 474
4:17 362
5:12 419
5:14 554
5:14-15 .... 144, 235
5:14-6:1 .... 167, 461
5:15 .... 260, 317
5:15-6:5 97
6:1-3 .... 251, 317, 482
6:6 .... 238, 241
6:9 361
7:11 482
7:12 554
7:16 554
8:7 267
8:9 482
9:6 164
9:7 96
9:9 255
9:15 557

9:16 56
10:10 557
10:12 .... 260, 375, 468
10:14 127
11:1-9 149
11:11 260
12:1 482
13:4-6 155
13:7 554
13:15 172
14:1 127
14:5 375
14:5-7 224

JOEL
1:10-12 202
1:12 201
1:13 290
1:15 34
2:1, 11 34
2:13 .... 186, 490
2:23 .... 365, 552
2:25-29 359
2:28-29 262
2:28-32 .... 45, 119, 262, 296, 358, 360
2:31 .... 34, 272
2:32 .... 44, 107, 408, 540
3:1-2 566
3:1-8 131
3:1-17 .... 206, 221, 240, 272, 414, 506, 529, 565
3:7 320
3:9-16 567
3:9-17 45
3:18 .... 251, 375, 466
3:18-21 .... 313, 423
3:19 .... 117, 273

AMOS
1:1 28
1:3 175
1:11-12 273
1:12 531
2:6-8 .... 24, 40, 52, 99
2:9 56
3:2 .... 159, 182, 330, 350, 428, 541
3:3 144
3:6 .... 218, 374
3:8 144
3:14-15 .... 40, 64
4:1 .... 40, 260
4:4-6 354
4:6-11 97
4:11 71
5:4-6 468
5:10 .... 24, 500, 559
5:11 554
5:11-12 .... 40, 52, 64, 99
5:13 500
5:18 .... 34, 58, 125, 235, 547
5:18-20 205
5:21-23 558
5:21-27 .... 20, 21
5:23 558
5:24 268
6:1 260
6:4-7 203
6:4-11 .... 40, 52
6:5-6 .... 53, 55
6:8 261
7:12 248
8:4 24
8:4-6 99
8:6 40
8:10 .... 42, 186
8:11 38

SCRIPTURE INDEX

9:7 138
9:8 414
9:8-10 .... 332, 428
9:11 147
9:11-12 117
9:11-15 .... 113, 263, 296, 313, 459, 493
9:12 .... 131, 178
9:13 .... 262, 423
9:16 47

OBADIAH
1:1 14
1-9 213
1:14 531
11-14 273
15-21 .... 313, 459
17 408
18 391
19 177
19-21 196
19:21 131

JONAH
1:3 .... 193, 508
2:9 119
3:5-8 491
3:6 290
4:2 .... 302, 508
4:11 78

MICAH
1:6 42
1:8 128
1:13, 4:8 19
2:1-2 40
2:1-9 52
2:2 24
2:11 184
2:12-13 .... 107, 296, 313, 317, 484, 493
2:13 269
3:1 .... 24, 184
3:1-4 337
3:1-9 258
3:1-11 355
3:9-10 263
3:9-12 .... 184, 337
3:4 20
3:6 241
3:9-12 232
3:10 51
3:11 38
3:12 64
4:1 550
4:1-5 94
4:2 .... 25, 423
4:3 .... 92, 212, 263
4:4 286
4:7 95
4:9-10 125
4:10-13 331
4:12 .... 209, 566
4:13 .... 175, 196
5:2 .... 73, 548
5:9 .... 24, 205
5:14 .... 388, 518
5:15 518
6:1 333
6:3 354
6:3-8 354
6:8 .... 238, 268, 472, 558
6:10 105
6:15 554
7:1 .... 24, 258, 513
7:1-4 477
7:1-6 268
7:2-4 .... 51, 498

7:3-4 260
7:14 267
7:18-19 .... 305, 354

NAHUM
1:1 14
1:3-8 252
1:10 391
2:7 500
2:9 103
2:10 125
3:8 158
3:10 127
3:13 165

HABAKKAK
1:6-11 .... 102, 103
1:13 86
2:4 .... 268, 504
2:6-17 102
2:13-14 375
2:14 115
2:19 322
3:2 .... 19, 236
3:3-7 .... 239, 539
3:3-15 252
3:8 564
3:16-19 306

ZEPHANIAH
1:1-3 565
1:7 .... 34, 125
1:7-9 273
1:12 559
1:13 554
1:14 34
1:15 499
2:3 221
2:8 148
2:9-10 .... 128, 142
2:14 135
2:14-17 269

2:15 203
3:1 25
3:8 221
3:10 167
3:11 203
3:12 .... 221, 515
3:12-20 313
3:14 .... 19, 365
3:14-17 .... 332, 427
3:14-20 92
3:15 269
3:15-17 317
3:16 125
3:17 553
3:20 526

HAGGAI
1:13 492
2:4-5 492
2:6 539
2:6-9 .... 196, 519
2:7 507
2:20 327
2:20-23 313
2:22 539

ZECHARIAH
1:12 173
1:14 501
1:17 130
2:5 .... 257, 317, 512, 564
2:6-7 400
2:6-13 176
2:7 .... 388, 410
2:8 .... 196, 255, 331, 342, 388
2:8-9 265
2:10 92
2:10-11 317
2:13 327
3:1-5 62

SCRIPTURE INDEX

3:2 .... 71, 156
3:4 .... 41, 430
3:5 .... 42, 525
3:8 .... 44, 113, 522
3:10 286
3:14-20 77
4:7 30
5:1-4 397
5:5-11 .... 136, 176
6:9 507
6:9-15 519
6:11-14 525
6:12 .... 44, 113, 522
6:15 509
8 493
8:1-6 422
8:1-8 117
8:2 502
8:3 .... 26, 30
8:4-5 320
8:4-8 460
8:11-13 168
8:11-15 244
8:12-13 520
8:13 215
8:13-23 511
8:18-23 .... 92, 509
8:20-23 .... 31, 115, 130, 296, 313, 378, 413
8:22 25
9:9 .... 19, 92, 365
9:14-15 564
9:16-17 90
10:8 57
10:8-12 .... 117, 408, 506
10:9-10 .... 296, 313, 460
10:11 226
11 169
11:2 267
11:7 .... 33, 140, 515
11:11 .... 140, 332
11:14 .... 98, 163
11:15-17 107
12:1 .... 206, 272, 322
12:1-9 .... 414, 506
12:1-9 .... 109, 331
12:1-13:1 45
12:10 .... 56, 64, 97, 107, 119, 221, 251, 262, 262, 269, 317, 332, 358, 380, 408, 439, 447, 483, 502, 548
12:10-13:1 560
12:10-14 432
12-14 313
13:1 .... 25, 97, 119, 225, 251, 262, 358, 483, 502
13:2 .... 115, 206
13:8-9 .... 25, 45, 46, 56, 64, 107, 221, 245, 380, 397, 513
13:9 .... 317, 408, 565
14:1 .... 34, 206, 240, 272, 506, 529
14:1-2 45
14:1-4 414
14:1-5 567
14:1-15 565
14:2 .... 566, 567
14:3 .... 221, 231, 331, 341
14:3-4 564
14:6-7 .... 125, 272
14:7 207

14:8 262
14:9 .... 30, 94, 269, 409, 415, 502
14:10 30
14:12 331
14:14 .... 507, 519
14:16 25
14:16-21 .... 30, 94, 167, 378, 567
14:20 196
14:20-21 528
14:21 430
14:26 221

MALACHI
1:1-4 567
1:2-3 273
1:2-5 531
1:8-11 186
1:11 .... 167, 375, 378, 408
1:12-13 149
1:13 354
2:7-8 475
2:15 17
2:16 498
3:1 317
3:1-3 25
3:1-4 .... 46, 313
3:1-5 64
3:1-6 56
3:1-7 547
3:3 .... 317, 397
3:4 535
3:5 24
3:6 .... 221, 357, 396
3:11 156
3:16 .... 45, 275
4:1 .... 56, 391
4:2 .... 251, 505, 506
4:5 34

4:5-6 .... 313, 317

MATTHEW
1:18-25 .... 73, 87
2:6 73
3:1-3 316
3:2 472
3:2-3 528
3:13-17 336
4:12-16 91
4:12-17 516
4:16 407
4:17 .... 472, 528
5:1-12 268
5:3-12 .... 210, 215
5:3 .... 332, 513, 558
5:3-4 290
5:3-12 483
5:5 .... 4, 216, 84, 513
5:11-12 257
5:18 .... 318, 366
5:35 .... 30, 94, 207, 394, 510
6:9 292
6:9-10 .... 210, 415, 502, 524
6:9-15 244
6:25-34 .... 155, 275
6:33 85
7:15 334
7:21-23 .... 472, 489
7:28-29 441
8:10-12 .... 211, 215
8:12 .... 206, 551
8:14-17 277

SCRIPTURE INDEX

8:17 336
8:18-25 113
9:13 21
9:36 150
10:5-6 407
10:23 546
10:28 .... 85, 155
10:29 323
11:2-6 516
11:5 277
11:14 316
11:21 290
11:27 233
11:28 .... 418, 465, 558
11:28-30 .... 380, 412, 518
12:13-21 338
12:18-21 336
12:29 414
12:39-45 546
13:11 .... 30, 241
13:39-43 206
13:41-42 115
13:42 551
13:43 115
13:49-50 .... 115, 206
13:50 551
15:8-9 241
15:24 407
16:16 515
16:18 .... 304, 453
16:19 188
16:20 515
16:27 207
17:10-13 317
18:25 416
19:28 94
20:28 .... 365, 401, 434, 445, 529
21:13 .... 290, 474
21:22 293
21:33-46 546
21:44 .... 85, 206
22:13 .... 206, 551
22:27-39 491
23:35-39 546
23:37 .... 233, 249, 255, 547
23:37-39 .... 57, 64
24:3-31 548
24:4-31 529
24:15-31 .... 46, 107
24:21 397
24:21-22 220
24:22 .... 45, 94, 484
24:29 .... 126, 272
24:30 163
24:31 .... 45, 94, 117, 226, 408, 506, 567
24:36-44 249
24:37-41 206
24:48-51 206
25:12-13 206
25:30 551
25:31 207
25:31-46 277
25:34 .... 45, 215, 221, 279
25:35-36 491
25:41 .... 221, 278, 380
25:46 221
26:42 362
26:53-54 449
26:63-64 515
27:42 449
27:43 447
27:57-60 451
28:6 407
28:10 330
28:19 408

28:20 330

MARK
1:1-4 316
1:10 336
9:1-3 .... 207, 318
9:23 306
11:17 474
13:31 318
15:42-46 451
25:41 206
25:43 115
25:46 206

LUKE
1:32-33 113
1:33 95
1:35 105
1:50-53 216
1:67-79 .... 113, 130, 408, 413
1:68-75 464
1:71-74 216
1:76 316
1:79 91
2:34 85
2:48 49
3:22 336
4:18 176
4:18-19 516
4:34 105
5:7 381
5:10 381
5:32 381
7:22 516
7:29 380
9:31 353
9:51 418
11:21 414
16:22-23 212
19:10 .... 338, 381
19:41 150
19:41-44 .... 316, 399, 444, 464

19:42 73
21:24 220
21:35 221
22:20 .... 338, 451
23:33-43 451
23:50-53 451
24:25-26 .... 438, 516
24:47 408

JOHN
1:1-3 321
1:4-5 499
1:9-11 407
1:11 .... 316, 341, 441
1:12 95
1:14 .... 147, 318, 405
1:23 316
1:29 448
1:32-34 336
1:41, 49 515
3:1-2 441
3:5 .... 119, 359
3:11 417
3:19 499
3:19-21 539
3:34 336
3:36 95
4:10-14 466
4:15 119
4:23-24 238
4:24 241
4:25 515
4:34 .... 337, 407, 417, 441
4:42 .... 339, 408
5:17 336
5:17-19 441
5:19 417
5:23 419

SCRIPTURE INDEX

5:24 346
5:30 .... 337, 407, 417, 441
6:29 105
6:37 475
6:38 .... 337, 407, 417, 441
6:44 475
7:1-4 337
7:37-38 .... 119, 466
8:12 .... 105, 339, 408, 420, 499
8:28 417
8:29 441
8:31-36 517
8:40, 45 232
8:46 .... 417, 441
8:56 220
8:58 399
9:5 .... 105, 339
9:34 559
10:11 452
10:11-16 320
10:15 452
10:16 .... 320, 474
10:17 452
10:18 452
10:27 .... 412, 453
10:28-29 346
11:25-26 .... 211, 220
11:47-53 .... 441, 451
12:26 453
12:35-40 499
12:37-41 .... 317, 341, 399, 475, 505
12:37-42 441
12:38 336
12:49 417
14:1-3 .... 434, 528
14:6 .... 111, 140
14:10 417
14:27 .... 330, 360
15 224
15:18-19 .... 257, 479, 557
16:23 293
16:33 .... 263, 298, 360, 409
17:1 340
17:5 318
17:22-24 318
17:24 .... 407, 453
19:7 446
19:30 437
19:38-40 451
20:19 360
20-21 441
22:37 336
23:33-34 336

ACTS
1:6 30
1:6-7 359
1:6-8 199
1:8 408
1:11 505
2:16-17 359
2:20 272
2:21 540
2:22-23 441
2:23 .... 32, 208, 241, 294, 317, 444, 452, 464, 516
2:36 455
3:14 105
3:25 .... 408, 530
4:12 140

4:27-28 .... 32, 208, 241, 294, 317, 441, 444, 452, 464, 516
8:27-39 473
8:30-35 436
10:34-35 380
13:47 408
13:48 45
14:15 380
14:24 216
15:19 380
16:31 120
17:27 499
26:17-18 338
28:26-28 241

ROMANS
1:4 407
1:5 .... 408, 472
1:18-21 63
1:19 241
2:28-29 353
2:29 359
3:2 .... 343, 441, 546
3:19-20 557
3:21 542
3:21-26 .... 40, 119, 339, 380, 432
3:23 212
3:23-24 408
3:29 408
3:30 159
5:1-11 386
5:12 .... 127, 313, 536, 553
5:12-20 211
5:12-21 275
5:14, 17 553
5:20-21 62
8:18 .... 127, 470, 519
8:18-27 .... 47, 114, 211

8:18-30 220
8:20 .... 275, 555
8:21 276
8:21-22 555
8:23 386
8:28 .... 102, 208, 295, 452
8:29 452
8:31 119
8:31-37 349
8:32 73
9:1-5 .... 182, 546
9:4 .... 343, 441
9:6 353
9:23 349
9:24 408
9:27 408
9:27-28 .... 45, 108, 513
9:27-29 113
9:29 19
9:33 .... 85, 513
10:2-3 489
10:11 513
10:12 408
10:13 .... 120, 380, 540
10:15 432
10:16 441
10:20-21 545
11:1-2 .... 330, 347
11:8 241
11:15 548
11:23-36 506
11:25 380
11:25-29 .... 19, 45
11:25-32 .... 64, 386, 408
11:25-36 .... 57, 130, 236, 245, 313, 349, 378, 548,

560
11:29 .... 250, 330, 460, 548
11:30 408
11:34 349
12:1 534
13:10 492
13:12 199
15:9-12 408
15:18-19 .... 408, 472
15:20-21 440
16:25-26 30
16:25-27 .... 408, 472, 545

I CORINTHIANS
1:9 241
2:9 539
2:14 536
2:16 349
7:29 199
8:4 384
10:11 199
10:20 384
10:21-22 550
15:3 445
15:12-57 211
15:32 184
16:22 199

II CORINTHIANS
1:21-22 386
3:18 275
5:1 304
5:5 387
5:8 212
5:21 .... 445, 450
6:1-2 409
11:3 223
15:8 230
16:14 187

GALATIANS
3:8 .... 408, 530

3:13 445

EPHESIANS
1:2-3 536
1:6 .... 245, 339, 556
1:11 .... 241, 444
1:12 .... 245, 339, 556
1:13-14 386
1:14 .... 245, 339, 556
2:11-22 30
2:11-4:16 359
3:1-9 30
4:30 .... 212, 386, 534
5:6-8 176
6:15 432

PHILIPPIANS
1:6 217
1:23 478
2:5-11 .... 339, 380, 519
2:9-11 .... 35, 438, 455, 456, 506
2:11 405
3:1-10 547
4:3 359
4:6 30
4:6-7 360
4:5 199
4:5-6 216

COLOSSIANS
1:15-17 321
1:26 .... 30, 545
2:11 359
3:5 52

I THESS
1:9 380
1:9-10 199
1:10 .... 144, 220
2:16 199,

221
4:13-18 212
4:14 211
5:1 144
5:1-2 107
5:1-3 221
5:1-9 199
5:9 144

II THESS
1:6-9 221,
265, 320, 501, 518, 564
2:8 114
2:8-12 221
2:11 .... 63, 241

I TIMOTHY
1:7 360
1:15 338
2:4-6 445
3:16 334
4:10 445
5:18 73
6:9-11 52
6:17 52
6:17-19 154

II TIMOTHY
1:10 211
2:11-13 330
2:13 346
2:21 62

TITUS
2:13 357
3:5 475

HEBREWS
1:1-3 321
1:2 29
1:14 .... 61, 464
2:3 464
2:5 464
2:9 120,
211, 445, 448
2:13-18 87
4:9 464
4:15 450
6:13-20 527

6:19-20 513
9:14-15 211
9:28 445,
464
10:19-25 111
10:25 199,
464
10:27 199
11:17-19 220
12:2 407,
453
12:11 225
12:16-17 177
12:18-20 539
12:18-22 61
12:28 464
13:5 330

JAMES
1:6 293
1:10-11 318
1:26, 27 21
2:13 389
2:18 21
4:6 558
4:14 318
5:8 .... 30, 199

I PETER
1:10-12 436
1:13 213,
222, 552
1:14-17 472
1:15-16 528
1:20 29,
317, 336
2:4 132
2:6 513
2:8 85
2:21-25 449
2:22 451
2:24 318,
432, 434, 445
3:1-6 41
3:7 497
3:13 257

SCRIPTURE INDEX

3:13-15 216
3:18 .... 434, 445
3:23 330
4:7 .... 30, 199
4:19 257
5:6-7 360
5:7 216

II PETER
1:21 334
2:1-3 334
3:3-10 249
3:7-11 .... 424, 552
3:9 .... 30, 36, 199, 380
3:11 199

I JOHN
1:9 22
2:2 445
2:1-2 448
2:8 29
2:15-17 163
2:18 .... 29, 199
3:5 450
3:13 .... 479, 559
3:17-18 492
4:1 334
4:10 .... 445, 448
4:14 .... 339, 408
5:14 293

JUDE
6 159

REVELATION
1:3 199
1:7 .... 163, 207
1:8 .... 361, 380
1:13 61
1:14-15 318
1:16 405
1:17 .... 62, 361
1:17-18 380
2:8 361
2:12, 16 405
2:17 552
2:26 94
2:28 483
3:7-8 189
3:12 552
3:20 211
3:21 94
4:4-11 61
4:6 61
5:3-5 455
5:8-14 .... 61, 94
5:9 204
5:9-10 305
6:7-8 202
6:9-11 209
6:12-14 272
6:15-17 204
7:1-8 .... 45, 221, 408
7:9 204
7:9-17 .... 204, 375, 380, 408
7:9-19 545
7:16 .... 210, 335
7:16-17 410
7:17 .... 119, 319, 335, 553
8:5 239
9:4 221
9:13-14 118
9:13-21 202
10:9-11 207
11:1-2 221
11:15 95
11:19 239
12:3 .... 133, 223
12:6 221,

408
12:9 223
12:11-17 408
12:14-17 .... 45, 221
12:15 223
13:7-9 204
13:8 45
14:1 .... 94, 221
14:1-5 204
14:5 340
14:6-8 199
14:8 126,
176, 428, 533
14:9-11 26,
207, 420
14:10 428
14:10-11 274
15:1-4 204,
209, 265, 341
15:8 61
16:4-7 209,
265, 320, 341, 517
16:8-11 272
16:12 118
16:12-16 272
16:12-21 93
16:13-16 206,
252
16:13-21 568
16:14 566
16:15 472
16:17 252
16:18 239
16:19 428
17&18 128,
136, 209
17:4 428
17:8 45
17:11-18 565
17:12-14 206
17:12-18 93
17:13-18 566
17:14-18 240
18:2 135
18:3 533
18:4 401,
410
18:6 428
18:9-19 203,
204
18:18 274
18:20 204,
209, 252, 320
19:1-6 252
19:1-10 209
19:2 320
19:3 274
19:11 277,
500, 504, 564
19:11-12 272
19:11-21 93,
206, 221, 318, 414, 505, 517, 528,
565, 569
19:13-15 532
19:14-21 114
19:15 405
20:1-3 115,
206, 223, 554
20:1-6 94
20:1-15 95
20:4 115,
204, 212, 552
20:10 207,
223
20:11-15 26,
207, 212, 420, 424, 485, 547
20:12 223
20:15 .... 45, 277
21&22 471,
554
21:1 424,
552
21:1-4 212,
410
21:1-5 279
21:4 211,
553
21:6 119,

SCRIPTURE INDEX

361, 379
21:23 207
22:1-5 ....279, 410
22:3 ....212, 270
22:5 ....95, 207
22:10 199
22:11 240
22:13 ....360, 380
22:14 401
22:17 ....119, 270, 401
22:18-19 334
22:20 199
22:20-21 ....30, 569

14
BIBLIOGRAPHY

Alden, Robert Alden. "*'oth*," ed. R. Laird Harris, Gleason L. Archer Jr., and Bruce K. Waltke. *Theological Wordbook of the Old Testament*, cited in electronic form with Logos Libronix. Chicago: Moody Press, 1999.

Alexander, Joseph. *Commentary on Isaiah*. Grand Rapids: Kregel, 1992.

Allen, Ronald B. "*'atsab*," ed. R. Laird Harris, Gleason L. Archer Jr., and Bruce K. Waltke. *Theological Wordbook of the Old Testament*, cited in electronic form with Logos Libronix. Chicago: Moody Press, 1999.

Archer, Gleason. *A Survey of Old Testament Introduction*. Chicago: Moody, 1994.

Austel, Hermann J. "*shmm*," ed. R. Laird Harris, Gleason L. Archer Jr., and Bruce K. Waltke. *Theological Wordbook of the Old Testament*, cited in electronic form with Logos Libronix. Chicago: Moody Press, 1999.

Blount, Douglas. "Providence." *Holman Illustrated Bible Dictionary*, ed. Chad Brand et al., cited in electronic form with Logos Libronix. Nashville, TN: Holman Bible Publishers, 2003.

Brand, Chad Charles Draper, et al., eds. "Aram-Naharaim." *Holman Illustrated Bible Dictionary*, cited in electronic form with Logos Libronix. Nashville, TN: Holman Bible Publishers, 2003.

Brown, Francis, and Samuel Rolles Driver, and Charles Augustus Briggs. *Enhanced Brown-Driver-Briggs Hebrew and English Lexicon*, cited in electronic form with Logos Libronix. Oxford: Clarendon Press, 1977.

Clines, D. J. A. "Cyrus," ed. Geoffrey W. Bromiley. *The International Standard Bible Encyclopedia, Revised*, cited in electronic form with Logos Libronix. Wm. B. Eerdmans, 1979–1988.

Coppes, Leonard J. "*qll*," ed. R. Laird Harris, Gleason L. Archer Jr., and Bruce K. Waltke. *Theological Wordbook of the Old Testament*, cited in electronic form with Logos Libronix. Chicago: Moody Press, 1999.

Culver, Robert D. Culver. "*chzh*," ed. R. Laird Harris, Gleason L. Archer Jr., and Bruce K. Waltke. *Theological Wordbook of the Old Testament*, cited in electronic form with Logos Libronix. Chicago: Moody Press, 1999.

Dockery, David S., ed. *Holman Bible Handbook*, cited in electronic form with Logos Libronix. Nashville, TN: Holman Bible Publishers, 1992.

BIBLIOGRAPHY

Editors. "Merodach-Baladan II." Encyclopaedia Britannica Online. https://www.britannica.com/biography/Merodach-Baladan-II. Accessed March 20, 2020.

Elwell, Walter A. and Philip Wesley Comfort. *Tyndale Bible Dictionary*, Tyndale Reference Library, cited in electronic form in Logos Libronix. Wheaton, IL: Tyndale House Publishers, 2001.

Freeman, James M, and Harold J. Chadwick. *Manners & Customs of the Bible*, cited in electronic form with Logos Libronix. North Brunswick, NJ: Bridge-Logos Publishers, 1998.

Gibson, J. C. L. *Davidson's Introductory Hebrew Grammar-Syntax*. Edinburgh: T&T Clark, 1994.

Grogan, G. W. "Isaiah." In *The Expositor's Bible Commentary*, ed. Frank E. Gaebelein, vol. 6. Grand Rapids: Zondervan, 1986.

Hamilton, Victor P. "*'ashr*," ed. R. Laird Harris, Gleason L. Archer Jr., and Bruce K. Waltke. *Theological Wordbook of the Old Testament*, cited in electronic form with Logos Libronix. Chicago: Moody Press, 1999.

Harris, R. Laird and Gleason L. Archer Jr., and Bruce K. Waltke, eds. *Theological Wordbook of the Old Testament*, cited in electronic form with Logos Libronix. Chicago: Moody Press, 1999.

_____. "*anag*." *Theological Wordbook of the Old Testament*, cited in electronic form with Logos Libronix. Chicago: Moody Press, 1999.

Holladay, William L., ed. *A Concise Hebrew and Aramaic Lexicon of the Old Testament*. Grand Rapids: Eerdmans, 1988.

Hughes, Robert B. J. Carl Laney. *Tyndale Concise Bible Commentary*. The Tyndale Reference Library, cited in electronic form with Logos Libronix. Wheaton, IL: Tyndale House Publishers, 2001.

Jamieson, Robert, and A. R. Fausset, and David Brown. *Commentary Critical and Explanatory on the Whole Bible*, vol. 1, cited in electronic form with Logos Libronix. Oak Harbor, WA: Logos Research Systems, Inc., 1997.

Kaiser, Walter C. *The Messiah in the Old Testament*. Grand Rapids: Zondervan, 1995.

_____. "*ntsr*," ed. R. Laird Harris, Gleason L. Archer Jr., and Bruce K. Waltke. *Theological Wordbook of the Old Testament*, cited in electronic form with Logos Libronix. Chicago: Moody Press, 1999.

_____. "*tsmch*," ed. R. Laird Harris, Gleason L. Archer Jr., and Bruce K. Waltke. *Theological Wordbook of the Old Testament*, cited in electronic form with Logos Libronix. Chicago: Moody Press, 1999.

Keil, C. F. and F. Delitzsch. *Keil and Delitzsch Commentary on the Old Testament*, vol. 7. Grand Rapids: Eerdmans, 1969.

Kidner, F. Derek. "Isaiah." In *New Bible Commentary: 21st Century Edition*, ed. D. A. Carson et al., 4th ed., cited in electronic form with Logos Libronix. Leicester, England; Downers Grove, IL: Inter-Varsity Press, 1994.

Koehler, Ludwig, et al. *The Hebrew And Aramaic Lexicon of the Old Testament*, cited in electronic form with Logos Libronix. Leiden: E.J. Brill, 1994–2000.

Langston, Scott. "Sidon and Tyre," ed. Chad Brand et al., *Holman Illustrated Bible Dictionary*, cited in electronic form with Logos Libronix. Nashville, TN: Holman Bible Publishers, 2003.

Lasor, W. W. "Tarshish," ed. Geoffrey W. Bromiley. *The International Standard Bible Encyclopedia, Revised*, cited in electronic form with Logos Libronix. Wm. B. Eerdmans, 1979–1988.

Martin, John A. "Isaiah." In *The Bible Knowledge Commentary: An Exposition of the Scriptures*, ed. J. F. Walvoord and R. B. Zuck, vol. 1, cited in electronic form with Logos Libronix. Wheaton, IL: Victor Books, 1985.

McComiskey, Thomas E. "*'nsh*," ed. R. Laird Harris, Gleason L. Archer Jr., and Bruce K. Waltke. *Theological Wordbook of the Old Testament*, cited in electronic form with Logos Libronix. Chicago: Moody Press, 1999.

McDowell, Josh. *Evidence That Demands a Verdict*. San Bernardino: Here's Life Publishers, 1972.

Myers, Allen C. *The Eerdmans Bible Dictionary*, cited in electronic form with Logos Libronix. Grand Rapids, MI: Eerdmans, 1987.

Mitchell, Elizabeth. "Doesn't Egyptian Chronology Prove That the Bible Is Unreliable?" https://answersingenesis.org/archaeology/ancient-egypt/doesnt-egyptian-chronology-prove-bible-unreliable/. Accessed Oct. 23, 2019.

Mitchell, Mike. "Cyrus," ed. Chad Brand et al. *Holman Illustrated Bible Dictionary*, cited in electronic form with Logos Libronix. Nashville, TN: Holman Bible Publishers, 2003.

Morris, Leon. *The Apostolic Preaching of the Cross*. London: Tyndale, 1955.

Motyer, J. Alec. *The Prophecy of Isaiah*. Downers Grove: IVP, 1993.

BIBLIOGRAPHY

Oswalt, John N. *The Book of Isaiah, 1-39*. The New International Commentary On The Old Testament, R. K. Harrison, Gen. Ed. Grand Rapids: Eerdmans, 1986.

_____. *The Book of Isaiah, 40-66*. The New International Commentary On The Old Testament, R. K. Harrison, Gen. Ed. Grand Rapids: Eerdmans, 1998.

Pfeiffer, Charles F. *The Wycliffe Bible Commentary: Old Testament*, cited in electronic form with Logos Libronix. Chicago: Moody Press, 1962.

Pratico, Gary D. and Miles V. Van Pelt. *Basics of Biblical Hebrew*, Second Edition. Grand Rapids: Zondervan, 2007.

Carl Schultz. "*'wh*," ed. R. Laird Harris, Gleason L. Archer Jr., and Bruce K. Waltke. *Theological Wordbook of the Old Testament*, cited in electronic form with Logos Libronix. Chicago: Moody Press, 1999.

_____. "*'ll*," ed. R. Laird Harris, Gleason L. Archer Jr., and Bruce K. Waltke. *Theological Wordbook of the Old Testament*, cited in electronic form with Logos Libronix. Chicago: Moody Press, 1999.

_____. "*'ur*," ed. R. Laird Harris, Gleason L. Archer Jr., and Bruce K. Waltke. *Theological Wordbook of the Old Testament*, cited in electronic form with Logos Libronix. Chicago: Moody Press, 1999.

Seow, C. L. *A Grammar for Biblical Hebrew*. Nashville: Abingdon, 1987.

Smick, Elmer B. "*nqm*," ed. R. Laird Harris, Gleason L. Archer Jr., and Bruce K. Waltke. *Theological Wordbook of the Old Testament*, cited in electronic form with Logos Libronix. Chicago: Moody Press, 1999.

Smith, Gary V. *Isaiah 1-39*, ed. E. Ray Clendenen. The New American Commentary, cited in electronic form with Logos Libronix. Nashville: B & H Publishing Group, 2007.

_____. *Isaiah 40-66*, vol. 15B. The New American Commentary, cited in electronic form with Logos Libronix. Nashville, TN: Broadman & Holman Publishers, 2009.

Steinmann, Andrew E. "The Chronology of 2 Kings 15-18." *JETS* 30:4 (1987): 391-397.

Swanson, James. *Dictionary of Biblical Languages with Semantic Domains: Hebrew (Old Testament)*. Oak Harbor: Logos Research Systems, Inc., cited in electronic form with Logos Libronix, 1997.

Unger, Merrill F. *Unger's Commentary on the Old Testament, Vol. II: Isaiah-Malachi*. Chicago: Moody, 1981.

Waltke, Bruce K. "*bzh*," ed. R. Laird Harris, Gleason L. Archer Jr., and Bruce K. Waltke. *Theological Wordbook of the Old Testament*, cited in electronic form with Logos Libronix. Chicago: Moody Press, 1999.

Waltke, Bruce K. and M. O'Connor. *An Introduction to Biblical Hebrew Syntax*. Winona Lake: Eisenbrauns, 1900.

Webb, Barry G. *The Message of Isaiah*. Downers Grove: IVP, 1996.

Weber, Carl Philip. "*hoy*," ed. R. Laird Harris, Gleason L. Archer Jr., and Bruce K. Waltke. *Theological Wordbook of the Old Testament*, cited in electronic form with Logos Libronix. Chicago: Moody Press, 1999.

Wilson, Marvin R. "*nchm*," ed. R. Laird Harris, Gleason L. Archer Jr., and Bruce K. Waltke. *Theological Wordbook of the Old Testament*, cited in electronic form with Logos Libronix. Chicago: Moody Press, 1999.

Wiseman, Donald J. "*chll*," ed. R. Laird Harris, Gleason L. Archer Jr., and Bruce K. Waltke. *Theological Wordbook of the Old Testament*, cited in electronic form with Logos Libronix. Chicago: Moody Press, 1999.

Wolf, Herbert. *Interpreting Isaiah*. Grand Rapids: Zondervan, 1985.

Wood, Leon J. "*chapats*," ed. R. Laird Harris, Gleason L. Archer Jr., and Bruce K. Waltke. *Theological Wordbook of the Old Testament*, cited in electronic form with Logos Libronix. Chicago: Moody Press, 1999.

Yamauchi, Edwin. "*tm'*," ed. R. Laird Harris, Gleason L. Archer Jr., and Bruce K. Waltke. *Theological Wordbook of the Old Testament*, cited in electronic form with Logos Libronix. Chicago: Moody Press, 1999.

Young, Edward J. *The Book of Isaiah, vol. 1*. Grand Rapids: Eerdmans, 1965.

_____. *The Book of Isaiah, vol. 2*. Grand Rapids: Eerdmans, 1965.

_____. *The Book of Isaiah, vol. 3*. Grand Rapids: Eerdmans, 1972.

Youngblood, Ronald F. "*t'h*," ed. R. Laird Harris, Gleason L. Archer Jr., and Bruce K. Waltke. *Theological Wordbook of the Old Testament*, cited in electronic form with Logos Libronix. Chicago: Moody Press, 1999.

Youngblood, Ronald F., and F. F. Bruce, and R. K. Harrison, Thomas Nelson Publishers, eds. *Nelson's New Illustrated Bible Dictionary*, cited in electronic form with Logos Libronix. Nashville, TN: Thomas Nelson, Inc., 1995.

Zemek, George. *A Biblical Theology of the Doctrines of Sovereign Grace*. Little Rock: B.T.D.S.G., 2002.

ABOUT THE AUTHOR

Tim Dane earned his M.Div. and Th.M. from the Master's Seminary (Sun Valley, CA) and his Ph.D. from Baptist Bible Seminary (Clarks Summit, PA). Tim has been in full-time pastoral ministry since 1995. He served 10 years in Torrance, California as the senior pastor of Anza Avenue Baptist Church, and has served as the senior pastor of Mesa Hills Bible Church in Colorado Springs, Colorado since 2011. Tim is the founding president of Front Range Bible Institute where he teaches on a regular basis, and has taught extensively in overseas seminaries such as Irpin Biblical Seminary in Kiev, Ukraine. Tim and his wife Karen have been married 34 years and have six children and eight grandchildren.

www.ingramcontent.com/pod-product-compliance
Lightning Source LLC
Chambersburg PA
CBHW050417240426
43661CB00055B/2179